THE LAW OF THE SOVIET STATE

THE LAW OF THE SOVIET STATE

Andrei Y. Vyshinsky

GENERAL EDITOR

TRANSLATED FROM THE RUSSIAN BY

HUGH W. BABB

*Professor & Head of the Department of Law
of the College of Business Administration,
Boston University*

INTRODUCTION BY

JOHN N. HAZARD

*Professor of Public Law,
Columbia University*

GREENWOOD PRESS, PUBLISHERS
WESTPORT, CONNECTICUT

Library of Congress Cataloging in Publication Data

Vyshinskiĭ, Andreĭ I͡Anuar'evich, 1883-1954, ed.
  The law of the Soviet State.

  Translation of Sovetskoe gosudarstvennoe pravo.
  Reprint of the 1951 printing of the ed. published
by Macmillan, New York, issued as no. 2 of the American
Council of Learned Societies Devoted to Humanistic
Studies, Russian Translation Project series.
  Includes bibliographical references and index.
  1. Russia--Constitutional law. I. Babb, Hugh
Webster, 1887-   II. Title. III. Series: American
Council of Learned Societies Devoted to Humanistic
Studies. Russian Translation Project. Series ; 2.
Law   342'.47   78-23524
ISBN 0-313-20765-8

Reprinted with the permission of Macmillan Publishing Co., Inc.

Reprinted in 1979 by Greenwood Press, Inc.
51 Riverside Avenue, Westport, CT 06880

Printed in the United States of America

10 9 8 7 6 5 4 3 2 1

81-7733

Foreword

THE Russian Translation Project of the American Council of Learned Societies was organized in 1944 with the aid of a subsidy from the Humanities Division of the Rockefeller Foundation. The aim of the Project is the translation into English of significant Russian works in the fields of the humanities and the social sciences which provide an insight into Russian life and thought.

In the difficult problem of the selection of books for translation, the Administrative Committee has had the counsel and cooperation of Slavic scholars throughout the United States and Great Britain. It is thought that the books chosen will be useful to general readers interested in world affairs, and will also serve as collateral reading material for the large number of courses on Russia in our colleges and universities.

Since Russian history is a continuum, the volumes translated are of various dates and have been drawn from both the prerevolutionary and post-revolutionary periods, from writings published inside and outside of Russia, the choice depending solely on their value to the fundamental aim of the Project. Translations are presented in authentic and unabridged English versions of the original text. Only in this way, it is believed, can American readers be made aware of the traditions, concepts, and ideologies by which the thinking and attitudes of the people of Russia are molded.

It should, of course, be clearly understood that the views expressed in the works translated are not to be identified in any way with those of the Administrative Committee or of the Council.

THE ADMINISTRATIVE COMMITTEE
JOHN A. MORRISON, *Chairman*
HAROLD SPIVACKE
SERGIUS YAKOBSON
MORTIMER GRAVES
W. CHAPIN HUNTINGTON

Introduction

E VERY Soviet student of government and law reads Vyshinsky's book.
Administrators and jurists use it for reference. It is, in a sense, the militant handbook of those engaged in government. It provides a guide through
the intricacies of the central and local levels of administration, an explanation of the Constitution, and a documented analysis of the laws relating to
the courts, elections, and rights and duties of citizens. It is designed also as
a means of instilling in the public official a firm conviction that he is a part
of a system of government which has no equal in the world outside.

Much of the determination of Soviet soldiers in the war just ended can
be traced to sources typified by this book. Much of the persistence and confidence evidenced by Soviet diplomats in international councils can likewise
be traced to the same sources. Vyshinsky and his team of collaborators
present the doctrine which Soviet men and women are taught in their schools
and general reading. In view of this fact, Vyshinsky's book provides one
avenue of approach to an understanding of the habit of thought which has
become characteristic of Soviet citizens.

Americans will find interest in this book not only because it is a statement
of a creed and an outline of the structure of the Soviet form of government:
the book is also revealing of Soviet pedagogical techniques. American readers will be introduced to the vigorous, uncompromising manner in which
Soviet teachers present their thesis. There is to be found the highly critical
and even scornful approach to non-Soviet systems of government. There is
to be found frequent repetition of ideas in varying forms. All of this is characteristic of the Soviet textbook, whether it be written for mass consumption
or for the advanced student in the professional school.

A brief statement of the setting in which the book was written may aid
the American reader who approaches Soviet political and legal literature for
the first time. It will be remembered that the year 1936 was a milestone in
Soviet constitutional history. A constitutional drafting commission under
Stalin's chairmanship brought forward a draft of a new constitution in June,
1936, to replace the constitution under which the Union of Soviet Socialist
Republics had come into being. The Draft Constitution was enacted by the
Eighth Congress of Soviets on December 5, 1936. It was heralded as a reflection of the changed economic and social conditions which had resulted from

the industrialization of the country under the five-year plans and the collectivization of agriculture.

The year 1936 was accepted as the date for which many had been waiting. It marked the end of many of the controls established by the Revolution to make certain that no combination of forces would arise which could threaten seriously the continued existence of the Soviet government and the political and economic system for which it had become known. Whole classes of the population had previously been discriminated against in legislation relating to education, military service, and even the obtaining of employment. The 1936 Constitution changed all of this by eliminating discrimination on the ground of social origin or occupation. Procedures, including the secret ballot and direct elections, were introduced, although the fundamental position of the Communist Party remained unchanged. To many an age of greater tolerance seemed to be dawning.

The process of establishing the Soviet government on a firm foundation had been long and arduous. Vyshinsky's book is a chronicle of the steps which were taken and the experiments which were tried. American readers will be able to learn much about the problems of Soviet government from the account. It may be helpful to bear in mind that Lenin maintained that Marxism provided no precise blueprint for the future government of revolutionary Russia. He foresaw the need for experimentation, and the record of the constitutional and legal history of the USSR has borne out his expectation. Various measures have been tried and abandoned to the accompaniment of bitter criticism, both within the USSR and abroad.

Vyshinsky's book was published two years after the adoption of the new Constitution. Much had occurred in those two years to affect the outlook of Soviet leaders. The imminence of the Second World War had become apparent to all. International tension had been reflected in the domestic life of the USSR. Production was the principal requirement for war, and the government had indicated that nothing was to be permitted to impede it.

Multicandidate elections, of which Stalin had spoken favorably to Roy Howard in 1936, had never materialized. A single candidate appeared on the ballot in electoral districts for deputies to the Supreme Soviets of the Union government and of the republics. Labor legislation had been enacted to place strict curbs upon labor turnover and to require discipline. Jurists who thought that the state should begin to "wither away" as socialism was achieved were denounced and removed from their positions.

The spirit of war psychology is clearly reflected in Vyshinsky's book. Outsiders have sometimes felt that restrictive legislation and practices were the result of a need to prepare for war and could have been explained to the public in such terms. Vyshinsky is, apparently, of a different view. He has fitted the tightening of controls into the general plan of his book as a logical development of the process of government, and has given little reason to suppose that they were to be abandoned with the coming of peace.

Events since the publication of Vyshinsky's book in 1936 have been momentous. In some ways they have definitely "dated" the book. There has been a world war and the beginning of a period of reconstruction. Every country of the world which participated in the war found it necessary to modify its governmental structure to meet the emergency. The USSR was no exception.

Changes in the Soviet structure concerned an increase in the number of commissariats to administer the new types of production required by the war. There also came into being immediately after the USSR was invaded in 1941 a State Committee for Defense with supreme authority over government and Communist Party agencies. In 1944 the relationship between the republics and the federal government was affected by amendments to the Constitution. The republics regained the authority which they had surrendered at the time of union in 1922, and in some cases earlier, to establish their own commissariats of foreign affairs and defense. The new commissariats were required by the amendments to follow the policies established by the commissariats of the same name in the federal government, but the change of 1944 affected the international status of the republics; two of them, indeed, the Ukrainian Soviet Socialist Republic and the Byelorussian Soviet Socialist Republic, even gained separate admission to the United Nations.

Since the end of the war, changes in the Soviet structure of government have continued to occur. The State Committee for Defense has been abolished, and the established agencies of government have resumed their constitutional functions. Elections have been resumed after having been postponed during the war. The commissariats in the federal government and in the republics were given the name of ministries by constitutional amendments in 1946. The Council of People's Commissars became the Council of Ministers. The Prosecutor of the USSR was renamed the Prosecutor General of the USSR. The number of members of the Presidium of the Supreme Soviet of the USSR has been reduced to make the body easier to assemble. At the same time the number of ministries has continued to rise. Molotov has explained that this was made necessary as new functions were assumed by government or as efficient administration demanded a splitting of a single industrial ministry in two, as was done with the Ministry of the Coal Industry.

Changes of the nature referred to have been largely matters of detail. Those who have familiarized themselves with the basic material in Vyshinsky's book will have no trouble keeping pace with these and the changes which can be anticipated in the future by following the pages of American political science reviews and comparative-government textbooks. Readers will do well to remember that the pace of translation and publication is always so measured that only those who can follow Russian language originals can hope to keep up to date.

A few words may be appropriate for those interested particularly in political theory. American readers will find that most of the great names in the history of political and legal theory will be found in Vyshinsky's book. Vyshinsky presents his interpretation of what the non-Marxists believed and taught; he then adds his criticism of their teaching. This technique is familiar in all Soviet textbooks for adult readers. Vyshinsky's aim is to acquaint the Soviet reader with what others have said and why he believes it to have lost validity. Such an approach is designed to bring the Soviet student to believe confidently in the strength of the political theory adopted by his country's leaders, and to understand why the theories proposed by others have been discarded.

Vyshinsky's method may have important effects upon international relations. His book aims to make certain that a Soviet student who reasons his way through the ponderous passages of this and similar works does more than memorize the fact that the accepted doctrine in the USSR is the preferred theory. From my own observation as a foreign student in a Soviet law school a decade ago, I believe that Vyshinsky's purpose was achieved with most of the students. If this is a correct observation, it explains the tenacity of Soviet citizens in argument with people of the West. The arguments of the West do not come to Soviet citizens for the first time when they are presented by diplomats, newspapers, radios, or in informal conversation between Soviet citizens and American students, government officials, businessmen, or tourists. The Soviet citizen has met these arguments before and is prepared with an immediate response. Consequently, few of them seem to be quickly moved by argument alone.

A final word is necessary about Andrei Yanuaryevich Vyshinsky. His reputation as Deputy Minister for Foreign Affairs of the USSR has already become so well established that he almost needs no introduction. Yet, because of this very fame in the diplomatic field his career as a jurist is sometimes overlooked. Before entering the Ministry of Foreign Affairs during the war he had been Prosecutor of the USSR. In this position he had supervised the preparation for, and conducted the prosecution in, the trials of Bukharin, Pyatakov, Kamenev, Radek, and their colleagues for treason against the USSR.

Vyshinsky has also evidenced qualities as a legal scholar by lecturing at the Moscow Juridical Institute and at meetings of Soviet jurists in Moscow and elsewhere. When the school of jurists, headed by E. B. Pashukanis, was ousted in 1937 because of its support of a program of progressive "withering away" of the state, Vyshinsky came forward as the principal organizer of the new jurisprudence. He became editor of the leading law review, *Sovetskoye Gosudarstvo i Pravo*. He was also named a member of the Academy of Sciences of the USSR and was a leader in the work of the Section of Economics and Law of the Academy.

In spite of his duties in the Ministry of Foreign Affairs, Vyshinsky has found time during and since the war to write and lecture extensively on law. In 1947 he was awarded a Stalin prize for a textbook on the law of evidence. In preparing the volume on Law in the Soviet State, Vyshinsky made use of his colleagues in the Institute of Law of the Academy of Sciences. The volume is a composite of their work, but Vyshinsky is well known in the USSR as an editor who takes great care with any manuscript on which his name appears. As a product of Vyshinsky's editing, this volume carries the weight of considerable authority.

The original Russian language edition of Vyshinsky's work contained no index. The index to the translation has been prepared by Kathryn and Henry Clarenbach to facilitate use of the volume by American political scientists familiar with American index headings and terminology. In consequence, the arrangement and choice of words may sometimes be unfamiliar to such Soviet jurists and American specialists on Soviet terminology as happen to examine this edition.

The translation of Hugh Webster Babb of Boston University has been prepared from a similar point of view. The Russian sentence structure has been changed in many instances to reduce the occasions in which American readers might have been hampered by an unfamiliar style. Professor Babb's effort to retain the original spirit and textual accuracy is notable, however. The translation reflects the translator's facility in Russian and legal scholarship.

JOHN N. HAZARD

THE RUSSIAN INSTITUTE
COLUMBIA UNIVERSITY

Contents

xi

Chapter VIII   The Court and the Prosecutor's Office

I

Introduction

SEC. 1: THE OCTOBER SOCIALIST REVOLUTION AND THE STATE

THE great October Socialist Revolution of 1917 destroyed the bourgeois state and created one of a new and higher type—the state of the proletarian dictatorship. Thereby it opened a new epoch in world history—the epoch of the socialist state of workers and peasants.

In doing away with the old bourgeois state machine, the Russian proletariat, under the guidance of the party of Lenin and Stalin, followed the great historical instructions of Marx and Engels, the founders of scientific socialism. On the basis of the experience of the Paris Commune, they established the proposition that "the working class cannot simply take possession of a state machine ready prepared and set it in motion for its own ends," [1] but must demolish and utterly break up this machine and build its own new state machine.

Lenin, on the eve of the great October Socialist Revolution of 1917, wrote on this same subject:

The revolution consists in the proletariat's *destroying* the apparatus of government and the *entire* state apparatus, putting in its place a new apparatus, composed of armed workers. . . . The revolution must consist not in the fact that a new class manages with the help of the *old* machinery of state, but in *smashing* the old and commanding and managing with the aid of new machinery.[2]

The violent seizure of authority by the proletariat, the demolition of the exploiting society's machinery of state, and the organization (in lieu of the old state machinery, now reduced to fragments) of a new state is the most important thesis of the Marxist-Leninist doctrine of proletarian revolution.

[1] Marx and Engels, *Manifesto of the Communist Party* (Russian ed., 1938), p. 6.
[2] Lenin, *Selected Works* (Russin ed.), Vol. XXI, p. 450.

This thesis is directly and immediately related to the most important problems of Soviet public law.

The greatest service of Lenin and Stalin is not only that they played the chief role in unmasking opportunist attempts to pervert this most important thesis of Marxism, but that they translated this doctrine into reality and led the Russian proletariat to shatter and demolish the bourgeois state apparatus, thus following the teachings bequeathed by the great founders of scientific socialism.

To *shatter* this machine, to *demolish* it—such is the real interest of the "people," of a majority of the people, of workers, and of a majority of the peasants; such as the "preliminary condition" of a free union of the poorest peasants with the proletarians; and, without this union, democracy is unstable and social reform impossible.[3]

The proletarian revolution transfers authority to the laboring people. Bourgeois revolutions had considered the "vast state edifice the chief spoil of the victor," [4] and handed it over to the bourgeoisie and its parties.

The bourgeoisie constantly improves this edifice, directing all its powers against the laboring people—the workers and the peasants. The pressure of bourgeois exploitation turns the peasants increasingly into a natural ally of the proletariat, destined to overthrow the bourgeois order.

Under the influence of sharpening class contradictions, which gradually enlightened even the most backward and politically undeveloped peasant minds, bourgeois demagogy (which had helped the exploiters lure the peasants into their nets with golden promises) lost much of its efficacy.[5] The bourgeois state was still more hostile to the interests of the proletariat which by the course of historical social development was ordained to become the gravedigger of the old, exploiting society.

The chief lesson drawn by the proletariat from the heroic seventy-three days of the Paris Commune was expressed in Marx's famous dictum of the necessity for the proletariat to destroy the machinery of the bourgeois state.[6]

[3] *Ibid.*, p. 396.

[4] Marx and Engels, *Selected Works* (Russian ed., 1934), Vol. VIII, p. 405.

[5] As early as 1852 Marx wrote that most of the French nation had turned into troglodytes, that sixteen million peasants live in dens, and that their houses have only one or two windows, rarely three, whereas "windows are to a house what the five senses are to the head." He went on to say: "The bourgeois order (which, at the beginning of the century, made the state watchman in the recent partitioning and dressed it with laurels) became a vampire, sucking its heart's blood and its brain, and casting it into the alchemist's retort of capital. The legal code of Napoleon is now merely a code to carry out court judgments, to levy execution on property and to sell it under the hammer." Marx and Engels (Russian ed., 1934), Vol. II, p. 324. (Note: All footnotes not otherwise attributed are those of the author, and are translated as they appeared in the original Russian edition. The abbreviation "Tr." is used to designate those footnotes supplied by the translator, and "Ed." for those supplied by the editor.—Ed.)

[6] See Marx's letter to Kugelmann, April 12, 1871 (Russian ed. of Marx's Letters, p. 289).

In its battle against the "parasite" (its bourgeoisie), the Paris Commune came to this conclusion. The necessity of destroying this machinery, as a condition precedent to the triumph of the national revolution, is explained by the characteristics of the bourgeois state machinery as a mighty instrument of repression and restraint. Without demolishing this machinery—without smashing the basic means whereby the exploiters oppose the national revolution—it is impossible to assure the revolution's success.

If the old state apparatus (the old institutions and the officials in them, the old working methods and practices, their old attachments and sympathies, the old ideas, views, notions, and wishes) is left intact, it is impossible to direct the state apparatus, the state, to the solution of new problems, to serve the interests of the new class which has come to power. The proletariat must, therefore, demolish and destroy the old bourgeois state machinery as it did in the great October Socialist Revolution.

The theory of Marx and Engels on the revolutionary overthrow and annihilation of the bourgeois machinery of state power is organically connected with the entire Marxist theory of the state. They debunked the pseudoscientific notion of bourgeois philistines and liberals concerning the state. They demonstrated the class origin and class nature of the state. At the same time, they showed that the proletariat, after seizing power, must of necessity utilize the state in order to continue its struggle for freedom, for the triumph of socialism.

The Soviets were the state form of the proletarian dictatorship revealed by Lenin—the new state form most closely corresponding to the requirements of the proletarian revolution and to the tasks of the period of transition from capitalism to communism.

Suppression and the use of force by the state are still essential during the transition period—force, however, exerted by the exploited majority upon the exploiting minority, different in type and new in principle. The indispensability of this force necessitates a special apparatus adapted to realize these purposes. The *Soviet state* is the particular apparatus, the special machinery, to crush enemies and all elements hostile to socialism.

The new Soviet state is a machine to crush the resistance of exploiters, to do away with exploitation and class domination by exploiters, to reinforce the class dominance of the proletariat and its leadership of the rest of the toiling masses to the end of finally liquidating classes in general and passing into communism.

"The state of armed workers," "the state of the Soviets of workers and peasants"—that is what distinguishes this new state (so unlike even the most "democratic" and "advanced" bourgeois state).

The Stalin epoch is marked by the final and irrevocable victory of the socialism which created the new constitution of the socialist state of workers and peasants.

The Soviet state played the decisive part in the achievement of these triumphs. It guaranteed the destruction of all the forces of bourgeois counterrevolution and the suppression of all attempts at restoration by the bourgeoisie and its Trotskyist-Bukharinist agents. In the fire of battle and in the heroism of socialist construction it consolidated the alliance between the working class and the peasants, under the guidance of the working class headed by the Communist Party of Bolsheviks. It defended and preserved all the gains of the proletarian revolution. It raised proletarian democracy to unprecedented heights.

The great October Socialist Revolution shattered to its very foundation the machinery of the bourgeois state—that frightful and monstrous mechanism for suppressing the toilers and insuring the dominance of the exploiters. It destroyed and demolished the old bourgeois state and erected in its place a new state—its Soviet state of workers and peasants. It made this state strong, and raised it to a gigantic height of historical development. Guided by the Lenin-Stalin Party, the proletariat built a new state—the socialist state of workers and peasants.

The Soviet state, whose first foundations were laid in the victorious October Socialist Revolution, grew and became a mighty proletarian power, an unassailable stronghold of communism—a gigantic force, guaranteeing the further victorious advance of our country's toilers to communism.

The organization, development and flowering of the Soviet state resulted from the heroic struggle of the laboring masses, from the victories of the inviolable union of workers and peasants, from the genius of the Communist Party led by Lenin and Stalin, in guiding the movement and the struggle of the masses—Lenin and Stalin, who had armed our proletariat with the invincible weapon of Marxism.

The Marxist-Leninist theory of proletarian revolution and of the Soviet state guaranteed the correct solution of the problems and methods of building the Soviet state, and of ways and means of realizing the triumph of socialism.

Without a correct understanding of the nature and essence of the state and of state power, proper guidance in the matter of building the state and the swift successes (unparalleled in the history of revolutions) attained by our country's toilers would have been equally impossible.

The genius of Marx-Engels-Lenin-Stalin provided a correct understanding of the nature and essence of the state, of its part in the history of human society and in the matter of the struggle of the proletariat for political and social emancipation, and finally of its historical development and historical fate.

Bourgeois theories of state and law—irrespective of the subjective aspirations and wishes of those who created those theories—serve the cause of exploitation. To expose their real nature is the first and most important problem of Soviet knowledge, dedicated, as it is, to the development of a theory of state and law.

The Marxist-Leninist theory of state and law in general, and of the Soviet state and law in particular, guaranteed the correct solution of all questions as to concrete problems, methods, and forms of building the Soviet state and Soviet law (including Soviet public law). We therefore begin our course on Soviet public law by examining a series of fundamental precepts of the Marxist-Leninist theory of state and law, as contrasted with bourgeois theories and all sorts of anti-Marxist perversions of questions related to a given branch of legal science.

SEC. 2: THE FOUNDATIONS OF THE MARXIST-LENINIST THEORY OF STATE AND LAW

The nature of the state is the most important question in the science of public law. The theory of the state is the basis not only of the science of state law but also of law in general, inasmuch as a scientific understanding of law is impossible without a correct understanding of the state. Law and state cannot be studied separately and apart from each other. Law draws its force, and obtains its content, from the state.

"Law is nothing without a mechanism capable of *compelling* the observance of legal norms." [1]

This fundamental precept of the Marxist-Leninist theory defines the relationship between law and state. We shall later discuss this precept in greater detail when we describe in their entirety the bases of the Marxist-Leninist theory of law and state.

This theory illustrates to the last detail all the falseness and pseudoscience of the various bourgeois "theories" of the state, which pervert the nature of the state to gratify the exploiters in order to perpetuate capitalist exploitation.

It reveals the artificiality and the unscientific character of bourgeois theories of law. Those theories portray their subject perversely and falsely.

[1] Lenin (Russian ed.), Vol. XXI, p. 438.

They disguise the class-exploiting character of bourgeois law. By phrases about "the general welfare" and "social" and "popular" interests, they strive to conceal the fact that bourgeois law, that subtle and poisoned instrument which defends the interests of the exploiters, is oppressive and hostile to the people.

Opposed to bourgeois theories of law and state, which are utterly arbitrary and developed in complete abstraction with no truly scientific content, stands the authentic Marxist-Leninist theory—the only scientific theory—of law and the state. Starting from its general methodology of dialectic materialism, the Marxist-Leninist theory presents a strictly scientific explanation of the origin and development of law and state.

Marx wrote as early as 1844:

My investigations have brought me to the conclusion that neither legal relationships, nor the forms of state, can be understood by themselves alone or by the so-called universal development of the human soul. On the contrary, they have their roots in the material conditions of life, the totality whereof Hegel (following the example of the English and the French in the eighteenth century) united under the name "civil society." The anatomy of civil society, however, must be sought in political economy, the study of which I began in Paris and continued in Brussels (where I moved following M. Guizot's order for my expulsion from Paris). The general conclusion to which I had come (and which served thereafter as the guiding thread in all my further investigations) may be briefly formulated thus: In the social production of their lives people enter into definite and necessary relationships which are independent of their will—production relationships, which correspond to the definite degree to which their material productive powers have developed. The totality of these production relationships constitutes the economic structure of society, the real basis upon which is built the juridical and political superstructure and to which definite forms of social consciousness correspond. The means of production of material life condition the social, political and spiritual processes of life in general.[2]

Here is a complete understanding of the fundamental laws of motion governing social development. Those laws similarly disclose the secret of the origin and the nature of law and state; and this revelation is one of the most important and original characteristics of Marxist-Leninist theory—its greatest strength.

Marxism-Leninism is forceful and vital in that in its practical activity it rests "specifically on the needs of society's material life to develop and is never separated from society's real life."[3]

Only by an analysis of the material conditions of human society can one

---

[2] Marx and Engels (Russian ed.), Vol. XII, Pt. 1, p. 6.
[3] *History of the All-Union Communist Party (of Bolsheviks): A Short Course* (Russian ed., 1938), p. 111.

understand the true nature of the law and state produced by "civil society," that is, by the totality of production relationships of society and of the social-economic relationships conditioned by it.

Criticizing Hegel's philosophy of law, with its idealistic interpretation of the relationship between society and the state, Marx wrote:

The family and civil society turn *themselves* into the state. They are the moving element. But according to Hegel they are *created by* an actual idea. Their unification into the state is not the result of their own development but is predetermined by the development of the idea. Family and civil society are the spheres wherein this idea is finite. Their existence is conditioned by another's spirit, not by their own spirit. They are not self-defining but are definitions introduced by a third element. For this reason they are also defined as "finite," as the particular *finiteness* of the "actual idea." The object of their existence is not this existence itself. The idea separates these premises from itself so as, "passing through their ideal nature, to be for itself an eternal, actual spirit;" that is to say, a political sovereign cannot exist without the natural basis of family and the artificial basis of civil society. These are conditions indispensable to the state. But in Hegel the condition is itself conditioned, that which defines is itself defined, and that which produces is the product of its product.[4]

Having disposed of Hegel's views of state and law, and disclosing their complete indefensibility, Marx and Engels laid firm and accurate foundations for a scientific world outlook which explains all the most complicated questions of sociology, history, and law. We know from Engels how Marx arrived at this new world outlook. He wrote:

Criticism of the debates in the Rhineland Landtag compelled Marx to the study of questions of material interests. He arrived at original views anticipated neither by jurisprudence nor by philosophy. Starting from Hegel's legal philosophy, Marx came to the conclusion that not the state (portrayed by Hegel as the "crown of the whole building") but rather civil society (which Hegel so disdained) was the sphere in which the key to an understanding of the process of man's historical development must be sought.[5]

What are the characteristics of that "civil society" which Hegel so disdained? According to Marx, in his *Holy Family*:

Natural necessity, qualities of the nature of man (however estranged they may seem), *interest*—these are what bind the members of civil society to each other. The *real* bond between them is not *political* life but *civil* life. Moreover, it is not the *state* which unites the *atoms* of civil society, but precisely the fact that they are *atoms* (only as it seems in the *heaven* of their imagination, whereas in *reality* they are beings differing most markedly from atoms) and the fact that they

---

[4] Marx and Engels (Russian ed.), Vol. I, p. 539.
[5] *Ibid.*, Vol. XIII, Pt. 1, p. 317.

are not *divine egoists* but *egoistic people*. In our time it is sheer *political preju-dice* to continue to imagine that the state unites civil life. The reverse is the fact: civil life unites the state.[6]

Studying the history of the development of human society, Marx and Engels came to conclusions which decisively changed and correctly evalu-ated all the views previously prevalent in science. This was particularly true of jurisprudence. Jurisprudence had floundered about, utterly impotent in a vicious circle of contradictions, which had actively influenced all bourgeois theories of law—even those of such authoritative and powerful thinkers of the bourgeois world as Kant and Hegel.

Marxism revealed the indefensibility of bourgeois scientific methodology, which was completely incapable of disclosing and formulating the basic laws of social development. Marxism revealed the pseudoscientific character of divers trends in the field of legal science. It put an end, once and for all, to the conceptions of formal jurisprudence and abstract idealism which had so completely muddled the idea of law and the state.

Marxism explained all the hitherto inexplicable questions and problems, and brought into a strictly scientific and logical system the solution to these questions, which were thus raised to the level of truly scientific theory. Marx and Engels showed that the state was the result of a definite plane of devel-opment of society's productive forces, that the state was founded on the ruins of the tribal regime, and that it experienced in its turn a series of cataclysms associated with the division of labor, the rise of classes, the appearance of private property in land, money, mortgages, and so forth.[7]

[6] *Ibid.*, Vol. III, p. 149.
[7] Engels, *The Origin of Family, Private Property and the State.* Concerning the social revolution in the tribal regime, Engels wrote: "The tribal regime was helpless against new elements which developed independently. It was postulated upon members of one *gens* or tribe living together in a single territory settled exclusively by them. This ceased long ago. Everywhere races and tribes were intermingled. Everywhere slaves, clients (*Schutzver-wandte*), and foreigners lived among free citizens. Localized settlement came only at the end of the intermediate stage of barbarism and was occasionally destroyed by the mobility and change of abode consequent upon trade activity, occupational change, and the aliena-tion of property in land. Members of tribal organizations could no longer meet to solve their common affairs—although there was perfunctory observance as to matters of small moment, such as religious festivals. Side by side with those demands and interests for whose disposi-tion tribal organizations were summoned and adapted, there came (as a result of the revolu-tion in conditions of production activity and the consequent changes in the social structure) new demands and interests not merely alien, but in every respect opposed, to the ancient tribal order. The interests of artisan groups which sprang up with the division of labor, and special demands of city as opposed to village, demanded new organs. And since each of these groups included people of different races, associations and tribes, and even foreigners, such organs had to come into being outside the tribal organization—side by side with it, and at the same time contrary to it. In every tribal organization in turn this conflict of interest found expression. It was sharpest where—within one and the same *gens* and one and the same tribe—rich and poor, usurers and debtors were united. There was the further addition of a mass of new population alien to the tribal groups, and capable (as in Rome) of becom-

The tribal form of society knew no antitheses within itself. But as Engels has said:

Here a society arose, doomed by all its economic conditions of life to split into free and slave, exploiting wealth and exploited poverty, and not only unable to reconcile these contrasts but bound to make them constantly sharper. Such a society could exist only in constant, open struggle between these classes, or under the domination of a third power which (supposedly standing above the contesting classes) puts down their open conflicts and (which is most important) permits class struggle only in the economic field, in its so-called legal form. The tribal form of society became obsolete. It was destroyed by the division of labor and the consequent division of society into classes. Its place was taken by the state.[8]

The whole course of the development of the state—as a force brought about by the very development of society and in no sense attached thereto from without—is here shown in its entirety and with marvelous clarity.

The state is the product of society in a certain stage of development. It is an acknowledgment that this society is inextricably involved in conflict with itself; that it has split into irreconcilable contradictions and is impotent to rid itself of those contradictions. And force became necessary in order that these contradictions, these classes with conflicting economic interests, might not devour each other and society in a fruitless struggle—force standing manifestly above society, force which would moderate the conflict, hold it within the bounds of "order." And this force, issuing out of society, but putting itself above society and ever more and more alienating itself from society, is the state.[9]

In the state, subjects settle throughout the territorial divisions, the state's social authority is established, exacting taxes, and consisting "not only of an armed population but also of material accessories, prisons and every sort of compulsory institution unknown to tribal society." [10] This authority is negligible where class contradictions are still not obvious (or not so obvious). Where they are sufficiently sharp and serious, however, the significance of authority and the part that it plays become stronger, and its influence grows in proportion. Authority here subordinates all persons to its influence. Its legal base is in statutes, by virtue of which those exercising the authority become particularly sacred and inviolable. Supreme power is here embodied

ing a force in the land. Moreover, this new population was too numerous to be included gradually in *gentes* and tribes related by blood. Opposed to this mass stood tribal groups— closed and privileged corporations. The natural democracy of primordial times became a hateful aristocracy. Finally, the tribal regime grew out of—and was only adapted to—a society which had known no antithesis within itself. It had no means of constraint other than social opinion." Marx and Engels (Russian ed.), Vol. XVI, pp. 143–144.

[8] Marx and Engels (Russian ed.), Vol. XVI, Pt. 1, p. 144.
[9] *Ibid.*, p. 145.
[10] *Ibid.*, p. 146.

in the coercive force of this authority which rests on the might of the class whose interest it serves.

The whole history of mankind proves that the state had its origin in class contradictions and conflicts created by the development of tribal society, in the need to "curb class opposition." It was precisely this fact that made the state the organ of the authority of the strongest—economically dominant—class which, with the support of the state, thus becomes the most powerful class politically as well. This in turn provides it with new means to crush and to exploit the oppressed class.

Such is the exploiter state of every sort—the ancient state, preeminently a slaveholders' state to crush the slaves and keep them in check; the feudal state, the organ of nobles and landholders to hold the peasant serfs in check; and the bourgeois state of our own time, the instrument whereby capital exploits hired labor.[11] "The state is an organization of the class of 'haves' to defend itself from the class of the 'have-nots.'"[12] "Political power, in the exact sense of the words, is organized force of one class to repress another."[13]

Marxism-Leninism gives a scientific explanation of the rise and development of the state, indicating its beginning and its end.

The state did not always exist. There were societies which got along without a state and without any conception of state or state authority. At a certain stage of economic development, necessarily connected with the split of society into classes, and by reason thereof, the state became a necessity. We are now fast approaching the stage in the development of production where the existence of these classes has not merely ceased to be a necessity but has become a direct impediment to production. The future disappearance of classes is just as inevitable as was their rise. With their disappearance, the state will inevitably disappear as well. Society, organizing production in a new way, on the basis of the free and equal association of producers, will relegate the whole state machine to what will then be its proper place—a museum of antiquities, with the distaff and bronze axe.[14]

Bourgeois political scientists strive, each in his own fashion, to prove that the state existed from the beginning. They assert that it stands above life and history, as it were—an eternal category of some sort. This assertion is utterly arbitrary, however. There was a period when there was no state—the time when there were no classes in society and therefore no division of it into exploiters and exploited.

Lenin says in his lecture "On the State":

Before the first form of man's exploitation by man, the first form of division

[11] *Ibid.*, p. 147.
[12] *Ibid.*
[13] Marx and Engels, *Communist Manifesto* (Russian ed., 1938), p. 52.
[14] *Ibid.*, Vol. XVI, p. 149.

into classes—slave-owners and slaves—there was the patriarchal (sometimes called the "clan") family ("clan" in the sense of "generation" or "gens" when people lived by races, by generations). Traces of these primordial times remained sufficiently well defined in the way of life of many primordial peoples. Take at random any work on primeval culture, and you always come up against more or less definite descriptions, indications, and reminiscences of how there was a time more or less like the primeval communism when there was no division of society into slave-owners and slaves. Then there was no state, no special apparatus, for the systematic application of violence and for subjecting people to it. Such apparatus is called the state.[15]

The state was always, and still is, an apparatus of constraint—of violence —with whose aid the dominant classes ensured the obedience of their "subjects." "The state is a machine to sustain the domination of one class over another." [16]

Under capitalism, as under feudalism and in ancient society, the state protects private property as the basis of exploitation and the interests of those who as exploiters hold private property. It serves to preserve and confirm the class interests of exploiters, dominant in that society. This is the part it plays, irrespective of forms of political organization.

The form of state domination may vary: capital manifests its force in one way where there is one form of domination and in another way where there is a different form. Power remains essentially in the hands of capital, however, whether a right is based on some qualification or otherwise, and whether or not the state is a democratic republic. Actually, the more democratic it is, the more crude and cynical is this domination by capitalism.[17]

Lenin pointed to the United States of America to illustrate this utterly cynical domination by capital:

Nowhere else is the power of capital—of a handful of millionaires—over all society manifested so crudely, with such open venality, as in America. Once capital exists, it dominates all society. Nor does any democratic republic, nor any right to vote, change the essence of the matter.[18]

Of course, the fact that the power of capital is dominant in modern bourgeois states in divers political forms does not exclude the necessity that the relation of the proletariat vary as does the form of bourgeois political domination.

Bourgeois-democratic republics and the regime of parliamentary representation, broader suffrage and more limited suffrage, fascist regime or bour-

[15] Lenin (Russian ed.), Vol. XXIV, p. 365.
[16] *Ibid.*, p. 369.
[17] *Ibid.*, p. 375.
[18] *Ibid.*

geois-democratic regime—these are not matters of indifference to the proletariat, which must differentiate in building its policy with reference to bourgeois states.

Under capitalism the proletariat is extremely interested in bourgeois-democratic "freedoms," and "civil rights," which ease the process of organizing its ranks and guiding its allies. "Without parliamentarianism, without the elective right, this development of the working class would be impossible." [19] The proletariat is interested in the movement of bourgeois society forward, not backward. Fascism drags this society backward from bourgeois democracy to the feudal state of lawlessness and to medievalism, perpetuating the slavery of the toiling class and dooming it to extinction and to eternal bondage.

The interests of the working class and of all toilers thus demand a decisive battle with the "totalitarian" state of fascism, and with fascism in its entirety. This does not derogate, however, from the significance of characterizing *every type* of bourgeois state—even the most "democratic"—as a machine to crush and to repress the toilers, as a bludgeon in the hands of the exploiters as against the exploited.

Marxism-Leninism rendered an enormous scientific service in defining and explaining scientifically the social nature of the state as an instrument of the socially dominant class, thus putting an end to the clerical-bourgeois notion of the state, and to the fiction that by nature it is superior to class and expresses and preserves the interests and the culture of all mankind alike.

The machinery called the state, before which people pause in superstitious reverence, giving credence to old tales to the effect that it expresses the will of all the people—this machinery the proletariat casts out with the words: "This is a bourgeois lie!" [20]

Marxism-Leninism thus draws a sharp line between the bourgeois and the proletarian viewpoint of the state—between bourgeois and proletarian theories concerning the state—and finally discloses as myth the proposition that the state is neutral and is above all classes.

Despite the idealistic and mechanistic notion concerning the state held by bourgeois and pseudo-Marxian politicians and political scientists, Marxism-Leninism showed conclusively the historical development of the state as emerging and disappearing at a certain stage of economic development.

Marxism plucked from the state the flowers of idealistic romanticism and showed its true nature as the instrument of the dominant classes, as a means of suppressing and enslaving the laboring masses—where exploiters are dominant; as the means and instrument of emancipation from suppression,

---

[19] *Ibid.*   [20] *Ibid.*, p. 377.

beggary, and enslavement by the exploiters—where the toilers are dominant.

The Marxist-Leninist doctrine of the state is not limited solely to an investigation of the nature of the origin and disappearance of the state, of its nature and characteristics. It also exhaustively elaborates and illuminates a series of other and most important questions connected with the state on the one hand, and problems and interests of the proletarian battle for emancipation on the other. Typical of such questions are those concerning the state of the period of transition from capitalism to communism, concerning the proletarian state as a state form of proletarian dictatorship, concerning state and democracy in general, concerning the Soviet state and socialist democracy in particular, concerning the forms and methods of reinforcing the proletarian state, concerning communism and the state, and, finally, concerning the state's disappearance or "withering away" in the highest phase of communism, complete and fully developed.

Marxism-Leninism gives a clear definition (the only scientific definition) of the essence of law. It teaches that legal relationships (and, consequently, law itself) are rooted in the material conditions of life, and that law is merely the will of the dominant class, elevated into a statute. It starts from the proposition that political, legal, philosophical, religious, and literary development is defined by—and is a superstructure over—economics.

Law is one of the superstructures above the totality of production relationships forming society's economic structure.

Marx wrote in a letter to Annenkov:

Take a definite stage of development of production, exchange and consumption and you get a definite social order, a definite organization of the family, of social orders, and of classes—in a word, a definite civil society. Take a definite civil society and you get definite political relationships, the official expression of civil society.[21]

Elsewhere (in *The German Ideology*) Marx says:

If, like Hobbes and others, we admit that force is the basis of law, then law, statutes, and so forth are merely a symptom, an expression of *other* relationships on which the authority of the state rests. In the material life of individuals (by no means dependent simply on their "will"), in their mode of production and the form of their community (these mutually condition each other), is to be found the real basis of the state, and this continues to be so (absolutely independently of the *"will"* of the individuals) in all states wherein division of labor and private property are still necessary. These actual relationships are in no way created by the authority of the state. On the contrary, they are themselves the force which creates state authority. Aside from the fact that the individuals domi-

[21] Marx, *Selected Works* (Russian ed., 1934), Vol. I, pp. 286–287.

nant in these relationships must constitute their force in the form of the *state*, they must give their will (conditioned by the definite relationships given) universal expression in the form of the state's will, in the form of a statute—an expression whose content is always given by the relationships of this class, as is proved particularly clearly by private (that is, civil) law and criminal law.[22]

Marx says further that a statute is "the expression of this will." But the existence of neither statute nor state depends upon this will.

In his *Critique of Hegel's Philosophy of State Law*, Marx brilliantly analyzes Hegel's understanding of law and reveals the indefensibility of Hegel's idealism.[23]

With extraordinary profundity, Marx reveals (in *The German Ideology*) the indefensibility of the idealistic notion that law and the state are generated by the "will" of the people. Here we read these notable words:

So long as productive forces are still insufficiently developed to make competition superfluous, and so long as competition would accordingly be produced thereby again and again—the hitherto subordinate classes would be wishing for the impossible if they had the "will" to abolish competition, and with it state and law.[24]

Law and legislation—and crime also—are generated by the condition of production forces and not arbitrarily.

The origin of crime—the struggle of the isolated individual against dominant relationships—like the origin of law, is not purely arbitrary. On the contrary, crime is rooted in the same conditions as is the governing power existing at the time.[25]

Marx satirizes the "visionaries" who see in law and legislation the dominance of some "independent," "general" will, and who

can perceive in crime a simple violation of law and legislation. In reality the state does not owe its existence to any dominant will, but on the contrary, growing out of the material way of life of individuals it has likewise the form of the dominant will. If that will loses its dominance, this means that not only the will, but also the material being and life of the individuals, have changed, and for this reason alone their will is changed also.[26]

State and law emerge from the material form of life of people and have only the form of the dominant will. In other words, they represent an expression of that will. Marx further unmasks the specific illusion of jurists and politicians who imagine, on the contrary, that legislation depends on

[22] Marx and Engels (Russian ed.), Vol. IV, p. 311.
[23] *Ibid.*, Vol. I, pp. 535–649.
[24] *Ibid.*, Vol. IV, p. 311.
[25] *Ibid.*, p. 312.
[26] *Ibid.*

the whim of people. Philosophers, says Marx, could conceive of a peculiar development and dominance of pure thought, by reason of which "political and civil history is ideologically dissolved in the history of the dominance of successive statutes."

In the history of the development of the courts Marx points out the close association between juridical relationships and the development of production forces and production relationships.

How close is the connection between juridical relationships and the development of these material forces arising out of the division of labor, is evident from the example of the historical development of the power of the courts and from complaints of feudal seigneurs against the development of the law (e.g. Monteille, fifteenth century). It was precisely in the transitional epoch between the dominance of the aristocracy and the dominance of the bourgeoisie, when the interests of both were clashing, when trade relationships between European races were growing and international relationships began accordingly to take on a *bourgeois* character, that the power of the courts began to increase. It attains the highest point under the dominance of the bourgeoisie, when this broadly developed division of labor becomes absolutely necessary. What those in bondage to the division of labor, the judges, or—most particularly—the professors of law, conceive therein is a matter of the utmost indifference.[27]

From the foregoing it is clear that Marx never confused juridical relationships either with the "material forces" arising out of the division of labor or with production relationships.

In *The German Ideology* he again emphasizes that law depends on, and is generated by, production relationships. He says in so many words: "Production relationships of individuals must likewise be expressed as legal and political relationships." [28]

Notwithstanding the extraordinary clarity of Marx's exposition of this question, we have several miscellaneous theories professing to be Marxism, yet representing a crude perversion thereof. Such anti-Marxist theories include that of Stuchka, who defined law as a system (or order) of social relationships and thus reduced it to economics. In his article, "Notes on the Class Theory of Law," he asserted that "Marx speaks of relationships of production" [29] or, "in juridical terms, relationships of property," [30] and claimed that the juridical and legal relationships are also production relationships. He either used an incorrect translation of the passage from the preface to Marx's *Critique of Political Economy*, however, or himself translated it incorrectly from the German. The expression of Marx which he translated "or, in juridical terms," should be translated, "or—which appears to be merely a juridical expression thereof." The difference is

[27] *Ibid.*, p. 326.
[28] *Ibid.*, p. 348.
[29] Marx, *Zur Kritik der politischen Oekonomie* (Russian ed., 1934), p. 5.
[30] *Sovetskoye Pravo* (*Soviet Law*) (1922), No. 3, p. 10.

obvious and eliminates any possibility of interpreting the famous instructions of Marx and Engels to mean that legal relationships are also, as it were, productive relationships, or a system of productive relationships. Confused in his analysis thereof, however, Stuchka tried to put the responsibility for his own confusion off upon Marx himself who had been brought up, as it were, on Roman law and on ideas of law for thirty years and was familiar with the terminology of Roman law. Stuchka went so far as to assume as an obvious matter that "now" Marx would speak another language. Complete confusion in defining the idea of law prevails also in bourgeois juridical science.

Because its representatives are not objective, and because of their class interest, bourgeois legal science is in no position to afford a correct and genuinely scientific explanation of the question. Furthermore, it is characteristic that, notwithstanding a great many utterly dissimilar and mutually exclusive theories, the bourgeois science of state law discloses with extraordinary clarity the ideological unity therein expressed. While each of the basic schools of bourgeois law refutes the other and attributes really scientific significance to itself alone, in reality all of them are unanimous in their obdurate yearning to veil the true essence of the bourgeois state as an instrument of class domination by a minority, to suppress and crush the people.

The contradictions distorting the science of bourgeois state law attest to the extraordinary weakness of the scientific propositions from which it starts, the fallibility of the fundamental sources and of the very bases of the scientific methodology of these schools.[31] Let us follow this into the ideas of individual representatives of bourgeois legal science. George Jellinek (1851–1911) was one of the most eminent of these representatives in the nineteenth century. Starting from his methodological ideas of principle, he deduces the very basis of the state, and knowledge of its purpose, from the general welfare. He defines the state as the expression of the inner unity of the nation. He speaks of the state as governed by the general will.

We have agreed that the tasks of the state are to preserve itself, to ensure the safety and development of its might, to organize and protect the law, and to cooperate with cultural interests. The guiding idea in this definition of purposes is the knowledge that *planned organization of safeguarding solidary national interests* (in so far as they require central guidance and can be satisfied by external means) can originate only in the most powerful of social factors, which is the state.[32]

[31] Even representatives of bourgeois legal science are forced to admit ·his. The "contemporary science of public law actually appears unstable in its foundations and in need of radical revision" according to Novgorodtsev in his preface to the Russian translation of Duguit, *Constitutional Law; A General Theory of the State.*

[32] George Jellinek, *A General Theory of the State* (St. Petersburg, 1908), pp. 170, 191–192. (Italics supplied by the compilers.)

The task of the state, therefore, according to Jellinek, is to be "guardian of the solidary national interests." (By "solidary national interests" he means the individual and national interests of mankind in general.) So he concludes that the state is

the dominant union of the people endowed with legal personality, satisfying (by means of planned and centralizing activity, operating with the aid of external means) the individual, national and solidary interests of mankind in general, in the direction of the progressive development of society.

This definition of state cannot withstand criticism.

Of course the bourgeois state, of which Jellinek is speaking, guarantees certain interests. But where is the proof that these are "solidary" and "national"? That the state and its activity exist specifically for the sake of satisfying these interests? Not only is this proposition not supported—it is categorically refuted—by history. It is without logical proof. Such an assertion is an abstraction and a fiction contradicting the facts of history.

Jellinek's definition of the state is extremely gratifying to the bourgeoisie, with its interest in glossing over class antagonisms and in propagandizing the view that the modern bourgeois state is to be regarded as the means of satisfying national needs and interests, an institution which preserves the rights of the people and guarantees to the people the development of their spiritual powers and the satisfaction of their cultural and material interests.

Jellinek clothes the state with legal form so as to give it the utmost authority in the eyes of the masses. The modern state, according to him, is a *Rechtsstaat*—a state bound and limited by statutes promulgated by itself. In defining the interrelation of law and state, he starts from the idea that law is a psychological phenomenon, existing only in our psyche, and calls it a certain part of the content of our consciousness. On the other hand, he proceeds to reason that law represents the totality of rules of human conduct, distinguished from rules of morality, from the imperatives of religion, morals, and the like, in that the purpose of law is to defend and to preserve human welfare and human interest. The legal norms are those issuing out of acknowledged external authority, and guaranteed, by external means at the state's disposal, to be obligatory. The entire legal order is, in his view, built on the conviction ("the average typical conviction of the people") that we are bound to follow these norms.[33] Such "conviction" of the people is construed by him as force not formed under the pressure of higher measures of a compulsive character, but influenced by another type of motivation which excludes constraint. The essential sign of the idea of law is thus not con-

[33] *Ibid.*, p. 244.

straint but *guarantee* (one of whose manifestations is constraint). Legal norms are less coercive than *guaranteed*.[34]

All this construing of "law" as a "guarantee" serves very well to suggest the idea that the people's subordination to their oppressors is voluntary, that inner morality approves this law, that the people morally excuse the violence inflicted upon them with the aid of the state and screened under the form of law.

Passing to the problem of law and the state, and seeking to answer the question whether or not the state is subordinate to the legal order, Jellinek starts from the fiction of a "general will"—making no distinction between the will of those who are dominant and that of those who are subject.

The will of the state is the human will. The question is thus reduced to the establishment of the presence of norms binding upon the human will representing the state. The existence of such norms must be considered as proved as soon as their being and operation are confirmed both by those in power and by those subject to power.[35]

Jellinek's own theory is basically merely an eccentric modernization of the old theory of so-called natural law, although he also declares his dissent from the theories of that law.

He objects to the principle that the state is not bound by law:

It follows from this theory that what is law for the subject (whether a private person, or an organ of the state) is not law for the state itself. In other words, if we look from the heights of the state at the lowlands of the law, we find only an empty place.[36]

He holds that the state is bound by law. The activity of the state is regulated by stable legal norms, binding upon state organs and upon the state itself. That even the state must be bound by legal norms is "a necessary condition of uninterrupted cultural development inasmuch as it alone also creates that social confidence without which mutual relationships between men would be possible only in the most elementary, rudimentary forms." [37]

The law is binding on the will of the state. The state creates all law, but finds in law its own self-limitation—a voluntary self-limitation, however, and therefore not prejudicial to its power, its sovereignty.

In the act of creating law—however this law arose—the state takes upon itself, with reference to its subjects, the obligation to apply and to effectuate this law.[38]

[34] *Ibid.*, p. 246. (Italics supplied by the compilers.)
[35] *Ibid.*, p. 247.
[36] *Ibid.*, p. 269.
[37] *Ibid.*, p. 270.
[38] *Ibid.*

Legal literature has already noted that this theory of the self-limitation of the state is clearly artificial and without scientific significance. It does not start from real facts but from assumptions, assumptions which have no place in actual practice. Of course, law and statutes, as one of the forms of expressing law, are binding even upon the state—or rather, upon state organs, institutions, and officials.

It is impossible to conceive the state as a definite organization of social order, social relationships, without acknowledging the obligatory character and the universality of statutes promulgated by it. To say that they are binding upon organs of state authority is not an expression of the "self-limitation" of any will. It is an expression of this will itself. The core of the question, however, does not relate to this but to the very essence of the state will. According to Jellinek, the essence—the content—of this will is "solidary" interests "of the people." But this is not so. As regards its subjects, the state is not bound in any manner whatever. It is not obligated—it rather *obligates* its subjects. State statutes are the form wherein the class dominant in a given society obligates all other classes to definite conduct—to the precise conduct advantageous and pleasing to that dominant class.

We may mention Hauriou and Duguit as representing the modern bourgeois science of public law.

Hauriou starts from the proposition that the state is possible only where the nation has become civil society, i.e., where political power has been separated from private property and has acquired the features of public power. He maintains, accordingly, that the feudal state is not a state at all in the true sense of the word; only the modern bourgeois state, supposedly representing the entire nation, is such a state. "The state is the juridical personification of a given nation, consequent upon the political, economic, and juridical centralization of the nation's elements to the end of realizing civil life." [39]

On this theory, the state is formed to the end of making civil life and civil society real and effective. The civil order or regime of "civil freedom" is *a regime of freedom and equality, established by a political organism [the state] in order that the automatism of economic society might be able to function within the state.* [40] What is this "automatism" of economic society? Apparently it is the famous laissez faire, laissez passer—"everyone who minds his own business is, almost inadvertently, minding society's business."

Hauriou's later exposition of the question reveals him as a bourgeois-reactionary, straining to prove that the highest realization of civil life is

[39] Hauriou, *The Foundations of Public Law* (Russian ed.), p. 294.
[40] *Ibid.*, p. 365.

manifested in the "middle class," as distinguished from "the rich" and "the poor."

In the spirit of narrow-minded, petty-bourgeois, sickly sentimentality, he outlines a seductive perspective of solving the "social question," by invoking the "common property" of employers and workers and at the same time preserving the "open bourgeoisie." Into the "open bourgeoisie" will pour the best of the working class (in proportion as it arrives at capitalist possession of land, money or enterprise), but there will always be reestablished therewith a class of toilers in the proper sense of the word.

The extraordinary banality of his ratiocinations regarding the essence of the state and the perspectives of its development is adequately shown by the tirade:

The Roman state became a state of patricians and plebs, and it is entirely possible that the bourgeois state will, after an indeterminate time—after revolutions, debates, and accords—become a bourgeois-workers' state. . . . If we allow the civil order (the bourgeois state) to finish its business, it . . . will (at extremely low prices) provide all the objects necessary for life and actually furnish each normal individual with a minimum of property—be it only property in the form of an official position—which will make him—practically, and not merely theoretically—a free man.[41]

Enough has been said to demonstrate the pitiful pass to which even prominent representatives of bourgeois science are brought when their purpose is to vindicate—at whatever cost—the bourgeois state, and to justify its parasitic and exploiting character.

The same may be said of Duguit (1859–1928), who, in his time, notoriously influenced even a number of Soviet jurists who portrayed his theory as if it were a socialist theory of law and sought to reconcile it with Marxism.

Duguit criticizes the juridical conception of the state, categorically objecting to the theory (of Ihering, Laband, and Jellinek) that the state is the sole source of law. He seeks an explanation of the state which would neither put it above the law nor make law dependent upon, or a derivative of, the state.

Human reason feels a strong need so to define the basis of law—understood as a social norm—that this norm be binding, not only upon individuals, but upon the state as well—however the state be understood, and irrespective of the fact that for us the modern state is above all the creator of norms (sanctioning obedience thereto by the material force at its disposal).[42]

He considers that his concept of law also solves the question of the state: the purpose of the state is to effectuate law.

[41] *Ibid.*, pp. 402, 408–409.
[42] L. Duguit, *Constitutional Law* (Moscow, 1908), p. 5.

The state is founded on force, but this force is lawful only when applied in conformity with law. We do not say (as Ihering does) that law is the policy of force. We assert that political power is force given over to serve the law.[43]

Duguit sees the principle of "social solidarity" as the basis of state and law alike, asserting that people are united by bonds of a social solidarity which embraces all members of the human race and is the source of law itself.

He sees the basis of legal form in the social obligations resting on each man, in his social role. Freedom is the right of man, but it is a right which man can realize only in proportion as he dedicates his activity to the realization of social solidarity. The very law of property is justified by the "social mission" supposedly resting upon the owner. A juridical act is a manifestation of will which conforms in purpose with social solidarity.

He rejects the idea that the state is a person, and looks at it from the point of view of factual possession of power, defining it in its most general sense as "every sort of human society wherein there is political differentiation between rulers and governed—in a word, political power." [44] He is particularly emphatic that the word "state" serves to designate specifically those societies where political differentiation has attained a certain degree of development and where, for that reason, political power presents definite and characteristic features.

He acknowledges that political power is a fact—a fact completely independent of the legality, or otherwise, of the power—and that this fact is a product of social evolution. He expressly declines to furnish philosophical justification of political power or to study all the details in the evolution of society in this direction. He confines himself to the task of merely showing the chief stage, and defining the most active factors, in the formation of society.

He defines the most important of these factors in a singularly inept manner. Some individuals, more powerful than others, make their will binding on the latter. They thus acquire definite political power with reference to those others. This political power, being factual, seeks no justification in the law. From the moment the conception of law is created in society, the idea emerges that the orders of this power are legitimate only in so far as they are in accord with the law; and that the application—by this political power—of material force is likewise legitimate only in so far as its purpose is to guarantee the sanction of the law.

Thus Duguit solves the question of the purpose of the state or of political power. This purpose is the realization of law. All the state does is done in

[43] *Ibid.*, p. 56.
[44] *Ibid.*, p. 25.

the interest of guaranteeing the law. The acts of the state must themselves be classified according to the action they exert in the world of the law—as an expression of the legislative, the judicial, or the administrative function of the state. At the same time, Duguit sees the state as possessing public power in the sense of a subjective right—the right to promulgate orders and forcibly to compel obedience to them—and also as a *Rechtsstaat*, as bound by law, as resting on a regime of legitimacy. The state is bound by statute, its legislative power is bound by objective law which is higher than the state and precedent thereto, or, more accurately, representative thereof.

The explanation of why the state is thus bound by the law is based neither on natural rights of individuals nor on the self-limitation of the state (Jellinek), but on the idea of social solidarity,[45] which is supposed to be the one foundation and the sole content of law and of legislation.

It is not difficult to show that this theory is indefensible. One need only point out that the very idea at the foundation of Duguit's entire conception of the state—"the more powerful individuals"—is utterly indefinite and devoid of scientific content. He was obviously in no position to explain the source of this "greater power" of some in relation to others. Unsuccessfully seeking to discover such source in the religious, economic, moral, or property advantages enjoyed by some in relation to others, he reveals his helplessness still more, being driven to confine himself to such lamentations as this: "The rulers always were, and are, and will be, those who are in fact the most powerful." [46] This explains nothing, for it does not explain the fundamental question—why some, rather than others, possess power.

His assertion that the aim of political power is the realization of law is completely arbitrary and devoid of historical content. His basic postulate—"social solidarity"—is itself artificial and metaphysical. But he begins from precisely this principle, considering that "solidarity is the life element of society of every sort." [47]

This "social solidarity" takes us back once again to the "general will" long cited by bourgeois philosophers and jurists in their efforts to conceal and gloss over the class and exploiting character of the bourgeois state. They strive to prove "solidarity" between bourgeoisie and proletariat—actually rather to subordinate the interests of the proletariat to the interests of the bourgeoisie.

The best possible refutation of these fables of "social solidarity" is the

[45] Conventional translations of Duguit into English designate the essence of his theory by the term "social contract." The Russian text, however, employs the term "social solidarity."—TR.

[46] L. Duguit, *Constitutional Law* (Moscow, 1908), p. 49.

[47] "To say that the state must guarantee its existence is to say that it must cooperate with social solidarity—and consequently with law, which is generated by that solidarity." *Ibid.*, p. 57.

annals of the state-political life of any capitalistic country taken at random. Fair illustrations refuting them may be found in an analysis of bourgeois statutes. Characterizing English legislation, Engels said:

Manifestly all legislation is directed to the protection of those who have as against those who have not. Statutes are necessary only because there are have-nots. . . . Hostility to the proletariat so regularly forms the basis of a statute that judges very readily acquire this sense—especially the inferior judges, who belong to bourgeois society themselves, and are the judges with whom the proletariat comes chiefly into contact.

When a rich man is summoned—or rather invited—into court, the judge expresses regret that the rich man had to inconvenience himself and tries in every way to turn the matter to the rich man's advantage; and if he must, despite everything, condemn him, he again expresses his infinite regret, and so on. But if some one of the poor has to stand before that judge, he nearly always has to spend the preceding night in jail with a mass of others like himself; he is looked upon as guilty from the very beginning. He is shouted at, and all his efforts to justify himself are met by a contemptuous, "Oh! we know these excuses." . . . On the one hand these Dogberries [inferior judges] interpret the laws only in the strictest sense therein contained. On the other, they are themselves bourgeois, and see the chief foundation of every kind of true order in the interests of that class above all else. And the police are the same as these judges. No matter what the bourgeois has done, the police are always civil to him and keep strictly to the statutes. To the proletariat they behave coarsely and cruelly. Poverty itself casts suspicion of every sort of crime upon the proletariat, at the same time depriving it of lawful means of defense against arbitrary authorities. Consequently the statute does not defend the proletariat—the police, without the slightest hesitation, burst into a proletarian's house, arrest him and deal with him at will.[48]

Such are "equality" and social solidarity in England—one of the most "democratic" of the bourgeois countries. At the time of the 1926 coal strike in this same England, the famous Habeas Corpus Act was temporarily shelved so as not to hamper the police in dealing with the strikers in their own way. A quantity of similar examples could be cited from the practice of any of the capitalist countries. All this refutes, with sufficient eloquence, the professorial babbling of the law as the expression of "social solidarity" and of the state as the savior of this sacred altar of universal well-being.

The idea of "social solidarity," which is fundamental to Duguit's entire juridical conception of the state, contradicts the fact of the class division of society, and of the class struggle which destroys that solidarity. Duguit does violence to facts and falsifies history. He declares war on the German school of juridical formalism, only that he may set off against it juridical normativism. He takes a certain objective norm, standing above positive law, and

[48] Marx and Engels (Russian ed.), Vol. III, pp. 558–559.

binding upon both subjects and rulers (the state) alike, as the key to the
solution of all questions of the modern building of state law. He operates
with ideas and formulae which lead to error as to their actual content. Objecting to individualism and defending social solidarity, he describes the
juridical norm as itself a means to compel the force at the disposal of the
rulers to react to the service of social solidarity—he portrays the state as force
put to the service of law.

This latter circumstance led the social reformists to see Duguit as representative of the new "social"—and all but "socialist"—trend, whereas in his
teaching he asserts the principles of bourgeois law—completely defends the
interests of capitalism.

Gumplowicz (1839–1909) claimed a still more socialist character for
his doctrine. He warred against juridical formalism more decisively than did
Duguit and flirted violently with "socialist" phraseology, although he did
not in fact advance a single step over his bourgeois predecessors and contemporaries in solving the problems of state law.

He opposed the prevailing individualist theories of such political scientists as Laband, Gierke, and also the theory of law and state of which we
spoke above. He sharply criticized the bourgeois science of state law as ten-
dentious, concerned only to justify a given state order in conformity with
the individual viewpoints of the authors and without taking the trouble to
know its actual nature. The extent of the material to be studied in no way
defined the difficulty of the scientific problem in this field, according to
Gumplowicz. On the contrary,

the difficulty of its task lies in the deceptiveness of this material. Nowhere, for
some reason or other, has there been so much concealed and obscured as in state
affairs. Nowhere is so much done for appearance as in public and in international
law. Nowhere has there been so much lying, so much said and written with
frank intent to deceive, as in this field. Nowhere is so much done on behalf of
convention. Nowhere are so many deliberate comedies played out, as here.[49]

All explanations of the essence of the state given by the bourgeois science
of law—from Welker, Robert von Mohl, Ahrens, Bluntschli, and Gerber to
Hegel and Kant—are completely unsatisfactory to Gumplowicz. He defines
correlation between state and law in these words: "Law is conceivable only
in a state. It exists and falls with the state." [50]

He asserts further that the state did not arise on the basis of law,
that law is not its cradle. Nor did it emerge by peaceful development out of
the idea of law or in any other peaceful manner. The state arose through
violence, which thus becomes the midwife of this new social phenomenon,

[49] Gumplowicz, General Theory of the State (Russian ed.), p. 16.
[50] Ibid., p. 28.

and not out of the family nor by way of the family's development. "No, the state emerges only from various human groups, from various tribes, and consists of them alone. The victors formed the ruling class—the vanquished and the enslaved, the class of workers and servants." [51] He finds in tribes the fundamental bases—the actual cornerstones—of the state. The state was created from tribes. They and they alone preceded the state. With the foundation of the state is created a bond between such tribes as join the state life. These state unions turn the tribes into a nation. . . . The chief sign of a nation is a single state authority, under the principle whereof the nation stands and to which it is subordinated.

The state will—not to be confused with national will—also corresponds to this state power. This state will, according to Gumplowicz and to the satisfaction of the "racists," is the will of the predominant tribes with sufficient means and enough force at its disposal to make itself in reality the dominant will. In the process of state development, he continues, tribes turn into castes or classes and devote themselves to certain occupations, which are handed down by inheritance. These classes are welded together by the force of the state—an organization of domination.

Consequently, domination—the government—takes this multiplicity in its grasp and forms a unity. The relationship of the elements dominant in the state toward those who are subject is expressed in the form of state organization. This form changes precisely as that relationship of domination changes and balances.[52]

Gumplowicz criticizes what has been done by such German jurists as Von Mohl, Stahl, and Lorenz von Stein, as well as the constitutional monarchy developed by Bluntschli—contrasting with it his own "modern *Kulturstaat.*" This *Kulturstaat*, incidentally, is notable, in his opinion, as resting on culture and contributing to the further development of culture.

The modern *Kulturstaat* is above all a state; and, as such, it is (like all states) always and everywhere an organization of domination, destined to support a certain legal order. Many years of development have resulted in remarkable mitigation of the forms of this domination. It now emerges in less severe shape. Old forms of slavery and servile dependency have disappeared, and "free" forms have appeared in their place. Their most important condition is that coercive domination is here realized on the basis of law, and not arbitrarily.[53]

There is, of course, no difference between the so-called *Kulturstaat*, so treated, and the so-called *Rechtsstaat*: law and statute operate in each alike as the supposed "court of last resort" of all social and state relationships. Gumplowicz sees the essential sign of this *Kulturstaat* in the fact that

[51] *Ibid.*, pp. 120–121.
[52] *Ibid.*, p. 209.
[53] *Ibid.*, p. 248.

state activity is itself nothing more than the exaction of taxes and the conduct of wars (in the interests of the ruling dynasty), and that this activity supposedly aims at "promoting the national welfare in every way and thereafter affords active support to the aspiration to all higher, ideal, human purposes." [54]

Gumplowicz depicts state officials themselves as bearers of culture—as warriors for culture and progress—acting in the name, and in the spirit, of the law. With their cooperation legislation likewise works toward culture, ceaselessly and ever more strenuously, wherefore, he says, the field of law becomes ever wider and richer in the modern *Kulturstaat* and public law develops to dimensions literally unprecedented. The "cultured" character of this modern state finds expression in the attraction of the middle and the working classes, to participate—side by side with the privileged class of nobles—in social and state affairs. Freedom of speech guarantees the influence of the educated classes upon social opinion, upon the election of national representatives, and thus upon the participation of the democratic strata of the population in legislation and in all state government. The *Kulturstaat* is concerned with the population, with the national economy, with the "ideal side of national life," with the sciences and the arts—in a word, contributes to the successful solution of all problems "common to humanity in general"—problems connected with neither more nor less than "the social forms of the future." Such is Gumplowicz's portrayal of this famous "modern *Kulturstaat*." His teaching as to this *Kulturstaat* was, in its turn, caught up by social reformism and—in a particularly monstrous form—by fascism.

In reality there never was—and there can never be—any such *Kulturstaat* in the history of exploiter-societies. Not a single one of the qualities so sentimentally described by Gumplowicz was, or could be, possessed by the modern bourgeois state—qualities of this sort are in direct and sharp contradiction to the true "class" and "exploiter" nature of that state.

The best refutation of the juridical and cultural illusions of Gumplowicz and his reformist followers is to consider any of the modern "bourgeois" states. At each step they afford an infinite number of examples of an inhuman, bestial relationship to the exploited masses of the people, of complete and utter unconcern for their needs and interests, of total aversion from dealing with the problems of mankind in general—those problems which have never appeared on the agenda of any bourgeois (and, in general, exploiting) state. This is sharply manifest in the activity of fascist states, which have in fact reached a stage of plain cannibalism.

The modern bourgeois state is an imperialist state, which, every day

[54] *Ibid.*, p. 248.

and every hour, sacrifices culture and the interests of cultural construction to its rapacious policy of wars and aggressions, fire and the sword. How can one possibly speak of the culture of the "modern" bourgeois state unless he chooses to close his eyes to the grievous barbarism created by it in every corner of the earth where the power of capital and of exploitation holds sway?

Gumplowicz was in no position to understand the actual nature of the state, the sources of its origin, the laws of its development. Even criticizing the theories of a formal-juridical trend, and attempting to contrast with it a new "scientific" teaching in the field of public law, he was utterly helpless in solving the fundamental problems of the science of public law. One of the causes of this impotence is his failure to understand the connection of state and law, on the one hand, with the class organization of society on the other; his failure to understand the organic connection between law, state, and politics; his failure to understand that the activity of law and the activity of the state cannot be understood and correctly appraised in isolation from politics—which is the expression, and the struggle for existence, of the class interests prevailing in a given society.

His understanding of the actual problems of scientific investigation is perverted and utterly incorrect. He makes it a necessary condition

of truly scientific and impartial investigation of political science to keep as far as possible from politics of every sort. . . . The political scientist must know how to draw the line between his science and politics. . . . It is for him to investigate the laws of political development in isolation from party life. Let . . . politicians and publicists quarrel among themselves as to *what conduct is proper*—study of the state is not occupied with such questions.

The attempts to explain the state from the viewpoint of juridical relationship are of significant interest. The chief representatives of this trend are the Germans: Loening and Affolter, and the (prerevolutionary) Russians: Korkunov, Lazarevsky, and others.

Criticizing the "will" theory of the state, Korkunov concludes that it begins with the explanation of the state from the fiction of a juristic person, whereas in reality "state domination is neither a fiction, nor a methodological mode, but the totality of real phenomena. . . ." Hence Korkunov considers that the scientific explanation of the idea of state power must relate to the establishment of domination as a particular group of the real phenomena of social life, rather than of a fiction of juridical construction. He correctly notes that all the phenomena of state life cannot possibly be reduced to the manifestation of any single will. He deems the very idea of a "single will" artificial—a juridical fiction. This is true, if we have in mind the will of all society. Korkunov—and others holding this theory—

believe that the idea of power does not coincide with the idea of will. Domination presupposes no dominant will. "Domination requires only the consciousness of dependence, not the reality thereof. If this is so, power is force conditioned by the subject's consciousness of dependence." [55] Thus reducing the whole matter to the "subject's" consciousness, this theory avoids answering the basic question: where and wherein must we see the forces of state power operating imperatively upon the consciousness of "subject" people? Unity of language, of customs, of culture (of which Korkunov speaks as though they were sources of the consciousness and of the bond of people with the state), ties of kinship, patriotism—these explain nothing here, since each of them requires to be itself explained.

"The state is a social union of free people with a peaceful order established by constraint by turning over the exclusive right of constraint to organs of the state alone." [56] The basic element of the state is, in his definition, independent coercive domination. "State power is force, conditioned by consciousness of dependence upon the state as a social union wherein peaceful order is established by constraint." [57]

Admitting that coercive state activity is the fundamental sign of state community, Korkunov emphasizes that another most important sign of state domination is domination over free people only.

It is pertinent to note that this is an obvious excuse for depriving of civil and political rights all who, by reason of the domination of exploiters, do not enjoy individual freedom. Korkunov frankly declares:

He who is not free, but subject to the private power of another, is thereby excluded from participation in state life. Only the free participate immediately in state community—only those for whom state power is not overshadowed by the power of private persons over them.[58]

Basic to Korkunov's theory of state is his definition of power, not as "will," but as force conditioned by consciousness of dependence upon the state. He holds that the state's unity is based on the unity, not of its (imaginary) will, but of incitement to subordination to state domination. But he further reasons that such unity is no longer unity of personality but unity of relationship—hence the definition of the state as a single juridical relationship. Examining the state from this point of view, Korkunov proves that the interests making up its content are limited by the adaptation of the object to joint enjoyment by separate individuals.

This proposition of Korkunov amplifies the other proposition that state

[55] H. M. Korkunov, *Russian Public Law* (St. Petersburg, 1908), p. 10.
[56] *Ibid.*, p. 27.
[57] *Ibid.*, p. 37.
[58] *Ibid.*, p. 38.

power, in order to remain such, must be an object of common enjoyment by all those who constitute the state. "If the state itself is a juridical relationship, *its subjects are all those who participate in the state community,* from the monarch down to the lowest member." [59]

Korkunov "does not see" the difference in the position occupied in the state by the monarch and that occupied by the "lowest subject." Nor does he see the class nature of the state, which guarantees domination over their subjects to various monarchs and to the social forces supporting them. His formula is a typical abstract juridical formula. It conceals the true class character of the state wherein the actual subject, who bears state power, is not "all those who participate in the state community" but only certain social classes which make use of the machinery of state for their own class interests.

Korkunov himself sees the artificiality of his thesis, and is in no position to deny that, even in bourgeois-democratic states, the extent of the rights of those participating in this state community varies so widely as to afford no basis for maintaining that any broad democratic group of the population participates therein with equal rights. Accordingly, he is compelled, with reference to certain separate groups of the population (of the degree of whose rights he is speaking), to reduce rights to obligations—which, of course, destroys the basis of his entire theoretic structure.

To eliminate the absurdities inherent in this construction, he has to resort to a new juridical construction—"orders in the interest of another," so-called. This he understands as the actualization of obligations resting upon organs of state power, whereas he construes the state domination itself not as unilateral domination—not as issuing from opposition of rulers and subjects—but as starting from the distribution of domination among all who participate in the state community. To be sure, he himself admits that some people attain in addition a predominance of power and others an obligation to obey; but he holds that this does not exclude the possibility of speaking of the state as a juridical relationship and of the inhabitants as the subject thereof. The rights comprising the content of the juridical relationship of state domination he reduces to the right to influence the realization of coercive power to this or that extent.

Thus from the legal point of view the state seems a juridical relationship of independent, compulsive domination, whose subject is the entire population of states, whose object is the compulsive power itself, and whose content is made up of rights to participate in domination and obligations to obey.[60]

Asserting that the state is "a real juridical relationship between ruler

[59] *Ibid.,* pp. 45–46.
[60] *Ibid.,* p. 48.

and subject," Korkunov and other advocates of this theory see this as a customary legal relationship resting on the principle that each side has equal rights—that the rights and obligations appertaining to each side are of equal range. This theory thus perverts the essence of relationships (which actually have place in the state) between rulers and subjects as relationships under which the dominant are not juridically—and are still less factually— equal with those whom they dominate. This alone is sufficient to refute completely the theory of the state as a juridical relationship and to demonstrate that it is a theory completely devoid of all scientific foundation and significance.

Even in its own time (the 1890's) Korkunov's theory, which regarded the state as a juridical relationship, provoked in legal literature a whole series of very substantial objections.[61] Korkunov characterized it as a theory of subjective realism, deducing the cause of subjection to state domination, neither from the individual will of the subjects nor from any metaphysical will having power over people, but from their own subjective (albeit "perfectly real") consciousness of their dependence upon the state.

To show the utter indefensibility of construing the state as a juridical relationship is a simple matter. It is enough to point out that, in reducing the cause of subjection to the subjects' consciousness of their dependence upon the state, Korkunov did not explain how this consciousness is defined and has therefore defined one unknown by another unknown. If the state were really founded upon the consciousness of individual people of their dependence upon the state, state unity would be utterly impossible. Consciousness is extraordinarily individual and diverse. It is defined by people's social position—by the place they occupy in production relationships, by their class position. Therefore consciousness (ideology) has of necessity a profoundly class character and so differs sharply in one class from the consciousness (the ideology) of another class. The theory of the state as a juridical relationship (it is still differently formulated as "community of domination") is vitiated by inner contradictions, insoluble if we remain within the field of so-called subjective realism. Critics of the theory point out, not without cause, that in the last resort it is a repetition, with certain modifications, of Montesquieu's theory of the separation of powers.

In the last resort the theory of the state as a legal relationship, beginning from the thesis that the entire population actualizes state domination, clearly contradicts historical facts. It has not the slightest confirmation in the slave-owning state, the feudal state or the capitalist state; in each of them the state power is actualized, not by the population, but only by an

[61] Profs. M. A. Dyakonov, A. S. Alexeyev, L. Z. Slonimsky, M. B. Gorenberg, V. V. Ivanovsky, and others.

insignificant minority which has concentrated in its hands economic domination over the majority, over the people.

The fundamental defect in the reasoning of Korkunov and other representatives of the "juridical relationship" school is the same as that of bourgeois scholars in general; they strive to deduce the idea of state and law out of themselves, to solve this problem with the aid of divers juridical constructions, of formal and abstract juridical thinking, or the formal structures of juridical logic. Meanwhile, the actual nature of state and law may be understood and defined from an analysis, not of juridical relationships *per se,* but of the relationships of social production, of which juridical relationships are only an expression. Attempts to cope with this problem—while keeping strictly within the sphere of juridical logic—are doomed to complete failure. Contemporary bourgeois science, however, is in no condition to emerge from the vicious circle of juridical scholasticism. Over it still hangs the weight of the prejudices of the trend of juridical formalism so characteristic of bourgeois jurisprudence in its entirety—irrespective of the differences between separate juridical schools, rivalling each other in subtlety and casuistry of juridical analysis.

Recent bourgeois juridical theorists modernize the ideas of Kant (1724–1804), who also erected his theory of law on the idea of the supremacy of human reason. According to him, the guiding principle of human activity is the demand of pure reason. The moral law or the categorical imperative is raised above all else. It prevails likewise in the field of law. Law itself is morality contemplated from the external side. Hence the fundamental requirement of legal rules: to act in conformity with the demand of the moral law, so that individual freedom be in consonance with the freedom of all other persons. The province of law is the province of external human relations. Therein operates private law (the law of tangible property, the law of persons, the law of marriage, and so forth) coercive in character, and defended in its totality by the common will which Kant defines as the state. But law of every sort has, according to Kant, the task of guaranteeing the actualization of law in general, and of the idea of justice.

The error of this reasoning is manifest: there never was, and there cannot be, any "idea" either of justice or of a "general" law endowed with a content independent of class. Hence to define law as the expression of any universal "idea," or of any abstract legal principle characteristic of law of every sort—law "in general"—is possible only if one is distracted from real social relationships, historically formed. Kant's "idea" of justice and "general law" or "law in general" is just as elusive as his *Ding an sich.*[62]

It is not difficult to perceive that Kant's basic legal ideas coincide with

[62] Lenin, *Materialism and Empirio-Criticism,* Vol. XIII, p. 82 *ff.*

those of Rousseau and the encyclopaedists, who started from the same abstract propositions as Kant—in particular, from the idea of the general will of the people. To Kant, law is the external expression of morality— merely a peculiar way of expressing morality.

A most important trend of bourgeois legal science formed under the immediate influence of Kant was *normativism*, which most sharply expressed Kant's fundamental idea, the separation of the juridical form from its social content. The most eminent representatives of normativism are Krabbe and Hans Kelsen.

The essence of normativism is in the complete dissociation of the juridical norm from social content—in asserting the supremacy of the juridical norm. Krabbe starts by admitting that "law is self-sufficient," and that "for law the principle of autonomy, and not of heteronomy, is operative." [63]

Consequently, the true and supreme criterion of law is found in law as such, not in phenomena lying outside it (economics, production relationships). Norms established by legislation are legal norms because the legal order acknowledges the legislator as an organ of law. The coercive force of this legal order is due to the conformity of its norms with the people's legal convictions. Legal norms are thus portrayed as expressing the legal convictions of the people and as such they are the supreme regulator of social and state life.

In clarification of the meaning of objective law Kelsen finds and construes the proper regularity of law. The state itself, from his point of view, is "the unity of the internal sense of legal propositions"—merely the personification of objective legal order, and properly to be understood "as a norm or order," as an idea identical with law or legal order. From the juridical point of view state and law are one and the same. Legal norms are absolute as ethical principles. Kelsen makes no distinction whatever between public and private law. He identifies the state with the legal order. He directly asserts that

the state is a legal order, but not every sort of legal order can be called a state. The legal order can be called a state only in case it establishes certain organs functioning on the basis of division of labor to settle and to execute the rules whereby it is formed. The legal order is called the state when it has attained a certain degree of centralization. The theory of three sorts of state power, or state functions, has as its object different stages of creating state order; state organs are understood only as organs of creating and actualizing law (*Rechtserzeugung*

---

[63] *Heteronomy* signifies dependence upon an external norm; in contrast, *autonomy* signifies dependence on a rule which the actor establishes for himself, G. F. Shershenevich, *General Theory of Law* (1911), p. 301.

und Rechtsvollziehung), and the state form is nothing but methods of creating legal order, figuratively called manifestation of the will of the state.[64]

Thus, normativism does not see the material content of social relationships, does not admit of the class structure of society—the struggle of social classes—and does not acknowledge the state as an organ of domination and repression. It excludes all this as metajuridical—lying outside juridical categories and normative ideas.

Normativism shows completely and logically the vacuity of neo-Kantian methodology which struggles only to disguise—by juridical norms and legal formulae—the class antagonisms destroying bourgeois society and the capitalist order. It is precisely for this reason that normativism became one of the havens of refuge for the spirit of reaction and for the trend of bourgeois juridical thought which expressed it.

By the examples of the chief bourgeois scholars of various tendencies we have shown that the theory of the state, created and developed by bourgeois science, was helpless to answer the fundamental questions of political science; that various attempts to do so ended inevitably in utter failure, and were essentially no more than attempts to rehabilitate the exploiter state because of hypocrisy and class interest—or from ignorance of what is described as representing and preserving the general welfare and general interests, the rights and interests of the people.

We observe the same picture of bankrupt bourgeois science in the field of legal theory also. Here, too, has accumulated a pile of scholastic rubbish, perverting the idea of law, its nature, its role in social history, its historic fate.

Even the works of outstanding scholars of the bourgeois world, who have left to later generations the best models of their investigation in the field of law (the school of natural law, Hegel, and the historic school of law), were likewise unable to lead bourgeois jurisprudence out of the labyrinth of contradictions, provisos, abstractions, fictions, and schemes. Kant had every reason to say of bourgeois science: "Jurists still seek a definition of the idea of their law." Gumplowicz noted that Kant's observation is valid even now.

Even at the present time jurists are seeking a definition of law, but they will not soon find it, for they have wandered into a false path and are in dreadful error, thinking to find their way from law to state, which they see as produced by law.[65]

And bourgeois legal science, pursuing this false path and moving along

---

[64] Hans Kelsen, *Reine Rechtslehre*, pp. 116–117.
[65] Gumplowicz, *General Theory of the State* (St. Petersburg, 1910), p. 355.

it, is in truth unable to cope with problems of truly scientific investigation. Suffice it to say, that so outstanding a representative of bourgeois philosophy (and especially of the philosophy and history of law) as Auguste Comte finds a way out of this position by the forthright denial of law itself—denial of its right to exist. He asserts that "human rights," advanced by metaphysics against theocracy, played only a negative part.

The word "law" must in the same measure be eliminated from our present political language as must the word "cause" from our present philosophical diction. Of these two ideas of metaphysical theology, the former is just as immoral and archaic as the other is irrational and sophistical. . . . In the positive state, which acknowledges no divine principle, the idea of law irrevocably disappears. Each is obligated before all others, but no one has rights as such. . . . In other words, no one possesses any right other than the right always to perform his duty.[66]

To the question: "What is subjective law?" Duguit replies: "This is an idea of purely metaphysical order. . . . The eternal quarrels as to the actual nature of subjective law are the best proof of all the artificiality and instability comprised in that idea." [67]

Karner, clearly disclosing his ignorance as to the most important question of the origin of law, puts the question as to the part played by law in society thus: "How does society create its law? How does law create its society?" He found nothing more intelligent to say of legal science than to cite Kant: "A purely empirical theory of law is a head—like the wooden head in the fable of Phaedrus—which may be beautiful but is, unfortunately, devoid of brains." Karner adds: "The science of law therefore begins exactly where jurisprudence ends." [68]

Shershenevich, having analyzed various legal systems, comes to this conclusion: "There is no hope of discovering the desired trait, applicable to law of every sort, and capable of serving to distinguish law from other manifestations of society." [69] Completely without hope of discovering the material content of law, he concludes that it is necessary to pass from the material side of law to its formal side.

Bergbohm, Gierke, Maier, Gumplowicz, Jellinek, Ihering, Anton Menger, Krabbe, Duguit, Petrazhitsky, Kelsen, Karner, and others define law, each in his own way, but none of them is able to take a single step forward or beyond the pitiful idealistic conception which flutters in the clutches of abstractions—"spirit," "idea," "will," "general will," "private will," "social

[66] Auguste Comte, Système de politique positive, Vol. I, p. 361.
[67] L. Duguit, General Reorganizations of Civil Law (State Publishing House, 1919), p. 13.
[68] Karner, The Social Functions of Law (Moscow, 1923), p. 11.
[69] G. F. Shershenevich, General Theory of Law (Moscow, 1910), p. 280.

solidarity," "social function," and so forth. All the impotence of bourgeois legal thought is expressed with particular clarity in the utter inability of bourgeois legal scholars in the matter of explaining the very origin of law.

Characteristic in this regard is the doctrine of Stammler, who, as he says, set out in defining the idea of law not from *a priori* judgments and notions, but from experience. He contemplates law as one side of social life, another side of which is economics. "The legal order and the economic order are absolutely one and the same. The material for every sort of social regulation is joint human activity directed at the satisfaction of needs"; and he explains that by "joint activity" is to be understood "social economy"—"all social life." [70] He sees law itself as coercive regulation (of the social life of people) subordinated to the idea of the human community. The superficiality of his definition of law is obvious.

Von Ihering, one of the most outstanding representatives of bourgeois legal science, also acknowledged legal compulsion to be a fundamental and most important sign of law. Von Ihering set forth his basic views on this question in a treatise which is, perhaps, the most famous of all the juridical works of the nineteenth century (*Der Zweck im Recht*). He starts by admitting that the basic source of law is human interest, protected by law as a special form of constraint. "A legal proposition without legal constraint is an inner contradiction—fire which does not burn, light which does not illuminate." [71] He regards law as one of the provisos guaranteeing the vital conditions of society. He starts from the idea of the self-limitation of state authority, assuming that it is specifically in law that the state, guided by the interests of all society, puts limits on its activity.

It goes without saying that this conception is no less artificial than that of Jellinek, who started from the abstract idea of "social solidarity" as the source of legal and state life. Ihering's theory undoubtedly answered burning questions of the contemporary bourgeoisie and served to justify the bourgeois state and law, concealing their true exploiter-nature.

In the juridical literature of prerevolutionary Russia the same absolutely unscientific views prevailed as in the bourgeois theory of western Europe. It is enough to point to such outstanding jurists of old Russia as Chicherin, Gradovsky, Korkunov, and Petrazhitsky.

Instead of setting out a concrete definition of law, Korkunov obliterates the boundary between law and morality and talks of delimitation of interests as the fundamental task of law. Understanding law as the delimitation of interests, he was clearly bound to remove public law, criminal law, and civil law beyond its boundaries.

[70] R. Stammler, *Wirtschaft und Recht* (St. Petersburg, 1907), pp. 170, 208.
[71] Ihering, *Der Zweck im Recht*, Vol. I, p. 322.

Petrazhitsky considers the nature of law incognizable. Its nature, he says, drives jurists upon a false road and permits no knowledge of itself. . . . Nevertheless, he stubbornly seeks the key to cognition of the law and finds it in . . . psychology. According to him, law is a psychological experience, consciousness, emotions. "We shall understand law, in the sense of a special class of real phenomena—as those ethical experiences whose emotions have an attributive character." [72] His law is "intuitive law" and "there are as many intuitive laws as there are individuals." [73]

It would hardly be necessary to spend time on this theory if there were not connected with it, in legal history of the postrevolutionary period, an entire group of crude perversions and antiscientific acrobatics by pseudo-Marxist jurists, whose idealistic, psychological, and other "theories" and "theorists" of every kind threatened to submerge Soviet juridical literature.

In this connection it is impossible not to mention Professor Reisner. [74] In his words on law he perverts Marxism in the most blatant way, unceremoniously substituting Machism for it. Not Marx, Engels, and Lenin, but Mach, Avenarius, and Bogdanov [75] are Reisner's actual teachers, although he elaborately strives to conceal this fact, giving out his own eclectic concoction as true Marxism.

Reisner considers that his merit in the field of legal theory is to have "revised" Petrazhitsky's theory of intuitive law, "in the sense of putting it on a Marxian basis," by reason of which intuitive law "was transformed into the most genuine *class law.*"

However, this perversion of intuitive, idealistic law into "class" law of the proletariat, of which Reisner speaks, really took place only in Reisner's own imagination. In historic fact, such a "metamorphosis" as idealism resting on a Marxist foundation has never occurred without—as happened in Reisner's case—that foundation itself being completely perverted.

Because of this radically mistaken (and diametrically anti-Marxist-Leninist) view of the essence of law, Reisner could tolerate the assertion that the foundation of our legal order, with all its special characteristics and class principles, was the application by the proletariat—victorious in 1917—of "intuitive law."

For Reisner there are no real legal phenomena in the sense of phenomena serving as intermediary links with social relationships. For him, the

---

[72] Prof. L. I. Petrazhitsky, *Theory of Law and the State in Connection with the Theory of Morality* (St. Petersburg, 1909), Vol. I, p. 85.

[73] *Ibid.* (1910 ed.), Vol. II, p. 480.

[74] M. Reisner, *Law: Our Law, Foreign Law, Common Law* (State Publishing House, 1925).

[75] Cf. Lenin, *Materialism and Empirio-Criticism,* Vol. II.

source of law is not production relationships, but the psyche, sensation, emotions, and ideas. He holds that law is a function of the psyche, and understandable only out of itself and of the human psyche as its basis. We are involuntarily reminded of the words of Marx:

Society does not rest on law. That is a phantasy of jurists. On the contrary, law—in contrast to the arbitrariness of the separate individuum—must rest on society, must be an expression of society's general interests and needs, as they emerge from a given material means of production.[76]

Reisner arrives at the assertion that the highest criterion of law is justice—understood as a self-sufficient, *a priori* category (of a universal character which allows justice to be made the starting point for absolute, categorical judgments).[77] Starting from these vicious theoretical propositions (a repetition of the crudely idealistic and antiscientific "truths" of Mach, Avenarius, Bogdanov, and Freud) Reisner construes his "class law" as the law of different classes, a compounding of ideological fragments of diverse class ideas, a "parti-colored fabric, created on the basis of the legal demands and views of the most diverse social classes." [78] He flatly objects to the Marxist understanding of law as the law of the *dominant class,* showing that side by side with the law of the dominant class there exists the law of the dependent and suppressed class. To positive state law he opposes the law of these other classes.

The reactionary character of Reisner's legal theory is particularly clear from his crudely anti-Marxist-Leninist understanding of Soviet law. Completely incapable (because of the viciousness of his initial viewpoint) to explain the correlation of the law of the Soviet state with that of the proletarian dictatorship, he seeks in defining law, a "social side" which would put some distinction between law and state constraint, between law and authority. Finding no such distinction, he doubts the necessity of law where there is a "firmly realized class interest."

Why legal regulation, once we have a firmly realized class interest and proper technical means to actualize it? . . . We remain as before in complete perplexity: thus we do not know *whether or not law is necessary to us, in what degree it is necessary to us,* and *whether or not we can put up with painting over the proletarian dictatorship and the class interests, for some reason, into enigmatic shapes and forms of law.*[79]

Such reasoning can be explained only by a completely perverted idea

[76] Marx and Engels (Russian ed.), Vol. VII, p. 254.
[77] M. Reisner, *Law: Our Law, Foreign Law, Common Law* (State Publishing House), p. 244.
[78] *Ibid.,* p. 184.
[79] *Ibid.,* pp. 33–34.

of law as "enigmatic shapes and forms of law." In fact law is no "enigmatic shape" but a living reality, expressing the essence of social relationships between classes on the basis of the dominance, domination, repression, and subjection, by the dominant classes, of other classes who are subordinate to this dominance.

It is precisely their failure to understand this basic phenomenon—this basic social fact—which explains the exceedingly crude perversions of the Marxist-Leninist doctrine of law and state and, in particular, of Soviet law and the Soviet state, in Reisner, Stuchka, and a group of other pseudo-Marxists who have spared no effort to litter our juridical literature with pseudoscientific rubbish.

SEC. 3: THE STATE AND THE LAW OF THE PERIOD OF TRANSITION FROM CAPITALISM TO COMMUNISM

The question of the period of transition from capitalism to communism was posed by Marx, and further exhaustively treated by Lenin and Stalin. As Marx showed, it occupies an entire period of history. A state of a special type—the revolutionary dictatorship of the proletariat—belongs to this period.

Between the capitalist and the communist society lies a period of revolutionary transformation of the former into the latter. A period of political transition corresponds to this, the government of which can be none other than *the revolutionary dictatorship of the proletariat.*[1]

Having conquered and cast down the bourgeoisie, won political power, and established its revolutionary dictatorship, the proletariat is not limited to victories already achieved. To consolidate them, and further to develop its successes, the proletariat requires a state, organized anew, and playing a most important part in the further proletarian struggle to realize its ultimate aims. In the course of this entire transitional period the state realizes its great mission of service in the building of socialism and the transition to communism.

Progress forward—that is to say, to communism—goes through the dictatorship of the proletariat. It can go no otherwise. *To shatter the resistance* of exploiter capitalists is impossible to anyone else and in any other manner.[2]

The pseudo-Marxists have put the matter as if, with the overthrow of

[1] Marx, *Selected Works* (Russian ed., 1934), Vol. II, p. 451.
[2] Lenin (Russian ed.), Vol. XXI, p. 430.

the bourgeoisie and the seizure of political power by the proletariat, the kingdom of universal freedom had come. Engels refuted this fantastic and sickly sentimentality when he pointed out that "the proletariat still *needs* the state, needs it in the interest, not of freedom, but of crushing its adversaries" and "when it becomes possible to speak of freedom, then the state as such ceases to exist." [3]

After the proletariat has grasped power, the class struggle does not cease. It continues in new forms, and with ever greater frenzy and ferocity, for the reason that the resistance of the exploiters to the fact of socialism is more savage than before. The triumph of the proletarian revolution, and the passing of power into the hands of the proletariat, do not end the struggle for socialism; they are only its beginning.

The overthrown exploiters cannot resign themselves to their defeat, to the loss of their economic and political domination. They hurl themselves into battle and do not hesitate to use any means whatever to seek the return of the lost paradise, of lost privileges, and former influence and significance.

The Marxist-Leninist doctrine is that the

dictatorship of the proletariat is the class struggle of a victorious proletariat which has possessed itself of political power, against the bourgeoisie, vanquished but not yet annihilated, which has neither disappeared nor ceased to resist, but has intensified its resistance. [4]

Stalin always warned—and still warns—against lack of understanding or denial of the continuance of the class struggle under conditions of triumphant socialist construction. For example, summing up the results of the first five-year plan, he recalled that:

The growth of the might of the Soviet state will intensify the resistance of the last remnants of the dying classes. For the very reason that they are dying and living their last days, they will pass from one form of attack to other and fiercer forms of attack, appealing to the backward strata of the population and mobilizing them against Soviet authority. There is no mischief or slander that these have-beens would not raise against Soviet power, and around which they would not strive to mobilize the backward elements. On this basis, shattered groups of the old counterrevolutionary parties of Social Revolutionaries,[5] Mensheviks or bourgeois nationalists in the central and border regions, may revive and stir, as may splinters of counterrevolutionary, opposition elements of Trotskyists and right-wing deviationists. This, of course, is no reason for alarm. But it must ever be kept in mind, if we wish to have done with these elements quickly, and without special sacrifices. [6]

[3] Marx, *Selected Works* (Russian ed., 1934), Vol. II, p. 463.
[4] Lenin, (Russian ed.), Vol. XXIV, p. 311.
[5] Hereinafter referred to as SR's.—Tr.
[6] Stalin, *Questions of Leninism* (10th Russian ed.), p. 510.

Stalin disclosed all the danger of interpreting incorrectly the thesis of the abolition of classes, of creating a classless society and of the withering away of the state. "Theoreticians" of the Trotskyist-Bukharinist stamp consciously perverted this thesis in order to achieve a weakening of the power of the Soviet state.

The abolition of classes is attained by intensifying—not by extinguishing—the class struggle. The withering away of the state will come, and not through weakening state power, but through the maximum intensification of it, necessary to finish off the remnants of the dying classes and to organize defence against capitalistic encirclement which is as yet far from being, and will not soon be, destroyed.[7]

The dictatorship of the proletariat, as a form of proletarian political power, has nothing in common with the power in a bourgeois state (the so-called "national," "universal franchise," "nonclass" or "supraclass" power) about which the bourgeois jurists prate. It is "the power of one class—the class of proletarians—which does not and cannot share that power with other classes." [8]

The state of the transition period from capitalism to communism is one which itself effectuates the political power of the proletariat, the dictatorship of the proletariat. It is differentiated sharply and fundamentally from the bourgeois state by a series of most important characteristics.

Under capitalism, we have a state in a peculiar sense of the word, a special machinery for one class (the minority) to crush another (the majority). Of course, the success of such a business as the systematic crushing of the exploited majority by the exploiting minority postulates extreme atrocity, ferocity of suppression, and seas of blood through which humanity—the slaves, the serfs, and the hirelings—goes on its way.[9]

The state of the transition period is of completely different character. During that period, the state is still necessary to the proletariat, because the majority—which was only yesterday the exploited—must now crush the exploiter minority.

The particular apparatus, the special machine of suppression, "the state," is *still* necessary. Already, however, it is a transition state—and no longer a state in the strict sense—since the suppression of the exploiter-minority by the hired slaves who were *yesterday's* majority is a matter so easy, simple, and natural by comparison that it will cost far less blood than crushing the uprisings of slaves, serfs, and hired workers—and be far cheaper for mankind.[10]

[7] *Ibid.*, p. 509.
[8] *Ibid.*, p. 110.
[9] Lenin (Russian ed.), Vol. XXI, pp. 431–432.
[10] *Ibid.*, p. 432.

Marxism-Leninism, as distinguished from anarchism, starts by admitting the necessity of proletarian utilization of the state for its purposes of emancipation. As distinguished from social reformists' and opportunists' views of the state, it starts by acknowledging the peculiar character—the particular nature—of the state of the transition period as a special machine to crush exploiters. The state which the proletariat won by conquest and organized is not only machinery to crush the exploiters—to destroy and annihilate their resistance. The organization of violence and repression with reference to exploiters and their agents does not complete the historic tasks of the state of the proletarian dictatorship. The latter is a special form of union of proletarian and nonproletarian working classes,

a special form of class alliance between the proletariat—the vanguard of the toilers—and numerous nonproletarian strata of toilers (the petty bourgeoisie, petty proprietors, peasants, the intellectuals, and so forth) or a majority of them, an alliance against—and for the complete overthrow of—capital, and for the utter crushing of bourgeois resistance and attempts on its part at restoration, an alliance for the purpose finally of building and consolidating socialism.[11]

The proletarian state is a special form of leadership of the remaining masses of toilers by the proletariat. For precisely this reason it represents the highest form of democracy possible in a class society. This democracy is expressed first of all in the very fact of participation by the working population in state government, in the fact that officials are all elected and can all be replaced, and in the extraordinarily simple forms and methods of state government, accessible to every worker.

Further developing this thought, Lenin emphasizes that this is one of the most important points of Marxism, the very point most thoroughly forgotten and perverted by opportunists.

Why is the proletarian state "not strictly a state"? Because any state other than the proletarian state is a *special power* in the hands of the minority to repress the toiling masses, whereas the new proletarian state of the transition period is *universal power* of the popular majority of workers and peasants to crush the exploiter-minority; it is the democracy of the oppressed classes.[12]

Bourgeois democracy, while progressive as compared with medievalism in the history of social development, remains narrow, curtailed, formal, and hypocritical—"a paradise for the rich, a snare and delusion for the exploited poor." [13]

In a bourgeois democracy, capitalists employ tricks by the thousand,

[11] *Ibid.*, Vol. XXIV, p. 311.
[12] *Ibid.*, Vol. XXI, p. 398.
[13] *Ibid.*, Vol. XXIII, p. 346.

artifices, outright swindles, forgeries, and violence to discourage the masses from taking part in government; this is required by bourgeois class interests whose defense is the *raison d'être* of the bourgeois state's functioning. On this score Lenin wrote:

> Participation in the bourgeois parliament (which *never* decides serious questions in bourgeois democracy—their decision is for the stock exchange and the banks) is *fenced off* from the toiling masses by thousands of barriers, and the workers know and sense, see and feel exceedingly well that the bourgeois parliament is an *alien* institution, a bourgeois *instrument to oppress* the proletarians, an institution of a hostile class—the exploiter-minority.[14]

Conversely, the proletarian state of the transition period is the Soviets— the Soviet state, the toiling masses' very own state.

It attracts the masses to state government. It rests upon them. It gives hitherto unprecedented breadth to democracy—democracy for the enormous majority of the people. This is proved with extraordinary clarity and brilliance by the great Stalin Constitution and by the first elections to the Supreme Soviet of the USSR and to the Supreme Soviets of the Union and Autonomous Republics. These indicated the political activity of the masses, and the indestructible moral and political unity of the Soviet people.

The Soviet state is the historically integrated form of the state during the transition period from capitalism to communism. It is the mightiest and most decisive factor of socialist construction. It guaranteed to the masses of the people such development of their creative powers in all fields of social, economic, and state construction as further conditioned the triumphs of socialism in the USSR—triumphs now a part of world history.

The foregoing does not, however, constitute an exhaustive survey of the special features of the Soviet state. That state has nothing in common with bourgeois-parliamentary states, with their apparatus of officials (opposed, as a special caste, to the people); with their dead, soulless state institutions (deaf to the needs of the toilers); with their privileges; with their wealth in the hands of a negligible handful of exploiters, and their masses—millions of workers and peasants—in monstrous beggary; and with their oppressed, exploited, and enslaved toilers—who have no rights.

The Soviets are the spontaneous organization of the toiling and exploited masses themselves, *facilitating* the possibility of themselves eliminating the state and governing it in every possible way. It is precisely the vanguard of toilers and exploited, the city proletariat, which has the advantage that it is best united by big undertakings—it is entirely easy for it to elect and to follow up elections. Automatically the Soviet organization *facilitates* the unification of all the toilers and the exploited around their vanguard—the proletariat. The old bourgeois

[14] *Ibid.*, p. 349.

apparatus—officialdom, the privileges of wealth, bourgeois education, connections, and so on (factual privileges differing in proportion to the development of bourgeois democracy)—all this disappears under the Soviet organization. Freedom of the press ceases to be hypocrisy, because the printing presses and paper are taken away from the bourgeoisie. The same occurs with the better buildings, the palaces, the private dwellings, and the landowners' houses. The Soviet authority took thousands and thousands of these better buildings from the exploiters straight away, and thus made a million times more democratic the right of masses to assemble—that right of assembly without which democracy is a delusion.[15]

This is why Leninism correctly affirms that Soviet democracy and the Soviet state are a million times more democratic than the most democratic bourgeois republic.

The essential and fundamental preeminence of Soviet democracy consists in the fact that for the first time in history the nation itself truly carries state government into effect in its own interests, depriving exploiters of all their privileges and advantages. Herein is also the fundamental feature of Soviet state order (the only truly democratic order) guaranteeing the satisfaction of all demands and needs, of all the interests and requirements of the popular masses of toilers. Actual freedom of the people consists precisely in this—not in so-called "rights" and "guarantees."

Actual freedom obtains only where exploitation is abolished, where there is no crushing of some by others, where there is no unemployment and beggary, where man does not tremble for fear that tomorrow he will lose his work, his dwelling, and his bread. Only in such society is personal—and all other—freedom possible, in reality and not merely on paper.[16]

The transitional state is a form of the dominance of the proletariat. Without the state, the proletariat cannot secure its successes and its victories—cannot guarantee to itself the success of the further movement toward communism.

"Socialism is unthinkable without the dominance of the proletariat in the state."[17] The proletariat can realize the overthrow of the bourgeoisie only by its metamorphosis "into the *dominant class,* capable of crushing the inevitable and desperate resistance of the bourgeoisie and of organizing for the new type of economy *all* the toiling and exploited masses."[18]

In the *Communist Manifesto,* Marx and Engels emphasize very decisively precisely this aspect of the matter, showing that "the first step in the workers' revolution is turning the proletariat into the dominant class,"

[15] *Ibid.,* p. 350.
[16] Stalin's interview with Roy Howard, March 1, 1936 (Party Publishing House, 1936), p. 19.
[17] Lenin, *Selected Works* (Russian ed.), Vol. XXII, p. 517.
[18] *Ibid.,* Vol. XXI, p. 386.

which means expropriating from the bourgeoisie all capital, instruments and means of production, and concentrating them "in the hands of the state, that is to say, the proletariat, organized as the dominant class." [19]

The suppression of exploiters cannot be represented, however, as a mechanical act or as the sum total of mechanical acts. The proletariat suppresses exploiters with the aid and by means of a whole system of measures—measures of direct violence as regards class enemies of the proletariat, and measures of economic and ideological organization, uniting, under the guidance of the proletariat, the nonproletarian masses, and guaranteeing to the proletariat the possibility of guiding these masses in the interests of socialist construction.[20]

To guarantee final victory in the struggle for socialism the proletariat must know not only how to crush its enemies but also how to guide its allies, how to unite around itself and under its banners millions of toilers from the nonproletarian classes, how to convince them that its cause is right, how to prove to them the significance of proletarian victory for their immediate interests, how to inspire them with confidence in victory, and how to lead them into battle for the triumph of the common interest.

Socialism was built in the USSR under conditions of a fierce class struggle which put its stern mark on the entire transitional period and on all the activity of the state during that period.

The "theory" that the kulaks would "peacefully" assimilate into socialism is a provocative snare of fascist agents of Japan and Germany, who strove to prepare the defeat of the proletariat, to corrupt its consciousness, to disarm it ideologically and to deprive it of its magnetic force. The entire twenty-year history of the October Revolution illustrates in infinite profusion the cruel resistance of our enemies to the cause of socialism.

The entire history of bourgeois counterrevolution in the USSR is connected with active efforts of the international bourgeoisie to overthrow the power of the Soviets. Not a single conspiracy—of any seriousness whatever—against the Soviet authority in the USSR has occurred without the direct and most active participation of foreign capitalists and militarists.

---

[19] Marx and Engels, *Communist Manifesto* (Russian ed., 1938), p. 50.

[20] One of the most brilliant examples of uniting measures of repression and measures of economic organization is the conduct (in the villages, under the guidance of the proletariat, 1929–1931) of the liquidation of the kulaks as a class, on the basis of complete collectivization. The mass kolkhoz (collective farm) movement arose on the basis of such measures as the development of socialist industry and the equipment of the country with machines and tractors, the organization of a network of sovkhozes (state farms), and machine and tractor stations, the development of agricultural cooperation and, finally, the decisive struggle with the kulaks.

"This is the foundation on which the mass kolkhoz movement of millions of poor and middle peasants arose. It began in the second half of 1929 and opened a period of great crisis in the life of our country." Stalin, *Questions of Leninism* (10th Russian ed.), p. 373.

In 1921 Lenin warned us: "We are encircled by the bourgeoisie of the entire world which is on the watch for every moment of vacillation so as to send back its own people, to reestablish the landowners and the bourgeoisie." [21]

Stalin is tireless in reminding us of the danger of capitalist encirclement, demonstrating that "the resistance of the dying classes of our country is not an occurrence isolated from the external world but is supported by capitalist encirclement." [22]

Is this not true also of the notorious Shakhty affair,[23] which was conducted primarily by Polish, French, and German capitalists united with the wreckers in a struggle against the USSR? Did not Dvorzhanchik, the Polish millowner, the French stockholders (Sanset, Remo, and Burcz), and the German AEG, and the militarists of a series of capitalist countries supporting them all, inspire that 1928 conspiracy so as, in concert with the general staffs of foreign countries, to drench our country with blood?

Is it not the same story with the notorious Industrialist Party affair, where the white émigrés Ryabushinsky and General Lukomsky, the English explorer Colonel Lawrence, and the French General Juanville (a well known collaborator in the northern intervention in 1919 and military attaché to Kolchak) played first violin alongside Ramzin and Chernovsky?

It is well known that the Shakhty people and those of the Industrialist Party not only were occupied with wrecking and preparing diversionary acts in case of war, but were carrying on systematic espionage. This was obvious in the Industrialist Party affair. Ramzin had even organized a special commission to carry on this work of espionage under the direction of the saboteur Professor Osadchy, at that time acting chairman of the State Planning Commission. The program of the Industralist Party stimulated interest in diversionary activities in Moscow, Leningrad, Donbas, and the Urals by blowing up bridges, destroying railroads, blowing up power stations, and causing the stoppage of works and factories.

Surely the devilish work of foreign scouts in our country is further evidenced by the affair of the English engineers, Thornton and MacDonald, and other agents of the "Intelligence Service," unmasked in 1933, who organized wreckings and diversions in various power stations—people who had prepared the support points for an impending intervention! Evidence of the same type of activity is finally afforded by the last court proceedings

[21] Lenin (Russian ed.), Vol. XXVI, p. 248.
[22] Stalin, *Questions of Leninism* (10th Russian ed.), p. 386.
[23] In 1928 the USSR Supreme Court had before it a case involving a number of engineering and technical workers in the coal-mining industry, charged with a plot to wreck that industry. These workers "belonging to the apex of the bourgeois intellectuals, were linked with the former owners and with foreign reconnaissance."

of 1936–1937 which unmasked monstrous crimes of spying, terrorist bands of followers of Trotsky and Zinovyev and other anti-Soviet elements, who put themselves at the service of foreign police organizations and were transformed into their spies and agents for diversion and terrorism.

To exactly the same effect is the utterly convincing evidence of the nightmarish crimes of these bandit gangs who were annihilated by the sentences of the Soviet court.

The proceedings against Zinovyev and Kamenev, against Pyatakov and Radek, and against a group of military traitors (Tukhachevsky, Yakir, and others) prove that our enemies do not plan quietly "to creep into socialism," as Bukharin, Rykov, and others associated with them proclaimed in order to conceal their foul and treacherous work, but they grab the most extreme, cruel, and filthy weapons for carrying on the struggle.

This was shown fully by the proceedings whose chief "heroes" were those who organized and inspired the anti-Soviet "Right-Trotsky bloc" —Bukharin, Rykov, Yagoda, and other traitors who were unmasked as inveterate enemies of the socialism of our country, of our people.

Capitalist encirclement is a real fact, whose significance for the entire cause of socialist construction in the USSR must not be in the slightest degree underestimated. Stalin set forth the essence of this question at the Sixteenth Party Congress (1930) when he showed that "capitalistic encirclement is not a mere 'geographical notion." [24]

Analyzing the shortcomings of Party work and pointing out measures for liquidating Trotskyists and other double dealers, Stalin said in 1937:

We are in the habit of chattering about capitalist encirclement but are unwilling to consider with care what kind of a thing it is. It is no empty phrase— it is an extremely real and unpleasant phenomenon. It means that there is one country—the Soviet Union—which has established within itself a socialist order, and that there are, beside, many countries—bourgeois countries—which continue to carry on the capitalist form of life and encircle the Soviet Union, awaiting an opportunity to fall upon it and to shatter it—or at least to undermine its power and weaken it. [25]

Some people do not understand, or fail to remember, this, intoxicated and captivated by all sorts of demonstrations, stupefied by the atmosphere of conceit and self-satisfaction zealously "diffused" by the enemies of the people. Stalin says of such people that they

forget certain essential facts of paramount significance for the fate of our country; they fail to observe such unpleasant facts as capitalist encirclement, new forms

---

[24] Stalin, *Questions of Leninism* (10th Russian ed.), p. 386.
[25] Stalin, *Concerning Shortcomings of Party Work and Measures for Liquidating Trotskyites and Other Double-Dealers* (Party Publishing House) 1937, p. 8.

of wrecking, and the dangers connected with our successes and the like. Capitalist encirclement? Absurd! What meaning can any capitalist encirclement have if we fulfill—and more than fulfill—our economic plans? New forms of wrecking? struggle with Trotskyism? All nonsense! What significance can all these trivialities have when we fulfill—and more than fulfill—our economic plans? The party rules, the elective character of party organs, the responsibility of party leaders to the party masses? Is all this necessary? Is it worthwhile to fuss with these trifles if our economy is growing and the material position of workers and peasants is constantly better and better? All this is nonsense! We are more than fulfilling our plans. Our party is not so bad. The Central Party Committee is likewise not so bad— What further stimulus do we need? Strange people sit there in Moscow on the Central Committee of the Party. They think up questions, they talk about some kind of wrecking, they do not sleep themselves and do not let others sleep.[26]. . . The Marxist-Leninist doctrine is that the state of the proletarian dictatorship can smash the resistance of exploiters and render harmless the influence of capitalist encirclement only if it is democratic and dictatorial in a new fashion.[27]

The state of the transitional period, the Soviet state, the socialist state, guarantees—on this basis of the joining of the proletarian dictatorship and proletarian democracy—a solution of all the historic problems connected with the proletarian battle for freedom.

The proletariat requires the state, state apparatus, a definite state order —the socialist legal order, which signifies the stability of socialist social relationships and of socialist discipline, respect for the rules of socialist life in common, respect and preservation inviolate of social, socialist property—the bases of the entire Soviet order, the observance of all Soviet laws. Special forms of the class struggle correspond to the epoch of the proletarian dictatorship, and the state during this period is confronted with special problems related to those forms and responsive to the demands of this period.

The sharpness of the class hatred of the exploiters and their remnants within the USSR toward the cause of socialism, the hostility and irreconcilable malice toward the USSR on the part of the capitalist encirclement, and particularly and especially on the part of the fascist countries which unceasingly prepare for military invasion of the USSR and form within it their spying-bandit bands of wreckers, diversionists, and terrorists out of the remains of the exploiter elements and the riffraff of Trotskyists and Bukharinists, SR's, Mensheviks and bourgeois nationalists—all this demands the intensification of the proletarian dictatorship. "A strong and mighty dictatorship of the proletariat is what we must have in order to scatter completely the last remnants of the dying classes and to smash their thievish machinations" is the teaching of Stalin, revealing all the harm to the cause

[26] *Ibid.*, pp. 17–18.
[27] Lenin (Russian ed.), Vol. XXI, p. 393.

of socialism in underestimating the problem of administration in the Soviet state, as the historic form of the proletarian state.[28]

The dictatorship of the proletariat solves the problems of the proletarian revolution both with the aid of law and with the assistance of measures strictly defined by statute, through administrative and judicial organs. The dictatorship of the proletariat is authority unlimited by any statutes whatever. But the dictatorship of the proletariat, creating its own laws, makes use of them, demands that they be observed, and punishes breach of them. Dictatorship of the proletariat does not signify anarchy and disorder but, on the contrary, strict order and firm authority which operates upon strict principles, set out in the fundamental law of the proletarian state—the Soviet Constitution.

The Soviet state faces the task of reinforcing the power of the proletarian dictatorship in all its incisiveness and strength. This task is interwoven with that of the further developing and reinforcing of proletarian, Soviet democracy.

The Soviet order is the maximum of democracy for workers and peasants. At the same time it signifies a break with *bourgeois* democracy and the rise of a *new type* of democracy in world history, that is to say, proletarian democracy or the dictatorship of the proletariat.[29]

The greatest expression of the development of proletarian democracy—and at the same time of the organic synthesis of the principles thereof and of the proletarian dictatorship—is the Stalin Constitution, which records in the form of law the brilliant and epoch-making triumphs of socialism. It is at the same time the greatest monument of Soviet socialist law, the greatest historical act, in which is expressed the will of the Soviet people, the will of the working classes. The Stalin Constitution signifies the ultimate strengthening of the Soviet order, of the proletarian dictatorship, which rests on a still more mighty socialist basis than had ever existed in the previous twenty years of the history of our socialist revolution. It reveals the ultimate essence of socialist democracy, which is the direct consequence of the triumph of the proletarian dictatorship and the integration of the development of the Soviet socialist state order.

The Soviet state represents the expression of the highest possible form of democracy. It represents the gigantic force of organization, education, training, and cultural growth of the national masses, the form "of *guiding* the huge mass of the population, the peasantry, the petty bourgeoisie, and the semiproletarians in setting up socialist economy." [30]

[28] Stalin, *Questions of Leninism* (10th Russian ed.), p. 509.
[29] Lenin, Vol. XXVII, p. 26.
[30] *Ibid.*, Vol. XXI, p. 386.

The transition to communism (to the highest phase of communism) can be accomplished only on the basis of gigantic development of productive forces. The Soviet state completely assures this development. The expropriation of the capitalists, taken by itself, has already vastly accelerated the development of the productive forces of human society. This development of productive forces attains ever increasing successes in proportion to the reinforcement and further development of the Soviet system, which rests on socialist property and leads to the complete annihilation of classes and the class division of society. Socialist property obliterates the boundaries between intellectual labor and physical labor, between city and country. At the same time, a new socialist attitude toward labor, society, and the fatherland is ever increasing. New cadres, new people grow up and are educated. The *new society* grows strong and develops. The Soviet state protects and assists this growth, purifying society of any capitalism that survives in the economy and the consciousness of the people. Here the role of the state as an organ of constraint and of education for discipline and self-discipline, for remaking human consciousness, for reinforcement and respect for the rules of socialist society, of respect for social and civil duty, emerges particularly sharply. Thus, gigantic problems confront the state of the transition period from capitalism to communism, problems whose solution guarantees to the proletariat the final triumph of socialism, in which the proletariat is vitally concerned. The solution of these problems is possible only upon condition of having a mighty and invincible state. The significance, for world history, of the teaching of Marx-Engels-Lenin-Stalin is that on that basis is fostered the revolutionary energy and socialist consciousness of the proletariat, convinced of the vast historic role of the state in the cause of socialist construction.[31]

The treachery of the Second International and its Trotskyist-Bukharinist agents was, in part, that these gentlemen—carrying out the will of their capitalist masters—suggested (and continue to suggest) to the working masses a perverted notion of the state, of its significance in the socialist revolution, and of the state policy of the proletariat. This perversion relates chiefly to two questions: that of the relation of the proletariat to the bourgeois state machine in winning power, and that of transforming political domination into the basis of the socialist reorganization of society.

These are the most important questions of the epoch of the transition

[31] In this regard, it is particularly necessary to emphasize the extraordinary character of the *History of the All-Union Communist Party (of Bolsheviks)—A Short Course,* published under the editorship of a commission of the Central Party Committee. This is a notable guide in the matter of education in the spirit of Bolshevism, in the spirit of the great ideas of Marx-Engels-Lenin-Stalin, under whose banner the toilers of our country have achieved the world-shaking victories of socialism.

period—their incorrect solution disarms the proletariat and hands it over to its foe.

Marxism teaches the necessities of using law as one of the means of the struggle for socialism—of recasting human society on socialist bases.

In the Soviet state, law is entirely and completely directed against exploitation and exploiters. Soviet law is the law of the socialist state of workers and peasants. It is invoked to meet the problems of the struggle with foes of socialism and the cause of building a socialist society. As socialist law, it puts these tasks into practice from the first moment of its rise.

Law is the totality (a) of the rules of conduct, expressing the will of the dominant class and established in legal order, and (b) of customs and rules of community life sanctioned by state authority—their application being guaranteed by the compulsive force of the state in order to guard, secure, and develop social relationships and social orders advantageous and agreeable to the dominant class.

Soviet law is the aggregate of the rules of conduct established in the form of legislation by the authority of the toilers and expressive of their will. The effective operation of these rules is guaranteed by the entire coercive force of the socialist state in order to defend, to secure, and to develop relationships and arrangements advantageous and agreeable to the toilers, and completely and finally to annihilate capitalism and its remnants in the economic system, the way of life, and human consciousness—in order to build a communist society.

We learn from Marxism that the proletariat requires the state also to crush exploiters and to guide the vast mass of the population in the matter of setting up the socialist economy. Here an exceptional role falls to the lot of such state organs as the court, whose activity is organically associated with legal norms, statutes, legal customs, legal views—with all of law.

The special character of social relationships during the transitional period makes it inconceivable to suppose that it is possible to solve the problems of restraint merely by administrative repression with the aid of extraordinary and exceptional measures and methods. The proletarian dictatorship acts also by legal means with the aid of courts, of procedural rules and orders. It organizes and sets in motion a court system resting on such procedural principles as publicity, immediacy, and contestation. Court and law are necessary to the proletariat, as are the criminal code, the civil code, and codes of procedure.

The criminal law of the proletarian dictatorship is not at all a "form of communion of egoistic, isolated subjects, bearers of an autonomous private interest or ideal property owners," as Pashukanis asserted. Soviet criminal law, in the name of the Soviet state, requires certain conduct, a certain relationship toward civil obligations—toward duty—the fulfillment of which is obligatory under sanction of criminal punishment.

Soviet criminal law explains and regulates by authority social relationships arising between the Soviet state and citizens in certain cases (defined by the state and in the name of the state)—under certain circumstances likewise defined by state authority. Like all socialist law, Soviet criminal law expresses the state will of the proletariat. ". . . The will, if it be the state will, must be expressed as *law* established by authority . . . otherwise the word 'will' is an empty concussion of air by an empty sound." [32]

Developing the doctrine of Marx and Engels, Lenin and Stalin teach proficiency in utilizing law and legislation in the interests of socialist revolution. Thus in October, 1922, Lenin, at the Fourth Session of the All-Russian Central Executive Committee, said with reference to the Civil Code adopted at that session:

Even here we have sought to observe the boundaries between the lawful satisfaction (of any citizen) linked with contemporary, economic trade turnover, on the one hand, and an apparent abuse of the New Economic Policy—which is legal in all states and which we do not desire to legalize on the other. [33]

According to Lenin, the Civil Code was directed against the "abuse of the New Economic Policy," that is, against the bourgeois principles and the bourgeois content of the civil codes of capitalist countries.

Stalin teaches the strengthening of socialist legislation, emphasizing the supreme importance of the stability of Soviet statutes as regards our further progress. This idea of the stability of statutes was reflected in the great Stalin Constitution, in its principle of referring the legislative function solely and exclusively to the competence of the Supreme Soviet, and in its delimitation of *laws, decrees, directives,* and *orders.*

Why is stability of statutes essential? Because it reinforces the stability of the state order and of the state discipline, and multiplies tenfold the powers of socialism, mobilizing and directing them against forces hostile to them.

The law not merely gives rights, it imposes obligations.

The annihilation of classes is our basic need. Without it, the annihilation of class domination is economically inconceivable. In place of "the equal right of all" I propose "the equal rights and *equal obligations* of all.". . . *Equal obligations* constitute an addition to bourgeois-democratic *equal rights* which is particu-

[32] Lenin (Russian ed.), Vol. XX, p. 532.
[33] *Ibid.*, Vol. XXVII, p. 319.

larly important for us—an addition which removes from the latter their specifically bourgeois meaning.[34]

This observation contains an extraordinarily important indication of the sense in which Marx speaks in his *Critique of the Gotha Program* of "bourgeois law" in the transitional period. He makes it clear (as against Lassalle) that in the first phase of communism there is as yet no "equality," no "equal rights" (no equal right of each to an equal product of labor). This law is still *unequal law* inasmuch as it starts by applying an equal and identical gauge to dissimilar persons, dissimilar in their needs and in their positions. Consequently, this law is still unequal and in this sense it is still "bourgeois" law.

Under socialism, however, the means of production became common property, and to this extent "bourgeois" law declined. In this society socialist principles are already realized—"he who does not work must not eat" and "an equal quantity of the product for an equal quantity of labor."

This distribution according to labor is an "injustice," still necessarily preserved, but being ever more and more mitigated and lessened. The socialist state corrects "unequal" law by sanatoria, rest houses, dispensaries, free (general and higher) training, pensions, a system of reliefs, and so on. "Meantime, individual people are not equal; some are stronger, some weaker; some are married, others unmarried; one has more children, another fewer children; and so on," [35] and into this "inequality" Soviet power introduces its corrections—easing the position of those with many children, with large families, and so forth. Thus does the Soviet socialist law ever increasingly develop.

As a means of control on the part of society, a means of regulating social relationships, a method and means of preserving the interests of socialist society and the rights and interests of citizens, Soviet law carries out a social function of gigantic importance—without which the socialist state could not get along until that time when it completely withers away.

Law—like the state—will wither away only in the highest phase of communism, with the annihilation of the capitalist encirclement; when all will learn to get along without special rules defining the conduct of people under the threat of punishment and with the aid of constraint; when people are so accustomed to observe the fundamental rules of community life that they will fulfill them without constraint of any sort. Until then, however, there is necessity for general control, firm discipline in labor and in community life, and complete subordination of all the new society's work to a truly democratic state.

[34] Marx and Engels (Russian ed.), Vol. XVI, Pt. 2, pp. 106–107.
[35] Lenin (Russian ed.), Vol. XXI, p. 434.

The central part of the Marx-Engels doctrine is that concerning the dictatorship of the proletariat—a doctrine reestablished and further elaborated by Lenin (who revealed Soviet power as the state form of proletarian dictatorship) and by Lenin's companion-in-arms, the genius Stalin (who enriched Marxism-Leninism with further development of the most important problems of the class struggle of the proletariat in various stages of socialist building). Marxism-Leninism, starting from the law of the inequality of capitalist development in the epoch of imperialism, teaches that socialism cannot be victorious *simultaneously* in all countries, but will be victorious originally in one or in some countries, while the others remain for a certain time bourgeois or prebourgeois.[36]

Lenin and Stalin unmasked the falsity of the counterrevolutionary Trotsky and Bukharin "theories," directed at snatching the victory away from socialism in our country. These "theories" were reflected also in denial of the socialist character of Soviet law, in attempts to portray Soviet law as bourgeois law—as law resting on the same bourgeois principles and expressing the same social relationships inherent in the bourgeois order. These persons trod the well worn path of Trotskyist-Bukharinist perversions, which transferred into the field of Soviet economy the laws of capitalist economy—the economic laws of capitalist society. Thus an adherent of the Bukharinist "law of labor payments," Stuchka—like Pashukanis (now unmasked as a spy and wrecker)—transfers the Bukharinist perversions of Marxism-Leninism from the field of economics to that of the law.

The wrecker character of the Bukharinist "law" of labor payments consisted in its carrying over into the socialist economy the legalities of capitalist society, in which relationships are regulated on the basis of the law of value. The law of value was in this way identified with the law of movement of Soviet economics, which meant reducing to zero the principle of planning in Soviet economy—cheapening the economic role of the proletarian dictatorship. But Stuchka cried: "Here before us is a ready scheme of the law of the present transitional period," [37] and declared that socialist development according to plan is *"in legal language"* simply the "law of nature" which, in a society where there is *anarchy of production* and of exchange, is manifested only elementally through endless crises.[38]

Stuchka crudely perverted the Marxist doctrine of law of the transitional period—robbed it of its revolutionary role and its essential fighting character —reducing the whole matter to a verification of our capacity to compete with

[36] *Ibid.*, Vol. XIX, p. 325.
[37] P. Stuchka, *State and Law in the Period of Socialist Building* (Russian ed., 1927), No. 2, p. 20.
[38] *Ibid.*, Vol. I, p. 165.

the owner of private property! He radically perverted the idea of Soviet law, treating it (after the fashion of Kautsky) as a *"compromise* between the idea of law" and "economics," and in the class sense—as a compromise between interests of classes—but with the *interests of the dominant class clearly and definitely paramount.*[39] He regards Soviet law, in particular Soviet civil law, as imported bourgeois law.

The entire distinction between our Civil Code and the bourgeois civil code he saw in the fact that there has been "injected" into ours "a new element—*socialist planning."* [40]

The reference to planning does not, however, change the matter. Stuchka's fundamental perversion in this question is that he reduced Soviet civil law to the sphere of production and barter. What then is to be done with the part of law which regulates marriage and family relationships? Or must these likewise be regulated from the viewpoint of "socialist planning?" Clearly civil law embraces a sphere of relationships broader than those of barter only (as Pashukanis asserts), or even those of production and barter only (Stuchka).

From this point of view the "theories" of Stuchka and Pashukanis are undoubtedly related and similar. It is not without reason that Stuchka in his time extolled and widely advertised the pamphlet of the wrecker Pashukanis, *The General Theory of Law and Marxism.*

Stuchka characterized Soviet civil law and the Soviet Civil Code as basically bourgeois phenomena. He flatly declared all the law of the period of the New Economic Policy to be bourgeois, asserting that we have simply "imported, borrowed, bourgeois law."

Our new (and we may say here our first) codes were to him the result of "concessions to bourgeois law," as "landmarks of retreat"—thus repeating the anti-Leninist fabrications of Zinovyev and Bukharin and transferring Trotskyist-Zinovyevist principles into the field of legal theory. In *The Revolutionary Role of Soviet Law,* Stuchka wrote that he had succeeded "with the help of his comrades" in formulating a new revolutionary dialectic conception of civil law in general and of our Soviet civil law in particular. This new conception, for whose invention Stuchka takes special credit, was the notorious theory of so-called "economic" law whereby, as everyone knows, Stuchka and some of his pupils understood a part of the civil law embracing questions of an administrative-economic character. The roots of this "economic" law lie in the rotten theory of the wrecker Pashukanis. The gist of this economic-administrative law was the cleavage of Soviet law (regulating economic relationships) into (1) civil law, covering relationships between

[39] *Ibid.,* pp. 16–17.
[40] *Ibid.,* p. 70.

state organs and private persons and between private citizens *inter se*, and (2) "economic" law, covering relationships within the state or the socialist section. As to its content, Stuchka said that administrative-economic law regulates economic relationships "of the socialist section, whereas the law of private economics, or civil (that is to say, private) law, regulates the property relationships chiefly of the section of private-property owners and, in part, intersectional" relations. Stuchka further explained that the difference between these two "laws" is that the first is distinguished by its planned character, and the second by the *anarchic* character of the freedom of competition at the basis of these relationships. A struggle was going on between these sections—and so between these laws, also—wherein one section sought to annihilate the other.[41] Obviously the same must occur also with "laws," one of which must "seek to annihilate the other."

The foregoing shows the limits to which Stuchka's confusion goes—in essence, actually approaching Reisner's "theory" of one's own and "another's" right.

As confirmation of the profound error of his position, Stuchka asserted that "purchase-and-sale will never be socialist . . . being a bourgeois institution, whereas socialism contemplates only direct supply (as distinguished from purchase and sale)," and that consequently "it is necessary to set aside in a special code that which now concerns not the civil law, but simply regulation of relationships of the socialist section." [42] Here everything is confused, from the smearing of Lenin's watchword: "Learn to trade," to the deliberate disregard of the familiar decisions of the Fourteenth Congress of the Bolshevik Party concerning the New Economic Policy and socialism. The "new, revolutionary-dialectic conception," proudly proclaimed by Stuchka, dwindled to the right-opportunist "theory" of "two-section law," merely contrasting the interests of socialist economy with those of the socialist man, and underestimating the civil law as law which regulates, affirms, and preserves the individual and property interests of the toiling citizens of the USSR, the builders of socialism.

This is a coarse perversion of the Marx-Engels-Lenin-Stalin theory of socialism—as to the place and part of individuality in socialist society.

Socialism does not deny individual interests—it amalgamates them with those of the group. Socialism cannot be isolated from individual interests—only socialist society can most completely satisfy them. Moreover, socialist society represents the only firm guarantee that individual interests will be preserved.[43]

[41] *Ibid.* (1931), Vol. III, p. 10.
[42] *ESYU* (*Yezhednevik Sovetskoy Yustitsy*) (The Daily Journal of Soviet Justice) (1929), Nos. 9–10, pp. 226–227.
[43] Stalin, *Questions of Leninism* (10th Russian ed.), pp. 226, 227.

These teachings of Stalin define also the path of development of Soviet civil law and the problems before us in this field—problems of developing and reinforcing Soviet civil law.

The extent of the perversions in the field of the Marxist-Leninist theory of law is particularly apparent in the liquidation of the discipline of Soviet civil law by Stuchka and his followers, who have now come actually to be wreckers and traitors. The whole depth of these perversions is particularly conspicuous in our time, when the greatest of human constitutions, the Stalin Constitution, allots a particularly honored place to the civil rights of Soviet people, when civil legal relationships are raised, in conditions of socialist society, to the highest degree of their development. Unfortunately the perversions of the Marxist theory of law went far deeper than would be inferred from the foregoing. A group of traitors, headed by Pashukanis and others, sat for a number of years in the former Institute of Soviet Construction and Law, and systematically practiced the distortion of the fundamental and most important principles of Marxist-Leninist methodology in the field of law.

Pashukanis with his *General Theory of Law and Marxism*; Volkov with his *Criminal Reflexology*; Ginsberg and Amfiteatrov with their *Course of Soviet Economic Law*; Krylenko with his anti-Marxist pamphlets on criminal law; Berman and Dotsenko with their "little theories" of the withering away of the law, and so forth—each in his field wrought not a little to pervert the great doctrine of Marx-Engels-Lenin-Stalin, so as to disarm Soviet jurists and expose them to the putrid vapor of all kinds of anti-Marxist, anti-Leninist "theories" whereby our enemies sought to sully the pure source of great and truly scientific thought. Because of the work of these wreckers over a period of years, the extremely rich scientific inheritance of Marx-Engels-Lenin, and the equally rich works of Stalin, which guarantee the further development of Soviet legal science, remained unutilized and insufficiently elaborated. Soviet legal science is confronted with the extraordinarily responsible tasks further of working out legal questions organically connected with problems of state and economic construction in the highest stages of development of socialism in the USSR.

Questions of the Soviet state as a form of proletarian dictatorship and socialist democracy (in conditions of capitalist encirclement and of further progress of the USSR toward communism), a multitude of questions of socialist administrative law, labor law, kolkhoz law, inheritance law, and so forth, and finally such basic questions as the problem of state and law in communist society—all these extraordinarily significant themes the wreckers pigeonholed and left inert. They denied the very possibility of the *development* of Soviet law as socialist law. They tried mechanically to transfer the legal institutions of one epoch (that of imperialistic capitalism) into another (that of socialism), perverting the basic methodological settings of Marxism-Leninism, which teaches that law, or the legal superstructure, can and must be explained in the last analysis out of the economic structure of society, out of its relationships of production.

It was not this penal code, which I hold in my hand, that created modern bourgeois society. On the contrary, bourgeois society, arising in the eighteenth century and continuing to develop in the nineteenth, found only its legal expression in this code. The moment it ceases to correspond to social relationships, it will become a mere package of paper.[44]

This statement is similarly an acknowledgment of the inevitability of the development of law. Law, however, has not a history of its own—the history of the development of law is organically connected with the development of "civil society"—that is to say, of the economic production relationships. The law and the entire legal (and, in general, the political) superstructure grow out of and on the basis of them.

For precisely this reason, law cannot be higher—nor lower—than the economic level of a given society. It must correspond to it or be inwardly in accord with it. This circumstance completely refutes the idea of legal development which starts from the possibility of mechanically transferring legal ideas and legal institutions from one economic epoch to another. From this point of view it is easy to unmask the anti-Marxian, pseudoscientific "theory" of the wreckers Pashukanis, Krylenko, and others who declared that Soviet law was simply assimilated and adapted bourgeois law. The viciousness and pseudoscience of such "theoretical" propositions lie in their perversion of the fundamental principles of the Marxist-Leninist theory of law.

When, for example, Pashukanis spoke of the two epochs of *culminating development* of general legal ideas—of Rome with its system of private law, and of the seventeenth and eighteenth centuries in Europe with the universalism of the bourgeois legal form—and from an analysis of precisely these forms tried to deduce a definition of law, he perverted the Marxist proposition that each historic epoch of class society has its own corresponding law and that exhaustive understanding of law must be sought and found in an analysis not of law (even though present in the most developed form), but of the social and production relationships which have generated a given form of law.

This is why it is a crude perversion of Marx's doctrine of law for the Pashukanises, the Bermans, and others of their ilk to assert that the transi-

[44] Marx and Engels (Russian ed.), Vol. VII, p. 254.

tion to developed communism was conceived by Marx not as a transition to new forms of law but as the withering away of juridical form in general —as emancipation from this legacy of the bourgeois epoch which was destined to outlive the bourgeoisie itself. Such a proposition would be possible if—but only if—the transition from capitalism to communism were without a transitional period, which is unimaginable without descending to utopianism.

We must pause briefly to consider also Reisner's anti-Marxist writings on questions of Soviet law. According to Reisner, law is a heap of ideological scraps of various classes. Starting from such an absolutely mistaken view of the nature and essence of law, he constructed his antiscientific, anti-Marxian statement of Soviet law as a law of compromise, as a law "of appeasement and reconciliation," going so far as to depict Soviet law as the totality of proletarian law, peasant law, and—on the basis of "tolerance and compromise"—bourgeois law.

Soviet law is thus a *complex legal order*, whose structure includes large segments of *socialist law of the working class and its proletarian class law*. Such is the dominant position of proletarian law by virtue of the dictatorship of the proletariat. The next place is occupied by *peasant class law*, embodied in the land code with its predominance of collective property. The *class law of the bourgeoisie*, with its civil code in the framework of trade turnover, is relegated to third place. But in one relationship the bourgeoisie may still celebrate its ideological victory. By reason of capitalist encirclement, our state socialism utilizes a market as an apparatus of distribution, and in view of this the Soviet order preserves in many cases the *forms of bourgeois individualist law*. The effect of this circumstance is heightened among us by the further fact that almost all the jurists employed by the Soviets for their codification had come out of the school of bourgeois jurisprudence or had been to a significant degree educated under its influence.[45]

According to Reisner, Soviet law is "triune law": proletarian, peasant, and bourgeois, with proletarian law occupying, so to speak, a dominant position in this system. No wonder Reisner saw the danger that Soviet law might turn into a reactionary force capable of paralyzing the struggle for socialism. This is literally what he wrote:

In the framework of our conditions, law is a vast apparatus of appeasement and reconciliation. It makes the proletarian dictatorship possible in an encirclement of great and small capitalism in internal as well as in external repercussions. *On the other hand the same law can become a reactionary force that will protect the transitional period in its New Economic Policy form over and above any actual necessity, and give to the scope of bourgeois law a breadth that can seriously prejudice the interest of the proletariat* and thereby either delay the course

[45] M. A. Reisner, *Our Law, Foreign Law, Common Law* (State Publishing House, 1925), p. 244.

of the "ingrowing" into communist society or necessitate a new revolution to free the proletariat from bourgeois snares which have imperceptibly wound around it.[46]

According to Reisner the result is that: (1) Soviet law "appeases and reconciles" the struggling classes; and (2) saves the proletarian dictatorship from collapse under the pressure of "encirclement by great and small capitalism." He considers this the positive side of Soviet law. But Soviet law apparently "risks" becoming a force of reaction, injurious to the "proletarian interest," delaying the process of "growing into" (?) communist society, and thus even causing some "new revolution" (?)! This is the negative side of Soviet law.

This discovery is extraordinarily characteristic of Reisner. It shows that bourgeois-Menshevik conceptions of law are, in him, closely connected and interwoven with counterrevolutionary Trotskyist slander as to the "regeneration" of the Soviet state, "the third revolution," and the like.

Lenin's words in the *Historical Fortunes of the Doctrine of Karl Marx* are justified: "The dialectic of history is such that the theoretic triumph of Marxism makes its enemies *change clothes* with Marxists. Inwardly corrupt liberalism essays to come to life again in the shape of socialist opportunism." [47] Reisnerism is one of the varieties of this opportunism, of the bourgeois vulgarization of Marxism, of the mutilation of Marxism by followers of Freud and Von Mach.

Marxism-Leninism contemplates the state as a historical category, thereby acknowledging that it will inevitably wither away. This matter is treated in the utmost detail by Marx in his *Critique of the Gotha Program*. There he showed that the necessity of the state as a special machine for repression disappears in proportion to the growth of the forces of production and to the spread of democracy to an overwhelming majority of the population. Commenting on this passage, Lenin wrote that exploiters cannot overwhelm the people without a most complicated machine, but *"the people can crush the exploiters with even a very simple 'machine,' almost without a 'machine,' without a special apparatus, by the simple organization of armed masses* (after the fashion of the Soviets of Workers' and Soldiers' Deputies, we may note by way of anticipation)." [48]

Marxism-Leninism teaches that, with the final triumph of communism in all advanced capitalist countries, the necessity for a state disappears and the excesses of individuals will be crushed by the armed nation itself "with

[46] *Ibid.*, p. 224.
[47] Lenin, (Russian ed.), Vol. XVI, p. 332.
[48] *Ibid.*, Vol. XXI, p. 432.

the same simplicity and ease with which any crowd of civilized people, even in present-day society, separates brawlers and prevents violence to a woman." Excesses in the form of violating the rules of community life have their roots chiefly, according to Lenin, in the exploitation of the masses, in their need and their beggary.

With this chief cause eliminated, excesses will inevitably begin to *wither away*. We do not know how quickly or by what degrees, but we do know that they will wither away. And with them the state *will wither away* also.[49] It will be possible for the state to wither completely away with society's realization of the rule: from each according to his capacities, to each according to his needs; that is to say, when people shall be so habituated to the observance of the fundamental rules of community life and their labor shall be so productive, that they will voluntarily labor *according to their capacities*.[50]

This process of the state's withering away is thus inevitably bound up with the highest development of the state—the highest flowering of the new economy and new productive forces. It presupposes a high level of communist culture and great labor productivity.

It is a protracted process, connected with the radical reorganization not only of the economy of human society but of human psychology as well. It will take place under complete communism, with the triumph of communism in all advanced capitalist countries, when "all shall learn to administer—and shall in reality administer—social production" without outside help, when the *necessity* of observing the simple, basic rules of all types of human society shall very quickly become *a habit*.[51]

The Marxist-Leninist doctrine of the withering away of the state has nothing in common with the anarchist theories of blowing up the state propagated by Proudhon, Bakunin, and Most (in the time of Marx) and by such traitors to socialism as Bukharin, who have sought to oppose their own "theory" of "blowing up the state" to the Marxist-Leninist theory. Nor has the latter theory anything in common with the perversions of opportunists who (after the manner of Kautsky) preach that the bourgeois state should be adapted to the needs of the proletariat.

Pseudo-Marxists, and those who simply betray the cause of the working class, consciously confuse and radically pervert the matter of the withering away of the state. They forcibly separate it from the question of how constantly to increase the development of democracy and to prepare the economic and social conditions under which the state will wither away. Whereas it is only and exclusively in this connection that the Marxist-

[49] *Ibid.*, p. 432.
[50] *Ibid.*, p. 436.
[51] *Ibid.*, p. 441.

Leninist formulation (of the question of the state's withering away) is comprehensible. Lenin emphasizes that the choice of the expression "the state withers away" is very happy, in that it indicates both the gradual nature and the elemental character of the process.[52]

Lenin and Stalin have emphasized more than once that only the habit of observing the rules of community life frees people from the necessity of employing a special apparatus (called the state) for constraint; that only the gigantic development of democracy, and of social relationships which radically recast human consciousness and foster a new relationship of people to labor and to society, will lead to the withering away of the state.

The withering away of the state is at the same time the withering away of democracy and of law—all these processes are organically connected with each other.

By what stages—through what practical measures—mankind will come to this higher goal, we do not and cannot know. It is important, however, to clarify for ourselves how infinitely false is the usual bourgeois notion that socialism is something dead, something that has set, something given once and for all. In reality, *only* with socialism will there begin swift, actual and genuinely mass motion forward in all fields of social and individual life, with the *majority*—and thereafter all—of the population participating.[53]

As to dates and forms of the withering away of the socialist state, a most important part must inevitably be played also by the external political setting, international relations and such facts as the capitalist encirclement. The vast successes of socialism, and the transition to the communist social-economic order exclude the slightest possibility of our state "withering away" with capitalist encirclement still preserved and present. The triumph of communism in the USSR cannot *per se* decide the question of relegating the state to a museum of antiquities. With a definite international situation—particularly, with the conditions of capitalist encirclement still preserved—the USSR will not be able, and will not have any right, to renounce such force as the socialist or communist state, which guarantees the stability and inviolability of the new communist society. In these conditions there can be no talk of any "withering away" of the state under victorious communism.

Thus the process of the withering away of the state is connected with the gigantic process of the development of socialism—the forward movement of human society—by overcoming such historical legacies as the state, law, and democracy.

[52] *Ibid.*, p. 431.
[53] *Ibid.*, p. 439.

Marxism-Leninism makes no schematic outline of the withering away of the state—it starts specifically from a scientific analysis of the conditions which pave the way for it.

Lenin scathingly ridiculed Bukharin's idea of the withering away of the state, which Bukharin presents in this form: "External coercive normalizations will begin to wither away: first the army and fleet as instruments of the most severe external constraint; then the system of punitive and repressive organs; then the coercive character of labor, and so on." Lenin wrote: "Is it not rather the reverse, first the third, then the second, and finally the first?" [54]

Stalin's teaching is that the withering away of the state will come not through a weakening of the state authority but through its maximum intensification, which is necessary to finish off the remnants of the dying classes and to organize defense against capitalist encirclement, which is now far from being—and will not soon be—destroyed.[55] Every other interpretation of the withering away of the state under present conditions is merely an attempt to disarm the proletariat, to weaken the authority of the proletarian state and the dictatorship of the proletariat—an attempt to justify the counterrevolutionary theory of the extinction of the class struggle. Stalin has said of the propounders of such theories: "These are degenerates, or double-dealers, who must be driven out of the party. The annihilation of classes is attained by intensifying, not extinguishing, the class struggle." [56]

Constantly by reinforcing the socialist state and law by every means, shattering one after another all the machinations of the enemies of the people, the enemies of socialism, and developing socialist democracy and culture, the toilers of our country will guarantee the building of the communist society and the triumph of communism.

SEC. 4: THE DEMOLITION OF THE MACHINERY OF THE BOURGEOIS STATE

The most important problem of the Marxist-Leninist doctrine of the state is, as previously indicated, that of demolishing the machinery of the bourgeois state and replacing it with new machinery.

[54] Lenin, Vol. XI, p. 400.
[55] Stalin, *Questions of Leninism* (10th Russian ed.), p. 509.
[56] *Ibid.*, p. 509.

What is the machinery of the bourgeois state but an apparatus to exploit, oppress, and crush the toilers? Alien to the people and to their interests, it is a frightful instrument—a dreadful octopus, entwining and exhausting with its multiple tentacles the living body of the people. Bourgeois, bureaucratic officialdom, bourgeois police, bourgeois courts, prisons, and army—all these are parts of that machinery, working like a mechanism wound up to go in the one direction of subordinating all life to the interests of the exploiters, and to the single end of strengthening and confirming their domination. The state is a subtle and complex system of heterogeneous organs and institutions, of laws and directives, of methods and manners of work, all specially selected to match this work of people with their views, practices, interests, and aspirations. The modern (bourgeois) "state is nothing but the organized, integrated power of the 'have' classes, the landowners and capitalists, directed against the exploited classes, the peasants and workers." [1] The middle of the nineteenth century saw the culmination of the fundamental reorganization of the bourgeois state into the so-called *national* state, which overcame the previously existing dismemberment and separation of its parts each from the other and therewith legislative separatism.

Disjointed legislation regulating trade and industry, diverse forms of law (including the law of negotiable instruments) disadvantageous to the turnover of trade and industry, of the state as a whole, various "police chicaneries, bureaucratic and fiscal *chevaux de frise*," [2] incongruous money systems and systems of weights and measures and the like—all this held back the development of the production forces of bourgeois society, with the resultant necessity for unity, for a single state high above the separate interests of these numerous "different-calibered" states (as Engels calls them). "The 'aspiration' to a single 'fatherland' had an extremely material basis." It was the aspiration of the practical merchant and industrialist "to sweep away all the provincial rubbish historically inherited by small states and which constituted a hindrance to the free development of trade and industry." [3] The attainment of this end completed the consolidation of the bourgeois national state, which turned into a "national instrument of the war of capital against labor" (Marx). The later development of the bourgeois state was merely the ever increasing centralization of state power and the ever more logical and irreconcilable repression of national masses and their revolutionary movements directed toward the defense of the life interests of the toiling people. Speaking of the Bonaparte monarchy (where

---

[1] Engels, *The Housing Question* (Party Publishing House, 1934), p. 70.
[2] Marx and Engels (Russian ed.), Vol. XVI, Pt. 1, p. 454.
[3] *Ibid.*, p. 456.

the government power was actually in the hands of a special caste of officers and bureaucrats), Engels emphasized that "the independence of this caste, which stands outside—and so to speak above—society, makes the state appear independent of society." [4]

But this independence is illusory, as illusory as the constitutionalism concealing the disintegration of the old absolute monarchy. It is no mere chance that even bourgeois political scientists are compelled to admit that it is extremely difficult to distinguish a constitutional monarchy from a bourgeois-democratic republic, and under certain historical circumstances, that the transition from the latter to the former is easy.

This disintegration of the old state occurs in full view of everyone. In its time, the Prussian state afforded a brilliant example of the old absolute state turning into the modern capitalist state with all the faults and caste peculiarities that make it incapable of solving the social question which has come to a head. In reality the officer-bureaucrat caste depends entirely and completely upon its "society," that is to say, on the exploiter cliques dominant in that society. Swiftly developing capitalist industry, stock jobbing, thirst for wealth, and feverish bank speculation—these increasingly attract into their sphere of influence different circles of capitalist society—from ministers, princes, and generals to priests, country nobles, and bureaucrats. Here is Engels's description of this process of development of the modern capitalist state:

The swift development of industry, and especially of stock manipulation, attracted all the dominant classes into a maelstrom of speculation. The mass corruption imported from France in 1870 is developing with unprecedented swiftness. . . . The country nobility—occupied from of old with such industries as sugar refining and distilling—have long since forgotten the good old days. Their names adorn directors' lists of all sorts of stock corporations—solid and otherwise. The bureaucrats more and more disdain embezzlement as the sole means of increasing their salaries, abandon the state to the tender mercies of fate and go off to hunt for far more lucrative posts as managers of industrial enterprises. Those still remaining in state service follow the example of their chiefs and speculate in shares or "participate" in railroads and similar enterprises. We even have a perfect right to suppose that lieutenants don't really mind a profit in certain speculations. In a word, the dissolution of all elements of the old state—the transition of an absolute into a Bonapartist monarchy—is in full swing. With a great crisis in trade and industry impending, the modern knave and the ancient Prussian state will go crashing down together.[5] And is this state—whose non-bourgeois

---

[4] Engels, *The Housing Question* (Party Publishing House, 1934), p. 71.

[5] "Even now (in 1886) only fear of the proletariat, whose growth since 1872 has been gigantic, as to both number and class consciousness, still sustains and unifies the Prussian State and its foundation—the union of big landowners with industrial capital—a union secured by protective customs duties" (Note by Engels to the second ed., 1887).

elements are becoming daily more bourgeois—to be called upon to solve the "social question" or even the housing problem? [6]

Of the bourgeoisie and the bourgeois state Lenin wrote: "I am entirely within my rights. I buy stocks. All the courts, all the police, all the standing armies and all the fleets in the world protect my sacred right to that stock." [7] Can such a state—devoted soul and body to the interests of the bourgeoisie and preserving its "right to shares of stock"—serve the interests of socialism? Of course it cannot.

Such a state would turn its weapons against the proletariat if the latter preserved that state—the most important lesson of the Paris Commune, as handed down by Marx and Engels, consists in precisely this truth. In his famous work, *The Eighteenth Brumaire of Louis Bonaparte*, Marx spoke of the bureaucracy and the military organization created by the French bourgeoisie—of this horrible parasite-organism winding like a net around the whole body of the absolute monarchy (an organization still further strengthened by Napoleon, who perfected this state apparatus). Marx wrote: "All the cataclysms have improved this machinery, instead of demolishing it"; [8] and with reference to these words Lenin wrote:

In this notable judgment, Marxism made a colossal forward step as compared with the *Communist Manifesto*. There the question of state is still put with extreme abstraction, in the most general ideas and expressions. Here it is put concretely, and the conclusion becomes extraordinarily exact and definite—and practically palpable: all the former revolutions improved the state machinery—whereas it must be shattered and demolished. This conclusion is the principal and basic teaching in the Marxist doctrine of the state.

In Marx' and Engels' preface to the German edition of the *Communist Manifesto* (1872), it is said that the Paris Commune "proved that the working class cannot simply take possession of a ready-made state machine and set it in motion for its own particular ends," [9] as Marx had written as early in 1871 in his *Civil War in France*. With reference to this citation from the latter work, Engels wrote twenty years later:

But in reality the state is nothing but a machine, whereby one class represses another—not a whit less in a democratic republic than in a monarchy; at best, the state is an evil transferred by inheritance to the proletariat which has won the victory in the struggle for class domination. Having won the victory, the proletariat (after the example of the Commune) will have immediately to ampu-

[6] Engels, *The Housing Question* (Party Publishing House), pp. 71–72.
[7] Lenin (Russian ed.), Vol. XXX, p. 341.
[8] Marx and Engels (Russian ed.), Vol. VIII, p. 404.
[9] Marx and Engels, *Communist Manifesto* (Russian ed., 1938), p. 6.

tate the worst features of this evil until a generation which has grown up in new
and free social conditions shall appear able to cast out all this rubbish associated
with the state. In recent times the social-democratic philistine again begins to
experience a salutary fear at the words: the *dictatorship of the proletariat*. Do you
wish to know, gentlemen, how this dictatorship looks? Look at the Paris Commune—that was the dictatorship of the proletariat.[10]

Is it an accident that the most vulgar and ignoble renegades of Marxism
—like the Kautskys, the Kunovs, and the Adlers—fall in such fury and frenzy
upon this doctrine of Marx relative to the demolition of the state machine?

Kautsky in his *Proletarian Revolution and Its Program* shamelessly
tried to prove that Marx, speaking of the necessity of shattering the bourgeois state machine, had in mind merely its bureaucratic-militaristic form,
wheareas (according to Kautsky) the democratic republic is perfectly suited
for the purposes of the proletarian dictatorship.

Marx by no means thought that the proletariat could in no case whatever
utilize the dominance it had attained without having first destroyed the state
apparatus it had inherited. Marx rejected only a particular form of this apparatus—its bureaucratic-militaristic form. . . . From Marx's own words it is apparent that his position had no relation to all the existing states. . . . Not every
kind of state apparatus is adequately suited for the proletariat to be able simply
to take possession of it and set it in motion for its own ends. A bureaucratic apparatus is unsuited for this. Only the *democratic republic* is suited for it! Where
this does not exist at the moment of the proletarian victory, the victorious proletariat must create it. In 1871, and for a long time thereafter, this task seemed
inevitable. Later years have brought an essential change in this regard. In almost
all the European countries, the triumphant proletariat will find a democratic
republic in ready shape. When it comes to power, it will not be necessary for it
to shatter the state machine in its entirety—only to eliminate the monarchist
remnants and the bureaucratic and military privileges.

And on another occasion (in his *Materialistic Understanding of History*) Kautsky tries to prove that at the present time the war-militaristic
state apparatus in capitalist countries is passing more and more into the
background, that now the state concentrates in its hands an increasing number of functions which are of real significance also for the exploited, and that
accordingly the exploited think ever less and less of weakening this state
but, on the contrary, rather of "taking possession of state power and making
it serve their own purposes"—of turning this apparatus from an apparatus
of dominance into an apparatus of emancipation.

A more cynical perversion of the Marxist doctrine of the state and the
proletarian dictatorship cannot be conceived.

[10] *Ibid.*, Vol. XVI, Pt. 2, p. 94.

Lenin and Stalin unmasked such perversions of Marxism and purified the Marxian doctrine from all the miscellaneous rotten and loathsome opportunism and counterrevolutionism.

Lenin's historical work on the *State and Revolution,* and Stalin's works dedicated to questions of the proletarian dictatorship, left not a single stone standing of the Kautsky, Trotsky, Bukharin, and other counterrevolutionary perversions whose treacherous blow is aimed at the very heart of the great theory.

Lenin, having cited the famous passage from Marx's *Civil War in France,* to the effect that "the proletariat must *shatter this machine* (army, police, bureaucracy)," continued:

Do not allow the police to be restored! Create out of the *people's militia* a militia *actually of all the people*—led by the proletariat—as "our state," upon condition that capitalists pay workers for days dedicated to service in the militia. *Supplement the marvels of proletarian heroism* (manifested *yesterday* by the proletariat in the struggle with tsarism and to be manifested *tomorrow* in the struggle with the Guchkovs and the Milyukovs) by *marvels of proletarian organization*. Here is the watchword of the moment! Here is the pledge of success.[11]

Zinovyev, Kamenev, Rykov, and their supporters were notoriously concerned with preserving in every way the inviolability of the bourgeois state apparatus. At the same time, Bukharin developed anarchist propaganda against utilizing the state in general, seeking renunciation by the proletariat of the use of the state apparatus for purposes of the further struggle for socialism.

As early as 1916 Bukharin defended views plainly anti-Marxian and anarchist with reference to the state, the proletarian dictatorship, and the class war. In an article published in that year, Lenin disclosed Bukharin's perversions of Marxism:

The author asks wherein do the relationships of socialists and anarchists as regard the state differ, and then answers quite another question as to the difference between their relationships as regards the economic foundation of future society. This is an extremely important and necessary question, of course. But it by no means follows that we can forget the *chief* matter in distinguishing the relationship of socialists and of anarchists toward the state. Socialists favor utilizing the modern state and its institutions in the struggle to free the working class and likewise for the necessary utilization of the state as a unique form for the transition from capitalism to socialism. The proletarian dictatorship is such a transitional form—and likewise a state.

The anarchists wish to abolish the state, to "blow it up" (*sprengen*) as it has been expressed (mistakenly attributing it to the socialists). Unfortunately the

[11] Lenin (Russian ed.), Vol. XXX, pp. 318–319.

author's citation of Engels' relevant words was incomplete. Socialists acknowledge
the withering away, the "gradual falling asleep," of the state *after* the expropriation of the bourgeoisie. . . . In order to "emphasize" the "principle of hostility"
toward the state, it is necessary to understand that hostility with real "clarity."
The author possesses absolutely none of this clarity. The phrase, "the roots of
the nature of the state," is completely confused, being neither Marxist nor
socialist. It is not "the nature of the state" which clashed with the denial of it;
it was opportunist policy (that is to say, the opportunist, reformist, bourgeois
relationship to the state) which clashed with the revolutionary social-democratic
attitude toward the bourgeois state and toward utilizing the state against the
bourgeoisie in order to overthrow the latter). These are utterly and completely
different things.[12]

Bukharin maintained complete silence with regard to Lenin's disclosures
until 1925, when—a year after Lenin's death—he collaborated with Pashukanis in an article on "The Theory of the Imperialistic State," in the collection of articles entitled *The Revolution of Law.* Lenin had refused to
publish this same article (as editor of *The Social-Democratic Collection of
Articles*). In a note to this article, Bukharin had the effrontery to declare
that in the controversy concerning the state he—and not Lenin—was right.
Stalin has said of the exceedingly crude perversions of Marxism by the
traitorous Bukharin: "The position of Bukharin—set out in his article in
International Youth—is that of negating the state in the transitional period
from capitalism to socialism." Thus Bukharin was surreptitiously propagat-
ing the anarchistic theory of "blowing up" the state, in place of the Marxist
theory of "demolishing," "shattering" the bourgeois state machinery. Unmasking Bukharin's anti-Marxist, counterrevolutionary theory of "blowing
up" the state, Stalin continued: "Lenin started specifically from the Marxist
theory of 'demolishing' the machinery of the *bourgeois* state, when he
criticized the anarchist theory of 'blowing up' and 'abolishing' the state
in general." [13]

Marxism-Leninism teaches the proletariat to utilize the state—having,
as a preliminary, completed the bourgeois state apparatus. In 1920 Stalin
said, in a ceremonial session of the Baku Soviet:

We knew in theory that the proletariat could not simply take the old state
machinery and set it in motion. This theoretical acquisition of ours from Marx
was completely confirmed by the facts when we encountered a whole wave of
sabotage on the part of officials in service and of the higher ranks of the proletariat, a wave of complete disorganization of state authority. The first and principal apparatus of the bourgeois state—the old army and its generals—was given

[12] *Ibid.*, Vol. XIX, p. 296.
[13] Stalin, *Questions of Leninism* (10th Russian ed.), pp. 273-274.

over to demolition. This cost us dear. As a result of this demolition, we had for a time to remain without an army of any kind. We had to sign the peace of Brest-Litovsk. But there was no other way out. History showed us no other way of freeing the proletariat.

Another equally important apparatus in the hands of the bourgeoisie, the apparatus of officialdom, was also destroyed and demolished. In the sphere of the economic control of the country, the most characteristic action was to take out of the hands of the bourgeoisie the basic nerve of bourgeois economic life, the banks. Banks were taken out of the hands of the bourgeoisie and it was left, so to speak, without a spirit. As for the future, the work of demolishing the old mechanisms of economic life and of expropriating the bourgeoisie goes on, taking factories and plants from the bourgeoisie, and giving them into the hands of the worker class. Finally comes the demolition of the old apparatus of food supply and the effort to build new ones capable of collecting grain and distributing it among the population. Last of all, the liquidation of the Constituent Assembly. These are approximately all the measures in the procedure of destroying the old mechanisms of the capitalist world which Soviet Russia was obliged to carry out during this period.[14]

The legislative memorials to this destruction of the old mechanisms of the capitalist state are the decrees (particularly of the first period) of the October Revolution. The decree concerning the courts (November 24, 1917) is one of them. It destroyed the old court system and replaced it by the new Soviet people's court. Other decrees concerned land (which destroyed the system of landholding by landowners and nobles), the organization of the Red Army, the Soviet militia, the nationalization of factories and plants, and so forth. Soviet legislation gave form and strength to the destruction of old bourgeois mechanisms and to the birth of new social relationships and a new state apparatus of the Soviets.

The decrees of this epoch played an enormous part in the work of propaganda and organization. At the Eighth Party Congress (1919) Lenin said:

Our decree is a challenge—but not in the earlier spirit: "Workers arise, overthrow the bourgeoisie!" No, this is a challenge to the masses, challenging them to practical action. *Decrees are instructions, summoning to mass practical action.* That is what is important. There may be in these decrees much that is unsuitable, much that will not be put into practice. But there is material for practical action, and it is the task of the decree to teach practical steps to the hundreds, the thousands, the millions of those who obey the voice of Soviet authority.

Such, however, is the part to be played not only by these decrees of Soviet authority but by each and every one of the measures directed at

[14] Stalin, *The October Revolution* (Party Publishing House, 1932), p. 27.

liquidating the remnants of serfdom in Russia, at annihilating the exploitation of man by man.

In a few months the first problem was solved. Then, as the years passed, the solution of subsequent problems followed, turning the Soviet state into a mighty socialist state of the workers and peasants who have built socialism and a new socialist culture.

SEC. 5: A STATE OF SOVIETS, NOT A BOURGEOIS-PARLIA-MENTARY REPUBLIC

In the history of society the nineteenth century is notable for the establishment, in almost all capitalist countries, of the constitutional (and particularly of the parliamentary) regime expressive of the dominance of the bourgeoisie.

England was the model constitutional-parliamentary state. According to the classical English formula, the highest and supreme power resides in Parliament, which is the union of three elements—the king, the House of Lords, and the House of Commons. The parliamentary regime is distinguished (a) by the so-called separation of powers (legislative, judicial, and executive), on the basis of subordinating executive power to the legislative body and (b) by the bicameral system.

The legislative houses are chosen on the basis of a right of suffrage completely guaranteeing the interests of the bourgeoisie (on account of election qualifications and all possible restrictive conditions) and not admitting the people to participate in fact in state government.

England served as model for a number of continental countries which borrowed from her the principles and ideas of organizing the parliamentary bourgeois democratic state.

Bourgeois jurists laud the parliamentary regime as the highest expression of democracy and popular power. Actually, the bourgeois democratic republics (even including parliamentary republics) only represent a form of the domination of the exploiter-minority.

In the epoch of imperialism, this feature of bourgeois parliamentarism is manifested with special force. The modern capitalist state is a "rentier-state," a state of parasitic and rotting capitalism.[1]

That "finance capital wishes domination, not freedom" had to be ad-

[1] Cf. Lenin (Russian ed.), Vol. XIX, p. 153.

mitted, even by Hilferding. The bourgeois-democratic parliamentary state guarantees to finance capital that domination. In the bourgeois parliament the chief part is played by the stock exchange and the banks. They constitute the true legislators.

Take the bourgeois parliament. Can we suppose that the learned Kautsky never heard how the more strongly democracy develops—the more effectively the bankers and the stock exchange subordinate bourgeois parliaments to themselves? Does it not follow from this that we must not employ bourgeois parliamentarism (and the Bolsheviks used it with a success hardly attained by any other party in the world—from 1912 to 1914 we won the entire labor division of the fourth Duma)? But from this it follows that only a liberal can forget the *limited* and *conditional* character of bourgeois parliamentarism in *history*—as Kautsky does. At each step in the most democratic bourgeois state, the oppressed masses encounter lamentable contradiction between the *formal* equality proclaimed by capitalist "democracy" and the thousands of factual limitations and complications making hired slaves of the proletarians. Just this contradiction opens the eyes of the masses to capitalism's rottenness, falsity, and hypocrisy.[2]

Marxism-Leninism teaches that bourgeois democracy was progressive in comparison with the Middle Ages. Even today it has important significance for the toilers in their struggle against fascism, but it is inadequate for the working class. "Now it is necessary to look forward, not back—to the *proletarian* democracy replacing bourgeois democracy."[3]

And even if the work preparatory to the proletarian revolution—the teaching and formation of the proletarian army—were possible (and necessary) *within the framework* of the bourgeois-democratic state, it would still be a betrayal of the interests of the proletariat and apostasy to limit it to that framework once the matter had reached the stage of decisive battles. The proletariat needs its state—not a parliamentary republic but a Soviet republic.

On the basis of his study of the experience of two revolutions in Russia, Lenin —starting from the theory of Marxism—concluded that the best political form of proletarian dictatorship is the republic of the Soviets, and not that of parliamentary democracy. On this basis, in April 1917—the period of transition from bourgeois revolution to socialist revolution—Lenin put forward the watchword of the organization of the Republic of the Soviets as the best political form of proletarian dictatorship. Opportunists of all countries began to cling fast to the parliamentary republic, accusing Lenin of departing from Marxism—of destroying democracy. But of course Lenin—and not the opportunists—was a true Marxist and possessed of the theory of Marxism, since he put forward the Marxist theory, enriching it

[2] *Ibid.*, Vol. XXIII, pp. 348–349.
[3] *Ibid.*, p. 361.

with new experience, whereas they dragged it behind them and turned one of its propositions into dogma.[4]

Marx contrasted the parliamentary republic with the Parisian Commune representing the prototype of the proletarian state.

Instead of deciding once in three years or once in six years what member of the dominant class should represent—and repress—the people in parliament, universal suffrage should be at the service of the people, organized into communes, to search out for the people's undertaking suitable workers, overseers, and accountants, as the individual right of choice serves every other sort of employer to this end.[5]

Lenin called this passage from *The Civil War in France* a notable criticism of parliamentarism and stated that here is expressed its real essence.

To decide once in several years what member of the dominant class will repress and crush the people in parliament is the actual essence of bourgeois parliamentarism, not only in parliamentary-constitutional monarchies but also in the most democratic republics.[6]

The proletariat needs no such parliamentarism but its escape therefrom lies not in annihilating representative institutions and elections but—in accordance with Marxism-Leninism—"to change representative institutions from talking shops into 'working' institutions." [7] Citing Marx's words, "the Commune should have been not a parliamentary, but a working, institution —legislating and executing statutes at one and the same time," Lenin says that these words ("not a parliamentary, but a working, institution") "hit the nail on the head as regards contemporary parliaments and the parliamentary 'lap dogs' of social democracy." [8]

Directing the full vigor of his sarcasm toward the unmasking of the Social Democrats' fraud on the people with their sonorous phrases about parliamentarism, Lenin continues:

Look at any parliamentary country you like, from America to Switzerland, from France to England or Norway and the others: the actual "state" work is done behind the scenes and carried into execution by departments, chancelleries, and staffs. In parliaments they only chatter—with the special purpose of duping the "simple people." This is true to such an extent that even in the Russian Republic—the bourgeois-democratic republic, before it succeeded in creating a

---

[4] *History of the All-Union Communist Party (of Bolsheviks), A Short Course* (1938), pp. 340–341.
[5] Marx and Engels, *Selected Works*, Vol. II, pp. 390–391.
[6] Lenin (Russian ed.), Vol. XXI, p. 400–402.
[7] *Ibid.*
[8] *Ibid.*

true parliament—all these sins of parliamentarism were expressed immediately. The heroes of the decayed petty bourgeoisie—the Skobelevs and the Tseretellis, the Chernovs and the Avksentyevs—knew how to defile even the Soviets and to turn them into empty talking shops after the style of the foulest bourgeois parliamentarism. In the Soviets the Messrs. "socialist" ministers swindle the trusting peasants with their flowery speech and their resolutions. In the government a parliament quadrille is in progress so that, on the one hand, as many of the SR's and Mensheviks as possible may take turns in sitting at the feast of lucrative and honorary places, and on the other, that the "attention" of the people may be "engrossed." And in the chancelleries, in the staffs, they "work" at "state" work! [9]

This fragment from Lenin's *State and Revolution* gives a crushing characterization of bourgeois parliamentarism—venal and rotten, as Lenin says—using the freedoms of parliamentary debates and other externals of bourgeois democracy for deceit, and as a curtain to veil infamous and knavish doings at the expense of the electors of various "parliamentarians."

Lenin contrasts this parliamentarism of bourgeois society with the organization of state authority under the dictatorship of the worker class, where true freedom and true democracy are guaranteed, where "parliamentarians must themselves work, must themselves execute their statutes, must themselves verify what is obtained in life, and must themselves answer immediately to their electors." [10]

The specific peculiarity of the state of the Soviets is that here there is no contrasting of the legislative body with the entire mass of the population immediately participating in state government and in building up the state.

The Soviet state is a new form of state organization, distinct in principle from the bourgeois-democratic, parliamentarian form. The Soviets differ radically—in many characteristics—from bourgeois-democratic parliamentary states. The gist of these characteristics is that the Soviets are truly the representative organs of the whole population—the only mass organizations embracing all previously oppressed toilers, the most all-inclusive mass organizations of the proletariat; the most mighty organs of the revolutionary struggle of the masses, "making participation in building and governing the new state as easy as possible for them and to the greatest extent releasing the revolutionary energy, the initiative and the creative capacities of the masses in the struggle to destroy the old way of life and for a new proletarian way of life." [11]

The Soviets have all the advantages over the parliamentary bourgeois-

[9] *Ibid.*, p. 402.
[10] *Ibid.*, p. 402.
[11] Stalin, *Questions of Leninism* (10th Russian ed.), p. 31.

democratic state: by their very nature and by all their qualities and characteristics, they completely answer the problems of the toiling masses' struggle for emancipation. It is just they that can—as a new form of organization of the proletariat—play the part of gravedigger of the machinery of the bourgeois state and not only smash that machinery but also replace bourgeois democracy with proletarian democracy and become the fundamental power of the proletarian state.

The Soviets guarantee the proletariat and all toilers the greatest development of their creative initiative, producing conditions most favorable for bringing up the working masses in the spirit of socialism and guaranteeing such unity of purposes as assures their success in the struggle and attainment of victories significant in world history.

The experience of the Paris Commune of 1871, of the Russian Soviets in 1905, and of the great October Socialist Revolution (which during the twenty-one years of its existence has built a gigantic new socialist state of workers and peasants and a new culture, has produced all the conditions for the manifold development of toiling humanity's spiritual forces of creation, has raised the material well-being of the popular masses to a great height, and has brought up a whole generation of new Soviet people) serves as the best proof of all the advantages of the Soviet system over the parliamentary system. This is why the proletarian revolution does not strive to improve the bourgeois-democratic—and in particular the parliamentary—state machinery, but shatters it with the iron hand of an upsurging proletariat and replaces it by a new socialist state—the state of the Soviets.

SEC. 6: SOVIET SOCIALIST PUBLIC LAW—ITS OBJECT AND ITS METHODS

Soviet socialist public law is one of the most important branches of Soviet socialist law, which we have previously defined as the totality of the rules of conduct, established in the form of legislation by the authoritative power of the toilers and expressing their will—the application of said rules being guaranteed by the entire coercive force of the socialist state to the end (a) of defending, securing, and developing relationships and orders advantageous and agreeable to the toilers, and (b) of annihilating, completely and finally, capitalism and its survivals in the economy, manner of life, and consciousness of people, with the aim of building communist society.

The specific mark of Soviet law, distinguishing it, radically and in principle, from the law of all other societies and epochs, is that it serves, in the true and actual sense of the word, the people—society—which for the first time in history comes into its own. In the USSR for the first time in history the people—the toiling national masses themselves—are the masters of their fate, themselves ruling their state with no exploiters, no landlords, no capitalists.

Here the socialist system of economy and socialist property in the means and instruments of production hold sway. They were confirmed as a result of the liquidation of the capitalistic system of ownership, of the abrogation of private property in the instruments and means of production, and of the annihilation of the exploitation of man by man. Here the land and its natural deposits, waters, forests, mills, factories, coal and ore mines, transport (by railroad, water, and air), banks, post, telegraph and telephones, big state-organized agricultural enterprises (sovkhozes, machine tractor stations, and the like), as well as municipal enterprises and the bulk of the dwelling houses in cities and industrial localities—all these are state property—the property of the entire nation.

The economic basis of the USSR—defended and preserved by our Soviet socialist law—is the socialist system of economy, socialist property in instruments and means of production. The political basis of the USSR—likewise preserved and defended by Soviet socialist law—is the Soviets of Workers' Deputies, which have grown and become strong as a result of the overthrow of the power of landlords and capitalists and in consequence of the conquest of the proletarian dictatorship.

These two circumstances, of world-wide historical significance, are, in themselves, sufficient to enable us to see the socialist content of Soviet law. Only traitors and those who betray the interests of socialism (like Pashukanis, Krylenko, and other apostates of our country) could deny the socialist nature of Soviet law, asserting that our law is a mere replica or adaptation of bourgeois law. Soviet law protects the interests of the toiling masses, who have been emancipated from exploitation and the weight of capitalism. It directs all its might at crushing and annihilating exploiters and the very possibility of exploitation.

The Soviet state, and Soviet law from the first days of its emergence defend the interests of labor against capital, the interests of popular masses—the overwhelming majority of the people—against a handful of exploiters and parasitic elements of the old society. Only in a socialist state of workers and peasants are the interests and rights of man defended at the same time, inasmuch as individual well-being rests on the social wealth—the property of the people.

For the first time in human history there is eliminated the conflict between social interest and personal interest, society and the state, and between society and the state (on the one hand) and individuality and individual interests (on the other). In 1922 Lenin wrote to Kursky of the relation of Soviet law to the capitalist elements in economy:

We acknowledge nothing as "private." For us *everything* in the province of economics is in the domain of *public law* and not of private law. We admit only the capitalism of the state. . . . Hence our task is to broaden the application of intrusion by the state into the relationships of "private law," to broaden the right of the state to abrogate "private" contracts, to apply not Corpus Juris Romani but our own *revolutionary legal consciousness* to "civil legal relationships," to show systematically, stubbornly, and insistently in a series of model processes *how* it is necessary to act with intelligence and with energy.[1]

On the same question Lenin wrote to Molotov:

We should acknowledge the chief task of the commission as being: completely to guarantee the interests of the proletarian state from the viewpoint of the possibility of controlling (subsequent control) all private enterprises without exception and abrogating all contracts and private agreements—as contradictory alike to the letter of the law and to the interests of the toiling mass of workers and peasants. Not slavish imitation of bourgeois civil law, but a series of limitations thereof in the spirit of our laws without embarrassment of economic or trading work.[2]

These words of the great Lenin emphasized the characteristic feature of Soviet law which was established to defend the interests of workers and peasants—to defend the Soviet state.

The content of Soviet law is made up, not of the Corpus Juris Romani —the gospel of capitalist society which rests on private property—but of revolutionary legal consciousness which defends the interests of the people —of millions of toiling masses. Soviet law is the law of the socialist state of workers and peasants, born in the fire of the October Revolution which cast down the authority of the bourgeoisie and confirmed the authority of workers and peasants. Soviet socialist law preserves and defends the interests of the Soviet state and of socialism, and the interests and rights of the toiling people.

We live in socialist society. 'The social organization which we have created may be called a Soviet, socialist organization—not yet completely built, but at root a socialist organization of society," as Stalin told Roy Howard. We still cannot proclaim the principle: "From each according to his capacities and to each according to his needs," but we can already say

[1] Lenin (Russian ed.), Vol. XXIX, p. 419.
[2] *Bolshevik* (1937), No. 2, p. 62.

(as does Article 12 of the Stalin Constitution) that labor in the USSR is a duty, and a matter of honor, for each citizen capable thereof, according to the principle: "He who does not work does not eat," and "From each according to his ability, to each according to his work." There is not the slightest doubt that each further success of socialism will see ever increasing obliteration of class boundaries, and that we shall build communism and be able completely to put into practice the communist principle "From each according to his ability, to each according to his needs." Already we embody in reality that whereof the best and noblest human minds have dreamed—Thomas More or Morelli, Saint-Simon, Fourier, Robert Owen.

Being socialist law, Soviet law expresses the victory and the triumph of socialist principles in all spheres of our life. Expressing the essence of new socialist relationships in the USSR, it grows and develops together with the whole country, with each year and each five-year period ever more completely and logically expressing in its institutes and its juridical formulae the principles of the socialism which is celebrating its triumph and preparing the transition to the highest phase of its development—to communism. It expresses the complete and final victory of socialist production and social relationships which found their embodiment in world history in the fundamental law of the USSR—the great Stalin Constitution.

The Stalin Constitution is the greatest act of Soviet socialist law which has consolidated the sum total of twenty years of triumphant development of the Soviet state and of twenty years of struggle for socialism waged by the proletariat and all those who toil in our land. It is the fundamental source of Soviet socialist law. Upon its basis must and can be worked out a system of Soviet socialist law, not hitherto worked out although all the necessary conditions were present.

The systematization of law presupposes the presence of a single, general guiding principle—unvarying for all legal institutes and branches of law. In Soviet law such a single and general principle is that of socialism—the principle of a socialist economic and social system resting on socialist property, annihilation of exploitation and social inequality, distribution in proportion to labor, a guarantee to each member of society of the complete and the manifold development of all his (spiritual and physical) creative forces, and true human freedom and personal independence. This is the principle of socialism! From the viewpoint of this principle Soviet statutes and entire branches of Soviet law can and must be brought into mutual interconnection, and the unity of the principles with which they are permeated can and must be shown. A general, legal idea—expressing the essence and the historical characteristics of the epoch of victorious socialism—can and must make them one.

The systematization of Soviet socialist law was decisively rejected by the people's enemies, who perverted socialist law and denied its creative role—predicting its "withering away" and "evaporation." It will, on the contrary, still further reinforce our law, for it will help each branch of law to take fresh stock of its weapons, to separate those that are of primary importance and to establish connections and transitions as between the different branches of law.

At present the science of Soviet socialist law lacks the necessary congruity and unity. Hitherto, for example, the development of public law, administrative law, and civil law among us has been parallel and almost without correlation and congruity of any sort. On the other hand, a series of problems (such as that developing contemporary kolkhozes) still await solution in each of these branches of law—often obtaining no proper answer from any one of them.

Soviet law is unitary because it expresses identical social relationships, serves identically the same purposes and problems, and employs identical methods in solving them. This is why, in speaking of Soviet public law, we must start by defining this idea from the Marxist-Leninist understanding of law in general and of Soviet law in particular. Soviet socialist state law is a branch of Soviet socialist law. It is distinguished by the same qualities and characteristics as is Soviet law in its entirety. Understanding of the essence and content of Soviet public law is possible only if we start from the Marxist-Leninist understanding of law in general.

In bourgeois science there is no unanimity of understanding of the content of public law. We have already seen how contradictory, and—above all else—how unscientific (and therefore fruitless) were the attempts of divers bourgeois scholars (and entire scientific schools and trends) to define the content of state and of law. This impotence of bourgeois legal science—and indeed of the rest of the bourgeois social sciences—is due to the vice and the ineptitude of the method ordinarily employed by bourgeois scholars. They invoke the aid of the theory of dogmatic jurisprudence to unriddle the secrets of social phenomena—a theory no more fit for this purpose than was the medieval theory of phlogiston [3] for the cognition of natural phenomena.

The formal-juridical method of investigation and cognition only conditions the manipulation of abstract ideas and notions instead of studying the phenomena concealed under the veil of such ideas and notions. It is a

---

[3] Phlogiston: a particular species of "imponderable fluid," by whose hypothetical existence chemists—down to the time of Lavoisier (1743–1794)—explained heat phenomena, and especially burning.

purely ideological method—a method which contemplates legal phenomena as self-contained entities, with their beginning and end originating within themselves and regardless of what exists in reality and in life outside of them. Hence the fallacy of its conclusions and the falsity of its judgments. It was no mere chance that Marx characterized the juridical method as *"juristisch—also falsch."* It is a method of ignoring the actual world of phenomena. It strives to know these phenomena by purely speculative analysis of them, not by disclosing the material causes which generated them.

Hence the fetishism of bourgeois law and bourgeois legal ideas, which also—in their systematized and generalized form—make up the content of the science of bourgeois law. Hence the arbitrariness of diverse "doctrines" and "theories" created by innumerable scholars of all sorts as applicable to their political tastes and to the demands of their capitalist masters.[4]

The juridical method of investigation is abstract and departs from the concrete peculiarities of the phenomenon under investigation. The more subtle distinctions of individuality depart from the view of judge and jurist, as Jellinek, for example, says:

> They are satisfied with Gaius and Titius,[5] plaintiff and defendant, representing something general, analogous to tone in acoustics or to colors in optics. In actual life, however, all agreements and delicts are individualized. Here the ancient rule is operative: *Si duo faciunt idem non est idem.* In the great majority of cases, all purchases and sales effected in the market are lumped by the jurist under one and the same category.[6]

A jurist employing the juridical method is not interested in the economic position of the various owners or in the diverse economic conditions of the agreements they make—the latter is the affair of economists, statisticians, sociologists, and so on. The juridical art of abstraction from "collateral" phenomena lying outside the legal field reigns here. Hence juridical thinking, one-sided and devoid of content, is replete with abstractions and alien to concreteness.

Herein is the reason why it is impossible to use the so-called dogmatic-

---

[4] Jellinek's observation on this score regarding the absence, in bourgeois legal science, of reasoned methodology is characteristic. "In the literature on the doctrine of the state there prevails in this regard the greatest confusion . . . right down to the present time, inconceivable fabrication in the sphere of state doctrine—if only presented with due aplomb—has attracted attention in literature and has been seriously considered. Assertions took the place of facts and convictions the place of proof. Vagueness passed for profundity, and arbitrary philosophizing for the highest knowledge. Chiefly for this reason, in the history of the literature of the doctrine of state there formed very recently so noticeable a gap that in the course of the last decades not a single systematic work has merited the slightest attention" (Jellinek, *General Theory of the State*, pp. 19–20).

[5] These are the conventional names of plaintiff and defendant in Roman law.

[6] Jellinek, *General Theory of the State*, p. 24.

juridical method for scientific investigation.[7] Even outstanding bourgeois jurists fail, however, to see the viciousness of the method they so widely employ, for which reason in large measure their scientific theories appear similarly vicious. The unsatisfactory character of such theories may be exemplified in any bourgeois conception of public law. Bourgeois science ordinarily defines the idea and content of public law by merely pointing at the aggregate norms defining the state organization.[8]

Such is the prevailing idea of the task and content of public law in bourgeois science, which elaborately avoids broadening the object of the science of public law (and of public law itself) to the point of contact with the "material substratum" of the state which serves as the foundation of each and every relationship, idea, and phenomenon of public law. The matter goes even further. A number of learned jurists hold that the tasks of the science of public law are limited to the study of a juridical nature of the so-called contemporary state alone.

The historian of law studies legal phenomena in their gradual development over prolongation of many centuries. He needs a definition that would help him distinguish the state from other cognate phenomena when he encounters diverse social unions in diverse epochs and among diverse peoples. . . . With such a purpose in view, he will give a definition studiously isolated from all the characteristics of the legal order of these diverse states—from that which is especially studied by legal dogma. . . . The dogma of public law of our time needs, therefore, not a definition which would embrace states of all times and all nations, but one which would serve as the starting point for an explanation of the juridical order of the contemporary legal state.[9]

The science of public law cannot, however, be limited to a narrowly juridical sphere of investigation—to a study of the state, solely and exclu-

[7] To avoid misunderstandings it should be emphasized that denial of the juridical method of investigation does not mean refusal to investigate an object from its juridical side (that is to say, from the point of view of what legal relationships are connected with a phenomenon).

[8] See, e.g., Yelistratov: "The aggregate of norms defining state organization will constitute public law. . . . The science of public law studies the norms which define state organization. . . ." (Public Law, pp. 54–55).

Korf: "The Science of Public Law is the name given to the discipline dedicated to study of the legal structure of the state" (Russian Public Law [1915], Pt. 1, p. 3).

By legal structure of the state is here understood the totality of the "legal phenomena which define the state organization of a given nation, the details of its state life, the essence and structure of the given state authority, its functioning, and so forth." Korf, however, considers it inevitable for the science of jurisprudence to utilize the data of political science; "otherwise it appears without foundation, unreal, utopian, and without life." (Op. cit., pp. 2–3).

"The task of the science of public law consists in examining the juridical principles which define the state's organization" (Korkunov, Russian Public Law [1908], Vol. I, p. 1).

[9] A. S. Alekseyev, Russian Thought (1894), Bk. XI, p. 59.

sively as a legal institute, a complex of certain juridical relationships. Science should start from actual social relationships. The nature of law and state cannot be understood by studying them isolatedly. The same is true if one seeks to understand and to portray how law and state arose, and how—and in accordance with what formulae—they developed. They may be understood and explained only on the basis of an analysis of social relationships, a study of the development of the latter (founded upon the production and distribution of material things in society), and a study of the history of the development of society and of the classes into which society split when private property in the form of instruments and means of production emerged.

The jurist, of course, is interested in the juridical nature of law and the state but has not the power to know that nature if he remains entirely within the limits of legal relationships and legal norms. Scientific cognition of the juridical nature of the state is possible only upon one condition: complete rejection of the formal juridical method of cognition, and unconditional transition to the method of dialectic materialism, which contemplates ideologies and other species of superstructure in connection with the production relationships upon which they are based. It contemplates state and law in connection with the life and development of all society, of all sides of its being—and above all that of its economic production.

The state as a form of organizing social relationships on the basis of dominance and subordination is to be explained only in the light of a study of its economic basis—of knowing the laws of historical development of society as the development of classes and class struggle. To separate the science of public law from the science of the economic development of society, away from sociology, history, and philosophy, is to leave a dead form, a dry skeleton affording no idea whatever of the entire organism—of the very essence of state and law. Juridical abstractions, illusions, and fictions flourish luxuriantly in this soil, giving off, like *ignes fatui*, their deceptive and lifeless glitter.

Bourgeois science of public law, following its vicious juridical methodology, portrays the object of public law incorrectly, limiting it as a rule to questions merely of state organization. From its point of view, of course, it is easy to understand the ignoring of questions of social organization and of the economic and political life and history of society and of the corresponding sciences. We categorically deny that these questions can be ignored. Only on the basis of the organic connection of legal science with these sciences can the study of problems of public law be fruitful and truly scientific. Only upon this condition can a solution of the questions attracting the attention of the science of public law be attained. Here, of course, method plays a decisive part. The only scientific method of cognition is the method of dialectic materialism.

In the *Eighteenth Brumaire of Louis Bonaparte* (1852), Marx wrote:

> Above the various forms of property, above the social conditions of existence, towers an entire superstructure of diverse and unique feelings, illusions, ideas, and world-views. The entire class creates and forms all this on the basis of its material conditions and the corresponding social relationships.[10]

Dialectic materialism was the key to cognition of society and of the essence of law and the state. From them it plucked the illusory flowers of idealist romanticism and showed them in their living shape and true light. Employing the method of dialectic materialism, Marxism-Leninism showed how, out of social life of one tenor, another develops because production forces have grown and production relationships have changed. The essence of the dialectic method is that it "requires that phenomena be contemplated, not only from the viewpoint of their being mutually connected and conditioned, but also from that of their moving, changing, developing— from the viewpoint of their emergence and their dying out." [11]

Marxism-Leninism scientifically illuminated all human history, all aspects of life of human society. It opened up and explained the history of the development of social relationships. It showed their true meaning and real essence. It revealed the perspective of the development and formulated the laws defining the trend and content of social relationships. Marxism answered all the most complicated—and hitherto seemingly inscrutable— questions of the history of philosophy, political economy, law and morality.

What was social science before Marx? "Pre-Marxian sociology" and historiography at *best* presented a desultory assemblage of crude facts and a portrayal of separate sides of the historic process. Marxism pointed the way to all-embracing, omnifarious study of the process of the emergence, development, and decay of social-economic formations. It contemplates the *totality* of all contradictory tendencies and reduces them to precisely defined conditions of the life and production of the various *classes* of society. It eliminates subjectivism and arbitrariness in choosing or interpreting separate "master" ideas. It exposes, without exception, the roots of all ideas and all different tendencies in the condition of material production forces. It is the people who create their own history. But how are their motives—and specifically the motives of the masses of people—defined? How are the collisions of contradictory ideas and aspirations evoked? What is the nature

---

[10] Marx and Engels (Russian ed., 1935), Vol. II, p. 273.
[11] *History of the All-Union Communist Party (of Bolsheviks): A Short Course* (1938), p. 101.

of the sum total of all these conflicts in the aggregate of human societies? What is the nature of the objective conditions of production of material life which create the basis of all the historic activity of people? What kind of law governs the development of these conditions? Marx directed his attention to all these questions, and pointed the way to the scientific study of history as one process, conforming in all of its diversification and contradiction to established principles.[12]

Marx and Engels turned socialism from a utopia into a science. They placed in the hands of the proletariat, struggling for emancipation, a new instrument which it had never seen before—scientific theory. Thus armed, the proletariat acquired the forces to conquer the old world and to build a new one—a new socialist society.

Marxism played a gigantic part in the development of all branches of knowledge, inasmuch as it provided a stable scientific foundation and an immensely powerful scientific method for cognition of phenomena—and, in particular, of social phenomena. It put an end to the mystification of social relationships and to the idealization of these. It showed that they result from a definite condition of productive forces, a definite state of economic development.

The economic order of society of each given epoch represents the real basis whose qualities explain in the last analysis the entire superstructure formed by the sum total of the legal and political institutions—and likewise of the religious, philosophical and other views—of each given historical period. Hegel freed the understanding of history from metaphysics. He made history dialectic, but his own view of history was essentially idealist. Now idealism has been driven out of its last refuge—the field of history. Now the understanding of history has become materialist. Now a road has been found to explain human self-consciousness by the conditions of human existence whereas the old explanation was that human self-consciousness explained these conditions.[13]

Juridical ideas are the form of this human self-consciousness. In themselves they are powerless to explain anything, precisely as we are powerless to explain the ideas themselves if we remain locked within a circle of juridical concepts.

Public law is concerned with legal questions—with juridical relationships, phenomena, and concepts—which, however, it can explain only if it abandons "legal" ground and passes to that of actual social relationships. Starting from what has been already expounded, we must define the object of public law with notably greater breadth, and differently as to methodological principle, than does bourgeois science. We see the object of public law in the

[12] Lenin (Russian ed.), Vol. XVIII, p. 13.
[13] Marx and Engels (Russian ed.), Vol. XIV, p. 26.

study of the legal norms and institutes which reflect, confirm, and develop the social and state order of a given society, the system of social and state institutions, the principles of their interrelations, the extent of their rights and obligations, the methods of their activity, and likewise also the study of various sorts of public-law institutes which define rights and obligations of citizens both in their relationship to society and the state and in their relationship to each other.

Soviet public socialist law studies the socialist order—social and state—of the USSR, its emergence and development, and the system of Soviet state institutions and organs, their powers, obligations and problems (and methods of solving them). It studies the rights of citizens of the USSR—preserved by Soviet legislation—and the obligations to country, society, and state laid upon citizens by the Soviet state.

State territory is not merely an expanded basis for "realizing the power of the state" [14]—it is the material expression of supremacy, independence, and inviolability of the people who inhabit that territory. Territorial supremacy is an organic part of state supremacy, defended with all the might of state and social forces and means, with all the might of moral— political and state—unity of the population.

The idea of inviolability of Soviet state territory as the basis of the supremacy of the Soviet state has been most excellently expressed by Stalin: "We do not wish for a single inch of foreign land. But of our own land we will give not one single inch to anyone." [15]

Soviet public law is concerned also with the idea of state authority. It contemplates *authority* in the state as the organization of the domination, of the guidance of the population with the aid of methods (characteristic of the state) of repressing and educating the subject classes of society in the spirit of protection of the interests of the dominant class.

Contemplating such qualities of state authority as sovereignty, or such forms of state domination as federation and autonomy, Soviet public law is mindful first of all of the relationships of class domination. These are apparent from an analysis of the aggregate of social relationships, namely as relationships of domination.

In place of the formal-juridical analysis of such categories as territory, authority, and population, Soviet public law employs dialectic materialism to explain them, thereby disclosing all the content of the object in its entirety, showing the dynamics of its development and its particular qualities, and explaining the actual substance of its outward forms and filling these in with material substance.

[14] G. Jellinek, *A General Theory of the State* (Russian ed., 1908), p. 289.
[15] Stalin, *Questions of Leninism* (10th ed.), p. 361.

In contrast to the methodology of bourgeois science, which rends an object into two unconnected parts—form and substance—dialectic materialism insists that form and substance are one and contemplates phenomena from the standpoint of that unity. Marx presented a model for analyzing phenomena from the point of view of unity of form and substance in a brilliant article dedicated to the question of substantive and procedural law.

If procedure represents nothing but empty form, then such formal triviality is of no independent value. From this point of view, Chinese law would become French law if squeezed into the form of French procedure. *Substantive law,* however, has its *necessary procedural forms inherent in it,* and as Chinese law must have a walking stick and mediaeval criminal law with its Draconian content required torture, so public, free procedure must necessarily have a substance which is public by nature and dictated by freedom—not by private interest. Procedure and law are just as closely connected with each other as, for example, the forms of plants and animals are with animal flesh and blood. One spirit must animate procedure and laws, since procedure is only *the form of the life of the law* and consequently a manifestation of its inward life.

The pirates of Tidong break the legs and hands of their captives so that they cannot escape. To guarantee themselves against timber thieves the Landtag not only broke the law's hands and feet, but even pierced its heart. In its application of our procedure to certain categories of crime we definitely see no merit whatever. On the contrary we must pay proper tribute to the openness and logic with which unfree form has been given to unfree substance. If private interest which does not endure the light of publicity is factually brought into our law, then it is necessary to give it accordingly such secret procedure as not to arouse and nourish, at least, any sort of dangerous and illusory self-gratification. We consider it the obligation of all Rhine citizens (and especially jurists) to devote their chief attention at the present moment *to the substance of law,* so that there should not be left among us in the last resort an empty mask. Form has no value if it is not the form of a substance.[16]

Soviet public law cannot, therefore, limit its study merely to the formal side of the object under investigation. It seeks to know phenomena from the point of view of their inward content as well as of their outward form.

The object of the science of Soviet socialist law is the material substratum of state relationships as well as juridical form—not only the juridical nature of the state, but also its social-economic nature as the foundation and determinant of the juridical properties and peculiarities of institutes of public law.

Public law may be understood both in a broad and in a narrow sense. In the broad sense it embraces criminal law, administrative law, procedural law, and the foundations of civil law and international law. Criminal law is

[16] Marx and Engels (Russian ed.), Vol. I, pp. 257–258.

part of public law in the broad sense, since it defines the conditions of civic responsibility in the criminal court and the order of application of punishment. Administrative law is part of public law, since it regularizes the relationships of government, defines the organization of government, the system of administrative organs—their powers and their responsibility, and the forms of their activity. Procedural law cannot be separated from public law; it studies the organization of justice, the forms of organization of court organs and organs of the prosecuting magistrates, the procedural order of the activity of state organs, the conditions and order of holding one to responsibility or freeing him from it.[17]

It is harder to establish the connection of public law with civil law. In part of the law of domestic relations and of inheritance, this connection and kinship are beyond question. But even in other parts—in the field of the law of property and of the law of obligations—it is impossible to deny the connection. Thus the law of personal property in the USSR can be neither deduced nor understood nor explained save in connection with the Constitution.

The right to labor—the basis of Soviet labor law—is an object of public law in the broad sense of the word. The same should be said also of international law, which is most closely related to the legal activity of the state.

Thus in essence all branches of law may be included within the orbit of public law if by the latter term is understood the study of all sides of development and activity of the state as manifested in various legal forms.

Public law in the narrow sense, however, limits the range of its study to those questions of which we have previously spoken in establishing the object of the science of public law.

The present course of Soviet socialist public law has also defined its object from the viewpoint of the foregoing definition of our science, having put at the basis of all its exposition—as the proposition wherein it originates —the unshakable principles of the greatest act of victorious socialism: the great Stalin Constitution.

[17] In the history of law this connection of procedural law with public law is brilliantly clear, e.g., from the fact that the fundamental act of the English Constitution is nothing but a simple procedural statute defining the conditions of the arrest of citizens if they are held to criminal responsibility.

II The Fundamental Stages of the Development of the Soviet Constitution

SEC. 1: INTRODUCTION

SOVIET constitutions represent the sum total of the historic path along which the Soviet state has traveled. At the same time, they are the legislative basis of the subsequent development of state life. Thus the development of Soviet constitutions is indissolubly linked with the development of the Soviet state. Changes in the social-political life of our country are reflected in the corresponding changes of Soviet constitutions accepted by the highest organs of state authority.

In Soviet constitutions we have the formal record and legal confirmation of socialist conquests won in the separate stages of the historical development of the Soviet state.

Soviet constitutions are not a program.

A program and a constitution are essentially different. A program speaks of that which is not yet and must still—in the future—be acquired and conquered. A constitution, conversely, must speak of what now is, already acquired and conquered now—in the present.[1]

It is impossible to understand the content of Soviet constitutions and their characteristics without analysis of the historic setting in which they were developed and adopted, and of the conquests whose formal record and legal confirmation they were.

The essence of the constitution is that the basic laws of the state in general, and laws relating to the right to elect to representative institutions (their powers and so on) express the actual correlation of forces in the class struggle. When legislation and actuality part, a constitution is a fiction; when they meet, it is not.[2]

[1] Stalin, *Report on the Draft of the USSR Constitution* (1936), p. 16.
[2] Lenin (Russian ed.), Vol. XIV, p. 18.

The historic road along which the Soviet state has traveled is one of un-interrupted struggle with exploiters, a struggle for the building of socialism. The correlation of class forces varied in separate stages of this historic road.

The first Soviet Constitution—the 1918 Constitution of the RSFSR [3]—and the first constitutions of the other Soviet Republics were confirmed in that period of existence of Soviet authority when only the first steps in building socialism were being taken. These constitutions were adopted in an atmosphere of violent civil war.

The 1924 Constitution of the USSR, on the basis of which the constitutions of the Union Republics were adopted, reflected the features of a historical situation that was still new. They were confirmed after the victorious ending of the civil war, when the Soviet Republics—united into a single Union state—successfully reestablished economy on the basis of the New Economic Policy. In this period the landowning class had already been finally liquidated, but there still existed classes in the city and in the country which carried on a violent struggle against socialism. Finally the Stalin Constitution, and the new constitutions of the Soviet Republics worked out on the basis of it, confirmed by law the complete victory of socialism in our country. They were adopted at a time when the working class and the toiling peasantry, under the guidance of the Communist Party, had successfully completed the struggle for socialist industrialization of our country and for collectivization of agriculture. They were adopted under the conditions of the victory attained by socialism in all branches of national economy, under conditions of a socialist society which had basically been established, in which all exploiter classes were liquidated—where flourished the mutual friendship of working class and peasantry, the fraternal friendship of nations in a system of a single, united socialist state.

Each stage of the development of Soviet constitutions was marked by a progressive broadening of socialist democracy. Even the first Soviet constitutions were the most democratic in the world, inasmuch as they confirmed by law the authority of the toilers and the participation of the broadest popular masses in state government. They were the legal bases for the further development of Soviet democracy in the period of transition from capitalism to socialism.

In the Stalin Constitution—the constitution of victorious socialism—socialist democracy found its most brilliant expression. Drawing ever broader masses of the people into the government of the state, constantly strengthening the bonds between the apparatus of authority and the people, reinforcing revolutionary legality—all this is a necessary consequence of the nature of the state of the proletarian dictatorship—the law of its development.

---

[3] Hereinafter used to designate the Russian Soviet Federative Socialist Republic.—Tr.

Soviet constitutions confirm genuinely democratic rights and freedoms in the toilers' behalf. For the vast majority of the population, the rights of citizens, as proclaimed by bourgeois constitutions, are merely mythical—in bourgeois states the conditions essential to a realization of these rights in behalf of the toilers do not obtain. Soviet constitutions, on the contrary, establish and emphasize material guarantees by virtue of which each citizen can realize the rights ceded to him by the state. From this viewpoint the development of the Soviet state represents an unbroken process of increasing material guarantees to actualize—to actualize in reality—and to extend rights and freedoms. This process is directly reflected in Soviet constitutions in the separate stages of their development. There follows an analysis of the basic characteristics of each of these stages.

SEC. 2: THE GREAT OCTOBER SOCIALIST REVOLUTION, THE FORMATION OF THE RSFSR AND THE FIRST SOVIET CONSTITUTION

1. *General characterization of the period*

The first Soviet Constitution, accepted by the Fifth All-Russian Congress of Soviets (July 10, 1918), is inseparably connected with the great October Socialist Revolution. This constitution was created in an extraordinarily complex and difficult setting. As a result of the October Revolution, the dictatorship of the proletariat had been confirmed in our country. For the first time in human history the worker class, which had won power, and the toiling masses of peasants—under the guidance of the worker class— set about translating Lenin's plan of building socialism in our country into reality.

"In our country socialism had been completely victorious in the *political* field as early as the October days of 1917." [1] In the economic field, however, the matter was more complicated. The Socialist Revolution proceeded in a country economically and culturally backward. In the period under consideration, the economy of the country was characterized (as Lenin pointed out) by the presence of five different social-economic types of life: the patriarchal (chiefly a natural economy), the production of small wares, the capitalism of private proprietorship, state capitalism, and socialism. "Russia is so vast and so variegated that all these different social-economic types are inter-

---

[1] Molotov, Address at the Grand Meeting in the Bolshoy Theater, Nov. 6, 1937, on the Twentieth Anniversary of the October Revolution (Party Publishing House, 1937), p. 28.

woven there. This is precisely what makes its position unique." [2] In the conditions given, the planned reorganization of this social and economic order—with its many types of life—into new socialist concord remained the historic task before the Soviet state, a program of actions calculated upon a prolonged interval of time, an entire *period of transition*. In complete conformity with this circumstance, the first Soviet Constitution delineated the characteristic features of the constitution of a state of the *transition* period from capitalism to socialism.

The Soviet Constitution of 1918 was created in circumstances of extraordinarily sharp conflict with enemies of the proletarian dictatorship, enemies of the Soviet state. The exploiter classes (the landowners and capitalists), who had been overthrown by the socialist revolution, sallied forth against Soviet authority, weapon in hand, with the purpose of overthrowing it and restoring capitalism. All breeds of Mensheviks and SR's, masking their subservience to the interests of capitalistic restoration under a sham "socialism" and crusade for "democracy," developed intensive counterrevolutionary activity. Despicable traitors and agitators representing the bourgeoisie in the ranks of the worker class, people from the camps of Trotsky-Bukharin and Zinovyev-Kamenev and Rykov and others, shaped their course for the restoration of capitalism. Indeed, in the first months of the October Revolution the Trotsky-Bukharin traitors formed a bloc with the so-called "left" SR's behind the backs of the party for the joint realization of a monstrous plan to murder the leaders of the worker class—Lenin, Stalin, and Sverdlov—to overthrow Soviet law and to reestablish the bourgeois-landowners' regime.

In the first stage of development of the Soviet state (from the Second to the Third All-Russian Soviet Congress), Soviet authority marched triumphant through the cities, towns, and villages of Russia, consolidated itself in almost all the immense territory of our land. In this period Soviet authority shattered the armed forces of internal counterrevolution (like Kaledin and Dutov) with comparative ease. Very soon, however, the Soviet Republic had to encounter a much more dangerous enemy—international imperialism.

From the very first days of the October Revolution, both groups of rapacious imperialists, German and Entente, though engaged in a common armed struggle to repartition the world, undertook a series of attempts—with no scruples whatever as to ways and means—to liquidate Soviet authority. German imperialism was, however, the greatest threat during this period.

In consequence of the foul provocation of Trotsky, the Soviet Republic (which had not yet succeeded in organizing its military forces) was subjected as early as February, 1918, to attack by the German militarists. Only the tactical genius of the revolutionary leaders, Lenin and Stalin, which

[2] Lenin (Russian ed.), Vol. XXII, p. 513.

succeeded in winning a peaceful breathing space, and the destruction (by the party and the laboring masses) of the Bukharins, the Trotskys, and the "left" SR's (who had provoked the war) saved the Soviet land from almost inevitable ruin at this period.

The conclusion of the peace of Brest-Litovsk made it possible: (1) for the party to win time to consolidate Soviet authority and to bring the economy of the country into order; (2) to take advantage of clashes in the imperialist camp (the continuing war between the Central Powers and the Entente), to disorganize the enemy's forces, to organize Soviet economy, and to create the Red Army; and (3) for the proletariat to reserve the peasantry for itself and to accumulate forces to destroy the White-Guard generals in the period of the civil war.

In the period of the October Revolution Lenin instructed the Bolshevik Party how essential it was to act fearlessly and decisively when the necessary conditions for such action existed. In the period of the Brest-Litovsk peace, he instructed the party how necessary is an orderly—and momentary—recession when the enemy's forces are known to exceed our own, so as with the greatest energy to make ready a new attack upon our enemies.

History has shown that Lenin's plan was correct in its entirety.[3]

The short breathing space, obtained by the Soviet authority through concluding the peace of Brest-Litovsk, was soon cut short when the Entente imperialists, too, came out openly against the Soviet Republic. Beginning with April, 1918, direct intervention by the "allies"—Japan, England, and France—developed in the Far East and in the north (Murmansk and Archangel). At the end of May, 1918, at the instigation, and with the direct support, of the Anglo-French imperialists, the so-called Czechoslovak Legions (the military divisions of Czechoslovak war prisoners of the World War) broke out against Soviet authority in the territory of Siberia, Ural, and the Volga provinces. Under the guidance and upon the instructions of the interventionists (and supported by the Trotsky-Bukharin traitors), the White Guards, the Mensheviks, the SR's and other anti-Soviet elements organized a whole series of counterrevolutionary uprisings, diversions, and acts of terrorism against the leaders of the Soviet state.

A wave of kulak uprisings rolled over the whole country. At this critical period the village kulaks maliciously sabotaged all the measures of Soviet authority—especially in the matter of provisions—and tried to strangle the revolution with the bony hand of hunger. The Soviet Republic was subjected to a unified attack by counterrevolution—external and internal. The ring of civil war fronts tightened around the Soviet country.

[3] *History of the All-Union Communist Party (of Bolsheviks): A Short Course* (1938), pp. 209–210.

The Constitution of the RSFSR of 1918 was thus born in an atmosphere of extraordinarily tense struggle of the toiling masses of our country against the interventionists, the White Guards, and other counterrevolutionary forces striving to restore capitalism.

2. *The October decrees and their constitutional significance*

The adoption of the first Soviet Constitution was preceded by a whole series of historic decrees of the Soviet government expressive of the subsequent fundamental triumphs of the toiling masses in various fields of state construction:

a) *The creation of the Soviet state and the concentration of entire and complete authority in the country in the hands of the Soviets as the organs of the proletarian dictatorship.*

This found constitutional formulation in the following acts: the Address of the Second All-Russian Congress of Soviets to Workers, Soldiers, and Peasants under date of October 25/November 7, 1917; [4] the decrees of the Second All-Russian Congress of Soviets: Concerning the Institution of the Council of People's Commissars, [5] and Concerning the Fullness of the Authority of the Soviets; [6] the address of Lenin as President of the Soviets of People's Commissars To the People; [7] the instructions of the People's Commissars for Internal Affairs: The Rights and Obligations of the Soviets; [8] the directives of the All-Russian Central Executive Committee: Concerning the Acknowledgment of All Attempts to Appropriate Functions of State Authority as Counterrevolutionary Action; [9] the decree of the All-Russian Central Executive Committee: Concerning the Dismissal of the Constituent Assembly; [10] the decree of the Third All-Russian Congress of Soviets as to changing the name of the Soviet government, [11] and others.

b) *The liberation of the Russian peoples and the proclamation of the Russian Soviet Federated Socialist Republic as a voluntary state union of these peoples, built on the basis of Soviet federation and Soviet autonomy.*

Here should be mentioned the decree of the Second All-Russian Con-

[4] Lenin (Russian ed.), Vol. XXII, p. 11.

[5] Cy. 1917, No. 1, Art. 1. (Abbreviations of references to legislation herein are: Cy: Collection of enactments and orders; Cz: Collection of statutes and orders; Cp: Collection of USSR Government directives and orders.)

[6] Cy. 1917, No. 1, Art. 5.

[7] Lenin (Russian ed.), Vol. XXII, p. 54.

[8] Cy. 1917, No. 12, Art. 180.

[9] Cy. 1918, No. 14, Art. 202.

[10] Cy. 1918, No. 15, Art. 216.

[11] Gazette of Worker-Peasant Government, No. 14 (5a) of Feb. 3/Jan. 21, 1918.

gress of Soviets: Concerning the Peace;[12] Stalin's Declaration of the Rights of Russian Peoples,[13] formulating the basic principles of the policy of Soviet authority as to nationalities; the directives of the Council of People's Commissars: Concerning the Acknowledgment of the Independence of the Ukrainian National Republic,[14] and Concerning the Republic of Finland;[15] the decree as to Turkish Armenia;[16] and in particular: the directive of the Third All-Russian Congress of Soviets: Concerning the Federal Institutions of the Russian Republic,[17] and the address of Stalin, as national commissar for matters of nationalities, to the Soviets of Kazan, Ufa, Orenburg, and others.[18]

c) *The actualization of Lenin's "first steps to socialism" directed toward the liquidation of private property in instruments and means of production, the possession of the proletarian state of commanding economic heights—the transfer of the land and the natural deposit therein, of factories, works, banks, transport, and so forth into property of the proletarian state—property of the entire people.*

The most important legislative acts in this field were the decree of the Second All-Russian Congress of Soviets: The Land;[19] the statute: Concerning Worker Control, adopted by the All-Russian Central Executive Committee;[20] decrees: Concerning the Supreme Council of National Economy;[21] Concerning the Nationalization of Banks;[22] Concerning the Annulment of State Loans;[23] Concerning the Nationalization of Foreign Trade;[24] Concerning the Nationalization of the Largest Enterprises of Industry and Transport,[25] and so forth.

d) *The conquest by the toiling masses of the most democratic rights and freedoms in the world.*

These rights and freedoms were proclaimed in the following decrees: The Eight-hour Work Day;[26] the Abolition of Social Orders and Civil Offi-

[12] Cy. 1917, No. 1, Art. 2.
[13] Cy. 1917, No. 2, Art. 18.
[14] Cy. 1917, No. 6, Art. 90.
[15] Cy. 1917, No. 11, Art. 163.
[16] Lenin-Stalin, *Selected Works of 1917* (1937 ed.), pp. 662–663.
[17] Gazette of the Temporary Worker-Peasant Government, 18/3: Jan., 1918.
[18] In the collection: *The Policy of Soviet Authority Concerning Matters of Nationalities for Three Years* (1920), pp. 8–9.
[19] Cy. 1917, No. 1, Art. 3.
[20] Cy. 1917, No. 3, Art. 35.
[21] Cy. 1917, No. 5, Art. 83.
[22] Cy. 1917, No. 10, Art. 150.
[23] Cy. 1918, No. 27, Art. 353.
[24] Cy. 1918, No. 33, Art. 432.
[25] Cy. 1918, No. 47, Art. 559.
[26] Cy. 1917, No. 1, Art. 10.

cials; [27] Social Insurance—a governmental communication; [28] Civil Marriage, Children, and Records of the Condition Thereof; [29] the Separation of the Church from the State, and of Schools from the Church.[30] The enormous majority of these decrees were published in the period of the triumphal progress of Soviet authority (October, 1917, to January, 1918). Their content was made general in the most outstanding constitutional act of the first stage of the development of the Socialist Revolution—the Lenin-Stalin Declaration of Rights of the Toiling and Exploited People,[31] the essence of which confirmed the conquests of the great October Socialist Revolution and was characterized by the genius of Lenin in the following words—referring to January, 1918: "We have already won: (a) the maximum of democracy; (b) the concrete realization of the first steps to socialism; (c) peace and land." On the basis of this notable "Declaration"—each line a triumph of the revolutionary creativeness of the toiling masses, and likewise of the directive: Concerning the Federal Institutions of the Russian Republic—the Third All-Russian Congress of Soviets (January 10–18/22–31, 1918) commissioned the All-Russian Central Executive Committee to draft the first Soviet Constitution.

3. *The development and confirmation of the First Soviet Constitution: Lenin and Stalin its creators*

The immediate realization of the Congress of Soviets' decision was hampered, however, by the attack of German imperialism and the concentration of the entire attention of the party and of the Soviet government upon the question of winning a breathing space of peace. Only after this had been guaranteed by the ratification of the Brest-Litovsk peace treaty by the Extraordinary Fourth All-Russian Congress of Soviets (March, 1918), was the Soviet government able immediately to proceed with the drafting of the constitution.

On April 1, 1918, the All-Russian Central Executive Committee at its fourth session authorized the formation of a constitutional commission to prepare the constitution. Sverdlov was chosen president of the commission. Stalin played the outstanding role in guiding the activity of the commission and in the development of the basic statutes of the Soviet Constitution.

On April 3, 1918, Stalin's interview with a correspondent of the *Isvestiya of the All-Russian Central Executive Committee* was published. In it Stalin

[27] Cy. 1917, No. 3, Art. 31.
[28] Cy. 1917, No. 2, Art. 17.
[29] Cy. 1917, No. 11, Art. 160.
[30] Cy. 1918, No. 18, Art. 263.
[31] Cy. 1918, No. 15, Art. 215.

noted the characteristic features of Soviet federalism as distinguished from bourgeois federation, pointed out the principles of the organization of the Russian federation, and characterized its structure, the rights of the federated regions and of national minorities, the construction of organs of Soviet authority, and the special characteristics of the Soviet system of suffrage.

The theses worked out by Stalin (by direction of the commission and accepted by it April 12, 1918) regarding the type of Soviet federation were particularly significant for the commission's work. In these emphasis was placed upon the significance of the proletarian dictatorship as an instrument for building socialism under the conditions obtaining during the transition period. Side by side with this, the theses pointed out that only regions distinguished by a special way of life and by a national structure—not regions in general and of every kind—may be subjects of the Soviet federation. Under Stalin's guidance, the commission rejected the anti-Lenin "project" (proposed by Reisner, a member of the commission) of federative organization of the Soviet Republic.

On the basis of his theses, Stalin drafted his project: General Proposals of the Constitution of the Russian Soviet Federative Republic, accepted by the commission at the session of April 19, 1918. In these "general proposals" the chief task of the Soviet Constitution was defined—to establish the dictatorship of the worker class in the form of the mighty All-Russian Soviet authority for the purpose of completely repressing the bourgeoisie, annihilating the exploitation of man by man, and building socialism.

It must be emphasized in this connection that it was precisely against this principle of proletarian dictatorship as the essence of the Soviet Constitution that all the enemies of Soviet authority fought with unprecedented ferocity. Our enemies from the camp of the "left" SR's and Trotsky-Bukharinist traitors who formed a bloc with them—all masquerading in the toga of "friendship" for Soviet authority and skulking behind ultraleftist "revolutionary" phrases—played an especially filthy part in this struggle.

The draft of the Soviet Constitution presented to the commission by Schreider (president of the "left" SR's) completely contradicted the principle of proletarian dictatorship and challenged the Soviets as mere political talking shops after the fashion of the ordinary bourgeois parliaments. To counteract the Bolshevik principle of democratic centralism, the "left" SR's put forward the watchword: "All possible decentralization of government!" This was merely an appeal for the independence of local Soviets with reference to the higher organs of Soviet authority—for local nonfulfillment of statutes and decrees of the proletarian state.

The constitutional commission declined this "left" SR draft of a constitution, precisely as it did the manifestly anarchistic project of a "constitution of a work-republic" proposed by the maximalists.[32]

The most important documents forming the bases of the draft of the constitution worked out by the Commission of the All-Russian Central Executive Committee were the Lenin-Stalin Declaration of Rights of the Toiling and Exploited People and Stalin's General Propositions of the Constitution of the Russian Soviet Federative Republic. After being revised (in a special commission of the Central Committee of the Bolshevik Party of Workers and Peasants) under Lenin's immediate guidance, the draft of the constitution came on for final affirmation by the Fifth All-Russian Congress of Soviets.

This congress was held in Moscow (July 4–10, 1918) in days of extraordinarily intense struggle with foreign interventionists and internal counterrevolution. On July 6–7, the "left" SR's (acting in complete agreement with the Bukharins and Trotskys) perpetrated, for political purposes, the murder of the German ambassador (Mirbach) and organized a counterrevolutionary *putsch* against the Soviet authority. The delegates to the Congress, under the immediate guidance of Lenin, took part in liquidating this *putsch* (which revealed, once and for all, the essentially counterrevolutionary nature of the "left" SR's). The Congress of Soviets completely approved the external and internal policy of the Soviet government, and in its final session (July 10) unanimously adopted and ratified the first Soviet Constitution in the name of the toiling masses of the entire Soviet land.

In his address to the congress (July 5), Lenin emphasized the fundamental peculiarity of this constitution as a document which recorded and formulated all that had already been created by the revolutionary experience —the revolutionary creativeness—of the toiling masses. Turning to the delegates of the congress, as the authentic representatives of the broadest masses of workers and peasants, he said:

If we are now able to propose a Soviet Constitution to this Congress, it is only because Soviets have been created and tested in every corner of our land, because you have created that constitution, you in every corner of the land have tested it. Only a half year after the October Revolution—hardly a year after the First All-Russian Congress of Soviets—we were able to put in writing what has already existed in practice.[33]

In its July 10th directive,[34] the Congress of Soviets ordained:

[32] The name of a group of SR's who split off from that party and put forward a "maximalist" program—by terror and expropriation to cause a national uprising and overthrow tsarism, and to open the way to a struggle for socialism; a semianarchistic organization of a group of frenzied members of the petty bourgeoisie.

[33] Lenin (Russian ed.), Vol. XXIII, p. 121.

[34] Cy. 1918, No. 51, Art. 582.

The declaration of rights of the toiling and exploited people, ratified by the Third All-Russian Congress of Soviets in January 1918, together with the Constitution of the Soviet Republic, ratified by the Fifth All-Russian Congress of Soviets, constitute the sole, fundamental law of the Russian Soviet Federative Socialist Republic.

The first Soviet Constitution consisted of six parts: Part I, the Declaration of Rights of the Toiling and Exploited People; Part II, the General Statutes of the Constitution of the RSFSR; Part III, the Construction of Soviet Authority; Part IV, the Active and Passive Right of Suffrage; Part V, Budget Law; and Part VI, the Coat of Arms and Flag of the RSFSR.

According to Article 1 of the constitution, the RSFSR was declared a Republic of the Soviets, all of the authority wherein belongs to the Soviets. In Article 2 was formulated the basic principle of the Soviet federation—the free union of free nations. Article 3 established that the decisive problem of the Soviet state is "the annihilation of every sort of exploitation of man by man, the complete elimination of the division of society into classes, the pitiless crushing of exploiters, the establishment of the socialist organization of society, and the victory of socialism in all countries. . . ."

Completely corresponding with the setting of the savage struggle of the proletarian dictatorship with class enemies, the constitution ordained that "there can be no place for exploiters in any one of the organs of authority" (Art. 7), and that the RSFSR "deprives separate persons and separate groups of rights exercised by them to the detriment of the interests of the socialist revolution" (Art. 23). In Article 9 it was pointed out that the basic task of the Soviet Constitution is to establish the dictatorship of the proletariat and the poorest peasants. Articles 11–12 established the principles of unifying national Soviet autonomies within the framework of the Russian federation and pointed out that the highest organ of authority of the RSFSR is the All-Russian Congress of Soviets and the Executive Committee chosen thereby. Articles 13–22 fixed the most important rights and obligations of the toilers —freedom of conscience, the guarantee of real freedom to express their opinions; freedom of assembly, meetings, processions, and unions; a guarantee to them of genuine access to knowledge; the obligations of all citizens to toil, to defend the socialist fatherland (and to universal military service); the giving of political rights to toiling foreigners; the right of asylum; and the equal rights of citizens (irrespective of their race and nationality). These Articles were particularly characterized by the fact that they were no mere declaration of the rights of citizens—these were, as well, material guarantees whereby the toilers could realize these rights in practice.

Subdivision 3 of the constitution established (a) the principles and order of organization of Soviet authority in the governing center and in the rural areas; (b) the competence of higher and local organs of Soviet authority; (c) the order of elections; (d) the rules of representation in Congresses of the Soviets; and so on. This subdivision was extraordinarily significant as regards strengthening the unity and introducing harmony throughout the system of organs of the Soviet authority, on the basis of the principle of democratic centralism.

To the end of guaranteeing the guiding role of the worker class in the Soviets, the constitution confirmed, in the election rules, certain advantages in its behalf as compared with the peasantry. Pursuant to Article 65 of the constitution, the exploiter elements—the landowners and the bourgeoisie—monks and ministers of religious cults, servants and agents of former police, the gendarmerie, the secret police, and so on, were deprived of voting rights.

The Constitution of the RSFSR of 1918 confirmed the foundations of Soviet authority already created by the toiling masses, and projected "a general perspective of further development of the land of the Soviets on the path to socialism" (Molotov). It was the banner of the struggle of the toiling masses for socialism, the legislative basis of the subsequent building of the Soviet state. It reflected the "ideals of the proletariat of the whole world." [35]

The first Soviet Constitution was brought into operation in the grim setting of foreign military intervention and civil war. But even in these conditions its character—as the most democratic constitution in the world—found its most brilliant manifestation.

In so difficult a time as that of war, when the action of European constitutions —established for ages and part of the folkways of western European man—have been almost entirely suspended, the Soviet Constitution (in the sense of the participation of the popular masses in government and in independent decision of matters of government in the Congresses and in the Soviets and in the reelections) was applied in the countryside in dimensions unequalled elsewhere in the world.[36]

When civil war flared up in November, 1918, the Extraordinary Sixth All-Russian Congress of Soviets adopted a special directive: Exact Observance of Laws [37] wherein was pointed out the enormous significance of exact observance of the Soviet Constitution and the laws of RSFSR "for the further development and reinforcement of the power of workers and peasants in Russia." The congress emphasized that "measures deviating from the laws of the Russian Socialist Federative Soviet Republic, or going beyond the

[35] Lenin (Russian ed.), Vol. XXIII, p. 150.
[36] Ibid., Vol. XXIV, p. 615.
[37] Cy. 1918, No. 90, Art. 908.

bounds thereof, are admissible only if called forth by special conditions of civil war and the struggle with counterrevolution."

Of the greatest significance in the processes of building the Soviet state on the basis of the first Soviet Constitution were the directives of the Seventh (December, 1919), Eighth (December, 1920), and Ninth (December, 1921) All-Russian Congresses of Soviets concerning the organization of the Soviet state structure. These (1) comprised the legislative formulation of the competence of the Presidium of the All-Russian Central Executive Committee as an organ representing the Committee in the period between sessions thereof summoned by the Presidium, and (2) emphasized the significance of the limitation of functions as between the Committee, its Presidium, and the Council of People's Commissars. It should be especially noted that in the directive of the Eighth All-Russian Congress of Soviets, for example, it was specifically pointed out that "no organs except the All-Russian Congress of Soviets, the All-Russian Central Executive Committee, its Presidium, and the Council of People's Commissars have the right to enact legislation of state-wide significance." [38]

Side by side with this, the foregoing directives formulated a series of most important proposals as to the work of the Soviets and of executive committees locally, summoning Congresses of the Soviets, and regulating the interrelation of central and local organs of Soviet authority on the basis of exact observance of the principle of democratic centralization, and so forth.

Directives of the Seventh, Eighth, and Ninth All-Russian Congresses of Soviets were adopted and put into effect—against a background of violent struggle with Detsists [39] and other anti-Party, counterrevolutionary elements, striving to undermine the guiding role of the Party in the system of proletarian dictatorship and to frustrate the building of the young Soviet state.

4. *The 1918 Constitution of the RSFSR and the constitutions of the other Soviet Socialist Republics*

The fundamental proposals of the 1918 Constitution of the RSFSR were models for the creation of constitutions of the fraternal Soviet Socialist Republics (Ukrainian SSR, the White Russian SSR, the Azerbaijan, Ar-

---

[38] Cy. 1921, No. 1, Art. 1.

[39] The name of an opportunist group headed by Sapronov-Osinsky, which came forward in 1919–1920 against Lenin's party-organization principles, against the guiding role of the Party in the work of the Soviets, against management on unitary responsibility, and against the creating of a strong centralized Soviet apparatus. The group screened their counterrevolutionary actions by demagogic watchwords: "handing over greater independence to the Soviet apparatus," "broadening the principle of collegia," and so on. The counterrevolutionary actions of this "faction of the noisiest vociferators" (Lenin) were supported by followers of Rykov, Bukharin, Trotsky, and other anti-Party groups.

menian and Georgian SSR) formed in 1917–1921 in the territory of the former Russian empire. These republics emerged with the direct, fraternal assistance of the RSFSR—of the great Russian people—many of whose best sons gave up their lives at the fronts during the civil war to emancipate the territories of the Ukraine, White Russia, Transcaucasia and other national borderlands from interventionists, White Guards, and the forces of nationalist counterrevolution.

On February 4, 1919, at the First Congress of the Soviets of White Russia, the first Constitution of the White Russian Soviet Socialist Republic was adopted. The Constitution of the Ukrainian Soviet Socialist Republic was adopted on March 10, 1919, in the Third All-Ukrainian Congress of Soviets. On May 19, 1921, the First Congress of the Soviets of Azerbaijan adopted the Constitution of the Azerbaijan Socialist Soviet Republic. On February 2, 1922, the First Congress of Soviets of Armenia adopted the Constitution of the Armenian Soviet Socialist Republic. In February of the same year, at the First Congress of Soviets of Georgia, the Constitution of the Georgian Soviet Socialist Republic was adopted.

In complete accord with the basic features of the Constitution of the RSFSR, the constitutions of the fraternal Soviet Socialist Republics were constructed upon the following principles: the establishment of Soviet authority as the state form of proletarian dictatorship, and the fundamental problems of that dictatorship—the transition from capitalism to socialism, the liquidation of classes, the annihilation of man's exploitation of man and of private property in land, the declaration that forests, natural deposits and waters are state property, the taking away of the political rights of exploiters, the building of organs of state authority on the basis of the principles of democratic centralism, and so forth.

The unity of the fundamental proposals of the Constitution of the RSFSR and of the constitutions of the other fraternal Soviet Socialist Republics demonstrated most brilliantly the international character of Soviet authority, which—on the principles of genuine democracy—rallies the toiling masses of various nationalities in the joint struggle against exploiters and for the building of socialism.

SEC. 3: THE FORMATION OF THE USSR AND THE FIRST UNION CONSTITUTION

1. *General characterization of the period of the formation of the USSR*

The mutual and brotherly friendship of the nations of our country was built on the foundation of the victory of the Soviets and the confirmation of the proletarian dictatorship. The very first measures of Soviet authority—relative to the emancipation of the formerly oppressed peoples—won for the Russian proletariat the faith of its brothers of other nations and created the ground for a close alliance between the numerous nations of Soviet Russia. The unifying movement of these passed through the following stages: 1917 to the middle of 1918—the period of liberation of the nations, when "the collaboration of the peoples had not yet a completely definite and rigidly fixed form":[1] the middle of 1918 to 1920—the period of foreign military intervention and civil war, when the existence of the republics was threatened with deadly danger and they were forced to have a united military policy in order to defend their existence; and 1921 to 1922—the victorious end of the civil war and the amplification of the military union of Soviet Republics by an economic union.

In October, 1922,

the Red army and the partisans of the Far East freed Vladivostok—the last bit of Soviet land in the hands of the interventionists—from the Japanese. Now, with all the territories of the Soviet land purged of interventionists, and the task of building socialism to defend the country requiring further reinforcement of the union of the nations of the Soviet land, the immediate question was of closer unification of the Soviet Republics in a single state union. All the national forces must be unified for the building of socialism. Strong defense of the country must be organized. All-sided development of all the nationalities of our land must be guaranteed. To accomplish this purpose, all the nationalities of the Soviet land must be brought into still closer proximity.[2]

The formation of the USSR—the only state comprising many nationalities—was the "final stage in developing the forms of collaboration which, on this occasion, assumed the character of military economy and political unification."[3]

[1] Stalin, *Marxism and the National-Colonial Question* (Party Publishing House, 1937), p. 105.
[2] *History of the All-Union Communist Party (of Bolsheviks): A Short Course*, p. 279.
[3] Stalin, *Marxism and the National-Colonial Question* (1937), p. 106.

In his address at the Tenth All-Russian Congress of Soviets, Stalin pointed out the following three causes for the inevitability and necessity of unifying the Soviet Republics into one Union state: (1) problems of rehabilitating the national economy, which demanded the rallying of all the forces of the Soviet Republics; (2) the constant threat from capitalist countries, the possibility of new attacks; (3) the very nature of Soviet authority—international in its essence—which had led the Soviet Republics along the road of unification. At the time of the formation of the USSR the Soviet Republics, which had defended their existence and independence in the civil war, concentrated all their efforts upon building a socialist economy and culture—on reestablishing the national economy. The transition to the New Economic Policy played a decisive part in that campaign. The Policy was calculated "upon (a) the admission of capitalism—provided the commanding heights remained in the hands of the proletarian state; (b) the struggle of capitalist and socialist elements; (c) the growth of the role of the socialist elements to the detriment of capitalist elements; (d) the victory of socialist elements over capitalist elements; (e) the annihilation of classes; and (f) building the basis of socialist economy." [4]

A two-year struggle to reestablish national economy on the basis of the New Economic Policy brought the country out of a condition of collapse. There was a steady rise, first in agriculture, and then in heavy industry. An economic basis for strengthening the union of the worker class with the peasantry through the development of turnover of goods was created. The leading role of progressive, socialist economy was strengthened in the entire national economy. The ruin caused by the war made the struggles of separate republics in the field of economic rehabilitation inadequate, however, and the further restoration of the national economy appeared impossible under a system of separate republics.

The growth of economy and the reinforcement of the might of the Soviet Republics were the most important factors in the acute crisis in the mutual relations of the Soviet Republics and the bourgeois states. Economic blockade and attempts at the immediate overthrow of the Soviet authority in open, armed struggle were replaced by de facto recognition of the Soviet state by capitalist states and the conclusion of trade agreements. The struggle of the two systems—capitalist and socialist—took on new and still more complex forms. Defeated in open political struggle and civil war, the class enemies of the proletarian dictatorship construed the transition to the New Economic Policy as an evolution toward the restoration of capitalism in our land and the beginning of the bourgeois regeneration of the proletarian state.

[4] Ibid., p. 106.

The exploiter classes and their political agents—Mensheviks, the SR's, the Trotskys, Bukharins, bourgeois nationalists and others—counted on the Soviet authority being compelled to open the road to private capital wider and wider. In this period there was a notable revival of activity of some bourgeois intellectuals, ill-disposed toward the Soviets and seeking to utilize certain legal possibilities for a struggle with Soviet authority. The Twelfth Party Conference (August, 1922) noted:

> Anti-Soviet parties and trends strive systematically to turn agricultural co-operation into an instrument of kulak counterrevolution, the professorial chair in higher educational institutions into a tribune of overt bourgeois propaganda, and lawful publishing into a means of agitation against the worker-peasant authority.

In connection with the introduction of the New Economic Policy, imperialistic chauvinism began to grow and to be intensified, "the idea of shifting boundary marks was born; there were vagrant desires to organize in the world order what Denikin failed to organize—that is, to create so-called 'one and indivisible;' local chauvinism also was intensified (Georgia, Azerbaijan, and Bokhara), . . . threatening to turn certain of our republics into an arena of nationalist squabbling and to undermine there the bonds of internationalism." [5]

Trotskyism developed a furious struggle against the policy of the Soviet authority, repeating, in fact, the watchwords of the counterrevolutionary boundary shifters—Mensheviks and SR's. In conditions when intensifications of party guidance of the country's economic life were needed, Trotskyism put forward the watchword of nonintervention by the party in the activity of economic organs. Trotskyism strove to develop measures threatening to breach the union of workers and peasants, and proposed "superindustrialization"—a policy of violently expropriating—of "devouring"—small commodity producers. For provocative purposes it strove for a policy of taxing the villages as much as possible and of screwing up the prices of industrial goods.

In these conditions of savage class struggle the USSR was formed, the first Union Constitution was worked out, and the movement to unite the peoples of the Soviet Republics, to which the laboring masses were led by "the very structure of the Soviet authority—international in its class nature—attained its culmination." [6]

---

[5] *Ibid.*, pp. 112–113.
[6] *Declaration Concerning the Formation of the Union of Soviet Socialist Republics* (1937), pp. 112, 113.

2. The development and confirmation of the Constitution of the USSR (1924)

At the end of 1922 the Soviet Republics of Transcaucasia, Azerbaijan, Armenia, and Georgia took the initiative in posing the question of unifying Soviet Republics into a single Union state. Almost simultaneously, the question of creating the USSR was posed in the Ukraine and in White Russia. The internationalism of Soviet authority and the preestablished bonds between the republics guaranteed the success of this unifying movement. In December, 1922, the Congresses of Soviets of the RSFSR, Ukraine, and White Russia, and of the republics of the Transcaucasian federation (Azerbaijan, Armenia, and Georgia) passed a decision that it was necessary to form the USSR, and assigned delegations empowered to work out and to accept a contract relative thereto. On December 29, 1922, there was a conference of these delegations which accepted the project of a "Declaration" and a "Compact Concerning the Formation of the USSR," and on December 30, 1922, the First Congress of Soviets of the USSR assembled, consummating the movement of the peoples of Soviet Russia to unite into a single state union.

The First Congress of Soviets of the USSR—after hearing the report of Stalin as to the formation of the USSR and considering the drafts of the Declaration and of the Compact Concerning the Formation of the USSR —adopted the following resolution:

1. To confirm in principle the declaration and the compact of union.

2. In view of the extraordinary importance of the declaration which has been adopted and the compact which has been concluded, and of the desirability of hearing the final opinions of all the republics entering the Union as to the text of the present compact, to transmit the declaration and compact for further consideration by the Central Executive Committees of the republics entering the Union—upon condition that the responses of such republics be furnished to the Central Executive Committee of the USSR at its next ordinary session.

3. To empower the next ordinary session of the Central Executive Committee of the USSR to consider the responses obtained, to confirm the text of the declaration and the Union compact, and immediately to put the same into operation.

4. To empower the Central Executive Committee of the USSR to prepare for the Second Congress of the Soviets of the Union a final text of the declaration and of the Union compact and to hand the same over for final affirmation by the Second Congress.[7]

[7] *Stenographic Report of the First Congress of the Soviets of USSR* (published by Central Executive Committee of USSR), Annex 1, p. 8.

On January 10, 1923, the Central Executive Committee of the USSR, chosen by the First Congress of Soviets, formed a Constitutional Commission. The commission was confronted with the task of working out—in conformity with the Leninist-Stalinist doctrine of Soviet federation—a Union Constitution completely reflecting the unity of the republics, their acknowledged equality of rights, and a plenary guarantee of their interests in the Union organs.

Stalin's report at the Twelfth Congress of the Bolshevik Worker-Peasant Party—"Nationalist Elements in the Structure of the Party and the State"— was of vast significance for working out the Union Constitution. Stalin indicated the forms and means indispensable to the realization of the development of the USSR as a single state of many nationalities:

1. The institution—in the system of higher organs of the Union—of a special organ representing all national republics and national regions, without exception and on principles of equality—an organ which would "reflect the special interests of nationalities, nations and tribes inhabiting the territories of the Union of Republics." [8]

2. The construction of commissariats of the Union on principles guaranteeing satisfaction of the needs and demands of the peoples of the Union.

3. The creation of the organs of national republics and regions preeminently from local people knowing the language, way of life, *mores* and customs of the respective nations, in order that Soviet authority in the republics might come to be understood and accepted by the masses of all republics (and especially of those backward in respect to economics and culture).

Stalin's report and the decisions of the Twelfth Congress of the Bolshevik Worker-Peasant Party based thereon lay at the foundation of the further development of the Constitution of the USSR. This constitution was drafted in the midst of an irreconcilable conflict with opponents of the unification of the Soviet Republics—the imperialist chauvinists and the bourgeois nationalists.

Under the guidance of Stalin, the Constitutional Commission rejected drafts of a Union Constitution worked out under the immediate influence of bourgeois nationalists and Trotskyists and contradictory to the fundamental propositions of the Compact for the Formation of the USSR, to the decisions of the Twelfth Congress of the Bolshevik Worker-Peasant Party and to the principle of democratic centralism—the basic organization-principle upon which the Soviet state apparatus was constructed.

The Fourth Conference of the Executive Committee of the Bolshevik Worker-Peasant Party, with responsible workers of the national republics

[8] Stalin, *Marxism and the National-Colonial Question* (1937), p. 123.

and regions (June 9–12, 1923), was of decisive significance in the final working out of the Union Constitution. The most important questions on the conference's agenda was that of the Union Constitution, particularly that of the structure and functions of the central organs of authority of the USSR, and that of the method of forming the second chamber of the Central Executive Committee—of the Council of Nationalities, its rights and jurisdiction. The conference expressed itself in favor of the necessity of equal representation of the autonomous and independent republics, of each chamber having equal rights—"preserving for each the right of legislative initiative and observing the condition whereby no single legislative proposal, introduced for consideration by the first or second chamber, could become a statute without the consent thereto of each chamber voting separately." [9] The conference noted the method of settling questions in dispute between the chambers (through a conciliation commission, sessions of the Central Executive Committee and the Congress of Soviets).

The conference rejected the proposal to create two presidia of the Central Executive Committee of the Union (to correspond with the two houses of the Central Executive Committee of the USSR) and expressed itself in favor of creating a *single* presidium.[10] "The formation of two presidia with legislative functions is a dichotomy of supreme authority which will inevitably create great difficulties in work. The houses must have their own presidia, but without legislative functions."

The conference pointed out that the presidium of the Central Executive Committee of the Union must be chosen by both houses of the Central Executive Committee, guaranteeing the representation of nationalities—or at least of the largest of them.

On the basis of these decisions and the directions of Stalin, the constitutional commission finished its work on June 16, 1923, having turned over the draft of the Union Constitution to the Commission of the Central Committee of the Bolshevik Worker-Peasant Party and to the Presidium of the Central Executive Committee of the USSR. The first subdivision of the draft was Stalin's Declaration Concerning the Formation of the USSR. The Compact Concerning the Formation of the USSR, adopted at the first Congress of Soviets of the USSR as a result of the work of the constitutional commission, was amplified and changed. A number of separate proposals and clauses of the Compact were elaborated into independent chapters of the constitution. The most important proposals resulting from the unity of the USSR were amplified: only the Congress of Soviets of the USSR have

---

[9] *The All-Union Communist Party (of Bolsheviks) in Resolutions and Decisions of the Congress, Conferences and Plena of the Central Committee*, Pt. 1, p. 539.
[10] *Ibid.*

the right to affirm and to change the fundamental principles of the constitution; the supreme organs of the Union have the right to regulate questions of changes of boundaries between Union Republics; and Union organs conduct all diplomatic relations and conclude political and other compacts with other states. As compared with the Compact, the jurisdiction of the Union organs was broadened. In June and July, 1923, this elaborated draft of the constitution was completely approved in sessions of the Central Executive Committees of the Union Republics and the republics of Transcaucasia.[11]

On June 6, 1923, the second session of the Central Executive Committee of the USSR—at its first convocation—approved a decision:

(1) To confirm the fundamental law (the Constitution) of the USSR and immediately to put it into operation; (2) to introduce for final approval by the second Congress of Soviets of the USSR the text of the fundamental law (Constitution) of the USSR, accepted by the present session of the Central Executive Committee of the USSR; and (3) until the formation of the Presidium of the Central Executive Committee of the USSR on the basis of Chapters IV and V of the Constitution of the USSR, all the powers given to the Central Executive Committee of the Union by the Constitution shall be reposed in the Presidium of the Central Executive Committee of the USSR—chosen at the first session of the Central Executive Committee of the USSR on the 30th of December, 1922, as a body of nineteen members.[12]

The activity of the all-union government began with the first convocation of the second session of the Central Executive Committee of the USSR which formed the Council of People's Commissars of the USSR under the presidency of Lenin. On July 13, 1923, Kalinin, President of the Central Executive Committee of the USSR, informed all the Central Executive Committees of the Union Republics of the beginning of the work of the Presidium of the Central Executive Committee of the USSR.[13]

After some days the Council of People's Commissars of the USSR entered upon its work.

On July 23 the government of the USSR informed foreign powers that it had assumed conduct of the foreign relations of the Soviet Republics.

The ratification of the Union Constitution at the Second Congress of Soviets of the USSR completed the legislative formulation of the USSR and

[11] Cf. Stenographic reports of the Second Session of All-Russian Central Executive Committee (June 29); and the Third Session of All-Ukrainian Central Executive Committee, seventh convocation (July 1–2). Cf. Code of Laws, White Russian SSR (1923, Nos. 13–14).

[12] Stenographic Report of Second Session, Central Executive Committee of USSR, p. 16.

[13] Herald of Central Executive Committee, Council of People's Commissars, and Labor-Defense Council of the USSR (1923, No. 1), Par. 11.

thereby created a firm basis for the nations of the USSR to live together in brotherhood and peace.

The Second Congress of Soviets of the USSR was held during the days when the entire nation was in mourning—Lenin died on January 21, 1924. The first session of the Congress, meeting on January 26, was dedicated entirely to his commemoration. He had ceaselessly reiterated "the necessity of the voluntary union of the peoples of our country, and of fraternal collaboration within the framework of the Union of Republics" [14] (Stalin). The climax of the first session of the Congress was the historical speech of Stalin—the genius who succeeded to and continued Lenin's work. The leader of the Bolsheviks took the following oath concerning the carrying out of Lenin's legacy: To hold high and to keep pure the great calling of party membership, to guard the unity of our party as the apple of his eye, to protect and consolidate the proletarian dictatorship, to strengthen with all his powers the union of workers and peasants, to strengthen and broaden the Union of Republics, to reinforce our Red Army and our Red Fleet, and to consolidate and broaden the union of toilers of the entire world—the Communist International.

On January 31, 1924, the Second Congress of Soviets of the USSR finally ratified the first Constitution of the USSR. In amplification of Paragraph 26, the Congress pointed out that the Presidium of the Central Executive Committee of the USSR is formed in joint session of the Soviet of the Union and the Soviet of Nationalities, but that their voting at this session is done separately.

The Second Congress of Soviets of the USSR was preceded by Congresses of Soviets of the Union Republics, which unanimously approved the Constitution of the USSR accepted by the second session of the Central Executive Committee of the USSR. At the Congress of Soviets it was emphasized that the Union Constitution—erected on principles of mutual confidence and collaboration—completely reflects the political, economic, and national characteristics of the Union Republics and guarantees the free development of national culture and a mighty advance of the economy of the peoples of the Soviet Republics. [15]

The 1924 Constitution of the USSR consisted of two parts—the Declaration Concerning the Formation of the USSR, and the Compact Concerning

[14] *Stenographic Report of the Second Congress of the Soviets of the USSR*, p. 27.

[15] Cf. *Izvestiya*, No. 127 of 1923 as to the Third Congress of Soviets of Azerbaijan SSR; No. 280 of 1923 as to the Third Congress of Soviets of the Armenian SSR; No. 5 of 1924 as to the Second Congress of Soviets of the Georgian SSR; No. 6 of 1924 as to the Transcaucasian Congress of Soviets; No. 17 of 1924 as to the Fifth Congress of Soviets of the White Russian SSR; No. 18 of 1924 as to the Eighth Congress of Soviets of the Ukrainian SSR; and No. 24 of 1924 as to the Eleventh All-Russian Congress of Soviets.

the Formation of the USSR, which comprised eleven sections: (1) the matters of concern to the supreme organs of authority of the USSR; (2) the sovereign rights of Union Republics and of Union citizenship; (3) the Congress of Soviets of the USSR; (4) the Central Executive Committee of the USSR; (5) the Presidium of the Central Executive Committee of the USSR; (6) the Council of People's Commissars of the USSR; (7) the Supreme Court of the USSR; (8) the People's Commissariats of the USSR; (9) the Unified State Political Administration (OGPU); (10) the Union Republics; (11) the Coat of Arms, Flag, and Capital of the USSR.

The 1924 Constitution of the USSR established the unification of Soviet Socialistic Republics into one Union state on the basis of the genuine brotherhood with confidence and equal rights of nations. It defined the method whereby separate Republics enter the Union—while preserving the right to withdraw freely therefrom—and likewise the method of organization and the jurisdiction of the Union organs of authority. It established the principle that the most important questions of the state's life, guaranteeing the USSR's unity of action in the field of external and internal policy (foreign affairs, defense, direction of foreign trade, transport, communication, and postal and telegraph matters), and the establishment of a single system of money and credit, and so forth, were to come under the jurisdiction of the organs of the USSR (Art. 1).

The sovereignty of the Union Republics is restricted only (1) by the limitations set forth in the present Constitution, and (2) with reference to matters referred to the jurisdiction of the Union. Outside these limitations, each Union Republic exercises its own state sovereignty independently. The USSR preserves the sovereign rights of the Union Republics.[16]

The supreme organ of power of the USSR was the Congress of Soviets; in the period between Congresses it was the Central Executive Committee of the USSR, consisting of the Soviet of the Union and the Soviet of Nationalities (Art. 8).

The Constitution provided that both chambers of the Central Executive Committee of the USSR were absolutely equal in respect of their rights.

The Soviet of the Union and the Soviet of Nationalities consider all decrees, codes, and directives which come to them from the Presidium of the Central Executive Committee and the Soviet of People's Commissars of the USSR, individual People's Commissariats of the Union, Central Executive Committees of the Union Republics, and also those which originate with the Soviet of the Union and the Soviet of Nationalities.[17]

[16] Constitution, Art. 3.
[17] Ibid., Art 16.

Legislative projects coming up to be considered by the Central Executive Committee of the USSR have the force of law only upon their acceptance both by the Soviet of the Union and by the Soviet of Nationalities.[18]

The Central Executive Committee of the USSR selects presidents of the Central Executive Committee of the USSR in accordance with the number of Union Republics—originally four (Art. 27). The Presidium of the Central Executive Committee of the USSR in the period between sessions of that committee is "the highest legislative, executive and directive organ of authority of the USSR" (Art. 29) and "publishes decrees, directives and orders" (Art. 33).

The Union Constitution established the responsibility and accountability of the Council of People's Commissars of the USSR to the Central Executive Committee of the USSR and its Presidium. The Council of People's Commissars of the USSR was formed by the Central Executive Committee of the USSR and was its executive and directive organ (Par. 37). Within the limits of the rights entrusted to it by the Central Executive Committee of the USSR, and on the basis of the regulation concerning the Council of People's Commissars of the USSR (Art. 38), the Council of People's Commissars issued decrees and directives.

In accordance with the jurisdiction of All-Union organs of state authority and government, the Constitution of the USSR defined the organization— for the immediate guidance of the separate branches of state government within the sphere of jurisdiction of the USSR Council of People's Commissars—of people's commissariats (commissariats of the Union in general) single commissariats for the whole USSR; and united commissariats, whose organs, in carrying out their tasks within the territory of the Union Republics, were the people's commissariats of the same name in those republics (Arts. 50–54).

The Supreme Court of the USSR—whose president, vice president, and members were designated by the Presidium of the Central Executive Committee of the USSR (Arts. 43–45)—was established in order "to confirm revolutionary legality" in the territory of the USSR under the Central Executive Committee of the USSR. In Articles 46, 47 and 63, the Constitution established that the Public Prosecutor of the Supreme Court of the USSR and his assistant be designated—and their activity defined—by the Presidium of the Central Executive Committee of the USSR.

Upon the Unified State Political Administration (OGPU), instituted under the Council of People's Commissars of the USSR, the Constitution of the USSR laid the duty of carrying on the struggle with political and

[18] *Ibid.*, Art. 22.

economic counterrevolution, espionage and banditry. Supervision over the legality of the action of the OGPU was exercised by the Public Prosecutor of the Supreme Court of the USSR (Arts. 61–63). The next six Articles (64–69) defined the structure of organs of state authority and government in the Union Republics.

Such were the fundamental proposals of the 1924 Constitution of the USSR. They conformed completely with the principles of the national policy of Lenin-Stalin and affirmed the equality of rights of the peoples of the Union Republics entering the USSR on a voluntary basis. It was the legislative formulation of the unification of Soviet Republics into one Union state. It demonstrated to the toilers of the whole world the solution of the question of nationalities in the spirit of proletarian internationalism—in the spirit of close collaboration of nations with equal rights. It was the basis of further development of Soviet democracy and of the growth of real possibilities for the successful economic social-cultural building of the Soviet Republics. It was the juridical basis for the later legal activity of the All-Union organs of authority. The third session of the Central Executive Committee of the USSR (November, 1923) confirmed the regulations as to higher organs of authority and government, as to people's commissariats, All-Union and unified, and as to the Supreme Court of the USSR; accepted the temporary regulation as to local finances; and solved the question of the order of governing industry which had All-Union significance and was within the jurisdiction of the Supreme Council of National Economy of the USSR. In October and December, 1924, the All-Union statutes concerned with the courts, finances and budget, external trade, and so forth, were adopted.[19]

3. *Changes in the Constitutions of Union Republics on the basis of the USSR Constitution*

The adoption of the USSR Constitution put before the Union Republics the question of revising the old constitutions hitherto in force. Article 5 of the USSR Constitution ordained: "The Union Republics, in conformity herewith, (shall) introduce changes into their own constitutions." During 1925 this work proceeded in the Union Republics. The revision was dictated not only by the fact that the USSR had been formed but also by the fact that in the first constitutions of Ukraine and White Russia there was no solution for a series of such exceedingly important matters as the juris-

[19] Specific references to the following are omitted: procedure (Oct. 29, 1924), criminal legislation and procedure and war crimes (Oct. 31, 1924), state income tax (Oct. 29, 1924), budget laws as between Union and constituent Republics (Oct. 29, 1924), the law as to customs duties (Oct. 25, 1924), and the distribution of state funds as between Union and Republics (Dec. 9, 1924).

diction of the Council of People's Commissars, the system of people's commissariats, and so forth. Aside from this, it was necessary to eliminate certain articles which reflected a stage of the struggle already passed and were already obsolete at the moment when the constitutions were revised (e.g., socialization of land, worker control, and so forth).

The revision of the constitutions in the Union Republics went on under conditions of struggle with the Trotsky (right) elements and their allies, the nationalists, who sought to take advantage of this revision for purposes of changing the bases of the proletarian dictatorship and the principles of building an apparatus of authority and government. They sought to obtain "constitutional guarantees" for the unobstructed development of capitalist elements under cover of the New Economic Policy, to hamper the development of socialism, and to facilitate conditions for restoring capitalism in the USSR.

Our party unmasked all these efforts. The new constitutions of the Union Republics, affirmed in Congresses of the Soviets in 1925 and 1927,[20] completely reflected the principle of unifying the multinational population into a single Union state on the basis of proletarian dictatorship. They introduced changes into the jurisdiction of the higher organs of republican authority and government in so far as a number of the most important questions was referred to the jurisdiction of All-Union organs. The new constitutions reflected changes in the budget law of the republics, in that their budgets were introduced as a constituent part into a single USSR budget. These changes, in turn, reflected new and essential elements, hitherto absent: the realization, by the appropriate people's commissariats, of directives of the United People's Commissariat of the USSR; the right of the Central Executive Committee of Union Republics to protest against directives of the Council of People's Commissars of the USSR and—under certain conditions—to countermand the orders of individual Union People's Commissariats, and so forth.

On the basis of the 1924 Constitution of the USSR, further organization of the structure of the multinational Soviet state took place. In 1924,[21] in connection with the national demarcation in Central Asia, new Union Republics were formed—the Uzbek and the Turkmen—which had expressed in their Congresses of Soviets a desire to enter, and had entered, into the

---

[20] The Constitution of the RSFSR was confirmed at the Twelfth All-Russian Congress of Soviets on May 11, 1925; that of the Ukraine SSR at the Ninth Congress of Soviets of the Ukrainian SSR, May 10, 1925; the Constitution of the White Russian SSR, April 11, 1927; and the Constitution of the Transcaucasian Socialist Federal Soviet Republic at the Third Transcaucasian Congress of Soviets, April 4, 1925. [References to specific enactments omitted.—TR.]

[21] Cz. 1924, No. 19, Art. 187.

structure of the USSR.[22] In 1929 [23] the seventh Union Republic entered the USSR—Tadjik, formed out of the autonomous Tadjik Soviet Socialist Republic. All this was confirmed in changes and amplifications of the Constitution of the USSR at the Third and Sixth Congresses of Soviets of the USSR.[24]

[22] Cz. 1925, No. 35, Art. 244.
[23] Cz. 1929, No. 75, Art. 717.
[24] Cz. 1925, No. 35, Art. 245; 1931, No. 17, Art. 162.

SEC. 4: THE VICTORY OF SOCIALISM IN THE USSR AND THE STALIN CONSTITUTION

1. *Changes in the mode of life in the USSR during the period 1924–1936*

The 1924 Constitution of the USSR was worked out during the period at the beginning of the New Economic Policy when the problem of reestablishing economy—ruined by the imperialistic and civil wars—was still undecided. This problem was solved in conditions of competition between two economic systems—the socialist and the capitalist.

This was the first period of NEP,[1] when the Soviet authority—while taking all measures for the development of socialism—admitted a certain revival of capitalism, and counted on organizing a preponderance of the socialist system over the capitalist system during the course of their competition. The task was to strengthen the position of socialism during the course of the competition, to attain the liquidation of capitalist elements, and to complete the victory of the socialist system as the basic system of national economy.[2]

The proportionate share of the socialist forms of economy in total industrial output was 76.7 per cent in 1923–1924; in retail turnover of goods, the share of the socialist sector was defined (in 1924) as only 47.3 per cent in all; while in total agricultural production it was utterly negligible—1.5 per cent.

At the beginning of the first five-year period—when the process of reestablishing economy was successfully completed and the national income exceeded prewar level—the proportionate share of the private-economy

[1] New Economic Policy.—Ed.
[2] Stalin, *Report on the Draft of the USSR Constitution* (1936), p. 7.

sector in industry (and especially in turnover of goods) appeared already significantly lower than in 1924. Yet at this moment (1928–1929), private economies yielded around 10 per cent of industrial production and distributed more than 20 per cent of the goods. As to the villages (in 1928), the predominant form of economy still continued to be the economy of the single peasant homestead, and the kulak still retained a substantial part of the grain in storage. In 1928 the sovkhozes and the kolkhozes furnished altogether only 3.3 per cent of gross agricultural production. The further period of development of our economy—the time of Stalin's great five-year plans—brought with it the final triumph of socialist forms of economy. The competition of two economic systems came to an end in this period with the complete liquidation of the private-capitalist sector in all branches of economy and the reduction of the role of small, noncapitalist private economies to a negligible minimum.

The tempestuous growth of the national income under the conditions of the Soviet authority during the years of the first and second five-year plans is unprecedented in the history of the economic development of a state. In 1936 the national income was estimated at 86 billion rubles at 1926–1927 prices, whereas in 1928 it had amounted (at the same prices) to 25 billion rubles, and in 1913—the highest point in the economy of tsarist Russia—to 21 billions. This vast economic rise was accompanied by radical structural changes in the field of national economy. If in 1928 the proportional share of socialist forms of economy in the total national income was computed at 44 per cent, in 1936 socialist (state and cooperative) enterprises furnished 99.1 per cent of the national income—only 9 per cent of the national income coming from private economies of the individual peasants and the homecraftsmen and artisans outside the cooperatives. The socialist economic system and socialist property in the instruments and means of production were finally confirmed as the constant economic basis of the USSR—the source of the wealth and power of our country and of the comfortable and cultural life of all toilers. "Social property (state, kolkhoz, and cooperative) is the basis of the Soviet regime. It is sacred and inviolate. Those encroaching thereon must be deemed enemies of the people." [3]

Hitherto a country economically backward, the USSR now became a mighty industrial power. The correlation of the country's industry and agriculture was most radically changed. In 1913 large-scale industry produced 42.1 per cent of the total output of national economy, whereas in 1937 the enterprises of large-scale socialist industry produced 77.4 per cent of the national economic output. Construction on a colossal scale occurred in all branches of industry, but because of the fulfilling of the five-year plans

[3] Cz. 1932, No. 62, Art. 360 (law of Aug. 7).

there was special growth of heavy industry—the basis of the economic and defensive power of the Soviet state. A whole series of new branches of large-scale industry was created. In some branches of industry the USSR stood first in world output; in its gross production—in 1936 more than seven times the prewar level—the USSR occupied first place in Europe.

The steady growth of the economy of the USSR, which knows no crises, made it possible to change all enterprises of industry and transportation to a seven-hour work day. This was carried into effect by putting into practice a directive of the Central Executive Committee and the Council of People's Commissars of the USSR (January 2, 1929).[4]

The number of workers and employees has increased from year to year. In 1936 it was 25.8 million, as against 11.4 million in 1914. In 1928 the labor exchanges estimated approximately 1.5 million unemployed; since 1931, unemployment in the USSR has been completely liquidated. The development of socialist economy made it possible truly to guarantee citizens of the USSR the right to work, no less than the right to rest and to have material provision for old age and upon loss of working capacity.

The socialist reorganization of the village—grand in range and in results—was realized in the years of the first and second five-year plans, making the USSR a land of socialist agricultural production, the greatest in the world, mechanized and with modern technical equipment. Millions of individual peasant homesteads joined the kolkhozes. In 1937 only 7 per cent of the peasant households were outside the kolkhoz associations. The land occupied by the kolkhozes was secured in their behalf for their free and unlimited use—that is to say, in perpetuity. This was given final, formal shape, in accordance with the directive of the Council of People's Commissars of the USSR[5] (July 7, 1935), by transferring special state documents to the kolkhozes.

In 1936 there were as many as 4,137 sovkhozes. There were 4,993 machine tractor stations with 289,000 tractors and approximately 30,000 combines. In 1937 there were already 5,617 machine tractor stations with 356,800 tractors and 96,300 combines. There were tens of thousands of trucks in the kolkhoz and sovkhoz fields.

The process of collectivizing agriculture was combined with that of complete liquidation of capitalist (kulak) economy in the village. The directive of the Central Executive Committee and the Council of People's Commissars of the USSR of February 1, 1930,[6] transferred to local organs of government (the regional and territorial executive committees and the govern-

[4] Cz. 1929, No. 4, Art. 30.
[5] Cz. 1935, No. 34, Art. 300.
[6] Cz. 1930, No. 9, Art. 105.

ments of autonomous republics) the right to put complete collectivization into operation in their districts. They were to take "all necessary measures in the struggle with the kulaks—even including the complete confiscation of their property and settling them outside the limits of separate districts and territories." The same directive suspended—in districts of complete collectivization—the operation of the law allowing the lease of land and the use of hired labor in the individual peasant homesteads. Capitalism was liquidated in agriculture as it had been in industry.

The victory of socialism in the field of industrial and agricultural production also made possible the liquidation of the private-economic sector in the field of trade and, at the same time, the swift acceleration of development of (state and cooperative) turnover of goods. In 1936 the turnover of goods in state cooperative and kolkhoz-peasant retail trade was 122.5 billion rubles, as against 47.8 in 1932. In 1936 the turnover of goods was 100 per cent in the hands of the state and the cooperative.

The complete victory of the socialist system in all spheres of national economy is thus an accomplished fact. What does that mean? It means that man's exploitation of man is abolished, liquidated, and that socialist property in the instruments and means of production is confirmed as the constant basis of our society.[7]

Such were the results of the steps taken ·to construct socialist economy (1924–1936)—results attained in the most savage struggle with capitalism (and its political agents) and with enemies of the people—the Trotskyists, the Bukharinists, the Zinovyevists, and the bourgeois nationalists. Under the guidance of the party of Lenin and Stalin, the toilers of the USSR achieved the complete victory of socialism in all branches of national economy.

Profound changes also occurred in the class structure of our society from the time when the first Constitution of the USSR was adopted. All the exploiter classes were liquidated. "There was no capitalist class in industry. There was no kulak class in agriculture. There were no merchants and speculators in the field of commodity-circulation."[8]

The liquidation of the exploiter classes occurred in conditions of savage struggle by their remnants against the proletarian dictatorship. Wrecking in all fields of economy, organized acts of terrorism against Party leaders and the government, betrayal of the fatherland, attempts to undermine the USSR's military might and sovereign independence and territorial inviolability, betrayals of state secrets, espionage in aid of foreign states—the class

[7] Stalin, Report on the Draft of the USSR Constitution (1936), p. 9.
[8] Ibid., p. 10.

enemy tried all these forms of struggle against the proletarian dictatorship. Soviet investigating agencies disclosed a whole series of counterrevolutionary organizations proposing to restore capitalism: the Shakhtintsy, the Industrial Party, the "union bureau" of Mensheviks, the Kondratyevtsy, the wreckers in power stations, and finally a series of organizations of the anti-Soviet Trotsky center and the anti-Soviet "Trotsky right bloc" which had gone over completely to the service of international fascism. Notwithstanding all the efforts of these counterrevolutionary organizations to obstruct the building of socialism, the historical task of the proletarian dictatorship— to liquidate the exploiter classes—was realized.

How powerfully the class structure of our country had changed during the time of the proletarian revolution is shown by the following table:

	Percentage of the Total	
	1913	1937
Workers and clerks	16.7	34.7
Kolkhoz peasants and village artisans organized in cooperatives	0.0	55.5
Single family peasants outside the kolkhoz (omitting kulaks) and village artisans not organized in cooperatives	65.1	5.6
Bourgeoisie (landowners, big and petty city bourgeoisie, traders, and kulaks)	15.9	0.0
Of these the kulaks were	[12.3]	[0.0]
The rest of the population (students, armed forces, pensioners, etc.)	2.3	4.2
	100.0	100.0

The worker class, the class of peasants, and the intellectuals were the social groups in the structure of the population of the USSR at the moment of the confirming of the Stalin Constitution—altogether different groups, however, from what they were during the period of capitalism.

Indicating the changes occurring in the class structure of Soviet society, Stalin says:

Whereof do these changes speak? They speak, in the first place, of the obliteration of boundaries, as well between the working class and the peasantry as between these classes and the intellectuals, and the disappearance of the old class exclusiveness—so that the distance between these social groups is constantly diminishing. Secondly, they speak of the decline and obliteration of economic contradictions between these social groups. Finally, they speak of the decline and obliteration of political contradictions between them.[9]

Analyzing the changes in the life of the USSR between 1924 and 1936, Stalin (in his report to the Extraordinary Eighth All-Union Congress of Soviets) noted the paramount significance of the question of the interrelations of nationalities in the USSR as a multinational state. The fourteen years of existence of the USSR prior to the moment of accepting the Stalin Constitution undoubtedly showed that

the experience of forming a multinational state, created on a basis of socialism, had been completely successful. . . . The absence of exploiter classes—the basic organizers of strife between nationalities; the absence of exploitation—the fomenter of distrust and inflamer of nationalist passions; the presence in authority of the worker class—the enemy of every sort of enslavement and truly the bearer of the idea of internationalism; the factual realization of mutual aid of peoples in all fields of economic and social life; and finally the flowering of nationalist culture of the peoples of the USSR, nationalist in form and socialist in content—all these and similar factors lead to the result that the whole face of the peoples of the USSR has radically changed; their feeling of mutual distrust has disappeared; a feeling of mutual friendship has developed among them and thus the present harmonious and fraternal collaboration of peoples in a system of a single Union state has ensued.

To the Extraordinary Eighth All-Union Congress of Soviets of the USSR, which affirmed the Stalin Constitution, the peoples of the Soviet Union—even the most backward, those formerly the most oppressed by tsarism—came with the greatest economic and cultural attainments. In such Union Republics (formed in the territory of colonies of the former Russian empire) as those of Transcaucasia and Central Asia, large-scale industry grew up and new cities—industrial centers—appeared as a result of the fulfilling of the five-year plans of national economy. In 1936 there was not a single Union Republic wherein industrial production increased less than 100 per cent as compared with prerevolutionary figures. In the Georgian SSR, it exceeded the 1913 level 18.6 times; in the Kirghiz SSR, 95 times, and in the Tadjik SSR, 116 times. The socialist reconstruction of agriculture guaranteed it a swift rise, mounting year by year. New lines of rail and air transport, radio, telegraph, and telephone connected the outlying regions of our state with its central regions in close economic and cultural bonds.

[9] *Ibid.*, p. 15.

The economic growth of the Soviet Union, and the unvarying concern of the Soviet authority for the cultural development of the masses, guaranteed the flowering of culture for all the nationalities of the USSR. The number of pupils in USSR elementary and intermediate schools in 1936–1937 was 28.8 millions as against 8 millions in 1914–1915. In many Union Republics it was tens and hundreds of times greater than in prerevolutionary times. The production of books and papers increased colossally, as did the number of theaters, libraries, and movie houses. Peoples formerly ignorant of their own language, and individually illiterate, acquired a rich literature in their native language and produced, from their own ranks, their own scholars, engineers, doctors, teachers, and so forth. Russian literature—all species of Russian art—became broadly accessible to all other peoples inhabiting the USSR, and for many millions of the Russian people, too, it became possible to know and to appreciate the cultural attainments of other nationalities.

By directive of the Central Executive Committee and the Council of People's Commissars of the USSR [10] (August 14, 1930) universal compulsory elementary training was introduced in the Soviet Union. State assistance of every sort made it possible for hundreds of thousands of pupils from the ranks of workers and peasants to finish the middle and the higher—as well as the elementary—schools. The right to education became the right of each Soviet citizen—indefeasible and genuinely guaranteed.

The entire period, from the moment of the acceptance of the first Constitution of the USSR, was signalized—as was the preceding period of the proletarian revolution—by the steady broadening of Soviet democracy, by the drawing into the building of the state of ever broader masses of the toilers. One of the most brilliant proofs of this is the heightened activity of voters at elections to the Soviets. Thus the percentage of voters taking part in elections for the Soviets was 50.8 in 1926 and 85 in 1934. The number of persons deprived of the right to vote declined from year to year. In 1929 it was 4.6 per cent of the total electorate, whereas in the election campaign of 1934 it had dropped to 2.5 per cent.

The development of Soviet democracy is indissolubly connected with the strengthening of revolutionary legislation. From 1924 to 1936, enormous work was carried through in this direction by the government of the USSR, the governments of the allied republics, and by all local organs of authority. A whole series of special directives—particularly that of the Third Congress of Soviets of the USSR (May 20, 1925),[11] that of the Central Executive Committee and Council of People's Commissars of the USSR: Concerning

[10] Cz. 1930, No. 39, Art. 420.
[11] Cz. 1925, No. 35, Art. 247.

Revolutionary Legality (June 25, 1932),[12] and that of the Soviet Control
Committee under the Council of People's Commissars of the USSR: Concerning the Consideration of Complaints of Toilers [13] (issued May 30,
1936) and so forth, were directed at every sort of measure to strengthen
revolutionary legislation . . . "one of the most important means of strengthening the proletarian dictatorship, defending the interests of workers and
toiling peasants, and struggling with class enemies of the toilers (kulaks,
second-hand dealer-speculators, bourgeois wreckers) and their counterrevolutionary political agents." An important step in the same direction was the
institution in 1933 of the Office of the Prosecutor of the USSR.[14]

2. The development and confirmation of the Stalin Constitution

The complete triumph of the socialist system in all branches of the national economy, the fundamental realization of socialism, the liquidation of
the exploiter classes, the annihilation of man's exploitation by man, the brilliant results in the creation of a union multinational state, the vast cultural
conquests, the attraction of the broadest popular masses into the building of
the state, the strengthening of revolutionary legality—all these factors evoked
the necessity of changing the Constitution of the USSR so that the new
Constitution should reflect all the changes which had occurred in the life
of the USSR since 1924.

Upon the motion of Stalin, the matter of changing the Constitution of
the USSR was set for consideration by the February (1935) Plenum of the
Central Committee of the All-Union Communist Party (of Bolsheviks). In
a resolution (adopted February 1) the plenum indicated the direction of the
changes to be introduced into the Constitution of the USSR. The plenum
commissioned Molotov to put forward such a proposal, in the name of the
Central Committee of the Party, at the Seventh All-Union Congress of
Soviets of the USSR which opened January 28, 1935. The Congress
acknowledged the proposal of the Central Party Committee as correct and
timely, and on February 6, 1925—upon a report by Molotov—directed the
introduction of changes into the Constitution of the USSR.[15]

In exact accord with the resolution of the Plenum of the Central Party
Committee, the Congress of Soviets pointed out that these changes must be
directed to

(a) further democratization of the elective system—in the sense of substituting
equal elections for elections not fully equal; direct elections for elections having

[12] Cz. 1932, No. 50, Art. 298.
[13] Cz. 1936, No. 31, Art. 276.
[14] Cz. 1933, No. 40, Art. 239.
[15] Cz. 1935, No. 8, Art. 69.

multiple stages; and secret elections for elections which were open; and (b) making more precise the social-economic bases of the Constitution—in the sense of bringing the Constitution into conformity with the present correlation of class forces in the USSR (the creation of new socialist industry, the destruction of kulaks, the triumph of the kolkhoz system, the confirmation of socialist property as the basis of Soviet society, and the like).

The Seventh All-Union Congress of Soviets proposed to the Central Executive Committee of the USSR the election of a Constitutional Commission to work out the new text of the Constitution and to present it for confirmation to a session of the Central Executive Committee of the USSR.

On February 7, 1935, the first session of the Central Executive Committee of the USSR (at its seventh convocation) chose a Constitutional Commission under the presidency of Stalin.

The first session of the Plenum of the Constitutional Commission (July 7, 1935) defined the order of further work of the commission and directed the creation of the following twelve subcommittees to conduct the preparatory work on the new text of the Constitution: (1) On general questions of the Constitution, (2) economic, (3) financial, (4) legal, (5) elective, (6) court organs, (7) central and local organs of authority, (8) popular education, (9) labor, (10) defense, (11) foreign affairs, (12) editorial. As President of the Constitutional Commission, Stalin also presided in the subcommittees on the general questions of constitutional and editorial matters. Thus Stalin carried on the general guidance of the work of creating the draft of the new Constitution of the USSR—as well as the immediate work on editing the final text thereof. He is the creator of the new Constitution of the USSR—the Constitution of victorious socialism, justly called the Stalin Constitution by the Soviet people.

In the summer of 1936, the draft of the new USSR Constitution was prepared. On May 15, in a regular plenum, the Constitutional Commission subjected the draft of the Constitution—presented by the editorial subcommittee—to elaborate scrutiny and approved the final text of its thirteen chapters.

On June 1, 1936, Stalin came forward with his report on the draft in the Plenum of the Central Committee of the Party. The plenum recorded fundamental approval of the draft of the Constitution of the USSR and recognized the necessity of convening an Extraordinary All-Union Congress of Soviets to consider and to confirm it.

On June 11, 1936, the Presidium of the Central Executive Committee of the USSR, having listened to Stalin's report on the draft of the new Constitution, passed the following directive: [16]

[16] Cz. 1936, No. 33, Art. 299.

(1) to approve the draft of the USSR Constitution presented by the Constitutional Commission of the Central Executive Committee of the USSR;

(2) to summon an All-Union Congress of Soviets to consider the draft of the USSR Constitution;

(3) to appoint the date for calling the Congress as November 25, 1936; and

(4) to publish the draft of the USSR Constitution for discussion by the whole nation.

On June 12, 1936, the draft of the USSR Constitution was published and the period for the discussion of it began. In this discussion millions of toilers took part. The draft was read with delight and discussed in all the industrial and transport enterprises, in sovkhozes and kolkhozes, and in government offices. Hundreds of thousands of written comments, supplements, and corrections came into the central and local government bureaus and newspaper offices.

Numerous responses came from different strata of people abroad, where the draft attained the widest publicity notwithstanding attempts by the capitalist press to silence it.

In the discussion by all the people of the draft of the fundamental law of our state—the Stalin Constitution—Soviet democracy found its most brilliant expression. Only in conditions of a socialist state of workers and peasants is it possible to draw many millions of the masses of toilers into the task of working out a constitution.

The Soviet people greeted the appearance of the draft of the new USSR Constitution with enormous enthusiasm and approved it with one accord. Proposals brought in by the toilers in connection with the discussion of the project were directed at making specific paragraphs of the Constitution more exact and detailed. The editorial commission of the Extraordinary Eighth All-Union Congress of Soviets considered these proposals in its work upon the final text of the draft. "In the working out and the final version of the Constitution of the USSR, discussion by all the people unquestionably brought vast benefit." [17]

The Extraordinary Eighth All-Union Congress of Soviets of the USSR opened on November 25, 1936. It had twelve sessions and continued through December 5.

The only question on the agenda of the Congress was consideration and approval of the draft of the Constitution. In connection with this question, Stalin came forward with his report. The Congress unanimously approved Stalin's draft of the Constitution, took it as the basis of its deliberations, proceeded to form an editorial commission—with Stalin as president—to con-

[17] Stalin, *Report on the Draft of the USSR Constitution* (1936), p. 47.

sider corrections and amplifications (introduced in the Congress itself and during the time of national discussion of the draft).

On December 5, 1936, after Stalin's report as president of the editorial commission, and as a result of voting on the draft paragraph by paragraph, the final text of the Constitution was unanimously approved by the Congress.

3. *The special characteristics at the foundation of the Stalin Constitution*

In his report to the Extraordinary Eighth All-Union Congress of Soviets, Stalin indicated in detail the special characteristics of the new Constitution.

(1) It is the integration of our achievements on the road we have traveled—of the conquests we have already won. Herein is the first of its special characteristics.

(2) The chief basis of the draft of the new USSR Constitution is the principles of socialism—its fundamental supports, already won and realized: socialist property in land, forests, factories, works and other instruments and means of production; liquidation of exploitation and exploiter classes; liquidation of beggary of the majority and luxury of the minority; liquidation of unemployment; work as an obligation and duty of honor of each citizen (capable of work) according to the formula: "He who does not work does not eat." The right to labor —that is, the right of each citizen to obtain guaranteed work; the right to rest, the right to education, and so forth. The draft of the new Constitution is supported by these and similar principles of socialism. It reflects them. It confirms them in legal order. This is the second of the special characteristics of the new Constitution.[18]

(3) Antagonistic classes have ceased to exist in our society—only classes friendly to each other have remained and are in authority—the working class which makes real its guidance of society (its dictatorship), and the peasantry. This is the third of the special characteristics of the Constitution.

(4) The Stalin Constitution—like the Soviet Constitutions preceding it —legitimatizes the principle that all races and all nationalities are completely equal in their rights. It is profoundly internationalistic. This is the fourth of the special characteristics of the Constitution.

(5) Consistent democracy sustained to the end—socialist democracy— characterizes the Stalin Constitution. It abolished what remained of limitations upon political rights—preserved in earlier Soviet constitutions from the time when the influence of the exploiter classes was still expressed with

[18] *Ibid.*, p. 18.

sufficient force and the Soviets were not yet strong. For the first time in the history of the existence of states, the Stalin Constitution introduced genuinely universal, equal, and direct suffrage with secret ballot. "The personal capacities and personal toil of each citizen define his position in society; not his position in terms of property, not national origin, not sex, not his position in terms of service." That is the fifth of the Constitution's special characteristics.

(6) The right to work; the right to rest and to material security in old age and in case of illness and loss of working capacity; the right to education; the same rights for women as for men in all fields of economic, state, cultural, and social-political life; freedom of conscience, of speech, of the press, of assembly and meeting, of street parades and demonstrations; the right to join social organizations; the guarantee of personal inviolability; legal preservation of the inviolability of dwelling and of one's papers—all this was genuinely realized in Soviet reality, legalized by the Stalin Constitution. The latter was not limited merely to fixing the formal rights of citizens, as is characteristic of bourgeois constitutions; it shifted the center of gravity to the matter of guaranteeing these rights—of means to make them real—and herein is still another of its special characteristics.

Such are the special characteristics at the foundation of the Stalin Constitution—the Constitution of victorious socialism.

The adoption of this Constitution was an act of universal historical significance. It

confirmed the universal-historical fact that the USSR has entered into a new phase of development, the phase of completing the building of socialist society and of the gradual transition to a communist society, where the guiding principle of social life must be the communist principle: "From each according to his capacities, to each according to his needs." [19]

In his report to the Extraordinary Eighth All-Union Congress of Soviets, Stalin—expressing confidence that the draft of the new USSR Constitution would be approved by the Congress—said:

This will be a historical document, treating simply and concisely—almost in protocol style—of the facts of socialism's victory in the USSR, of the emancipation of the toilers of the USSR from capitalist slavery, of the victory in the USSR of democracy expanded and consistent to the last detail. This will be a document attesting the fact that the USSR has already realized that whereof millions of honest people in capitalist countries have dreamed and still dream; and that what

[19] *History of All-Union Communist Party (of Bolsheviks): A Short Course* (1938), p. 331.

has been put into practice in the USSR can perfectly well be put into practice in other countries too.[20]

The Stalin Constitution mobilizes the masses of toilers of all countries for the struggle against fascism. It is the banner—the program of action—in that struggle. It confirms faith in its forces among the toilers of the USSR and mobilizes them to struggle for the complete triumph of communism. "The Constitution of the USSR will be an indictment of fascism and an assurance of the invincibility of socialism and democracy." [21]

4. The creation of new constitutions of Union Republics on the basis of the Stalin Constitution

Immediately upon the publication of the draft of the Stalin Constitution, the highest organs of state authority of the Union Republics began working out new constitutions for those republics. To this end, in June and July, 1936, constitutional commissions were created in all the Union Republics. After the drafts of constitutions presented by constitutional commissions were confirmed by the presidia of the Central Executive Committees of the Republics, they were published and approved in final form by Extraordinary Congresses of the Soviets of the Republics, as shown in the table herewith.

The new constitutions of the Union Republics were built on the basis of the Stalin Constitution and in complete conformity therewith. At the same time, they take into account the special characteristics of each republic.

The chapters concerning the social organization in all the constitutions spring in their entirety from the paragraphs of Chapter I of the Stalin Constitution and as a rule reproduce them almost verbatim. Certain textual differences are here conditioned merely by the presence of historical features in the development of a given Soviet Republic. Most of these differences refer to Articles 2 and 4. Thus in Article 2 of the constitutions of most of the Union Republics it is emphasized that the Soviets of Deputies of Toilers grew and became strong as a result of the overthrow of the power of landowners and capitalists—the conquest by the dictatorship of the proletariat—and so as a result of the proletarian dictatorship freeing the population of a given republic from the national weight of tsarism and of the Russian imperialist bourgeoisie, and destroying nationalist counterrevolution. Side by side with these, the constitutions of the Turkmen, Uzbek, and Tadjik SSR's note such an important element as the reunion—into a state of workers and peasants—of the parts of their respective peoples formerly torn asunder by tsarism.

[20] Stalin, *Report on the Draft of the USSR Constitution* (1936), p. 45.
[21] *Ibid.*, p. 46.

Republic	Constitutional Commission Formed	Draft of Constitution Approved by Presidium of Central Executive Committee of Union Republic	Extraordinary Congresses of Soviets of the Union Republics Confirming the Constitution	Constitution Confirmed by Congress of Soviets
RSFSR	July 1936	Dec. 23, 1936	Seventeenth Extraordinary All-Russian Congress of Soviets	Jan. 21, 1937
Ukrainian SSR	July 1936	Dec. 31, 1936	Fourteenth Extraordinary Congress of Soviets of Ukrainian SSR	Jan. 30, 1937
White Russian SSR	June 1936	Dec. 30, 1936	Twelfth Extraordinary Congress of Soviets of White Russia	Feb. 19, 1937
Azerbaijan SSR	June 1936	Feb. 20, 1937	Ninth Extraordinary Congress of All-Azerbaijan Soviets	March 14, 1937
Georgian SSR	June 1936	Feb. 1, 1937	Eighth Extraordinary All-Georgian Congress of Soviets	Feb. 13, 1937
Armenian SSR	July 1936	Feb. 22, 1937	Ninth Extraordinary Congress of Soviets of Armenian SSR	March 23, 1937
Turkmen SSR	June 1936	Feb. 16, 1937	Sixth Extraordinary Congress of Soviets of Turkmen SSR	March 2, 1937
Uzbek SSR	June 1936	Feb. 8, 1937	Sixth Extraordinary Congress of Soviets of Uzbek SSR	Feb. 14, 1937
Tadjik SSR	June 1936	Feb. 20, 1937	Sixth Extraordinary Congress of Soviets of Tadjik SSR	March 1, 1937
Kazakh SSR	June 1936	Feb. 3, 1937	Tenth Extraordinary All-Kazakh Congress of Soviets	March 26, 1937
Kirghiz SSR	June 1936	March 11, 1937	Fifth Extraordinary Congress of Soviets of Kirghiz SSR	March 23, 1937

In Article 4 of the constitutions of the Turkmen, Uzbek, Tadjik, Kazakh and Kirghiz SSR's, in closest conjunction with the special historical characteristics of their economic development, it is pointed out that the socialist system of economics and socialist property was confirmed as a result of the liquidation, not only of the capitalist, but also of the *feudal*, system of economy.

Again, the chapters of the constitutions of Union Republics dedicated to state organization fixed the following proposals in complete conformity with Chapter II of the Stalin Constitution:

(a) The basic motives and purposes of the entry of a given republic into the structure of the USSR (unification with other Soviet Socialist Republics having equal rights, "to the end of realizing mutual aid along economic and political lines, and also that of defense").

(b) The guarantee in behalf of the USSR—as personified by its highest organs of authority and of state government—of the rights defined by Article 14 of the Constitution of the USSR.

(c) The sovereign rights of a Union Republic—in the realization of state authority—as to all questions not within the bounds of Article 14 of the Constitution of the USSR.

The chapters of the constitutions of the Union Republics dedicated to the questions of higher organs of state authority and state government also basically coincide. The negligible differences are concerned entirely with numbers of the population and peculiarities in the organization of the administrative territory of a given Union Republic. The following differences should be noted: (*a*) in rules of representation in the Supreme Soviets,[22] and (*b*) in the number of vice presidents and members of the presidia of the Supreme Soviets.[23]

[22] In the RSFSR, one deputy for each 150,000 of the population; in the Ukrainian SSR, one deputy for each 100,000 of the population; in the White Russian SSR, one deputy for each 20,000 of the population; in the Azerbaijan SSR, one deputy for each 10,000 of the population; in the Georgian SSR, one deputy for each 15,000 of the population; in the Armenian SSR, one deputy for each 5,000 of the population; in the Turkmen SSR, one deputy for each 5,000 of the population; in the Uzbek SSR, one deputy for each 15,000 of the population; in the Tadjik SSR, one deputy for each 5,000 of the population; in the Kazakh SSR, one deputy for each 20,000 of the population; in the Kirghiz SSR, one deputy for each 5,000 of the population. [Local constitutional citations omitted.—Tr.]

[23] The RSFSR has 17 vice presidents of the presidium of the Supreme Soviet (corresponding to the number of Autonomous Republics) and 20 members of the presidium.

The Ukrainian SSR has two vice presidents of the presidium of the Supreme Soviet and 15 members of the presidium.

The White Russian SSR has two vice presidents of the presidium of the Supreme Soviet and 15 members of the presidium.

The Azerbaijan SSR has two vice presidents of the presidium of the Supreme Soviet (the number of Autonomous Republics and provinces) and 13 members of the presidium.

It is especially necessary to point out the differences in the structure of the people's commissariats of the Union Republics.[24]

The constitutions of the Union Republics almost completely coincide with one another and all spring from the USSR Constitution as regards such important questions as suffrage, courts, and prosecuting magistracy, and rights and obligations of citizens.

Certain amplifications in formulating the articles concerned with the rights of women should be noted in the constitutions of the Turkmen, Uzbek, Tadjik, Kazakh, and Kirghiz SSR's. Side by side with the general formulation of the principle that women have equal rights with men, there are in the constitutions of these republics, special additions reflecting special characteristics in the position of women and emphasizing that Soviet law stands guard over their factual emancipation.[25]

In all the constitutions of the Union Republics, the indestructible moral-political unity of the multinational Soviet people finds its brightest expression. At the same time they concretely disclose the essence of the Stalin Constitution—the most democratic in the world. They are the legislative basis for further successes in the construction of socialism—for the triumphant advance to communism by the united and brotherly family of the peoples of the USSR.

The Georgian SSR has two vice presidents of the presidium of the Supreme Soviet (the number of Autonomous Republics) and 13 members of the presidium.

The Armenian SSR has two vice presidents of the presidium of the Supreme Soviet and 9 members of the presidium.

The Turkmen SSR has two vice presidents of the presidium of the Supreme Soviet and 11 members of the presidium.

The Uzbek SSR has three vice presidents of the presidium of the Supreme Soviet and 13 members of the presidium.

The Tadjik SSR has two vice presidents of the presidium of the Supreme Soviet and 11 members of the presidium.

The Kazakh SSR has two vice presidents of the presidium of the Supreme Soviet and 15 members of the presidium.

The Kirghiz SSR has two vice presidents of the presidium of the Supreme Soviet and 11 members of the presidium.

[24] The Tadjik SSR has no People's Commissariat of forest industry, or of state grain and livestock farms; the Turkmen SSR has no People's Commissariat of forest industry; the Azerbaijan and Armenian SSR's have no People's Commissariat of state grain and livestock farms.

[25] As an example we may cite the final paragraph of Article 99 of the Turkmen Constitution: "Resistance to the factual emancipation of women—giving them in marriage while they are still of tender years, selling them into marriage, organizing resistance to drawing them into studies, agriculture and industrial production, state government and social-political life—is punished by law." There are similar supplementary provisions in the constitutions of the Uzbek, Tadjik, Kazakh and Kirghiz SSR's.

III   *The Social Organization of the USSR*

SEC. 1: INTRODUCTION

AS hereinbefore pointed out, Soviet public law embraces the legal rules and relationships which confirm and organize as well the social arrangement of the USSR—that is to say, the order of socialist relationships in the economic, political and cultural fields of social life.[1]

The principles, forms, and character of our social organization are defined in the Stalin Constitution (in the chapter on Social Organization) in the most amplified, exact, and classical shape. The class structure of Soviet society, its political and economic bases—that is to say, that which in its entirety also constitutes social organization—are defined in extraordinarily sharp, and classically exact, juridical form.

In the bourgeois public law and bourgeois constitutions there is no section concerned specially with social organization. Separate matters of social organization are, to be sure, treated therein, but they are scattered about in the utmost diversity. As a general rule the most important matters of social organization—those concerned with the class structure of society and the class essence of the state—are obscured in bourgeois public law. Lastly, and most important, bourgeois public law poses and "resolves" questions of social organization absolutely unsuccessfully, pervertedly, and in complete contradiction with social-economic and political reality.

It is not difficult to disclose the causes and essence of the difference between Soviet public law and bourgeois law in this regard. It is rooted in the class antithesis of these two historical types of law. Soviet law reflects and confirms social orders agreeable and advantageous to the toiling classes—the

[1] In the Stalin Constitution, "social order" and "social organization" express essentially the same content—the socialist order existing in our land.

129

absolute majority of society. It is a means to crush the opposition of exploiter classes. Frankly and openly it formulates its class principles and asserts the class character of the Soviet social order. Naturally it contemplates questions of social organization in a special section dedicated to that problem.

Bourgeois law reflects and confirms social orders agreeable and advantageous to the exploiter class—an insignificant minority of society. It is a means to repress the toiling classes by force. It is accordingly constrained to conceal from the masses its true class character. Carefully it skirts those questions wherein is the greatest danger of its class essence being revealed—in the first instance, questions of social organization. Accordingly everyone knows that in bourgeois public law these questions are silenced as far as possible.

The famous bourgeois political scientist Jellinek thus notes the round of questions forming the object of bourgeois constitutions:

The constitution of the state thus embraces the entirety of the legal proposals defining the highest organs of the state, the order of calling upon them to function, their mutual relationships and jurisdiction, and likewise the principles of the individual's position as regards state authority.

We see that questions of social organization are here absent—which bourgeois political scientists consider perfectly normal.

Scientific principles form the basis of Soviet law—principles of scientific socialism, the doctrine of the transition period from capitalism to communism. These principles are embodied in expanded and exhaustive form in the chapter on Social Organization in the Soviet Constitution, with special emphasis upon firmness of principle and Soviet socialist law's unity of theory and practice.

Bourgeois public law is devoid of true scientific foundation. It operates with antiscientific ideas. Its ideological function is to deceive the people. It *particularly* manifests these qualities in matters of state organization, since here are the most important and basic matters of law in general and of public law in particular.

Texts of bourgeois constitutions are adapted to the task of befogging, clouding over, and perverting the essence of the matter—particularly as concerns social organization. Thus the Declaration of Independence of 1776, decisively influential upon subsequent epochs of bourgeois revolutions, formulates the principles of social order: "We hold these truths to be self-evident,—that all men are created equal; that they are endowed by their Creator with certain unalienable rights; that among these are life, liberty, and the pursuit of happiness."

Bourgeois revolutionary declarations in their time played a progressive role mobilizing the masses to struggle with feudalism, proclaiming the abolition of feudal servile orders and of class privileges, proclaiming political freedoms and separation of church from state, and so forth. At the same time the actual historical and class content of these declarations and specifically their defense, in the last analysis, of the economic and political domination of the bourgeoisie were submerged in their showy phraseology concerning "man" in general, "citizens" in general, and "society" governed by "natural" laws supposedly outside all history. Only when the bourgeoisie defended its domination and found itself face to face with the worker class and the toiling masses—upon whose enslavement and repression the bourgeois domination was based—was this fully disclosed. The real historical content of bourgeois constitutions, as distinguished from their phraseology, is the defense and consecration of capitalist exploitation.

The idea of "social organization," as a public law idea having distinct and clear formulation and scientific basis, is inherent in Soviet public law alone. The science of that law studies questions of social organization (in so far as the latter is reflected and protected in corresponding juridical, public-law acts, institutions, and relationships), approaching questions of social order specifically from this point of view—being a special branch of legal science. It starts here from methodological proposals of general theory, proposals furnished by the Marx-Lenin doctrine of society, and particularly of social-economic formations. It works with absolutely exact, scientific categories, speaking of definite classes, definite species of property, definite means of production and distribution, of the definite class essence of state authority, and so forth.

In Soviet public law, as in Soviet constitutions, questions of social organization are given first consideration and occupy therein the chief position—in the earlier Soviet constitution as well as in the Stalin Constitution now in force.[2] Herein is made manifest the chief and decisive significance attributed to questions of social organization in the Soviet public law. And this is perfectly understandable. For the correct appreciation of separate concrete questions of public law (the formation and activity of organs of state authority, the rights and obligations of citizens, and so forth) a correct appreciation of the nature and character of Soviet social organization is of decisive importance.

[2] One of the first fundamental constitutional Acts of Soviet authority—the Declaration of Rights of the Toiling and Exploited People, adopted Jan. 31, 1918—was basically dedicated to questions of the social organization of the newly arisen Soviet Republics. In the Constitution of RSFSR (1918) the Declaration was included in its entirety as the first subdivision. The same should be said, for example, of the White Russian Constitution; this, too, begins with the Declaration.

The changes introduced into this division of public law by the Stalin Constitution are of the greatest and most decisive significance also with reference to the remaining subdivisions of public law. The changes of principle introduced into them can be correctly explained only in the light of these changes. Accordingly the subdivision concerning social organization serves as a basis—an introductory part—of the whole system of public law.[3]

SEC. 2: THE SOCIAL ORDER OF THE USSR—THE ORDER OF SOCIALIST SOCIETY

The USSR is a socialist state—a state of socialist society. The confirmation therein of the socialist social order results from the socialist reorganization of the country which started the moment the power of capitalists and landowners was overthrown and the proletarian dictatorship established.

From its very first steps Soviet authority proclaimed that its task was to build socialist society, guided by the Leninist-Stalinist doctrine as to the possibility of socialism being victorious in one country taken separately. This doctrine Lenin and Stalin established and defended even in the period of preparation for the proletarian revolution. In the Sixth Party Congress, in a resolution (on the question of policy position) proposed by Stalin, it was established that the task of the proletariat and of the poorest peasantry was to win state authority so as to approach the socialist reorganization of society in union with the revolutionary proletariat of advanced countries. Against this resolution, Preobrazhensky came forward to defend the Trotsky "theory" of the impossibility of socialism being victorious in one country taken separately.

Unmasking this "theory," Stalin said: "The possibility is not excluded that Russia will herself be the country to open the road to socialism. . . .

---

[3] It is interesting in this regard to contrast with our Constitution the Weimar Constitution (abolished by the fascists) which in its time enjoyed popularity among the adherents of bourgeois democracy as a "social constitution." In its fifth subdivision—"Economic Life"— are points touching upon the economic regime of the country. This subdivision occupies the very last place (after the subdivisions "Separate Personality," "Religion and Religious Societies," "Education and Schools"). It is further characteristic that it appears in the part of the constitution concerned with "Fundamental Rights and Obligations of Germans." Economics, it thus contemplates, not as a basis for civil rights and obligations, but only as a manifestation—a consequence—thereof. This expresses the constitutional triumph of the individualist bourgeois conception of law, which treats society and the state as a "union of persons" irrespective of the class to which they belong, and contemplates legal problems in the light of the interrelations of separate individuals (among themselves or with society), "abstracted" from the decisive fact of the division of bourgeois society into antagonistic classes.

We must cast away the outworn idea that only Europe can show us the way. There exist both dogmatic Marxism and creative Marxism. I stand on the ground of creative Marxism." [1] And the most important principle of creative Marxism—and consequently, of Leninism—is the doctrine of the possibility of socialism being victorious in one country taken separately. As early as the first day of the existence of Soviet authority—October 25 [2]/-November 7, 1917—Lenin, reporting on the problems of the authority of the Soviets, said, at a session of the Petrograd Soviet of Workers' and Soldiers' Deputies: "From now on, progress is through a new domain of Russian history. In the final analysis the present third Russian revolution must lead to the victory of socialism." [3]

In one of the first historical documents of Soviet authority, his address, "To the Population," the President of the Council of People's Commissars said (of the victory of the October Revolution and the problems of struggle in the country): "Gradually, with the accord and approval of the majority of peasants and as indicated by their *practical* experience and that of the workers, we shall proceed firmly and undeviatingly to the victory of socialism. . . ." [4]

As the foundation of the first most important historical measures of Soviet authority—the abolition of private property in land, the confiscation of banks, the introduction of control over production, universal labor service, and organization of the Red Army—the Third All-Russian Congress of Soviets (1918) put forward the basic task:

The annihilation of every sort of exploitation of man by man, the complete elimination of the division of society into classes, the pitiless repression of exploiters, the establishment of a socialist organization of society, and the victory of socialism in all countries. [5]

In the Declaration of Rights of the Toiling and Exploited People, the principles and demands of scientific socialism and proletarian dictatorship were put forward in clear and distinct form as the most important constitutional act of the new socialist power. The proletarian Declaration of Rights, baldly and openly proclaiming the struggle against exploiter classes, summoned the working masses to create a new socialist society. In his final words before the close of the Congress, Lenin said:

Now, with historic rubbish cleared away, we will erect the mighty and shining edifice of socialist society. A new and historically unprecedented type of state

[1] Lenin and Stalin, *Selected Works* (Russian ed., 1917), pp. 294–295.
[2] Oct. 25, 1917, Old Style (Gregorian) Calendar.—Ed.
[3] Lenin (Russian ed.), Vol. XXII, p. 4.
[4] *Ibid.*, p. 56.
[5] Cy. 1918, No. 15, Art. 223.

authority is being created, called by the will of the revolution to purify the earth from every sort of exploitation, violence and slavery.[6]

The practical measures, decrees, and directives of Soviet authority in the very first period of its existence signified a planned struggle against capitalist classes—a struggle to implant and to develop socialist forms of economy, and to educate and reeducate the masses politically in a spirit of socialism.

The Address of the People's Commissariat for Nationalities (April, 1918), signed by Stalin as People's Commissar, characterizes the activity of Soviet authority at that time in the following words:

The last two months of the revolution's development in Russia—especially after the conclusion of peace with Germany and the crushing of the bourgeois counterrevolution at home—may be characterized as a period of stabilizing Soviet authority in Russia, and a beginning of the planned reorganization of the defunct social-economic regime into a new socialist concord.[7]

The Soviet state was socialist from the moment of its emergence, setting as its basic task the creation of a socialist society—having noted the correct ways, and working practically upon the realization of this basic and chief problem: "The expression 'Socialist Soviet Republic' signifies the decision of Soviet authority to realize the transition to socialism, and in no wise admits that the new economic orders are socialist." [8]

The Soviet state acted upon the general Leninist-Stalinist plan of building socialism. This included not simply and merely the reestablishment of the national economy destroyed by imperialist and civil wars, but the reconstruction of the country on the basis of socialist industrialization; the collectivization of agriculture; the establishment of the dominance of the socialist system of economy and socialist property; the liquidation—on this basis—of all capitalist elements, including the last capitalist class—the kulaks; the complete annihilation of exploitation of man by man and the very roots and every possibility of such exploitation. The fulfillment of this plan step by step —particularly as a result of Stalin's heroic five-year plans—actually guaranteed also the victory of socialism.

The principles at the root of the socialist society built in the USSR were fixed in Chapter I of the Stalin Constitution—Social Organization. Each of the twelve articles of this chapter expresses and confirms some separate aspect or principle of the socialist social organization formed among us. This is an organization whereunder the Soviets of the Deputies of the Toilers constitute the political basis of society. All authority belongs to all toilers as

[6] Lenin (Russian ed.), Vol. XXII, p. 223.
[7] *The Policy of Soviet Authority Regarding National Matters* (Nov. 1917–1920), p. 8.
[8] Lenin (Russian ed.), Vol. XXII, p. 513.

personified by these Soviets. Economy is built according to the socialist system. Property in the instruments and means of production belongs to society. The exploitation of man by man is annihilated and exploiter classes are liquidated. Society consists of toiling citizens, to whom toil is an obligation and a matter of honor, and whose personal and general interests in all fields of life are organically united and preserved by law.

It is an organization which guarantees the elevation of the citizens' material well-being, and the development of all their creative capacities and powers. All these characteristics of the social organization of the USSR are apparent, in one form or another, in all the chapters of the Constitution. To study the Stalin Constitution also means, in the first instance, to examine how *socialist* social relationships in all their multiformity are reflected and protected by legislation in our country.

The chief characteristic of the Stalin Constitution is that it is the constitution of a socialist society. It speaks of socialism as something "that already is, that has already been attained and won, now, at the present time." In the Stalin Constitution socialism emerges as an order of economic, social relationships—reinforced, entering into the real, daily life, and way of life, of the population. "Our Soviet society has already attained fundamental realization of socialism and created a socialist order—that is to say, it has realized what the Marxists call the first or lower phase of communism." [9] Thus the triumph of the Marxist-Leninist doctrine of socialism (as the first phase of communism) found in the Constitution of the USSR (and especially in the chapter concerning social organization) its distinct expression in public law. Defending the social relationships of the first phase of communism, the Stalin Constitution thereby strengthened and makes easier the further forward movement of our society along the road of socialism to the highest phase of communism—the communist order.

SEC. 3: THE CLASS STRUCTURE OF THE USSR

The idea of a social class as an exact, scientific idea—applied in law and in legal science—is peculiar to Soviet public law. Bourgeois public law ordinarily and in general hushes up the most important and decisive fact— the division of capitalist society into opposed and antagonistic classes—and operates by categories—population, citizens, nation, people, and so forth—

[9] Stalin, *Report on the Draft of the USSR Constitution* (1936), pp. 16–17.

"abstracted" from the class structure of society.[1] Bourgeois public law produces the thesis that the bourgeois state is supposedly concerned only with individual citizens—or with the unification of citizens—irrespective of their belonging to a class. In fact, bourgeois constitutions—in all their essence reflecting and protecting the division of society into classes and the class domination of exploiters—start of course from the class antagonism of bourgeois society, but pass it by in silence and suppress it. "Bourgeois constitutions start from the tacit hypothesis that society consists of antagonistic classes, of classes possessing wealth and classes possessing no wealth. . . ." [2]

The question of the social class structure of Soviet society is posed and decided in Soviet public law as the basic question of social organization. In complete accord with the Marxist-Engels-Leninist-Stalinist doctrine concerning society and the state in general, and society and the state of the transition period from capitalism to communism in particular, Soviet public law starts from the point that classes will exist during the whole period of transition to communism (the highest phase). Only under complete communism can and will the complete annihilation of all class differences in society—the complete classlessness of society—be attained. The process of annihilating classes, with the help of the dictatorship of the worker class, constitutes the decisive side —the social essence—of the whole period of transition to classless, that is to say, communist society.

The Soviet state sets as its task the complete annihilation of the class division of society and of the classes themselves. Its policy started and starts altogether from the facts (1) that friendly classes of workers and peasants exist in our society, and (2) that exploiter classes and their remnants and agents are antagonistic to socialism. Reinforcing the fraternal union of workers and peasants, and pitilessly crushing the resistance of exploiters, the Soviet state attained the essential and real successes which guarantee complete and final solution of the problem of building classless, communist society.

The October Socialist Revolution liquidated the authority of landowners

---

[1] The word "class" appears in certain postrevolutionary bourgeois constitutions or other public law acts. There is obviously nowhere, however, the slightest mention of exploiter capitalist classes as dominant in bourgeois society. If bourgeois constitutions do speak of classes, it is in the incorrect and antiscientific sense of shading away or directly denying irreconcilable class contradictions. For example, in the Weimar Constitution (Art. 164) the following "social category" figures: "The independent middle class in agriculture, industry, and trade . . ." In the fascist constitution of Portugal, there is shamefaced and misty talk about "the least guaranteed social classes." All this reflects the sharpness of class contradictions and the class struggle in bourgeois society—characteristic of the epoch of the general crisis of capitalism. This is done by the bourgeoisie with the demagogic purpose of deceiving the masses with words as to the bourgeois state supposedly standing for the defense of the toiling classes.

[2] Stalin, *Report on the Draft of the USSR Constitution* (1936), pp. 18–19.

and capitalists in our country, and transferred authority into the hands of workers and peasants. The final liquidation of the landowner class resulted from the triumph of the proletariat and the peasantry in the civil war. The class of capitalists—the big industrialists and traders—was likewise liquidated fundamentally at this same time. The expropriation of big capitalist property in the instruments and means of production, the winning by Soviet authority of commanding heights in industry, the political regime established in the Soviet state with reference to exploiter classes—all this guaranteed the liquidation of the industrial urban bourgeoisie as a class.

In the first period of the New Economic Policy the Soviet authority carried on, with reference to the kulaks, a system of limitation and dislodgment "because in the country we had not as yet the bases—in the form of a broad net of sovkhozes and kolkhozes—from which to maintain a decisive attack on the kulaks." [3] After the great crisis of 1929, that policy of limitation and dislodgment was replaced by one of liquidating the kulaks as a class, on the basis of complete collectivization of agriculture. With the development of this policy came the liquidation of the last exploiter capitalist class—the kulaks. "All exploiter classes thus appeared liquidated, and there remained: (1) the working class, (2) the peasant class, and (3) the intellectuals." [4]

Strengthening the proletarian dictatorship and the brilliant successes of socialist building resulted in radical alterations in the toiling classes—the worker class and the peasantry—of our country. The worker class has radically changed. Under capitalism it was a class—the proletariat—without instruments and means of production, exploited by capitalists to whom these belonged. Now in the USSR it is completely and finally freed from exploitation and the possibility of exploitation. The instruments and means of production are in the hands of the state whose guide is the worker class. Consequently the worker class—together with all the people—has possession of them.

The worker class was formerly a class of society without rights, and oppressed. It has become free—and the guiding class of a society that knows neither enslavers nor oppressors. It was formerly pushed aside and prevented in every way from participating in state government. It has become active as builder, organizer, and guide of the most powerful state in the history of the world. It has grown immeasurably in political and cultural respects. It directs Soviet society along the road of communism. Finally it has grown quantitatively—it has sharply increased its proportional share in the general mass of the population. All this signifies that "the worker class of the USSR

[3] Stalin, *Questions of Leninism* (10th Russian ed.), pp. 314-315.
[4] Stalin, *Report on the Draft of the USSR Constitution* (1936), p. 10.

is a completely new worker class, saved from exploitation. The history of mankind has never yet known such a class." [5] All this signifies that it is now incorrect to call our worker class the "proletariat" in the old and ordinary sense of the word. This term has a perfectly concrete historical content. It is applicable to the past—but by no means to the present—worker class of our country. As employed in the Stalin Constitution, it reflects the historic fact that "the proletariat of the USSR has become a completely new class—the worker class of the USSR—which has annihilated the capitalist system of economy and confirmed socialist property in the instruments and means of production, and directs Soviet society along the path of communism." [6]

The peasantry, too, has been subjected to radical changes. Formerly it represented small producers subjected to exploitation by landowners, kulaks, buyers, speculators, usurers, and the like. Now it is liberated, completely and finally, from this exploitation. It consisted of millions of small proprietors scattered over the whole country—slaves of private property—of drudges helpless, in their backward technique, to rise to a comfortable and cultural life. Now it consists, in overwhelming majority, of members of kolkhozes— possessors of social cooperative-kolkhoz property; of workmen of large-scale socialist agriculture which is equipped with the most advanced and mighty technique in the world; and of toilers to whom the kolkhoz structure guarantees a comfortable and cultural life. Under the guidance of the worker class, it shakes off the individualist psychology of the petty proprietor, and is permeated by collectivist psychology, taking in and assimilating socialist methods of labor and socialist forms of community life. Thus Soviet peasantry is a completely new peasantry, the like of which the history of man has never known.

Finally, the intellectuals have likewise undergone fundamental changes. Soviet intellectuals of the present day—unlike prerevolutionary intellectuals —are (nine-tenths of them) persons from the ranks of the workers and peasants and other strata of the toilers. The character of their activity has also changed radically.

Formerly they had to minister to the wealthy classes—they had no other way out. Now they must serve the people—there are no more exploiter classes. For this very reason they are now members of a Soviet society with equal rights. There— in teamwork with the workers and peasants—they carry on the building of the new classless socialist society.[7]

The group of Soviet intellectuals formed and grew in the process of the creation and growth of the socialist culture which has embraced broad

[5] *Ibid.*, p. 11.
[6] *Ibid.*
[7] *Ibid.*, p. 12.

masses of the toiling population. The creation of Soviet intellectuals cost the Soviet state enormous material means and intense political and organizational struggles. It occurred in conditions of sharp conflict between hostile classes which, for counterrevolutionary purposes, sought to find support in certain strata of the intellectuals. Carrying on the correct Leninist-Stalinist policy as to the latter, the party and Soviet authority knew how to turn the basic and best section of the old intellectuals into the path of socialism. What is most important, they knew how to hammer out the new and numerous group of Soviet intellectuals—"a completely new, toiling intelligentsia, the like of which is not to be found in any country of the world." [8] The intellectuals are, in our society too, a stratum. They never were nor can they be a class. As a social group, they represent an organic and constituent part of our socialist society.

The changes in class interrelations, resulting from the building of socialist society, are also clear from this. Stalin has given a classic characterization and formulation of these changes:

Whereof do these changes speak? (1) Of the fact that the boundaries between the worker class and the peasantry—as also between these classes and the intellectuals—are effaced, and the old class exclusiveness has disappeared, so that the distance between these social groups is constantly lessening. (2) Of the fact that economic contradictions between these social groups decline and are effaced. (3) Of the fact, finally, that political contradictions between them decline and are effaced. Such is the state of affairs as to the changes in the field of *class structure* of the USSR. [9]

The class structure of our society is reflected in Article 1 of the Constitution of the USSR. As to this Stalin pointed out:

Whereof does the first paragraph of the draft of the Constitution speak? It speaks of the class structure of Soviet society. Can we Marxists avoid in the Constitution the question of class structure of our society? We cannot. Everyone knows that Soviet society consists of two classes—workers and peasants. The first article of the draft of the Constitution treats precisely of this. Consequently it correctly reflects the class structure of our society. [10]

The first article of the Constitution (as it appeared in the draft of the Constitution) says: "The USSR is a socialist state of workers and peasants." In that sentence is fixed precisely what is at this moment distinct from what was in the recent past and what will be in the future. In the recent past, the kulaks still existed as an exploiter class and socialist society was not as yet built, the proletariat was not as yet raised to the height of political might—

[8] *Ibid.*, p. 13.
[9] *Ibid.*, pp. 13–14.
[10] *Ibid.*, p. 34.

to the lofty condition of socialist organization and culture—which it has now attained, and the peasantry was not yet kolkhoz by an overwhelming majority (as it now is). In the future all differences now existing between classes will disappear, "classes shall no longer be, and workers and peasants will become toilers of a single communist society." [11]

The expression "socialist state of workers and peasants" is found in the earlier Soviet constitutions prior to 1936 (in that of the RSFSR, 1925; of the Turkmen SSR, 1931; and of the Uzbek SSR). It then signified that the Soviet state—as the authority of workers and peasants—puts before itself the task of building socialist society; that the workers and peasants, with the help of the Soviet state, build socialism. Article 1 of the USSR Constitution of 1936 characterizes the present social structure of our Soviet society. The expression "socialist" as applied to our state signifies now that the socialist society is already fundamentally constructed—that ours is now a state of fundamentally socialist society. Article 1 says that the class structure of our society is characterized as socialist.

We have hereinbefore cited comparative figures as to the class structure of the people of our country. These must be further amplified by pointing out that the general number of workers and employees rose from 11.4 million in 1913 to 25.8 million in 1936—more than 200 per cent.[12] It will increase even further both absolutely and relatively—in consequence of the trend of our country's economic development.

Such definition of the class structure of our society is accordingly extremely important and significant in principle. It is important for understanding how at a given stage the most important questions of the structure and activity of the organs of state authority in the USSR are solved—questions of the further development of socialist democracy, of the strengthening of the dictatorship of the worker class, of rights and obligations of USSR citizens, and so forth. Accordingly, the Constitution of the USSR speaks first of all specifically of the class structure of the USSR.

SEC. 4: THE POLITICAL BASIS OF THE USSR

The political basis of society means, in the first instance: (1) to what class or classes of that society does state authority belong? and (2) in what form is this authority carried into effect—whether or not the masses take

[11] *Ibid.*, p. 37.
[12] *Twenty Years of Soviet Authority* (1937), p. 11.

part in governing the state and if so to what degree? The political basis of
the USSR is the *Soviets of the Deputies of the Toilers*. All the authority in
the USSR belongs to the toilers of city and country as personified by them.
Through them the toilers are the direct administrators of the state. They
are the state form of proletarian dictatorship, won in the USSR by the
worker class allied with the basic peasant masses and under the guidance
of the Bolshevik Communist Party.

1. *The rise and confirmation of the authority of the Soviets*

The Soviets passed along a great and extraordinarily complicated and
heroic road of historic development. As expressed in Article 2 of the USSR
Constitution they grew and became strong "as a result of the overthrow of
the power of landowners and capitalists and the conquest of the proletarian
dictatorship."

The Soviets of Deputies came into being first in our country, appearing
in the bourgeois-democratic revolution of 1905 as organs of the principal
mass revolutionary struggle of the worker class. They emerged in the greatest
proletarian centers of the country (St. Petersburg, Moscow, Baku, Ivanov-
Voznesensk, Rostov on Don, and so forth). By the popular creativeness of
the proletarian masses they were brought forth as the basic organs of revolutionary uprising which, ideologically and organizationally, was prepared
and guided by the Bolshevik Party.

The Soviets of Workers' Deputies, representing the assembly of delegates from all the factories and plants, were an unprecedented mass political
organization of the worker class. The Soviets which first came into the world
in 1905 were the *prototype* of the Soviet authority created by the proletariat
under the guidance of the Bolshevik Party in 1917. Soviets were a new revolutionary form of the people's creativeness. They were created solely by
revolutionary strata of the population, in violence of all the laws and regulations of tsarism. They were the manifestation of the self-help of the people,
who had arisen to struggle against tsarism.[1]

Lenin evaluated at one stroke the historical significance of the Soviet.
He pointed out that they are the organization of the struggle of the worker
class to overthrow tsarist autocracy, that their task was to establish a new
revolutionary authority (at that historic period—the revolutionary-democratic
dictatorship of the proletariat and peasantry). In an article, "The Dying
Autocracy and the New Organs of National Authority" (printed in December, 1905), Lenin wrote of Soviets of Workers' Deputies as the new organs
of popular authority.[2]

[1] *History of the All-Union Communist Party (of Bolsheviks)* (1938), p. 75.
[2] Lenin (Russian ed.), Vol. VIII, p. 408.

Concerning the burning traces of the revolution of 1905, generalizing the experience of the Soviets, Lenin wrote of them (at the beginning of 1906 in a pamphlet *The Victory of the Cadets and the Tasks of the Worker Party*): "These were undoubtedly the embryos of a new national—or, if you please, revolutionary—government." With the utmost force Lenin showed the extremely broad democracy characteristic of the Soviets of that period as the rudimentary form of the new people's power:

The new authority, as the dictatorship of the vast majority, could hold and did hold out solely with the aid of the confidence of the vast mass, solely because it attracted the whole mass to participate in authority in the freest, broadest, and strongest manner. Nothing concealed. Nothing secret. No regulations. No formalities. Are you a worker? Do you want to struggle to deliver Russia from a little handful of violent police? You are our Comrade. Choose your deputy. This is authority issuing directly from the mass—the direct and immediate organ of the popular mass and its will.[3]

The Mensheviks, who in 1905 and in the following period came out against armed uprising (contending for the subordination of the proletariat to the guidance of the bourgeoisie), sought to turn the Soviets into purely representative organs in the bourgeois-parliamentary sense of the word—organs which would merely help the bourgeoisie attain political power and grow strong therein, on the one hand—and into organs of local self-government, on the other.

Lenin disclosed in the Soviets (erected by the revolutionary creative power of the people) a concrete historical form of the revolutionary-democratic dictatorship of the proletariat and peasantry, and defended with the utmost resolution the task of creating and developing Soviets in the future revolution as organs of the state authority of that dictatorship.

In 1915 Lenin, speaking of the immediate task—of the conquest of the revolutionary-democratic dictatorship of the proletariat and peasantry—pointed at the Soviets as the state form of this dictatorship: "The Soviets of the Workers' Deputies and like institutions must be viewed as organs of insurrection—organs of revolutionary authority." [4]

In accordance with the doctrine (developed by Lenin in 1905) of the bourgeois-democratic revolution growing into a socialist revolution, the Bolsheviks viewed the Soviets as the state organization of the revolutionary-democratic dictatorship of the proletariat and peasantry, with whose help the transition to the latter and higher stage of the revolution—the conquest of the proletarian dictatorship—would occur. This Bolshevik setting in the matter of Soviets was completely triumphant—as we shall see hereafter—

[3] *Ibid.*, Vol. IX, pp. 117–118.
[4] *Ibid.*, Vol. XVIII, p. 312.

in the period of preparation for the October Revolution and its victory. The appearance of the Soviets in the historical arena in 1905 was a "dress rehearsal" for their appearance in 1917.

The February bourgeois-democratic revolution of 1917 overthrew the autocracy of the tsar and the power of the landowners, the serf-holders who had governed the vast country for hundreds of years. The extreme reaction of their power was manifested with particular force at the beginning of the twentieth century. Tsarist Russia was an absolute monarchy. Supreme authority in the state belonged to the monarch (the Romanov line), the Russian emperor who ruled autocratically. The whole apparatus of state authority—from the Council of Ministers to the village policeman—was built on the principle of a bureaucratic, military-police centralization which had attained monstrous proportions. The tsarist official was in fact omnipotent with reference to the toiling population.

Imperial laws essentially encouraged arbitrary exercise of authority by bureaucrats over the people. The police, the gendarmerie, the courts dealt pitilessly with all who sought to defend the interests of the toilers. The people were bereft of elementary civil and political rights. The stupid tsarist censorship ran wild, stifling every sort of manifestation of living and progressive thought. . . . Active revolutionists—in the first instance and principally the Bolsheviks—were subjected to the fiercest persecutions by the police, tortured and exterminated in prisons and at hard labor.

Protected by the military-police power, the capitalist and landowning exploiters pressed with all their weight upon the toilers. Attempts to protest against intolerable exploitation—workers coming out against industrialists and peasants against landowners—were crushed by tsarist authority with extraordinary measures, with the aid of punitive expeditions, shootings, mass murders, arrests, and so on. The shooting of workers during the peaceful demonstration of January 9, 1905, and the Lena shooting on April 4, 1912, were particularly memorable. Class privileges of the aristocrats of the higher nobility—with the tsarist family at the top—were preserved and guarded by law, as were the privileges of the landowners, by occupancy of state positions and in elections to the Duma, to organs of self-government, and so on. Class barriers (of the orders of nobles, bourgeois, and clergy) were artificially sustained.

At the beginning of World War I capitalism in Russia had attained a high stage of development. The monopolist and imperialist bourgeoisie (the Ryabushinskys, the Konovalovs, and so forth) played a leading role in the economic life of the country, but politically that bourgeoisie was helpless. Political control was in the hands of the serf-owning landowners, in the person of an autocratic sovereign. The bourgeoisie was reconciled with the autocracy because it feared a decisive political struggle; behind its back stood the proletariat, already formed as a class and growing in revolutionary strength. The bourgeoisie relied on autocracy as a cover from attacks by the proletariat.

One of the reasons that impelled the tsarist government to meddle in World War I was its longing to retard the growth of revolution. In that war, however, the Russian state of serf-owning landowners, profoundly hated by the population and guided by unintelligent, venal, and morally decayed officials and bureaucrats, found its grave. Shattered and disorganized by defeats on the military fronts, leading the country to the verge of hunger and economic collapse, the tsarist autocracy was cast down by the revolutionary onset of workers and soldiers in February, 1917.

Although they had wrested authority out of the hands of the tsarist government, the workers and peasants could not at once take it into their own. Authority passed to the bourgeoisie, which was sufficiently organized to utilize, in its own class interests, the then existent revolutionary setting and to take authority into its own hands. In time of war the autocracy had perforce to rely in a certain measure on the help of the bourgeoisie, having broadened its rights and permitted its initiative and self-help to develop more broadly.

The bourgeoisie had received the right to organize divers societies and social enterprises in the interests of war mobilization of resources. Guided by busy bourgeois politicians like Konovalov, Ryabushinsky, and Lvov, social organizations (such as the Union of Zemstvos [5] and Cities [Zemgor] greatly expanded their activity throughout the country. "The War-Industry Committees," through which war orders were distributed, emerged in the summer of 1915, being likewise political and organizational support points for the bourgeoisie. During the course of the war, the bourgeoisie became more active as its economic importance expanded under the conditions of war economy, and because of the manifest failure of the government apparatus of autocracy (whose utter unpreparedness and decay became constantly more obvious) to cope with the problems of carrying on the imperialist war.

The bourgeoisie was anxious about the outcome of the war, and with regard to the deterioration of the internal political situation. Its fear that the tsarist autocracy and the tsarist government apparatus would not know how to crush the growing revolutionary movement was well founded. This was the basis of the opposition moods which developed in the bourgeois upper circle. The most powerful industrialist—Ryabushinsky—declared in the Congress of Representatives of the War-Industry Committees: "We must direct attention to the very organization of government authority—that authority

[5] Units of rural self-government in prerevolutionary Russia.—ED.

has not risen to the emergency." [6] The bourgeoisie had significant influence also in the Fourth Duma, which represented the interests of a bloc of serf-owning landowners and the bourgeois apex (the former predominating).

The bourgeoisie had its political parties (the party of "Cadets," the "Progressive" party, in which there were eminent politicians like Milyukov, Shingarev, Konovalov, and others) and was closely connected with the government apparatus. In all these organizations the bourgeoisie was preparing for itself the basis of the future apparatus of authority. When the revolutionary workers and soldiers actually overthrew autocracy, the bourgeoisie—relying upon its organizations—at once formed its government. On February 27 the State Duma formed the Temporary Committee, having for a time taken upon itself governmental functions. On February 28 the Temporary Committee appointed commissars to the city Dumas and to the ministries. On March 2 the Provisional Government was formed, with Prince Lvov as president and a ministry composed chiefly of the "Cadets" and "Progressive" parties.

Having been confirmed in authority, the bourgeoisie set for itself the task of halting or retarding the growth of the revolutionary movement in the city and in the country, and of continuing the war "to a victorious end." It advanced the watchword of deferring the solution of fundamental questions of state order until the summoning of the Constituent Assembly. The aims of the bourgeois parties were to establish in the country "firm order and powerful authority" by the time of the Constituent Assembly (if it were summoned). That is to say, their aims were to crush the revolution spreading over the land—relying upon the petty-bourgeois parties (the Mensheviks and the SR's) which supported the bourgeoisie with all their strength.

Simultaneously with the Provisional Government as an organization of the authority of the Russian bourgeoisie, another power—another unique government—emerged: the government of workers and soldiers, personified by Soviets of Workers' and Soldiers' Deputies. The bourgeois leaders at once appreciated the significance of these Soviets, and set themselves the task of rendering them impotent—as militant political organizations of toilers—and thus reducing them to naught so as later to be delivered from them completely. The Provisional Government proceeded to develop this policy—maneuvering and double-dealing, and from time to time elaborately concealing its hostility to the Soviets behind democratic phrases about "the unity of the forces of democracy," enjoying therein the complete support of the Mensheviks and the SR's.

These parties clung to the view that, after the overthrow of the autocracy, only the bourgeoisie could create an apparatus of state authority and govern

[6] *History of the Civil War*, Vol. I, p. 16.

the state. The old Menshevik Potresov wrote frankly that it was specifically for the bourgeoisie that the role of master and managing director is prepared "in the immediate—though it be a brief—period of history, while the developed capitalist order is reinforced in the land." [7] The Mensheviks developed the point of view that "all the forces of democracy" must aid the bourgeoisie to repair, under its guidance, the state machine out of the ranks of "specialists," that is, of the old bureaucracy—those who were active in the Zemstvos, the bourgeois city self-governments, and the bureaucratic apex of the petty bourgeois parties (including, of course, the Mensheviks). The Mensheviks, considering that the revolution must end by confirming the bourgeois republic, and above all else fearing the development and the deepening of the revolution—believing neither in the force and state capacities of the masses nor in those of the worker class to rally the peasantry behind it—cynically false to the interests of workers and peasants, resolutely opposed the transfer of authority to the Soviets.

The First All-Russian Congress of Soviets (which opened June 3, 1917), with an overwhelming majority of SR's and Mensheviks, and other fragments of the petty bourgeoisie trailing along, adopted a resolution:

The transfer of all authority to the Soviets of Workers' and Soldiers' Deputies, in the period of the current Russian revolution, would significantly weaken the powers of the revolution, prematurely repel from it the elements still capable of serving it, and threaten it with collapse.[8]

Meantime, threat of revolution came from another side—that of the bourgeois counterrevolution, spreading under the dominance of the Provisional Government. Struggling for its own sole power and to destroy the duality of powers, the bourgeoisie sought to liquidate the Soviets—intensifying its auxiliary organizations. Aside from the War-Industry Committees—whose activity was significantly extended—other organizations of social and semistate character were created. These include the so-called "shock battalions" (of reactionary militarists and reactionary bourgeois elements) intended for punitive operations in crushing revolutionary outbreaks in the rear and at the front.

Thus, at the beginning of the Kornilov adventure, there were at the front thirty-three shock battalions and one division. At the end of October, in eighty-five of the biggest centers of the country, there were staffs for the formation of punitive detachments of this sort. The counterrevolutionists had at their disposal forty shock battalions and one division—more than 50,000 excellently armed and equipped soldiers. "Battalions of Cavaliers of St. George," "Battalions of Death," and so on, were created with analogous

[7] Ibid., p. 79.
[8] Ibid., p. 134.

purpose. The bourgeoisie hastily created its bourgeois White Guard—an apparatus for terrorist crushing of the revolutionary popular masses.

The other big counterrevolutionary organization was the "Union of Officers of the Army and the Fleet," with its chief committee in the quarters of the commander-in-chief. This carried on the work of unifying reactionary officers and assembling active cadres of counterrevolution, devoting special attention to military schools of ensigns and cadets. The cadet groups were later among the chief forces which came out with arms in their hands against the dictatorship of the proletariat, against the Bolshevik Soviets.

The bourgeoisie strenuously prepared the apparatus of military terrorist dictatorship which was bound to destroy not only the Soviets but all other organizations of the toilers.

Lenin, in his April Theses reporting to the All-Russian April conference of Bolsheviks, and in numerous articles in the subsequent period, proved conclusively, in the practical experience of the revolution, that a completely new form of state (radically different from all forms of state hitherto known in history), personified by the Soviets, was growing up and the apparatus of a new and higher type of state—the state of the proletarian dictatorship—emerging.

Lenin showed the historical connection and successorship of the 1917 Soviets with those of 1905 and with the Paris Commune of 1871. In the light of recent experience of the Soviets he showed the vast historical significance of the Paris Commune as the first attempt of the proletariat to create its own special apparatus of state authority. With special force he unmasked Kautsky, who—perverting the facts—tried to prove that the experience of the Paris Commune supposedly tells against the dictatorship of the proletariat. Lenin shows how Kautsky extols the Commune for its mistakes (its irresolution and illogicality in developing necessary state measures to crush counterrevolution, to intensify the economic might of the Commune, to establish connection with the provinces, and so forth), and seeks to discredit it as a new historical form of authority. Lenin reestablishes Marx' and Engels' characterization of the Paris Commune as the prototype of the proletarian dictatorship.

Lenin depicted the special characteristics of the state organization of the Paris Commune as the following: (1) the annihilation of the bureaucratic apparatus of officialdom, police, and army; (2) their replacement by democratic organs with officials broadly elective and controlled and paid no more than a good workman; and (3) the abolition of bourgeois parliamentarism and the unification of representative and executive functions in one state organ. He went on to show that the Soviets of Deputies reproduce, in a new historical setting and in a higher stage, these distinguishing features of the Paris Commune. He put forward as the most important question on revising the party program "the demand of a state organization in the form of a commune" [9] (that is, the state whose prototype was afforded by the Paris Commune).

Lenin showed that the solution of the immediate, fundamental questions of the revolution—questions of peace, land, and bread—was impossible if the old state apparatus was preserved. That apparatus must be smashed, and a new state apparatus must be created by the Soviets to replace it.

Lenin and Stalin unmasked the class nature of the Provisional Government and contrasted the Soviets with it. In the very first days of the bourgeois-democratic revolution of 1917 Lenin characterized the Soviets of Workers' and Soldiers' Deputies as the rudimentary form of proletarian dictatorship. The chief point in the famous Lenin thesis of "duality of power" was that the Soviets were put forth as an organization of future state authority of the dictatorship of the proletariat. Lenin and Stalin called the proletariat to strengthen and develop the Soviets in every way as organs of the genuinely revolutionary authority of workers and peasants.

Two days after his return from exile Stalin put forward as the most important task (*Pravda*, March 14, 1917): "To strengthen . . . the Soviets, to make them ubiquitous, to bind them *inter se*—with the Central Soviet of Workers' and Soldiers' Deputies at their head—as an organ of the revolutionary power of the nation." [10] In its relationship to the Soviets, the party of Bolsheviks started from Lenin's plan as to the democratic-bourgeois revolution "growing over" into a socialist revolution—a plan worked out by him as early as 1905. Lenin's plan started from the fact (established by him) that at this period the country was in a condition of transition "from the first stage of revolution, which gave authority to the bourgeoisie (by reason of the proletariat being insufficiently conscious and organized), to the *second* stage of revolution which must transfer authority into the hands of the proletariat and the poorest strata of the peasantry." [11]

Everyone knows that a frenzied struggle against Lenin's program of conquest by the dictatorship of the proletariat was carried on by traitors to the worker class—agents of the bourgeoisie—Zinovyev, Kamenev, and Rykov. Repeating in essence the Menshevik arguments against the proletarian dictatorship, they showed the necessity of not going beyond the bounds of establishing a bourgeois-democratic republic, having subordinated the Soviets to this task and turned them into an organization to realize this purpose. Thus as early as the first stage of the struggle for authority of the

[9] Lenin (Russian ed.), Vol. XX, p. 89.
[10] Stalin, *On the Paths to October* (State Publishing House, 1925), p. 2.
[11] Lenin (Russian ed.), Vol. XX, p. 78.

Soviets, these traitors—later proven enemies of the people—declared them-selves strike-breakers and traitors to the proletarian state.

The course of events entirely confirmed this. The Provisional Govern-ment strove to utilize as far as possible the old apparatus and its bureaucratic cadres to prosecute their class policy of hostility to the people. Setting itself the task of prolonging the predatory war contrary to the wishes and will of the masses, it sought to preserve a reactionary set of generals as leaders of the army and the old principles of army-building. It contemplated using the army to crush the antiwar—and, in general, revolutionary—outbreaks of the masses.

The nation could gain peace—and the counterrevolutionary plans and doings of the bourgeoisie be nipped in the bud—only by winning the army over to the side of the people—that is, in the last analysis, by creating in place of the old army (which was functionally and structurally hostile to the people) a new, people's army. It was necessary to arm the people. The Soviets of Workers' and Soldiers' Deputies were distinguished by the fact that, from the very beginning, they enjoyed the support of broad soldier (that is to say, armed) masses of the people, and actually possessed a vast armed force—especially the Soviets of Petrograd, Kronstadt, and Moscow. In the words of Lenin they represented "the people in arms."

To give the land to the peasants—that is to say, to take it by violence from the landowners and change it into property of the state, having handed it over to be used by the toilers of the country—was possible only with the help of such authority and such state organization as would stand to the defense of the interests of the peasantry—would go out from the core of the working class and the peasantry and everywhere realize their inter-ests. Such authority was, once again, the authority of the Soviets.

The Provisional Government, with its capitalist ministers (Konovalov, Guchkov, and others), persons active in the War Industry Committees (Palchinsky and others), and "socialist" ministers (Tseretelli, Skobelev and others), not only took no measures whatsoever to combat the crisis in pro-visions and general economy (then raging) and the madly growing specu-lation, but on the contrary organized and encouraged that crisis, to the end that the bourgeoisie, the landowners, and the kulaks might profit by it.

The Provisional Government not only prosecuted no struggle of any kind with economic sabotage by capitalists who closed enterprises and halted production so as to stifle the revolution by "the bony hand of hunger" (an expression of Ryabushinsky's), but on the contrary encouraged this counterrevolutionary sabotage. To avert the economic bankruptcy in preparation by the capitalists, it was essential unhesitatingly to take pro-duction under the control of the entire state and to smash sabotage by the capitalists. Such control could, however, be realized only by the state authority of the toilers, that is to say, the *Soviets*. Only they could actually realize such control in the interests of the toilers and practically organize it with the forces of the worker mass. Only by establishing the authority of the Soviets could this most important question of the revolution be solved in the interests of the toilers. Accordingly, as early as April, 1917, the Bolshevik Party, under the guidance of Lenin and Stalin, put forward the watchword: "All power to the Soviets!"

The Mensheviks and the SR's were dominant in the Soviets at this initial period of the revolution and were the leaders in most affairs. Putting forward the watchword: "All power to the Soviets!" the Bolsheviks set as their task the clarification for the masses of the treachery of the Menshevik-SR policy carried on by the Soviets, so that the masses might in their own political experience be convinced of the necessity of transferring to the Soviets complete and full authority and of realizing—in the form of the Soviets—the dictatorship of the proletariat. Moreover, the Bolsheviks proceeded from the possibility at that time of the peaceful development of the revolution and the painless transfer of authority to the Soviets.

In the course of revolutionary events, however, the Soviets—still constantly under the guidance of Mensheviks and SR's—finally meandered into the camp of the bourgeoisie. They not only refused to assume authority, they also supported the Provisional Government in its attack upon the revolution—in smashing the July demonstration, organizing prosecution and pogroms of the Bolsheviks, disarming detachments of the Red Guard, and so on. Unity of authority—that of the counterrevolutionary bourgeoisie—took the place of duality of authority. In this connection the Bolsheviks, at the Sixth Congress of the Party, temporarily suspended the use of the watchword: "All power to the Soviets!" That Congress put forward the immediate preparation for an armed uprising. "The watchword: 'All power to the Soviets' must be discontinued after the July days," said Stalin. "Temporary discontinuance of this watchword, however, by no means signifies refusal to struggle for the power of the Soviets. It is a matter, not of Soviets in general as organs of revolutionary struggle, but only of certain Soviets which are guided by Mensheviks and SR's." [12]

Lenin and Stalin put before the Party the most important task—the Bolshevization of the Soviets—a task successfully solved by the Party. In conditions of the mighty revolutionary uplift evoked by the struggle of the toiling masses led by Bolsheviks against the forces of Kornilov, there developed "a zone of revitalization and renovation—of *Bolshevization*—of the Soviets. Factories, works, and military units reelecting their deputies

[12] *History of the All-Union Communist Party (of Bolsheviks)* (1938) p. 188.

sent to the Soviets representatives of the Bolshevist Party, in place of Mensheviks and SR's." At the end of September, 1917, the Soviets were already Bolshevist. They became the organs for the immediate and direct struggle of workers and of the poorest peasants to grasp state authority. When this was attained—when adherents of the Bolsheviks began to predominate in the Soviets—the party again put forward its war cry: 'All power to the Soviets!' [13]

Under this watchword the Bolsheviks succeeded in organizing the overthrow of the Provisional Government and the victory of the proletarian dictatorship in October, 1917. In the period before the Bolsheviks assumed authority, Bolshevization of the Soviets signified (1) the arming of the worker masses by the Soviets and the rallying around them of revolutionary soldiery ready to support the Soviets by armed attack upon the bourgeois administration; (2) the strengthening and development of the proletarian militia—chiefly in the form of the Red Guard, which organized and preserved revolutionary legal order; (3) that the Soviets had begun in fact—through arrangement by their own officials—to establish a significant degree of control over production, foiling sabotage by the proprietors, breaking up their lockouts, carrying the eight-hour work day into effect, and so on. The Bolshevization of the Soviets meant that the Soviets began to control the activity of various organs concerned with food supply and to employ revolutionary measures (of confiscation and requisition) in the struggle with speculation, and so forth.

Under the leadership of the Bolsheviks, the worker class, in the course of its struggle against the bourgeois dictatorship, making ready the Socialist Revolution, thus created—in the form of the Soviets—the apparatus of its future state authority. The watchword: "All power to the Soviets!" was the concentrated and militant expression of the Bolshevik plan forcibly to overthrow the Provisional Government and the bourgeois-nationalist governments in the borderlands—a plan of revolutionary seizure of authority by the worker class and the poorest peasantry and of establishing the proletarian dictatorship.

With the triumph of the October Revolution came also the practical realization of this plan. The revolution transferred authority to the Soviets, which, having assumed it, became in turn sovereign organs of the state authority of workers and peasants—a mighty state organization, essential to reinforce the conquests of the revolution and its further development. On the day following the victory of the Socialist Revolution, the worker class—in the form of the Soviets—already possessed, in general features, the foundation of the state apparatus created in the struggle against the power

[13] *Ibid.*, p. 194.

of capitalists and landowners. In the course of the revolution the worker class smashed the old state apparatus of mass strangulation and repression alien and hostile to the people—and developed and strengthened the new Soviet apparatus of authority which had grown out of the peoples and serves the people. This was the result of the struggle of the Bolshevik Party. guided by Lenin and Stalin, for the conquest of the proletarian dictatorship.

Only after creating such state organization as the Soviets could the worker class establish and stabilize its dictatorship. On the other hand, only the victory of the dictatorship—the political domination of the proletariat—made possible the uninterrupted development and strengthening of the Soviets as the political basis of the new society of the transition from capitalism to communism.

Characterizing the Soviets as the new type of state authority, Stalin says: "The Republic of Soviets is thus the political form—long sought after and finally found—within whose framework must be accomplished the economic emancipation of the proletariat—the complete victory of socialism." [14]

A description and portrayal of the organization and activity of the Soviets require particularly the disclosure of the concrete content of this Stalin formula. In a preceding chapter we have shown how the development of the Soviets was reflected in the history of the Soviet Constitution. In subsequent chapters we shall clarify specific phases of the organization and activity of the Soviets as organs of authority, of the state government realized by the toiling masses of our socialist state. We shall now pause to set out the manner wherein Soviet public law reflects and confirms the general and characteristic principles of the Soviet state as a state of a new and higher type.

2. The Soviets—a state form of the dictatorship of the worker class

The Soviets have been defined in Soviet law, always openly and frankly, as state organs of the proletarian dictatorship. Such is the frank characterization of our state in Soviet constitutions since the first constitution of the RSFSR in 1918.[15] Only Soviet public law—in contrast with bourgeois law—answers directly and faithfully the question of the class character of state authority. This particular and specific feature of proletarian, socialist, public law attracts the sympathies of the toilers of the whole world.

[14] Stalin, *Questions of Leninism* (10th Russian ed.), p. 33.
[15] Cf. Constitution of RSFSR (1918) Art. 9; of the White Russian SSR (1919) Art. 4; of the Ukrainian SSR (1919) Art. 2; of the Azerbaijan SSR (1921) Art. 1; of the Armenian SSR (1922) Art. 11; of USSR (1924), subdivision 1; of RSFSR (1925) Art. 1; of the Turkmen SSR (1931) Art. 1; of the Uzbek SSR (1931) Art. 1; and others.

Specifically by reason of its having stated openly that everything is subordinated to the dictatorship of the proletariat—that it is a new type of state organization—Soviet authority has won for itself the sympathy of the workers of the whole world.[16]

Thus Soviet constitutions scientifically define in principle the class essence of the Soviet state, emphasized in the program of the Bolshevik Party in the following words:

In contrast with bourgeois democracy—which conceals the class character of its state—Soviet authority openly acknowledges the inevitable class character of every sort of state, until the complete disappearance of the division of society into classes and therewith of all state authority of every sort.

The matter of the class essence of the Soviet state as a proletarian dictatorship was exhaustively developed in the works of Lenin and Stalin. The classic reference is Stalin's famous proposition as to the three fundamental sides of the proletarian dictatorship.[17] These sides were also reflected in Soviet public law.

a) Crushing the resistance of class enemies

From the moment of its emergence and down to the present time, the Soviet state has clashed—and still constantly clashes—in fierce conflict with the overthrown exploiter classes and their toadies. Counterrevolutionary sabotage by industrialists and bourgeois intellectuals in 1918 was one of the earliest stages and methods of resistance by the exploiter classes. Swiftly Soviet authority entered into still more savage struggle against the White Guard and interventionist armies and all sorts of bandit gangs organized by the kulaks to overthrow Soviet authority. Routed in the civil war, the exploiter classes did not cease—they merely changed in forms and methods their resistance to socialism. The organization of anti-Soviet counterrevolutionary parties and conspirator groups (the "Industrialist Party," the "United Center," the Trotsky-Bukharin bands, nationalist organizations, and so on) brought wrecking, diversions, espionage, and acts of terrorism to bear upon persons active in behalf of the Soviets . . . all as a continuation of the savage class struggle by representatives of the dying capitalist world against the socialism which was being built.

Guided by Lenin and Stalin, the Soviet state always started from the position that the perishing classes would resist with all their powers until the last moment, and that their pitiless repression would therefore always constitute an imprescriptible and necessary task of the proletarian dictator-

[16] Lenin (Russian ed.), Vol. XXIV, p. 307.
[17] Stalin, *Questions of Leninism* (10th Russian ed.), pp. 112–113.

ship. Accordingly, as early as the Declaration of Rights, the pitiless repression of exploiters was openly proclaimed as one of the basic tasks of Soviet authority.[18] In conformity with this principle of the proletarian dictatorship, Soviet authority takes substantial and definitive measures to crush the resistance of exploiter classes and their elements. It expelled them from all organs of state authority and cut off from them any access thereto. The Declaration of Rights frankly established that "exploiters can have no place in any organ of authority." Their organizations were prohibited and liquidated, and attempts to reestablish them were—and are—pitilessly crushed by Soviet authority. This is one of the basic tasks of the proletarian dictatorship, wielding the drawn sword of retribution created by the revolution—the Cheka,[19] the OGPU,[20] and the NKVD.[21] The exploiter elements and their assistants were deprived of political rights—particularly the right of suffrage. *"Guided solely by interests of the worker class, the Russian Socialist Federative Soviet Republic deprives individuals and groups of rights utilized by them to the detriment of the interests of the socialist revolution."* [22]

The class and *historical* sense of thus depriving defined social groups and persons of rights was solely and specifically to *crush the resistance* of class enemies of the toilers *insofar* as they could utilize those rights to struggle against the Soviet order. At the present moment—with socialism victorious—depriving any social group of political rights is entirely abrogated. That signifies, however, the abrogation only of a certain *concrete form* of repressing resistance of the enemies of socialism; *repression* itself, as a function of the proletariat state, remains—and will remain—so long as such resistance—in whatever form—continues. Only the concrete conditions and forms of repression change.

In the present period, as everyone knows, primary and especially outstanding significance attaches to international capitalist encirclement, which stimulates and organizes the counterrevolutionary and anti-Soviet activity of the last of the exploiter groups and elements in the USSR. Their basic method of resistance to socialism at the present time is the pillaging and destruction of socialist property—wrecking, diversion, and espionage in aid of foreign bourgeois states, terror, attempts to undermine the military and

---

[18] 1918, No. 15, Art. 215. As in the Constitutions of all the Soviet Republics, e.g., that of the Azerbaijan SSR (1921) speaks of "the complete repression of the bourgeoisie"—a formula found in other constitutions.

[19] The All-Russian Extraordinary Commission for the Suppression of Counterrevolution, Sabotage, and Speculation.

[20] Unified State Political Department.

[21] People's Commissariat for Home Affairs.

[22] Constitution of RSFSR (1918), Art. 23. For analogous articles compare the constitutions of the Azerbaijan SSR (1921), Art. 14; the Turkmen SSR (1921), Art. 17; and others. The Armenian SSR Constitution provides that "exploiter classes are deprived of political rights in general, and of the right to occupy political posts in particular" (Art. 5).

political might and state unity of the peoples of the USSR, and the like. Hence follow the specific tasks of crushing the enemies of socialism and the particular significance of such methods of exposing and annihilating them as intensification of the revolutionary vigilance of the toiling masses and organs of proletarian dictatorship, intensified guard of the boundaries of the USSR, intensification of measures to thwart counterrevolutionary activity, and so on.

To intensify the repression of enemies of socialism—enemies cf the people—it is necessary to strengthen the dictatorship of the worker class. "A strong and mighty proletarian dictatorship is what we need now to dispel the last remnants of the dying classes to the winds and to shatter their thievish machinations,"[23] Stalin said at the beginning of 1923, and even now his words are completely significant. Furthermore, they have acquired peculiar and real force in contemporary conditions.

What is the dictatorship of the proletariat? Lenin defined it as the domination of the proletariat over the bourgeoisie—unlimited by law and resting on force—enjoying the sympathy and support of all the toiling masses. The task of that dominance is completely and finally to crush the shattered exploiters' resistance to socialism. At the present moment a significant part of that task is already completed. But in its entirety it remains, and will always constitute an imprescriptible side of the proletarian dictatorship.

b) *The strengthening of the union of the worker class with the peasantry*

In Soviet public law the role and significance of the union of the worker class and the peasantry is particularly emphasized. It is spoken of in Soviet constitutions, in all the most important constitutional acts, and directives of Union and Republic Congresses of Soviets. It is evidenced by the daily activity of the Soviet worker-peasant government. The very construction and daily policy of the Soviet government as a worker-peasant government is the practical embodiment of the union of the worker class and the peasantry under the guidance of the worker class.[24] The task of strengthening the union of the worker class with the peasantry and the guiding role of the worker class are especially emphasized in separate directives of Congresses of the Soviets.

Thus, for example, the directive of the Third All-Union Congress of Soviets of 1925, Concerning Soviet Construction,[25] a directive particularly keenly edged against Trotskyist attempts to break the party line and the

[23] Stalin, *Questions of Leninism* (10th Russian ed.), p. 509.
[24] This matter is especially and exhaustively illuminated in Stalin's answer to Dmitriev. Cf. *Questions of Leninism* (1932), pp. 238–244.
[25] Cz. 1925, No. 35, Art. 247.

government line in this matter, points out that the fundamental task in attracting broad masses of workers and peasants "consists in striving for ever greater solidarity of workers and peasants, and also of the laboring (particularly the village) intellectuals—teachers, agronomists, and doctors— around the Soviets, and in reinforcing the union of workers and peasants."

At the end of this directive is the following statement:

At the same time the Third Congress of Soviets of the USSR deems it necessary to remind workers and peasants of the fundamental legacy of Lenin, that the victory of socialism in our country is possible only if actual guidance of the peasantry by the working class is realized on the basis of strengthening the union of workers and peasants.

The realization of the Lenin-Stalin plan of socialist industrialization of the country and collectivization of agriculture enormously intensified—and gave a new and mighty basis to—the union of the worker class and the peasantry.

A directive of the Fourth Congress of Soviets of the USSR [26] in accordance with the report of Kalinin Concerning the Basic Tasks of Agriculture in Connection with the Development of National Economy and Industrialization of the Country states:

Successes in industrializing the country will create a new and still more favorable condition for further confirmation of the bond between city and country, agriculture and industry, for strengthening the union of workers and peasants, for stabilizing the dictatorship of the proletariat and for the further advance to socialism.

In the spring of 1929—the year of the great crisis—the Fifth Congress of Soviets of the USSR adopted an extremely important directive, Concerning Ways of Raising the Level of Agriculture and Building Cooperatives in the Villages.[27] Here were noted definitive measures preparing the transition to mass rural collectivization beginning in the summer of that year. In that directive is found the following statement:

The Congress of Soviets considers that the solution of the tasks it sets in the field of agriculture can be only on the basis of activating farm laborers and the poor and middle class peasant masses, this to be under the proletarian guidance of the peasantry, and accompanied by the consolidation and organization of these three groups, in order to improve farming and reorganize it on socialist lines, based on a still further strengthening of the union of the worker class with the peasantry.

Finally, the Sixth Congress of Soviets of the USSR,[28] in the directive,

[26] Cz. 1927, No. 21, Art. 240.
[27] Cz. 1929, No. 35, Art. 312.
[28] Cz. 1931, No. 17, Art. 161.

Concerning the Building of Kolkhozes, stated and confirmed the new and higher level of the worker-peasant union attained by the brilliant success of collectivization on the basis of the new correlation of class forces. In this directive we find:

The triumphant kolkhoz movement decisively changes the correlation of class forces in the USSR. . . . On the basis of the expansion of uninterrupted collectivization, Soviet authority has gone over to a policy of liquidating the kulaks as a class and has been successfully carrying this policy into effect for the past year. The middle-class peasant, entering the kolkhoz, becomes—side by side with what were formerly poverty-stricken hirelings—the veritable and stable foundation of Soviet authority in the country. Thereby the union of the worker class with the peasantry is vastly strengthened, and the basis of worker-peasant power—for which henceforward the basic and chief foundation in the country is the kolkhoz peasantry—is broadened.

The efficient union of the worker class with the peasantry leads to the final triumph of the kolkhoz order in the country, and the colossal growth in the kolkhoz peasantry of political consciousness and of socialist organization and culture—and all this at the same time promotes further and uninterrupted strengthening of that union under the guidance of the worker class. This union finds expression in the highest foundation—the foundation of socialist social organization—the Stalin Constitution of 1936.

It is reflected in Article 1, which defines our land as a socialist state of workers and peasants. It is emphasized by the definition of the Soviets as "Soviets of Working People's Deputies," instead of "Soviets of Worker, Peasant, and Red Army Deputies." This definition of the Soviets, wherein workers and peasants are united under the general idea of "workers," indicates that in political state life workers and peasants are united still more closely, that in the given relationship also—that of their part in the construction of the state—the boundaries between them fall away and are effaced. Such a definition indicates in particular that in the formation of the Soviets—in their elections—the former distinction between workers and peasants as to standards of representation is eliminated. The political significance of that elimination is, in the first instance, that the influence of the worker class upon the peasantry—the state guidance of the peasantry by the worker class—was immensely strengthened.

Raised to a new and higher level, the union of the worker class and the peasantry is emphasized in Article 3 of the Constitution of the USSR, wherein it is pointed out that state authority in our country belongs to "the workers of town and country." It is reflected and confirmed in the following articles of Chapter I which speak of the economic basis of socialism —victorious alike in city and in country—in the interests of workers and peasants, and essentially in all the Chapters of the Stalin Constitution—that basic law of our socialist *worker-peasant* state.

The guiding role of the worker class has its roots in the very essence of the Soviet social order—in the historic mission of the worker class, summoned to annihilate capitalism and to build a new socialist society. That role exists because of the real relationships existent between worker class and peasantry, formed during the historical development in conditions of socialist revolution, civil war, and expanded building of socialism. It will be preserved as the most important principle of the worker-class dictatorship so long as that dictatorship—that is to say, so long as class differences in socialist society—continue to exist. The guiding role of the worker class is acknowledged by our peasantry, conscious of the decisive signifiance of that leadership for realizing the general interests of all toilers. Precisely this is the decisive point and the essence of the matter.

As to the special advantages of the worker class as compared with the peasantry—advantages confirmed in legislative order and directed at facilitating the working class' fulfillment of its leading role—they were never of decisive significance. Expressed basically in workers' advantages in the election law, they had a temporary character only, as was pointed out in the program of the Bolshevik Party; their practical significance constantly diminished, and now they are completely abrogated by the existing Constitution. The fact of their abrogation is particularly evident in the circumstance that guidance of the peasantry by the worker class has entered firmly into life and the manner of living, and is completely and fully guaranteed by the actual position of the worker class in society, its acknowledged authority as leader in the midst of all the toilers, and the further circumstance that the worker class has no need of any constitutional advantages in carrying out its leading role.

Thus from this aspect also, the dictatorship of the worker class grows strong and will in the future grow still stronger, and the necessity of constant intensification of the dictatorship of the working class is likewise clear. Soviet public law completely serves this task, reflecting service to this great historic purpose in its institutes and in its solution of various problems.

c) *The dictatorship of the worker class as an instrument for building communism*

A special characteristic of the Soviet state in point of principle is that it comes forward as organizing the economic and cultural life of our society[29] as the most important and decisive means of building communist society.

[29] Cy. 1918, No. 15, Art. 215.

In the Declaration of Rights "the establishment of the socialist organization of society" is put forward as one of the basic tasks of the Soviet state. The Constitution of the RSFSR [30] proclaims "the installation of socialism" as one of its fundamental tasks. An analogous formula is contained in the constitutions of other Soviet republics.[31]

In the Stalin Constitution the building of socialism is fixed and confirmed as an historic fact. Having confirmed the first phase of communism already fundamentally attained, the dictatorship of the worker class thereby confirms the basis for further socialist building—for the transition to the higher phase of communism, employing in full measure the conquests of socialism for the winning of new victories of communism. From the fact that this dictatorship is a necessary and fundamental means of building communist society, the conclusion is absolutely clear that its maximum intensification is for the basic interests of all the toilers who create that society.

d) The leading role of the Communist Party

The political basis of the USSR comprises—as the most important principle of the worker-class dictatorship—the leading and directing role of the Communist Party in all fields of economic, social, and cultural activity. The works of Lenin and Stalin develop exhaustively the theoretical and the organizational practical aspects of this matter.[32] A series of decisions of the Bolshevik Party firmly established the organization forms whereby the party's guidance of state organs is effectuated. Therein is likewise established a delimitation of the functions of party and state organs, starting from this principle: "The party must develop its decisions through Soviet organs *within the framework of the Soviet Constitution*. The party seeks to *guide*— not to replace—the activity of the Soviets." [33]

[30] Cy. 1918, No. 51, Art. 582.
[31] Compare the Constitutions of the White Russian SSR of 1919 (Arts. 2 and 4) and of the Azerbaijan SSR of 1921 (Art. 1 and others). The Ukraine SSR provides (Art. 2): "The task of this dictatorship is to realize the transition from a bourgeois order to socialism by developing socialist reorganizations." The Armenian SSR Constitution (1922, Art. 11) proclaims that the dictatorship of the proletariat "has as its purpose putting an end to the capitalist order and realizing socialism with the aid of revolutionary overturn" (i.e., the bold and decisive reorganization of society to harmonize with socialism). The Constitution of the Georgian SSR (1922) says: "The task of the dictatorship is to realize the transition from the bourgeois order to socialism by undeviating and planned utilization of socialist reorganizations."
[32] Cf. Lenin (Russian ed.), Vol. XXII, p. 457, Vol. XXIII, p. 326, Vol. XXV, pp. 34–36, 185–190; Stalin, *Questions of Leninism*, pp. 62–72, 113–131, 578–598. In the Stalin Constitution (Art. 126) the leading and directing role of the All-Russian Communist Party (of Bolsheviks) in the Soviet state is defined with all clearness.
[33] From a resolution of the Eighth Congress of the Bolshevik Worker-Peasant Party, cited in *The All-Union Communist Party (of Bolsheviks) in Resolutions* (1936), Pt. 1, p. 315.

Practically, the party's guidance of the Soviets is actualized as follows: (1) First of all, the party seeks to advance its candidates into the basic posts of state work in our country at elections for Soviets—its best workers, devoted to the concerns of socialist building and enjoying the broadest confidence of the popular masses. In this the party succeeds, "since workers and peasants have confidence in the Party. It is no accident that those who guide the organs of authority among us are Communists, since these leaders enjoy vast authority in the land." [34] This is brilliantly illustrated by the results of the elections to the Supreme Soviets in 1937 and 1938, conducted for the first time in accordance with the elective system introduced by the Stalin Constitution. (2) "The Party verifies the work of the organs of government and the organs of authority correcting unavoidable mistakes and shortcomings, helping them develop the decisions of the government and trying to guarantee them support of the masses—and not a single important decision is taken by them without corresponding directions of the Party." (3) "In developing a plan of work of a given organ of authority—whether along the line of industry and agriculture or that of building trade and culture—the Party gives general guiding directions defining the character and direction of the work of these organs during the time when these plans are operative." [35]

Of important significance in principle and practice is party guidance of elections to the Soviets, made real by the elective bloc of Communists and nonparty members at all stages of the election campaign. Party guidance of the Soviets is guaranteed particularly by the fact that the party teaches the toilers—organized into Soviets—socialist methods of state work, and nonparty workers of the Soviets are also convinced in practice of the correctness of the party directions.

The uninterrupted growth and strengthening of the Bolshevik Party and of its influence on the masses and ties with them, and its guidance of the state are the chief guaranty of strengthening and development—toward the highest phase of communism—of the dictatorship of the worker class, the reliable political foundation of Soviet socialist society.

3. *The Soviets of the deputies of the toilers—the highest type of democracy*

a) *Soviet democracy as democracy of the highest type*

The foregoing relates to a characterization of the class essence and the historic tasks of the worker-class dictatorship. Analysis of the specific state form, wherein the proletarian dictatorship of the Soviets of the Deputies

[34] Stalin, *Questions of Leninism* (10th Russian ed.), pp. 174–175.
[35] *Ibid.*

of the Toilers manifests itself, makes possible the conviction that the Soviet state is a state democratic *after a new fashion*—a democracy of a higher type.

That the proletarian socialist democracy is a democracy of a special and higher type was basically worked out in theory by Lenin and Stalin even before the Bolsheviks assumed authority. It was under their guidance that the Bolsheviks came to the events of October with their plan of a new socialist-democratic organization of state authority already prepared. This plan was brilliantly realized in practice in the precise and definitive historic form wherein it was projected—that of Soviet authority.

From the very moment of its emergence—from its first practical steps— Soviet authority, as the state form of proletarian dictatorship, showed itself the most democratic form of authority in the history of the world. This is due to its class essence—to the historical mission of the worker-class dictatorship, which cannot exist as state authority save in the form of the most elevated and authentic democracy.

Lenin completely unmasked—and devastatingly criticized—the "theories" (of Kautsky and others) that dictatorship and democracy "in general" are incompatible and mutually contradictory, wherefore the dictatorship of the proletariat established in our land is supposed to exclude democracy "in general." In reality the bourgeois—like every other exploiter—dictatorship is incompatible with true and real democracy.

The proletarian dictatorship excludes bourgeois democracy, but it is not only compatible with—it is in fact impossible without—authentic (viz., proletarian) democracy. All three sides of the proletarian dictatorship neces-sarily presuppose—and essentially signify—proletarian democracy. The union of worker class and peasantry, and state guidance of society by the worker class, cannot be realized without attracting into the factual government of the state, and drawing into active and conscious political life, the broadest masses of the toilers. The same should be said of the task of building social-ist society. This can be accomplished only in the event of the broadest possible masses being summoned and moved into proximity to guidance by the state of the entire process of reorganizing society and recasting the people's way of life and psychology. Whereas even the task of violently crushing exploiter resistance cannot be accomplished by the undemocratic method.

Lenin and Stalin entirely and completely refuted the reactionary asser-tions that violence is "in general" incompatible with democracy. Genuine democracy—democracy of the toilers—is incompatible with the violence of the exploiter classes dominant in society. In exploiter society—in a setting of particularly savage class struggle and imminent proletarian revolution— the bourgeoisie ever more and more limits and frustrates bourgeois democracy, extirpating it violently and—in certain conditions—replacing it completely by the naked, reactionary, counterrevolutionary violence of fascist terrorist dictatorship.

Proletarian revolutionary violence is democratic in the true sense of the word—both by its social essence and by the forms wherein it is realized. It is democratic in social essence because it is directed to the defense of the interests of the majority of the toilers against the exploiter minority. It becomes, accordingly, ever more democratic in proportion to the development of a socialist society which ever increasingly consolidates and unites the overwhelming majority of the population and wherein the last of the exploiters become ever more and more a miserable handful. Proletarian revolutionary violence is democratic in form, because it is realized with the most active participation of the broadest strata of the population from whose mass workers, devotedly and courageously defending the interests of society, emerge and grow. Surely the civil war—the heroic struggle of the toilers of our country against counterrevolution in all its forms—was the highest manifestation of true democracy as to both its purposes and the forms and methods whereby it was carried on. Surely it rallied the majority of the toilers of all peoples and nationalities of our great country, raised the political consciousness and the culture of the toiling population—oppressed and backward before the revolution—and brought forward from the depths of the nation tens and hundreds of thousands of persons to govern the state.

Civil war against the bourgeoisie is the war—*democratically* organized and carried on—of the poverty-stricken masses against the minority, the haves. But since it is war, it must inevitably put violence in the place of law. Moreover, violence exerted in the name of interests and rights of the majority of the population is distinguished by a different character: it tramples on "rights" of exploiters—of the bourgeoisie; it *cannot be realized* without democratic organization of troops and the rear. Civil war violently expropriates—at one stroke and first of all—the banks, the factories, the railroads, the big agricultural properties, and so on. But, precisely *for the purpose of* expropriating all this, it is essential to introduce also the choice by the people of all officials and officers, *the complete merging* of the army (which carries on the war against the bourgeoisie) with the mass of the people, and complete democracy in the matter of disposing of provisions—and of their production and distribution, and the like.[36]

The state consciousness and activity of the toiling masses who have come to authority is, in accord with the principles of proletarian democracy, an elementary condition for successful struggle against the enemies of the people—against representatives of the destroyed exploiter classes. The most important means of successful struggle against every sort of counterrevolu-

[36] Lenin (Russian ed.), Vol. XXX, pp. 260–261.

tionary wrecker activity of anti-Soviet organizations and persons is, in the first instance, such democratic means as *revolutionary vigilance of the masses themselves and their activity* in inveigling and rendering harmless the enemies of the people.

Lenin and Stalin revealed with finality the fallacious and antiscientific contrasting of democracy "in general" with violence "in general." Precisely because democracy is a form of political organization of the state, it is unachievable without violence. "Democracy is a state which acknowledges the subordination of the minority to the majority. It is an organization for systematic *violence* of one class—of one part of the population—exerted upon another." [37] So long, therefore, as democracy is present, violence in some form or other will also be present. As regards violence, the peculiarity of socialist democracy is that it is a means of building society without classes, without a state, and consequently without violence, whereas bourgeois democracy conceals and seeks to perpetuate the class violence of exploiters upon exploited.

Trotskyists, Bukharinists, and other traitors and enemies of the people, with the purpose first of frustrating the creation of our state and then the strengthening of it, likewise essayed the contrast of proletarian dictatorship to proletarian democracy. Trotskyists—despicable restorers of capitalism—feigned adherence to the proletarian dictatorship, which they themselves conceived as a system of bare administration, disregard of the masses, bureaucratic centralization, and other antidemocratic methods in reality profoundly alien and hostile to the proletarian dictatorship. At the same time they demagogically demanded "democracy," possibly aiming at carrying on their subversive anti-Soviet activity directed against the dictatorship of the proletariat and true proletarian democracy. The Bukharinists—Rightist restorers of capitalism—campaigned for "democracy," but in such form as to create the possibility of "the kulaks growing into socialism" (that is, of reestablishing capitalist exploitation), of "easing class contradictions" (that is, of liquidating the dictatorship of the proletariat and proletarian democracy), and of reestablishing the power of landowners and capitalists.

Having shattered the Trotskyists, Bukharinists, and other counterrevolutionary anti-Soviet organizations, the Party and the whole Soviet people annihilated the irreconcilable and sworn enemies of proletarian, socialist democracy. Despite their resistance and the gloomy expectations and predictions of all sorts of sceptics and persons of little faith, the USSR witnessed the undeviating development of the might of the worker-class dictatorship and of the strength and breadth of proletarian socialist democracy. These were as the two sides of one and the same phenomenon and process:

[37] *Ibid.*, Vol. XXI, p. 426.

socialist reorganization of society by means of the Soviet state—a state of a new and higher type.

In the Stalin Constitution the plenitude of proletarian socialist democracy found its highest reflection and confirmation in public law.

We will proceed to clarify particular questions of socialist democracy in the USSR.

b) *All authority in the USSR belongs to the toilers*

Article 3 of the Constitution of the USSR provides that "all authority in the USSR belongs to the toilers of the city and country, personified by Soviets of the Deputies of the Toilers," confirming the fact of world history in our country that authority is actually in the hands of the toilers—they in reality govern the state and all the affairs of state. Bourgeois public law starts from the principle that the people cannot and should not themselves govern the state—only those enjoying the right to vote can express their state will through parliament and its legislative activity. The state, however, should be governed by special executive and judicial mechanisms consisting of particular officials—a bureaucracy—functioning in everyday activity independently of the masses and without their participation in separate branches of state building. The people cannot and should not themselves execute the work of the state. They delegate authority—belonging to them only in principle—to special state organs empowered to carry out all the work of governing the state in the strict sense of the word.

In one form or another this principle finds foundation in the theory of bourgeois public law. The prevailing bourgeois concepts of "national sovereignty" developed the idea that authority starts only from the people—that supremacy of authority "is rooted in the people," and so forth. But in practice the work of the state is executed by special institutions and officials authorized therefor. Precisely in this sense many bourgeois constitutions proclaim "national sovereignty," [38] the bourgeois conception whereof—suprem-

[38] Thus, according to the Constitution of Greece (1927), Art. 2: "All authority issues from the people, exists for their welfare and is realized in the order prescribed by the Constitution." Even in the fascist Constitution of Portugal (Art. 71) is the following: "Sovereignty resides in the nation." In the Constitution of Belgium (Art. 25): "All powers emanate from the nation and are realized in the order established by the Constitution." In the fundamental law of the republic of Turkey (1924, Art. 3): "The supreme authority, with no limitations or conditions whatsoever, belongs to the people." The Constitution of Latvia (1922, Art. 2) provides that "the sovereign authority in Latvia belongs to the Latvian people." The Constitution of Lithuania (1928, Art. 1): "The supreme state authority belongs to the people." In the Constitution of Finland (1919, Sec. 2): "Supreme authority in Finland belongs to the people." In the fundamental law of Estonia (1933, Sec. 1): "Estonia is an independent republic whose state authority is in the hands of the people," and so forth. It must be noted that when bourgeois constitutions become fascist,

acy of the authority of the people—is false in its very foundation. It gives out as the real possession of authority the right of a limited circle of electors to vote for deputies to the bourgeois parliament (which is not an actual and deciding organ of state government and wherein, moreover, the bourgeoisie —to the extent that it remains the dominant class in society—guarantees itself a majority by artificial means). This concept is built on a negation of the incontestable truth and fact that authority—the fullness of authority, moreover, the supremacy of authority in bourgeois society—belongs to the capitalists in alliance with the landowners, and not to the people.

In contrast with the false, hypocritical and antiscientific declarations of bourgeois states as to "authority of the people," the Soviet state made real —and Soviet public law has confirmed—that authority is actually and totally in the hands of the toilers—genuine national sovereignty, on the basis of the Lenin-Stalin doctrine as to the proletarian state.

Having seized authority and built it on absolutely new foundations, the worker class in the very first days of the existence of this authority declared, through Stalin in his report at the Third All-Russian Congress of Soviets (January 28, 1918): *"To us, who represent the lowly workers, it is necessary that the people not only vote but rule as well. Those who rule—not those who choose and elect—are the ones in authority."* [39]

From the very first days of its existence, the central task of Soviet authority was that of the broadest possible attraction of toiling masses to govern all the affairs of state; upon this the chief attention of the Bolshevik Party, headed by Lenin and Stalin, was focused. They always put this problem forward into first place. In his famous address, "To the Population," Lenin, President of the Council of People's Commissars,[40] said:

Comrade-toilers! Remember that *you yourselves* now govern the state. No one will be able to help you if you yourselves shall not unite and take *all matters* of the state into *your* own hands. *Your* Soviets are henceforward organs of state

---

the proclamation of "national sovereignty" is eliminated. Thus in the Constitution of Poland (1921, Art. 2): "The supreme authority in the Polish Republic belongs to the people." State organs are here called "popular organs." In the fascist constitution of 1935, this democratic phraseology is openly cast away. Article 2 says: "(1) At the head of the state stands the president of the republic. (2) Upon him rests responsibility before God and history for the fate of the state." In the Constitution of the German Empire (1919)— the so-called Weimar Constitution—Article 1 says: "The German Empire is a republic. State authority issues from the people." Fascists, as everyone knows, abrogated the Weimar Constitution. If the principle preached in this field by fascist political scientists were formulated, it would have to be set out as follows: "The Third Reich is an authoritarian state (that is to say, a terrorist-military-police state). State authority starts from the Fuehrer and the head of the government."

[39] Stalin, *Articles and Speeches Concerning the Ukraine* (Party Publishing House, 1936), p. 38.

[40] Lenin (Russian ed.), Vol. XXII, p. 55.

authority—organs with complete authority and decision. Rally around your Soviets. Make them strong. Take hold of affairs yourselves from below, with no tarrying for any one. . . .

Bourgeois ideologists often try to embellish and shade off the fictitious character of national sovereignty under capitalism by an ideological fiction —the theory of "the separation of powers." [41] The most general variant of this theory is that "national sovereignty" is *immediately* embodied in a parliamentary legislative organ whose power must be *separated* from the executive and judicial "powers." Representative elective organs, accordingly, cannot, and must not, possess any sort of executive power, or all power—"powers"—must be "separated."

Under capitalism parliaments are essentially one of the state levers for the repression of the masses by the ruling bourgeois classes. The latter conduct their own policy of hostility to the masses through parliament also, forming and defending that policy by legislative Acts issued by parliament. Herein the bourgeoisie succeeds by reason of its economic and political domination in the land (owing to its bribery of petty-bourgeois parliaments), and by its greater political organizations as compared with the worker class and the toiling peasantry, thanks to its bold use and cultivation—with the aid of the church, a venal press, the movies, and so on—of religious and political prejudices in the masses. As a result of all this, and however great the successes of the parliamentary struggle of the revolutionary proletariat, parliament remains—and cannot but remain—under capitalism a bourgeois state institution, an institution to deceive, oppress, and crush the masses.

From the moment when a change in the correlation of the real forces of the struggling classes in the land and in parliament leaves the bourgeoisie no longer in a position to develop its policy further through parliament, when parliament ceases to be a support, and becomes an obstacle, to bourgeois domination, the bourgeoisie makes the state system fascist, liquidates parliamentarism and puts in its place the open dictatorship of military police.

Realization of popular sovereignty requires the annihilation of the bourgeois state and of bourgeois parliamentarism—an instrument to oppress and crush the masses. The proletariat—being in authority—creates its own new system of *representative* state organs to replace bourgeois parliamentarism. The Soviets are truly democratic representative organs—organizations of socialist parliamentarism—at once representative organs (for they, and they only, actually represent the people) and working organs as well—organs with whose help the people immediately executes the leading state work.

---

[41] This theory is associated with the name of Montesquieu (1689-1755), who saw in the division of state powers into legislative, judicial, and executive, a guarantee of reasoning and just state government and of citizens' personal rights and freedoms.

In the form of the Soviets, the worker class makes true popular sovereignty real, having called the people to govern the state and made them alone the bearers of all state authority.

All authority belongs to the Soviets—such is the formula of our socialist state since the very first day of its existence. The historic address of the Second All-Russian Congress of Soviets (October 25/November 7, 1917) proclaimed: "The congress takes authority into its own hands . . . It directs: all authority in the country passes to the Soviets of worker, soldier, and peasant deputies, who must also guarantee genuine revolutionary order." [42]

To actualize this decision, the Council of National Commissars published a decree three days later, *The Completeness of the Authority of the Soviets,* which provided: "All authority belongs henceforth to the Soviets. Commissars of the former Provisional Government are dismissed. Presidents of the Soviets confer immediately wtih the Revolutionary Government." [43] As early as the first two or three months of its existence, the youthful revolutionary worker-peasant authority passed in triumphal march through the cities and villages of the country. This most important fact was reflected and confirmed in the first instance in the Declaration of Rights and then in the first Constitution of the RSFSR with its proclamation that Russia is declared a Republic of the Soviets of Worker, Soldier, and Peasant deputies. "All authority—central and local—belongs to these Soviets" (*Izvestiya,* January 4/17, 1918). This formula entered into the constitutions of all the Soviet Republics. Furthermore, this principle is underlined still more categorically in the declaration: "Authority must belong entirely and exclusively to the toiling masses and their authorized representative—the Soviets of Worker, Soldier, and Peasant deputies."

The Soviet state created a democratic apparatus of authority. Local Soviets are links of one unbroken chain of organs of state authority. All the distance of the heavens from the earth separates them from the municipal and communal organs of self-government in bourgeois countries, which are in fact completely subordinated to administrative organs of state authority (which do not appear as such). Local Soviets, as we shall hereinafter show, form the most important part—the mighty foundation—of all the Soviet state organization.

The activity of the Soviets extends to everything which enters into the building of the country's economic and cultural structure. During the civil war they carried out extraordinarily complex and difficult tasks in defense of the country, having created a mighty, invincible rear, and

[42] Cf. *Pravda* of that date.
[43] Cy. 1917, No. 1, Art. 6.

strengthening the unbroken foundation of the socialist state. With the transition to peaceful construction, they expanded the work of reestablishing industry and transportation—of economic and cultural aid to the country. During the socialist industrialization and the collectivization of agriculture, the economic-cultural activity of the Soviets attained an extraordinary pitch. In this tense, creative state work they grew powerfully and became strong as organs of the authority of the toilers.

Practical participation in the work of the Soviets—not only by workers but by peasants and intellectuals also—grew in enormous measure. The kolkhoz peasantry and the new Soviet intelligentsia represent the unwavering support of the Soviets. Under the guidance of the worker class, they are drawn in ever greater degree—through the Soviets—into everyday government of all phases of the building of the state. The special characteristic of the Soviets as an *all-encompassing* mass organization, embracing all toilers, is manifested with extraordinary force in the conditions of socialist society. The definition of Soviets as "Soviets of Deputies of Toilers," in place of the former definition, "Soviets of Worker, Peasant, and Red Army deputies," reflects the fact that the attraction of *all* toiling masses to govern the state through the Soviets has been raised to a new and loftier level with the triumph of socialism.

The successful development of the dictatorship of the worker class— and only this—could and did make true popular sovereignty an historic reality, and the Soviets are thus the sole state form wherein that sovereignty can be realized.

c) *Soviet authority as authority which embodies the will of the people*

Democracy signifies literally "the authority of the people." Only that state authority which is guided in its activity by the will of the people, and embodies that will in practice, is truly democratic. Hence only the Soviet authority can be considered truly democratic. Bourgeois ideology— bourgeois theories of public law in particular—operate with the idea of a "general will" or "will of the majority" supposedly defining the essence and everyday policy of the bourgeois state. The ostensibly "universal" or "popular" will materializes as in reality the will of an insignificant, social minority —the dominant exploiter classes. By the methods of bourgeois democracy— parliamentarism, elective latitude and so on—the capitalists try to create a semblance of the "will of the majority," to which state authority is supposedly subordinate. Even fascist oppressors of the people try, by dramatizing all sorts of "plebiscites" and "national elections," to represent the matter as if their barbarous actions are coincident with "the will of the people."

Clearly, in conditions of bourgeois society, we are concerned with the falsification of this will, the will of the majority of society. In conditions where antagonistic classes exist, a single "popular will" is, in general, impossible. Bourgeois authority expresses and realizes the will of the dominant capitalist classes, acting in fact against the will of the majority and fastening the class will of the ruling minority upon this oppressed majority of the people. In conditions of capitalism the so-called "general will," which Rousseau advanced as the basic motive power of the democratic state, remains—and cannot but remain—a fiction, a false ideological pendant to the bourgeois state apparatus of class oppression.[44]

The program of our Party [45] states:

The bourgeois republic—even the most democratic, consecrated by watchwords of the will of all the people, or of the nation in general, or of non-class will—inevitably remained in fact a dictatorship of the bourgeoisie, a machine for a handful of capitalists to exploit and crush the vast majority of the toilers. This is because of the existence of private property in land and other means of production.

Those who guide bourgeois governments speak in the name of the majority of the people, frequently on the "basis" that they succeed in obtaining the approval of a majority in parliament. But from this it follows merely that most of the deputies in parliament stand in bourgeois positions—not reflecting the actual will of the majority of the people.

It is Lenin's doctrine—and the experience of history completely confirms it—that

if political authority in a state is in the hands of a class whose interests coincide with those of the majority, the government of the state can then actually accord with the will of the majority. But if political authority is found in the hands of the class whose interests diverge from those of the majority, every sort of administration according to the majority then inevitably turns into deception or repression of that majority.[46]

The question of the will of the majority must be put concretely: In what setting and with what correlation of class forces does "the manifestation of will" take place? For the will of the majority to be capable of becoming a law for authority, it is necessary "to destroy the bourgeois setting, its real conditions of motivating the will." [47] Contemplated from this point of

[44] Jean Jacques Rousseau (1712–1778) was a famous French writer and thinker, an ideologist of the radical petty bourgeoisie. His famous *Du Contrat Social*, wherein his views as to public law are developed, exerted an enormous influence on the development of the bourgeois liberal-democratic theory of the state as the incarnation of the "general will."

[45] 1936 ed., p. 13.

[46] Lenin (Russian ed.), Vol. XXI, p. 52.

[47] *Ibid.*, Vol. XXV, p. 9.

view, the most important task of the class struggle of the proletariat is: (1) to unite its own ranks by a single class will, and (2) to convince the nonproletarian masses of toilers that the proletarian will embraces the rooted interests of all toilers—the majority of the people—and that, being realized in state order, the will of the proletariat will guarantee the realization of those interests. The will of the worker class—and so the will of the majority of the people—can be turned into a law of the state only through the victory of the proletarian revolution.

Preparing the socialist revolution, Lenin wrote:

In order that the majority of the people may become a true majority in governing the state—actually ministering to the interests of the majority, actually guarding the rights of the majority, and so on—for this a definite class condition is necessary, viz., the incorporation, at least at a decisive moment and place, of a majority of the petty bourgeoisie in the revolutionary proletariat." [48]

Under the guidance of Lenin and Stalin, the Bolsheviks, by their work among the masses on the way to the October Revolution, aimed at and attained the incorporation of a majority of the toiling peasantry into the revolutionary proletariat. Having overcome the resistance of Mensheviks, SR's, Trotskyists, Bukharinists, and other traitors who demonstrated that the majority of the people were supposedly against all the fullness of authority passing to the Soviets—against the dictatorship of the proletariat— the Bolsheviks won over most of the toilers and brought them to the side of the socialist revolution. It is the will of this majority to which the Soviets gave expression.

In complete accord with the true state of affairs, the Second All-Russian Congress of Soviets, in the first constitutional act of Soviet authority—the Address to Workers, Soldiers, and Peasants—concerning the October Revolution and its immediate problems proclaimed: "Resting upon the will of the vast majority of workers, soldiers, and peasants—upon the triumphant uprising of the workers and the garrison, accomplished in Petrograd—the Congress takes authority into its hands." [49] Resting upon the will of the majority of the toilers, Soviet authority promoted the most important measures in their interests: it declared peace, transferred lands to the peasants, nationalized the banks and enterprises, and approached the task of socialist building. Resting upon the will of the majority, Soviet authority in turn strengthened and tempered that will—the will to struggle against the old world, to build a new society.

In the Declaration of the Provisional Worker-Peasant Soviet Government of the Ukraine (1919) is the following: "In the ranks of the Red

[48] *Ibid.*, Vol. XXI, p. 53.
[49] *Ibid.*, Vol. XXII, p. 11.

Army, behind the loom in the factory, on the railroad, in the mines, everywhere, the revolutionary will of the proletariat and peasantry to have done with the old world and to erect a new socialist order, must be felt." In the Declaration of the First White Russian Congress of Soviets (February, 1919) the Socialist Soviet Republic is proclaimed "to manifest to the whole world the inflexible will of worker-peasant White Russia, directed at final annihilation of the dominance of capital and for the establishment of the socialist order."

According to the will of the majority of the people, the Soviet authority, giving effect to this will, realized industrialization and collectivization, liquidated the kulaks as a class, created a mighty defense of the country, developed—and still develops—a policy of peace, created favorable conditions for science, culture, and art to flourish, and so forth. No, there never was, and there can never be, a single measure of the Soviet authority going counter to the interests and will of the majority. This is defined by the fundamental fact that between worker class and peasantry there never was, and there could not be, antagonism of any sort—their relations are based on community of fundamental interests—and that socialist reorganization of society is in the interests of workers and peasants.

The worker class guided the peasantry behind it, helped the peasantry correctly to understand its actual interests as peasants and the ways of realizing them—despite agitation of the kulaks and vacillations of the wavering and unstable elements in the peasantry. By clarification and persuasion, the worker class united the peasantry to itself in fundamental, decisive questions. It did not coercively fasten its own will upon the peasantry, but helped the peasantry, practically and by deeds, to form and temper its own will in the struggle for the common concerns of workers and peasants. In addition, it rested upon the strata of the peasantry which were progressive in political respect—on the poor peasants and the progressive part of the middle-class peasants. As a result, the will of the worker class and of the peasantry basically coincided, blending into a general will of the overwhelming majority of toilers, guided by the worker class. Of course, this was a complex and dialectic process. It cost no little exertion to both the worker class and to the peasantry. But under the guidance of the Party it went forward ever more and more successfully in close connection with the successes of socialist building.

The victory of socialism—the liquidation of the kulaks as a class—signalizes a new phase in this regard also. If, in conditions of the existence of exploiter classes, the will of the worker class and peasantry, and likewise of the toiling Soviet intellectuals, was the will of the *majority of the people*— so in present conditions this is *the will of the entire Soviet people*. Speaking

of will in the social or political sense, we have in view neither the mechanical "sum total of wills" of separate persons, nor the mythical "national will"
(existing only in the imagination, or rather as portrayed by every sort of
bourgeois liberal or reactionary sociologist and political scientist). Following the Marx-Lenin doctrine, we have in mind the will of social classes.
To the extent that exploiters in Soviet society are liquidated as a class, we
have a right to speak of *a single will* of the Soviet people, of the popular
will in the authentic socialist sense of this word, and of Soviet authority as
its true exponent.

One further special characteristic of Soviet authority must be pointed
out. In multinational bourgeois states it is impossible to speak of the *"general will"* as the basis of authority, for the further reason that in conditions
where national rights are not equal, and where national contradictions and
disparity are found, this is the will of the great-power nation oppressing
other nations and fastening its will—the will of the dominant nation, or
rather of its ruling classes—upon them. In contrast to this, in the Soviet
socialist state the single will of the people is the single will of all the
peoples of the USSR united by common purposes and common interests.
Soviet authority in the USSR—as the state form of the multinational socialist state—expresses and realizes the will of the entire multinational single
Soviet people.

d) The Soviets as the truly democratic mechanism of state authority

The mechanism of the socialist state, personified by the Soviets, was
created in the course of the proletarian revolution of toilers of our country.

At a session of the Petrograd Soviet of Worker and Soldier Deputies
(October 25/November 7, 1917), on the first day of the victory of the
revolution, Lenin said:

What is the significance of this worker-peasant revolution? First of all, the
significance of this overturn is that there will be among us a Soviet government—
our own organ of authority—without participation of any sort whatever by the
bourgeoisie. The oppressed masses will themselves create the authority. The old
state mechanism will be utterly smashed and a new mechanism of government—
personified by Soviet organizations—will be created.[50]

The plan of creating a state mechanism of proletarian authority in the
shape of Soviets, developed upon a manifold foundation by Lenin and
Stalin in the course of preparation of the socialist revolution, was brilliantly vindicated and practically realized during the revolution, in the

[50] *Ibid.*, Vol. XXII, p. 4.

first period of the existence of the socialist state. Resting upon the Soviets, which the revolution turned into organs of unified and complete power of the toilers, the worker class, supported by the peasantry, smashed the old state mechanism and created a completely new apparatus, contrasted in essence and in organizational forms to the bourgeois (and all other exploiter) types of state apparatus.

This is the first time in history that a mechanism has been created without the participation—and in spite—of the exploiters, and for the purpose of crushing the exploiters. And for the first time in history a mechanism has been created to free the toilers (to whom it is closely akin), not to oppress them, as if it were their enemy; to attract the masses in every way to the management of state matters, not to remove them from that management; most closely bound to the people and merging with them, not fenced off from them as by a closed circle. It is a mechanism without officialdom or privileged bureaucracy, and without police and army to be guided by an aristocratic officer caste to wreak bloody vengeance upon the people.

The basic and distinctive peculiarity of the Soviet state mechanism is first of all its human structure: it grew—and continuously grows—out of the midst of the toilers. Through the Soviets, broad masses of the toiling population are elevated to guide the state, whereas prior to the revolution in our country they were—as they are still in capitalist countries—only an object (but in no measure whatever a subject) of state government. They did not govern. They were governed—that is, oppressed—by state authority. "The essence of Soviet authority is that the constant and sole basis of all state authority—of the whole state mechanism—is the mass organization of precisely those classes which were oppressed by capitalism." [51]

In this sense Soviet authority is truly popular authority. Speaking as People's Commissar for Nationalities, Stalin wrote (in April, 1918): "Authority in the center has already become really popular authority growing out of the very midst of the toiling masses. Herein is the strength and the might of Soviet authority." The development of Soviet authority ever proceeded, and still proceeds, specifically toward the broadening and strengthening of its *popular character*—its true democratic character—and toward the attraction of ever broader strata of the people into the building up of the state in its most diverse branches and forms.

The development of the bourgeois state—particularly in the epoch of the universal crisis of the capitalist system—proceeded, and still proceeds, in exactly the opposite direction. The state apparatus of capitalism is *antipopular, antidemocratic*, filled with a bureaucratic caste, a professional bureaucracy especially schooled to execute specialized functions of crushing the

[51] *Ibid.*, Vol. XXIV, p. 13.

people, to remove the people from control—in whatever form—of the actions of the organs of authority. The bourgeoisie tries to strengthen its state mechanism by intensifying its bureaucratization and militarism. In a particularly sharp and crude police form it produces fascism.[52]

True, for purposes of social and national demagogy, the German fascists chatter about the *Völkische Staat*, which their bloody, imperialist clique dictatorship over the people is supposed to be. But their demagogy so pitifully contradicts the facts, politics, and practice of fascism that many "theoreticians" of fascism consider it possible to speak openly of guidance of the state by a "chosen" minority. For example, the reactionary political scientist Forsthoff, having become a fascist, writes:

A particular stratum, living by its own special laws and subject to a special historical responsibility, must stand out from the mass of the people. The qualitative peculiarity of this stratum of the chosen makes it a true social order, fostered for its own preservation in indescribably savage struggle for the state.[53]

Another fascist "political scientist," a specialist in matters of the "race theory of law," wrote that the tiny apex of the fascist party, chosen according to the criterion of race, must guide the state. This he calls *Fuehrertum* and describes it as the "elite" of the minority, called to domination by force of its spiritual and practical (*leistungmässigen*) excellence.[54] Insofar as he directly speaks here of the fascist clique, it is scarcely necessary to comment on his words. What "spiritual excellence" of fascist barbarians can there be to talk about?

"Intensifying" the bourgeois state mechanism by such means is very relative indeed, and evokes in the toiling masses still greater enmity and hatred for that state.

The second most important special characteristic of the Soviets is that through them the toilers in fact govern the state. The party struggled, and still struggles, against attempts of every sort to pervert this Soviet principle.

There is a petty bourgeois tendency to pervert members of the Soviets into parliamentarians or into bureaucrats. We must struggle against this. We must attract *all* members of the Soviets to take a practical part in government.[55]

Further development of Soviet state organization must consist (1) in each member of the Soviet being obligated to work constantly in governing the state, side by side with participation in assemblies of the Soviet; and (2) in the entire

[52] A particular illustration of this may be found in the practice of German fascist legislation on the matter of the so-called "professional bureaucracy" (cf. e.g., the law of 1933).
[53] *Der totale Staat*, p. 33.
[54] Nicolay, *Rasse und Recht*, p. 69.
[55] Lenin (Russian ed.), Vol. XXII, p. 465.

population without exception being attracted gradually to participate in Soviet organization (upon condition of subordination to organizations of the toilers) and likewise to serve in the state government.[56]

Soviet authority made completely real what was already projected by the Paris Commune as to abolishing the negative sides of bourgeois parliamentarism with its representative institutions remote alike from the masses and from the work of the state.[57]

Factual participation by the masses in state government sharply increased during the period of socialist industrialization and collectivization of agriculture. In the first instance and chiefly because the party and the government knew how to organize, and systematically to raise, the state activity of the broad masses, our state could carry through the gigantic work accomplished by it at this period. Only with the help of such state mechanism as that of the Soviets, and with active and immediate participation by the masses in state government, was it possible to reorganize the country in all respects in such a short time as was required in the USSR. Here we approach still another (the third) distinguishing feature of Soviet state mechanism from the viewpoint of attracting the masses to state government: such attraction proceeds through our mass social organizations and societies of the toilers as well as through the Soviets.[58]

Soviet legislation guarantees all the conditions essential to the successful development of our social organizations and societies of the toilers, and to fulfillment by them of the tasks of drawing the masses into state government. Compare particularly Articles 125, 126, and 141 of the Stalin Constitution.

The fourth special characteristic of the Soviet state mechanism—as being of the most democratic and highest type—undeviatingly puts into practice specific Soviet principles which embody socialist democracy in the building and functioning of state authority. Such is the principle of *democratic centralism,* as contrasted with bourgeois bureaucratic centralism. Such are the principles of the election and recall of elected persons, the social control over the activity of Soviet organizations, and broad criticism and self-criticism— that most important and specific principle of Soviet state building: "the watchword of self-criticism is the basis of our party action, the means of

[56] *Ibid.,* Vol. XXII, p. 372.

[57] In the directive of the Seventh All-Russian Congress of Soviets adopted on the matter Concerning Soviet Construction (Dec. 9, 1919), it is emphasized: "The Soviets must work not only as an apparatus of agitation and information but also as a businesslike mechanism. Each member of the Soviet is with the least possible delay drawn to the fulfillment of definite state work" (Cy. 1919, No. 64, Art. 578).

[58] For a notable characterization and formulation of this method of drawing the masses into state government see Stalin, *Questions of Leninism* (9th Russian ed.), pp. 147–150.

strengthening the proletarian dictatorship, the soul of the Bolshevik method of fostering cadres." [59]

4. *The Soviets and proletarian internationalism*

Internationalism is the most important distinguishing feature of the Soviets as a new and higher form of state authority. Bourgeois states, even the most democratic, develop open or concealed nationalism, preserve and strengthen—as to nationalities—inequality of rights and oppression in internal and external politics as well as in building and organizing the activity of the state mechanism. In contrast to them, the Soviets—expressing the unity of interests of the toilers of all nationalities—firmly develop the principles of proletarian internationalism. The concrete forms wherein this internationalism is practically embodied by the Soviet are:

a) The state unification of peoples upon voluntary principles of equal rights in a socialist union state—the USSR. Union and autonomous Soviet republics, as well as autonomous regions, are the definitive state forms wherein proletarian internationalism is developed with all logic and clarity.

b) The Soviets guarantee the actual and complete equality of the rights of peoples and nationalities in all fields of the economic, cultural, and political life of the country, pursuant to Article 123 of the USSR Constitution.

c) Proletarian internationalism is embodied in the everyday activity and in the building of the organs of state authority and government, from the Supreme Soviet of the USSR to the village or hamlet Soviet.

d) It is embodied in the external policy of the Soviet state, directed at defending the interests of the toilers of all the peoples and nationalities of the USSR, and at bringing them closer to the peoples of the whole world in united struggle against imperialist aggressors.

e) It is embodied in the public law institute of the right of asylum (Article 129 of the USSR Constitution) afforded to foreigners persecuted for their participation in the struggle for national liberation—an institute made real only in the Soviet state.

Such are the basic features of the socialist democracy of the Soviets—of the political basis of the USSR.

SEC. 5: THE ECONOMIC BASIS OF THE USSR

A definite means of producing and distributing products—that is to say, a definite system of economy, and a form of property in the instruments and means of production corresponding thereto—forms the eco-

[59] Stalin, *Questions of Leninism* (10th Russian ed.), p. 228.

nomic basis of any social order. At the basis of slave-owning society was ancient property based on exploitation of slave labor and trade in slaves.

Under the slave-owning system the basis of production relationships is the property of the slaveowner in the means of production and likewise in the production worker—the slave, whom his own can sell or buy or kill like a beast. Here the slaveowner is, first and basically, a full-value owner. Rich and poor, exploiters and exploited, persons with full rights and persons with no rights, and a savage class struggle between them—such is the picture of the slave-owning system.[1]

The basis of feudal society was feudal property, whose chief characteristic was the feudal serf-owner's property in the land and the exploitation of the labor of the peasant serfs.

Under the feudal regime, the basis of production relationships is the ownership by the feudal lord of the means of production and his qualified property in the production worker—the serf, whom he can no longer kill but whom he can buy and sell. Side by side with feudal property exists the individual property of the peasant and craftsman in instruments of production and in his private economy based on personal toil. Such production relationships fundamentally answer to the condition of the production forces in this period.

Further improvement in the smelting and working of iron; the spread of the iron plow and the weaving loom; further development of agriculture, gardening, viniculture, and butter-making; the appearance of manufacturing enterprises side by side with master craftsmen—such are the features characterizing the condition of production forces. New production forces require workmen with some initiative in production and disposition and interest to work. Hence the feudal lord abandons the slave as a workman not interested in labor and completely without initiative, and prefers to have dealing with a serf who has his own economy, his own instruments of production and a certain interest in the toil necessary to cultivate the land and pay the feudal lord in kind out of his harvest. Private property here attains its furthest development. Exploitation is almost as fierce as under slavery—it is only somewhat mitigated. The basic feature of the feudal order is the class struggle between exploiters and exploited.

The economic foundation of bourgeois society is the capitalist system of economy and capitalist property—with exploitation of the hired labor of proletarians and semiproletarians. Under the capitalist order, production relationships are based on capitalist property in the means of production with no property at all in the production workers—hired slaves whom (because they are free from personal dependence) the capitalist can neither beat nor sell, but who are without means of production and must therefore (to avoid death by hunger) sell their working force to the capitalist and bear upon their necks the yoke of exploitation.[2]

In all these societies, property belonged—as it still belongs—to the ex-

---

[1] *History of the All-Union Communist Party (of Bolsheviks): A Short Course* (1938), pp. 119–120.
[2] *Ibid.,* p. 120.

ploiters. It was, as it still is, the basis for the social and political (and likewise ideological) dominance of the exploiters over the exploited. Changing
the forms of property in exploiter society signified merely changing the
means of exploiting labor—that exploitation was taking a new historical
(feudal or capitalist) form.[3] The transition from the dominance of feudal
property to that of capitalist property signified only a transition from
the dominance of one form to that of another form of *private* property. The
form of private property as the economic basis of exploiter society changed,
but its dominance and exploitation were preserved and strengthened.

In contrast to this, the confirmation of the dominance of the socialist
system of economy and socialist property signifies the creation of an economic basis of society wherein private property is abrogated, instruments
and means of production become the property of the entire nation, and
man's exploitation of man—and the possibilities thereof—are completely and
forever abolished.

1. *The confirmation of the socialist system of economy and socialist property in the USSR*

The building of the economic basis of socialist society in the USSR
was the integration of a prolonged and intense struggle of the worker class
and of all the toilers who had taken authority into their hands. The confirmation of the dominance of socialist property under the dictatorship of
the proletariat was radically different from the manner of confirmation of
the dominance of capitalist property as the basis of bourgeois society. If
capitalist property was already created in the very core of feudal society and
the bourgeois revolution removed the obstacles to its development, socialist
property only begins to exist and to develop after the victory of the proletarian revolution and the creation of the proletarian state. If the dominance
of the capitalist property begins already to form gradually in conditions of
feudal society and the bourgeois state forms and confirms that dominance,
socialist property becomes dominant in the national economy because the
proletarian state logically develops an all-embracing plan of radical reorganization of economy.

Furthermore, it has to overcome the active and sharp resistance of the
forces of counterrevolution and restoration, as well as economic traditions
and habits formed by thousands of years passed in the conditions of exploiter
society. The Soviet state elevated the national economy to ever new heights,
extirpating, liquidating, and abrogating capitalist forms of economy, stub-

[3] For the historical development of forms of property, cf. Marx and Engels (Russian ed.)
Vol. IV, pp. 12–25.

bornly implanting and uninterruptedly confirming socialist forms of economy—state and cooperative—kolkhoz enterprises.

Application of all the actively effective, creative, and reformative force of the proletarian state was essential to the end that, every sort of obstacle and difficulty having been overcome, socialist property should attain a dominant position, the remnants of capitalist economy be completely liquidated, and man's exploitation of man be annihilated. In the very first days of its existence, Soviet authority proclaimed the principle: The wealth of the country must become social property. Addressing the people as President of the Council of People's Commissars (November 5/18, 1917) Lenin said: "Guard and preserve as the apple of your eye the earth, the grain, the factories, the instruments, the products, transportation—all this will henceforth be *completely* yours—social property." [4]

As a result of the imperialist war, the economy of the country had by the time of the revolution been undermined. Bureaucrats of the old ministries—headed by SR's and Mensheviks—tried by organized sabotage to thwart the first successes of Soviet authority. The problems of preventing economic catastrophe and rehabilitating national economy made particularly pointed the question of turning capitalist and landowner property into state property.

To undermine the economic force of the bourgeoisie and to organize Soviet national economy, first of all—to organize the new Soviet industry—banks, railroads, foreign trade, the merchant fleet, and all big industry in all its branches were nationalized: coal mining, metallurgy, oil, chemistry, machine tools, textiles, sugar refining, and so on. To the end of freeing our country from financial dependence and exploitation by foreign capitalists, foreign Russian loans concluded by the tsar and the Provisional Government were abrogated. The peoples of our country did not wish to pay for debts incurred in prolonging the predatory war and putting our country into servile dependence upon foreign capital. [5]

From the very beginning, Soviet authority adopted the principle of forcible alienation and confiscation of capitalist and landowner property without compensation. As carried out, this necessitated taking into account all conditions of a political as well as an organizational and administrative character, particularly as regards the matter of order and preliminary steps for promoting nationalization in separate branches of national economy. In the first instance, landowner property in land was completely abrogated (the Decree Concerning Land, October 26/November 8, 1917). [6]

[4] Lenin (Russian ed.), Vol. XXII, p. 55.
[5] *History of the All-Union Communist Party (of Bolsheviks)*, p. 205.
[6] Cy. 1917, No. 1, Art. 3.

With reference to industry, transport, and financial enterprises, worker control over production was advanced as a transition form. This was essentially state control—control in behalf of a class which had established its own dictatorship. Realized in the interests of the toilers—resting on revolutionary state activity of the worker class and reinforced by the coercive power of the proletarian state—Soviet worker control of production became a real and actual control over the process of production by the producers themselves, although the proprietors still owned the means of production. It was introduced by the state as a means of preparing for nationalization. Its problem was that the worker class, having begun factually to govern economy, and accumulating experience of government, should practically prepare the transition to complete "statification"—the nationalization of enterprises—and to the immediate management thereof on a state-wide scale. The sabotage of capitalists accelerated the transition to nationalization. From worker control the state passed to nationalization, depending upon the special necessity therefor in a given branch of economy. First the nationalization of banks was realized.[7]

Six weeks later (January 26, 1918) the directive of the Council of People's Commissars of the RSFSR: Concerning the Nationalization of the Merchant Fleet,[8] was published. Industrial enterprises were nationalized later. However, in cases where the proprietors or their managers refused to yield to worker control, the enterprises were transferred into state property.[9]

The Declaration of Rights ratified the abrogation of private property in land and turning the land into the property of the entire people. It also confirmed the law as to worker control as the first step to the complete passing of factories, works, mines, railroads, and other means of production and transportation into the property of the Soviet Worker-Peasant Republic, to the end of guaranteeing the authority of the toilers over the exploiters.[10]

Realization of worker control, organization of the Supreme Soviet of National Economy and its local departments, and gradual assumption of possession of the state mechanism and economic guidance were in preparation for the transition to nationalization. In the realization thereof, the Council of People's Commissars of the RSFSR (June 28, 1918) published

[7] Cf. the directive of the All-Russian Central Executive Committee (December 14, 1917): Concerning the Nationalization of Banks (Cy. 1917, No. 10, Art. 250).

[8] Cy. 1918, No. 19, Art. 290.

[9] Thus as to the stock company of the Kyshtym mountain district, the directive of the Council of People's Commissars stated: "In view of the refusal of the works management of the company to submit to the decree of the Council of National Commissars as to introducing worker control over production, the Council has directed the confiscation of all the property of the company of whatever nature, and the declaration thereof as property of the Russian Republic" (Cy. 1917, No. 13, Art. 192).

[10] Cy. 1918, No. 15, Art. 215.

a directive as to the nationalization of the biggest enterprises of industry and transportation.[11]

By the end of the civil war (which continued for three years in the central part of the RSFSR and still longer in its borderlands and in other Soviet Republics), the economy of the country was in still more deplorable condition than at the beginning. From the end of 1920, Soviet authority set about the reestablishment of national economy. One of the acts in this connection was the final *culmination* of the nationalization of enterprises.[12] By nationalizing land and enterprises of finance, transportation and industry—turning them into state property—the economic basis of the Soviet state was created. It then remained for the production forces of the country— freed from landowner-capitalist fetters and resting upon and aided by that economic basis—to move forward in the direction of socialist reorganization. Guided by the Lenin-Stalin Party, Soviet authority came forth to organize the country's economic advance.[13]

Brilliantly, and in a brief historic period, the Soviet state grappled with the problem of reestablishing national economy. Soviet law manifested therein its vast power as an active reformative influence upon economy as a mighty instrument of the proletarian dictatorship. In ever greater degree that active influence encompassed the processes of economic life, piercing them ever more and more deeply as the organization and regulation force of the socialist state increased, and the socialist sector—and its influence in national economy—grew.

Party and government directives on economic matters comprised the expanded programs of socialist building, indicating forms and methods of organizing the toiling masses, through state organs, to make these programs real. Soviet law stood strongly to the defense of the state's economic policy with its point directed, during the first period of the New Economic Policy, against the extremes of war communism and confirming socialist property against would-be wreckers and despoilers of that property. Soviet law was thus put to serve the socialist reorganization of economy and moved into the struggle with the enemies of socialism.

The decisive factor of successful struggle for the domination of socialist

[11] *Ibid.*, No. 47, Art. 559.

[12] A directive of the Supreme Council of National Economy (Nov. 29, 1920): Concerning the Nationalization of Enterprises provides: "(1) All industrial enterprises in the possession of private persons or companies whose workers number more than five with mechanical motive-power—or ten where there is not—are declared nationalized. (2) All property, things, and capital of such enterprises—wherever this property may be found or whereinsoever it may consist—are declared property of the RSFSR" (Cy. 1920, No. 93, Art. 512).

[13] Compare in this regard the directive of the Eighth All-Russian Congress of Soviets: Concerning the Order of Worker Red Banner (Cy. 1921, No. 1, Art. 7) and the address of that Congress to the toilers (App. 3).

property was that from the very beginning the worker-peasant state held in its hands the commanding heights in the national economy—heavy and medium industry, the state bank and transportation. Under the guidance of Lenin and Stalin the Soviet state at one stroke put itself on the road of fortifying these commanding heights in the struggle against the capitalist social-economic way of life. It strengthened them so as to create and to elevate ever higher and higher the economic union of city and country under the guidance of the city, of industry and of the proletariat.

This was clearly indicated in the Ninth All-Russian Congress of Soviets in the following words:

Now the struggle between communist economy and private economy is transferred to the economic field—to the market—where nationalized industry, concentrated in the hands of the worker-state, must—in application to circumstances of the market and the methods of competition therein—win for itself decisive dominance. The bolder and more systematic the planning in accordance wherewith the proletariat manages the vast instruments of production (concentrated in its hands as a result of the October Revolution), the stronger the union of proletariat and peasantry (resting on barter between city and village), and the more rapidly the progressive elements of city and country toilers learn to conduct the struggle (on the new field, with new methods, utilizing the new setting, and becoming leaders of new branches of work), the more decisive will be the victory.[14]

At the decisive stage of the struggle to confirm socialist property—in periods of industrialization and collectivization—the role of Soviet law and Soviet legislation grew vastly, embodying the undeviating will of the worker class and its aspiration to win a complete victory in the organization of socialism. It constituted a powerful instrument in the hands of the toilers of the USSR in their intense, unselfish and heroic struggle (guided by the worker class and the Communist Party) for the full victory of the socialist system of economy and for confirmation of the complete domination of socialist property in instruments and means of production.

This was a struggle against class enemies—against enemies of the people: Trotskyists, Bukharinists, bourgeois nationalists, remnants of Menshevik-SR's, and other anti-Soviet organizations and groups striving by any kind of wrecker action to thwart the liquidation of capitalist property and the affirmation of socialist property. The execution of Stalin's five-year plans brought this struggle to complete victory for the socialist way of life in the country's economy. The following figures [15] clearly illustrate this:

[14] Cy. 1922, No. 4, Art. 43.
[15] *Twenty Years of Soviet Authority* (1937), pp. 3, 9.

PRODUCTION FUNDS IN USSR ACCORDING TO THE FORMS OF PROPERTY (IN PERCENTAGES)

	1928			1936		
	Industry	Agriculture	Total National Economy	Industry	Agriculture	Total National Economy
1. Socialist property a) State property	(97.9) 96.6	(63.6) 62.6	(77.8) 76.5	(99.95) 97.35	(96.3) 76.0	(98.7) 90.0
b) Property of separate kolkhozes and cooperative associations	1.3	1.0	1.3	2.6	20.3	8.7
2. Personal property of the members of the kolkhozes (excluding the exploitation of others' labor), being the element subsidiary to socialist kolkhoz property		0.1			3.1	1.1
3. Petty private property of single peasant families and craftsmen, based on personal labor and being the basic source of existence	2.0	31.9	19.6	0.05	0.6	0.2
4. Capitalist private property based on exploitation of another's labor	0.1	4.4	2.6			
	100.	100.	100.	100.	100.	100.

PROPORTIONATE SHARE OF SOCIALIST ECONOMY
(IN PERCENTAGES)

	1928	1936
In the national income	44.0	99.1
In the gross production of all industry	82.4	99.8
In the gross production of agriculture (including the individual subsidiary economy of members of the kolkhozes)	3.3	97.7
In the retail turnover of trading enterprises	76.4	100.0
In the production funds of the entire national economy	77.8	98.7

Thus in 1936, 98.7 per cent of all instruments and means of production were social property of the Soviet people; capitalist property was completely liquidated; and petty-labor private property constituted only 0.2 per cent. This also signifies the abolition of private property and the passing of instruments and means of production into social property, the annihilation of man's exploitation of man and of the economic foundation of the possibility thereof.

In order for all instruments and means of production to become social property, it was necessary to effect a radical technical reconstruction of the entire national economy, industrial and agricultural, at the same time. This task was complicated by specific difficulties evoked by the country's technical-economic backwardness in the recent past, by hostile capitalist encirclement, and so on. In successfully overcoming these, the vast creative organizing might of the Soviet state and law was manifested with extraordinary force. In *The Principles of Communism,* Engels wrote:

Is it possible to bring about the abrogation of private property at one stroke? . . . No, it is just as impossible as to increase at one stroke the available means of production in such bounds as are essential for creating social production. Hence the revolution of the proletariat—which most probably will occur—will know only how gradually to reorganize existing society and to abrogate private property only later, when the requisite means of production will have been amassed.[16]

"The basic means of production were amassed" as a result of industrialization. This could be developed in the interests of the toilers—and in such brief historic limits of time—only with the aid of the Soviet state, on the basis of social property as the foundation of the socialist economy. For this reason the foes of socialism strove in every way to undermine that social property—injuring, despoiling, and annihilating it. This struggle of

[16] Marx and Engels (Russian ed.), Vol. V, p. 474.

the people's foes against social property attained particularly sharp and extreme forms during the liquidation of the kulaks as a class. Concerning the despoilers of socialist property Stalin wrote: "They feel—as if by a class instinct—that the basis of Soviet economy is social property, that it is precisely this basis that must be shaken in order to befoul the Soviet authority—and they actually try to shake social property through organizing mass thievery and plundering." [17]

The worker class dictatorship, that knew how to create and uninterruptedly to multiply social property, knew also how to manifest the necessary firmness and pitilessness to its enemies, defending that property from those who would despoil it.[18] The Stalin Constitution (Art. 131) confirmed and ratified this principle of Soviet authority as an unwavering principle of the defense of socialism's economic basis.

2. Two forms of socialist property in the USSR

According to the Constitution of the USSR (Art. 5): "Socialist property in the USSR has the form either of state property (property of the entire nation) or of cooperative-kolkhoz property (property of separate kolkhozes—of cooperative societies)." This definition expresses, first of all, the unity of the social nature of state property and cooperative-kolkhoz property alike as socialist property. At the same time the difference between them, as two forms of socialist property, is here developed.

Under the Soviet social order, property in the hands of the state is socialist property. It constitutes property of the entire people, which possesses and operates it in its interest—in the interest of the toilers—by means of the socialist state. It is radically different from state property in bourgeois countries where, both by its social-economic content (as an instrument to defend the interests of exploiters) and by the methods of its utilization, state property is a variety of capitalist property.

Property in instruments and means of production, in the hands of the proletarian state as socialist property, was the decisive economic basis for reorganizing the entire national economy on socialist principles.

Enemies of socialism—especially Trotsky-Bukharin wreckers like Sokolnikov and others—sought to assert that our state enterprises bear the character of state capitalism and not of socialism. They demanded that the methods of capitalist economy be implanted in state industrial enterprises and banks,

[17] Stalin, Questions of Leninism (10th Russian ed.), p. 508.
[18] Cf. Directive of the Central Executive Committee and the Council of People's Commissars of the USSR (Aug. 7, 1932) Concerning the Guarding of the Property of State Enterprises. Kolkhozes and Cooperatives and the Confirming of Social (Socialist) Property. (Cz. 1932, No. 62, Art. 360).

coming out against the state plan, state discipline, and Soviet cost accounting—with the purpose of frustrating the building up of socialism and liquidating the state guidance of the national economic life. Apologists for state
property from the ranks of bourgeois jurists asserted that the passing of
means of production into the hands of the state meant annihilation of every
kind of property in the USSR—that under the Soviet regime there would
be "no property of any kind at all."

State property in the USSR is the highest form of socialist property. It
bears a logically socialist character in the sense (1) of the social relationships
and types of the organization of labor formed on its basis, and (2) of a form
of distributing industrial products and fostering on the basis of that distribution a new labor psychology and discipline. All this defines the content
of Soviet law in that part of its tasks which is concerned with strengthening
and developing state property. The public character of state property means
that it belongs to all the Soviet people taken as a whole. The subject bearing
the right to this property is the Soviet state in its entirety. Separate state
(economic or administrative) organs or social organizations (as commissioned by the state) carry out, in conformity with the law, divers functions
in managing a given object of state property. Separate organs of state authority, administrative and economic agencies and enterprises, carry out
various functions in the management of state property. They possess corresponding jurisdiction and fulfill defined obligations entrusted to them. They
themselves are not the owners of objects of state property, however. The
owner of state property, its sole owner, in all these cases remains the entire
socialist nation personified by its state.

The decisive characteristic of state property in the USSR is the unity
of all the resources of this property as expressed in the management of the
property on a state-wide scale. This means, for example, that the highest
organ of state authority of the USSR has the right, in accordance with law,
to transfer any part of state property from one institution to another gratis,
for use and management. The constitutional regulations in this regard are
in Articles 4 (k, l, m, n, o, p) and 68 (a, b and e) of the Constitution of
the USSR, and in corresponding paragraphs of those of union and autonomous republics. Directives of the Central Executive Committee and the
Council of People's Commissars of the USSR (April 29, 1935): Concerning
the Transfer of State Buildings, Enterprises and Constructions,[19] and (of
February 15, 1936)[20] Concerning the Method of Transferring State Buildings, Enterprises and Structures, contain definitive indications of the order
of transfer of state properties from one institution to another—the right

[19] Cz. 1935, No. 28, Art. 221.
[20] Cz. 1936, No. 11, Art. 93.

to such transfer being realized by the Council of People's Commissars of the USSR.

The unity of production stocks forms the basis of a single state-wide stock for distribution (á wage fund, a social insurance fund, and others) in the shape of a state-wide plan, and also of special directives of higher organs of state authority and organs of government of the USSR.

Still another extremely important characteristic of the USSR state property is that its objects include those in which the right of property belongs exclusively to the state. Such are the earth and the natural deposits therein, the waters, the forests, and the railroads. They are the exclusive property of the state throughout the entire USSR and cannot be objects of property of cooperative-kolkhoz organizations (and still less of separate persons), but can merely be utilized by these organizations (and likewise by separate persons) in the method established by the law of the USSR. They do not circulate in commercial trade. According to Article 6 of the USSR Constitution, state property includes: the earth and the natural deposits therein, the waters, the forests, factories, works, mines, coal mines, transportation by rail, air, and water, banks, means of communication, large agricultural enterprises organized by the state (sovkhozes, machine and tractor stations and the like) and also municipal enterprises and the bulk of the dwelling houses in cities and industrial localities.

Defining the cooperative-kolkhoz property in the USSR as socialist, the Constitution of the USSR reflects and confirms the actual character and essence of this property. It is socialist property because: (a) it is the social property of the collective of toilers; (b) it is the basis upon which are liquidated the exploiter elements, man's exploitation of man and the very possibility thereof; (c) on it as a basis is realized the socialist principle: "From each according to his capacity, to each according to his toil," for all those working in cooperative-kolkhoz production; (d) on it as a basis is built largescale collective production (with the application of contemporary industrial technique) working according to a state-wide socialist plan and guaranteeing unlimited possibilities of elevating the material well-being and cultural level of the toilers working in this branch of production.

All these sides of Soviet production cooperation are integrated under the active influence of the proletarian state, under state property in land, and with the enormous material—technical and organizational—aid of state socialist enterprises (especially machine and tractor service stations).

Characterizing the special characteristics of the development of cooperation in the conditions of the Soviet social order, Lenin wrote:

Under private capitalism, cooperative enterprises, as collective enterprises, are distinguished from capitalist enterprises, which are private enterprises. Under state capitalism, cooperative enterprises are distinguished from state-capitalist enterprises as (1) private enterprises and (2) collective enterprises. Under our existing social order, cooperative enterprises are distinguished from private-capitalist enterprises as collective enterprises; but they are not distinguished from socialist enterprises if they are based on the land, with means of production belonging to the state—that is to say, to the worker class.[21]

From the very first steps of its organizational and legislative activity, Soviet authority put before itself the task of collaborating in every way for the development of production cooperation, especially in agriculture. The Law as to the Socialization of Land [22] (January 31, 1918) states (Art. 35):

> The Russian Federative Soviet Republic, to the end of most speedily attaining socialism, cooperates in every way (in the form of cultural and material aid) for the general cultivation of the earth, giving preference to labor communist, artel and cooperative enterprises over those of the individual peasant.

The Soviet state—as we see—from the very first days of the socialist revolution, summoned the peasantry to organize kolkhozes. Under the transition to peaceful economic building (in 1921), Soviet authority set about the development of practical measures to create and confirm cooperation.[23]

The Lenin-Stalin cooperative-kolkhoz plan was one of turning the petty labor property of tens of millions of (middle and poor) peasants, which was broken up into small parcels, into socialist, social property by the voluntary unification of the toiling, separate peasant-homesteaders into a social kolkhoz economic organization. The realization of this plan during the first, and especially the second, five-year period resulted in cooperative-kolkhoz property becoming completely dominant in the country and also in the petty craftsman industry, side by side with the mighty state property of socialist society. Property of kolkhozes and cooperative organizations comprises: "Social enterprises in kolkhozes and cooperative organizations with their inventory (living and otherwise), products of kolkhozes and cooperative organizations as well as their social structures" (Constitution of the USSR, Art. 7). Accordingly, Soviet law guards all the rights of kolkhozes and cooperatives in their property and in the management thereof. Their internal affairs are decided by themselves in accordance with their regulations.

Of outstanding constitutional significance is the model regulation of

---

[21] Lenin (Russian ed.), Vol. XXVII, p. 396.

[22] Cy. 1918, No. 25, Art. 346.

[23] The Ninth All-Russian Congress of Soviets (Dec. 28, 1921) adopted a special directive concerning agricultural cooperation, clearly developing the idea of Lenin's cooperative plan. It said: "Organizational forms of concentrating the forces of the small agricultural units are given historically to the cooperatives. With the development of the New Economic Policy, Soviet authority makes the creation and development of agricultural cooperation one of the basic elements of its agricultural policy" (Cy. 1922, No. 5, Art. 48).

the agricultural artel created under the immediate guidance of Stalin, accepted at the Second All-Russian Congress of Kolkhoz Shock Workers, and confirmed by the Council of People's Commissars of the USSR and the Central Committee of the All-Union Communist Party (of Bolsheviks) February 17, 1935.[24] According to Stalin's definition it is "the highest law—the fundamental law—of building new society in rural areas." It is built on principles of socialist democracy and constitutes the fundamental juridical basis of kolkhoz democracy. It clearly established the problems and order of activity of the kolkhozes—especially the order of governing the economy of the kolkhoz, the admission and expulsion of members, the order of dividing the income among the members according to their work days, the rights and mutual obligations of the members and the kolkhoz, and so forth.

The most important matters of kolkhoz life: the acceptance of basic production plans of the kolkhoz, the admission and expulsion of members, the confirmation of plans for dividing the income, building, and the like must be decided by a general assembly of the kolkhoz members. The assembly is considered competent to decide particularly important questions only if a qualified majority is present. The administration of the kolkhoz is an elected, standing, directing organ, responsible to the general assembly. All members of the kolkhoz—without distinction of sex, age, nationality or social origin—have equal rights and obligations in the kolkhoz. Female members are given the right of freedom from work during the period of pregnancy and childbirth without loss of their work days (at the rates established by regulation).

On the basis of the model regulation of the agricultural artel, each kolkhoz works out its regulation with the active participation of its members and taking into account special local characteristics of production and manner of life. The regulations are adopted by a general assembly of members of the agricultural artel and affirmed and recorded in established order by the state organs.

Soviet law firmly defends the rights of the kolkhoz and of its members. Illegal obtrusion into the life and ways of the kolkhozes and their members in any manner whatsoever by administrative organs or separate officials is forbidden. The law establishes responsibility for infraction of kolkhoz democracy (breach of the principles of the elective character of organs of administration of the kolkhozes and of responsibility of kolkhoz members to the assembly, violation of rights of kolkhoz members and the like) and for arbitrary management of the property, money resources and landed capital of the kolkhozes.

The mutual relationships of kolkhozes and state organs are built on the

[24] Cz. 1935, No. 11, Art. 82.

basis of planned state guidance of kolkhozes and every sort of state aid to them. The most important task of the state organs for guiding the kolkhozes is to control the observance of kolkhoz regulations. Daily work in this direction must be carried on by village and district Soviets, resting upon inspection committees of the kolkhozes (the staff of these committees is confirmed by the executive committee of the district). The village Soviets and the district executive committees guide the development of basic agricultural campaigns in the kolkhoz (plowing, sowing, harvesting, and so on) and the fulfillment of obligations due from the kolkhozes to the state.

The village Soviets have the right to suspend—and the district executive committees to abrogate—unlawful enactments of the kolkhozes. The basic economic and organizational technical guidance of the kolkhozes and aid to them are realized by the state's organization in the village of enterprises of a logically socialist type—machine and tractor service stations, which emerged in 1928—1929. The juridical relations of kolkhozes and machine and tractor service stations are regulated by contracts between them containing an enumeration of the mutual obligations of the parties (the order of using the tractor park, payment of technical personnel, payment of disbursements according to the content of the park, organizational-economic aid to the kolkhoz, and so on). The parties are responsible for breach of contract. Controversies over these contracts are decided in the order established by law. In 1937 the number of machine and tractor service stations reached 5,617, and the quantity of tractors amounted to more than 350,000 (more than six and a half million horsepower). In 1937 the stations served 91.5 per cent of the entire kolkhoz acreage under crop.

Kolkhozes are bound to carry out the programs (of taxation, grain storage, and the like) established for them by the state. Having fulfilled these programs in the order provided by law, the kolkhozes are free to manage what they have produced—their natural and financial resources. Part of the income they distribute between the members according to their work days; part they turn into indivisible funds (including funds for capital building, and so forth), part they convert into cash in the market according to the prices obtaining in the market, and part they allocate to the fulfillment of contracts whereby they are obligated to state or cooperative trade organizations, and so forth. All this must be developed in complete accordance with the regulation of the agricultural artel.

The Stalin Constitution, as we have seen, makes a distinction between the two forms of socialist property. State property is the higher form of social property—the form more nearly consistent with socialism. Whereas state property is the property of the entire Soviet people, cooperative-kolkhoz property is property of the separate kolkhozes—of the separate cooperative societies. State property emerged originally by violent expropriation, nationalization, and confiscation—by coercive alienation of property of the exploiters. On the other hand, property of the cooperative-kolkhoz societies emerged from voluntary socialization of the means of their members (the joint adventurers). State property constitutes a single state-wide (nationwide) fund. Property of cooperative-kolkhoz societies forms no single statewide fund. The subject of the right of property in cooperative-kolkhoz societies is these separate societies.

In precisely the same way, too, the division of produce between members of the cooperative-kolkhoz society takes place out of the resources of each such society separately; thus work days in kolkhozes are paid for on the basis of the income of each kolkhoz separately. Finally kolkhoz property, in distinction from state property, presupposes that side by side with the socialist social economy there exists individual, subsidiary economy of the kolkhoz member—which, in the given circumstances, furnishes the best union of individual and collective interests of kolkhoz members.

The funds of state and cooperative-kolkhoz property exist independently. The transition from state to cooperative-kolkhoz societies (and vice versa) of objects of property is achieved on the basis of mutual reckoning and not gratuitously.

State property played—and still plays—a leading and guiding part in the entire national economy: the development of cooperative-kolkhoz property necessarily postulated its strengthening and broadening on the basis of the latest technical achievements. This made it economically and technically possible to liquidate capitalist society in the rural districts and to collectivize agriculture. In dimensions and proportional share, state property slightly exceeds cooperative-kolkhoz property (cf. the table above).

The Soviet state creates conditions most favorable for the development of the cooperative-kolkhoz form of economy, for uninterrupted increase of the productivity of socialist agricultural labor, and—on this basis—for material and cultural well-being to flourish among the peasantry. In this connection it is particularly important to point out the second part of Article 7 of the Stalin Constitution:

Each kolkhoz household—aside from its basic income from the social kolkhoz enterprise—has for its individual use a small parcel of land appurtenant and—as its individual property—a subsidiary proprietorship thereon—a dwelling, livestock, poultry and a small agricultural inventory—according to the regulation of the agricultural artel.

The circumstance that this proposition is especially established in the Constitution emphasizes its vast significance in principle. It is an extraordinarily essential part of the legislative confirmation of the agricultural artel as the basic form of the kolkhoz movement at a given historical stage. The right of the kolkhoz member to a parcel of land appurtenant, to personal subsidiary proprietorship, and so on, is very important for strengthening the kolkhoz, for guaranteeing its members a comfortable life, and for uniting individual and social interest. The Soviet state draws a hard and clear line regarding the agricultural artel as the basic form of the kolkhoz movement at the given period of time. (Cf. directive of the Sixth Congress of Soviets of the USSR—1931—Concerning Kolkhoz Organization.) [25]

In the process of complete collectivization (during the period 1930–1931), there were in practice hostile perversions—often of a provocative character and consisting of attempts mechanically to transfer to the kolkhozes the system of government established in sovkhozes. The Soviet state acted with decision to cut short attempts of this sort as politically and organizationally harmful. The distinction between sovkhozes and kolkhozes as two forms of socialist agriculture must be kept firmly in mind.[26]

Article 8 of the Constitution of the USSR provides that "the earth occupied by kolkhozes is confirmed in their behalf, to be enjoyed by them without payment and without limit of time—that is to say, in perpetuity." The basic juridical act, securing for the kolkhoz the earth allotted to be enjoyed by it, is "State Act for Perpetual Enjoyment of the Land." This act accurately points out the dimensions and boundaries of property in the earth, with its appanages, handed over to the given kolkhoz to be enjoyed in perpetuity and without payment. All rights of the kolkhoz (flowing from the confirmation in its behalf of the land occupied by it) are completely preserved by Soviet legislation, any invasion of them whatsoever by any institutions or persons being most strictly forbidden.

Transfer to the kolkhozes, and confirmation in their behalf, of the land (in perpetuity and without payment) is one of the basic specific institutes of Soviet public law as socialist law. Its historical significance is enormous. In all countries of the world except the USSR, when land is in the hands of big proprietors it serves as an instrument of the most cruel exploitation of hirelings and the poor, and, when it is in the hands of small work-proprietors, it cannot serve as a basis to guarantee life and most frequently turns into a heavy burden. Having created the necessary conditions for productive and profitable socialist economy of toiling peasants (united into kolkhozes) the Soviet state turned over to them the earth to be used gratuitously and in perpetuity. No bourgeois revolution has realized—or could realize—the

[25] Cz. 1931, No. 17, Art. 161.
[26] Cf. Sovkhoz Organization, a directive of the Sixth Congress of Soviets of the USSR (Cz. 1931, No. 17, Art. 160).

actual nationalization of the earth and its transfer into gratuitous enjoyment by the toilers thereon. During the struggle against feudalism, such demand was advanced by representatives not only of the peasantry but also of radical circles of the revolutionary bourgeoisie, but it was never realized anywhere. Even at the present time the land problem is the most insistent question in most capitalist—and especially colonial—states. For demagogic purposes bourgeois constitutions have sometimes expressed pious wishes as to "the just enjoyment of the land," but they remain empty wishes.[27]

3. Small private economy of individual peasants and craftsmen

Side by side with the socialist scheme of economy—the predominant form of economy in the USSR—the law permits the small private economy of individual peasants and craftsmen based on personal toil and not including exploitation of another's labor (Art. 9 of the Constitution of the USSR).

Although at the present moment the proportionate share and practical significance of private economy in the USSR is already absolutely negligible (only 0.2 per cent of all the production stocks in 1936), the Constitution dedicated a special article to private economy. In that article is manifested a special characteristic of Soviet government policy regarding small private enterprises of individual peasants and craftsmen: the transfer of such small private economy into largescale socialist economy is by the voluntary choice of the petty producers themselves, convinced of the advantages of socialized economy aided by the state in every way, under the guidance of the worker class. This emphasizes the fact that the Soviet state is a complete stranger to methods of coercive socialization of the private-labor economy, notwithstanding slanders of enemies, Trotsky-Bukharin bandits, and similar counterrevolutionary elements, and their provocative attempts to break the line of the Party and of the government in this regard.

The formula "the law permits" signifies that all attempts whatsoever from any quarter to suppress the peasant's or craftsman's small private economy, or artificially, by administrative means, to limit or to hamper his activity, contradicts the Constitution and Soviet public law, with all the con-

---

[27] Thus the Weimar Constitution (Art. 155) says: "The distribution of land and the enjoyment thereof are under the supervision of the state, which forbids abuse and strives to guarantee to each German a healthy dwelling and to all German families—particularly those with many children [to encourage the then low birth rate in Germany] to guarantee a domestic hearth and roof for work corresponding to their needs." All these turgid and false expressions remained empty words. The earth is in the hands of Prussian landowners (including the richest of them, the former Kaiser Wilhelm II) as it was then and remains to this very day. Far from ceasing, the ruin of the toiling peasantry went on at a much faster tempo. The "supervision of the state" of the Weimar Constitution consisted in millions being remitted in loans to the landowners while peasant enterprises—mortgaged to the state and banks—were sold under the hammer.

clusions deriving therefrom. On the other hand, it reflects the real and incontestable fact that in the USSR, at the present epoch of triumphant socialism, the place of small private economy is by way of being taken by big socialist economy, but the former "is permitted by law" insofar as it continues to exist.

The small private economy of individual peasants and craftsmen is permitted in the USSR upon condition that individual labor be utilized without the exploitation of another's toil.[28] In direct and immediate form and in legislative order the exploitation of man by man is thus here abrogated and forbidden. (In socialist economy, exploitation is excluded by the very character of that economy.)

4. The right of private property in the USSR

The constitutional definition of this right is to be found in Article 10 of the USSR Constitution. The right of citizens to individual ownership of their labor income and savings, of a dwelling house and subsidiary domestic economy, of objects of household economy and use, of objects of personal use and convenience as well as the right to inherit the individual property of citizens is protected by law. The right, like every right possessed by citizens of the Soviet state, is guaranteed, really and in all its fullness, by our entire social order, by the actual conditions of life created by the socialist reorganization of the country for all its citizens. The socialist method of production and distribution in the USSR created the firm and stable basis whereon such personal property of the citizens may grow and expand.

The theoretical side of the matter of personal property under socialism was most profoundly and exhaustively illuminated by Marx and Engels. They established (particularly in their economic works) that personal consumption is defined by the means of appropriation, and consequently by the means of production, prevailing in a given society. Annihilating the capitalist means of production and appropriation of products, the proletariat produces a complete overturn as regards personal consumption in the character of personal property.

Bourgeois and petty bourgeois apologists for capitalist private property in means of production sought to represent the case as if the abrogation of such property meant the abrogation of individual property of all sorts—the "abolition of personality." Marx and Engels answered:

[28] Cf. in this connection the Law as to the State Tax on the Horses of Individual Economies, adopted by the Supreme Soviet of the USSR on Aug. 21, 1938.

From the moment when labor can no more be turned into capital, money, land rent (more briefly, into a social force which can be monopolized)—that is to say, from the moment when individual property can no more become bourgeois property—from that moment, you declare that personality is abolished. Consequently you are conscious that by personality you acknowledge none other than the bourgeois, the bourgeois proprietor. Such personality must actually be abolished. Communism takes from no one the power of appropriating to himself social products. It takes away only the power of subjugating the labor of another to himself by means of this appropriation.[29]

Bourgeois ideologists state the alternative: Either private property—and then "just" property—guaranteed for all; or the abolition of private property, and then property of every kind will inevitably be abolished for all. This alternative is false from start to finish. (1) The dominance of private, that is, capitalist, property presupposes that an absolute majority of society are without property in the means of production. "We wish to abolish property; it presupposes, as a necessary condition, the absence of property in the vast majority of society." [30] (2) Personal property, property in means of consumption in conditions of capitalist property, is for workers limited always to the extreme minimum of means necessary for their mere existence as a working force serving to bring about the enrichment of capitalists:

That which the hired worker appropriates by his activity suffices only to reproduce his existence. By no means do we wish to eliminate this individual appropriation of the products of labor which serve immediately to reproduce life —an appropriation which leaves no net income whatever that could create power over another's toil. We wish only to eliminate the beggarly character of such appropriation, under which the worker lives only to increase capital and only insofar as this is required by the interests of the dominant class.[31]

Here we see Marx and Engels sharply distinguish between individual appropriation by the worker (appropriation of a consumer character)—which excludes the possibility of exploiting another's labor—and the individual appropriation of the capitalist, based on exploitation of another's labor. Capitalist appropriation presupposes that the majority of society is without private property in the means of production and exists on an extremely low and beggarly level of personal property as regards objects of consumption. Speaking of the impending and historically inevitable annihilation of capitalist property, "the hour of capitalist private property is striking, the expropriators are being expropriated," [32] Marx makes it clear that this will

[29] *Communist Manifesto* (1938, Russian ed.), p. 44.
[30] *Ibid.*, p. 43.
[31] *Ibid.*, pp. 42–43.
[32] Marx, *Das Kapital* (Party Publishing House, 1937), Vol. I, p. 834.

lead, not to the reestablishment of private property (that is to say, property in the means of production) for the workers, but to the abolition (on the basis of social property) of the beggarly level of personal appropriation of the toilers, to the compass and level of this appropriation being constantly higher when freed from the clutches of capitalist exploitation.

The capitalist means of appropriation (flowing out of the capitalist means of production)—and consequently capitalist private property also—is the first negation of individual property based on one's own labor. This itself effects a negation of capitalist production with the inevitability of a process of natural history. This is the negation of a negation. It again creates individual property, but on the basis of acquisitions of the capitalist era—of the cooperation of free workers and their communal possession of the earth and the means of production which they have produced.[33]

This scientific prognosis of Marx was brilliantly realized with the triumph of socialism in the USSR. Individual property of the toilers, in the form of labor income of workers, kolkhoz members and intellectuals, has under it a firm economic basis. We have no unemployment and no crises. We have no capitalist appropriation or parasitism. Distribution is upon the socialist principle: "From each according to his capacity, to each according to his toil." The productivity of labor in state and cooperative-kolkhoz enterprises has steadily grown, with consequent raising of wages and of the value of the work day. All this makes up the material postulates and guarantees of the unbroken growth of the material blessings constituting the individual property of USSR citizens. Individual property in the USSR originates entirely in labor—nothing is appropriated to it except by labor (that is to say, by exploiter appropriation which contradicts the socialist social and legal order and socialist laws).

Accordingly, Soviet law provides for struggle with the utilization of private property for nonlabor, exploiter appropriation. Such is the legislation against speculation (directive of the Central Executive Committe and Council of People's Commissars of the USSR, August 22, 1932: Concerning the Struggle with Speculation,[34] and Article 107 of the Criminal Code of the RSFSR and corresponding articles of the criminal codes of other allied republics) and likewise against agreements directed at exploiting another person (Art. 33 of the Civil Code of the RSFSR). Legislation limits the extent of individual property (for example, in dwelling houses: Civil Code of the RSFSR, Art. 182) to the end of not permitting individual property to become nonlabor property—a means of exploiting another's work— whereas there is no legal limitation of the size of citizens' individual property

[33] Ibid.
[34] Cz. 1932, No. 65, Art. 375.

as labor property in so far as it is not employed for nonlabor purposes and has a "consumer" or "use" character.

In all cases, Soviet legislation on the matter of individual property starts logically from the principle of socialism—to each according to his toil—firmly preserving all the labor acquisitions of the citizens.

In the USSR there can be no antithesis of individual property to social property. Individual property is not only in no contradiction with social property, on the contrary it corresponds harmoniously. The growth of social property conditions the growth of citizens' individual property. The growth of individual property in turn promotes the rise of culture and of the production and social activity of the toilers, and thereby the growth and strengthening of social property as well. Socialism actually harmonizes the interests (including the material interests) of separate individuality and of all society. The rise of personal, material well-being among us takes place by reason of the rise of material well-being of the entire collective, in contrast to the wolf law, "the strong devours the weak," prevalent in exploiter, and particularly in capitalist, society. "Collectivism—socialism—does not deny individual interests. Rather it combines individual interests with those of the collective. Socialism cannot be abstracted from individual interests. *Socialist society alone* can give the most complete satisfaction to *these individual interests.*" [35]

Article 10 of the Stalin Constitution realizes, in public law form, this basic principle of socialism in the domain of property rights of citizens of the USSR, making the idea of individual property definitive in such a way that its *socialist labor character* comes out perfectly clearly and distinctly, with no possibility of any idle talk. This refers also to subsidiary domestic economy. Subsidiary economy is described as individual, not private, property in Article 7 of the Constitution of the USSR. It is subsidiary property in the sense that it fills in the consumer stock of its owner. It does not, however, constitute any parallel and special form of economy, with any special form of property in the means of production. Being *subsidiary* to the labor of its possessor in socialist economy (and constituting moreover an absolutely insignificant magnitude in the national economy: only 1.1 per cent in the production resources of the USSR in 1936), the domestic economy of kolkhoz members is, in its way, an element subsidiary to socialist property.

The definition of subsidiary domestic economy as individual property gives distinct starting points to our legislation, particularly to the codes, in which the right of individual property must in the USSR find its further confirmation. The law protects the individual property of USSR citizens from encroachment by anyone whatsoever. The criminal sanctions directed

[35] Stalin, *Questions of Leninism* (10th Russian ed.), p. 602. Emphasis supplied.

at its preservation must be particularly indicated (Arts. 162—169 of the Criminal Code of the RSFSR and analogous articles in the Criminal Codes of other Union Republics). Soviet law—as socialist law—is characterized by the firm revolutionary defense of individual property, by strict suppression of all breaches of every kind as well as of crimes against rights of individual property, and by respect for individual property of USSR citizens.

The right of inheritance in the USSR issues out of all that has been hereinbefore said as to the social nature of individual property (its labor origin and consumer function), and concretely expresses the right of individual property. It differs radically from the right of inheritance in conditions where capitalist private property (one of the instruments for the preservation and strengthening whereof it is) prevails. The right of inheriting individual property in the USSR is an institution completely corresponding to the interests of citizens as testators and heirs. Being one of the incitements to labor, to productive industry of USSR citizens, it cooperates to strengthen both individual and social property and to elevate the level of the welfare both of individual citizens and of socialist society as a whole.

5. State planning of the national economic life of the USSR

"The economic life of the USSR is defined and directed by the state plan of national economy for the purposes of increasing public wealth, steadily raising the material and cultural level of the toilers, and strengthening the independence of the USSR and intensifying its power of defense." This Article (11) of the Stalin Constitution reflects and confirms the decisive characteristic of our socialist social order—that national economy is planned; all its branches are subordinate to a single state-wide plan. That socialist economy shall be an economy organized and planned, as distinguished from an anarchic, elemental, and plannless economy under capitalism, was exhaustively established in theory and predicted by Marx and Engels.[36]

In the epoch of imperialism, Lenin analyzed the processes of capital concentration and developed the views of Marx and Engels on this matter, showing that in the stage of imperialism capitalism prepares organizational-technical postulates in the form of superpowerful trusts and syndicates for the transition to planned organization of economy, under condition of the passing of means of production from the hands of separate industrialists and societies into the hands of the state, to be managed by society. This cannot be effected merely by the forcible intrusion of the new revolutionary authority, the proletarian state, into the right of private property. Organized planned economy is impossible so long as the means of production remain

[36] Cf. Anti-Dühring (Russian ed.), pp. 201–204.

for the time being in the hands of the capitalist-owners. The scattered, diminutive individual economies of peasants and craftsmen must also be socialized if the entire national economy is to be embraced by a single state plan.

In the program of the All-Union Communist Party (of Bolsheviks), the Marx-Lenin doctrine of transition to a planned economy under socialism found expression in the teaching that "one of the fundamental problems is the maximum unification of all the country's economic activity according to one state-wide plan." [37]

Guided by Lenin and Stalin, the Soviet state from the very beginning projected a distinct line as to planning the national economy, putting it firmly into practice and overcoming the hostile line and activity of Trotskyists and Bukharinists (with their "theory of labor payments" built upon an essential negation of the possibility of socialist planning of economy, and their Rykov "two-year periods" directed at subordinating national economy to the market element, liquidating socialist planning, and so forth). That line it firmly developed in struggle against the bourgeois Menshevik-SR specialist wreckers and numerous economic difficulties and difficulties of organization and technique in the practical realization of state plans of national economy which were being worked out.

The question of the practical approach to the manifold planning of the national economy was posed at one stroke at the beginning of the transition to peaceful economic building. In a resolution of the Ninth Congress of the Bolshevik Worker-Peasant Party (March–April, 1920) Concerning the Immediate Tasks of Economic Building, it was said: "A fundamental condition precedent to the country's economic renaissance is the undeviating development of a *single economic plan* calculated upon the immediate historical epoch." To realize this, the famous plan for the electrification of Russia—GOELRO [38]—was projected, a plan already proposed by Lenin and Stalin in 1920.

The Eighth All-Russian Congress of Soviets (December, 1920) especially considered the plan of electrification of the country and in a directive [39] on this matter said: "The Congress appreciates the plan of electrifying Russia worked out—upon the initiative of the Supreme Soviet of National Economy—by the State Commission for Electrification as the first step of a great economic undertaking."

First to be transferred into principles of systematic planning was large-scale state industry which, as a commanding economic height in the hands

[37] *Program of the All-Union Communist Party (of Bolsheviks)* (1936), p. 49.
[38] The State Commission for the Electrification of Russia.
[39] Cy. 1921, No. 1, Art. 11.

of the proletarian dictatorship, must become the basis of the switch to a plan of complete national economy. Regarding the New Economic Policy and industry, the Ninth All-Russian Congress of Soviets (December, 1921) directed:

Economic calculation and state-wide planning of industry—based on an exact accounting of the resources of production and a budget of each state enterprise separately and of all of them in the aggregate—must lie at the basis of the conduct of all state industry.[40]

Practice confirmed the correctness of the purpose of the Soviet state to develop state industry with all its powers by putting into practice a definite plan of restoration, and then of reconstruction, of that industry.

The Tenth All-Russian Congress of Soviets pointed out (Concerning the Report on the Condition of Industry, 1922)[41] that

the preparation of a production plan for the future must be based upon calculation of the necessity of intensifying further the work of state industry and by the actual guarantee of this plan by essential transportation, finance, production and other resources.

The principle of planning increasingly took root in the country's economic life. The plan embraced ever broader fields of national economy. Its role of regulator and director constantly increased. The state-obligatory character of the plan was increasingly confirmed economically by the growth of the socialist sector in national economy. The real force of socialist planning grew in proportion to the growth of the political and organizational power of the proletarian state. A clear definition of the nature of our plans was given by Stalin, in particular, at the Fifteenth Party Congress. He pointed out in his report that "ours are plans neither of prognosis nor of guesswork. They are *directive* plans, *binding* upon the guiding organs, and—upon the scale of the *entire* country—*defining* the direction of our *future* economic development." [42]

Establishing the plan in the core of economic life and actually subordinating all branches of economy to state planning demanded colossal efforts and Bolshevist tenacity on the part of the organs of authority, as well as taking wholly into account the definitive economic setting in the country, the achievements of the national economy at the given moment, and the separate branches and sectors of that economy from the point of view of

[40] Cy. 1922, No. 4, Art. 43.
[41] Cy. 1923, No. 28, Art. 367.
[42] *Stenographic Report of the Fifteenth Party Congress* (State Publishing House, 1928), p. 69.

the possibility of their subordination to plan. Speaking of planning in the specific setting of 1928, Stalin pointed out that "it must not be forgotten that—aside from elements subject to the influence of our planning—the structure of our national economy comprises as well other elements (not for the time being subject to planning) and, finally, classes hostile to us which mere state planning cannot overcome." [43]

The matter stood entirely differently after the kulak economy had been liquidated and most of the peasant economies collectivized, when socialist economy, built according to plan, had attained unlimited domination. In these conditions the principle of state planning becomes completely applicable to agriculture as well. Herein is expressed the vast force of state planning influence upon collectivized agriculture. Upon the People's Commissariat for Agriculture (organized since 1930) the government placed the duty of "working out a general plan for the development of agriculture in perspective, with yearly control figures." [44]

State planning is one of the most important forms of state direction of the kolkhoz economy. Economic plans, constructed by separate kolkhozes and cooperative associations, start from plans worked out for the cooperative-kolkhoz economy of the whole country by state organs (the Council of People's Commissars, the State Planning Committee and the People's Commissariat of Agriculture). In the aggregate they represent in the final analysis a detailed state-wide economic plan, concrete in time and space, for the cooperative-kolkhoz sector of the entire national economy of the country.

The construction and realization of the five-year plans are the basic and chief form of planning national economy of the USSR. They brilliantly justified themselves historically. The first five-year plan (1928–1933) was, as everyone knows, not only fulfilled but more than fulfilled before the expiration of the period, that is, in four years, at the end of 1932. The second five-year plan (1933–1937) was likewise fulfilled and, in certain particulars, more than fulfilled. The period of national economic life of the USSR from 1938 to 1942 is the period of the third five-year plan which is likewise in process of successful realization. [45]

The five-year plans of developing national economy—the yearly and quarterly plans projected for national economy in its entirety and for its separate branches—have the force of obligatory state acts with all the consequences flowing from such acts, including particularly the establishment of criminal sanctions for opposing the execution of the plans, for the col-

[43] Stalin, *Questions of Leninism* (10th Russian ed.), p. 210.
[44] Cz. 1929, No. 75, Art. 718.
[45] In 1938, date of Russian edition.—ED.

lapse of plans and of their qualitative and quantitative elements,[46] and likewise for the inaction of officials responsible for the fulfillment of the plan.

To defend and to strengthen in the national economic life the principle of planning—planned discipline and a system of organization—is the most important task of Soviet law. The guarantee of development according to plan—of the fulfillment of plans concerning separate branches of national economy by separate economic societies and enterprises, is one of the basic elements of the content of Soviet law as socialist law.

Not only does Soviet law in no wise contradict the principle of development according to plan—as has been asserted by traitors like Pashukanis, Ginsberg and company, who declared that the intensification of planning leads to the "fading out" of legal form, to the withering away of the legal principle in economic life, to the "crowding out" of the law by the plan, and the like—it is a powerful and effective means of intensifying that principle, just as the stabilizing of that principle cooperated in turn to strengthen in its entirety the socialist legal order (one of whose basic constituent elements is the planned development of economy). Contract and contract relationships of an economic order, in particular, contract discipline, in the USSR serve as a practical means of carrying out the plan within the established time limits and with observance of the corresponding requirements as to quantity and quality.

Plans of national economy in the stages of their elaboration and of their fulfillment alike represent the result of the state creativeness (economic and organizational) of broad masses of toilers, whose life interests constitute the essence of these plans. Around their fulfillment as measures of state obligation, the Party and the government as well as mass social organizations (trade unions, the Young Communist League and others), organize the production initiative and self-help of the masses.

Soviet planning combines state discipline with the self-help of the masses, brilliantly expressing socialist democracy, the participation of the masses in state government. Drawing the masses into the elaboration and execution of plans is one of the most essential factors of their realism.

It would be stupid to suppose that a production plan is a mere enumeration of figures and problems. It is in reality the living and practical activity of millions of persons. The realism of our production plan is the millions of toilers who are creating a new life. The realism of our program is the living persons—you and

---

[46] Cf. Art. 128A of the Criminal Code of the RSFSR and corresponding articles of the criminal codes of other Union Republics.

I—our will to labor, our readiness to work in a new fashion, our determination to carry out the plan.[47]

The advantages of the socialist system of economy over the capitalist system are manifested with special force in the unbroken growth of actual development according to plan in all our national economy.

Bourgeois politicians of the biggest capitalist states resort to "planned" demagogy, declaring that with the preservation of private capitalist property the bourgeois state must—and is in condition to—organize planned economy. This "planned" demagogy attained specially significant dimensions in the period of the world economic crisis (1929–1933) when the anarchy of capitalist production manifested itself with monstrous force in crises.

The only realism behind the "economic plans" and "planned economy" of fascist dictatorships—for example, in the form of the fascist four-year periods—is the intensification and improvement of planned robbery of the toiling masses, by monopolist capital with the supplementary aid of a police-military-bureaucratic-imperialist state, for economic preparation for war. This is the militarization of economy under the slogan: "Guns instead of butter." It cannot be otherwise so long as the dominance of capitalist property is preserved. Under capitalism anarchy, absence of plan and economic life of an elemental sort are inevitable. Under capitalism "plannedness"—development according to plan—is the confirmation of mass hunger and beggary.

Only in the USSR is true "planning" realized in the interests of increasing social wealth, constantly raising the material and cultural level of the toilers, confirming the independence of the USSR and increasing its defensive capacity. The specific content of any plan of national economy in the USSR, whether a five-year plan, or an annual or quarterly plan, completely corresponds to these interests.

The incentive of the capitalist economy (preserved by bourgeois state law) is the egoistic capitalist aspiration for individual enrichment through exploitation. Production interests the capitalist only from the viewpoint of how (at its expense) his own personal wealth may be increased. The elemental and anarchic character of capitalist production, the dominance of capitalist production by the market, the aspiration to gain to the utmost profit as the sole stimulus of capitalist economy—all this results in ever sharper conflict between interests of developing production forces and capitalist production relations.

Bourgeois public law, which sanctifies and preserves these relationships, is reactionary and profoundly hostile to the interests of the broad masses

[47] Stalin, *Questions of Leninism* (10th Russian ed.), p. 466.

of the toilers. Under capitalism there is no social wealth in the true sense of the word, wealth belonging to all society and utilized in the interests of society consciously, rationally, and in accordance with plan. Under socialism social wealth grows constantly and in accordance with plan at a pace incomparably swifter than that of increment of the general mass of wealth under capitalism—even in periods most propitious and favorable for such increment.

In the imperialist stage, capitalist economy is characterized not only by holding back and retarding the increment of national wealth but frequently by outright destruction of values acquired by national toil (such as the stores of goods which cannot be disposed of in the market, or crops that have been sown, or reducing the acreage under crop) in a situation when the vast masses of toilers are being systematically deprived of necessary consumer products. The interests of capitalist accumulation of wealth by the exploiter minority are radically hostile to those of the overwhelming majority of society, to interests of raising the material well-being and cultural level of the toilers. In the USSR, on the contrary, the material and cultural interests of all toilers are the decisive factor of all economic activity directed by a single plan of the socialist state embodying this will.

Under capitalism the toilers serve as a means of individual exploiter enrichment. Under socialism social wealth, constantly growing, serves as a means of satisfying in ever increasing measure and in planned order the material and cultural demands of the toilers. The fundamental interests of our socialist society (which finds itself encircled by capitalism)—as indeed of all toiling humanity, in its struggle against world capitalism and imperialist wars and aggression—are those of strengthening the independence and defensive capacity of the USSR. Putting these interests at the foundation of its plan of national economy and realizing them through public law, the USSR comes forward in this respect also as a state of a new and loftier socialist type.

SEC. 6: THE REALIZATION OF THE SOCIALIST PRINCIPLE: "FROM EACH ACCORDING TO HIS CAPACITY, TO EACH ACCORDING TO HIS TOIL"

"Labor in the USSR is an obligation and a matter of honor of each citizen capable thereof, upon the principle: 'He who does not work does not eat.' In the USSR is realized the socialist principle: 'From each according to his capacity, to each according to his toil.'" (Constitution of the USSR, Art. 12). This article of the Stalin Constitution expresses in the finely chiseled formula of scientific communism—and confirmed in public-law form—the most important consummation of the socialist reorganization of our society, the victory of the socialist organization of labor and of the socialist distribution of the products of labor. It contains a sort of generalization and culmination of the principles of social organization of the USSR given in the first eleven articles of the Stalin Constitution. Actually the principles contained in Article 12 could be vitalized only on the basis and in the process of successfully building up socialism. It neither was nor could be otherwise. On the other hand, realization of these principles constitutes the most important and decisive feature of socialist society, the first phase of communism.

The basic principle of this phase of communism is, as everyone knows, the formula: "From each according to his capacity, to each according to his toil." Should our Constitution reflect this fact—the fact that socialism has been achieved? Should it be based on this achievement? Unconditionally, it should. It should, inasmuch as socialism is for the USSR something which has already been attained and won.[1]

The practical realization of these principles signifies the triumph of the Marx-Engels-Lenin-Stalin doctrine as to communism—as to the two phases of communism and their distinguishing characteristics.[2]

From the very beginning Soviet authority inscribed on its banner the socialist principle: "Let him who toils not, eat not," proclaimed as early as the first Soviet constitutions.[3]

The Soviet state put before it the greatest task in the history of the universe—to annihilate parasitism and sloth, to unite the whole population for socially useful, productive activity. Liability to universal labor service in the first period of Soviet authority was introduced "to the end of abolishing the parasitic strata of society and organizing economy."[4] This measure played its political and economic part (1) in conditions when Soviet authority, taking its first steps to organize the state direction of economy, encountered economic sabotage, and (2) thereafter, as applied to the problems of war economy during the period of war communism. Complete extirpation of the economic roots of parasitism as a social phenomenon was possible, however, only after reorganization of the entire national economy

[1] Stalin, Report on the Draft of the USSR Constitution (1936), p. 17.
[2] Cf. Marx, A Critique of the Gotha Program, and Lenin, The State and Revolution, Chap. 5.
[3] That of the RSFSR (1918, Art. 18); of the White Russian SSR (1919, Art. 12); and the Azerbaijan SSR (1921, Art. 9); etc.
[4] Declaration of Rights, Chap. 2(f).

to harmonize with socialism. After liquidating the capitalist elements in the country's economy and annihilating the possibility of man's exploitation by man, we annihilated the ground for parasitism as well. Having, on the other hand, guaranteed to all citizens the possibility of laboring, and made labor the sole source of income for all, we made for all citizens their obligation to labor realistically capable of execution.

In form, bourgeois public law evades the question of parasitism as a social phenomenon inevitable in exploiter society. Essentially and in fact, however, it sanctifies and confirms parasitism in that it sanctifies and preserves capitalist private property which, especially in the epoch of imperialism, is as inseparable from parasitism as is a cause from its proximate consequence. Soviet public law openly and proudly reflects and confirms the greatest fact in the history of the universe: the final annihilation of parasitism and the metamorphosis of all the country's population into toilers and workers in the interests, and for the welfare, of socialist society.

Toil in the USSR has become a matter of honor for each citizen capable of toiling. The principle of the socialist organization of labor is a conscious, labor, socialist discipline as contrasted with the forced hard-labor discipline supported by the threat of hunger under capitalism. This is the socialist rivalry of conscious and free toilers, resulting in the elevation of the national economy in the general interests of all the toilers.

Socialist rivalry, called to life by the mighty labor uplift, by production enthusiasm in the ranks of the worker class, organized and directed by the party according to the teachings of Lenin [5] and Stalin,[6] is preserved by law and actively supported among us by means of the state organization. Emerging as early as the period of civil war, it developed and acquired vast sweep and creative force during the Stalin five-year plans. Its significance in turning labor into a matter of honor for the Soviet citizen is extraordinarily great. State cooperation and encouragement of socialist rivalry are established in legislative form and confirmed in a whole series of directives.[7] To the end of encouraging the unselfish and heroic activity of citizens of the USSR in all fields of labor, the Soviet state adopted the practice of bestowing the Orders of Lenin, of the Red Banner of Labor, and of the Symbol of Honor, and also other sorts of symbols of encouragement and distinction, such as the Badge of Distinguished Shock Workers, recording a name on the roll of honor, presenting valuable gifts, and so on.

[5] Cf. Lenin, *The Great Beginning.*

[6] Cf. Stalin, *Political Report of the Central Committee to the Sixteenth Congress of the All-Union Communist Party (of Bolsheviks);* and Speech at First All-Union Conference of Stakhanovites.

[7] See, for example, the directive of the Sixth Congress of Soviets of the USSR Concerning the Report of the Government (Cz. 1931, No. 17, Art. 159).

Encouragement of heroism and enthusiasm by the Soviet state is brilliantly expressed in the establishment of the title "Hero of Labor," awarded to persons who have particularly distinguished themselves in the lists of labor over a long period of time, and the title "Hero of the Soviet Union," awarded for exceptional heroism and achievements in carrying out the socialist duty to the state.

Only in the USSR is there encouragement of creative, socially beneficial labor, of which there is—and of course can be—none in bourgeois countries, where the preservation and protection of the legal order (under which labor is enslaved) constitutes the state's most important function. In the USSR, state organs, economic and administrative, must encourage and defend socialist labor, especially in its higher forms of socialist competition and shock-working. Furthermore, Soviet law provides for the criminal prosecution of persons designedly impeding the development of socialist organization of labor.

The victory of socialism in the USSR was signalized by the elevation of socialist competition and shock-working to its highest pitch in the form of the Stakhanovite movement which since 1935 has embraced all branches of national economy. The historical significance of this movement is that it contains the embryo of that cultural-technical rise of the toilers which creates the material conditions for the transition to the higher form of communism.[8] Accordingly the Soviet state takes measures to strengthen it. The principle of socialism: "From each according to his capacity, to each according to his toil" is, in the USSR, the dominant principle of organizing labor and distributing its products.

The capitalist system of labor dulls and crushes the capacities of the majority of the toilers, depriving them of the real possibility of best applying their capacities (in particular the possibilities of choice of profession) and of systematic improvement of work habits and technical knowledge. The toiler cannot, under capitalism, develop his creative powers and capacities. The Soviet regime completely guarantees to the toiler this possibility by a system of training (beginning at the school bench) and by affording a real possibility of choosing a profession through encouragement of higher qualifications and the like. All this combines the conditions essential for turning labor completely into a natural need of mankind in the higher phase of communism where quantity and quality—that is, the measure of the labor which each citizen will give to society—will be defined solely by the organic demand for labor and by his (the citizen's) own individual capacities. The measure of reward will not act as a stimulus to labor, since it will be defined only by the needs of each member of society.

[8] Compare Stalin's speech at the First All-Union Conference of Stakhanovites.

The transition to the realization of the principle of communist distribution: "To each according to his needs," is possible only on the basis of originally putting into practice the principle of socialism: "To each according to his toil."

Under socialism, distribution is not yet just in the communist sense of the word, as Marx and Lenin point out. It still remains in a certain sense "unjust." The injustice is that society gives to people—who are unequal in capacity, family position, and so on—an equal quantity of products for what is in fact an unequal quantity of labor.[9] This form of division according to labor—"unjust" from the viewpoint of communism—is inevitable under socialism. The state must scrupulously follow the development of this rule of distribution so that each may obtain exactly as much as he is supposed to have, no more and no less, according to the labor imposed by the state for social production. Soviet socialist law firmly preserves this rule from all violations whatsoever. This is absolutely necessary and inevitable because it is impossible (without falling into utopianism) to suppose that, after overthrowing capitalism, people will learn at one stroke to work for society *without rules of law of any sort,* and the abolition of capitalism *does not at a stroke give* economic premises of *such* change.[10] But the edge of this "injustice" is taken off by various measures of the Soviet government, which establishes supplementary rewards, prizes, and exemptions, for example, in favor of mothers having many children (law of June 27, 1936).[11]

The socialist character of Soviet legal rules, even in this field of distribution of products, stands out absolutely clearly.

1. The development of this rule—to each according to his toil—for the whole population is feasible only if capitalist forms of economy are completely abolished, if unlimited dominance of the socialist system of economy is established.

2. The development of this rule is the most important factor of the uninterrupted strengthening of conscious socialist discipline of labor, of the uplift of labor enthusiasm of members of socialist society forever freed from nonlabor capitalist appropriation—from man's exploitation by man. Thereby it is the most important factor of the mighty growth of the production forces of society, of the creation of ample abundance of consumer products and of turning labor into "the first need of life" (Marx). And this makes feasible the complete abolition of all legal rules whatsoever, regulating the distribution of products in society (in the highest phase of communism).

Thus the legal guard over the principle: "To each according to his toil," subserves the further development of socialist society to its transition to the highest phase of communism.

[9] Lenin (Russian ed.), Vol. XXI, p. 434.
[10] *Ibid.*, p. 435.
[11] Cz. 1936, No. 34, Art. 309.

The principle of rewarding each according to his labor is concretely realized in the form of labor pay for those at work and in service and by distributing income according to work days, according to the model charter of the agricultural artel in the kolkhozes. The Stalin Constitution (Art. 12) confirms the juridical basis for the regulative activity of organs of the Soviet state in this field. The goal of these organs must be that in the practice of institutions and of the corresponding officials, the socialist principle of distribution be strictly observed and that deviations therefrom of whatsoever sort be cut down. There should in particular be elimination of tendencies to petty bourgeois wage-leveling, having nothing in common with the principle of payment according to labor—with the socialist understanding of equality.[12]

Only so can (and should) the realization in the USSR—and confirmation by the Stalin Constitution—of the authentic and great equality of people on the basis of socialist toil be understood. Only this equality of members of socialist society can serve as the basis for gradual transition to the higher condition of equality, the equal right of all toilers to receive according to their needs under communist society.

[12] For the classical formulation of the socialist principle of equality compare Stalin's report to the Seventeenth Party Congress concerning the work of the Central Committee of the All-Union Communist Party (of Bolsheviks), *Questions of Leninism* (10th Russian ed.), p. 583.

IV The State Organization of the USSR

SEC. 1: INTRODUCTION

STATE organization of the USSR—treated in Chapter II of the Stalin Constitution—embraces a number of questions associated with the voluntary unification of peoples into one union socialist state. In the struggle of two mutually opposed worlds and systems, this state represents "a Union of Soviet Republics of developed lands and colonies that have fallen, and are falling, away from the imperialist system of economy, opposing itself to the world capitalist system in its struggle for world socialism." [1]

State organization, according to Chapter II of the Stalin Constitution, is the public-law organization of a state of a new type, the Soviet multinational state which guarantees: (a) the voluntary unification of the toilers of numerous nationalities into one Soviet Union state, and (b) the broadest possible drawing of the toiling masses of all nationalities of the USSR into the administration of the Soviet state.

Chapter II of the Stalin Constitution, concerning the state organization of the USSR, establishes (1) the structure of the USSR as a Union state formed on the basis of voluntary unification of Soviet Socialist Republics having equal rights; (2) the structure of Union Republics and their territorial organization; (3) the sovereignty of the Union and of the Union Republics; the delimitation of rights and jurisdiction between them; and (4) the fundamental principles of citizenship of the Union and of Union Republics.

This truly democratic state organization, unique in history, could be realized only in consequence of the overthrow of the power of capitalists and landowners and the establishment of the worker-class dictatorship. It completely answers the purposes and problems of that dictatorship in creating

[1] Stalin, *Questions of Leninism* (9th Russian ed., 1932), p. 338.

fraternal and mutual friendship and collaboration of peoples. State organization of capitalist countries offers a sharp contrast thereto. Most modern bourgeois states, particularly those with colonies, are multinational as regards the structure of their population. In them the sovereign nation—the exploiter apex of which oppresses and exploits other nations which are in a subordinate position—plays the dominant role. Frequently national inequality is further confirmed by rules of law defining the activity of state authority for that inequality.

In colonies a special colonial law operates, depriving the people even of the "constitutional guarantees" ordinarily found in constitutions of bourgeois states. Thus the French bourgeoisie, while still a revolutionary class, proclaimed in its Declaration of Rights: "People are born free and equal in rights." But in its first constitution (1791), consisting in part of the Declaration of Rights, the bourgeoisie noted (in Subdivision 7) that "the present constitution has no reference to French colonies and possessions in Asia, Africa, and America, although they constitute a part of the French Empire."

A special colonial law operates in the colonies of England, France, Belgium, Holland, Italy, and other states.

One of the most eminent contemporary French political scientists (Duguit, who died in 1928) wrote:

In the majority of states they say the people consist of various nationalities—not of course forming a nation—hence it cannot be asserted that a "nation" is a general constituent element of the "state." To this it is answered that—notwithstanding diversity of nationalities subject to a single public authority—there may exist a central core of the population which forms a united nation and that the existence of such a "nation" is necessary for the presence of the "state"—if, for example, we contemplate France, the French nation forms the *substratum* of the French state as a subject of law; and the nationalities distinct from the French nation do not contribute to the formation of a subjective unity of the French state, being simply an object of the power borne by the French state. On the contrary, the French nation in its present structure forms an element of the personality of the French state.[2]

In the France of which Duguit was writing, only the territory between the Rhine and the Pyrenees—the mother country—is governed on the basis of the French Constitution and the parliamentary laws, whereas the colonies (with a population of sixty millions) are governed according to presidential decrees published on the basis of proposals of ministers and their subordinate officials. Only the population of the mother country are counted as citizens.[3]

---

[2] Duguit, *Constitutional Law*, p. 110.
[3] Political rights are enjoyed only by males who satisfy the requirements of various qualification laws.

But the population of the colonies—with negligible exceptions—are considered merely subjects.

Individual bourgeois political scientists openly defend the imperialist state organization aimed at crushing and subordinating the oppressed nations of the colonies and of the mother country. The famous jurist Hauriou considers that the constitutional (state) organization is the political and juridical centralization of peoples that have attained the level of nations. Only in behalf of the chosen apex of the people, the "elite" occupying a dominant position in the nation, does he acknowledge the right to be considered a nation. The right of independent statehood and state organization must be refused to people who have not grown to the level of a nation as he understands it. Their fate will be "the concern" of those who have attained the level of nations. "It cannot be asserted that all races and all mixtures of different races—for example the Papuans—create nations capable of taking in the state regime." [4] The basis of state organization (according to bourgeois political scientists) there accords with the interests of the imperial bourgeoisie's dictatorship and its administrative convenience.

Fascism establishes state organization to accord with monopolist capital's bestial terrorist dictatorship over the toiling and oppressed nations. In Italy this is characterized by the creation of a new "Italian Empire" after the seizure and enslavement of Abyssinia. German fascists by piratical violence seized Austria and united it to the German Empire and, in company with the Italian fascists, organized the intervention in Spain, military aggression against Czechoslovakia, and the like. In order to unify the state government of the country, the imperial federation was abolished by fascist methods and all the formerly independent "lands" (Bavaria, Würtemberg, Baden and the like) are now under the arbitrary domination of Hitler's deputies (*Staathälter*). The fascist state perpetrates the most barbarous and unbridled oppression of nationalities as attested by various "race" laws, and especially the "Nuremberg Laws" (1935), which divided the German population into "imperial citizens" and state subjects. With the aid of the fascist state (centralized after the military-police pattern), monopolist capital, making ready for new wars, strives to subordinate to itself other nations which must become objects of exploitation by the "higher" German race (in fact, by German monopolist capital).

[4] Hauriou, *Public Law*, p. 320.

SEC. 2: THE BASES OF THE STATE ORGANIZATION OF THE USSR

The USSR is a multinational socialist state which was formed, grew, and became strong as a result of the annihilation of the oppressive imperialist state of tsarist Russia (the erstwhile "prison of the peoples"), the abolition of pressure upon nationalities and inequality of rights, and the unification (by the state) of the peoples of our country on the basis of principles of the Lenin-Stalin policy as to nationalities.

In their works on nationalities, Lenin and Stalin disclosed the special historical conditions leading to the formation, from time to time, of multinational states in eastern Europe, where the awakening to national life on the part of many peoples lagged behind the formation of centralized states unified by the dominant apex of some more powerful single nationality. In Russia this was a dominant apex of Russians; in Austria, of Germans; and in Hungary, of Magyars. This apex subordinated to its own class interests those of all other peoples of the state. Even in eastern Europe, however, developing capitalism shattered the old economic relationships and therewith promoted the formation of subordinate peoples into nations, intensifying (by its oppression of nationalities) their dissatisfaction and their aspiration to create their own national statehood. "But although they have awakened to independent life, nations that have been driven out no longer form into independent national states: on their way they encounter stronger resistance from the directing strata of the commanding nations that have long since come to head the state. They are too late." [1]

In old (prerevolutionary) Russia and in Austria-Hungary there was an age-old struggle of oppressed nationalities for their freedom from imperialist oppression and for the creation of their nationalist statehood.

Throughout its history the Lenin-Stalin Party was, as it remains, the most logical and genuine champion of the equal rights of nationalities. As early as the first draft of the Party program, which he wrote in prison (1894–1896), Lenin emphasized the requirement of "equality of rights of all nationalities" as part of the general policy of the program [2] and of the struggle for the proletarian dictatorship. The point as to the matter of nationality in the third version of Lenin's draft, he formulated as "the acknowledgment—in behalf of all nations entering into the structure of the state—of the right of self-determination," [3] and this became an essential

[1] Stalin, *Marxism and the National-Colonial Question* (1937), p. 11.
[2] Lenin (Russian ed.), Vol. I, p. 15.
[3] Lenin, *Collected Works*, Vol. II, p. 46.

point (the ninth) in the program of the Russian Social-Democratic Worker
Party. The Party always interpreted it as the right of nations to self-determination, including the right of withdrawal.

Lenin and Stalin unmasked the opportunism which, veiled under "revolutionary" phraseology, in fact sowed nationalism in the international worker
movement, and carried on a bitter struggle against Austro-Marxist projects
of "autonomy of national culture," showing that they were reactionary and
chauvinistic. This was the project of "solving" the problem of nationalities by
starting from the interests of the integrity of the tattered Hapsburg monarchy and the predominant position in Austria of Germans (in fact, the
German bourgeoisie), and differentiating cultural from state-wide questions
by the creation of so-called corporations of entire nationalities wherein nationalist "collaboration of classes" was to be made real.

It denied the right of nations oppressed by Austria, such as the Czechs,
to self-determination. It put forward niggardly "reforms" to embarrass and
frustrate a solution of the nationality problem by revolution. In Russia the
most characteristic adherent of such "autonomies of nationalist culture" was
the Bund. It reduced the problem of nationality to problems of nationalist
culture. Culture was thus torn out from the general bundle of economic and
political matters, in opposition to the Marxist views that the school, and
matters of culture in general, are most closely connected with the economic
—and so with the class—struggle. Contemplating the nation as a category
outside classes, the Eighth Bund Conference expressed itself in favor of
utilizing the Hebrew religious commune as the basis of a Hebrew "autonomy
of nationalist culture" and reorganizing it by means of legislation as a
secular institution. In August, 1912, the Trotsky-liquidator conference, at
the insistence of Caucasian liquidators, declared in its turn that the "autonomy of nationalist culture" does not run counter to the Party program
adopted in 1903.

In contrast to all these alien views which sought confirmation in the
midst of the workers, the Party of Bolsheviks, guided by Lenin and Stalin,
came forward still more decisively to defend the watchword of the right of
nations to self-determination (including the right of withdrawal). This was
emphasized at the August Conference (of 1913) of the Central Committee
of the Russian Social Democratic Worker Party with the responsible
workers, in Lenin's articles of the period, and in Stalin's classical work
Marxism and the National-Colonial Question. Defending the inalienable
right of nations to self-determination (including the right of withdrawal),
the party by no means supported as inevitable in every case the separation
of nations from a big state—already formed—representing a broader arena
for the struggle in behalf of socialism. "Social-democracy is bound to con-

duct such agitation and so to influence the will of the nations that the latter may be organized in the form most in accord with the interests of the proletariat." [4]

Overcoming chauvinism and opportunism in the midst of the workers, the Party carried on as well a struggle against the theories of Rosa Luxemburg, who viewed the question of nationalities outside its concrete historical setting and spoke out against the slogan: "The right of nations to self-determination," asserting that there cannot be nationalist wars in the epoch of imperialism. Holding that the proletariat can aid the peasantry, she was nevertheless unwilling to understand Lenin's revolutionary formulation of the matter of the alliance of the worker class with the peasantry, in which the peasantry of oppressed nationalities plays a vast role. Trotsky, Bukharin, Pyatakov, Radek, and others took up her theory for counterrevolutionary purposes in the struggle against Leninism. Lenin proved the revolutionary significance of the demand by the oppressed nationalities for a nationalist state and demonstrated that it is directed against the imperialist state and causes it to totter.

To counterbalance Lenin, and starting from interests of "world economy"—factually from the interests of monopolist capital—Trotsky asserted that it was time in general for the nationalist state to be smashed and, altogether in the interests of the imperialist state, denied the right of oppressed nationalities to their independent state.

At the time of the World War, Lenin was for a civil war of the proletariat against its bourgeoisie, for a proletarian revolution which must likewise free the oppressed peoples of the mother country and of the colonies. The Trotskyists and Bukharinists, at the same time, came out with their "United State of Europe," a slogan directed in fact toward cooperation with capitalism to confirm its shaken positions and to guarantee the big European imperialists the right to plunder the colonies and to dominate over them.

Lenin proved the progressive and revolutionary significance of nationalist wars, and showed that a proletariat must advance unconditionally the demand that nations have the right of self-determination (including withdrawal) "although the chance of withdrawal was possible and feasible prior to socialism in only one in a thousand cases." [5] The Trotskyists and Bukharinists came out against Lenin's revolutionary watchword: "The right of nations to self-determination, including withdrawal." In fact, they supported the right of imperialists to oppress nations, to pursue a barbarous policy of colonization, to retard the progressive development of backward nations and colonies. Their aim was to weaken the international positions of the prole-

[4] Stalin, *Marxism and the National-Colonial Question* (1937), p. 39.
[5] Lenin (Russian ed.), Vol. XIX, p. 262.

tariat, to thwart its union with the vast masses of oppressed nations of the mother countries and the colonies. Coming out against the right of national self-determination, they joined ranks with counterrevolutionary nationalist elements after the victory of the proletarian state and the Lenin-Stalin national policy with the purpose of estrangement from the union socialist state of national republics and of reestablishment of capitalist serfdom in the interests of bloody and barbarous fascism.

We demand freedom of self-determination—independence . . . freedom of oppressed nations to withdraw—not because we have dreamed of economic dismemberment or of an ideal of petty state, but because, on the contrary, we wish big states and the approximation, even the blending, of nations—on a truly democratic and internationalist base, however, which is *nonsensical* without freedom of withdrawal.[6]

The victory of the Lenin-Stalin line in the nationalist question was expressed with particular clarity after the February Revolution of 1917. That question became one of the most important matters of the revolution's further development. The border lands were dappled with divers "national Soviets" proclaimed by the bourgeoisie and its intellectuals. The imperialist position of the Provisional Government and its supporting parties merely deepened the distrust of the oppressed nationalities toward the government and served to intensify nationalism.

Numerous "national Soviets," proclaimed by the bourgeoisie of each nationality and ready to trade with the Provisional Government about "autonomy," "federation," and so on in proportion to the intensification of the proletariat's contest for power, used nationalist slogans for the struggle against the Russian revolutionary worker class. The slogan of "the right of nations to self-determination" was given a nationalist interpretation by the bourgeoisie of separate nations, agitating for separation from revolutionary Russia, and directing all their efforts to the creation of a barrier between the revolutionary proletariat of the center and the toilers of the borderlands.

At the time of the February Revolution Lenin and Stalin came out in fiery defense of demands by Finland and the Ukraine for the right to self-determination.

We are no partisans of little states. We are for the closest union of the workers of all countries against capitalists and their ilk and of all countries in general. But precisely in order that this union be voluntary, the Russian worker—not for a single minute trusting either the Russian bourgeoisie or the Ukraine bourgeoisie in any respect whatsoever—stands now for the right of the Ukrainians to with-

[6] *Ibid.*, Vol. XVIII, p. 328.

draw, not *obtruding* his friendship upon them but *winning* theirs by a relationship as to an equal—as to any ally and brother in the struggle for socialism.[7]

The establishment of friendship between the Russian proletariat and the toilers of the former oppressed nationalities—such were the real results of the Lenin-Stalin national policy which contributed to draw the toilers of all nations into the channel of socialist revolution.

The Bolshevist slogan: "The right of nations to self-determination," in combination with all the other Bolshevik slogans of the October Revolution —particularly those of the agrarian revolution—became one of the greatest factors in *uniting the toiling masses of the nationalities in one proletarian state,* thereby vindicating the words of Stalin at the Seventh April Conference (1917) that after the overthrow of tsarism "nine tenths of the nationalities will not wish to withdraw." [8]

Specifically because the peasantry, the basic mass of former oppressed nationalities, felt still more heavily than did the Russian peasantry the pressure of the landowners, the wealthy landowners of Central Asia, the bureaucracy, and so on, the proletariat, deciding the national question correctly (under the guidance of the Bolshevik Party), could raise the multimillion masses of national peasantry to struggle for peace, for land, and other revolutionary needs. This struggle raised the masses of toiling nationalities against their own landowners, the bourgeoisie, the wealthy landowners of Central Asia, and the imperialist interveners who strove to separate the border lands from revolutionary Russia.

In the heroic civil war, the formerly oppressed nationalities decided the question of their national self-determination. They created the Soviet authority and in their Congresses of Soviets triumphantly proclaimed their inflexible will to struggle—together with the Russian worker class and peasantry—for the general interests of the toilers.

The toiling masses, freed from the yoke of the bourgeoisie, *will strain* with all their powers for union and merger with the large and advanced socialist nations for the sake of this "cultural help," provided only yesterday's oppressors do not affront the highly developed democratic feeling of self-respect of the long oppressed nation, provided only they give it equality in everything—including state building, experience to build "their own" state.[9]

The great October Socialist Revolution confirmed Lenin's foresight and realized the yearnings of the toilers of all the formerly oppressed nationalities for land, peace, and their own national statehood. The latter was created solely in democratic fashion, on the basis of Soviet federation ex-

[7] *Ibid.,* Vol. XX, p. 535.
[8] Stalin, *Marxism and the National-Colonial Question* (1937), p. 48
[9] Lenin (Russian ed.), Vol. XIX, p. 256.

pressing the mutual confidence of the toiling masses of the various nationalities and their voluntary aspiration for alliance within the limits of one multinational socialist state. In his address at the Extraordinary Eighth All-Union Congress of Soviets, Stalin noted that, creating the multinational socialist state, the "Soviet authority could not but see the difficulties of this matter, having before it the unsuccessful experiences of multinational states in bourgeois countries, including the old Austro-Hungarian experiment that has miscarried." [10]

The modern political map of the world shows no Austria-Hungary. The experience of this state graphically supports all the instability of the capitalist multinational state. The dominant classes of Austria-Hungary had forcibly to overthrow and crush nationalist aspirations of oppressed nationalities (Czechs, Poles, Ukrainians, Croats, Serbs, Italians, and others). The result was the collapse of old Austria-Hungary in October, 1918, under the burden of class and national contradictions. But, as Stalin noted in his report at the Extraordinary Eighth All-Union Congress of Soviets: "We now have in the Soviet Union a completely formed multinational socialist state which has sustained all trials, whose stability might well be envied by any national state in any part of the world." [11]

The socialist revolution made possible the consolidation of all nationalities into nations on the Soviet basis. Many of them, such as the Kirghiz people, the Kalmyks, the Turkmens, the northern nationalities, and others, lived prior to the socialist revolution as dispersed tribes in conditions of the patriarchal way of life, without a written literature and (many of them) without even an alphabet. Representatives of the dominant classes spoke of many of them as "peoples without a history," meaning that they must not cherish any hope of regeneration.

Hunted into steppes, Arctic fens, mountains, and forests, far from the centers of culture, abandoned to the arbitrary caprices of merchants, priests, and bureaucrats, many of them were doomed to hunger, beggary, disease, lack of culture, and gradual extinction. These were peoples—Ukrainian, White Russian, Georgian, Armenian, and others—whom tsarism had vainly sought to Russify. There were others, too, who had not yet attained the rank of nations, of whom scarcely anyone even knew, such as the Itelmens, the Nenets, the Koryaks, the Evenks.

Only the socialist revolution brought out into the social arena many forgotten and formerly humiliated nations and inspired in them faith in their right to exist. Only the victory of socialist forms of economy shattered the former tribal seclusion, annihilated the remnants of the patriarchal way of

---

[10] Stalin, *Report on the Draft of the USSR Constitution* (1936), p. 14.
[11] *Ibid.*, p. 15.

life, and rallied the dispersed and often nomad groups into nations. "The October Revolution, having burst the old chains and put forward upon the scene a whole procession of forgotten peoples and nationalities, gave them new life and new development." [12]

The development of all the peoples of our country, including the large nations which had formed earlier, took place in bitter class struggle. In the contest for their class interests the toilers of all the Soviet peoples burst nationalist, ethnic, tribal, and religious bonds which had formerly allowed a negligible handful of the rich to exploit the masses, giving out their class interests as national interests. The toilers of all the nations, under the guidance of the Bolshevik Party, struggled against attempts by their bourgeoisie and other representatives of formerly privileged classes to manipulate for their own advantage the people's rights proclaimed by the socialist revolution and broadly utilized them to create and to strengthen their Soviet national statehood and (with the help of the dictatorship of the worker class) advanced the development of national culture.

The brevity of the periods wherein new nations were organized under the dictatorship of the worker class is unmatched in the history of the capitalist world. In the recent past the Uzbeks, the Turkmens, the Tadjiks, were still disunited, being formed within the boundaries of old Russia in various territories and regions and even in different states (Bokhara, Khiva). After the victory of the socialist revolution, the Turkestan autonomous republic was created—the first step on the road toward the national-state organization of the nations of Central Asia.

In 1924 the national demarcation of peoples of Central Asia was carried out, with the result of creating two Union Republics, Turkmenistan and Uzbekistan, and later Tadjikistan and Kirghizia. "To reunite Poland the bourgeoisie required a whole series of wars. To reunite Turkmenistan and Uzbekistan the communists required only a few months of clarifying propaganda." [13] Because they rested firmly on the will and confidence of the broadest masses of the people, the communists succeeded in deciding swiftly a matter so complicated as was the delimitation of the nations of Central Asia. The socialist revolution overthrew all the "arguments" of the nationalists as to the emancipation of nations being feasible only through separation from the state. The actuality of socialist building showed that nations can flourish in mutual friendship only in the Soviet state on the basis of Soviet federation.

[12] Stalin, *Marxism and the National-Colonial Question* (1937), p. 158.
[13] *Ibid.*, p. 157.

SEC. 3: FEDERATION IN THE TEACHING OF MARX AND LENIN

Marx and Engels opposed bourgeois federation, considering it a survival of feudal dispersedness and a brake on economic and cultural development. In 1891 Engels wrote that for Germany "to become a federalist Swiss canton would be a great step backwards." Even under capitalism, however, Marx and Engels admitted federation in the conditions of a multinational state. They contemplated federation as a means of struggling with national oppression and of establishing international bonds between the toilers of different nations, so as to accelerate thereby the process of proletarian class self-determination within the framework of the nation. Starting from this, Marx, for example, considered that not only in the interests of the Irish people but in its own interests as well, the English worker class should not only cooperate with the Irish but should assume the initiative in dissolving the alliance of 1801 and replacing it by a free union on federative principles.[1]

Marx and Engels did not view the Irish question as an isolated question. They associated it with problems of the English proletarian class struggles, of winning the peasantry to their side, and of attracting into the revolutionary stream the most oppressed hirelings in England and peasants of Ireland. The Irish question is linked with questions of agrarian revolution, with the peasant question. If, after they had dealt with the Chartists, the English ruling classes felt themselves victorious over the proletariat, the Irish national movement—which is linked with the agrarian movement—could significantly strengthen the position of the English proletariat.

Coming out in favor of federation with the aim of solving the national question, Marx and Engels opposed the federalism of followers of Proudhon and Bakunin, who considered that state power, after being first parcelled out upon the principle of federalism, could then easily be annihilated, and whose federalism flows immediately out of the petty bourgeois essence of their ideas. The Proudhon federation, at the basis of anarchic federation in general,[2] is a "free contract" whereby families, communes, groups of communes, and so on will be mutually obligated upon definite matters con-

[1] Marx and Engels (Russian ed.), Vol. XVI, Pt. 2, p. 110.
[2] Proudhon (1809–1865) voiced the interests of the petty artisans defended from big industry. The fundamental idea of his theory is "just barter": the purchaser is contrasted with the producer. Author of the phrase "property is thievery," he came out, not in fact against property, but in behalf of making the barter "just" (according to the labor expended) through banks and gratuitous credit which were to help workers to become owners and producers.

sequent upon barter.[3] Each side preserves its complete freedom of action. In such relationships there are more features of confederation than of federation.

Such contracts on confederation principles, according to Proudhon and his followers, must liquidate the class struggle, strikes, and conflicts in general between capitalists and workers. "Socialism" will thus, according to his theory, grow out of voluntary cooperative societies, under capitalism, whereas political struggle will seem superfluous and unnecessary. Proudhon was thus for the reconciliation of classes through the federative (confederative) principle. The same petty bourgeois basis upon which this theory with its federalism (confederalism) grew served as the ground for Bakunin's later theory of anarchism which veiled its petty bourgeois character under "revolutionary" phraseology.

Bakunin (1814–1876) advanced the idea of free federative unification of separate personalities in a commune as a counterpoise to the state. Furthermore, his followers—like all anarchists—had an extremely obscure idea of how exactly to replace the state. In the center of the anarchist theory is the "free personality" which must establish its relations toward society. Anarchists—in place of a state—advanced such unreal and nonsensical formulae as "free community life on the basis of mutual contracts." Individuals are united into communes, communes are federated into regions, regions into nations, and nations into United States of Europe and then of the whole world. Such was Bakunin's scheme of "the emancipation of personality" without any sort of state coercion and without annihilating classes.

Anarchists do not in words admit a national question of any sort, considering that it is related to the field of political struggle wherewith they are, in general, not occupied. In reality this "abstention from politics" is itself politics, proceeding, however, in the interests of the imperialist oppressors of the nation. Marx and Engels struggled keenly against this disdain of the national question.[4] Coming out against anarchist ignoring of the national question, they also came out at the same time against the imperialist centralism of the nationalist who, while seeking confirmation amongst the workers, subordinated worker class interests to bourgeois nationalist interests. Hence the struggle of Marx and Engels against Lassalle.[5]

Lassalle was a nationalist. As to the unification of Germany and the

---

[3] Marx and Engels (Russian ed.), Vol. XVI, Pt. 2, p. 110.

[4] Marx and Engels, Letters (1931), pp. 258–259.

[5] Lassalle (1825–1864) was an outstanding representative of the opportunist wing of the German labor movement of the nineteenth century. He tried—by agreement with the German government (Bismarck), and in fact at the price of betraying the revolutionary proletariat—to wrest at least some concessions, to the end of bettering the worker class position.

centralization of its government, he stood opposed to Marx and Engels, starting from bourgeois nationalist ideas rather than from problems of revolution. He subordinated the interests of other nations as well to "his" state —proclaimed by the Junkers and headed by Bismarck. He came out against the slogan of the right of nations to self-determination, against the democratic slogans developed by Marx and Engels. His proposed centralization was that Prussia forcibly subordinate to itself, not only all of Germany, but the neighboring countries as well. He was for war with Denmark so as to subordinate Schleswig-Holstein forcibly to Prussia. This he even made a matter of trade with Bismarck, promising Bismarck the aid of the workers in the war against Denmark in return for the introduction of universal suffrage. Marx and Engels were in favor of Poland's unqualified right to self-determination, not only in the interests of the Poles but also in the interests of European democracy as a whole, since the development of the latter was in the interests of the proletariat. But Lassalle was for unifying Russian and Prussian Poland within the limits of Prussia and under the latter's protectorate, so that he was in fact in favor of Prussia's absorption of Poland.

Lenin and Stalin developed the Marxist position on federation, having raised it to a great revolutionary height and introducing into it much that was new in the conditions of proletarian revolution. They established that national-territorial autonomy, resting on actual democratic centralism, must aid the equality of rights of nationalities, their unification and solidarity in correspondence with the class interest of the proletariat. Capitalism develops chauvinism, seeks to poison the toiling masses with it, to split their class unity, to evoke among them nationalist conflicts and quarrels. "Only in the realm of socialism can complete peace be established. But even within the framework of capitalism it is possible to reduce the national struggle to a minimum, to undermine it at the root, to make it supremely innocuous for the proletariat." [6] "For this, however, it is necessary to democratize the country and to make free development possible for the nations." [7] The struggle against nationalist oppression is therefore the struggle for democracy.

The sole means of rallying the toilers of all nationalities around their class tasks is the revolutionary formulation of the right of nations to self-determination, including withdrawal. Stalin, emphasizing the sovereignty and equality of rights of nations, wrote (in 1913) that "a nation can be organized according to its wish. It has the right to organize its life on the principles of autonomy—to enter into federative relationships with other nations." [8]

[6] Stalin, *Marxism, and the National-Colonial Question* (1937), p. 15.
[7] *Ibid.*, p. 14.
[8] *Ibid.*

The struggle for these rights of nations infallibly becomes a struggle against the imperialist states—the common enemy of the proletariat and of oppressed nations—promotes drawing the toilers of oppressed nationalities into the stream of the proletarian class struggle, and strengthens the alliance between the toilers of all nations.

As long ago as July, 1903, Lenin wrote:

We must always and unconditionally aspire to the *closest* alliance of the proletariat of all nationalities and only in particular and exceptional cases can we put forward and actively support demands inclining toward the creation of a new class state or toward replacing the complete political unity of the state by a weaker federative unity, and the like.[9]

The party was thus in principle against federation. Lenin regarded it as a "type unsuitable for a single state" [10] inasmuch as it weakened economic bonds, but at the same time Lenin admitted federation in separate exceptional cases.

Thus, starting from special and definitive conditions of history, Lenin put the matter of the Balkan Federation. In the Balkans, broad masses of the people were under a twofold yoke—the yoke of their own dominant classes of landowners and bourgeoisie and the yoke of foreign imperialists. Each of the rival imperialist groups sought support from the dominant classes of separate Balkan states (Serbia, Bulgaria, Montenegro, Greece, and Turkey), setting one nation on another and evoking national conflicts and wars. In October, 1912, Lenin wrote: "The actual *freedom* of the Slav peasantry in the Balkans—like that of the Turkish peasantry—can be guaranteed *only* by complete freedom within *each* country and a complete and final federation of democratic states." [11] In Russia the Bolsheviks defended the right of nations to self-determination, the right to separate and to form an independent state. For nations preferring to remain within the framework of a single multinational state, the Party put forward regional autonomy.

A new situation was created in 1917. The imperialist policy of the Provisional Government and its parties evoked the dissatisfaction of oppressed nationalities and contributed to the intensification of nationalist tendencies among them. Numerous "national Soviets"—proclaimed by the bourgeoisie as the proletarian struggle for authority became intense—used their influence upon the toilers to develop a policy of separation from the proletarian revolution and thereby to create a barrier between the proletarian center and the toilers of the borderlands.

[9] Lenin (Russian ed.), Vol. V, p. 337.
[10] *Ibid.*, Vol. XVII, p. 90.
[11] *Ibid.*, Vol. XVI, p. 161.

Here all the force of the Lenin-Stalin dialectic was expressed in formulating the question of federation. Still more decisively the Lenin-Stalin Party opposed its program slogan: "The right of nations to self-determination, including withdrawal," to the imperialist policy of the Provisional Government and its supporting parties. At the same time it summoned the toiling masses of all nationalities to join the Russian worker class in the struggle for peace, for land—a struggle which, under the guidance of the proletariat, drew the toilers of all nationalities into the channel of the socialist revolution.

The organizational side of the task confronting the proletariat—to unify the toilers of all nations—Lenin had in view in his *State and Revolution*. In an analysis of definitive historical conditions evoked by war and revolution, the Party—after October, 1917—put forward federation as a means of holding the masses of the nationalities in the camp of the proletarian revolution, as a way of strengthening the confidence between the toilers of all nationalities and of unifying their forces against common class enemies.

The common struggle brought together the toilers of all nations, creating mutual confidence between them, strengthening the consciousness that their revolutionary conquests could be defended only by close unification of forces. Federation was the expression and the guaranty of the voluntary character of the union of peoples in the conditions of proletarian dictatorship.

Lenin and Stalin effected the theoretical basic and practical organization of the new type of federation—the Soviet type, radically different from the bourgeois type of federation. Because it made real the slogan: "The right of nations to self-determination, including withdrawal," Soviet federation intensified the close voluntary bond between the toilers of all nationalities.

Two elements play a most important part in insuring the stability of the multinational state: (1) the economic bonds of separate national parts of the state and (2) national collaboration. These two elements, incompatible in the capitalist state, are democratically united in the Soviet federation.

Stalin has noted that the realization of the Soviet federation was conditioned by the following circumstances: (1) at the time of the October *coup d'état,* a whole series of nationalities appeared in reality completely separated and dissociated from each other, in view whereof federation seemed a step away from the dispersed condition of their toiling masses and a step forward toward those masses being brought together and unified; (2) the very forms of federation projected in the course of Soviet building seemed far less incompatible with the purposes of bringing the toiling masses of the nationalities together economically than might earlier have appeared

—indeed they seemed not at all incompatible with those purposes, as subsequent practice proved; and (3) the comparative strength of the nationalist movement seemed far more serious, and the way to uniting the nations far more complex, than it could earlier appear in the prewar period or in the period before the October Revolution.[12]

The building of the Soviet federation proceeded in conflict with hostile elements striving to pervert the essence and the meaning of Soviet federation.

Who should be the subject of the federation? Stalin came forward against proposals which, in their lowest terms, would create the federation upon the principle of geography.

This is not a matter of the geographical position of any regions or of the separation of parts from the center by expanses of water (as in Turkestan) or by a mountain range (as in Siberia) or by steppes (as in Turkestan). . . . Poland and the Ukraine are not separated from the center by a mountain range or by expanses of water. None the less no one would think of asserting that the absence of these geographical signs excludes the right of these regions to free self-government.[13]

Lenin and Stalin came out against a draft federation starting from the "left-SR circles," who proposed to create a federation of separate autonomous regions. These proposals were redolent of petty-bourgeois provincial rule and the theory of Proudhon. Thus the federation proposed by the "left" SR's said, among other things: "Upon the principles of federation the Soviets of cities and villages form a close fraternal Union of Soviets called a Socialist Federative Republic." Stalin emphasized that "not all sorts of parcels and units, not every sort of geographical territory should—and can—be the subject of the federation—only definite regions naturally uniting within themselves peculiar ways of life, unique national structure, and a certain integral minimum of economic territory." [14]

The Tenth Congress of the Party, taking account of the experience of organized national Soviet Republics and regions, noted that:

The Federation of Soviet Republics, based on military and economic community, is the general form of state union which makes feasible: (a) a guaranty of the integrity and economic development of separate republics as well as of the federation in its entirety; (b) the inclusion of all the diverse ways of life, cultures and economic conditions of the different nations and nationalities (being in different stages of development) and (in conformity therewith) the application of this or that species of federation; and (c) the advancement of the harmonious life

[12] Stalin, *On the Way to the October Revolution* (State Publishing House, 1925), pp. 21–22.
[13] *Izvestiya* (April 3, 1918), interview with Stalin.
[14] *Ibid.*

together and the fraternal collaboration of nations and nationalities that have in one way or another united their fate with that of the federation.[15]

Soviet federation is not dogma; its forms cannot be frozen and established once and for all but must evolve, changing to the extent required by the concrete environment. The new period of peaceful building, begun after the triumphant finish of the civil war, demanded still greater confirmation of the bond of all the Soviet Republics. This was evoked by conditions of capitalist encirclement, by the necessity of better utilizing—to advance their common purposes—all the resources historically distributed among the separate Soviet Republics, and finally by the very character of Soviet authority, international in its nature, striving to bring together the toilers of all nations for more successful attainment of purposes jointly planned—the building of socialism.

In this is the greatest world significance of the Soviet federation which, side by side with other factors, guaranteed the power and the might of the proletarian state and made it a model for all future proletarian revolutions.

Noting the significance of *Soviet* federation, Lenin, in his "Original Sketch of Theses on National and Colonial Questions," said:

Acknowledging the federation as a transitional form to complete unity, it is necessary to strive for ever closer federative union having in view: (1) the impossibility of defending the existence of Soviet Republics—encircled by imperialist powers of the entire world, of incomparably greater military might, without the closest union of Soviet Republics; (2) the necessity of close economic union of the Soviet Republics, without which it is not feasible to rehabilitate the production forces destroyed by imperialism and to guarantee the welfare of the toilers; and (3) the tendency to create a single universal economy as an entirety, regulated according to general plan by the proletariat of all nations—a tendency perfectly clearly manifested already under capitalism and unconditionally subject to further development and complete culmination under socialism.[16]

These teachings of Lenin in 1920 served later as the basis for organizing the USSR. The development of Soviet federation occurred during violent conflict with the remnants both of imperialist chauvinism and of local nationalism, intensified in connection with the New Economic Policy. The imperialist chauvinism was overcome by destruction of all the privileges of the former sovereign nation, by the struggle for the factual equalization of nationalities. Guided by Stalin, the Party struggled against overestimating national special characteristics and underestimating proletarian class inter-

[15] *The All-Union Communist Party (of Bolsheviks) in Resolutions* (Party Publishing House, 1936), Pt. 1, p. 393.
[16] Lenin (Russian ed.), Vol. XXV, p. 287.

ests—which could only hamper the uniting of the proletariat and all the toilers of the various nationalities. It rejected and overcame the nationalist importunities of the Georgian nationalists, later disclosed as enemies of the people, having already, at that time, termed their coming forward and demanding a privileged position for Georgia a hostile, nationalist sortie.

Defending the creation of a single Union Soviet state, Stalin came out also against the Ukraine project defended by nationalists and Trotskyists, directed at construing the USSR as a union of separate republics, a confederation, rather than as a single union state. True, the nationalists and Trotskyists did not dare to come out openly against a unity for which there was so strong a mass movement.

The Ukrainian bourgeois nationalists and Trotskyists perverted the meaning of the Contract and the Declaration accepted at the First Congress of Soviets of the USSR. In their own "draft" of a Constitution of the USSR, they repeated the introductory part of the Contract Concerning the Formation of the USSR, but the words: "They conclude the present contract concerning unification into a single union state," they replaced by the words: "They conclude the present contract concerning the formation of a Union of Soviet Socialist Republics." Thus the words about "unification into a single union state" were apparently thrown out, the essence of the USSR as a single state thereby emasculated, and it was given the character of a union of states, of a form approximating a confederation. From that it followed also that in their counterrevolutionary draft the Ukrainian nationalists and Trotskyists proposed to leave the directive (and not to merge) the most important organs whereby the USSR maintains relations with the outside world—the People's Commissariat for Foreign Affairs and the People's Commissariat for Foreign Trade. This emphasized still further the character of the draft of nationalists and Trotskyists as a confederation. Hence their proposal concerning the creation of a special Presidium for each chamber of the Central Executive Committee of the USSR. In their draft, they threw out the words about the Presidium of the Central Executive Committee as bearing supreme authority in the intervals between the sessions, having divided authority between the Presidia of the two chambers.

The Soviet federation rejected all nationalistic "theories" to the effect that the freedom and independence of nations can be acquired only by isolating them, and proved all the advantages of a big socialist state which in no wise whatever contradicts the Soviet national statehood personified by the Union and autonomous Soviet Socialist Republics. "In the Soviet social order the proletariat found the key to the correct solution of the national question. It opened therein the road to the organization of a stable multinational state on the principles of national equality of rights and free will." [17]

The essence of Soviet federation consists in the peoples' being rallied in a single state union on the basis of common interests of socialist social reorganization, and the spontaneity and equality of the constituent parties. Herein is the fundamental distinction between the Soviet state (as a federation of national republics) and the bourgeois multinational state (under which such federation is impossible by reason of the essentially oppressive character of the state and its nationalist-bureaucratic structure.)

There, in the West, in the world of bourgeois democracy, we are concerned with the gradual dissolution and decline of multinational states into their constituent parts (like Great Britain—as to which I do not know how it will arrange its affair with India, Egypt, and Ireland; or like Poland—as to which again I do not know how it will arrange matters with its White Russians, Ukrainians, Germans and Jews). But here in our federation—which unites no fewer than thirty nationalities—we, on the contrary, are concerned with the process of strengthening state bonds between independent republics—a process leading to ever closer approximation of independent nationalities into one independent state! Here are your two types of state unions, of which the first—or capitalist type—leads to the collapse of the constituent parts of the state, while the second—the Soviet type—leads on the contrary to gradual but stable approximation of formerly independent nationalities into one independent state.[18]

Such are the bases of the Marxist-Leninist doctrine as to federation—the key to the unification of peoples and organization of the unity of all toiling humanity on a socialist basis.

SEC. 4: THE PRINCIPLES OF BUILDING THE SOVIET UNION STATE

"The Union of Soviet Socialist Republics is a union state formed on the basis of the voluntary unification of Soviet Socialist Republics having equal rights. . . ." This definition in Article 13 of the Stalin Constitution stresses three characteristic features of the USSR: (1) it is a *union* state (2) formed on the basis of *voluntary* unification (3) of Soviet Socialist Republics *having equal rights*.

This defines the political form of the state organization of the USSR.

The Union State. The Soviet Union State is a federative state. Both by its class essence and by its organizational structure it is sharply distinguished

[17] *The All-Union Communist Party (of Bolsheviks) in Resolutions*, Pt. 1, p. 503.
[18] Stalin, *Marxism, and the National-Colonial Question*, p. 93.

from all existing forms of federation, confederation, and unitarism formerly or now existing in the capitalist world. It is a type of state without a precedent in history. It emerged from the problems of the worker class dictatorship in a multinational country. It is the realization and expression of the general will and mutual confidence of the toilers of nations with equal rights.

The nationality principle at the basis of the creation of the Soviet Union State is the distinctive characteristic of the Soviet type of federation. The toilers of each nation of the USSR are independent in deciding upon the national forms of their participation in the general socialist building. Soviet national statehood is the national form of the worker class dictatorship. For each nation, resting on the help of that dictatorship, it became—and continues to be—genuinely possible to raise its economy, to develop its culture, national in form and socialist in content, and to put it to the service of socialist building. In each national-state unification, the state mechanism (the organs of authority, the court, the administration, the organs of economy) is "radicated"—it consists of representatives of local "root" nationalities thoroughly acquainted with the language, manner of life, psychology, and needs of the local population.

Each national state unification was an instrument to raise the economy and develop the national culture (national school, press, clubs, and other forms of enlightened work), and to draw the broadest masses into the administration of the Soviet state and into the building up of socialism.

Soviet authority had first of all to become understood by them before it could become their own. Hence it is necessary that all Soviet organs in the borderlands —court, administration, organs of economy, organs of immediate authority (and of the Party)—consist so far as possible of local people knowing the way of life, the *mores*, the customs and the language of the local population, that into these institutions be attracted all the best persons from the indigenous masses of the people, that the local toiling masses be drawn into all fields of government of the land—including also the field of military formations—and that the masses see that Soviet authority and its organs are a matter of their own exertions and personify their desires.[1]

The eradication of the state mechanism is a constituent part of Soviet socialist democracy and, at the same time, one of the conditions of constant democratic control of that mechanism by the masses.

The union form of the USSR state organization is a political organization of peoples united on the basis of the socialist social organization inscribed in Chapter I of the Stalin Constitution, with the purpose of further developing this social organization and strengthening its defense in con-

---

[1] Stalin, *Marxism, and the National-Colonial Question,* p. 62.

ditions of capitalist encirclement. Thereby is its content distinguished from
the content and essence of all bourgeois union states. Their constitutions
speak only of external forms of union statehood. They establish jurisdictional boundaries of organs of authority—the administrative-territorial division of the state—but they emasculate the class content and essence of the
state and shade out the class and national contradictions of social organization.[2]

The Soviet Union State is built on principles of democratic centralism
sharply opposed to the bureaucratic centralism of the capitalist states. It
takes maximum account of the singularity and the demands of separate parts
of the state, it strives to unify these parts by a common conscious will, by
common interests and tasks. It not only does not exclude local self-help, on
the contrary, it assumes it, making it broadly possible for rural areas to
utilize the most suitable means (comprehensible to the population) and
ways to realize general problems. Finally it eliminates contradictions between separate parts of the state, including those between different national
districts.

Thus democratic centralism makes real that which the bureaucratic
centralized capitalist state—pursuing the opposite course of sharpening contradictions between city and country, between different regions, and between
nations—could never make real. Employed to crush the weak nations (forcibly included within the boundaries of separate states), bureaucratic centralism intensifies chauvinism and nationalism, and renders international
collaboration and worker class solidarity difficult.

Democratic centralism presupposes centralism in basic questions: in
general guidance, in the maximum unification of all economic activity according to one state-wide plan, in guiding production to the end of rational
and economic utilization of all the country's material resources. Far from
excluding, it presupposes local independence, upon condition of developing
the creative self-reliance and initiative of the local population (with its
differing languages, ways of life, and economic relationships) for the best
possible fulfillment of general plans of economic and cultural building.

Democratic and socialist centralism has nothing in common either with the
setting of a pattern or with the establishment of uniformity from above. Unity in
the basic, the radical and the essential is not destroyed. It is rather guaranteed by
multiformity in details, in local special characteristics, in methods of *approaching*
the matter, and in the *means* of realizing control.[3]

[2] Obscuring the exploiter character of the state, the Constitution of the U.S.A. (1787)
points out that it is published "to form a more perfect Union, establish justice, insure
domestic tranquillity, provide for the common defence, promote the general welfare, and
secure the blessings of liberty to ourselves and our posterity. . . ."
[3] Lenin (Russian ed.), Vol. XXII, p. 166.

Far from excluding local self-government and the *autonomy* of regions distinguished by peculiar economic and life conditions and peculiar national structure of population, democratic centralism necessarily requires *both the one and the other*.[4]

It affords national districts the broadest possibilities of utilizing the means and methods most suitable and intelligible to the population to realize the purposes confronting the districts themselves and the state as a whole. At the same time it presupposes that all organs of authority are necessarily elected and broadly accountable to their electors and that subordinate organs are obligated to execute the decisions of those above them.

Soviet federation, built on principles of democratic centralism, permitted all the diversity of ways of life, culture, and economic condition of various peoples in different stages of development to be embraced. Its distinguishing feature is the elasticity of its forms as applied (*a*) to concrete problems of the socialist state in raising the economic-cultural level of each people separately, and (*b*) to the conditions of the class struggle at each separate historical stage. The forms of federative bonds existing in bourgeois federations are alien to it.

Soviet Republics became the basis of state and national regeneration of the nationalities in forms most intelligible and suitable to each separate nation. As early as 1921, before the formation of the USSR, Stalin noted the distinction of these forms of federation:

> Russia's experience with the application of various species of federation, with the transition from federation based on Soviet autonomy (Kirghiz, Bashkiria, Tatar, Gortsy, and Dagestan) to federation based on contract relations with independent Soviet Republics (Ukraine, Azerbaijan) and with the admission of interstitial stages between them (Turkestan, White Russia)—entirely confirmed the complete expediency and elasticity of federation, as the general form of the state Union of Soviet Republics.[5]

Federation based on contract relations between independent Soviet Republics was a stage on the road to federation based on their unification into a single union state. While still in the course of its building in the period of civil war, Soviet federation confirmed all the political, economic, strategic and other advantages and preferences of a big Soviet state for the toilers of the Soviet Republics unified thereby. This was emphasized with special importance in conditions of capitalist encirclement.

Russia, as Stalin said in 1920, represents a boundless, vast country in whose territory it is possible to hold out for a long time, retreating—in case of failure—into the depth of the land, so as to muster forces and again go over to the offen-

[4] *Ibid.*, Vol. XVII, p. 155.
[5] Stalin, *Marxism, and the National-Colonial Question*, p. 69.

sive. Were Russia a tiny country like Hungary, where a powerful attack by the adversary quickly decides the country's fate, where it is difficult to maneuver and there is no scope for retreat, Russia could, as a socialist country, scarcely hold out for a long time. Then there is still another condition, likewise of a constant character, contributing to the development of socialist Russia: Russia represents one of a few countries in the world having within itself an abundance of all species of fuel, raw materials and supplies; a country independent of, and able to get along without, foreign countries with reference to fuel, supplies and so on. No doubt if Russia lived by foreign grain and fuel—like Italy, for example —she would have fallen into a critical condition on the day following the revolution, since merely to blockade her would suffice for her to be left without bread and without fuel. As it was, the blockade of Russia undertaken by the Entente struck at the interests, not of Russia alone, but of the Entente itself, since the latter was deprived of Russia's raw materials.[6]

The legal form of Soviet federation, created after the organization of the USSR, reduces basically to the following: the USSR is a *voluntary* unification of Union Republics having equal rights, in which separate republics (such as RSFSR, the Ukrainian SSR, and others) comprise in their turn autonomous republics, autonomous regions and national districts. "By the Declaration and the Contract Concerning the Formation of the USSR" (December 30, 1922), the Union Republics acknowledged the necessity of creating a single central Union authority to which—having contracted among themselves—they handed over a number of their rights and functions concerning the most important matters of defense, foreign relations and economics, voluntarily limiting themselves in aid of the Union authority. The contract was thereafter confirmed by a basic law (the Constitution) binding upon all constituent parts (Union Republics) of the Soviet Union State. Upon the basis of the USSR Constitution, laws of Union authority, in accord with the rights and jurisdiction appropriated to it, are binding upon all the Union Republics. The Union Constitution defines the jurisdiction of Union authority and that of the authority of the Union Republics. State unity was confirmed also by a single Union citizenship.

Union Republics have their own constitutions which they have the right to change independently. They publish statutes which are of binding force within the territory of the given Union Republic. These sovereign rights of Union Republics are confirmed by the further right of a Union Republic to unilateral withdrawal from the Union, written into both the USSR Constitution and the constitutions of the Union Republics, and further confirmed by the fact that the territory of a Union Republic cannot be changed without its consent. Constitutions of Union Republics, like all

[6] Stalin, *The October Revolution* (Party Publishing House, 1932), p. 22.

their legislation, must conform with the USSR Constitution and with Union legislation.

The voluntariness of the union of peoples in the Soviet Union State flows from principles of Soviet authority, from the Lenin-Stalin national policy, from the active, voluntary aspiration of toilers for unification into one Soviet Union State. "We wish a *voluntary* union of nations—such union as would be based on the most complete confidence, on clear consciousness of fraternal unity, on completely voluntary accord." [7] "No union of peoples—no unification of peoples into a single state—can be firm unless it is completely voluntary at its foundation, if a given people—if the peoples themselves—wish not to be united." [8] This sharply distinguishes the Soviet Union State from all the bourgeois union states.

The voluntary character of the Soviet federation is distinctly and clearly expressed in the Declaration of Rights of the Toiling and Exploited People which proclaims that

the Soviet Russian Republic is instituted upon the basis of a free union of free nations, as a Federation of Soviet National Republics. The Third Congress of Soviets is limited to the establishment of the root principles of the Federation of the Soviet Republics of Russia, leaving it to the workers and peasants of each nation to make a decision independently in their own plenipotentiary Soviet Congress as to whether or not they wish to participate in the federal administration and in the remaining federal Soviet institutions—and if so upon what bases.[9]

Bourgeois union states, emerging at first as a unified alliance of little states, in the process of their further development maintained state "unity" over the members of the union by force. In an interview with a correspondent of *Izvestiya* (in April, 1918) concerning the matter of organizing the RSFSR, Stalin, characterizing bourgeois federation (union states), noted that their process of development "passed successively through violence, oppression, and national wars." [10]

Thus in the U.S.A. in the 1860's, the leading reactionary cliques of the Southern states, in consequence of economic dissensions with the Northern states as to freedom of trade, formulated the matter of their withdrawal from the Union—a question decided by arms in the Civil War by the victory of the North over the South; that is, by military violence. One of the greatest commentators on the American Constitution, James Bryce, wrote:

The victory won by the North will discourage like attempts in the future. This is so strongly felt that it has not even been thought worthwhile to add to

[7] Lenin (Russian ed.), Vol. XXIV, p. 657.
[8] Stalin, *Marxism and the National-Colonial Question*, p. 114.
[9] Cy. 1918, No. 15, Art. 215.
[10] *Izvestiya*, No. 64, April 3, 1918.

the Constitution an amendment negativing the right to secede. The doctrine of
the legal indestructibility of the Union is now well established. To establish it,
however, cost thousands of millions of dollars and the lives of a million of men.[11]

But even before the Civil War, the territory of the union state (the
United States of America) was extended not at all by reason of the voluntary wish of the population of the territories that were added, but by way
of trade agreements and wars. In 1803 the United States *bought* Louisiana
from France. In 1819 the United States *bought* Florida from Spain. In
1845 it finally annexed Texas as a result of *war* with Mexico.

Another example is the creation of the Swiss Union State. In 1847 the
union of seven cantons—the so-called Sonderbund (Wallis, Luzerne, Uri,
Unterwalden, Freiburg, Zug, and Schwytz)—under the influence of reactionary clerical Catholic circles raised the question of separation from the
remaining cantons. Undoubtedly this contradicted the interests of the
capitalist development of Switzerland, whose industrial bourgeoisie aspired
to centralize the national market and the state; and the question was decided here also by war, by violence, by the military defeat of the Sonderbund in that year (1847).

In precisely the same way the North German Union was created in
1867 through the war between Prussia and Austria, as a result of Austria's
defeat. Thereafter Austria was knocked out of the union of German states
by Bismarck and obligated not to obstruct the creation of the North German Union under the hegemony of Prussia.

Thus it is not seemly to talk of the "voluntariness" of the union in bourgeois union states.

The voluntariness of the USSR was emphasized in the Stalin Constitution by the provision that "in behalf of each Union Republic is preserved
the right of free withdrawal from the USSR" (Article 17). The significance
of this article was pointed out in Stalin's report to the Extraordinary Eighth
All-Union Congress of Soviets: "To exclude from the Constitution the
article concerning the right of free withdrawal from the USSR would be
to violate the voluntary character thereof." [12]

Precisely because the Union is of this voluntary character, the Union
Republics have strengthened their mutual bond ever more closely. This is
explained also by the fact that the peoples of each of the sovereign Union
Republics really feel and are conscious of the very great advantages of the
Union which has made it possible for them to pass the stage of a national
economic and cultural regeneration unprecedented in history and has guaranteed the conditions of their further forward movement.

[11] James Bryce, *The American Commonwealth*, Vol. I, pp. 378, 379.
[12] Stalin, *Report on the Draft of the Constitution of the USSR*, p. 36.

The *equality of rights* of Union Soviet Socialist Republics flows immediately out of that of the nations which they unify. "Equality of nationalities and of states!" This was the watchword frequently put forward by reformists and seized upon by bourgeois nationalists. Everyone knows, however, that under imperialism there can be no talk of any sort of equality of rights of nations and states. The utopia of a "peaceful union of nations having equal rights" is often confirmed by representatives of imperialism, upon condition of veiling the serfdom of weak nations by the dominant classes of powerful nations. The same interest is served also by various international nonstate institutions (international tribunals and so on) organized on the basis of modern bourgeois international law. The capitalist world is sharply divided into oppressor nations and oppressed nations. Only the great October Socialist Revolution proclaimed "the equality and sovereignty of the peoples of Russia" and made these principles real indeed.

Soviet authority, starting from these same principles, denounced all the unequal international contracts fastened by the former tsarist government upon other nations (Iran, Turkey, and China), and concluded with them new contracts on principles of equal right and friendship. Legal equality was the great conquest of the victorious worker class and the toilers of the formerly oppressed nations united around it. Legal equality lay at the basis of the USSR—all the Union Republics which have entered the USSR, irrespective of the size of their territory and the numbers of their population, possess equal rights. All enjoy the blessings of the Union in like measure and all alike renounce in its favor certain rights to advance their own interests as well as those of the Union as a whole.

Legal equality is further confirmed by the participation of all nations in creating the Soviet of Nationalities—the second chamber of the highest organ of authority—the Supreme Soviet of the USSR. Every statute accepted by the Soviet of the Union requires confirmation also by the Soviet of Nationalities. This emphasizes the necessity that statutes, as the expression of the will of the entire Soviet people, be responsive to the special interests of nationalities as well as to the general interests of the toilers. Through the Soviet of Nationalities, and likewise through their deputies in the Soviet of the Union, the peoples of the USSR participate likewise in creating the Presidium of the Supreme Soviet of the USSR, in which there are eleven vice-presidents—the number of Union Republics. They participate in forming the Government of the USSR, in elections to the Supreme Court of the USSR, in designating the Public Prosecutor of the USSR, and the like.

Legal equality is guaranteed to the nations and the nationalities of the USSR in all spheres of social-political life. But, as Stalin noted as early as the Twelfth Party Congress: "We have proclaimed and are developing legal equality, but, all the same, from legal equality—which has in itself the greatest significance in the history of the development of Soviet Republics—it is a very great distance to equality in fact." [13] The introduction of the element of factual equality side by side with legal equality into the national question sharply distinguishes the Bolshevik formulation of the national question from all formulations thereof by reformists.

What is factual equality? It is not only political equality but economic and cultural equality as well. National equality would be incomplete if the Party and Soviet authority did not strive to give a stable economic and cultural basis to political equality. In this regard the national question is solved in the USSR by analogy to that of women—merely to proclaim that women have rights equal with the rights of men would be inadequate; a woman must further be armed economically and culturally, so that she can in fact take advantage of the equality given to her.

As to the national question, the problem is to raise the economic and cultural level of numerous peoples who by reason of national oppression experienced in the past are in a backward condition. Bourgeois ideologists strive to perpetuate this backwardness by "theories" of a supposedly inevitable difference between "civilized" and "uncivilized" nations. Reactionary bourgeois, particularly fascist, ideologists strive also to devise "qualitative" differences between nations. Thus German fascists spread a "theory" of "higher" and "lower" races to justify their bandit policy and their aggression against other peoples. The so-called "uncivilized" character of backward nations is conditioned by definitive, historical causes, and particularly by national-colonial imperialist pressure artificially retarding the economic and cultural development of backward peoples. The logical putting into practice of the Lenin-Stalin national policy proved that in the conditions of the worker class dictatorship are found all the conditions precedent to the equalization of backward with advanced nations.

In the USSR the backwardness of peoples formerly oppressed is shaken off with the aid of the worker class of the advanced districts, aid economically guaranteed by the planned organization of the socialist economy. Direction of a single centralized economy by the Soviet Union State, personified by its higher organs of authority and administration, makes feasible the conduct of planned work to raise formerly backward peoples economically and culturally. This helped to make it possible for nations formerly in precapitalist conditions and now sustained by the worker class dictatorship to avoid the capitalist stage of development and to embark upon the road of socialist development.

[13] Stalin, *Marxism, and the National-Colonial Question*, p. 117.

The struggle for factual equality—already signalized by the greatest victories in the history of the universe—is at the same time a protracted struggle where the Party and Soviet authority exert all their energy to complete it in the shortest possible time, inasmuch as backwardness is a serious obstacle to further and swifter progress of all peoples along the road to communism.

The development of each nation is based on the stable material foundation put under it by socialist economy. The national republics (Uzbekistan, Kazakhstan, and others), formerly merely colonial, raw-material appendages of the industry of the central regions, are now industrial-agrarian republics. Labor in their agriculture—on the basis of kolkhozes and sovkhozes, equipped with new technique—becomes ever more and more a variety of industrial labor. New cities are built and old cities, formerly the bulwark of colonial oppression, are reconstructed. New qualified cadres of workers from the indigenous nationalities grow up. On the basis of successes attained, the welfare of each Soviet people and of the USSR in its entirety grows and develops.

At this moment, all the peoples of our boundless country are flourishing and are experiencing regeneration unprecedented and impossible in their previous history. On the basis of the new socialist economy they mutually enrich each other with new cultural experience. Swiftly, national cultures —national in form and socialist in content—grow and develop.[14] The toiler of each nation of the eleven Union Republics—in the city, in the hamlet, in the mountains, in the steppe, in the Caucasian village—is proudly conscious that he is a citizen (on the basis of equal rights) of the great socialist Union State which has guaranteed the growth of individual and national freedom, exchanged stagnation for progress, and shattered the fetters of ignorance.

The greatest expression of this union of peoples is the Stalin Constitution.

SEC. 5: FORMS OF BOURGEOIS STATE ORGANIZATION

1. Bourgeois federation

In his criticism of the Erfurt program of 1891, Engels wrote:

Two points distinguish the Union State from the completely unitary state: (1) each separate state entering into the Union—each canton—has its own civil and criminal law, its own legal procedure; (2) side by side with the popular cham-

---

[14] Figures showing this growth may be found in the statistical collection, *Twenty Years of Soviet Authority* (1937), pp. 95–106.

ber is the chamber of representatives from states, in which each canton—be it
large or small—votes as such. The first point we have fortunately overcome and
shall not be so childish as to introduce it again; but the second is present in the
shape of the Union Council, without which we can get along excellently, and in
general our "Union State" is already a transition to the unitary state.[1]

The aspiration to unify the judicial system and civil and criminal legislation finds expression in all bourgeois federations. This flows out of the
centralizing policy of the bourgeoisie, which starts from requirements of a
centralized market and from problems of confirming its political and class
dominance.

In almost all federations representative organs are built on the bicameral
system. Irrespective of their size, separate territorial parts of the federation
(states or cantons) enjoy formal "equality of rights"—ordinarily with the
further conceded right to participate upon equal principles in the composition of the so-called "second chamber." In the U. S. A. the Congress consists of a House of Representatives made up on the principle of representation from the states on the basis of population, and a Senate consisting of
two senators from each state. The ideologists who drafted the Constitution
of the United States of America (Hamilton, Madison, and so on) considered the equality of state votes in the Senate a recognition of the share of
sovereignty still remaining in the states, and furthermore—and this is most
important—the Senate, built on less democratic principles than the House,
will restrain the latter from being carried away by all sorts of "enthusiasms."

Following the foregoing example, representative organs were created
in Switzerland where the Union Assembly is made up of a National Council "whose representatives are chosen on the basis of population (one for
every 22,000), and a Council of States (with two representatives from
each canton).   Such "equality" of states is in fact illusory. Capitalism develops contradictions between separate districts (between industrial and
agricultural and the like), and leads to economic exploitation of some districts (states or cantons) by others. In fact, the elective machinations of
bourgeois parties of monopolist capital, extending their activity and influence into many states—often into the whole country—reduce the formal
"equality" of states to naught.

Bourgeois federation may be a democratic republic (as in Switzerland
and the U.S.A.) in which the citizen—on the basis of existing rights of
suffrage—is supposed to "direct" the policy of his state, canton, and federation in its entirety.

A federation may be semiparliamentary where the republican form veils
a significant mass of feudal survivals; such are the federative republics of

[1] Marx and Engels, Vol. XVI, p. 110.

Latin America (Argentina, Brazil, Chile, and so on). In these the dictatorship of creatures of foreign (chiefly Anglo-American) finance capital and of big local landowners is developed by crude antidemocratic methods and is based on class and race exploitation—on feudal colonization.

A federation may be also monarchic, representing a union of bourgeois landowner classes with semifeudal dynasties against the worker class and the toilers. Such was Germany prior to the 1918 Revolution. Whatever the forms of bourgeois federation, a state based on its principles is merely an instrument of the exploiter classes.

Separate union constitutions provide a definite political form of unified parts of a union state. Thus the constitutions of the U.S.A. (Art. IV, Sec. 4), Weimar (Art. 17) and Switzerland (Art. 6) provide a republican form for governing parts of the federation. In the old German Constitution of 1871, the union state was based on a contract of the monarchs for "eternal union." In addition, however, separate parts of the union (such as Hamburg or Bremen, which were free Hanseatic cities) were republics within the limits of a monarchical union state. The dominance of capitalism tolerates both political forms.

In all republican federations—for example, the U.S.A.—there is a single head of the state, a president of the republic, who is distinguished from a constitutional monarch only in that he is chosen for a definite term, whereas the office of the monarch is limitless and hereditary.

Some federal constitutions have detailed reservations as to the jurisdiction of union power. Thus in the Constitution of the U.S.A. (Art. 1, Sec. 8) the union power has jurisdiction over taxes and loans, money, courts subordinate to the Supreme Court, army and fleet, declaration of war, and so on. The tenth amendment (1791) declares: "The powers not delegated to the United States by the Constitution, nor prohibited by it to the States, are reserved to the States respectively, or to the people."

Other federal constitutions contain detailed reservations as to the jurisdiction of parts of the federation. Thus the Canadian Constitution (Art. 92) establishes in detail the jurisdiction of the provinces which, under Article 91, must not go beyond the boundaries of Article 92.

A third type of federal constitution, signifying a further transition to unitarism, gives the central authority the right in case of necessity to appropriate to itself separate spheres of the jurisdiction of the separate parts. Such was the Weimar Constitution (Arts. 10–13).

In general the union authority in all independent union states has jurisdiction over relations with other states, the army, war, and peace, over legislation (binding on all parts of the union state) and, in particular, matters of war, finance, foreign trade, customs, and so on.

Since the end of the nineteenth century the general tendency of the development of union states shows an extraordinary broadening of the jurisdiction of central organs of union authority at the expense of the parts of the union. As the interests of capitalists of separate states or cantons in the national market became more and more interwoven, and they aspired to win foreign markets—and conversely to fence off the national market from being conquered (albeit by "peaceful" means) by capitalists of foreign countries—and as the proletariat grew in numbers and its class struggle intensified, there was ever increasing centralization of the most important state functions in the hands of union authority at the expense of territorial authority, with the result that the differences between the bourgeois federative state and the bourgeois unitary state were in fact effaced. In an interview in April, 1918, with a correspondent of *Izvestiya*, Stalin noted that: "Of all the existing federative unions, the American and the Swiss federations are most typical of the bourgeois-democratic order. Historically they were formed out of independent states—through confederation to federation—and furthermore they became in fact unitary states, preserving merely the forms of federalism."[2] This is completely confirmed by the historical development of bourgeois union states.

The tempestuous expansion of capitalism during the entire nineteenth century led to ever greater unification and centralization of economy, but at the same time to ever increasing centralization of state administration. Under the influence of capitalism, cities continued to grow at the expense of the village, big industry at the expense of little industry, big banking associations at the expense of separate and scattered banks. The state mechanism became the direct instrument of separate cliques of the monopolist capital, which developed at the end of the nineteenth century and put their own people at the head of the state and its local organs. By coalescence of the central and local state mechanism with capitalist monopolies, the latter define the activity of the entire state. The monopolist stage of capitalism extraordinarily increased the might of the state itself as an instrument of class constraint and of repression of the proletariat and the oppressed nations, uniting this might with corruption and deceit. With the cooperation of the state, monopolist capital ever more strongly and cruelly seizes all the territory of the state, breaks down every sort of local obstacle, and develops its policy of centralization.

Bourgeois centralization is bureaucratic centralization which takes into account neither local peculiarities nor the interests of separate nations within the boundaries of the state. All reciprocal relationships of the center and rural areas are subordinated to the interests of monopolist capital. Under

[2] *Izvestiya*, No. 64, April 3, 1918.

imperialism the attitude toward local—especially national—peculiarities became ever increasingly disdainful.

In the U.S.A. formal federation conceals a plutocratic centralization; finance capital is essentially centralist. States have long since passed out of the stage of self-sufficient economic districts. Big trusts extend their influence into a number of states and define the policy of state governments. The power of big bourgeois parties, expressing the interests of separate cliques of big finance and industrial capital, dominates the states and centralizes them, putting bureaucrats in them from top to bottom. Party "bosses" (the real masters of the bourgeois parties) manage the filling of jobs in each state and bring to naught its "sovereignty" and "autonomy." They also guide the elective "kitchen" which by thousands of machinations and tricks eliminates broad masses of the people from voting. The system of corruption in elections, the venality of the capitalist press, the "clarifications" and interpretations of the Constitution by the Supreme Court—all these taken together make illusory every sort of autonomy of the states and "will of the people" as personified by the parliaments of the states.

Lenin emphasizes that "nowhere is the power of capital—the power of a handful of billionaires—over all society manifested so crudely and with such open corruption as in America."[3]

The so-called "sovereignty" of the states is limited also by "interpretations" of the Constitution by the Supreme Court. There has been little fundamental change in the Constitution of the U.S.A. since its framing in 1787, hence its development is characterized by Supreme Court "interpretations" always adapted to the interests of American capital. But from the viewpoint of the Constitution, the Supreme Court decides controversies between federal power and the states, between the states themselves, and so forth, in form merely "equalizing"—on the basis of the "separation of powers"—legislative and executive authority, but in fact having the power to declare unconstitutional any statute or any directive of the executive authority. At the same time, it has never raised the question of the unconstitutionality of such reactionary chauvinist directives as those of Southern states in regard to negroes or of measures limiting their voting rights.

Bourgeois union states were historically created on the principle of unifying administrative-territorial provinces, not nations. Thus the United States Constitution was adopted after the victorious struggle for national freedom by the bourgeoisie of the former North American colonies against England. But after winning this struggle that bourgeoisie preserved national oppression—slavery. Engels wrote: "The American Constitution—the first which acknowledged the rights of man—also asserted at the same time the existence

[3] Lenin (Russian ed.), Vol. XXIV, p. 375.

of slavery of the colored races there: class privileges were abolished—race privileges sanctified." [4] Slave trade was confirmed in the Constitution and slavery was preserved for more than six decades after the Constitution was adopted.

During the Civil War (1861–1865) the abolition of negro slavery was proclaimed. In 1870 the fifteenth amendment to the Constitution was adopted as follows: "The right of the citizens of the United States to vote shall not be denied or abridged by the United States or by any State on account of race, color, or previous condition of servitude." [5] In fact, the burden of nationality has not even at the present time been removed from negroes (of whom there are thirteen millions—more than 10 per cent of the population of the U.S.A.). From 1890 on, constitutions of separate states, especially of the South, have included a succession of amendments striking at civil rights of the "colored" population (chiefly negro). [6]

From 1881 to 1907 Southern states published a succession of other laws and directives to the effect that persons of African origin (negroes) must in railroad cars and trams occupy places especially partitioned off. In twenty-nine of the forty-eight states, marriages between white and "colored" persons are forbidden. Negroes are often outside the law; extra-judicial executions (lynch law) are perpetrated upon them. In April, 1937, the (national) House of Representatives passed an antilynching bill. In February, 1938, it was considered in the Senate, but by reason of *obstruction* by the Southern *senators* it was removed altogether from further consideration. One of the obstructionist Southern senators—Ellender—argued against the bill because "to give negroes equal social rights would mean the bankruptcy of American civilization."

The development of federation in Switzerland is likewise characteristic. Finance capital has embraced all branches of the Swiss national economy. It plants its creatures in the organs of Swiss central and cantonal government, thereby in fact centralizing the country under its control. It devotes special attention to the central organs of authority. Legislative functions of federal government were increased many times at the expense of those of the cantons which are now in fact ordinary administrative regions.

From the time of the last serious revision of the Constitution (1874) to the end of 1935 there were in Switzerland thirty-six partial modifications of the Constitution. Most of them aimed at intensifying the jurisdiction of union authority at the expense of the cantons. Such centralization—bringing the Swiss federation near to the unitary form of state and accompanied by the

[4] Marx and Engels (Russian ed.), Vol. XIV, p. 106.
[5] See U. S. Constitution, Section IX, Par. 1.
[6] Cf. Mississippi (1896), South Carolina (1895), Louisiana (1898), North Carolina (1900), Alabama (1901), Virginia (1901), Georgia (1908), Oklahoma (1910).

interweaving of interests of representatives of authority with those of capitalist monopolies—makes it easier for the bourgeoisie to utilize the state apparatus for the development of its policy.

As long ago as the time of the World War, Lenin emphasized that "the bourgeois government" of Switzerland—thanks to the numerous ties of Swiss banking capital—is not only a "bourgeois government" but an "*imperialist* bourgeois government." [7] In form Switzerland is still called a "confederation," but in fact it has long since been passing along the path from a union (federative) state to a unitary state. The factual power of cliques of monopolisitic capital has imposed a reactionary stamp upon the policy of the Swiss Government, which explains the still hostile position of the Swiss Government toward the USSR (with which it does not maintain ordinary diplomatic relations). It even protects all sorts of white bandits who organized an attempt on representatives of the USSR (Vorovsky and others).

The tendency of a federation to develop toward unitarism has found especially graphic expression in Germany. Under the Constitution of 1871, Germany became a federation of German states under the hegemony of Prussia. The Weimar Constitution of 1919 was a great step forward on the road to unitarism. Articles 6 and 7 established the jurisdiction of the imperial authority, while Articles 8–11 added that in case of need the empire could relate to its own jurisdiction a succession of legislative rights appropriated to the provinces, and Article 12 unambiguously emphasized that only "so long and in so far as the empire does not use its legislative rights do the provinces preserve their legislative authority."

In the interests of the concentration of power in the hands of separate protégés of monopolist capital, fascism has "solved" in its own fashion the question of utilizing the earlier union state. In order to unify the territorial dictatorship of fascism, Hitler abolished the former rights of the provinces (Bavaria, Württemberg and others) and abolished their parliaments and their special governments and constitutions. He designated for all the other provinces his own vicegerents (*Staathälter*) who—in the interests of strengthening the fascist terror and arbitrariness—carried out a bureaucratic, military-police centralization of the state from top to bottom and to the most extreme degree.

2. *Confederation*

The history of the emergence of bourgeois union states shows that their problems consisted in organizing and broadening the national market and defending the interests of the dominant classes in external relationships with other states.

[7] Lenin, *Collection*, Vol. XVII, p. 129.

Union states, promoting centralization and the development of big production, were a progressive step as compared with the earlier feudal dispersion and the backward forms of small production. State centralization promoted also the increase of proletarian cadres and organization of the proletariat into an independent class with class interests. The most characteristic modern federations developed from confederation.[8]

The term "confederation" means a union of separate independent states unified for certain purposes only. This union may at any moment be broken by each member of the confederation. There is no higher legislative authority extended to all members of the confederation. Each member state of the confederation legislates independently within its territorial limits. Members of the confederation have the right to conclude agreements with foreign states on matters not lying within the jurisdiction of the confederation. Even if general organs of the confederation exist, their activity is limited by agreement and they have no right to broaden their jurisdiction without the consent of each separate member of the confederation. The limited circle of matters which do lie within the jurisdiction of organs of the confederation is solved in practice through organs of the confederated states whose assent is necessary to the passage of general measures. In a confederation there is no citizenship of the entire confederation as well. A confederation was possible in conditions of weakly developed capitalism.

Using the example of Switzerland, Engels disclosed very distinctly the causes which impelled the bourgeoisie to the transition from confederative to federative bonds.

If feudalism, patriarchal methods and the burgher regime of the cities successfully develop in isolated provinces and separate cities, then the bourgeoisie demands the broadest possible territory for its development. In place of twenty-two tiny cantons, it required a big Switzerland. The sovereignty of cantons—formerly the political form most suited to old Switzerland—fettered the bourgeoisie with intolerable shackles. The latter required a central authority which would be sufficiently strong to direct the legislation of separate cantons according to a defined and general pattern and to smooth out by its influence the difference in their state organization and statutes. It had to eliminate the remnants of feudal, patriarchal and burgher legislation and energetically defend the interests of the Swiss bourgeoisie in external relationships.[9]

We will glance at the organization system of the German Confederation as it existed from 1815 to 1867. It was based on Acts of the Vienna Congress

[8] Germany from 1815 to 1867 (prior to the formation of the North German Union) and 1871 (before the creation of the empire) was a confederation of German states. Precisely the same is true of Switzerland to the end of the eighteenth century, and thereafter from 1815 to 1848. The U.S.A. was a confederation from 1776 to 1787.

[9] Marx and Engels (Russian ed.), Vol. V, p. 244.

of thirteen powers (1815), supplemented in 1820 and in the following years. It consisted of thirty-eight (later thirty-three) independent states united for "external and internal security" and mutually guaranteeing to each other the inviolability of their possessions. Only German lands, so-called, entered the confederation. As to Austria: the Italian possessions of Austria at that time, Hungary and the lands of the Slav peoples were not counted as participating in the confederation. The same is true as to Prussia in respect of Poznan and East and West Prussia. At the same time, the King of Denmark was a member of the confederation, being at that time Prince of Holstein and Lauenberg. The same is true of the King of Holland as Possessory Prince of Luxemburg and Limburg. The organ of the confederation was the Sehm, consisting of plenipotentiary states sitting in Frankfort, and having a standing council (Engerer Rat) and plenary sitting (Plena), the presidency of both belonging to Austria. Matters within the jurisdiction of the Sehm were: international interests of the entire confederation, the right to send and to receive envoys, declaration of war and conclusion of treaties, and mediation in case of a claim asserted by a foreign power against a member of the confederation. The states entering the confederation were at the same time independent and autonomous as to matters of their internal and external policy.

There are no longer any confederations. The nineteenth, and particularly the twentieth, century saw the development of big capitalist industry and mass production. Changes in economy furnished the impetus for ever increasing centralization of the market—and therewith also of state authority, as expressed in the transition of separate confederations (U.S.A., Switzerland, and Germany) to federations and to unitarism.

3. The Unitary State

A unitary state is one centralized state, not divided into independent parts, and admitting only a degree of local communal self-government based upon a law worked out by the central authority. Expanding capitalism, interested in centralization of the market and oneness of legislation for the whole state, stood by the cradle of modern unitary states (France, Belgium, Switzerland, Denmark, and others) and conditioned the solidarity of nations and nationalist states as well as bourgeois revolutions which strengthened bourgeois political authority in the state. Most characteristic in this regard was the French Revolution of 1789, which created the classical type of bourgeois unitary state. The first French Constitution (1791) provided that: "The French kingdom is single and indivisible. Its structure consists of eighty-three departments, each divided into districts, each of which is divided into cantons." [10] Such was the laconic design of the bourgeois centralized unitary state.

Relying upon the masses, the French bourgeoisie conquered feudalism and absolutism and attracted to the channel of its struggle masses not only of French nationals but of other nationalities as well (Germans, Flemings, Basques, Catalonians, Bretons, Italians, and others), using lands of the aristocracy and of the church to balance accounts with the masses for their support. The more strongly and stoutly the revolution beat upon feudalism, the greater was the sympathy it evoked not only among the French nationalities but also in lands to which the victorious revolutionary armies brought with them the ideas of the French Revolution. Delegations from Nice, Savoy, Belgium, the Netherlands, Nassau, Zweibrücken, and elsewhere petitioned the Convention and the Jacobin clubs for the preservation of their territory for the "revolutionary fatherland." [11] The French unitary state most democratically solved the transition from feudalism to capitalism—and in a significant degree the national question as well, in the sense that it created a single state which defended the interests of the bourgeoisie of all France (including bourgeoisie of other nationality).

Further development of capitalism, and of the bourgeois state standing upon its defense, made class contradictions ever deeper and deeper. The revolution made all the peasantry equal in form. After having freed even the peasantry of another nationality from the feudal yoke, the French bourgeoisie handed it, as well as all the French peasantry, over to be exploited by capitalists. We have already noted that the Revolution of 1789 preserved the national oppression of peoples of the colonies. Such in brief was the process of creating the unitary state in western Europe.

In eastern Europe, the process of creating unitary centralized states was carried into effect differently. Here the development of capitalism was significantly slower. But interests of defense (from Turks, Mongols, and other nations whose attack threatened the weaker tribes and peoples) compelled their union into a single centralized state headed by a single more developed and powerful nation (whose dominant classes still further extended the state by subsequent wars).

"Inasmuch as the appearance of centralized states in eastern Europe proceeded more swiftly than the formation of people into nations, mixed states were there formed—consisting of nationalities that had not yet coalesced into nations but had already become unified into a common state." [12] States of this sort were (1) Russia prior to 1917 and (2) Austria-Hungary prior to 1918.

[10] *Legislative Acts of France* (1905), p. 33.
[11] Marx and Engels (Russian ed.), Vol. XVI, Pt. 1, pp. 489–490.
[12] Stalin, *Marxism, and the National-Colonial Question*, p. 73.

We will take up briefly the development of the Russian unitary state. The process of turning the Russian unitary monarchy into a bourgeois monarchy was not finished even by 1917. In a certain degree the landowners admitted the bourgeoisie also to authority. These two exploiter classes unified their mutual interest in the struggle against the worker class, the peasantry and oppressed nationalities. Finance capital united the interests of landowners and of capitalists under one roof. Imperialism striving to subordinate and to exploit new peoples and to seize their territories acquired in Russia a specific expression which Lenin characterized as war-feudalism, under which the monopoly of war power "partly completes and partly replaces the monopoly of the contemporary, most recent finance capital." [13] The bourgeoisie supported the state organization of tsarist Russia, starting from its interests in predatory exploitation of numerous oppressed nationalities and in crushing the proletariat and the national-emancipation movements in the country. The highest authority in the state was considered to pertain to the tsar, representing a combination of big agriculture with the capitalist, monopolist apex.

The fundamental laws of April 23, 1906, proclaimed: "The Russian state is single and indivisible [Art. 1]. . . . To the Emperor of all the Russias belongs supreme and autocratic power. . . . Obedience to his power—not only from fear but from conscience also—is commanded by God himself [Art. 4]. . . . The Emperor affirms laws—without such affirmance no law can become operative [Arts. 9 and 86]." The will of the tsar was the highest law—above the Imperial Duma and the Imperial Council.

Unitarism and state centralization bore a clearly expressed bureaucratic character adapted to the police-fiscal system of absolutism. This system came down particularly heavily upon the numerous nationalities living chiefly in the Russian borderlands. In those regions there survived—right down to the great October Socialist Revolution—the greatest number of feudal remnants of an economic and legal character, and as regards the manner of living—all of them putting a brake upon the local economic and cultural development. There, too, particularly in Central Asia and in the North Caucasus, diverse local civil statutes were preserved.

The administrative-territorial division of Russia also corresponded with the bureaucratic state organization. The basic division of tsarist Russia was into guberniyas.[14]

At the head of the governments were the governors, appointed and re-

---

[13] Lenin (Russian ed.), Vol. XIX, pp. 309–310.

[14] These (guberniyas) were introduced under Peter I. In 1703 eight of them were organized. By the end of the reign of Catherine II their number had reached forty. In the period immediately before the revolution there were seventy-eight (forty-nine administered on the basis of general rules and twenty-nine with deviations therefrom—ten Polish, seven

placed by the tsar upon reports by the Ministry of the Interior (to which they were subordinate). The governor preserved the interests of the nobility and the Church, striving to link their interests with those of the bourgeoisie. He had jurisdiction over all matters of internal government (including the police), crushed proletarian revolutionary movements and the dissatisfaction of oppressed nationalities. Besides governors, there were governors-general appointed by the tsar to certain governments populated chiefly by non-Russian nationalities (such as Turkestan, the steppes, and others) which caused the government special uneasiness. A governor-general possessed greater rights than did ordinary governors.[15]

The Caucasian territory was governed by a deputy with special powers and supreme authority in all questions of territorial administration.[16]

This entire state system stifled local social initiative, crushed the aspiration of the oppressed nationalities to create their own statehood, and was a brake also upon economic and cultural development. It was the arbitrariness of nobles and landowners raised to a principle of state organization.

As to Austria-Hungary, the "historical crown lands" enjoyed autonomy of an extremely relative sort. Local parliaments had the right to publish statutes on local matters, but bureaucratic unitarism was expressed in the requirement of imperial sanction and countersignature by the Austrian minister in respect of all laws. Local statutes were thus merely acts of the imperial will, expressing authority and its reactionary and bureaucratic arbitrariness which made the national question pointed and acute.

The bourgeoisie adapts bureaucratic unitarism to all forms of its political dominance. The modern unitary state may be monarchical (like Belgium) or republican (like France): in either case it remains imperialist, aimed at crushing the worker class and sustaining national pressure upon subordinate nations of the motherland and the colonies.

Caucasian, eight Finnish, and four Siberian). In addition there were nineteen provinces.

[For purposes of this text, the effort has been made to use the following translations with a uniformity not always paralleled in the Russian authorities, whose meaning is sometimes conjectural: guberniya = government; uyezd = province, a subdivision of a guberniya; oblast' = region or area; kray = territory; okrug = district or area; and rayon = district.—Tr.]

[15] The fundamental distinction between governors-general and governors was that the former had the right to report to the tsar directly whereas the latter were subordinate to the Ministry of the Interior; all relations of governors with central organs in places where there were governors-general passed through the latter; the opinion of the governor-general was indispensable to passage by the central organs of measures touching separate territories.

[16] An imperial ukase of February 26, 1905, defined the rights of the deputy of the Caucasus thus: (1) to assume the highest authority in all spheres of civil government in the territory entrusted to him; (2) to be, by reason of his official position, a member of the Imperial Council and of the Council and Committee of Ministers, Commander in Chief of the forces disposed within the boundaries of his territory, and Military Deputy Ataman of the Caucasian Kazakh troops (Cy. No. 36, Art. 262, March 3, 1905).

SEC. 6: THE DEVELOPMENT OF FORMS OF FEDERATIVE UNIFICATION OF THE SOVIET REPUBLICS

1. *The foundations of Soviet federation: The right of nations to self- determination*

The history of the formation of the Soviet federation shows the development of forms of fraternal and voluntary cooperation between nations upon the basis of equal rights. As early as the first Act of Soviet authority, issued (October 25/November 7, 1917) by the Second All-Russian Congress of Soviets—in the address to workers, soldiers, and peasants with reference to the passing of power to the Soviets—declared that Soviet authority "guarantees to all the nations dwelling in Russia the genuine right of self-determination." [1]

In the decree concerning peace (issued October 26/November 8, 1917) the Bolshevik understanding of the right of nations to self-determination was formulated with complete definiteness as the renunciation of annexation of every sort, of every species of violent incorporation or restraint of any nation in the boundaries of existing multinational states, irrespective of the time of its incorporation within the given state.

To develop the Lenin-Stalin policy as to nationalities, the same Congress formed (October 26, 1917) a special People's Commissariat for Nationalities for the Affairs of Nationalities, headed by Stalin—thus attesting the great significance attached by the Party and Soviet authority to the correct development of the Bolshevik policy as to nationalities.

The official Act of a constitutional character, containing an acknowledgment of the right of nations of Russia to self-determination and the basic principles of the policy of the Soviet authority as to nationalities, was the Declaration of Rights of the Peoples of Russia written by Stalin and signed by Lenin and Stalin (November 2/15, 1917). This declared that one of the chief tasks of Soviet authority was to set free the peoples held in serfdom by Russian tsarism and the imperialist bourgeoisie. It formulated the principles and program of Soviet national policy.

Pointing out the conclusions of the First and Second Congresses of Soviets, it declared:

Fulfilling the will of these Congresses, the Council of People's Commissars has resolved to place at the foundations of its activity relative to Russian nationalities the following principles: (1) the peoples of Russia are equal and sovereign; (2) the peoples of Russia have the right to free self-determination—including

[1] Lenin (Russian ed.), Vol. XXII, p. 11.

the right to withdraw and to form an independent state; (3) all privileges and limitations of nationalities, and of national religions of every sort, are abrogated; and (4) the national minorities and ethnographic groups inhabiting the territory of Russia shall develop freely.

Definitive decrees ensuing hereupon will be worked out immediately after the formation of the commission for affairs of nationalities.

These definitive decrees were quickly published. On December 4/17, 1917, the Council of People's Commissars issued a decree concerning the acknowledgment of the Ukraine's right to self-determination, including withdrawal. On December 18/31 it acknowledged the state independence of Finland by a directive confirmed by the All-Russian Central Executive Committee (upon the report of Stalin) on December 22, 1917. One week later a decree was published concerning Turkish Armenia containing a renunciation by Soviet authority of Turkish Armenia (which had been occupied by Russians during the war) and an acknowledgment of its right to self-determination. Even earlier (November 20/December 3, 1917) an address, "To All the Toiling Mussulmans of Russia and the East," written by Stalin and signed by Lenin and Stalin, was published. In that address the Soviet authority declared the annulment of all the imperialist contracts subscribed by tsarist Russia concerning the division of Turkey and Iran.

In the first months of the existence of Soviet authority the results of this policy were already expressed, as attested by the growing gravitation of the toilers of all nationalities to unification with Soviet Russia. Soviet federation was put forward as the state form of unification. On November 23, 1917 (old style), Stalin declared:

As to the national question, the views of the central authority elected by the Second All-Russian Congress of Soviets and acknowledged by the recently formed congress of peasants are as follows: the right of nationalities to complete self-determination, including withdrawal and the formation of an independent state, is acknowledged. The will of the nation is defined by referendum or or national constituent assembly. If the will of the nation shall be expressed in favor of a federative republic, the Council of People's Commissars can have nothing against it. That is the right of each nation. Therewith will the government reckon. [2]

The Soviet government in the aforesaid decree concerning the Ukraine (December 4/17, 1917) accordingly acknowledged the right of the Ukraine to withdraw completely from Russia, at the same time expressing its readiness to enter into negotiations concerning the establishment of federative and analogous relations between Russia and the Ukraine. On December 12/25, 1917, Stalin, in a document issued from the People's Commissariat

[2] Stalin, *Articles and Speeches on the Ukraine* (1936), pp. 14–15.

of Nationalities, declared that the Council of People's Commissars was "ready to acknowledge the federative organization of the political life of our country in the style, let us say, of the United States of Russia, if the toiling population of the Russian regions shall demand it." [3]

The formation, as early as the end of 1917, of the Soviet Ukrainian government, which in fact established federative relationships with the Russian Soviet government, played a great part in forming the principle of federation as the shape of organization of the Soviet State—a principle finally confirmed and formulated in the Declaration of Rights of the Toiling and Exploited People (affirmed by the Third All-Russian Congress of Soviets January 25 and 31, 1918, new style). The second point of Subdivision 1 of the Declaration proclaimed that "the Russian Soviet Republic is instituted on the basis of a free union of free nations as a federation of Soviet national republics."

The Declaration concluded with a statement that it was made possible for the workers and peasants of each nation to "take an independent decision in their own plenipotentiary Soviet Congress as to whether or not they wish—and, if so, on what bases—to participate in a federal government and in the other federal Soviet institutions." This point was made concrete in a directive adopted (January 28) by the same Congress of Soviets upon the report of Stalin: Concerning Federal Institutions of the Russian Republic, according to which the means of participation in the federal government by Soviet Republics—by separate regions distinguished by a special way of life and a national structure—and also the delimitation of spheres of activity of federal and regional institutions of the Russian Republic, is defined forthwith according to the formation of regional Soviet Republics by the All-Russian Central Executive Committee and the Central Executive Committees of said republics.[4]

With the then enormous differences in the internal and international positions of the separate nationalities (in their geographical situation, number and density and in the relationships between the nationalities themselves) any single form of federative union of these nationalities was impossible. In one case this unification assumed the character of some form of alliance, in another that of an autonomy.

2. Military and economic unification of independent Soviet Republics

The organization of independent Soviet Republics, and the integration of the original forms of their unification in the shape of a military union, occurred under conditions of foreign military intervention and civil war.

[3] *Pravda*, No. 213, Dec. 13/26, 1917.
[4] *Gazette of the Temporary Worker-Peasant Government*, No. 11 (56), Jan. 18/31, 1918.

The revolution which had begun in the center could not long be confined within the framework of that narrow territory. Victorious in the center, it must inevitably extend to the borderlands. And actually, from the very first days of the *coup d'état,* the revolutionary wave from the north flooded all of Russia, gaining possession of borderland after borderland.[5]

The affirmation of Soviet authority in the borderlands clashed with stubborn resistance by the local national bourgeoisie which had joined ranks with imperialist interventionists. Imperialism, which regarded the national borderlands as a drill ground for stifling the proletarian revolution in the center and as objects of colonial exploitation (its own possible bases for oil, cotton, coal, and provisions), actively supported the nationalist counterrevolution from the very beginning, using it as a screen to establish (with the aid of the local bourgeoisie) its uncontrolled management in the borderlands. This is what was really back of the "independence" of the Ukraine, of the Hetman and Petliura, the Menshevik Georgia, the Dashnak Armenia, and the Mussavat Azerbaijan.

"Of whom is the government of Gegechkora independent?" asked Lenin in May, 1918. "Of the Soviet Republic—yes. It is a bit dependent, however, upon German imperialism, and that is natural." [6] Imperialism repaid the national bourgeoisie by outright military repression of the worker and peasant uprisings (this was the role of German troops in the Ukraine and Georgia) and by supporting it in the armed struggle against the Soviets.

For their true national independence and their emancipation from exploitation of every sort, the toiling masses of the national borderlands struggled stubbornly against imperialist interventionists and their agents, the traitorous counterrevolutionary nationalist bourgeoisie. Enjoying the fraternal support of the most powerful Soviet Republic (the RSFSR), the toiling masses of the borderland achieved in this struggle a decisive victory and the establishment of Soviet authority in the forms of national Soviet statehood.

As early as the end of 1918 and the beginning of 1919, the collapse of German intervention and the emancipation of the western provinces occupied by German troops led to the reestablishment of Soviet authority in the Ukraine and the formation of a succession of independent Soviet Republics.

In accordance with the principle of the nations' rights to self-determination, the government of the RSFSR forthwith acknowledged the independence of these republics. Thus as early as the beginning of February, 1919, it had acknowledged the independence of Soviet White Russia, at the same

[5] Stalin, *Marxism, and the National-Colonial Question,* p. 53.
[6] Lenin (Russian ed.), Vol. XXIII, p. 12.

time declaring its readiness "to render aid and support of every sort to the toiling masses of White Russia in their struggle against the dominance of exploitation and oppression and in their defense of their freedom and independence from attempts of foreign conquest."[7]

From the very first day of their emergence these Soviet Republics had to carry on a desperate struggle for existence against imperialist intervention and internal counterrevolution. This, and the correct Lenin-Stalin national policy of the Soviet government, quickened the realization by the toiling masses of these republics of the necessity of establishing the closest military union with the Russian Republic. Acknowledgment of their complete independence on the part of the RSFSR established genuine and mutual understanding between the peoples of the Soviet Republics and promoted their gravitation toward the voluntary union of all Soviet Republics.

The temporary worker-peasant government of the Ukraine (formed in November, 1918) proclaimed the struggle of the masses against German intervention, and announced (in the declaration of January 26, 1919) "the necessity of unifying the Ukrainian Soviet Republic with Soviet Russia on the principles of a socialist federation whose forms will be established by plenipotentiary representative at the All-Ukrainian Congress of Soviets."[8]

Unification of the independent Soviet Republics in civil war conditions began with unification of their military forces. The Ukrainian government assumed the initiative in this matter, having addressed to all the Soviet governments (January 28, 1919) a summons "to conclude a close defensive union against attempts of every sort to overthrow the worker-peasant authority established at the price of such heavy sacrifices."[9] This summons met a warm response at the First White Russian Congress of Soviets.

The Constitution of the Ukrainian SSR (adopted in March, 1919) emphasized once again the decision of the Ukrainian toilers to enter into the closest political union with the other republics (cf. particularly Art. 4).

In May, 1919, when the threat to the Ukraine and to the RSFSR from Denikin and his followers was already completely evident, the Ukrainian Central Executive Committee, jointly with Ukrainian organizations, directed that "a proposal be addressed to the Central Executive Committees of all the Soviet Republics to work out concrete forms of organizing a single front of revolutionary struggle."[10]

Finally, on June 1, 1919, the All-Russian Central Executive Committee

[7] Cy. 1919, No. 3, Art. 31.
[8] Cy. of the Ukrainian SSR, 1919, No. 4, Art. 46.
[9] *Policy of Soviet Authority Regarding the National Question for Three Years* (1920), p. 43.
[10] Lenin (Russian ed.), Vol. XXIV, p. 814.

passed a directive concerning the unification of Soviet Republics for the struggle with world imperialism. In that directive the committee, referring to the decision reached by other Soviet Republics, acknowledged the necessity of close unification (1) of military organization and military command, (2) of councils of national economy, (3) of railroad management and economy, (4) of finances, and (5) of commissariats of labor.[11]

The direction of these People's Commissariats was necessarily transferred into the hands of single departments. Unification had necessarily to be reached by accord between the RSFSR and the governments of the other Soviet Republics. If, therefore, from November, 1917, to the fall of the first Ukrainian Soviet government (as a result of the German occupation of the Ukraine), relations between the independent Soviet Republics had no longer "a completely definite and strictly established form," [12] collaboration between the republics nevertheless did, during the civil war, take on the character of a military alliance. It was military considerations that in the first instance then evoked the anticipated unification of Economic People's Commissariats.

The attack of Denikin and the White Poles, and the resulting enemy occupation of territories of the Soviet Republics (except the RSFSR) postponed the realization of this union, although directives concerning it, adopted by the highest organs of authority of the RSFSR and the Ukraine, remained in force. The Seventh All-Russian Congress of Soviets, already able to welcome the beginning of the emancipation of the Ukraine from the followers of Denikin and the interventionists, emphasized that "at the present time the relations between the Ukrainian SSR and RSFSR are defined as a federative bond based on resolutions of the Central Executive Committee of the Ukraine (of May 18, 1919) and the All-Russian Central Executive Committee (of June 1 of the same year)." [13]

In its first proclamation to the workers and peasants of the Ukraine (December, 1919), the new Soviet government of the Ukraine, the Revolutionary Committee of the Ukrainian SSR, confirmed anew the stability and firmness of the union concluded "in the difficult days of failure by directives of the Central Executive Committees of the Ukraine and of Russia." [14] The proclamation pointed out that in a future Congress of Soviets of the Ukraine, it would be possible for the Ukraine workers and peasants "to define with finality the form of the relations between the Ukrainian SSR and the RSFSR." [15]

[11] Cy. 1919, No. 21, Art. 264.
[12] Stalin, Marxism, and the National-Colonial Question (1937), p. 105.
[13] Cy. 1919, No. 64, Art. 580.
[14] Policy of Soviet Authority on the National Question for Three Years, p. 117.
[15] Ibid., p. 117.

Actually the Fourth All-Ukrainian Congress of Soviets, in its directive of May 20, 1920, having emphasized the membership of the Ukrainian SSR in the All-Russian Socialist Soviet Federative Republic, asserted that the Central Executive Committees of the Republics were in accord concerning the unification of the People's Commissariats, and directed the initiation of negotiations with the All-Russian Central Executive Committee concerning the representation of the Ukraine therein. Accordingly that committee (June, 1920) directed the introduction into its personnel of thirty members of the Ukrainian Central Executive Committee.

As early as July, 1920, the successes of the Red Army in the war with Poland had led to the emancipation of White Russia. The new Soviet government of White Russia, having proclaimed the independence of the White Russian SSR (in its declaration of August 1, 1920), announced at the same time "the transfer of all its armed forces to be disposed of by the single command of the armed forces of all the Soviet Republics, the accord of its external policy with that of the RSFSR, and its intention to set about the establishment of a single economic plan with the RSFSR and other Soviet Republics which have emerged or may emerge." [16]

This declaration already reflected the significance of economic collaboration, a significance that had particularly increased in the period after the end of the civil war and during the transition to peaceful work in the rehabilitation of national economy, when "questions of the rehabilitation of production forces destroyed by war were first and foremost." [17] The economic collapse consequent upon the many years of war could be overcome only along lines of economic collaboration between the republics. Expansion of the significance of such collaboration of independent Soviet Republics required more distinct formulation with the aid of compacts. The form of such compacts was first applied in relations between the RSFSR and the Azerbaijan SSR (formed in April, 1920, as a result of the overthrow by the Azerbaijan toiling masses of the Mussavatist government). These two republics concluded a compact (September 30, 1920) concerning a military and economic union which contemplated the unification of (1) military organization and military command; (2) organs having jurisdiction over national economy and foreign trade; (3) organs of supply; (4) railroad and water transportation and the post and telegraph department; and (5) finances.

To the compact were annexed special accords concerning the unification of the food policy and of the administration of post, telegraph, telephone, and radiograms, an accord on finance matters, an accord on matters

---

[16] *Soviet White Russia*, pp. 8–9.
[17] Stalin, *Marxism, and the National-Colonial Question*, p. 106.

of foreign trade, and an accord on the conduct of single economic policy.[18] All these establish the general lines of collaboration between the republics, giving general guidance over to the corresponding People's Commissariats of the RSFSR which had its own representatives in the Council of People's Commissars of the Azerbaijan SSR. However, there were preserved also the Azerbaijan People's Commissariats of Post and Telegraph and Foreign Trade, which had acquired the right to carry on trade with the contiguous eastern countries independently. The compact established the forms of unification and collaboration of organs of the RSFSR and the Azerbaijan SSR. Following this, analogous compacts were concluded between the RSFSR and other independent Soviet Republics, including the Soviets of Armenia and Georgia, formed later (in December, 1920, and February, 1921) as a result of the victory of the toiling masses over the Dashnaks and Mensheviks, respectively.

On December 28, 1920, a union worker-peasant compact was concluded between the RSFSR and the Ukrainian SSR, providing for a military and economic union and the unification of seven People's Commissariats: Military and Naval Affairs, the Supreme Council for National Economy, Foreign Trade, Finance, Labor, Transport, and Post and Telegraph. The unified People's Commissariats were incorporated into the Council of People's Commissars of the RSFSR and were represented in the Ukraine SSR Council of People's Commissars by delegates confirmed and controlled by the Ukraine Central Executive Committee and Congress of Soviets.

On January 16, 1921, a compact was concluded on the same bases between the RSFSR and White Russian SSR.[19] On May 21, 1921, a compact and an accord on financial matters were concluded between the RSFSR and the Georgian SSR. On July 26, 1921, an accord on financial matters was concluded between the RSFSR and the White Russian SSR; and on September 30, 1921, between the RSFSR and Soviet Armenia.[20]

The process of bringing the Soviet Republics together found its expression in the formation of the Transcaucasian federation (unifying the independent Soviet Republics of Georgia, Armenia, and Azerbaijan), whose creation was dictated by conditions which had then taken shape in Transcaucasia by reason of the former management of the Mensheviks, Dashnaks, and Mussavatists, because of the fact that national interrelations had become acute, and by economic collapse. These conditions required closely coordinated action by the three Soviet Republics of Transcaucasia and

[18] Cy. 1920, No. 85, Art. 426.
[19] All-Russian Central Executive Committee News (April 6, 1921), No. 74.
[20] People's Commissariat for Internal Affairs, Collection of Compacts in Force, pp. 5–6, Issues II (1921), pp. 3–6, III (1922), pp. 20–22.

special measures to overcome conflicts between the nations. In each of these respects the Transcaucasian federation played an enormous and positive role. It was no accident that formation of the federation encountered such fierce opposition from the Georgian national-deviators—later proven traitors to the peoples of Transcaucasia, and agents and spies of the imperialist powers.

The formation of the Trancaucasian federation passed through several stages. By direction of Stalin the unification of railroads and foreign trade was carried through during 1921. On November 28, 1921, Lenin gave the following instructions with reference to the Transcaucasian federation: (1) to acknowledge the Transcaucasian federation as absolutely correct in principle and to be realized unconditionally but in the sense of the immediate, practical realization of preliminary propaganda and development from below, requiring some weeks of consideration; and (2) to propose to the Central Committees of Georgia, Armenia, and Azerbaijan to put this resolution into practice.

Lenin accepted an amendment proposed by Stalin to change the words "requiring some weeks for consideration" to the words "requiring a certain period of time for consideration." [21]

At a conference of delegates of the three Transcaucasian Republics (on March 12, 1922), the Federative Union of Transcaucasian Republics was founded. At the First Transcaucasian Congress of Soviets (December 13, 1922), the Federative Union of Transcaucasian Republics was reorganized into the Transcaucasian Socialist Federative Soviet Republic. The highest organs of authority of the Republic were declared to be the Transcaucasian Congress of Soviets and the Transcaucasian Central Executive Committee; and the Transcaucasian Council of People's Commissars was formed.

This very first Transcaucasian Congress of Soviets directed the entry of the new Soviet Republic into the USSR.

3. The origin and development of Soviet autonomies

Side by side with the formation of military and economic collaboration between independent Soviet Republics, there also took shape, in the period preceding the formation of the Union, the Soviet autonomy.

Soon after the Third All-Russian Congress of Soviets the question of building Soviet autonomies came up in connection with the successes of the sovietization of the eastern districts. Among the eastern nationalities, aspirations for autonomy were strong even from prerevolutionary times; demands for autonomy were advanced in particular by bourgeois nationalist parties, who in a number of cases even succeeded in attaining leadership

[21] Lenin (Russian ed.), Vol. XXVII, p. 94.

of a part of the masses under the slogan of autonomy. The task of the Soviet national policy consisted in indoctrinating these nationalities in logical socialist principles of Soviet autonomy—expressive of the interests of the toilers—and in utilizing it to strengthen Soviet authority among these nationalities in a form corresponding to their specific conditions and needs. This task was put before the local Soviet organizations with all distinctness in April, 1918, by the People's Commissars for Nationalities in its address, signed by Stalin, to the Soviets of Kazan, Ufa, Orenburg, Yekaterinburg, to the People's Commissars of the Turkestan territory, and others.

In this address, the Commissar indicated autonomy as a necessary means "for attracting the toiling and exploited masses of these borderlands into the process of revolutionary development" [22] for raising the masses to Soviet authority. The address emphasized the fundamental character of this autonomy as Soviet autonomy—to counteract bourgeois autonomy.

It is necessary only to build this autonomy on the basis of local Soviets; only thus can authority be popular and truly belong to the masses—that is to say, it is necessary only that autonomy guarantee authority not for the apex but for the nether parts of a given nation. Herein is the entire essence of the matter.[23]

The address finally defines also the content of autonomy as "an organization of local organs of authority, of local social, political, and educational institutions, with a guaranty of the completeness of the rights of the local language—native to the toiling masses of the country—in all spheres of social-political work." [24]

Some practical steps in organizing Soviet autonomies also took place in this period. The Fifth Congress of the Turkestan territory (April 30, 1918) proclaimed the formation of the Turkestan Republic. Still earlier (March 23, 1918), the People's Commissariat of Nationalities had confirmed the regulation concerning the Tatar-Bashkir Republic and had worked out also a regulation as to the Kazakh (Kirghiz) and other autonomous republics.

Soviet autonomy obtained a basis in principle in the works of the constitutional commission of the All-Russian Central Executive Committee, and in particular in Stalin's notable proposals concerning the type of federation of the Russian Soviet Republic and his General Regulations of the Constitution of the Russian Soviet Federative Republic. These were at the basis of the Constitution of the RSFSR (adopted July 10, 1918), which precisely formulated the principles of Soviet autonomy in Article 11.

[22] *Policy of Soviet Authority on the National Question During Three Years*, p. 8.
[23] *Ibid.*, p. 9.
[24] *Ibid.*

In July, 1918, the Transbaikal area Executive Committee passed a resolution for forming the Buriat-Mongol autonomy.

In October, 1918, immediately after the emancipation of the Central Volga lands, a directive of the Council of People's Commissars formed (in districts of the German colonies of the Volga lands) a territorial unification with the character of a work commune.

In February, 1919, pursuant to a compact with the Bashkir nationalist government, which had passed to the side of Soviet authority under the pressure of the toiling masses, the Bashkir Autonomous Soviet Republic was formed.

In 1919 and 1920 victories of the Red Army freed broad eastern districts of the RSFSR, and in these national districts autonomous Soviet Republics and regions were formed.

By a decree of July 10, 1919, a revolutionary committee was formed to govern the Kirghiz territory (now the Kazakh SSR) to which passed the government of the freed regions of Kirghizstan: "thenceforward until the calling of a general Kirghiz Congress . . . and the declaration of the autonomy of the Kirghiz territory." [25]

The Karelian work commune was formed in the western part of the RSFSR in 1919.

In 1920 the Autonomous Tatar [26] and Kirghiz [27] Republics, and the autonomous Chuvash,[28] Mari,[29] Votyak [30] (Udmurt) and Kalmyk [31] regions were formed.

In 1921 in RSFSR were formed the republics of Dagestan [32] and Gorsk,[33] the autonomous Crimean SSR,[34] the autonomous regions of Komi [35] and Kabardino [36] (the latter being separated from the Gorsk Autonomous SSR). In 1922 was formed the Yakutsk Autonomous SSR [37] and the Karachay-Cherkessy,[38] Kabardino-Balkaria,[39] Chechen,[40] Mongol-Buriat,[41] Oirot,[42] and Cherkess (Adighey) [43] autonomous regions.

After 1921 national republics and regions appear also in other Union Republics beside the RSFSR; thus the autonomous republics of Adjaria and Abkhazia were formed in Georgia in 1921.

The People's Commissariat of Nationalities played an enormous historical part in developing Soviet federation. It had jurisdiction over the

[25] Op. cit., p. 42.
[26] Cy. No. 51, Art. 222.
[27] Cy. No. 76, Art. 359.
[28] Cy. No. 59, Art. 267.
[29] Cy. No. 87, Art. 436.
[30] Cy. No. 87, Art. 437.
[31] Cy. No. 87, Art. 435.
[32] Cy. No. 5, Art. 39.
[33] Cy. No. 6, Art. 41.
[34] Cy. No. 69, Art. 556.
[35] Cy. No. 61, Art. 438.
[36] Cy. No. 63, Art. 457.
[37] Cy. No. 30, Art. 370.
[38] Cy. No. 6, Art. 63.
[39] Cy. No. 11, Art. 109.
[40] Cy. No. 80, Art. 1009.
[41] Cy. No. 6, Art. 59.
[42] Cy. No. 39, Art. 450.
[43] Cy. No. 47, Art. 596.

entire sphere of interrelations of the Soviet government and nationalities. It initiated the entire Soviet legislation on the matter of nationalities, including the acknowledgment of independent Soviet Republics, the establishment of autonomous Soviet Republics, measures concerned with the economic and cultural uplift of nationalities, and so forth. As an operating organ, the Commissariat established close bonds with the communist organizations and the worker masses of different nationalities and took an active and leading part in organizing independent and autonomous republics and regions. With the growth of the number of these, the Commissariat became one of the most important organs of unifying Soviet Republics.

A directive of the All-Russian Central Executive Committee (May 19, 1920) provided for the formation within the structure of the People's Commissariat of Nationalities of a Soviet of Nationalities from representatives of the autonomous republics and regions. The Soviet of Nationalities was characterized by a regulation (May 26, 1921) Concerning the People's Commissariat of Nationalities as a consultative representative organ. In the Soviet of Nationalities of the People's Commissariat of Nationalities, all measures touching specific interests of nationalities were considered; it had the right to go with its conclusions and proposals through the People's Commissariat of Nationalities to the All-Russian Central Executive Committee and the Council of the People's Commissars. True, only autonomous republics and regions were represented in the Soviet of Nationalities, but the activity of the People's Commissariat of Nationalities touched also the relations between the RSFSR and the republics which were bound by compact.

The regulation concerning the People's Commissariat of Nationalities charged it to "see to it that all the nationalities and tribes of the RSFSR, as well as the friendly Soviet Republics bound by compact, live together in peace and in fraternal collaboration." Accordingly, that Commissariat "issues conclusions upon all measures proposed by individual People's Commissariats of the RSFSR touching the autonomous and Soviet Republics bound by compact." [44]

Of particular significance is the point that "to the end of generalizing the experience of developing the policy of Soviet authority in autonomous regions, republics, and in the republics bound by compact, and for overseeing the fulfillment of directives (issued by the Central Federative Authority of the RSFSR in developing Article 22 of its Constitution) protecting the rights and interests of national minorities, the People's Commissariat of Nationalities has its representations with the governments of autonomous and compact-bound republics and also with the executive com-

[44] *Source Book of People's Commissariat for Nationalities* (1921), p. 5.

mittees of autonomous regions." Thus, the People's Commissariat of Nationalities extended its activity not only to the autonomous republics but also to the compact-bound republics, having as its task "to oversee the putting into practice of the national policy of Soviet authority." [45]

4. *The formation of the USSR*

By their very essence, compact relations between Soviet Republics represented a stage preparatory to a closer unification in the form of a single union state—a genuine, stable "state union of Soviet Republics" [46]—as the single form in which realization of the grandiose task of reorganizing the Soviet multinational society on socialist principles was feasible.

By the end of 1922, the necessity of forming the Union had already matured completely. This period is signalized by the end of the retreating (which began in 1921) and the transition to attack upon the capitalist elements along the lines of the New Economic Policy. Clear signs of economic uplift were noted (the gold-backed ten-ruble-note issue, and the growth of industry and agriculture). The successes attained in the struggle to rehabilitate economy could be confirmed and extended only by the creation of organizational premises for single guidance of the economy of all the Soviet Republics.

The political and economic collaboration which had developed between the Soviet Republics conditioned the complete solidarity and unity of their foreign policy interests. Aside from this, although the union compacts left questions of foreign policy within the jurisdiction of separate independent Soviet Republics, interests of self-defense from capitalist encirclement led in fact to the establishment of actual and close collaboration by them in the field of external policy also.

Thus a compact between the RSFSR and Turkey (March 16, 1921) served as a basis for the Kars compact between the Soviet Republics of Georgia, Armenia, and Azerbaijan (parties of the one part) and Turkey (party of the other part) signed October 13, 1921 (in the Kars Conference in which the RSFSR took a most active part) and for the compact between the Soviet Republic of the Ukraine and Turkey (January 21, 1922). The collaboration of Soviet Republics in the field of external policy was demonstrated still more clearly by the protocol (February 22, 1922) between the RSFSR on the one hand and the Soviet Republics of Armenia, Azerbaijan, Georgia, White Russia, Ukraine, Khorezm, Bokhara and the Far East on the other, concerning the transfer to the RSFSR of representation from all Soviet Republics to the pan-European economic conference in Genoa.

---

[45] *Ibid.*, pp. 5, 8–9.
[46] Stalin, *Marxism, and the National-Colonial Question*, p. 69.

Convinced of the impossibility of conquering the Soviet Republics by armed intervention and the hunger blockade, the capitalist world passed to new methods of struggle: diplomatic and economic pressure, manifested with particular distinctness at the Genoa Conference and the subsequent Hague Conference, when the capitalists strove to fasten upon the Soviet Republics payment of tsarist debts, compensation for "damage" inflicted upon the foreign owners of nationalized enterprises, unilateral concessions, and so on.

New conditions demanded the complete unification of the external policy of all the Soviet Republics to the end of exerting resistance to the onset of imperialism against their political and economic independence. Only by the joint exertions of all the republics and utilization of the resources of each and of the division of labor that had historically developed would disorder be overcome, the country led along the line of expanded development of socialism, and its defensive capacity and international positions strengthened in the face of world imperialism. But the compact system, supplemented by accords from time to time on individual questions, did not keep pace with the mounting inclination for greater unity. Genuine unity of political, economic, and military direction of the Soviet Republics could be assured only by creating permanent all-federative organs clothed with complete state authority in the territory of all Soviet Republics—that is to say, by forming a single union state.

Now when all the territory of the Soviet land had been purged of interventionists, and the tasks of building socialism and defense of the country required further strengthening of the union of peoples of the Soviet land, the immediate question was closer unification of Soviet Republics in a single state union. All the people's powers must be unified for the building of socialism. Strong defense of the country must be organized. All-sided development of all its nationalities must be assured. To accomplish this all the peoples of the Soviet land must be brought still closer together.[47]

In his report to the Tenth All-Russian Congress of Soviets (December 26, 1922), Stalin pointed out that the necessity of creating a union state was conditioned by "facts touching our inner economic condition . . . facts connected with our external position," and facts associated "with the character of the building and with the class nature of Soviet authority." [48] In the first group were facts associated with the current paucity of economic resources, the division of labor that had historically developed, and interests of transport and finances. In the second group of facts were foreign trade,

[47] *History of the All-Union Communist Party (of Bolsheviks)*, p. 249.
[48] Stalin, *Marxism and the National-Colonial Question*, pp. 90–92.

military needs, and the foreign policy relations of Soviet Republics. In the third group was the fact that "Soviet authority is so built that, international in its inner essence, it promotes in every way in the masses the idea—itself impels them along the road—of union." [49]

The campaign for unification of the Soviet Republics in the form of a single union state, initiated by Lenin and Stalin in the second half of 1922, stimulated the masses in all the Soviet Republics.

In his report at the Tenth Congress of Soviets of the RSFSR, Stalin pointed out:

The campaign means that the old compact relationships—the convention relationships between the RSFSR and the other Soviet Republics—have exhausted themselves, have shown themselves to be inadequate. The campaign means that we must inevitably pass from old compact relationships to relationships of closer unification, relationships postulating the creation of a single, union state with corresponding union organs (executive and legislative) and with a Central Executive Committee and Council of People's Commissars of the Union. In brief, it is now proposed, in the course of the campaign, to form as something permanent what has hitherto been decided spasmodically within the framework of convention relationships. [50]

In the summer and autumn of 1922, the question of unifying the republics was considered in the directing organs of the Party. On October 6, 1922, theses on the matter of unification—signed by Stalin, Ordzhoni-kidze, Molotov, and Myasnikov—were proposed and approved by the Plenum of the Central Committee of the Russian Communist Party of Bolsheviks. On December 13, the first Transcaucasian Congress of Soviets directed the sending of its representatives to the Congress of Socialist Soviet Republics, furnished with mandates to subscribe the contract of Organization of the Union. On December 13, the Declaration Concerning the Formation of the Union was adopted by the Seventh All-Ukraine Congress of Soviets; on December 16 a similar directive was passed by the Fourth Congress of Soviets of the White Russian SSR, and on December 26 by the Tenth All-Russian Congress of Soviets.

On December 30, 1922, the Declaration and Contract Concerning the Formation of the Union upon voluntary principles and with equal rights and comprising the foundations of the organization of the Soviet Union State, projected and worked out by Stalin, were adopted by the First Congress of Soviets of the USSR upon Stalin's report. "The creation of the USSR signalized the strengthening of Soviet authority and a great victory

[49] *Ibid.*, pp. 90–92.
[50] *Ibid.*, p. 90.

of the Lenin-Stalin policy of the Bolshevik Party on the matter of nationalities." [51]

The Twelfth Congress of the Party (April, 1923) and the fourth session of the Executive Committee, with responsible workers of the national republics and regions (summoned in June, 1923, upon the initiative of Stalin), played a decisive part in working out the forms of the Union Federation of Republics and of the first Union Constitution.

In his report at the Twelfth Congress of the Party (April 23, 1923), Stalin pointed out the circumstances which at that period retarded the unification of the republics, impeded such unification: the imperialist chauvinism of the national majority, factual inequality, and local nationalism. The conditions of the New Economic Policy promoted a certain excitation of both imperialist and local nationalism. Nationalism played upon the fact "that this was a period when relations between peoples were not yet properly harmonious, remnants of the distrust for Great Russians had not yet disappeared, and centrifugal forces still continued to operate." [52]

Bourgeois nationalism through its agents, who had made their way into Party and Soviet organizations, tried to frustrate the unification of the republics and the creation of a Soviet Union state during the preparation for the First Congress of Soviets of the USSR and the working out of its first constitution. Not venturing to come out openly against the proposal (which enjoyed the support of the toiling masses), the local nationalists strove to pervert the essence of this unification and to give the Union the character of a "free confederation."

We have already noted that the Ukrainian nationalists and Trotskyists insisted on preserving Republic People's Commissariats for Foreign Affairs and People's Commissariats for Foreign Trade, with the proviso that the Union People's Commissariats for Foreign Affairs and for Foreign Trade have the character not of All-Union, but of unified, directive People's Commissariats. Thus, as is now clear, they wished to preserve the legal possibility of contact with their masters—the big imperialist powers and Poland—so as to betray their people and the Union in its entirety.

Striving to utilize the geographical advantages of Georgia, the Georgian nationalist-deviators demanded special privileges for Georgia, as compared with the other Transcaucasian republics.

The great power chauvinists tried to interpret the formation of the Union as the restoration of the "single and indivisible" Russian Empire.

Guided by Lenin and Stalin, the party shattered these Trotsky-Bukhar-

[51] *History of the All-Union Communist Party (of Bolsheviks): A Short Course* (1938), p. 249.
[52] Stalin, *Report on the Draft of the USSR Constitution* (1936), p. 14.

inist and bourgeois-nationalist plans, accepting in its entirety the Stalin plan of creating a single union state, built on the principles that all members entering that state did so voluntarily and were equal.

The Constitution of the USSR, adopted at the second session of the Central Executive Committee (July 6, 1923), was finally affirmed by the Second All-Russian Congress of Soviets on January 31, 1924. It provided for the creation of All-Union legislative and executive organs: a Congress of Soviets, a Central Executive Committee of the USSR, and a Council of People's Commissars of the USSR.

5. *National delimitation of Central Asia: extension of the Union*

In his report to the Tenth All-Russian Congress of Soviets concerning the unification of Soviet Republics, Stalin noted that

two independent Soviet Republics, Khorezm and Bokhara—being People's Soviet, but not Socialist, Republics—remain for the present outside the framework of this Union solely and exclusively because they are not yet socialist. I have no doubt—and I hope you too have no doubt—that, in proportion to their internal development toward socialism, they likewise will enter the structure of the union state now being formed.[53]

The Khorezm and Bokhara People's Republics were formed in 1920 as a result of the overthrow by the toilers of their feudal despots. Compacts of union concluded by these republics with the RSFSR (September 13, 1920, and March 4, 1921) differed sharply from those between Soviet Socialist Republics hereinbefore described, inasmuch as they did not provide for unification of certain branches of administration and economy.

The development of Soviet People's Republics did indeed continue along the line pointed out by Stalin. As early as October, 1923, the Khorezm People's Republic was reorganized by the Fourth Khorezm Assembly (kurultay) into a Socialist Republic which proclaimed a dictatorship of the proletariat and poorest peasantry (Dekhkanstvo) and deprived exploiter classes of their voting rights. The Central Executive Committee of Bokhara (in extraordinary session, August, 1923) likewise went along the line of limiting the political rights of exploiter classes, depriving of their voting rights the former emir bureaucrats, usurers, merchants, and those occupied with big trade. (Under the old constitution only agricultural and financial magnates had been deprived of voting rights.) There was increased representation of trade union members in organs of the republic. In September, 1924, the All-Bokhara assembly (kurultay) proclaimed the Socialist Republic of Bokhara. Obstacles to the union of these republics with the USSR thereby disappeared.

[53] Stalin, *Marxism and the National-Colonial Question* (1937). p. 93.

An essential step on the road to joining Khorezm and Bokhara to the USSR was their economic unification (in 1923) with the Turkestan Autonomous SSR by the creation of a single supreme economic organ for all three, notwithstanding overt and latent resistance by nationalist elements.

The national delimitation of all of Soviet Central Asia, however, had to precede entry of the Central Asia Republics into the USSR. Khorezm and Bokhara and also the Turkestan Autonomous SSR were not national but multinational republics. Each of them united a number of nationalities. Each of the big nationalities of Central Asia was dispersed over various republics (Uzbeks and Turkmens in Bokhara, Khorezm and Turkestan; Tadjiks in Bokhara and Turkestan; and Kazakhs in Turkestan and Kazakhstan). Such a situation, reflecting old political divisions which had resulted from the policy of Russian imperialism and of the Bokhara and Khiva (Asiatic) despots, promoted the persistence of antagonisms between the peoples (such as the Uzbek-Turkmen internecine strife in Khorezm), retarded the process of national consolidation of the Central Asiatic nationalities, and obstructed the creation of Soviet statehood close to the masses, national in form and socialist in content.

Problems of Soviet socialist building in Central Asia could be solved only by the national delimitation of that region, by reorganizing multinational Soviet Republics into national republics—which realized the important historical problem of national unification of its peoples.

The delimitation of Turkestan is, first of all, reunion into independent states of disrupted parts of these lands. If thereafter these states wished to enter the Soviet Union, as members having equal rights, this merely attests the fact that the Bolsheviks have found the key to the deepest yearnings of the national masses of the East, and the further fact that the Soviet Union is the only voluntary union in the world of the toiling masses of various nationalities.[54]

The national delimitation of Central Asia and the entry into the USSR of new republics, prepared by decisions of Party organs, was made real by the free manifestation of their will by the peoples of Bokhara, Khorezm, and Turkestan.[55] As a result of the national delimitation, the

[54] *Ibid.*, p. 157.

[55] Directives of the Fifth All-Bokhara Kurultay, the Central Executive Committee of the Khorezm Republic, the extraordinary session of the Central Executive Committee of the Turkestan Autonomous SSR in Sept., 1924, confirmed by directive of Central Executive Committee of the USSR Oct. 27, 1924 (Cz. 1924, No. 19, Art. 187).

February 17, 1925, the Tenth Congress of Soviets of Uzbekistan adopted a declaration concerning the formation of Uzbek SSR and its voluntary entry into the structure of the USSR.

Feb. 20, 1925, an analogous declaration was adopted by the First All-Turkmen Congress of Soviets.

May 13, 1925, the Third Congress of Soviets of the USSR directed the reception of the newly formed republics into the structure of the USSR, starting from the principle

regions of the Turkestan Autonomous SSR, Bokhara and Khorezm—settled by the Uzbeks and Turkmens—constituted the Uzbek and Turkmen SSR; the regions of the Turkestan Autonomous SSR and Bokhara—settled by Tadjiks—became the Tadjik Autonomous SSR within the Uzbek SSR. The part of Turkestan Autonomous SSR inhabited by Kazakhs was united with Kazakh Autonomous SSR, and another part—inhabited by Kirghiz—formed the Kirghiz autonomous region within the RSFSR. The region settled by Kara-Kalpaks formed the Kara-Kalpak autonomous region in the structure of the Kazakh Autonomous SSR.

During the years 1923 to 1925 there was further growth of Soviet autonomies. The Moldavian Autonomous SSR was formed within the Ukrainian SSR, and the Nakhichevan Autonomous SSR and the Nagorno-Karabakh autonomous region were formed within the Azerbaijan SSR. This period was characterized not only by the appearance of a succession of new autonomous state formations, but also by inception of the process of reorganizing autonomous regions into autonomous republics (such as the reorganization of the Karelian and the German labor communes and cf the Chuvash and Kirghiz autonomous regions into autonomous Soviet Socialist Republics).

During the years 1924 to 1926, by accord between the RSFSR and the White Russian SSR, there were joined to the latter the western districts of the RSFSR having a population predominantly White Russian with consequent significant increase of the territory, population, and economic resources of White Russia.

A constituent part of the process of development of the Soviet autonomy was the liquidation of multinational autonomous formations. These had already played their historic role, having united the backward tribes and nationalities and drawn them into the channel of the tasks of Soviet authority. In 1924 the Gorsk Republic was divided into the North Ossetian and Ingush autonomous regions, and the city of Vladikavkas (now Ordjonikidze) and the Sunzhensky district were set off.[56]

The Turkestan Republic was, as we have seen, liquidated with the national delimitation of Central Asia in 1924.

6. *The development of the Soviet Union State prior to the Stalin Constitution*

In 1923, in his proposals to the Twelfth Party Congress, Stalin emphasized as one of the immediate tasks of the Party after formation of the

---

(established by the Declaration Concerning the Formation of the USSR) that access to the Union was open to all Socialist Soviet Republics whether now existing or to emerge (Cz. 1925, No. 35, Art. 244).
[56] Cy. 1924, No. 66, Art. 656.

Union the task of overcoming the existing national inequality, economic and cultural, "by actual and continued aid by the Russian proletariat of the backward peoples of the Union in the matter of their economic and cultural prosperity." [57]

The task of liquidating the age-old backwardness of national republics was solved by the Party and by the Soviet state along lines of socialist reconstruction of economy, erection of new socialist industry, and socialist reorganization of agriculture.

During the struggle for industrialization and collectivization, the surface of the national republics was completely transformed. Hundreds of machine and tractor service stations and tens of thousands of tractors appeared and the basic mass of economics was collectivized. Vast successes in industrialization were achieved by the republics. In certain republics production of industry increased tenfold. New branches of heavy and light industry were created. Big industrial enterprises, equipped with the last word in technique, appeared in what had been the most backward, formerly the colonial, borderlands.

Not less striking were the cultural attainments of the republics. Nationalities, reckoned as late as the 1925 census at 1 per cent to 2 per cent literate, raised the percentage of literacy to 70 or 80. Universal instruction was realized in all the republics. Literature, printing, the theater, and motion pictures made marked progress. The culture of the peoples of the USSR, nationalist in form, socialist in content, flourished.

Guided by Stalin, the peoples of the Soviet Republics won these tremendous victories in pitiless struggle with the remnants of the exploiter classes—bourgeois nationalists, Bukharinists, Mensheviks, SR's—with all the agents of fascism who had laid plans to wrench the national republics from the Union and to give them over as serfs to imperialism with wreckers of industry and agriculture, and so on. The unmasking and destruction of the people's enemies opened perspectives wherein the Soviet Republics would flourish still more brilliantly.

The profound upheavals in the economy of the Soviet Republics were accompanied by like upheavals in class structure: liquidation of exploiter classes, and changes in the worker class, the peasantry, and among the intellectuals. All of this necessarily entailed as well profound upheavals in national interrelations—necessarily led to the further strengthening of the Soviet multinational state.

The absence of the exploiter classes who are the basic organizers of quarrels between the nations; the absence of the exploitation which cultivates mutual distrust and inflames nationalist passions; the presence in authority of the

[57] Stalin, *Marxism and the National-Colonial Question* (1937), p. 107.

worker class—the foe of every sort of enslavement and loyal bearer of the idea of internationalism; the factual realization of mutual aid of the peoples in all domains of economic and social life; finally the exuberance of national culture of the peoples of the USSR—national in form, socialist in content—all these and similar factors have wrought radical and apparent changes in the peoples of the USSR. Their feeling of mutual distrust has disappeared, the feeling of mutual friendship has developed—and the present fraternal collaboration of peoples in the system of a single union state has thus been brought into working harmony.[58]

The course of socialist building has completely vindicated the form of one union state defined by the 1924 Constitution—"the experiment of forming a multinational state, created on the basis of socialism, has completely succeeded." [59]

The changes occurring in economy, class structure and national interrelations not only did not require any changes of principle as regards the Soviet Union State system itself, but, on the contrary, promoted further strengthening of that system. This did not exclude the introduction of more or less essential correctives and supplements (as to details of that system, particularly as to interrelations between organs of the Union and organs of the republics within the framework of the union state), reflecting new facts of the social and economic life of our Union and evoked by the necessity of adapting the state system to these new facts—to the new tasks of socialist building.

These new tasks and the new elements in the social-economic life of the USSR demanded further unification, planning, and guidance of the economic and cultural building on an All-Union scale, further centralization of this guidance. Toward this centralization worked not only the essential requirements of building, but also the facts of the economic interdependence that had grown on the basis of the new economy and culture, and the economic and cultural bonds that had developed between different parts of the Union.

This increased role of Union organs, however, not only did not exclude, it actually presupposed, further development and strengthening of national state organizations and the intensification of their operative independence and self-help. The unity of the socialist economy and socialist planning—the socialist division of labor between parts of the state—is based on the most complete and manifold development of the industrial and agrarian resources and possibilities of each part of the Union. The Party emphatically rejected reactionary and nationalist projects to turn separate republics into

[58] Stalin, *Report on the Draft of the USSR Constitution* (1936), p. 15.
[59] *Ibid.*

closed economic agglomerates as well as plans for implanting a single culture in each separate republic.

The vast economic growth of national republics and regions puts before their organs new and complex tasks and demands that those organs be strengthened.

The economic and cultural rise accelerated the process of consolidating nations "under the aegis of Soviet authority," [60] and led to the development into independent nations of the nationalities formerly the most backward. This could not but be reflected also in the further growth of national state organizations.

The tasks of socialist building required the utmost bringing of state organs near to the masses, the utmost attraction of masses into Soviet organs and into socialist culture's orbit of influence, and in connection with this the role of national republics and regions grew ever greater. In his political report at the Sixteenth Party Congress, Stalin pointed out:

We have established the unity of economic and political interest of the peoples of the USSR. But does this mean that we have annihilated thereby national differences, national languages, culture, manner of life, and so on? Clearly it does not. If national differences, language, culture, manner of life, and so on remain, however, is it not clear that the demand for the annihilation of national republics and regions in a given historical period is a reactionary demand, directed against the interests of the proletarian dictatorship? Do our deviators understand that to annihilate the national republics and regions now is to deprive millions of the masses of the peoples of the USSR of the possibility of obtaining education in their *own* language, of having a school, a court, administration, social and other organizations and institutions in their *own* language, of joining socialist building? [61]

New elements in the mutual relations between the Union and its members found legislative expression in a whole succession of separate Acts of a constitutional character.

Growth of Soviet Republics and regions in this period is attested by the further reorganization of autonomous regions into autonomous republics.

At the end of 1934 the Kara-Kalpak,[62] Udmurt [63] and Mordovian [64] autonomous regions were reorganized into autonomous republics, and at the end of 1935 the Kalmyk [65] autonomous region was so reorganized.

In the period since 1925 the following new national autonomous organizations were formed: the Gorny-Badakhshan autonomous region (1926), the Cherkessy autonomous regions (reorganized in 1928 from the Cherkessy

---

[60] Stalin, *Marxism, and the National-Colonial Question* (1937), p. 158.
[61] *Ibid.*, p. 193.
[62] Cy. 1935, No. 9, Art. 95.
[63] Cy. 1935, No. 2, Art. 10.
[64] Cy. 1935, No. 1, Art. 1.
[65] Cy. 1936, No. 2, Art. 5.

national district, divided in 1926 from the Karachay-Cherkessy region),[66] the Mordovian Autonomous SSR [67] (reorganized in 1934 from the Mordovian autonomous region), the Khakass autonomous region (reorganized in 1930 from the Khakass district formed in 1925),[68] and the Jewish autonomous region (formed from the Birobidjan district in 1934).[69]

In the same period, a new form of national-state organization developed, the national district, making possible the union of the most backward nationalities of the North with the Soviet construction in national forms.

In 1929 the Tadjik Autonomous SSR, a component part of the Uzbek SSR, was reorganized into a Union Republic, and entered immediately into the USSR;[70] this was confirmed by the Sixth Congress of Soviets of the USSR in 1931.[71]

The strengthening of the independence of the republics was reflected in such acts as the elimination (in 1924) of the All-Central-Asiatic Party organs (the Central Asia Bureau of the Central Committee of the All-Union Communist Party (of Bolsheviks)) and the economic organs (the Central Asia Economic Council),[72] and the directive of the Central Committee of the All-Union Communist Party (of Bolsheviks), 1931, concerning the Transcaucasian Federative Soviet Republic. This directive aimed at increasing the independence of its constituent republics, which prepared the conditions for its liquidation (which occurred in 1936), and in the formation of new Republic People's Commissariats for Local Industry [73] and People's Commissariats for Economy.[74]

Intensification of the principles of single All-Union direction was reflected in changes (in the sphere of jurisdiction of the USSR and the Union Republics) adopted by the Sixth Congress of Soviets in 1931, in forming new All-Union and Union Republic (unified) People's Commissariats as component parts of the Council of People's Commissars of the USSR, and in forming a Union prosecuting magistracy (1933)[75] and an All-Union Commission of Soviet Control (1934)[76] in place of the (liquidated) unified People's Commissariat of Worker-Peasant Inspection.

The new elements in the mutual relationships between the Union and Union Republics were reflected most clearly, exhaustively, and logically in changes in the organization of our union state established (in 1936) by the Stalin Constitution.

[66] Cy. 1928, No. 49, Art. 371
[67] Cy. 1935, No. 1, Art. 1.
[68] Cy. 1930, No. 55, Art. 660.
[69] Cy. 1934, No. 19, Art. 114.
[70] Cz. 1929, No. 75, Art. 717.
[71] Cz. 1931, No. 17, Art. 162.

[72] Cz. 1934, No. 6c, Art. 441.
[73] Cz. 1934, No. 42, Art. 325.
[74] Cz. 1931, No. 65, Art. 426.
[75] Cz. 1933, No. 40, Art. 239.
[76] Cz. 1934, No. 9, Art. 58.

SEC. 7: LEGAL FORMS OF THE SOVIET UNION STATE

1. *Composition and boundaries of the USSR*

By the time the new Constitution was adopted in 1936, seven Union Republics had entered the USSR. Into the structure of the Union the Stalin Constitution introduced changes of the greatest historical significance: (1) in connection with the new problems confronting them, the hitherto autonomous Kazakh and Kirghiz Republics were reorganized into Union Republics; and (2) the Transcaucasian Federation was liquidated and the three constituent Soviet Socialist Republics—Azerbaijan, Georgia, and Armenia—became Union Republics.

The Transcaucasian Federation had fulfilled its historic mission and successfully solved all the tasks put before it. For the fourteen years of its existence, it had assured the economic and cultural development of its republics and their conversion into advanced socialist states. It had fulfilled its mission also in that it had liquidated the struggle between the nations and put in its place friendship and peace between the toilers of its different nationalities.

To solve the question of the transfer of autonomous republics into the category of Union Republics, there must be present the three signs of which Stalin spoke in his *Report on the Draft of the USSR Constitution*: "It is impossible to justify the transfer of autonomous republics into the category of Union Republics by their economic and cultural maturity, just as it is impossible to justify leaving this or that republic in the list of autonomous republics by reason of its economic or cultural backwardness."[1]

Having noted that such approach would be neither Marxist nor Leninist, Stalin pointed out the following three signs as affording the basis for transferring autonomous republics into the category of Union Republics:

(1) It is necessary that the republic be a borderland, not encircled on all sides by USSR territories. Why? Because if there is preserved in behalf of a Union Republic the right to withdraw from the USSR, then it must necessarily be possible for this republic—having become a Union Republic—logically and in fact to put the question of its withdrawal from the USSR. But such a question can be put only by a republic which, let us say, borders on some foreign state and is accordingly not encircled on all sides by USSR territory. Of course we have no republics which would in fact put the question of withdrawing from the USSR. But once the right of such withdrawal remains in behalf of a Union

[1] Stalin, *Report on the Draft of the USSR Constitution* (1936), p. 37.

Republic, it is necessary that the setting of the matter be such that this right become no empty and senseless piece of paper. Take, for example, the Bashkir or Tatar Republic, and assume that these autonomous republics have passed into the category of Union Republics. Could they—logically and factually—put the question of their withdrawal from the USSR? No, they could not. Why? Because on all sides they are surrounded by Soviet Republics and regions, and out of the structure of the USSR they have, strictly speaking, nowhere to go. Hence the transfer of such republics into the category of Union Republics would be incorrect.

Stalin further pointed out:

(2) It is necessary that the nationality which gave the Soviet Republic its name represent therein a more or less compact majority. Take, for example, the Crimean Autonomous Republic. It is a borderland republic, but the Crimean Tatars are not a majority in it; on the contrary, they represent a local minority. Accordingly, it would be incorrect and illogical to transfer the Crimean Republic into the category of Union Republics. (3) It is necessary that the republic be not very small in the sense of the number of its population; it must have a population, let us say, of not less, but more, than at least a million. Why? Because it would be incorrect to assume that a tiny Soviet Republic—with a minimum population and an insignificant army—could count on independent state existence. There can scarcely be any doubt that rapacious imperialists would promptly appropriate it.

I think that without these three objective signs being present, it would be incorrect at this moment of history to put the question of the transfer of any autonomous republic into the category of Union Republics.[2]

At the present time the Soviet Union is a single, union, multinational state consisting of eleven Union Soviet Socialist Republics which in their turn unify twenty-two autonomous republics, nine autonomous regions, and eleven national districts. The total population of the USSR has attained almost 170 millions.

The territory of the Soviet Union, occupying the eastern half of Europe and the northern third of Asia, constitutes more than 21 million square kilometers—that is to say, approximately one-sixth of all the dry land of the world. Its territory is two and one-half times the size of that of the U.S.A. and forty-five times the size of that of Germany. From north to south—from the shores of the Arctic Ocean to the Black Sea—it stretches 4,500 kilometers; and from west to east—from the Baltic Sea to the Pacific Ocean—10,000 kilometers. The length of its boundaries is 60,000 kilometers: 43,000 on the sea and 17,500 on the land. It borders on twelve countries: Finland, Esthonia, Latvia, Poland, Rumania, Turkey, Iran, Afghanistan, China, the Mongolian People's Republic, the Tuvan People's Republic, and Japan.

[2] *Ibid.*, pp. 38–39.

The North European part of the Union—the Archangel region and the Kola Peninsula—are washed by the waves of the White Sea and the Bering Sea. The boundary with Finland runs from north to south. As far as Lake Ladoga it goes through the Kola Peninsula and Karelia, then it intersects Lake Ladoga and the isthmus uniting it with the Gulf of Finland, and goes along the Gulf to the mouth of the Narva. From the Gulf of Finland the boundary passes along the right bank of the Narva and along Lake Chud (in 1242, Russian troops, led by Alexander Nevsky, won their famous victory upon the ice of this lake, wiping out the Teutonic Knights —those currish knights, as Marx called them—who were trying to seize the Russian land).

From Lake Chud the boundary runs south again and intersects the Western Dvina not far from the station of Bigosovo. In this section it divides the USSR (the Leningrad and Kalinin regions of the RSFSR and the northwest part of the White Russian SSR) from Esthonia and Latvia. Then starting from the banks of the Western Dvina and extending to the banks of the Black Sea the boundary runs with Poland and Rumania. The White Russian and the Ukrainian SSR border on Poland, and the Ukrainian SSR on Rumania.

The Soviet-Turkish boundary begins on the shore of the Black Sea south of Batum and passes along the mountain ridges of the Georgian and Armenian SSR.

To the southwest of Erevan (capital of Soviet Armenia), along the Arax (a tributary of the Kura), the boundary runs between the Armenian SSR and Iran, and then between the Azerbaijan SSR and Iran. The Turkmen SSR also borders upon Iran. The boundary here stretches from Mount Hassan-Kuli (on the east bank of the Caspian Sea) along the river Atrek, along mountains of Kopet-Daga and the river Tedjen.

From the Tedjen and then along the Amu-Darya and the Piandj the boundary of the Turkmen, Uzbek, and Tadjik Union Republics goes with Afghanistan. The Gorny-Badakhshan autonomous region, a constituent part of the Tadjik SSR, is separated only by a narrow strip of Afghan territory from the English colony of India.

From the Soviet-Afghan border northeast along the Pamir Mountains, the glaciers of Tianshan, and the mountains of east Kazakhstan, intersected by river valleys, as far as Altay, extends the boundary of the Tadjik, Kirghiz, and Kazakh Union Republics with that of Sinkiang of western China.

Along the Sayan Mountains goes the boundary of the USSR with the Tuva People's Republic, separating this republic from the Krasnoyarsk territory and the Irkutsk region of the RSFSR.

Further, along the Altay, the Sayan Mountains and the low mountains of eastern Siberia, runs the boundary between the USSR and the Mongolian People's Republic, followed by the boundary with Manchuria—turned by the Japanese into the colony of Manchukuo. South from Vladivostok along Cape Posiet, the USSR boundary touches that of the Japanese colony of Korea, and on the island of Sakhalin another Japanese colony—South Sakhalin. More than 20,000 kilometers of Far Eastern sea boundaries go along the Maritime and Khabarovsk territories. In the north, not far from the boundary of the USSR, are the possessions of the U.S.A., the Aleutian Islands (in the Bering Sea), and Alaska.

The northern shores of the Asiatic part of the USSR are washed by the waters of the North Arctic Ocean.

Soviet boundaries are sharply guarded by our heroic border troops. To guard them there are also four mighty Soviet fleets—the North Fleet, the Baltic Fleet, the Black Sea Fleet, and the Pacific Fleet. Any enemy effort to violate these boundaries will encounter the most energetic resistance from the Red Army, the Red Fleet, and all the multinational Soviet people—such as was encountered by the insolent Japanese Samurai, who were soundly beaten by our noble Far-Eastern border troops in the historic battles near the island of Khasan. We "do not wish a single inch of another's land. But of our own land we will not yield an inch to anyone."[3]

Herewith is a table showing the dimension, territory, and external boundaries of each Union Republic separately.

Within the USSR each of the Union Republics borders upon the following Union Republics: RSFSR upon the White Russian, Ukrainian, Georgian, Azerbaijan and Kazakh SSR; the Ukrainian SSR upon the RSFSR and the White Russian SSR; the Georgian SSR upon the RSFSR, and the Azerbaijan and Armenian SSR; the Armenian SSR upon the Georgian and Azerbaijan SSR; the Turkmen SSR upon the Kazakh and Uzbek SSR; the Uzbek SSR upon the Turkmen, Kazakh, Tadjik and Kirghiz SSR; the Tadjik SSR upon the Uzbek and Kirghiz SSR; the Kazakh SSR upon RSFSR, and the Turkmen, Uzbek and Kirghiz SSR; and the Kirghiz SSR upon the Kazakh, Uzbek, and Tadjik SSR.

Changes in the structure of the USSR—that is to say, the growth of the number of Union and autonomous republics—signify the further development of Soviet federalism, and strengthening of the USSR and the further growth of its national state organizations.

2. Sovereignty of the USSR

In the science of public law, sovereignty means the supremacy of state authority, by virtue of which that authority appears unlimited and autono-

[3] Stalin, *Questions of Leninism* (10th Russian ed.), p. 361.

Name of Soviet Socialist Republic	Capital	Dimensions of territory (in thousands of square kilometers) and in percentage to the entire territory of the USSR	Contiguous foreign countries
RSFSR	Moscow	16510.5 78 per cent	Finland, Latvia, Esthonia, the People's Republic of Mongolia, the Tuvinian People's Republic, China, Manchuria, and Japan.
Ukrainian SSR	Kiev	445.3 2.09 per cent	Poland and Rumania
White Russian SSR	Minsk	126.8 .6 per cent	Poland and Latvia
Azerbaijan SSR	Baku	86 .4 per cent	Iran
Georgian SSR	Tiflis	69.6 .33 per cent	Turkey
Armenian SSR	Erevan	30 .14 per cent	Turkey and Iran
Turkmen SSR	Ashkhabad	443.6 2.11 per cent	Iran and Afganistan
Uzbek SSR	Tashkent	378.3 1.75 per cent	Afghanistan
Tadjik SSR	Stalinabad	143.9 .68 per cent	China
Kazakh SSR	Alma-Ata	2744.5 12.97 per cent	China
Kirghiz SSR	Frunza	196.7 .93 per cent	China

mous within the land and independent in foreign relationships. In the USSR sovereignty belongs to the multinational Soviet people. Through their socialist state, personified by its highest organs of authority, the people effectuate that sovereignty. It was affirmed in obdurate class struggle against foes within and without. Formed independently by the will of the toilers of all nationalities, defending its independence of imperialist states, the Soviet state existed at the beginning without being acknowledged by any of them. Its later acknowledgment by most of them expressed its universally admitted might and authority in the international system of states. This was brilliantly attested likewise by its being invited into the League of Nations (September, 1934) by thirty-seven states.

Existing in a system of states, the USSR is completely independent of all in foreign relationships in its external policy. "We formerly were—and are now—orientated to the USSR and only to the USSR," [4] as Stalin said in his report at the Seventeenth Party Congress.

The stable, economic basis of the sovereignty of the Soviet people, personified by their union state, is the socialist system of economy and socialist property in instruments and means of production.

The USSR sovereignty finds its concrete expression and its juridical confirmation in the plenary powers possessed by it (as personified in its higher organs of state authority and state government) and fixed by Article 14 of the Union Constitution. We have already spoken in detail of the jurisdiction of the USSR. We will now pause only on the question of the interrelation of the Union sovereignty and that of the Union Republics.

Each Union Republic is a sovereign state. Its sovereignty is assured by a whole series of special legal guarantees provided by the Constitution of the USSR (the right of free withdrawal from the Union, its own Constitution, the inadmissibility of territorial change without the consent of the Union Republic concerned, and so on). The sovereignty of the Soviet Union State is not opposed to the sovereignty of Union Republics. Each amplifies and confirms the other. The sovereignty of the Union could not possess adequate power, did it not preserve and reinforce the sovereignty of the Union Republics. Conversely, the sovereignty of the Union Republics would not be guaranteed, did it not rest on the military power and material resources of the entire Union.

In the bourgeois science of public law, sovereignty in the federative state—who bears this sovereignty therein—is a moot question. (1) Some of the most eminent bourgeois political scientists (such as De Tocqueville and Weitz) consider that the central—the Union—authority divides its sovereignty with the constituent parts of the federation, with the authority of the states or cantons. (2) Others (such as Calhoun and Seidel) starting from the "indivisibility" of sovereignty and from the fact that the union state was historically created by its parts (the states), assert that sovereignty is the property of the parts of the union state which only temporarily hands it over to the federal authority. (3) Finally, there are still others (Laband, Jellinek) who consider that sovereignty in the union state belongs only to

[4] *Ibid.*, pp. 550–551.

the center (as in a unitary state) and that states, cantons, lands, and so on may be considered a state and not as possessing sovereignty but as having only such sign of authority as independent legislation.

Whether developing one point of view or the other, bourgeois jurists focus their attention chiefly on the formal-juridical relationships between the union authority and the parts of the federations, and contemplate these only in the shape in which they are expressed in constitutions. Meantime, constitutions of bourgeois states, as everyone knows, always lag behind actual legal relationships, which are extremely mobile and are most closely connected with, and dependent upon, the changing conditions of capitalist development and the development of the class struggle. When the first of the three groups listed above assumes that union authority divides sovereignty with parts of the federation,[5] it only formally fixes that which is inscribed in constitutions, without analyzing the social-economic conditions impelling the bourgeoisie to create the union state. But these conditions were such as, in spite of constitutions, to evoke progressively greater centralization of authority—the approximation of federal authority to unitary authority—and an almost monopolist domination of central authority expressing the interest of big capital. The viewpoint of the second group—that sovereignty belongs only to the parts of the federation which have handed it over to federal authority temporarily and while they consider it advantageous for themselves to be in the union—factually reflects the contradictory interests of the bourgeoisie of different districts of the capitalist union state. The bourgeoisie strives to preserve its sovereignty in its own state or canton, upon condition of opposing the bourgeoisie of other states and cantons.[6]

The assertion of the third group—that sovereignty belongs only to the center, signifies nothing but a defense of specific interrelations formed after 1871 in the German union state under Prussian hegemony, whereas the other "states" (like Bavaria, Baden, and Württemberg) were in fact in the position of not having rights equal with those of Prussia.

Confirming the sovereignty of the Union Republics, the Constitution of the Soviet Union State preserves their sovereign rights and guarantees their factual realization. As in all else, it is not divorced from life, and it fixes the actual interrelations between the Union and its constituent parts.

In bourgeois federative states the interrelations between the union authority and members of the union state are actually made up otherwise than would appear in the constitutions of the states. The Swiss Constitu-

[5] In particular, De Tocqueville, who bases his views on the example of the U.S.A. (Cf. his book, *Democracy in America*.)

[6] The theory of one of these jurists, Calhoun, was accepted by the bourgeoisie of the Confederate States which, during the Civil War, sought to withdraw from the Northern States.

tion, for example, proclaims (in Article 3) that "the cantons are sovereign in so far as their sovereignty is not limited by the union constitution," whereas Article 16 of this constitution—based on Article 2—grants to the central authority the right of intervening in canton matters in case of disturbances.[7] The class essence of Article 16 consists in the fact that the central authority deals with striking workers on a "legal" basis. So it was, for example, when (in 1875) the bourgeoisie sent troops to crush strikers during the building of the Saint Gotthard Tunnel. Thereafter such intervention of union power in the affairs of the cantons became a system. That the parts of the bourgeois federation are not sovereign, and that the constitutions are remote from reality, is attested likewise by the fact that the "sovereign" cantons in Switzerland and the sovereign states in the U.S.A. have not the right to withdraw from the union. Attempts of this sort invariably encounter the most decisive resistance from union authority, as exemplified by the war against the Sonderbund in Switzerland (1847) and the Civil War in the U.S.A. (1861–1865).

In international life bourgeois jurists regard the states as juridical persons. In point of form it is considered that just as a person within the state must respect the rights of another person, so one state-personality must respect the rights of another state-personality. In international intercourse, sovereignty in relations between states is fixed by compacts. Moreover, there is ordinarily formal admission of the principle of state equality. In fact, however, the big capitalist powers obtrude their conditions and their will upon the weaker states. The sovereignty of imperialist states does in fact create consequences, including often legal consequences, such as limit the sovereignty of the weaker states and reduce it to naught. "Such already is the law of the exploiters—the 'wolf law' of capitalism—to beat the backward and the weak. You are backward, you are weak—that means you have no rights and accordingly you may be beaten and enslaved."[8]

We may be convinced by many examples that the sovereignty of such weak states, in conditions of imperialism and where constitutions do not coincide with reality, is of formal significance only. Thus in the Constitution of Iraq: "Iraq is a sovereign state—independent and free." Notwithstanding formal attributes of a sovereign state—wherewith it was endowed by England—and although in the "union compact" between England and Iraq (June 30, 1930) the latter is designated a "high contracting party" having equal rights, Iraq is wholly dependent upon England and is in fact a mandated state. Egypt is in the same category as Iraq. In the Egyptian Constitu-

[7] Art. 2: "The Union has the purpose of guaranteeing the independence of the fatherland from foreign states, preserving internal quiet and order within the land, safeguarding the freedom and rights of members of the Union, and heightening their common prosperity."

[8] Stalin, *Questions of Leninism* (10th Russian ed.), p. 445.

tion is literally the same phrase about "sovereignty" and "independence," whereas everyone knows that the true master of Egypt is the same England. The position of Syria is analogous: Article 1 of its Constitution (1930) says: "Syria is an independent and sovereign state," but the presence of France's mandate to govern Syria makes the sovereignty of the latter just as ephemeral as it is in the other two cases just cited.

3. *Jurisdiction of the USSR*

Matters assigned to the jurisdiction of the USSR (Art. 14 of the Constitution) may be fundamentally reduced to four groups: first, questions flowing out of the fact of the capitalist encirclement in which the Soviet Union finds itself—questions of foreign relationships and defense of the state. The necessity and inevitability of creating a single front of Soviet Republics in the presence of capitalist encirclement was, as we have seen, one of the causes of their unification into the USSR, into a single union state able to guarantee external safety and also internal economic development and freedom of national development of the peoples. The Union Republics composing the USSR have empowered the latter, personified by its supreme organs of authority, to have jurisdiction over questions of foreign relationships and defense of the country (as was stated in the 1924 USSR Constitution), Art. 1, Pars. *a, b, c, d, e, f, g, j*).

The 1936 Constitution leaves questions of external relationships (diplomatic and economic) and matters concerned with the defense of the land to the unlimited jurisdiction of the Union as before. That jurisdiction, according to Article 14 of the Constitution, includes the following: (1) representation of the USSR in international relationships, the conclusion and ratification of treaties with other states; (2) matters of war and peace; (3) organization of the defense of the USSR and direction of all its armed forces; (4) foreign trade—on the basis of a state monopoly; and (5) preservation of the security of the state.

To this group of Union powers is related likewise the right of the Presidium of the Supreme Soviet of the USSR to proclaim "martial law in separate localities or throughout the Union in the interests of defense of the Union or of assuring social order and state security." This right was given to the Presidium by the first session of the Supreme Soviet of the USSR (January 15, 1938) and fixed as point "P" in Article 49 of the Constitution.[9]

The *second* group, the broadest, comprises questions related to the field of socialist economy and resulting from the fact that the Soviet state is not

[9] Prior to the acceptance of the Stalin Constitution, the method of initiating a state of war was established by a Regulation Concerning Extraordinary Measures of Defense of Revolutionary Order affirmed by the Central Executive Committee and the Council of People's Commissars of the USSR, April 3, 1925 (Cz. 1925, No. 25, Art. 167).

only a political but also a managing subject.[10] Matters within this group emanate from the dominance in our country of socialist property in the instruments and means of production, from socialist planning of the Soviet scheme of economy. In the same way as its plenary powers in the fields of war and diplomacy, the plenary economic powers of the Union were formed historically. We have already pointed out that as early as the period of compact relationships, the Soviet Republics concluded accords with the RSFSR concerning not only a military—but also and at the same time an economic —union.

The compact for the formation of the USSR, and then the Constitution of the USSR (1924), defined the circle of economic matters within the jurisdiction of the Union, being naturally and first and foremost precisely the same matters as those about which (prior to the formation of the Union) compacts and accords were entered into between the RSFSR and other republics. We may judge of the economic jurisdiction of the Union under the 1924 Constitution by the catalogue of the People's Commissariats of USSR. The division of these into two categories, All-Union and Unified, and (by the Stalin Constitution) All-Union and Union Republic, attests the fact that some branches of economy are within the exclusive jurisdiction of the Union, while as to others this jurisdiction is distributed accordingly between the Union and the Union Republics.

The apportionment of authority as between the Union and Union Republics expresses the principle of the stipulated collaboration between the federation (the Union) and its members—one of the most important characteristics of the USSR as a union state.

The broad range of jurisdiction of Union authority in the USSR (by virtue of the socialist character of the Soviet Union and the centralized planning of all national economy realized thereby) shows the unity of the Soviet state and the extremely close solidarity of the Soviet Republics. Centralized administration of the branches of economy upon democratic principles not only does not destroy—but operates the better to satisfy—the special interests of separate republics.

[10] Herein is one of the fundamental distinctions between the Soviet state and every sort of bourgeois state, a happy definition of whose functions and relationship to economy was given by Stalin in an interview with the English writer, H. G. Wells (July 23, 1934). Pointing out the impossibility of realizing the principles of planned economy in the conditions of capitalism—when the economic basis of capitalism (private property in the instruments and means of production) is preserved in the state—and the consequent futility of Roosevelt's attempts to apply these principles in the U.S.A., Stalin said: "We must not forget about the functions of the state in the bourgeois world. It is an institution for organizing the defense of the land—the defense of order—a mechanism for collecting taxes. But the capitalist state is little concerned with economy in the proper sense of the word—economy is not in the hands of the state—on the contrary the state is in the hands of capitalist economy."—Stalin, *Questions of Leninism* (10th Russian ed.), pp. 601-602.

In the economic sphere, the Stalin Constitution assigns to the jurisdiction of the Union (Art. 14): (1) establishment of the national economic plans of the USSR; (2) confirmation of a single state budget of the USSR as well as of taxes and revenues going into Union, republic and local budgets; (3) administration of banks, industrial and agricultural establishments and enterprises, and also of trading enterprises of All-Union importance; (4) administration of transport and communications; (5) direction of the money and credit system; (6) organization of state insurance; (7) concluding and granting loans; (8) establishment of basic principles for the use of land and of natural deposits, forests, and waters; and (9) organization of a single system of economic statistics.

As distinct from the first group of matters referred in their entirety to the exclusive jurisdiction of the Union, the second group comprises questions of which one part is referred to the exclusive jurisdiction of the Union, whereas jurisdiction with reference to the other part belongs to both Union and Union Republics.

The USSR realizes its undivided direction in the following branches of national economy: all means of communication, water transport, heavy and defense industry, machinery building, and food supply. Direction of these branches belongs to the corresponding All-Union People's Commissariats which effectuate that direction either directly or through organs designated by them (in accordance with Art. 75 of the Constitution).

Branches wherein jurisdiction is apportioned by the Constitution between the Union and the Union Republics include: food supply, light industry, timber industry, agriculture, state grain and livestock farms, and finance and trade. Directing these branches through the corresponding Union Republic People's Commissariats, the Union leaves to Union Republics where there are People's Commissariats of the same name, an important measure of self-help. These commissariats, subordinate to the Supreme Soviets of the Union Republics, carry out the directives and tasks of the corresponding People's Commissariats of the USSR, which in their work rest on Union Republic People's Commissariats of the same name. By way of exception, the latter commissariats exercise also the *immediate* direction of certain enterprises within the bounds of the branch of state administration entrusted to them, but the number of such enterprises is strictly limited to the list specially affirmed by the Presidium of the Supreme Soviet of the USSR (Art. 76 of the Constitution).

The *third* group consists of matters relating to the social-cultural field, matters of education, preservation of health, and labor. As to the first two, the Union has the right to establish "basic principles," as to labor, to establish "bases of legislation." This means that in these matters the Union Republics have greater independence.[11]

The *fourth* group of Union powers embraces matters touching the inter-relations of Union and Union Republics, conditioned by general principles of Union supremacy, including: admission of new republics into the structure of the USSR; control over observance of the USSR Constitution and insuring that the constitutions of Union Republics correspond with the Union Constitution; confirmation of boundary changes as between Union Republics; and confirmation of the formation of new territories and regions and of new autonomous republics within the Union Republics.[12] All these plenary powers are realized solely by organs of the Union. By their very nature they cannot belong to Union Republics.

In addition to the matters enumerated, the Union has jurisdiction of: legislation concerning the structure of the courts and legal procedure, criminal and civil codes, laws concerning Union citizenship and the rights of foreigners, and, finally, the publication of All-Union acts of amnesty.

The Stalin Constitution introduced a series of changes in the delimitation of the Union and Union Republic jurisdiction established by the 1924 Constitution. These changes reflect the strengthening of socialist economy and the need for unification of direction and legal rules thereby entailed. At the same time they attest the strengthening of fraternal collaboration and mutual aid between the republics. Thus the 1924 Constitution gave the Union jurisdiction only to establish the *bases* and the general plan of all national economy, *bases* of court structure and legal procedure and criminal and civil legislation, and *basic* legislation in the field of Union citizenship (and, moreover, only in regard to rights of foreigners). Formulation in the new Constitution of the plenary powers of the Union in these fields is characterized by a heightening of the role of the Union and a further strengthening of the unity of the Soviet Union State.

According to the formula of the 1924 Constitution, organs of the Union realized *direction* of foreign trade, whereas the Stalin Constitution places foreign trade under the exclusive jurisdiction of the Union. The 1924 Con-

---

[11] As to the preservation of health, Union jurisdiction is not limited to the mere establishment of "basic principles" as it is with reference to popular education. The Union exerts direct guidance of the preservation of health through the Union Republic People's Commissariat of Preservation of Health. (Until 1936, this People's Commissariat was one of the Republic Commissariats; it became a Union Republic Commissariat on June 20, 1936—Cz. 1936, No. 40, p. 337.)

[12] Here the Constitution has in view also new autonomous regions. The constitutions of the Union Republics which comprise autonomous regions include indications that the Supreme Soviets of these republics submit for confirmation by the Supreme Soviet of the USSR the formation likewise of new autonomous regions also in the number of other administrative-territorial units.

stitution, reflecting the then inadequate economic connection between the republics, acknowledged the right of Union Republics to conclude external and internal loans upon permission of organs of the USSR. According to the Stalin Constitution, this right belongs only to the USSR. The new Constitution included among the objects of jurisdiction of higher organs of the Union the affirmation of the formation within Union Republics of new territories, regions and autonomous republics. This element reflects the necessity for greater stability of the basic administrative divisions.

The new Constitution perfected the structure of the Soviet Union multinational state, adapted it to the conditions of the victorious socialist order in our country, and reinforced the might of the Soviet state in the presence of the steadily increasing threat of military attack on the USSR by aggressive fascist powers.

The Stalin Constitution is the Constitution of the completely formed multinational socialist state, which has withstood all trials, "whose stability any national state in any part of the world might well envy." [13]

4. The legal position of Union Republics and their jurisdiction

The sovereignty of the Union Republics is limited only within the bounds pointed out in Article 14 of the Union Constitution; outside these bounds each Union Republic carries state authority into effect independently. The USSR protects the sovereign rights of the Union Republics.

The basic signs of the sovereignty of the Union Republics are that: (1) each Union Republic has its own constitution; (2) the right to free withdrawal from the Union is preserved in behalf of each Union Republic; and (3) the territory of Union Republics cannot be changed without their consent. These most important principles of Union Republic sovereignty are reinforced in Articles 16 through 18 of the Stalin Constitution. To them must be added a fourth: within the bounds of its jurisdiction the realization of state authority by a Union Republic is independent.

Constitutions of Union Republics are constructed in complete accord with the Union Constitution, as required by Article 16 of the latter. And this is perfectly natural. In order to realize mutual aid—economic, political, and defensive—the Soviet Socialist Republics have been voluntarily united into a union state, the USSR.[14] Therefore the oneness of the purposes of the USSR and of the separate Union Republics—the oneness of the Soviet socialist system—must be and is reflected both in the Constitution of the Union and in the constitutions of the Union Republics. While it cor-

---

[13] Stalin, *Report on the Draft of the USSR Constitution* (1936), p. 15.
[14] Cf. Art. 13 of the Constitution of the RSFSR and similar provisions in those of other Union Republics.

responds with the Union Constitution, the constitution of each Union Republic reflects at the same time the specific interests and national special characteristics of that republic. Constitutions of Union Republics thus unite the general interests of the state with the special interests of the USSR nationalities. Herein is the pledge of the stability and might of the USSR as a socialist multinational state.

The right of free withdrawal from the USSR, proclaimed in Article 17 of the USSR Constitution, expresses one of the most important principles of the Lenin-Stalin national policy—the voluntary character of the union between the nations. An amendment to the draft of the Constitution of the USSR, introduced while it was being considered by the entire people, proposed to exclude Article 17 from the draft. Stalin pointed out in his report at the Extraordinary Eighth All-Union Congress of Soviets that this proposal was wrong and should not be adopted by the Congress. "The USSR is a voluntary union of Union Republics having equal rights. To exclude from the Constitution the Article concerning the right of free withdrawal from the USSR is to destroy the voluntary character thereof." [15]

Of course we have not a single republic which would wish to withdraw from the structure of the USSR; that would not be in its own interests.

Under socialism the toiling masses themselves will nowhere consent to isolation for purely economic . . . motives, but diversity of political forms, freedom to withdraw from the state, the experience of state building—all this will (until every sort of state shall in general wither away) be the foundation of a rich cultural life, a pledge that the nations shall the more quickly come together voluntarily and merge.[16]

Article 18 of the Constitution also expresses the sovereignty of the Union Republics, declaring inadmissible any change of the territory of Union Republics without their consent, and thereby stabilizing and strengthening the economic basis of the development of each. Everyone knows that territory is a necessary concomitant of every sort of state. Without definite territory there cannot be a state. But if in the bourgeois state the significance of territory is merely that it is the boundary of that state's authority in terms of space, it has in the Soviet state another significance also and is defined by still another relationship of the state to the earth (territory): the Soviet state is the proprietor of the entire earthly expanse constituting the territory of the USSR. It has been that proprietor since the moment of its emergence in consequence of the October Socialist Revolution which destroyed private

---

[15] Stalin, *Report on the Draft of the USSR Constitution* (1936), p. 36.
[16] Lenin (Russian ed.), Vol. XIX, p. 256.

property and land, in consequence of which, territory (the earth) became not only the boundary in space of the expanding Soviet authority but also an object of socialist economy, an arena of socialist building.

Bearing the supreme right of property in land, the USSR possesses broad and plenary powers in managing land territory. The Constitution of the USSR (Art. 14) charges organs of the Union to establish fundamental principles for the use of land (and of natural deposits, forests, and waters), to confirm changes of boundaries between Union Republics, and so on. Notwithstanding all this, however, organs of the Union cannot change the territory of Union Republics without their consent thereto, and this in no-wise contradicts what has been said previously as to rights of the Union in regard to territory. Article 18 of the Constitution of the USSR represents a guarantee of the sovereignty of Union Republics which amplifies the funda-mental guarantee thereof—the right of withdrawal from the Union. At the same time this Article signifies that each Union Republic, as a state, has definite state territory, whose boundaries have precisely established the limit in space of the state authority of that republic and which is the basis of its economic activity.

Article 15 of the USSR Constitution limits the sovereignty of Union Republics only within the bounds indicated in Article 14. Such limitation flows immediately out, and is a consequence, of the very fact of the unifica-tion of Union Republics into one union state. "Unification of every sort is some limitation upon rights theretofore possessed by those united." [17] This limitation—the renunciation of certain of their rights of independence—is alike for all the Union Republics, which fact—and the further fact that they all in like degree enjoy the blessings of the Union—expresses the legal equality of the Union Republics.

Guaranteeing to the USSR (as personified by its higher organs of authority and of state government) the rights defined by Article 14 of the USSR Constitution, the Union Republics have also their own jurisdiction in matters within the scope of the Union's jurisdiction. True, their jurisdic-tion is here limited by the bounds established by Article 14 of the Union Constitution and by Union legislation (including the "fundamental prin-ciples, bases of legislation," and so on). Even with this proviso, however, powers of the Union Republics are significant, particularly as to national economy.

Pursuant to its constitution, each Union Republic carries into effect within its territory the following measures: (1) it affirms the plan of national economy and the budget of the republic; (2) it establishes, in con-formity with USSR legislation, state and local taxes and levies, and other

[17] Stalin, *Marxism and the National-Colonial Question* (1937), p. 115.

income; (3) it manages insurance and savings; (4) it establishes the order of using the land, its natural deposits, the forests and waters—guided therein by basic principles established by Union organs; (5) it actually controls and superintends the administration and condition of enterprises subordinate to the Union (a particularly graphic illustration of the activity of Union Republics within the sphere of Union jurisdiction); and (6) it accomplishes the building of roads and directs local transport and communications.

In the field of social-cultural measures, the jurisdiction of the Union Republic includes: legislation concerning labor, direction of the care of public health, and of primary intermediate and higher education.

Outside the bounds indicated in Article 14 of the USSR Constitution, Union Republics exercise state authority independently, having an adequately broad basis for independent state activity. In *the economic field,* for example, they direct the preparation and fulfillment of the budgets of autonomous republics and the local budgets of territories and regions (those republics having no territorial and regional division) the budgets of areas, districts, and cities; they administer banks, industries, agricultural and trade enterprises (subordinate to the republics), and likewise direct local industry; to them belong direction of housing and communal economy, the construction of houses, and the good order of cities and other inhabited places.

In *the cultural-social field* the Union Republics direct the cultural-educational and scientific organizations and institutions of the republics and administer the cultural-educational and scientific organizations and institutions of All-Republic significance. They direct social insurance. To them belong likewise the direction and organization of physical culture and sport, the organization of republic court organs, the conferring of rights of citizenship of a given republic, and amnesty and pardoning of citizens condemned by courts of the republic.

In *the field of administrative-territorial organization* the Union Republics have the right of confirming the boundaries and districting of autonomous republics and autonomous regions and of establishing the boundaries and districts of territories and regions (or, where there are none, the general administrative-territorial division of the republic). As to forming new territories and regions, and likewise new autonomous republics and regions, the formation thereof is proposed by Union Republics for confirmation by the Supreme Soviet of the USSR.

The system of republic organs of state administration also corresponds completely to the compass of the plenary powers of the Union Republics. For the administration of such branches of economic and cultural-social organization—although they are within the jurisdiction of the Union Republic—as are also within the jurisdictional bounds set by Article 14 of the Union Constitution,[18] the Union Republics (as has already been noted) have their own commissariats subordinate both to the Council of People's Commissars of the USSR and to the corresponding Union-Republic People's Commissariat of the USSR.

Direction of those branches of economy and cultural-social organization in which the activity of Union Republics is most independent is exercised by Republic People's Commissariats subordinate immediately to the Council of People's Commissars of the Union Republic. Each Union Republic has four such autonomous People's Commissariats not analogous to any of the People's Commissariats of the Union; these are the People's Commissariats for Education, for Local Industry, for Communal Economy, and for Social Insurance.

5. The USSR as protector of the sovereign rights of Union Republics

The USSR guards the sovereign rights of the Union Republics (Art. 15 of the Constitution of the USSR). Against what and by what means are these sovereign rights guarded? (1) Against any possible violation (by separate organs or individuals) of any law of the Union authority assuring these rights. Such protection is made real by organs of state authority and organs of state administration of the USSR and also by the Public Prosecutor of the USSR. The supreme organs control fulfillment of the Constitution of the USSR; the Presidium of the Supreme Soviet abrogates directives of the Council of People's Commissars of the USSR and of Union Republic Councils of People's Commissars if they do not conform with law; the Supreme Soviet of the USSR (when it deems necessary) appoints committees of inquiry and investigation on any matter (Art. 51), and consequently on questions touching a breach of the sovereign rights of Union Republics. The Public Prosecutor of the USSR exercises supreme supervision over exact fulfillment of the laws by all the People's Commissariats and the institutions subordinate to them (Art. 113). (2) Against attempts (military and of every other sort) upon the Union Republic by capitalist states. A mighty means of defense against such attempts is the Worker-Peasant Red Army and Navy. Each Union Republic is assured that it will be defended, in case of attack upon it, by the might of the entire Union. An important part in guarding the sovereignty of the Union Republics belongs likewise to the People's Commissariat for Internal Affairs. The proceedings against the anti-Soviet "right-Trotsky bloc" revealed that the fascist states yearn to wrest

[18] Reciting that "the jurisdiction of the USSR"—personified by its highest organs of state authority and of government—covers a list of twenty-three matters.

from the Soviet Union the majority of the Union Republics and turn them into colonies of their own.

Union Republics are thus sovereign states with their supreme legislative organs and organs of state administration. The sovereignty of each Union Republic is expressed in the fact that it: (1) has its own basic law, its constitution, established by itself; (2) has at its disposal definite territory which cannot be changed without its consent; and (3) enjoys the right of free withdrawal from the Union.

Aside from this, each Union Republic participates on equal principles with all the others in the creation and activity of the supreme organs of authority of the USSR through which it can forcefully influence the legislative activity of the Union and exercise state authority independently within the bounds of its own jurisdiction. Union Republics themselves voluntarily limit their own sovereignty in aid of the Union in those fields, plenary jurisdiction whereof on the part of the Union in fact reinforces the strength of the republics themselves. Union authority utilizes the rights given to it by the Union Republics in order (by unifying the most important resources) to guarantee the growth and development of the republics themselves and the unity of the Soviet Socialist State—a factor of its indestructible might and steady development.

6. Laws of the USSR as expressing the unity of the socialist state

The nature of the USSR as a single, union, socialist state determines and conditions the solution by the Union Constitution of the matter of its laws. The rights transferred to the Union by the Union Republics include that of All-Union legislation on questions of Union jurisdiction. The Constitution of the USSR establishes the immutable rule (Art. 19) that "laws of the USSR have like force in the territory of all Union Republics." They are binding upon each Union Republic and have binding force in its territory.

As Union sovereignty is inconceivable without All-Union laws (including those in the form of "bases," "basic principles" and the like) binding upon the Union Republics, so also the sovereignty of the Union Republics necessarily presupposes their own legislative activity on matters within the bounds of their jurisdiction. As to a series of questions, the Constitution of the USSR leaves to the Union the right of establishing only "general principles" and "bases of legislation" (the use of land and of the natural deposits therein, and of forests and waters, education, preservation of health, and labor). This means that in all these provinces the Union Republics can develop broad independent activity, including legislative activity. The laws of Union Republics must not deviate, however, from those of the Union; otherwise the All-Union law prevails (Art. 20).

The Soviet system of economy and administration is so built as to afford the maximum assurance of the interests of the toilers and the successes of socialist building. This purpose is subserved by laws of the Union, which play an enormous part in the planned prosecution of the policy of the Soviet government, in the regulation and direction of all economic-political life of the country in the interests of socialism. And if some law of a Union Republic deviates from the corresponding Union law, that means that the law of the republic has violated the law of the Union. Article 20 of the USSR Constitution has precisely in view only such concrete cases as the legislation of separate Union Republics going beyond the bounds of their jurisdiction or contradicting (violating) fundamental principles established by Union legislation. Neither the one nor the other can be admitted; otherwise this would be a breach of the agreed activity of Union and republic organs of authority and a violation of the principle of planned development (contrary to the interests of the Union Republics themselves).

For a further reason it is inappropriate to speak of the priority of All-Union legislation as violating the sovereignty of Union Republics; they themselves participate in that legislation through their representatives in the Supreme Soviet of the USSR (in particular, in the Soviet of Nationalities).

The Stalin Constitution guarantees observance of the unity of Soviet socialist legality in the territory of the entire USSR.

7. Citizenship of the USSR and of the Union Republics

Citizenship means that a person belongs to a certain state, which conditions the extension to him of all laws regulating the positions of citizens in the state, their rights and obligations. By virtue of belonging to a certain state, he also enjoys diplomatic protection by it when he is abroad. In the constitutions of some capitalist states, the matter of citizenship is treated in the subdivisions regulating the rights and obligations of citizens (Japan, Poland—in its Constitution of 1921—and Yugoslavia). But citizenship is not a right in itself; it is only a condition, a premise, which makes it possible for all the laws defining the legal position of citizens of this or that state to apply to a given person. So it is not accidental that the USSR Constitution and the constitutions of the Union Republics treat the matter of citizenship in the chapter concerned with state organization rather than in that dealing with fundamental rights and obligations of citizens.

At the basis of the Soviet system of citizenship lie the principles of the internationalism and unity of the Soviet Union State, expressed in the formulation of Article 21 of the USSR Constitution. "A single Union citizenship is established for citizens of the USSR. Each citizen of a Union Republic is a citizen of the USSR." The constitutions of Union Republics establish in turn that each citizen of a given republic is a citizen of the USSR. At the same time they point out that citizens of all the other Union Republics enjoy in the territory of a given republic like rights with the citizens of that republic.

These statutes (1) characterize the actual unity of the socialist union state, and (2) attest the absence of national antagonisms, estrangements and distrust as between peoples, and certify that in national relations the USSR is now dominated by fraternity, mutual friendship, and the feeling of mutual respect of peoples struggling to attain a single end—communism. The existence of citizenship of the separate Union Republics side by side with Union citizenship emphasizes the state independence of these republics.

On August 19, 1938, at the second session of the Supreme Soviet of the USSR, a new Law of Citizenship of the USSR was adopted, starting first of all from the principle (confirmed by the Constitution) of both formal and factual equality of rights of Soviet citizens in the socialist state, irrespective of their nationality and race, as well as of sex—so that in the USSR women are given equal rights with men in all fields of economic, state, cultural and social-political life. Article 1 reproduces in their entirety the statutes of Article 21 of the USSR Constitution establishing single Union citizenship and the rule that each citizen of a Union Republic is a citizen of the USSR. Article 2 points out precisely who are citizens of the USSR: (a) all who were on November 7, 1917, subjects of the former Russian Empire and have not lost Soviet citizenship, and (b) "persons who have acquired Soviet citizenship in the legally established order."

According to the new law, the definition of possessing Soviet citizenship of the USSR is thus essentially different from the definition given by former regulations concerning citizenship (1924, 1931), which established that every person found in the territory of the USSR is acknowledged to be a citizen of the USSR in so far as it is not proved that he is a citizen of a foreign state.[19] In particular, as concerns foreigners contemplated by Paragraph b of Article 2, the fact of a foreigner being found in the territory of the USSR and not being proved to be a citizen of a foreign state is now not enough for him to be considered a citizen of the USSR. This requires in addition the (affirmative) acquisition of Soviet citizenship in the order established by Soviet law. This order is provided in Article 3 of the new law: "Independently of their nationality and race, foreigners are taken into

[19] Cf. Cz. 1924, No. 23, Art. 202, Par. 3; and Cz. 1931, No. 24, Art. 196, Par. 3.

citizenship of the USSR upon their petition therefor by the Presidium of the Supreme Soviet of the USSR or by the Presidium of the Supreme Soviet of the Union Republic within whose bounds they live."

The regulation of USSR citizenship (1931) admitted a simplified order of acquiring Soviet citizenship by foreigners in a series of cases. The right of admitting foreigners to USSR citizenship was given not only to territorial and regional executive committees but in certain cases even to separate district executive committees and likewise to city Soviets of cities divided into independent administrative-economic units. Such a simplified order of admitting foreigners to Soviet citizenship was not infrequently used by capitalist states surrounding the USSR as a means of sending their spies and diversionists into the Soviet Union. Naturally the former order of admission to Soviet citizenship could not be left in force in conditions of capitalist encirclement of the new, complicated international situation. This is a matter not of local, but of general political and statewide significance, and requires greater vigilance than hitherto. For this reason the right of admission to Soviet citizenship under the new law, and in correspondence with the USSR Constitution and the constitutions of the Union Republics, belongs solely to the Presidium of the Supreme Soviet of the USSR and the Presidia of the Supreme Soviets of Union Republics.

No less important is the political and state significance of withdrawal from citizenship. As distinguished from the former regulation (which permitted in this regard the same simplified order as in acquisition of citizenship), and likewise in distinction from the order established by the new law for admission to citizenship, withdrawal from citizenship is permitted according to the new law only by the Presidium of the Supreme Soviet of the USSR (Art. 4).

Article 5 of the law establishes that: "Matrimony by a citizen of the USSR with one not such a citizen entails no change of citizenship." This proposition remains unaltered since the time of the October Socialist Revolution, when women were given equal rights with men, including free choice of citizenship in case of marriage, whereas in prewar time it was ordinarily considered in capitalist countries that the citizenship of the wife followed that of the husband. The difference between the new law and the previously existing regulation is that marriage with a Soviet citizen now ceases to be, as it previously was, cause for the simplified admission of a foreigner into USSR citizenship.

Article 6 regulates the matter of the citizenship of children. If the parents' citizenship changes so that they both become citizens or both withdraw from citizenship of the USSR, the corresponding change of citizenship of their children may automatically occur only in case the latter have not attained the age of fourteen. The solution of the question of citizenship of children from fourteen to eighteen years of age depends—under the conditions hereinbefore indicated—upon the consent of the children themselves. In other cases, a change of citizenship of children who have not attained the age of eighteen may follow only in the general order.

Article 7 distinctly establishes the cases wherein a person may be deprived of Soviet citizenship: (1) by sentence of a court in cases provided by law, and (2) by virtue of a decree, special in each case, by the Presidium of the Supreme Soviet of the USSR. Such an arrangement assures the correct solution of the matter of depriving persons who shall prove unworthy to bear the lofty designation of Soviet citizen, of USSR citizenship.

Article 8 introduces a new statute into our legislation regarding citizenship by providing a category of persons without citizenship. To that category are relegated persons who, living in USSR territory and not being citizens thereof, have no proof that they possess foreign citizenship. Thus, that a person has no proofs of foreign citizenship is no longer basis for acknowledging him, as heretofore, a citizen of the USSR, inasmuch as acquisition of Soviet citizenship cannot occur automatically. Such a person will enjoy all the rights of citizens assigned by the Stalin Constitution, and bear all the obligations provided for therein, excepting, however, political rights (for example, the right to elect, and to be elected) and obligations (military service in the Worker-Peasant Red Army) which only USSR citizens possess.

8. *Administrative-territorial organization of Union Republics*

As distinguished from the Constitution of 1924, the new USSR Constitution not only enumerates the Union Republics embodied in the Union (Art. 13) but also establishes the structure of the separate Union Republics (Art. 22–29).[20] This is done for the first time and has profound significance in principle and in practice.[21] Stalin explained the meaning in his *Report on the Draft of the Constitution* at the Extraordinary Eighth All-Union Congress of Soviets. Demonstrating the inadmissibility of the proposal (introduced during the consideration of the Constitution by the entire nation) to strike out in Articles 22 to 29 the detailed enumeration of the division of Union Republics into administrative departments, Stalin said:

[20] Except the Armenian, Turkmen, and Kirghiz SSR's, which have in their structure no territories, regions, or autonomous republics.

[21] In the 1924 Constitution there was merely an enumeration of Union Republics without indication of their structure, the only exception (due to the somewhat different position and historical past of the Soviet Socialist Republics embodied therein) being the Transcaucasian Federation.

In the USSR there are people who are ready—with the utmost willingness and assiduity—to rehash territories and regions, thereby introducing into our work confusion and uncertainty. The draft of the Constitution puts a curb on these people, and this is excellent because here—as in much else—we require an atmosphere of confidence, as well as stability, and clarity.[22]

The USSR Constitution has solved the task of putting an end to the recarving of territories and regions, with consequent confusion and uncertainty in the work, and of stabilizing the division into administrative territories (and thereby to create an atmosphere of confidence in the work).

The 1924 Constitution of the USSR referred to the jurisdiction of the Union—side by side with the alteration of external boundaries of the Union —the regulation likewise of questions of changing boundaries between the Union Republics. The impossibility of changing the territory of Union Republics without their consent, as established by Article 6 of the same constitution, emphasized the sovereignty of Union Republics with reference to their state boundaries.

As regards constitutions of the republics, that of the RSFSR, for example (1925), established that the general administrative division of territory of the RSFSR and the confirmation of territorial and regional unifications were subject to the jurisdiction of the All-Russian Congress of Soviets and the All-Russian Central Executive Committee (Art. 17c). Notwithstanding such regulation—or rather, because it was insufficiently rigid—changes of territory of the Union Republics could (in so far as they were connected with no change of the Constitution) be made by republic organs with comparative ease.[23]

It is different according to the Stalin Constitution. Leaving in force the necessity of consent by Union Republics to a change of their territory, the new USSR Constitution now no longer limits the activity of Union organs to questions of "regulation" alone. The plenary powers of the Union are now broader and more exactly defined, and the matter of administrative division of territory of Union Republics is more centralized. Whereas previously a Union Republic (the Congress of Soviets or Central Executive Committee)

---

[22] Stalin, *Report on the Draft of the USSR Constitution* (1936), p. 39.

[23] The very formulation of the RSFSR Constitution—"The affirmation of territorial and regional unification"—presupposed a certain independence of local organs in work of theirs, the results of which were subsequently proposed by them for confirmation by the All-Russian Central Executive Committee. The independence of this clause was not infrequently so abused that the committee had to adopt special resolutions with criminal sanctions for altering administrative-territorial boundaries of autonomous Soviet Socialist Republics, territories, regions, and districts without permisson of the Presidium of the Committee. (Cf., for example, directives of the Committee on May 9, 1923, June 6, 1924, and Nov. 12, 1928: Cy. 1923, No. 41, Art. 448; Cy. 1924, No. 51, Art. 492; and Cy. 1928, No. 141, Art. 928.)

had the right itself to confirm the formation of territories and regions, such changes in the administrative-territorial division of Union Republics may now occur only with the affirmation of the Supreme Soviet of the Union and pursuant to the provision for changing Union and republic constitutions.

The USSR Constitution establishes an exact catalogue of territories, regions, autonomous republics, and areas of each Union Republic in which such administrative territorial units are embodied. The same catalogue is contained also in constitutions of the corresponding Union Republics. The constitutions of those having no territories or regions fix the structure of autonomous republics and areas, cantons, districts, and cities subordinate to the republic. Consequently in these republics, even changes in district divi-

Name of the Union Republic	Number of Administrative-Territorial Units Embodied in the Republic			
	Territories	Regions	ASSR	Autonomous Regions
The RSFSR	5*	28 †	17	6
The Ukrainian SSR	—	12	1	—
The White Russian SSR	—	5	—	—
The Azerbaijan SSR	—	—	1	1
The Georgian SSR	—	—	2	1
The Uzbek SSR	—	5	1	—
The Tadjik SSR	—	—	—	1
The Kazakh SSR	—	11	—	—
The Armenian SSR ⎫ The Turkmen SSR ⎬ The Kirghiz SSR ⎭	⎰ No administrative territorial units: division only ⎱ into districts and, in the case of the Turkmen ⎰ and Kirghiz SSR, into areas.			
The USSR in its entirety	5	61 ‡	22	9

* By decree of the Presidium of the Supreme Soviet of the USSR (Oct. 20, 1933), the Far Eastern Territory is divided into the Maritime and the Khabarovsk territories; thus in the RSFSR (and in the USSR in its entirety) there are at present 6 territories.

† This number is exclusive of 7 regions, into which, because of the breadth of their territory, are divided the Maritime territory (Maritime and Ussuri) and the Khabarovsk territory (Khabarovsk, Sakhalin, Kamchatka, Lower Amur, and Amur). By decree of the Presidium of the Supreme Soviet of the USSR (Oct. 3, 1938), the Sverdlovsk region was divided into two (Sverdlovsk and Perm: cf. *Izvestiya*, Oct. 4, 1938, No. 232); thus at the present time the RSFSR has 29 regions, and in all of the USSR there are 62 regions.

‡ Since the division of the Sverdlovsk region (Oct. 3, 1938) into two (Sverdlovsk and Perm), there are 62 regions in the USSR.

sion must evoke changes in the constitutions of the republics. What is the motive for requiring the stability of the territorial division of Union Republics to be guaranteed by the Constitution? The answer must be sought in the part played in the USSR by territory as an object of socialist management. The purpose of stabilizing territorial division is to create for each territory, region, and district an atmosphere of confidence, clarity, and stability of the conditions for the planned and most effective development of local economy.

The possibility of stabilizing further administrative-territorial division and the realization of this possibility at the present time are evolved from all the preceding development of the USSR. The culmination of the process of division into districts—the defined economic specification of separate economic districts of the country and the clear perspective of their further development—allows the utmost stability and definiteness to be given now likewise to the administrative-territorial organization.

Turning immediately to the present structure of Union Republics, we must first of all note the great diversity in administrative-territorial division inevitable in view of the immensity of the USSR. The structure of the Union Republics includes territories, regions, autonomous republics, autonomous regions, areas (national and administrative) and districts. For all this diversity, the basic forms of division are region and district. The USSR Constitution establishes the following structure of the separate Union Republics.

Thus the most complex division is in the RSFSR, and the simplest is in the Armenian, Turkmen, and Kirghiz SSR, to which belongs also the Tadjik SSR, which has in its structure one autonomous region. In the constitutions of most Union Republics (independently of the regions, autonomous Socialist Soviet Republics and autonomous regions embodied in them) there are enumerated also areas, districts, and cities which are independent administrative units not embodied in the districts. In the constitutions of the RSFSR, the Ukrainian, the White Russian, the Uzbek, and the Kazakh SSR, however, are enumerated only those constituent parts of these republics indicated in the USSR Constitution, chiefly because these republics have a greater number of other administrative divisions (especially districts, the enumeration of which in the constitutions would be difficult).[24]

Besides what is indicated in the USSR Constitution, republic constitutions of the republics hereinafter enumerated establish their structure as follows:

[24] In the RSFSR there were (on Sept. 15, 1938) 9 administrative areas, 11 national areas, and 2,267 districts; in the Ukrainian SSR, 502 districts; in the White Russian SSR, 90 districts; in the Uzbek SSR, one area and 111 districts; and in the Kazakh SSR, 171 districts.

Name of Republic	Administrative Areas	Districts	Cities Not Embodied in Districts
Azerbaijan	—	50 *	1
Georgia	—	64 †	5
Armenia	—	37	2
Tadjikistan	3	35 ‡	7
Turkmenia	2	47	11
Kirghizia	4	47	5

* The districts embodied in the Nakhichevan ASSR and Nagorny-Karabakh autonomous region (11) are not specially indicated in the Constitution of Azerbaijan.

† This includes the districts (separately enumerated in the Constitution) of the Abkhazian (5) and Adjarian (4) autonomous republics and of the South Ossetian autonomous region (4).

‡ The districts embodied in the Gorny-Badakhshan autonomous region (8) are enumerated specially and are included in the figure 35. The districts entering into the structure of the areas (31) are not enumerated in the Constitution.

Altogether in the Union Republics, including the RSFSR, the Ukrainian SSR, the White Russian SSR, the Uzbek SSR, and the Kazakh SSR, there were (on September 15, 1938) nineteen administrative areas,[25] eleven national areas,[26] and 3,463 districts.

The existing administrative-territorial division of Union Republics is based on a consideration of national characteristics of the population and scientific-economic data. These principles were unknown in the territorial organization of the former Russian Empire. The administrative division at that time, already established in the time of Catherine II and preserved in its fundamental features right down to the October Revolution, was based on what was convenient for police administration and treasury interests. To these ends the country was bureaucratically divided into parts—governments—approximately equal in population, and the governments were subdivided into districts and volosts. From the point of view of jurisdictional administration, such mechanical division was not always convenient, but the inconvenience was compensated by a supplementary division of the country into departmental areas: military, judicial, customs, educational, and so on. The interests and needs of the population itself were not taken into account in this respect. Lenin, in his article "Critical Notes on the Na-

[25] Narym, Kingisepp, Pskov, Kizliar, Opochet, Tar, Astrakhan, Pechora, Tobolsk (RSFSR), Kerky, Tashauz (Turkmen SSR), Garm, Kuliab, Leninabad (Tadjik SSR), Osh, Djalal (Abad, Issyk), Kul, Tien-Shen (Kirghiz SSR), and Syr-Darya (Uzbek).

[26] Komy-Perm (Sverdlovsk region), Nenets (region of Archangel), Agin, Buriat-Mongolia (Chita region), Koryak, Chukotka (Kamchatka region, Khabarovsk territory), Ostyako-Vogulsk, Yamalo-Nenets (Omsk region), Taimyr, Evenky (Krasnoyarsk territory), Karelia (Kalinin region), Ust-Ordynsk, Buriat-Mongolia (Irkutsk region).

tional Question" (1913), called the old administrative divisions of Russia "medieval, feudal, and exchequer-bureaucratic." [27]

9. *Legal position of autonomous republics in the USSR and in the Union Republic: their jurisdiction*

The first Soviet Constitution (1918) contained only general proposals defining in terms of principles the fundamental lines of building federative autonomy.[28] There were no concrete indications in it of the state organization, the state mechanism or the plenary powers of the autonomous state organizations. At the moment when the Constitution was adopted there was no one of these in the RSFSR structure. The first autonomy, the Labor Commune of the Germans of the Volga Lands, emerged as we have already seen, on October 19, 1918, after the adoption of the first constitution.

Thus, while the Russian Soviet Socialist Republic was called a federative republic in the constitution it was not then actually a federation.[29] The federation was proclaimed as a plan of state organization; a federation upon the principles of Soviet autonomy was still to be created in the future. The RSFSR was in fact formed as a federation during the period from 1920 to 1924, when the development of autonomies was carried on with particular energy.[30]

By the time the Twelfth All-Russian Congress of Soviets had adopted the second Constitution of the RSFSR (1925), sufficiently significant experience of autonomous federative building had been accumulated so that it was already possible to generalize in the Constitution. For this reason, we find in the Constitution of the RSFSR (1925) more detailed indications regarding autonomies (Arts. 44–48, 51, and 80). In basic features it defined the legal position of autonomous republics and their mutual relations with

[27] Lenin (Russian ed.), Vol. XVII, p. 156.

[28] These proposals were reflected in a series of legislative acts and other documents relative to the period preceding the adoption of the first Constitution: the Declaration of Rights of the Peoples of Russia (2/15 Nov. 1917); the Address (of the Council of People's Commissars and the People's Commissariat of Nationalities) to All the Toiling Mussulmans of Russia and the East (20 Nov./3 Dec. 1917); the Decree (of the Council of People's Commissars) Concerning Turkish Armenia (Dec. 29, 1917/Jan. 11, 1918); the Declaration of Rights of the Toiling and Exploited People (Jan. 25, 1918); the Directive of the Third All-Russian Congress of Soviets Concerning the Federal Institutions of the Russian Republic (Jan. 28, 1918); the Address of the People's Commissar of Nationalities to the Soviets of Kazan, Ufa, Orenburg and Yekaterinburg, to the Council of People's Commissars of the Turkestan territory, and others (April, 1918).

[29] That it is constructed as a federation had already been indicated earlier in the Declaration of Rights of the Toiling and Exploited People, adopted by the Third All-Russian Congress of Soviets, Jan. 25, 1918.

[30] By the beginning of 1925 there were already 11 autonomous republics and 13 autonomous regions embodied in the RSFSR.

the RSFSR, and in part, though in the most general form, established the jurisdiction of autonomous Socialist Soviet Republics. Regulation of state organization and administration, as well as of questions of the jurisdiction of autonomous republics, was contained also in directives of the All-Russian Central Executive Committee concerning the formation of a particular autonomous republic, although even here only the foundations—and even they only in general features—were established.[31]

The USSR Constitution (1924) assigned relatively little space to autonomous republics and regions, but what was said therein about them (Art. 15) is of extraordinarily great significance in characterizing their legal position in the Union. They were spoken of in connection with the structure of the (bicameral) Central Executive Committee and the method of its formation, and the immediate representation of autonomous republics and regions in the Soviet of Nationalities was established. The fact that immediate representation in the supreme organ of state authority of the Union was settled in behalf of autonomies (within the structure of the USSR) not directly, but through the appropriate Union Republic, indicates the extraordinary attention to autonomous national-state formations evinced by the Union.

Between 1924 and 1936 there were great changes in the structure of the autonomies: (1) four autonomous republics were reorganized into Union Republics; (2) eleven new autonomous republics, newly formed and reorganized out of autonomous regions, emerged; and (3) nine new autonomous regions were created.

All autonomous republics are now embodied, without exception and directly, in Union Republics, avoiding territorial unification—testimony to their economic and cultural growth and their strengthened independence.[32]

The development of autonomies, paralleling their economic and cultural growth and at the same time portraying the elasticity of Soviet autonomy, is reflected both in the Stalin Constitution and in constitutions of the Union Republics. The new USSR Constitution, preserving the bicameral system, left in force the direct representation of autonomies in the highest organ of state authority of the Union—the Supreme Soviet of the USSR.

[31] E.g., the Decree of the All-Russian Central Executive Committee and the Council of People's Commissars of the RSFSR Concerning the Formation of the Crimean Autonomous SSR (Cy. 1921, No. 69, Art. 556.).

[32] Down to 1936, and partially down to 1937 (that is to say, down to the reorganization of some territories into regions and the division of others), only five of the autonomous republics of the RSFSR were incorporated directly into the RSFSR and were directly subordinate to its higher organs as to all questions. The remaining twelve autonomous republics were incorporated in territorial unifications. The conditions of this incorporation and of the interrelation of autonomous republics with territorial organs of authority were defined by a directive of the All-Russian Central Executive Committee (June 28, 1928, Cy. 1928, No. 79, Art. 544).

Unlike the 1924 Constitution, the Stalin Constitution set out rules for increased representation: from five to eleven deputies for autonomous republics, and from one to five deputies for autonomous regions. Furthermore, representation in the Soviet of Nationalities from national areas—which were given one deputy each—was introduced (cf. Art. 35). There is a special chapter (Chapter VII) concerning the highest organs of state authority of autonomous republics, portraying the remarkable independence of the latter.[33]

The legal position of an autonomous republic in a Union Republic is exhaustively depicted by new constitutions of the Union Republics—the RSFSR, and the Ukrainian, Azerbaijan, Georgian and Uzbek SSR—as well as by constitutions of the autonomous republics themselves.

In accordance with Article 92 of the USSR Constitution, the constitutions of Union Republics confirm in behalf of the autonomous republics the right to their own constitutions, pointing out that the latter must be built in complete accord both with the USSR Constitution and with that of the Union Republics. The constitution of the autonomous republic is confirmed by the Supreme Soviet of the Union Republic, of which mention is made in constitutions of Union Republics and also in those of the autonomous republics themselves. This circumstance particularly emphasizes the Union Republic's responsibility for the economic and cultural development of each nationality organized into an autonomous administrative-territorial unit and being a constituent part of that republic.

An autonomous republic is one having the same external signs as those of a Union Republic: its constitution, its right to legislate, its supreme organs of state authority, and the like,[34] but possessing a jurisdiction less broad than that of the Union Republic. It has no special representation in the Supreme Soviet—the supreme organ of state authority of the Union Republic—being represented therein on general grounds by choosing deputies to the Supreme Soviet according to the regulation existing in a given Union Republic. However, one of the vice chairmen of the Presidium of the Supreme Soviet of a Union Republic is a representative of the autonomous Republic and the constitutions of Union Republics provide as many vice chairmen as there are autonomous republics therein. Thus in the RSFSR the Supreme Soviet

[33] Aside from Chaps. III and VII, autonomous republics are also referred to in Chap. IX as to courts of the autonomous republics, Arts. 102 and 107, and as to the appointment of Public Prosecutors of the autonomous republics by the Public Prosecutor of the USSR, Art. 114; and in Chap. XI as to elections of deputies to the Supreme Soviets of autonomous republics by electors on the basis of universal, equal and direct suffrage and secret ballot, Art. 134.

[34] In their constitutions, autonomous republics are denominated "socialist states of workers and peasants."

chooses seventeen vice chairmen of the Presidium of the Supreme Soviet, in accordance with the number of autonomous republics (Art. 31).[35]

The constitutions of the Union Republics say nothing about territory of the autonomous republics except that the Union Republic has the right to confirm boundaries and district divisions of autonomous republics and is bound to propose the formation of new autonomous republics for confirmation by the Supreme Soviet of the USSR. But the existence of the autonomous republic as a state formation naturally presupposes its existence in a defined territory not subject to change without its consent. Constitutions of Union Republics may take this for granted, but constitutions of the autonomous republics themselves specifically note it.

As to the jurisdiction of autonomous republics, the Union Republic constitutions establish only the following rights of the Supreme Soviet of an autonomous republic: (a) adoption of the constitution of the autonomous republic and introducing it for confirmation by the Supreme Soviet of the USSR; (b) establishment of the district division of the autonomous republic and the boundaries of districts and cities, and introducing them for confirmation by the Supreme Soviet of the Union Republic; (c) confirmation of the economic plan and budget of the autonomous republic; and (d) appropriation of honorary titles of autonomous republics. (Cf. the Constitution of the RSFSR, Art. 59.)

As for the rest, the plenary powers of autonomous republics are defined by their own constitutions, in each of which it is pointed out that, outside the limits of Article 14 of the USSR Constitution and the corresponding article of the constitution of the Union Republic, the autonomous republic "exercises state authority upon autonomous principles."

The constitutions of all the autonomous republics keep strictly to the constitution of the corresponding Union Republic in enumerating the objects of their jurisdiction. In defining the range of its powers, the article of the constitution of each autonomous republic makes concrete that which is noted in general form in the article of such Union constitution, which discloses the heading of state organization and declares the right of the autonomous republic—outside the limits of Article 14 of the USSR Constitution and the corresponding article of the Union Republic constitution —to exercise state authority upon autonomous principles. This autonomous character is expressed in the fact that the autonomous republic legislates

___

[35] The number of vice chairmen of the Presidium of the Supreme Soviet, according to the number of autonomous republics, with indication thereof in constitutions, is established also in the Georgian SSR (2) and in the Azerbaijan SSR (2), whereas in the latter there are in view one autonomous republic and one autonomous region. In constitutions of the Ukrainian SSR and the Uzbek SSR there is provision for choosing vice chairmen without mentioning autonomous republics and autonomous regions.

in all fields of economic and cultural building within the limits of its jurisdiction, possessing its own highest organs of state authority and organs of
state administration, built according to the type of the corresponding Union
Republic organs.

Legal relationships as between the autonomous republic and the Union
Republic (aside from what was said previously as to the constitution of the
autonomous republic, its territory, and its representation in the Supreme
Soviet of the Union Republic) are characterized likewise by the interrelations between the Union Republic Council of People's Commissars and
that of the autonomous republic, and likewise by the system of People's
Commissariats of the autonomous republic and their mutual relations with
those of the Union Republic.

The Council of People's Commissars of the Union Republic has the
right to suspend directives and orders of autonomous republic Councils of
People's Commissars, and the Presidium of the Supreme Soviet of the
Union Republic can abrogate them, along with decisions and orders of
territorial and regional Soviets of Deputies of the Toilers, if they do not
correspond with the law. (Cf. Arts. 33 and 46 of the RSFSR Constitution).

In autonomous republics there are no People's Commissariats if there
are not in the Union Republic [36] Commissariats of the same name: in other
words autonomous republics have no autonomous People's Commissariats
subject solely to a Council of People's Commissars of an autonomous
republic.

All People's Commissariats without exception—aside from the Council
of People's Commissars of the autonomous republic—are likewise subject
also to the corresponding People's Commissariats of the Union Republic
(including Republic People's Commissariats of Education, of Local Industry, of Communal Economy, and of Social Security). Thus the system of

---

[36] But not all Union Republic People's Commissariats have the same name as People's
Commissariats of autonomous republics. According to the Constitution of the RSFSR (Art.
69), the People's Commissariats for Food, Forest, and Light Industry (all, or merely some of
them) may be formed in an autonomous republic only contingently upon the special characteristics of the economy of the given autonomous republic and confirmation by the Supreme
Soviet of the RSFSR. Consequently, certain autonomous republics of the RSFSR lack one
or two or even all three of such People's Commissariats (thus the Udmurt and Karelian
autonomous republics have no People's Commissariat for light industry, Dagestan has none
for forest industry, and the Crimea none for light and forest industry; North Ossetia has
none of the three). The Constitution of Georgia provides for the formation of these People's
Commissariats under the same conditions as in the RSFSR. The Ukrainian Constitution
provides only for a People's Commissariat for Food Industry of the number of such People's
Commissariats of the Moldavian autonomous republic, and the Azerbaijan Constitution for
People's Commissariats for Light and Forest Industry (for the Nakhichevan ASSR). According to the Constitution of the Uzbek SSR, the Kara-Kalpak Autonomous SSR has none of
the three People's Commissariats. Moreover, no autonomous republic of any of the Union
Republics has a People's Commissariat for State Grain and Livestock Farms.

dual subordination is extended without exception to all autonomous republic People's Commissariats.

Having exclusive powers in no single branch of economy and administration, the autonomous republics yet possess broad powers in all fields of cultural-economic building. In their territory they immediately direct primary and intermediate education, preservation of health, social security, and housing and communal economy. They administer industrial, agricultural and trade enterprises and organizations subordinate to the republic. They achieve the building of roads and the management of local transport and local communications. They control and oversee the condition and administration of enterprises subordinate to USSR and Union Republic organs, and so on. It is completely practicable, and within their rights, for them to reach independent decisions within the bounds of their powers upon questions of internal administration.

Being republics incorporated in Union Republics, autonomous republics are basically distinguished from the latter by the facts: (1) that they do not possess all three, or certain, of the signs characteristic of the formation of the Union Republics; (2) they have not the right of free withdrawal from the USSR; and (3) they are required to propose their constitutions for confirmation by the Union Republic Supreme Soviet whereas the constitution of the latter is adopted by its Supreme Soviet, and is not confirmed by the highest organs of the USSR.

Jurists of the old school, adapting to Soviet autonomous republics the pattern of bourgeois science, try to discern the fundamental peculiarity of autonomous republics—and their distinction from Union Republics—in that they are supposed not to have the right of self-organization, that their existence is based on the principle of a grant or concession of autonomy. To confirm this conclusion they ordinarily cite decrees of Soviet authority concerning the organization of autonomous republics where, in a number of cases, it was said that such and such an autonomous Soviet Socialist Republic is to be formed. This ignores the extremely essential fact, however, that directives of supreme organs of authority of Union Republics are, as a rule, preceded by a manifestation of the will of the toiling masses of this or that nationality concerning their organization into an autonomous republic.

It is perfectly possible for nations formed into autonomous republics to develop Soviet national statehood—their own national culture—on condition of putting them at the service of socialist building. In this respect autonomous republics are in the same position as are Union Republics.

All nations in the USSR have equal rights. The equality of the rights of national autonomous republics is confirmed by laws of the Union and of the Union Republics. Moreover, autonomous republics themselves take part in confirming the laws of the Union (through the Soviet of Nationalities) and it is also possible for them to influence the legislation of a Union Republic.

10. *The coat of arms, flag, and capital*

A *state's coat of arms* is the official emblem of the state graphically describing some idea or series of fundamental ideas of an historical-political order corresponding with the character of the given state. The portrayal of this emblem in all its details is confirmed by special legislative act.

On the coats of arms of capitalist states birds of prey and beasts—eagles, hawks and lions—are most widely depicted, characterizing the rapacious policy of the state's dominant classes.

Prior to the October Revolution, the state coat of arms of Russia portrayed the two-headed eagle, with tsarist crowns on the heads, with scepter and orb in its claws, and coats of arms of subject lands, peoples, and tribes on its wings; [37] on the eagle's breast was portrayed George the Victor seated on a horse and striking a dragon-snake with a lance.[38] The coat of arms of tsarist Russia was the emblem of Russian imperium, an emblem reflecting the grasping policy of tsarism which resulted in the forcible annexation to Russia of Siberia, the Caucasus, Poland, Finland, Crimea, Turkestan, and so forth. The coats of arms of these countries, principalities and regions summed up, as it were, the long history of imperial policy developed by tsarism over many centuries.

Soviet authority, having fundamentally destroyed the old bourgeois-landowner order, put an end to the policy of oppressing nationalities, and freed the peoples of Russia from capitalist slavery. It annulled the emblem of this order, together with the order itself—the state coat of arms with its black eagle and a multiplicity of attributes of all sorts. Soon after the great October Socialist Revolution, the coat of arms of the RSFSR was established (1918), at the basis of which was put the emblem of the new social order. The coat of arms of the RSFSR had as its design a crossed sickle and hammer framed by a wreath of ears of corn, with the device below: "Proletarians of all countries, unite!"

After the formation of the USSR, the second session of the USSR

[37] Scepter and orb are symbols of tsarist power, the former depicted as a staff, and the orb as a sphere crowned with a cross.

[38] This has been the Russian coat of arms for some time. Under Ivan III at the end of the fifteenth century, a new state coat of arms appears, portraying a two-headed eagle borrowed from Byzantium. At first George the Victor was placed on the reverse side of the new coat of arms, but later the old coat of arms was placed on a small shield on the breast of the eagle.

Central Executive Committee's first convocation (July 6, 1923) confirmed also the design of the USSR coat of arms: a sickle and a hammer on a globe surrounded by a wreath of ears of corn bound with a scarlet ribbon, with devices thereon in six languages (Russian, Ukrainian, White Russian, Georgian, Armenian and Turkish-Tatar) of the watchword: "Proletarians of all countries, unite!" Below—where the branches of the wreath are united—is the rising sun illuminating the globe with its rays. Above the coat of arms is a five-pointed star.

According to the Stalin Constitution (Art. 143), the state coat of arms of the USSR likewise consists of a sickle and hammer upon a globe, depicted in the rays of the sun and framed by ears of grain, with the device in the languages of the eleven Union Republics: "Proletarians of all countries, unite!" Above, over the globe, is a five-pointed star.

The design of the USSR coat of arms was confirmed on March 17, 1937, by a directive of the Presidium of the Central Executive Committee of the USSR.[39]

The sickle and hammer, the emblem of toil, portrayed on the USSR state coat of arms embody the indestructible union of workers and peasants who have destroyed the capitalist social order and have, under the guidance of the Lenin-Stalin Party, rebuilt their own state in which there is no exploitation of man by man. The emblem attests the rule in our country of the law of socialist toil. The Soviet coat of arms is a symbol of the unity of the peoples, a symbol of the union of eleven Soviet Republics having equal rights and of the peaceful and voluntary union of toilers. This union is indissoluble and invincible. Anyone who shall wish to attack one of the republics will have to deal with all of them; of this the star of the Red Army—burning at the top of the coat of arms—is a menacing reminder. The toilers of all nationalities have, by their common, friendly efforts, built socialism in our land. What they have won, they have won for the whole world. It is for this reason that on the Soviet coat of arms the sickle and hammer are portrayed on the globe.

Repeated in the languages of the eleven Union Republics, the slogan: "Proletarians of all countries, unite!" summons the proletarians of all countries to unite after the examples of these republics so as, following the same example, to have done once and for all with the rapacious laws of capitalism and to establish new laws, the laws of socialist society. This slogan emphasizes the universal solidarity of the toilers, and the portrayal of the sickle and hammer on the globe, twined with ears of corn, anticipates as it were the peaceful organization of socialist economy unconstrained by state boundaries.

[39] *Izvestiya of the Central Executive Committee*, March 20, 1937.

Each of the Union Republics has its own state coat of arms, all based on that confirmed by Lenin in 1918. All have a common emblem, the sickle and hammer, and are distinguished from each other only by certain details reflecting special characteristics of the nature and economy of the given republic.[40]

The state flag, a width of cloth of one color or of many colors, is a symbol of state sovereignty. A description of the flag, as of the coat of arms, is fixed in legal order. The first Soviet flag was the red flag of the RSFSR, portraying in the upper left-hand corner the gold letters "RSFSR" in Slavonic script, and edged below and on the right with a gold border. After the formation of the USSR, its flag was established which, according to the 1924 Constitution (Art. 71) and the directive of the USSR Central Executive Committee (August 29, 1929), consisted of a red rectangular cloth portraying in the upper left-hand corner the golden sickle and hammer, and above them the red five-pointed star framed with a golden border. According to the new USSR Constitution (Art. 144), the state flag of the USSR is of red cloth on which, in the upper corner near the staff are portrayed a golden sickle and hammer and above them a red five-pointed star framed with a gold border. The proportion of length to breadth is as two to one.

State flags of the Union Republics have certain differences in the portrayals upon them. Thus the flags of the RSFSR, and of the Georgian, Turkmen, Uzbek, and Kirghiz SSR, consist of red cloth with the name of the republic set out in the upper left-hand corner in gold letters; whereas on the flags of all the other Union Republics, in addition to the names of the republics, are placed also the sickle and the hammer; and on the White Russian SSR flag there is also a red star edged with a golden border.

Each state has its own officially acknowledged principal city, the state *capital*. Ordinarily the capital is the permanent residence of the chief of the state and of the administration.[41] Down to 1712 the capital of the Russian state was Moscow. From 1712 it was St. Petersburg, which name was changed (August, 1914) to Petrograd, and Moscow was considered the second capital. After the October Revolution, the capital of the Russian Socialist Soviet Republic was Petrograd for some time. In 1924 the name was changed to Leningrad, after Lenin, the leader of the proletarian revo-

[40] Thus, for example, on the coat of arms of the Azerbaijan SSR an oil derrick is portrayed in addition to the sickle and hammer; the wreath consists of ears of corn and cotton. On the coat of arms of the Georgian SSR are portrayed snow-capped mountains, on both sides of which are arranged ears of corn and vines with clusters of grapes.

[41] There are a few exceptions: thus, in imperial Germany the residence of Wilhelm II was Potsdam, whereas the capital of Germany was Berlin; in the erstwhile Russian Empire, the abode of Nicholas II was in Tsarskoe Selo, whereas the capital was St. Petersburg; and in England the capital is London, but the king lives in Windsor.

lution. In connection with the immediate threat that the Germans would capture Pétrograd, the All-Russian Central Executive Committee at its third session directed the transfer of the capital to Moscow whither (March 11–12, 1918) the highest organs of government moved.

The Extraordinary Fourth All-Russian Congress of Soviets, the first Soviet summoned in Moscow, confirmed this decision. Concerning the revolutionary expediency of transferring the capital from Petrograd to Moscow, *Pravda* (March 10, 1918) made the following comment: "Any honorable opponent of the worker-peasant revolutionary social order will admit that here is a measure dictated by political considerations of whose entire persuasiveness all who understand the difficulty of the present situation are completely conscious." This article was directed against the Mensheviks, who came out against the transfer of the capital and slanderously propounded its supposed effect of discrediting the revolution in the eyes of European workers and creating the impression in Russia and in all the world that Soviet authority was "capitulating." Lenin well knew, and explained, that the workers would understand the revolutionary purpose of the transfer, and that the change of government to Moscow would also be intelligible to the international proletariat. Remaining the capital of the RSFSR, Moscow, from the time of the formation of the USSR, became also the Union capital, as is recorded in its 1924 Constitution (Art. 72) and later in the Stalin Constitution (Art. 145).

Moscow is the center of political, economic, and cultural life of the country—made so by the great October Socialist Revolution. In the time of tsarism, it was a typical city of nobles and merchants, bearing all the marks of the old order. In the center were situated the luxurious private dwellings of nobles and merchants. On the outskirts, in close, dark, damp and half-ruined lodgings, generally in the cellars, workers and the rest of the "have-nots" found shelter. In the center and on the outskirts alike were many churches and monasteries. The city was striking for its unfavorable and absurd planning. During the years of Soviet authority Moscow has been literally transformed, and has become completely unrecognizable for those who knew it before. A great quantity of beautiful social buildings, homes, schools, and so on, have been constructed. Entire streets have been built anew. The outskirts of the city are now not far behind the center; in many cases they even transcend it in their excellent order. Most of the streets and squares of Moscow are paved with asphalt. Movement of automobiles, buses, and trolley buses, as well as of trains, has developed. Two lines of the best subway in the world are already built—the pride of the capital. During the Stalin five-year plans, Moscow saw the building and reconstruction of many of the biggest industrial enterprises. The population at the end of 1938 was almost four millions, as against 1.16 millions in 1912 and 2.026 millions in 1926.

The Soviet government, the Central Committee of the Bolshevik Party, and Stalin devote enormous attention to the reconstruction of Moscow and to the maximum creation of facilities for the toilers. As a result of the completion of the ten-year plan of reconstruction, Moscow will become the most beautiful and best ordered city in the world. Its center is the ancient and majestic Kremlin where the great leader of the people, Stalin, lives and works. To this center are directed all the thoughts and feelings of the Soviet people and the hopes of the toilers of the whole world. The Kremlin adjoins the historic Red Square, the center of mass popular demonstrations and ceremonial parades. Here in a marble mausoleum rests the dust of the genius who led the world proletariat—Lenin. Upon the towers of the Kremlin the five-pointed red stars burn brightly. Their light, as Molotov has said: [42]

shines afar and faithfully. They say that these stars are visible from all the ends of Moscow. They say further that they are all but visible from the ends of the Soviet Union. . . . In case of military attack upon the Soviet Union, the attacker will experience both the force of our iron self-defense and the force of the light of Soviet red stars which shine far beyond the boundaries of our country.

Capitals of the Union Republics, like that of the USSR, also flourish: Kiev, Minsk, Alma-Ata, Baku, Tiflis, Erevan, Tashkent, Ashkhabad, Frunze, and Stalinabad. In certain of the Union Republics, the capital cities were created over a period of years in a completely vacant place. Thus, where formerly there was the village of Diushambe, whose little dark huts clung to the recesses of the mountains, there is now the city of Stalinabad, the capital of the Tadjik SSR, with a population of more than 40,000, with broad clean streets and pretty new houses. It has a sewing factory, a leather works, a printing combine, and other enterprises. A railroad has been developed there and a series of paved highways have been laid out in places formerly impassable.

[42] *Pravda*, Dec. 9, 1937.

V

The Supreme Organs of State Authority of the USSR and of the Union and Autonomous Republics

SEC. 1: THE SUPREME SOVIET—THE HIGHEST ORGAN OF USSR STATE AUTHORITY

THE highest organs of USSR state authority are the state organs embodying the will, and completely and entirely realizing the sovereignty, of the entire Soviet multinational people. They are chosen by the entire Soviet people and are its highest representative institutions. From the highest representative institutions of capitalist countries, bourgeois parliaments, the highest Soviet representative institutions are distinguished both by their class nature and by their organizational form. "To decide once in several years what member of the dominant class will crush and repress the people in parliament is the real essence of bourgeois parliamentarism—not only in parliamentary-constitutional monarchies but in the most democratic republics as well." [1] By the will of the entire Soviet people the Soviet supreme representative organs are invoked to preserve and to protect the interests of toilers, and to reinforce and to defend victorious socialism which has made an end of every sort of exploitation of man by man. Such is the essential difference between the two types of highest representative institutions.

But there is a difference between them, too, as regards organizational form. In England the highest organs of authority are the hereditary crown, the House of Lords and the House of Commons. Bourgeois political science theoretically "proves" that the Lords—sitting in the House of Lords by right of "noble" birth or by royal appointment, and the House of Commons, chosen on the basis of universal suffrage with the ordinary qualification limitations—constitute a single parliament, a single supreme Soviet, representing the interests "of all the nation." The old English theory explains

---

[1] Lenin (Russian ed.), Vol. XXI, p. 400.

parliament as the personal council of the king. King and parliament are inseparable. "The king in parliament" is the laconic old English formula.

In France the highest organs of authority are: (1) a Chamber of Deputies chosen on the basis of "universal" suffrage, with the limitation—customary in bourgeois countries—upon the toilers' right to vote; (2) a Senate chosen by a narrow circle of persons—chiefly from the well-to-do classes—and rejecting every progressive law at all responsive to the toilers' interests; and (3) a President of the republic who, on the basis of the French Constitution, can hold back a law passed by parliament and, with the consent of the Senate, can even dissolve the Chamber of Deputies.

Such is the organizational structure of the supreme organs of authority supposed to represent the "will of the people" in bourgeois-democratic countries. In reality, all these organs of authority represent only the will of a handful of exploiters. Parliament is in form considered omnipotent. Everyone knows the saying: "The English parliament can do anything except make a man a woman." In reality, the rights of "popular representation" personified by the House of Commons are limited by rights of the House of Lords and of the king as head of the state. In England a law passed by parliament still needs confirmation by the king. Statutes in France and the U.S.A. are sanctioned by the President of the republic; if he is not in accord with a statute he can send it back to the legislature for second consideration.

One of the most eminent contemporary bourgeois political scientists of France, Hauriou, frankly declares: "At first parliament—and then the elective body—was thought to be the people itself. These illusions had to be abandoned. At the present time it must be admitted that every created political organization, by virtue of the fact that it is an organization, is removed from the people."

All forms of existing bourgeois parliamentarism are instruments of dominance over the people. When the bourgeoisie concludes that parliament is becoming a brake on its domination, it passes to open forms of dictatorship—to fascism, which liquidates parliaments and other attributes of democracy. In capitalist countries, capital is omnipotent, holding in its hands the state and all the state organs, and blindly executing the will of the people's oppressors—not of the people.

The matter is different in principle in the USSR where, personified in the highest organs of state authority, the will of the people—of the masses of millions of workers, peasants, and intellectuals—finds expression. On the basis of Article 30 of the Stalin Constitution, "the highest organ of USSR state authority is the Supreme Soviet of the USSR." This, on the basis of Article 31 of that Constitution, "exercises all the rights vested in the USSR in conformity with Article 14 of the Constitution, in so far as they do not (by virtue of the Constitution) come within the jurisdiction of organs of the USSR accountable to the USSR Supreme Soviet: the Presidium of the Supreme Soviet of the USSR, the Council of People's Commissars of the USSR, and the People's Commissariats of the USSR."

The objects of USSR jurisdiction are hereinbefore set out in the chapter concerned with state organization. According to the 1924 Constitution of the USSR, the supreme organ of authority of the USSR was the Congress of Soviets and, in the period between Congresses of Soviets, the Central Executive Committee of the USSR, consisting of the Union Soviet and the Soviet of Nationalities. Inasmuch as the Central Executive Committee sat only during sessions, the highest legislative, executive, and administrative organ of Union authority (in the intervals between sessions) was the Presidium of the Central Executive Committee of the USSR.

The Stalin Constitution establishes that "the legislative authority of the USSR is exercised solely by the Supreme Soviet of the USSR" (Art. 32). "Solely" means that, independently of the Supreme Soviet of the USSR, there are and can be in the USSR no other organs of authority with the right to issue acts having legislative force. According to the first (1924) Constitution of the USSR, however, the right to publish such acts was possessed not merely by Congresses of Soviets of the USSR, the Central Executive Committee of the USSR and its Presidium, but also by the Council of People's Commissars of the USSR. The 1924 Constitution of the USSR (Art. 18) pointed out, however, that "all decrees and directives defining general rules of USSR political and economic life—and likewise introducing radical changes into the existing practice of USSR state organs —must necessarily come up for consideration and affirmance by the Central Executive Committee of USSR."

This assured democratic control over legislation by the Central Executive Committee as the organ of authority chosen by the Congress of Soviets of the USSR and the highest organ of authority in intervals between sessions of the Soviets. In the person of the Supreme Soviet of the USSR, chosen on the basis of universal, equal, and direct suffrage, with secret ballot, by all USSR citizens who have reached the age of eighteen, the genuine will of the Soviet people is manifested.

Expressing the sovereign will of the Soviet people, laws of the Supreme Soviet of the USSR are of binding force in all the territory of the USSR. Soviet laws are near and dear to each Soviet person, because they are created by the will of the people and subserve the people's happiness and welfare.

All organs of authority in the USSR are subject to law; they must precisely and undeviatingly observe laws established by the highest organ of state authority, the Supreme Soviet of the USSR. From the laws of the Supreme Soviet of the USSR, all the other organs of authority draw instructions for their activity.

The completeness of the authority of the Supreme Soviet of the USSR is further emphasized in the Constitution by Article 51: "The Supreme Soviet of the USSR—when it deems necessary—appoints commissions of inquiry and investigation upon any matter. All institutions and officials must carry out the demands of these commissions and produce for them the necessary materials and documents."

SEC. 2: THE THEORY OF THE (SO-CALLED) "SEPARATION OF POWERS"

Side by side with the principle of "popular" representation, a fundamental principle of bourgeois theories of the "constitutional" and "legal" state is that of the separation of powers. The most logical expression of the doctrine is that of Montesquieu (1689–1755), who asserted that the union of powers in a single person or state organ leads to lawlessness, whereas separation of powers supposedly "checks" separate powers, "equalizes" them, and averts all possible abuses. Starting from this, Montesquieu considered the separation of powers (into legislative, executive, and judicial) essential. According to him, the essence of the matter is not whose hands hold the authority, whether those of the monarch or those of the people, but that the said three powers, constituting the supreme power, be concentrated in different hands.

The French bourgeoisie supported the principle of the separation of powers as early as the time when it came forward within the framework of the "third estate." Coming forward under absolutism as champion of the "rights of personality," the bourgeoisie sought in every way to limit absolute authority. The system of the separation of powers, like that of checks and balances, was to decentralize and weaken absolute power. Struggling for power, the bourgeoisie included in its watchwords also the principle of "the separation of powers" as a principle of "just power." [1] With this doctrine, the bourgeoisie approached the revolution of 1789. Victorious

---

[1] "At such a time, for example, and in such a country—with royal power, aristocracy, and bourgeoisie quarreling for domination, and dominance thus divided—the prevailing thought appears to be the doctrine of the separation of powers, spoken of as an eternal law" (Marx and Engels, Russian ed., Vol. IV, p. 37).

in the revolution, they, on the contrary, subordinated the power of the king and the executive power under him "to popular representation." In its Declaration of Rights of Man and Citizen, the bourgeoisie noted that "every society, wherein the guarantee of rights is not secured and the separation of powers not established, is without a constitution." [2]

True, the king was given the right of suspensive veto (the right merely to halt laws of the parliament), but each attempt on his part to realize this right evoked the indignation of the people, who were then marching behind the bourgeoisie, and the people impelled the legislative power to more decisive steps leading to the traitor king (who had conspired with the enemies of the revolution against the people) being sent to the scaffold.

The concentration of the power, and the aspiration to subordinate the executive power to the legislative power, came out later still more sharply in conditions of the rise of the revolution. The Convention at its very first meeting (September 2, 1792) abolished the royal power and concentrated all the government in its own hands. It ordained that legislative power give the orders and executive power carry them out. The law of December 4, 1793, emphasized that the Convention is the "sole center of governmental activity," but put all the executive power under the immediate supervision of the Committee of Public Safety.

If the democratic Constitution of 1793 had in principle employed every method of advancing popular representation in the form of legislative organs [3] into first place, the Thermidor reaction of 1794, on the contrary, sought under the form of "separation of powers" to simplify the executive power and to make it independent of parliament. This tendency of the reactionary bourgeoisie, victorious in July, 1794, passed later by way of inheritance to other constitutions, in which the bourgeoisie sought to limit democracy.

The Constitution of 1795 was a reaction against the "omnipotence of the legislative assembly." "Popular representation" was still further relegated to the background by the Constitution of 1799. The legislative body and the tribunate were mere playthings in the hands of the first consul. The empire of Napoleon I finally gave the executive power the character of unlimited dictatorship. All this, with sundry deviations, is characteristic also of the later regimes of France. Marx, in his *Eighteenth Brumaire*, notes that "the immediate and palpable result was the victory of Bonaparte over

---

[2] *New History in Documents and Materials* (Social-Economic State Publishing House, 1934), p. 121.

[3] In proportion, however, as the position at the fronts and within the country became more complicated, the Committee of Public Safety, consisting at first of nine and later of twelve members of the Convention, together with the Committee of General Security, directed all the power and headed the revolutionary dictatorship.

parliament, of executive power over legislative power, of force not veiled with phrases over the force of the phrase." [4]

In reality the history of bourgeois society knows no separation of powers, nor did such separation ever exist in history. Not "separation of powers" but predominance of executive power characterizes the organization of the state government of capitalist countries. But why did the bourgeoisie need to preserve in form in their constitutions the principle of "separation of powers"? For the same reason that obtained as to the formally noted principles of bourgeois democracy, principles of the separation of powers were to implant in the popular masses illusions as to the "justice" of power, the impossibility of arbitrary powers, the "legal state" in which no single power can by its arbitrariness solve the most important questions: that the powers are supposedly "equalized" and control each other. The principle of the separation of powers was to strengthen the idea of class bourgeois power as power elevated above classes—"popular sovereignty," supposed to distribute the functions of the legislation and administration reasonably and impartially among divers state organs.

In reality, however, the class dictatorship of the bourgeoisie developed alike in all the organs of authority under the hegemony of the executive power. Nowhere and never did the bourgeoisie "separate" powers as equal and self-sufficient forces of the state. Nowhere were there in reality the "dynamic resultants" of which Montesquieu wrote. [5] In the bourgeois state all organs of power are organs of bourgeois dictatorship. Delimitation of their functions, given out as the separation of powers, is nothing more than the hegemony of the executive power over the legislative, a limitation of the rights of parliaments.

As to legislative power, the bourgeoisie broadened or narrowed the rights of popular representation according to the sharpness of the class struggle and the pressure of popular masses. Even at the very time when it was compelled to make concessions and to broaden the circle of electors, the bourgeoisie exerted all its powers to turn parliaments into "talking-shops," keeping the center of authority in bureaucratic ·executive organs. From the beginning of the last quarter of the nineteenth century this was especially clearly expressed from the inception of the development of monopolist capital, and particularly in the postwar period of the universal crisis of capitalism.

Look at any parliamentary country you like, from America to Switzerland,

[4] Marx and Engels (Russian ed.), Vol. VIII, p. 403.
[5] Cf. Marx, *The Eighteenth Brumaire of Louis Bonaparte, Concerning the 1848 Constitution* (Russian ed., 1935), pp. 22–23.

from France to England, Norway and so on, the real "state" work is done behind the scenes and carried out by departments, chancelleries, and staffs. In parliaments they merely babble—with the special purpose of fooling "simple folk." [6]

Such is the "art" of bourgeois government. Contingents of professional politicians, lawyers, and businessmen specialized in this "art," making their living out of the confidence of the popular masses. Each bourgeois party strives to take into its own hands the most important posts in the state in legislative, executive, and judicial organs so as to develop the policy of the dominant class from the point of view of its group interests.

In England, whose example Montesquieu followed, it is held in theory that parliament is omnipotent, that it can at any given moment change that "holy of holies," the English Constitution. And all the same, this parliament yields to the premier, of whose rights there is not a word in any English constitutional act. The parliamentary majority, whose representative and leader is the premier himself, enables the latter to manage parliament completely, as if it were his own property, and to promote his own measures, clothing them in the form of statutes and thus usurping the rights of parliament. Actually the government, as the cabinet of ministers, often legislates itself.

In England there are orders in council signed by the king, in addition to statutes issued by parliament. Such order should in principle introduce no essential changes into legislation. In reality, however, the government expedites through parliament propositions broadly interpreted in principle, and then employs "orders in council," turning them into statutes. Such orders are framed by officials from the ministerial machine. Often they are considered in departmental or royal commissions, with the participation of "experts" from the world of finance and industry. This "personal" governmental parliament behind the scenes plays in fact a greater part than does the true parliament. In form, parliament can—but the obedient majority does not—protest various directives of the government. Moreover, as a rule the parliamentary majority includes in all acts (at all important) special points empowering a ministry to issue directives which in fact acquire the force of law.

At the time of the financial crisis in England (August-September, 1931), parliament adopted a directive permitting the government to effectuate "economy" (in fact, to legislate on finance matters) by means of orders. In England the government, resting on its parliamentary majority, can resort the more rarely to extraordinary legislation in that the obedient

[6] Lenin (Russian ed.), Vol. XXI, p. 401.

majority makes it completely possible for the government to legislate independently of parliament.[7]

Extraordinary legislation was expanded also in France. Almost each new government in recent years begins by demanding unlimited power to legislate independently of parliament by means of so-called decretal laws. The basic motive of extraordinary legislation is the desire to be freed from parliamentary control.

The dominant position of executive power may be illustrated from the activity. practiced by the supreme state organs of all capitalist countries. Thus, bourgeois political scientists consider that the principle of the "separation of powers" is most logically expressed in the Constitution of the U.S.A., adopted in 1787. Theoretically the Congress, as it were, bears the national sovereignty. Bourgeois class policy superadds two further institutions personified by (a) the President (who can hold back the realization of an act accepted by Congress), and (b) the Supreme Court (which can "clarify" a law and declare it unconstitutional, thereby annulling it). "The equalization of powers" existing in the U.S.A. thus puts forward into first place the President (head of the executive authority and not responsible to the Congress). Furthermore, the bourgeoisie insures itself against all sorts of undesirable laws by the Supreme Court (whose members are designated by the President with the consent of the Senate). If a majority in the Supreme Court is hostile to the policy of the President, the latter can appoint an additional number of judges to assure himself a majority in the Supreme Court.

The bourgeoisie in all countries esteems the executive power as more "elastic," more closely integrated with the interests of the dominant classes than the "chattering" parliaments.

The part played by the state machinery itself must also be considered. Ministers come and go, but the heads of departments, the bureaucratic machinery, remain in their entirety. Over a period of many years the apparatus is chosen from elements most trustworthy and devoted to capitalism. The routine established in this apparatus cannot be changed by the temporary presence of this or that "progressive" minister at the head of a min-

---

[7] How broadly this practice has actually taken root is attested by the old English Liberal and president of the Liberal party, Ramsay Muir, who says in his book *How Britain Is Governed:* "Some idea of the dimensions attained by this practice may be afforded by figures as to 1927. In that year parliament passed forty-three statutes. Of most of them society heard either nothing at all or very little. They were proposed by ministers and adopted after negligible discussion. Twenty-six contained points empowering the appropriate minister to issue directives having the force of law. In the same year (1927)—which witnessed the passage of forty-three acts of parliament—ministers published no less than 1,349 binding directives and orders. These were just as much a constituent part of legislation as were the acts of parliament" (Russian ed., 1936, p. 72).

istry. The bureaucracy concentrated in the apparatus loathes control and hates parliament. "The entire history of bourgeois parliamentary countries —even of bourgeois constitutional countries in a significant degree—shows that a shift of ministers means very little, since the real work of administration lies in the hands of the gigantic army of officials." [8]

Moreover, the state apparatus serves as a means to install in offices— wherefrom they may extract income—a notable number of representatives of the bourgeoisie.

Material interests of the French bourgeoisie are most closely and definitely bound up with the preservation of this vast machinery of state with its manifold ramifications. Here the bourgeoisie settles its superfluous population and supplements by official salaries what does not drop into its pocket by way of gains, percentages, rents, and salaries.[9]

In the U.S.A. the custom is already established that there are new appointments and changes when a new President is chosen. Bourgeois parties take advantage of this in election campaigns for pressure in the first instance upon state servants. For these servants elections are a sort of lottery in which their fate and their career are decided. In the U.S.A. such a system is called the "spoils system." Each bourgeois party coming to power divides the spoils among its supporters.[10]

The state machinery and the bureaucracy at its head work remote from the people and outside popular influence. Yet they embrace the entire life of society and direct it along the desired path. In February, 1934, the former prefect of the Paris Police Chiappe aided fascist provocation attacks in the streets of Paris, graphically proving how the bureaucratic machinery can develop the policy of the bourgeoisie against the will of ministers and despite parliament.

The fiction of the "separation of powers" attained its most graphic expression in the period of the postwar crisis of capitalism, when the class struggle became intense. Preserving its dictatorship and legal order, the bourgeoisie—with democratic constitutions and parliaments existing—passed (at the moment when the class struggle became acute) to extraordinary legislation, so-called, on the basis of which the executive power, independently of parliament, issues laws.

The practice of pre-Hitler Germany also affords a characteristic example. The Weimar Constitution created in form a series of "checks" and "bal-

---

[8] Lenin (Russian ed.), Vol. XXI, p. 144.

[9] Marx, *The Eighteenth Brumaire of Louis Bonaparte* (Russian ed., 1932), pp. 45–46.

[10] James Bryce, the well known commentator on the American Constitution, wrote that "those, however, whose bread and butter depend on their party may be trusted to work for their party, to enlist recruits, look after the organization, play electioneering tricks from which ordinary party spirit might recoil." (*The American Commonwealth*, Vol. II, p. 141.)

ances" for legislative and executive power. According to Article 43, the President of the Republic could be dismissed from his post by popular vote upon motion by two-thirds of the deputies of the Reichstag. But according to Article 25, the President of the Republic could dismiss the Reichstag. Furthermore, under Article 48, the President could issue laws without the Reichstag under certain conditions. During the entire existence of the Weimar regime, there was no opportunity for the bourgeois parliament to express itself in favor of a change of President. Moreover, there were not a few cases when the President dissolved parliament. Furthermore, the bourgeois majority in parliament itself helped the President realize rights, given to him by Article 48, to legislate independently of parliament.

Where, in conditions of the postwar crisis and the preparation for a new imperialist war, class contradictions between capitalists and the worker class have reached high tension, the bourgeoisie altogether casts off all democratic veils, including the fiction of the "separation of powers," and passes to unbridled and open terror and force—to fascism. Fascist power is built on the principle of the unlimited dominance of the executive power, concentration of that power in the hands of individuals who are the creatures and agents of monopolist capital.

From top to bottom the Soviet social order is penetrated by the single general spirit of the oneness of the authority of the toilers. The program of the All-Union Communist Party (of Bolsheviks) rejects the bourgeois principle of separation of powers.[11] The unity of the authority of the toilers, embodied in the highest organs of that authority, expresses their democratic nature and the sovereignty of the Soviet people. Under the bourgeois principle of so-called "separation of powers" into three or four powers, these powers are separated from, and factually dominate over, society.[12]

In the USSR, authority has its beginning in the genuine popular sovereignty personified by the Supreme Soviet of the USSR. This is not incompatible with limiting the jurisdiction of authority as between separate organs. Such limitation flows out of the extraordinarily complex functions of the Soviet state machinery governing both people and economy.

As early as 1918 Lenin, pointing out the vast significance of the

[11] "Holding for the toiling masses the assurance—incomparably greater than is possible with bourgeois democracy and parliamentarism—of conducting the elections and recall of deputies in a manner most easy and accessible to workers and peasants, Soviet authority at the same time abrogates the negative sides of parliamentarism, especially the separation of legislative and executive power, the remoteness of representative institutions from the masses, and so on" (*The Party Program*, Par. 5).

[12] The idea of four powers, legislative, executive, judicial, and the king, as a balancing power, was put forward by Benjamin Constant (1767–1830), and is completely embodied in the Constitution of Portugal of April 29, 1826.

creativeness of the masses, considered it at the same time necessary to introduce discipline into the fulfillment of the precepts and orders of authorities,
and to augment the personal responsibility of all persons bearing any executive functions. He emphasized that the masses must choose leaders and
control them. At the same time, however, he considered it essential to
distinguish control by the masses over the passage of legislative enactments
from the functions of such passage.

The masses can now—the Soviets guarantee it to them—take all authority into
their own hands and exercise it. But in order that the division of power and the
irresponsibility from which we suffer incredibly at the present time may not
result, it is indispensable that for each executive function we know precisely
and exactly what people—having been selected for the office of responsible
leaders—bear responsibility for the functioning of the whole economic organism
in its entirety.[13]

All this is still more important at the present time. The total dominance
of socialist economy both in the city and in the country has importantly
multiplied the functions of the machinery of the state and increased the
branches of state administration. The state machinery carries on directly
the work of organizing economy, increasing labor productivity, strengthening socialist labor discipline, and rallying workers and kolkhoz groups
around the most urgent concerns of our socialist building. This makes it
essential in building the organs of higher authority and administration
carefully to delimit their functions. This may be followed historically even
before the adoption of the first Constitution of the RSFSR (1918).[14]

The 1918 Constitution pointed out in Article 31 that in the interval
between Congresses of the Soviets, the All-Russian Central Executive
Committee of Soviets is the supreme legislative, executive, and controlling
organ of the RSFSR: [15]

The All-Russian Central Executive Committee of Soviets gives general
direction to the activity of the Worker-Peasant Government and of all organs

[13] Lenin (Russian ed.), Vol. XXII, pp. 420–421.
[14] Nov. 17, 1917, upon the motion of Sverdlov, the All-Russian Central Executive Committee adopted a decree-constitution: "(1) according to the decision of the Second All-Russian Congress, the Council of People's Commissars is responsible to the Central Executive
Committee; (2) all legislative acts—also directives of great and general political significance
—are presented for consideration and affirmation by the Central Executive Committee; (3)
measures for struggle with counterrevolution may be passed by the Council of the People's
Commissars immediately (but upon condition of their responsibility to the Central Executive
Committee); (4) once a week each member of the Council of the People's Commissars
renders an account to the Central Executive Committee; (5) enquiries of the Central Executive Committee should be answered forthwith. Enquiries are decreed to have been proposed
if fifteen members of the Central Executive Committee have expressed themselves in favor
of them." (Protocols of sessions of the All-Russian Central Executive Committee, second
convocation, 1918, p. 71.)
[15] Cy. 1918, No. 51, Art. 582.

of Soviet authority in the land, unifies and harmonizes work on legislation and administration, and sees to the putting into practice of the Soviet Constitution and of directing of the All-Russian Congresses of Soviets and of the central organs of Soviet authority. The Committee considers and affirms projected decrees and other proposals introduced by the Council of People's Commissars or by separate departments, and likewise issues its own decrees and orders" (Art. 32, 33).

Thus the RSFSR Constitution established the rights of the All-Russian Central Executive Committee which, in the period between Congresses, was the highest legislative authority in the republic.

As to the Council of People's Commissars, the 1918 Constitution established (Art. 37) that "general administration of the affairs of the RSFSR belongs to the Council of People's Commissars. In realizing this task, the Council issues decrees, orders, and instructions and, in general, adopts all measures necessary in order that the life of the state may flow on with ordered swiftness" (Art. 38). Concerning all its decisions and directives, the Council of People's Commissars communicates forthwith to the All-Russian Central Executive Committee (Art. 39). Further articles (39–41) point out that the latter committee has the right to change or to suspend any directive or decision of the Council whatsoever, and, further, that such directives and decisions of the Council as have great social-political significance are presented to be considered and affirmed by the All-Russian Central Executive Committee.

Thus the supreme legislative organ, the All-Russian Central Executive Committee, stood above the Council of People's Commissars. Lenin pointed out that "of course if the Council of People's Commissars should violate directives of the All-Russian Central Executive Committee, it would be subject to court prosecution." [16]

With the expansion of socialist building, Lenin emphasized the necessity for the supreme legislative organs, personified by the All-Russian Central Executive Committee, to work with proportionately greater intensity. At the Eleventh Party Congress he said:

It is necessary to attain the result that the All-Russian Central Executive Committee work more energetically and meet correctly in sessions which should be more extended. The sessions should consider statutory projects sometimes hurriedly introduced without compelling necessity in the Council of People's Commissars. It is better to delay and to give local workers an opportunity for attentive consideration, and to establish more strict requirements than we now do as to proponents of laws. If sessions of the All-Russian Executive Committee of Commissars are more prolonged, they will be divided into sections and

[16] Lenin (Russian ed.) Vol. XXV, p. 116.

subcommittees and will know how to verify the work more strictly, striving for what—in my judgment—is the nub and the essence of the present political moment: transferring the center of gravity to the selection of people—to the verification of factual fulfillment.[17]

In the spirit of these views of Lenin, and under the guidance of Stalin, the first USSR Constitution was later created. All decrees and directives defining the general rules of political and economic life of the USSR must (under Art. 18) come up for consideration and affirmation by the Central Executive Committee of the USSR. Further practice has likewise established that a statute defining general rules of political and economic life was published over the joint signatures of the Central Executive Committee and the Council of the People's Commissars. If such statute appeared at the same time a party directive of importance, then practice has established that it be signed also by the Secretary of the Central Committee of the All-Union Communist Party (of Bolsheviks) side by side with the signature of the leader of the highest Soviet organ.

As previously noted, the total dominance of socialist economy in the city and in the country multiplied the branches of administration, dictating the necessity of an elaborate delimitation of the functions of organs of authority.

According to the Stalin Constitution, entire and complete authority (state sovereignty) is concentrated in the Supreme Soviet of the USSR, which is also the sole USSR legislative organ, chosen by the people of the USSR.

The masses realize the broadest democratic control by truly democratic elections, on the basis of universal, equal, direct and secret suffrage. Such control is guaranteed also by the right to recall deputies, by referenda which the Presidium of the Supreme Soviet conducts upon its own initiative or as required by one of the Union Republics, and so forth.

The Council of People's Commissars of the USSR is responsible to the Supreme Soviet of the USSR. As hereinbefore indicated, the Presidium of that Soviet may abrogate a directive of the Council of People's Commissars (if it does not correspond with law), relieve individual People's Commissars of their obligations and nominate new ones subject to subsequent confirmation by the Supreme Soviet of the USSR (Art. 49, Pars. *e* and *f*).

The Council of People's Commissars of the USSR issues decisions and orders on the basis and in pursuance of laws in operation and supervises their execution (Art. 66).

Thus, in the activity of the supreme organs of authority and administration of the USSR there is a distinct delimitation of jurisdiction with

---

[17] *Ibid.*, Vol. XXVII, p. 259.

complete supremacy of legislative authority as embodying the will of the entire Soviet people.

SEC. 3: THE BICAMERAL SYSTEM OF THE USSR SUPREME SOVIET

The Supreme Soviet of the USSR consists of two chambers: the Soviet of the Union and the Soviet of Nationalities (Art. 33). The bicameral system of representation exists also in capitalist countries. Thus in England, parliament includes a lower house (the House of Commons) and an upper house (the House of Lords). In the U.S.A., Congress includes the House of Representatives and the Senate. In France, parliament includes the Chamber of Deputies and the Senate, and so forth.

As to the so-called "first" or "lower" chambers, the exertions being put forth by the bourgeoisie to insulate their activity from the influence of the broad popular masses are indicated below. Representatives (deputies) are in form elected to this chamber by the people. In reality the bourgeoisie strives to limit the voting rights of the broad popular masses so as to attain the most conservative possible representation in the "first" or lower chamber.

As to upper chambers, their function is to guarantee the bourgeoisie against the adoption of laws disadvantageous to it, if they have passed the lower house. "Ordinarily the upper chamber degenerates into a center of reaction and a brake upon forward movement." [1]

Both houses are considered in capitalist countries to have in form equal rights. They have in form equal rights in the consideration and adoption of laws, and in the realization of control over the activity of the government. In fact, however, the second chamber "is not infrequently given greater rights than the first chamber, and furthermore it is as a rule organized undemocratically—not infrequently by the appointment of its members from above." [2]

In reality, upper chambers enjoy in all capitalist countries the advantage that they can hold back and delay a law that has passed the first or lower house.

Second chambers also have special privileges. Thus in France the President of the Republic can, with the consent of the Senate, dissolve the lower house, whereas the upper house, the Senate, cannot be dissolved. The reactionary role of the French Senate may be characterized by its

[1] Stalin, *Report on the Draft of the USSR Constitution*, p. 40.
[2] *Ibid.*

action in the matter of giving voting rights to women. The Chamber of Deputies passed a law for giving voting rights to women in 1922, 1932, and 1935, but each time the law was sidetracked by the Senate. In the U.S.A., the President of the Republic must in many important matters, such as the conclusion of international treaties or the appointment of higher officials, receive the sanction of two-thirds of the Senate only—not of the House of Representatives.

Starting from the conception of the second chamber as the organ restraining the legislative "transports" of the lower chamber, the bourgeoisie finds it necessary to assure that upper houses are made up of their faithful and trustworthy people. In England, for example, the upper house, the House of Lords, consists of representatives sitting by right: (1) of "noble" birth, (2) of election by the higher nobility and the landholding class, (3) of holding the highest offices, and (4) of appointment by the king.

More than half of the lords acquired their title and right to sit in the House of Lords through inheritance, as eldest sons.[3]

In precisely the same way in Japan, also, the upper chamber is composed basically of members appointed or sitting by right of inheritance.

Even where upper chambers are elected, as in France and the U.S.A., elections proceed on the basis of higher electoral qualifications both for electors and for candidates.

Upper chambers are ordinarily formed for a longer period than are lower chambers, on terms of representing the ruling bourgeois clique for a longer time. Moreover, elections of members of upper and lower chambers occur at different times: (1) because the times of expiration of the terms of the deputies of the first and second chambers do not coincide, and (2) most important, because the bourgeoisie tries to create a continuity of policy of upper houses. So in France, for example, only one-third of the Senate is renewed each three years, while in the U.S.A. one-third of the Senate is renewed each two years. In Holland one-half of the upper house is renewed every three years; in Denmark one-half every four years; in Switzerland one-eighth every year.

In France the second chamber (the Senate) consists of 314 senators, elected from persons who have attained the age of forty years. The elections are thus so realized that only candidates of the bourgeoisie can for the most part be elected. Elections are not by the people but by departmental colleges, consisting of members of the general council of the department, members of district councils, deputies of the chamber of each department, and representatives of municipal councils. The elective system is so constructed

---

[3] At the beginning of 1934, the House of Lords consisted of 768 members: 24 dukes, 27 marquesses, 131 earls, 73 viscounts, 453 barons, 26 archbishops and bishops, and 34 others.

as to give advantages to the kulaks of the rural districts at the expense of the cities—at the expense of the proletariat.

In Russia, prior to 1917, the second chamber was the State Council, which existed, up to the beginning of the twentieth century, as a consultative organ under the tsar. After the Revolution of 1905, when a "parliament" was created in Russia in the form of the State Duma, additional functions were appropriated (by the law of April 24, 1906) to the State Council as a second chamber. It consisted of approximately two hundred persons. One hundred were nominated by the tsar from representatives of high society and the higher bureaucracy, and approximately a hundred were "elected" upon the following principle: from the clergy, six; from landowners, fifty-six; from societies of the nobility, eighteen; from industrialists and traders, two; from the Academy of Sciences and higher educational institutions, six; and from Finland, two. The members of this essentially landlord-noble assembly must have reached the age of forty. Members designated by the tsar were irremovable, but they were called to sit in the legislative chamber by a nominal tsarist law from a standing contingent of members of the State Council, whose number exceeded the number of those present by designation. The "elected" members of the State Council obtained authority for nine years, whereas the period of authority of members of the State Duma was five years.

Historically, the forms of creating the second chamber attained their development in England and were borrowed from England by other countries. In capitalist countries they are survivals of old political forms, remains of former privileged classes and groups, of privileges issuing out of the feudal and absolute monarchy. Hence the rights, lasting for life and passing by inheritance, of the ancestral aristocracy in the upper house in England, Japan, and elsewhere, rights which (in proportion to the strengthening of the bourgeoisie) were later extended also to the money aristocracy and the plutocracy. The conservative nature of the membership of upper houses in capitalist countries conditions the conservatism and reaction of their policy, whose function is to hamper the passage of statutes not to the liking of the dominant classes.

The bicameral system of the USSR Supreme Soviet is radically different from the capitalist bicameral system, both in its class essence and in its structure.

Both houses of the USSR Supreme Soviet are chosen by Soviet citizens according to the only truly democratic system of suffrage in the world, according to electoral areas on the basis of universal, equal, direct suffrage with secret ballot. Rules of representation are defined in Articles 34 and

35 of the Stalin Constitution. They point out that the Soviet of the Union is selected according to electoral areas in accordance with the rule: one deputy for each 300,000 population; while the Soviet of Nationalities is chosen according to the rule: twenty-five deputies from each Union Republic, eleven from each Autonomous Republic, five from each Autonomous Region, and one from each National Area.

Both houses of the Supreme Soviet of the USSR, the Soviet of the Union and the Soviet of Nationalities, are elected for four years and at the same time. Consequently, in neither house of the Supreme Soviet in the USSR is there, or can there be, the advantages (associated with the dates of powers and of election) hereinbefore referred to as enjoyed by second chambers of capitalist countries. Both houses of the USSR Supreme Soviet have equal rights—genuinely equal rights. In the Soviet system there are no "higher" or "lower" houses, nor can a situation arise in which the second chamber could hold back or put a brake on legislative proposals of the first. The class nature and essence of both chambers of the Supreme Soviet is the same: both are chosen by all the toilers of the USSR. Each of them has alike a single goal: the strengthening of socialism. Both enjoy a like measure of legislative initiative; a statute is deemed affirmed if adopted by both houses by simple majority vote of each.

Joint sessions of both houses are conducted in turn by the President of the Soviet of the Union and by the President of the Soviet of Nationalities. The Presidents and their two Vice-Presidents are chosen separately by each house. Statutes adopted by the Supreme Soviet of the USSR—that is to say, having passed both houses—are automatically published by the Presidium of the Supreme Soviet of the USSR in the languages of the Union Republics, over the signatures of the President and Secretary of the Presidium of the Supreme Soviet of the USSR. The USSR Constitution of 1936 points out (Art. 47) that in case the houses do not agree, controverted questions are transferred to be decided by a board of conciliation made up of equal representation of both houses. If this board does not arrive at a harmonious decision, or if its decision fails to satisfy one of the chambers, the question is again considered in the chambers. If this time a harmonious decision of two houses is still lacking, the Presidium of the Supreme Soviet dissolves the houses and directs new elections. Controversies between the houses are thus solved by turning to the voters who finally solve the disputed matters. This feature specifically characterizes Soviet democracy and Soviet popular sovereignty. In this regard the Stalin Constitution introduced changes as compared with the 1924 Constitution whereby, if no accord was reached between chambers (the Soviet of the Union and the Soviet of Nationalities) in the commission and at the joint session of both houses, the contested question must, upon the demand of a chamber, be transferred for solution by an ordinary or extraordinary Congress of the Soviets of the USSR, which was also bound to decide the question once and for all (Art. 24).

The presence of the second chamber, the Soviet of Nationalities, in the structure of the Supreme Soviet of the USSR brilliantly expresses Soviet democracy, in which the starting points of all enactments are the specific national (no less than the general) interests of all the USSR toilers. Thereby the mutual faith and collaboration of nations are strengthened, and national peace is guaranteed.

Specifically for this reason, Stalin came forth at the Extraordinary Eighth All-Union Congress of Soviets against amendments to the projected USSR Constitution, which proposed to liquidate the Soviet of Nationalities and to preserve only one chamber.

Among us there is a supreme organ where the *general* interests of all toilers of the USSR—irrespective of their nationalities—are represented. This is the Soviet of the Union. But, in addition to their general interests, the Nationalities of the USSR have *also their own particular, specific* interests, connected with their national characteristics. Is it possible to disregard these specific interests? No, it is not possible. Is there necessity for a special supreme organ which would reflect precisely these specific interests? Yes, absolutely. There can be no doubt that it would be impossible without such an organ to administer such a multinational state as the USSR. Such an organ is the Second Chamber —the Soviet of Nationalities of the USSR.[4]

Historically the prototype of the present Council of Nationalities was created even before the organization of the USSR. From the very first days of the October Socialist Revolution, there was created in the RSFSR, as we have seen, among the administrative organs (People's Commissariats) the People's Commissariat for Nationalities, headed by Stalin. This People's Commissariat is a child of the October Socialist Revolution. Its activity is to achieve the principles of the Lenin-Stalin nationalist policy in practical realization of the principles of Soviet autonomy. When the Autonomous Republics and Regions of the RSFSR grew strong as national state organizations, the People's Commissariat of Nationalities, upon the proposal of Stalin, was reorganized by directive of the All-Russian Central Executive Committee of May 19, 1920.[5] Through its Congress of Soviets, each nationality designated its own representation to the People's Commissariat of Nationalities. With the People's Commissariat of Nationalities itself was formed the Soviet of Nationalities, which became the guiding

---

[4] Stalin, *Report on the Draft of the Constitution of the USSR*, p. 40.
[5] Cy. 1920, No. 45, Art. 202.

organ of the People's Commissariat. The Soviet of Nationalities consisted of representatives of national republics and regions and was headed by a People's Commissar—Stalin.

With the People's Commissariat of Nationalities, the Soviet of Nationalities considered and gave its conclusions upon all matters touching the activity of all People's Commissariats in the national republics and regions, worked out legislative projects concerning nationalities with which it entered into the highest organs of the RSFSR, studied the needs and demands of each separate nationality, worked out legislative projects satisfying these needs, and so on.

Through its delegates, the People's Commissariat of Nationalities was connected not only with autonomous organizations of the RSFSR but also with the constituent Soviet Republics, giving the latter the experience of the national building of the RSFSR.

In proportion to the ever increasing strength of the autonomous republics and regions, the growth of Soviet federation and the establishment of a closer bond between the independent Soviet Republics, the People's Commissariat of Nationalities, by its successful activity in organizing the nationalities, historically prepared its own liquidation. In the Soviet of Nationalities it gave a concrete model of representation of the interests of nationalities, a model taken into account also in the building of the supreme organs of the USSR.

Defending the principle of equality of nations in the Soviet of Nationalities, Stalin—even before the Twelfth Congress of the Party (1923)—came out sharply against the nationalist-Trotskyist project of creating supreme organs of authority. Their proposal was, in its lowest terms, that only representatives of the four republics which had concluded a compact of union should enter the Second Chamber (the future Soviet of Nationalities of the Central Executive Committee of the USSR). Thus representation from autonomous republics and regions was absolutely excluded. The nationalist essence of the project of the nationalists and the Trotskyists was further expressed in the fact that those who initiated it promoted a radical difference in rights (between the Ukraine on the one hand and the Tatar, Bashkir, and other autonomous republics and regions on the other) as to participation in the formation of the supreme organ of authority—the Soviet of Nationalities.

Upon the report and motion of Stalin, the Twelfth Congress of the Bolshevik Worker-Peasant Party directed that

side by side with the existing central organs of the Union—representing the toiling masses of the entire Union (irrespective of nationalities)—there should be created a special organ to represent the nationalities on principles of equality.

Such organization of central organs of the Union would make it perfectly feasible to listen responsively to the needs and demands of the peoples, to render them timely and necessary aid, to create a setting of complete mutual confidence, and thus to liquidate—with the least pain—the afore-mentioned inheritance.[6]

The Fourth Council of the Central Committee of the Worker-Peasant Party of Bolsheviks, with responsible workers of national republics and regions, meeting June 9–12, 1923, upon the report of Stalin as to realizing the decisions of the Twelfth Party Congress on the national question, defined the practical measures in conformity with the decision as to the bicameral system of the Central Executive Committee. It established also the designation of the two chambers of a single Central Executive Committee of the USSR—the Union Soviet and the Soviet of Nationalities. The Soviet of Nationalities is the only second chamber in the world formed according to the index of nationality; the deputies elected December 12, 1937, represented fifty-four nationalities.

In bourgeois union states—even the most democratic, such as the U.S.A. and Switzerland, the second chamber is formed from administrative-territorial units: two deputies from each state (as in the U.S.A.) or canton (as in Switzerland). With this arrangement, national interests are not taken into account, so that the national pressure upon weak peoples—the negroes and Indians in the U.S.A., and so on—is intensified.

In second chambers of bourgeois union states, the right of representation is enjoyed only by the immediate members of the union (states or cantons). In the USSR, not only the immediate members of the Union, Union Republics, but also their constituent autonomous republics, regions, and national areas are represented in the Soviet of Nationalities. This strengthens the Lenin-Stalin principle of the equality of nations.

In the Stalin Constitution, the equal rights of Union Soviet Republics are expressed in an extremely striking and clear manner. The small White Russian SSR and the vast RSFSR enjoy in the Soviet of Nationalities the same rule of representation—twenty-five deputies each. This equality of right exists also as between autonomous republics (eleven deputies), autonomous regions (five deputies), and national areas (one deputy)—regardless of size and population (Art. 35). How broadly the representation of nationalities is assured is attested by the fact that of 574 deputies in the Soviet of Nationalities 275 fall to the lot of Union Republics, and 299 to the lot of autonomous republics, autonomous regions, and national areas. Moreover, the latter participate as well in elections of deputies to the

[6] The All-Union Communist Party (of Bolsheviks) in Resolutions, Vol. I, p. 506.

Soviet of Nationalities from the Union Republic of which they are component parts.

It is a special characteristic of the equality of rights of nationalities in the USSR that the obligatory representation in the Soviet of Nationalities of even the tiniest national formations is assured. Take, for example, such tiny national areas as Koryak (with a population of 13,000) or Evenki (with a population of 6,000), and others. In elections of deputies to the Soviet of the Union, they must be united with the neighboring districts to form one elective district embracing 300,000 population. But in the Soviet of Nationalities, the Stalin Constitution confirms representation on the basis of one deputy from each of the existing national areas. That is a special characteristic of the second chamber of the USSR Supreme Soviet.

SEC. 4: THE PRESIDIUM OF THE SUPREME SOVIET OF THE USSR

Pursuant to Article 48 of the USSR Constitution, the Supreme Soviet of the USSR, at a joint sitting of both chambers, elects the Presidium of the Supreme Soviet of the USSR, consisting of a president of the Presidium of the Supreme Soviet of the USSR, eleven vice presidents, a secretary and twenty-four members of the Presidium.

The Presidium of the Supreme Soviet of the USSR: (a) convenes sessions of the Supreme Soviet of the USSR; (b) interprets operative USSR laws and issues decrees; (c) dissolves the Supreme Soviet of the USSR (in accordance with Art. 47 of the USSR Constitution), and orders new elections; (d) conducts referenda on its own initiative or upon demand of one of the Union Republics; (e) annuls directives and orders of the Council of People's Commissars of the USSR and of Union Republic Councils of People's Commissars in case of their nonconformity with law; (f) in the period between sessions of the Supreme Soviet of the USSR relieves of their posts and appoints separate People's Commissars of the USSR on the recommendation of the President of the Council of People's Commissars of the USSR, subject to later confirmation by the Supreme Soviet of the USSR; (g) awards decorations and confers titles of honor of the USSR; (h) exercises the right of pardon; (i) appoints and removes higher commands of armed forces of the USSR; (j) in the period between sessions of the Supreme Soviet of the USSR proclaims a state of war in case of armed attack upon the USSR or whenever necessary to fulfill international treaty obligations for mutual defense against aggression; (k) orders general or partial mobilization; (*l*) ratifies international treaties; [1] (*m*) designates and recalls plenipotentiary representatives of the USSR in foreign states; (*n*) receives credentials and letters of recall of accredited diplomatic representatives of foreign states; and (*o*) declares in separate localities or throughout the USSR martial law in the interests of defense of the USSR or assurance of public order and state security.[2]

From this enumeration it is clear that the Presidium of the Supreme Soviet of the USSR is charged chiefly with such functions as are appropriated in bourgeois states to the head of the state, the king, or the president of the republic as contrasted with the "popular" representation. But the Presidium of the Supreme Soviet fulfills its functions, being "accountable to the Supreme Soviet of the USSR for all its activity" (Art. 48). This is something which does not exist in capitalist states, where heads of states are not responsible to "popular" representation. The democratic essence of the Presidium of the Supreme Soviet, and its distinction from all the so-called "heads of states" in capitalist countries, derives from its class essence, from the fact that it is an organ of a *socialist* state of workers and peasants.

The Presidium of the Supreme Soviet is, by the definition given to it by Stalin in his report to the Extraordinary Eighth All-Union Congress of Soviets, *a collegium president*,[3] chosen by the Soviet of the Union and the Soviet of Nationalities in joint session. The President of the Presidium of the Supreme Soviet of the USSR has no such special rights as characterize individual presidents of bourgeois states. His rights flow out of his position as president of a collegium institution of socialist authority. Over his signature are published statutes adopted by the Supreme Soviet of the USSR. He presides at sessions of the Presidium of the Supreme Soviet of the USSR. He signs its laws and other acts, receives in its name accredited emissaries of other states, and oversees the execution of decisions adopted by the collegium.

[1] The second session of the Supreme Soviet of the USSR adopted a Law Concerning the Order of Ratification and Denunciation of International Contracts of the USSR as follows: "Art. 2. Treaties of peace, of mutual defense from aggression, and of mutual nonaggression—concluded by the USSR—are subject to ratification, as are international treaties wherein the respective parties have stipulated therefor. Art. 3. The denunciation of ratified international treaties is achieved on the basis of laws of the Presidium of the Supreme Soviet of the USSR."

[2] The last point was supplemented in Art. 49 of the USSR Constitution at the first session of the Supreme Soviet of the USSR (Jan. 12–19, 1938).

[3] I do not believe that any mere *translation* would make clear what the text is, I think, supposed to mean. There had been a proposal to amend Art. 48 to the effect that the President of the Presidium of the USSR Supreme Soviet be elected by the whole population, so that he would be on the level of—and able to put himself in opposition to—the Supreme Soviet. Stalin's report rejected that proposal, saying, in substance, that "the President of the USSR is a Collegium: the Presidium of the Supreme Soviet, including the President of that Presidium—elected by (and accountable to) the Supreme Soviet."—TR.

The Presidium of the Supreme Soviet of the USSR is built in conformity with the international principles of our multinational Soviet state, principles of the friendship and the unity of the USSR peoples. In any bourgeois republic, the president is necessarily a representative of the sovereign nation. It is inconceivable that the bourgeois U.S.A. would admit a negro or a representative of another oppressed nationality as President or Vice-President.

In the USSR there are, aside from the President, eleven Vice-Presidents, according to the number of Union Republics. Speaking of the amendment to the proposed Constitution (introduced at the time of the consideration by the entire nation) of Vice-Presidents of the Presidium of the Supreme Soviet of the USSR according to the principle of representation (by one each) from the Union Republics, Stalin in the Extraordinary Eighth All-Union Congress of Soviets said: "I think that this amendment could be adopted—it would be an improvement and can not fail to strengthen the authority of the Presidium of the Supreme Soviet of the USSR." [4] The collegium character of the Presidium of the Supreme Soviet of the USSR reflects also the equality of nations of our Union. This principle is placed also at the basis of the formation of Presidia of Supreme Soviets of those Union Republics having autonomous republics and regions.[5]

But the particularly distinctive feature of Soviet collegium president is its place in the system of higher organs of authority of the USSR. First it must be noted that, starting from the democratic structure of higher organs of authority, the Presidium of the Supreme Soviet of the USSR is, as we have noted, completely accountable in all its activity to the Supreme Soviet of the USSR. The latter, as the supreme organ of authority, may at any moment have a new election of its Presidium. Therein it is sharply distinguished, for example, from the President of the U.S.A. who, conformably with the principle of so-called "separation of powers," not only is not answerable to Congress but has in fact advantages over Congress as well: the right of so-called "delaying veto" (of returning to Congress for fresh consideration an act adopted by Congress).

The Soviet collegium president is distinguished from all capitalist state heads, contrasted in one form or another with the principle of "popular sovereignty," even in the form of bourgeois parliaments so little representative of the actual interests of those who make up the true people. In the Soviet system of building the higher organs of authority, there can be no talk of any "veto" by the Presidium of the Supreme Soviet of the USSR of

[4] Stalin, *Report on the Draft of the Constitution of the USSR*, p. 42.
[5] Constitution of the RSFSR, Art. 31; of the Georgian SSR, Art. 34; and of the Azerbaijan SSR, Art. 31.

laws adopted by the Supreme Soviet. The Presidium cannot send back for reconsideration a statute already adopted by the Supreme Soviet, as can the presidents of France, the U.S.A., and others. A statute adopted by the Supreme Soviet of the USSR becomes operative without further action. The Presidium of the Supreme Soviet of the USSR publishes this statute in the languages of the Union Republics over the signatures of the President and Secretary of the Presidium of the Supreme Soviet of the USSR (Art. 40).

The essential democracy of the building of the higher organs of USSR authority is expressed also in the fact that, according to the Constitution, the Presidium of the Supreme Soviet of the USSR publishes decrees as distinguished from statutes; it only gives interpretations of operative statutes. This emphasizes the supremacy of socialist law, issued only by the highest organ of power, the Supreme Soviet of the USSR.

The Presidium of the Supreme Soviet of the USSR keeps watch that all directives and orders of executive governmental organs conform with the USSR Constitution and laws. We have already seen that it annuls directives and orders of the Council of People's Commissars of the USSR, and of Councils of People's Commissars of Union Republics, if they do not conform with law (Art. 49, Par. e).

The subordination of all organs of authority to socialist law is a special characteristic of the Stalin Constitution. The matter stands otherwise in capitalist countries. For example, the German President had the right (under Art. 48 of the Weimar Constitution) to legislate independently and in spite of parliament. When the draft of the Stalin Constitution was under consideration by all the people, there was a proposal to supplement Article 40 by pointing out that the Presidium of the Supreme Soviet is granted the right to issue provisional legislative acts. Stalin expressed himself against this proposal:

I think this addendum is wrong and should not be adopted by the Congress. It is necessary at last to put an end to a situation where legislation is not confined to any one organ alone but is performed by a whole series of organs. Such a situation is antagonistic to the principle of statutory stability—and statutory stability is necessary to us now more than ever before. Legislative authority in the USSR must be realized by one organ only—the Supreme Soviet of the USSR.[6]

The broad personal rights of the president in bourgeois republics are often explained by the fact that he is supposed to be chosen by the people (as in the U.S.A., pre-Hitler Germany, and so on). History affords many

---

[6] Stalin, *Report on the Draft of the Constitution of the USSR*, p. 41.

examples of a president utilizing such a motif, not merely setting himself in opposition to parliament, but even establishing his own personal dictatorship (Napoleon III, December 2, 1851). Reaction specifically explained also the broad rights of President Hindenburg by the fact that he was supposed to have been chosen by the people. The same reasoning also justified the practice of broadly utilizing Article 48 of the Weimar Constitution, in accordance with which the president legislated even independently of parliament.

When the draft of the Constitution of the USSR was under consideration by all the people, there was introduced an amendment proposing that the President of the Presidium of the Supreme Soviet of the USSR be chosen directly by the electors rather than by the Soviet of the USSR. Stalin, at the Extraordinary Eighth All-Union Congress of Soviets, came forward to defend the proposed Constitution, emphasizing the subordination and accountability of the Presidium of the Supreme Soviet of the USSR to the Supreme Soviet of the USSR, which expresses the sovereignty of the people. "The experience of history shows that such is the most democratic structure of supreme organs—guaranteeing the country against undesirable vicissitudes." [7]

Many bourgeois-democratic constitutions grant the president the right to dissolve parliament immediately (the Weimar Constitution) or with the consent of the senate (the French Constitution). Under Article 47 of the Stalin Constitution, it is provided that in case of disagreement between the two chambers, and if accord cannot be reached, the Presidium of the Supreme Soviet of the USSR dissolves the Supreme Soviet of the USSR and directs new elections. It effectuates such dissolution, however, solely in the case provided by the Constitution and not at its own discretion: specifically, when a disagreement, having arisen between the Soviet of the Union and the Soviet of Nationalities, is not eliminated in the method established by the Constitution, and when, by virtue thereof, dissolution of the Supreme Soviet and new elections are necessary. From this it is clear that the Presidium of the Supreme Soviet of the USSR exercises only the organizational functions of (1) dismissing the Supreme Soviet of the USSR and (2) ordering new elections, making it possible for the electors themselves to resolve the dispute between the chambers.

In case of the premature dissolution of parliament in bourgeois republics, presidents remain. But the Presidium of the Supreme Soviet of the USSR orders elections within a period not exceeding two months from the date of dissolution of the USSR Supreme Soviet (Art. 54). Moreover, the newly chosen Supreme Soviet of the USSR is convened by the outgoing

[7] *Ibid.*

Presidium of the Supreme Soviet of the USSR not later than one month after the elections (Art. 55). In case of premature dissolution of the Supreme Soviet of the USSR, the Presidium itself retains its powers only until the formation, by the newly chosen Supreme Soviet of the USSR, of the new Presidium of the Supreme Soviet of the USSR (Art. 53) to which it gives place.

The role of the Presidium of the Supreme Soviet of the USSR is particularly significant in the period between sessions of the Supreme Soviet with particular reference to control over governmental activity. Everyone knows of the pressure exerted upon the court, policy, and legislation by the President of the U.S.A., for example, since he not only has the veto power but (with the consent of the Senate) appoints judges to the Supreme Court, who both judge and interpret the Constitution (often abrogating statutes). The democratic essence of the Presidium of the Supreme Soviet is expressed also in the fact that it has no right to designate judges. "Judges are independent and subject solely to the law" (Art. 112). The people's judges are chosen on the basis of universal, direct, and equal suffrage by secret ballot (Art. 109). They are responsible to their electors and are bound to render an account to them. The Supreme Court of the USSR and special courts are chosen by the sole bearer of sovereignty of the Soviet people, the Supreme Soviet of the USSR (Art. 105). Supreme courts of Union and autonomous republics are chosen in precisely the same way by the Supreme Soviets of these republics (Arts. 106, 107).

In bourgeois states such as the U.S.A., the designation of higher officials is by the President with the consent of the Senate. As to ministers (or secretaries), the President designates them at his own discretion. In practice there has never been a case when the legislative chambers disputed this right of the President of the U.S.A. The President of France formally designates the premier and the other higher officials.

In the period between sessions of the Supreme Soviet, the Presidium of the Supreme Soviet of the USSR relieves from office and designates separate People's Commissars of the USSR upon recommendation by the President of the Council of People's Commissars of the USSR, but these appointments are subject to subsequent confirmation by the Supreme Soviet of the USSR (Art. 49, Par. f).

In relations between the Supreme Soviet of the USSR and its Presidium there are no such "messages" as those whereby the presidents of the United States, France and other bourgeois republics strive to direct legislation from the point of view of the policy they follow. The Presidium of the Supreme Soviet of the USSR is an organ working daily, accountable and subordinate to the Supreme Soviet of the USSR. This solves also the matter of the responsibility of the Presidium of the Supreme Soviet as contrasted with the nonaccountability of presidents of the bourgeois republics. The directing line of the Presidium of the Supreme Soviet is exclusively that charted by the statutes of the Supreme Soviet.

Functions of the Presidium of the Supreme Soviet also include the holding, upon its own initiative or upon the demand of one of the Union Republics, of a referendum, an interrogation of the people concerning proposed legislation, also called "direct popular legislation" as distinguished from legislation through representative organs. As direct popular legislation it was preserved only in certain backward cantons of Switzerland, where it is a survival of antiquity, when custom occupied the place of statute and the people decided all matters directly. In other countries and in certain cantons of Switzerland itself, the referendum in various forms—obligatory or "facultative" (conditional, when required by a certain number of voters and so forth)—exists side by side with "national representation" (parliaments). When a legislative proposal is considered in representative organs, amendments may be introduced as to separate points; they may be adopted, rejected and replaced. In referenda this becomes extremely complicated; then the consideration of proposed legislation can be only preliminary—in assemblies and in the press—whereas the proposed legislation is itself ordinarily voted on in its entirety and by a mere Yes or No answer of acceptance or rejection. While a referendum is one form of solving a question democratically, the practice and the fate of all species of referenda in capitalist countries are analogous to those of voting in parliamentary elections, with all their limitations and abuses.

Various postwar bourgeois democratic constitutions (the Weimar Constitution, and the constitutions of Czechoslovakia, Lithuania, Esthonia and others) contain a formal inclusion of various species of referenda side by side with parliaments. In some countries no referendum has ever been held. In others referenda have been rare. Reaction—being in authority—has more than once utilized referenda for its own purposes to the accompaniment of governmental terror, high-pressure preparation for the voting, crushing of its adversaries, and direct manipulation in totalling the voting figures. Hitler himself sometimes uses referenda in precisely this way after having forcibly deprived a significant part of the German population of their voting rights (communists and antifascists in general, and the so-called non-Aryans, who have been deprived of the right of citizenship). All fascist "referenda" take place in conditions of the most cruel terror and the prosecution of persons suspected of being "unreliable." In bourgeois-democratic countries (Switzerland and the U.S.A., where the referendum exists in separate states), the bourgeoisie holds tightly in its hands the direction of referenda.

All the limitations upon suffrage in bourgeois democratic lands (denial of voting rights to women, divers voting qualifications and so on) are shown by practice to be extended to referenda also. The interrogation is addressed only to those who enjoy voting rights—not to the entire adult population. Moreover, all the means of pressure by the dominant classes, exerted by them in elections (the role of the press, radio, corruption, and so on), are exerted also in referenda. In the USSR the referendum is a different matter. In the land of socialism it will be effectuated not (as in capitalist countries) in a setting of class contradictions, but in Soviet conditions, in a setting where exploiter classes have been liquidated and there are only friendly classes of workers and peasants in the USSR, fraternally bound in an indestructible union. With this situation, participation by the USSR population in referenda will be veritably universal. Finally, a Soviet referendum is introduced in conditions when the press, lodgings for assemblies, and all the instruments of agitation and propaganda, utilized in capitalist lands against the toilers, are in the USSR utilized in their interests. Only in these conditions can there be truly *democratic* interrogation of the entire Soviet people or of a part thereof, a sovereign Soviet Republic, on matters of Soviet legislation.

The foregoing brilliantly characterizes the position of the Presidium of the Supreme Soviet in the system of highest organs of USSR authority, built on principles of socialist democracy, of genuine sovereignty of the Soviet people.

SEC. 5: STATUTE, DECREE, STATUTORY INTERPRETATION

We have already pointed out that the Stalin Constitution distinctly limits the functions of organs possessing unitary state authority. Statutes are issued only by the Supreme Soviet of the USSR.

A statute is of juridical force higher than that of other state acts; it is the highest juridical form in which state authority is manifested. For this very reason, it is affirmed by the highest state authority, the Supreme Soviet of the USSR, and can be abrogated or amended only by its directive.

In bourgeois society, a statute expresses the will of the dominant class, the dictatorship of a negligible minority over the majority. There a statute guards the interests of capitalist private property, its exploiter system. It is social coercion "concentrated and organized." [1] In the conditions of worker class dictatorship, a statute guards the interests of the toilers—the overwhelming majority of the population that has overthrown capitalists and landowners and built socialist society wherein there is no longer place for man's exploitation of man. In socialist society a statute is the highest act of state authority, responsive to the interests of the broadest masses of the people. The growth of the consciousness of the masses augments the force of a Soviet statute. In contrast to the ever increasing part played in capitalist countries by executive authority at the expense of legislative authority, the Stalin Constitution emphasizes the supremacy of the socialist statute as expressing the will of the sovereign Soviet people. While the old state apparatus was being broken up, and during the civil war which soon followed, the Soviet statute, as the expression of the will of the dictatorship of the worker class (the broadest masses of the people), was directed chiefly at crushing the resistance of class enemies. It rallied the masses under the guidance of the worker class. It was also significant from the viewpoint of propaganda. "We had a zone when decrees served as a form of propaganda." [2]

At the same time, however, the statute also strengthened the basis for socialist building, of which it was the expression. Without this, victory in the civil war was impossible. From the very first day of the victory of Soviet authority, Soviet statutes were socialist statutes. During the victory of socialism, the statute pointed sharply toward organization of the toilers for the further strengthening of socialism. A brilliant example is the statute (of August 7, 1932) issued before the adoption of the Stalin Constitution, confirming socialist property and proclaiming it the sacred and inviolable "basis of the Soviet social order." [3] But this by no means removed the tasks of crushing the hostile elements striving to undermine socialist building. "Will —if it be the state will—must be expressed as a *statute*, established by *authority*—otherwise the word 'will' is an empty concussion of air by empty sound." [4] This defines the important significance attributed by the Stalin Constitution to the socialist statute, emanating from the enormous and influential role of the Soviet state in the further triumphant development of socialism, of its reinforcement and defense.

Statutes for the most part prescribe general regulations, define the general rules established in the interests of the toilers by the supreme organs of state authority. A statute takes account of experience and generalizes mass conduct, directing it to a definite goal. It thus not only records experience,

[1] Marx, *Das Kapital* (Russian ed., 1936), Vol. I, p. 821.
[2] Lenin (Russian ed.), Vol. XXVII, p. 225.
[3] Cz. 1932, No. 62, Art. 360.
[4] Lenin (Russian ed.), Vol. XX, p. 532.

it also synthesizes experience and draws inferences therefrom, to the end of further changing social relationships to accord with socialist problems of the worker-class dictatorship. A statute is not everlasting; it can run its course to the extent that the cases for which it was created are disposed of, whereupon it is abrogated, or replaced by a new statute. The reality of the socialist statute is assured by the prestige of the highest authority (chosen by the people themselves) which issues statutes, and its support by the broadest masses. A statute and its effectuation by the masses are one; this is the distinguishing feature of the single Soviet legality put by Lenin as a condition of culture.

Writing to Stalin, Lenin said: "If we do not effectuate this most elementary condition for the establishment of unitary legality—at whatever cost —in the entire federation, there can be no talk of any guard or of any creation of a state of culture." [5] In his article: "The Question of the Policy of Liquidating the Kulaks as a Class," Stalin pointed out that the Fifteenth Party Congress still left in force the statute as to leasing land and hiring labor in the rural districts, notwithstanding that the policy of there restricting the exploiter elements was intensified. But from the year 1929 the development there culminated in the direction of eliminating the kulaks as a class on the basis of complete collectivization.

Do these laws and these directives contradict the policy of *eliminating* the kulaks as a class? Unconditionally, *Yes!* These statutes and these directives we shall now—in districts of complete collectivization, the sphere of whose expansion increases not merely every day but every hour—have accordingly to put on one side.[6]

In accordance with the definitive tasks of socialist building, statutes may be issued for a definite time, after which their action is either continued by special directives or terminated.

On the basis of the Stalin Constitution, "the right to initiate legislation belongs alike to the Soviet of the Union and to the Soviet of Nationalities equally" (Art. 38). All proposed legislation introduced into the Supreme Soviet is considered in sessions of both chambers and is deemed affirmed if adopted by both chambers of the Supreme Soviet by mere majority vote in each (Art. 39). To amend the fundamental law—the Constitution—a different and more complicated method of voting is established; this (Art. 146) requires a majority of not less than two-thirds of the votes in each chamber of the Supreme Soviet of the USSR.

Statutes cannot possibly provide in advance for all the manifold diversity of the phenomena of life. That which explains an operative statute—no less

[5] *Ibid.*, Vol. XXVII, p. 299.
[6] Stalin, *Questions of Leninism* (10th Russian ed), p. 320.

than that which is directly stated in it—has universally obligatory force. Accordingly, the Presidium of the Supreme Soviet of the USSR is charged by the Constitution of 1936 to watch that the law be correctly applied in conformity with the demands of life. As stated in the Stalin Constitution (Art. 49, Par. *b*), it "interprets operative laws of the USSR and issues decrees."

Interpretation of a statute is elucidation of its purposes and content, and of the conditions of its most correct application (in conformity with questions of socialist building), and also of its separate propositions (or of the whole statute) as applied to the concrete facts of life. According to the Stalin Constitution, the legislator himself establishes who is to interpret the laws. In the USSR that right is given to the Presidium of the Supreme Soviet of the USSR, the collegium president, an organ accountable to the Supreme Soviet. Thus, the utmost identity (authenticity) of statutory interpretation with the statutes themselves, as expressing the will of the entire Soviet people, is guaranteed. Thereby social legality is strengthened and stabilized, and the character of statutory interpretation in the USSR, its subordination to the statute, is foreordained. Interpretation neither creates a new rule nor goes outside the compass and bounds of the statute under interpretation. It merely reveals the meaning and content of the statute, the obligations imposed thereby, starting from concrete circumstances, from the unity of socialist purposes and from socialist law presently in force.

In bourgeois countries the right to interpret statutes is in most cases appropriated to organs not responsible to parliament. Thus, in the U.S.A., according to the theory of so-called "separation of powers," the courts are granted the right to interpret statutes or, in simple words, to control acts of Congress in respect of their conformity with the meaning of the Constitution. If a statute or a single paragraph thereof is admitted to be in conflict with the Constitution, it is declared unconstitutional, and therefore inoperative, by the court, and no rights can for the future be based upon it. Thus, the rights of the Supreme Court are opposed to the rights of the Congress representing "the will of the people."

In the U.S.A. neither the Constitution nor the laws of Congress, but the interpretations and constructions of statutes by the Supreme Court, are in fact—in most matters—the operative rule. Constitutional control by the Supreme Court of the United States thus in fact creates new legislation. Moreover, it must be noted that judges opposed to Congress are nominated by the President, with the assent only of the Senate; the House of Representatives has no part in the appointment of judges. Another characteristic feature must also be noted: the "control" and "interpretation" of statutes are not a systematic function of the Supreme Court of the United States. Every sort of statute is considered as having force until it occurs to some private person or capitalist enterprise to file a petition in court to have it, or a separate paragraph of it, declared unconstitutional. Naturally this right is broadly used by monopolist cliques of exploiters to obtain a declaration of "unconstitutionality" as to laws running counter to their interests.

Bourgeois political science obscures the class essence of juridical chicanery in statutory interpretation by a system of formal interpretations.

Interpretation is sometimes based on an investigation of the statuory text by etymological and syntactic—grammatical—analysis of words and separate phrases in the text. This is called *grammatical* interpretation. Indications of the process of forming the statute, of the course of events which evoked the necessity of issuing it, are sometimes cited as the basis of interpretation. This is called *historical* interpretation. A third species of interpretation is to compare one paragraph of a statute with another in calculating the entire aggregate of existing rules: interpretation of the content of a certain statute by comparing it with general legislation. Bourgeois political scientists call this *systematic* interpretation.

According to the Stalin Constitution of 1936, the method of interpreting statutes is established by the Presidium of the Supreme Soviet itself; it is free in the choice of means of interpretation. According to the Constitution of 1924, the right of interpreting statutes belonged to the USSR Supreme Court. According to that Constitution, the functions of the Supreme Court of the USSR included:

a) giving to the Supreme Courts of Union Republics explanatory directions as to matters of All-Union legislation; and . . .

c) giving its conclusions—as required by the Central Executive Committee of the USSR—as to the legality of directives of Union Republics from the viewpoint of the Constitution (Art. 43).

Thus, according to the (1924) Constitution, the functions of the USSR Supreme Court included elucidations of questions of All-Union legislation and interpretation of the Constitution (upon request by the Central Executive Committee of USSR). According to the USSR Constitution of 1936, the right of interpreting statutes belongs solely to the Presidium of the Supreme Soviet of the USSR and, as regards republic statutes, to the Presidia of the Supreme Soviets of Union and Autonomous Republics.

Details of the development of social relationships cannot possibly be anticipated by legislation nor can it, even in general form, furnish rules for all concrete cases. It enunciates general principles, leaving the details of the statements of principle to be developed in the form of decrees. A decree is an act of higher administration based on a statute. It makes easier the development and realization of statutes, their application to concrete cases. Decrees assure that the statute shall be applied in conformity with the changing conditions of life. By means of decrees a statute is extended to all the cases embraced by its meaning and content.

Decrees are of varying content. A decree can be issued regarding the organization of state institutions, the method of their activity, the functioning of responsible leaders (People's Commissars and others), on the basis of the Constitution and published statutes; it can create rules of conduct for citizens (declaration of a state of war in the interests of defense, and the like). It can be an act of reward or pardon on the basis of rights granted by the Constitution to the Presidium of the Supreme Soviet of the USSR. Finally, it can be an act preliminary to the work of higher organs of authority (designating elections, summoning legislative chambers, and so on). In all cases a decree can be issued only on the basis of a statute, and must neither contradict it nor deviate from it.

Separate decrees issued as matters of higher administration and related to the jurisdiction of the USSR (as personified by its highest organs of authority and state administration) require confirmation by the Supreme Soviet of the USSR. Thus Article 14 of the USSR Constitution points out that to the jurisdiction of the USSR (as personified by its highest organs of authority and organs of state administration) is submitted the "confirmation of the formation of new territories and regions, and also of new autonomous republics within Union Republics" (Par. *f*). On the basis of this, the first session of the Supreme Soviet of the USSR affirmed the directives of the Central Executive Committee of the USSR, and the second session confirmed decrees of the Presidium of the Supreme Soviet of the USSR as to the division of territories and regions of Union Republics. In accordance therewith, changes in Articles 22, 23, 26, 28 and 29 of the USSR Constitution were adopted at the first and second sessions.

According to Article 49 of the Constitution, the Presidium of the Supreme Soviet of the USSR, "in the intervals between sessions of the Supreme Soviet of the USSR, relieves of their posts—and appoints—People's Commissars of the USSR, upon recommendation of the President of the USSR Council of People's Commissars, subject to later confirmation by the Supreme Soviet of the USSR" (Par. *f*). Accordingly, the second session of the Supreme Soviet of the USSR affirmed decrees of the Presidium concerning relieving individual People's Commissars of their duties, the appointment of new People's Commissars, and the appointment of Kaganovich as Vice-President of the Council of People's Commissars of the USSR.

Article 14 (Par. *v*) of the Constitution of the USSR points out that the jurisdiction of the USSR (as personified by its highest organs of state authority and organs of state administration) includes the establishment of "laws concerning citizenship of the Union; laws concerning the rights of foreigners." The law concerning citizenship of the Union, adopted by the second session of the Supreme Soviet of the USSR, refers to the jurisdiction of the Presidium of the Supreme Soviet of the USSR: the admission of foreigners into citizenship upon their petition,[7] permission to withdraw from citizenship, and deprivation of USSR citizenship by virtue of a decree of a Presidium of the Supreme Soviet of the USSR—a special decree in each case.

In capitalist countries it is likewise held that a decree must not contradict a statute, but this is so only in theory there. In fact, as the bourgeois political scientist Korkunov admits, where decrees are issued it is sometimes impossible to get along "without violating the constitution, just as it is without violating ordinary statutes." [8] Examples previously cited of the English practice as to decrees have already indicated how the government employs decrees so as to legislate independently of parliament and in the teeth of the constitution. Bourgeois political scientists explained this government policy by saying that parliament works slowly and fails to keep pace with the demands of a life which has become extraordinarily complicated. Of course it is undeniable that the circle of matters entering into the sphere of modern legislation has increased many times in comparison with what it was at the beginning of the century. Fundamentally, however, this fact is associated with the development of class struggle, and in particular with the efforts of bourgeois government to be freed from the control of parliamentary institutions. This is the basic reason for the growth of administrative decrees at the expense of statutes. In individual countries, decrees issuing from the head of the state are the only supreme rules for separate parts of the territory of that state, especially for colonies. Thus, in France, acts of the legislature extend chiefly to metropolitan France. As to colonies, decrees of the President of the Republic, formulated by bureaucrats of the separate departments, are operative.

To the foregoing must be added the extraordinary decrees which have been broadly expanded in the postwar period. In prewar time, extraordinary decrees were particularly widely used in Russia (on the basis of Art. 87 of the Basic Statutes of 1906). But in the postwar period, as previously noted with reference to the application of Article 48 of the Weimar Constitution, extraordinary legislation (*Notverordnungen*) was extensively applied in pre-Hitler Germany. It is sufficient to note that in 1931 the Reichstag

---

[7] The right of admitting foreigners into USSR citizenship is possessed also by presidia of the Supreme Soviets of the Union Republics within whose boundaries the foreigners are domiciled.

[8] H. M. Korkunov, *Decree and Statute* (1894), p. 227.

affirmed thirty-five statutes, while there were forty-three extraordinary statutes issued independently of the Reichstag, on the basis of Article 48 of the Weimar Constitution. In 1932 the Reichstag adopted five statutes in all, whereas fifty-nine extraordinary statutes were adopted. On the basis of these extraordinary statutes, the ponderous burden of the crisis was transferred to the shoulders of the worker masses, and the policy of despoiling workers, of curtailing social incomes, was pursued.

In the war and postwar period, extraordinary legislation (*décret-loi*) was broadly expanded in France and other capitalist countries. In Switzerland, for example, in the period during and immediately after the war, there were issued 1,004 extraordinary laws, many of which were in conflict with the Swiss Constitution. This occurred notwithstanding the fact that, according to Article 89 of the Swiss Constitution, "union statutes, decrees, and orders can be issued only with the consent of both chambers." In addition, according to the same article of the constitution, union statutes are submitted to the people for acceptance or rejection (to a referendum) if 30,000 active citizens or eight cantons so require. The basic motive of extraordinary legislation is to be free from parliamentary tutelage and control. Fascism introduced "extraordinary legislation" into a principle and a rule, reverting to the arbitrary fiat of the absolute monarch. By its "decree" policy, and without control of parliament, it was exceedingly easy to give a semblance of "legality" to what was in fact the illegal, terrorist, rightless and arbitrary conduct of fascist governments.

SEC. 6: SESSIONS OF THE USSR SUPREME SOVIET

In accordance with the Stalin Constitution, ordinary sessions of the Supreme Soviet of the USSR are, as we have already noted, summoned twice a year. Sessions of both chambers begin and end at the same time. They are summoned by the Presidium of the Supreme Soviet of the USSR which is accountable for its action to the Supreme Soviet of the USSR. The chambers of the Supreme Soviet of the USSR themselves establish the order and time of their work, and the date of the end of the session. Extraordinary sessions of the Supreme Soviet of the USSR are summoned by the Presidium of the Supreme Soviet at its discretion or upon demand by one of the Union Republics, emphasizing still once again the equality of rights of the Union Soviet Republics.

The radical distinction between sessions of the Supreme Soviet of the USSR and those of bourgeois parliaments flows out of the radical distinction between the Soviet representative system and the bourgeois representative system, between a deputy of the Soviet parliament and a deputy of the bourgeois parliament.

The indissoluble unity of the entire Soviet people, confidently advancing along the socialist road under the guidance of the Lenin-Stalin Party, is most brilliantly expressed also in the work of deputies of the USSR Supreme Soviet. The utter and complete absence of party quarrels (characteristic of bourgeois parliaments) makes the work of the sessions of the Supreme Soviet of the USSR active and fruitful, and the deputies' criticism efficient. This accounts also for the joint work during the sessions of the two Soviet chambers possessing equal rights, a single class nature, and only socialist goals.

The matter is otherwise as to sessions of bourgeois parliaments. These, in monarchical countries, are summoned by the monarch at his pleasure. In tsarist Russia, Article 99 of the "Fundamental Laws" provided that "the duration of the yearly business of the Imperial Council and Imperial Duma—and the dates of the interruption thereof during the course of the year—are defined by the decrees of H. M. the Emperor."

In England the king, as the saying is, reigns but does not rule. His ministers, and particularly the Prime Minister, rule. Neither king nor ministers need protracted work by parliament. But constitutional tradition demands that the budget and certain important laws be affirmed yearly by parliament. Parliament is itself already broadening the circle of matters which it considers at each session. The Prime Minister, however, as leader of the parliamentary majority, as hereinbefore noted, is in fact a dictator in parliament. He passes the necessary legislative projects without any particular difficulty, legislating without parliament by tacit consent of the parliamentary majority.

France is a Republic in which the President is granted the right to summon sessions of parliament. The French Constitution provides that the Senate and Chamber of Deputies assemble yearly on the second Tuesday of January unless earlier summoned by the President of the Republic. The latter, however, has the right to adjourn, to close, a session of parliament and, with the consent of the Senate, to dissolve the Chamber of Deputies altogether. Naturally he acts in all these cases at the instance of the government and, in the first instance, of its head, the Premier. Under the French Constitution, the President of the Republic is bound to summon the chambers in the interval between sessions if so required by an absolute majority of the members of each. Thus in the Chamber of Deputies there are 612 members, so that no less than 307 signatures are necessary to legalize the demand for a summons. A majority of the *nominal* membership of the chamber being required, deputies who are dead or have left are not excluded from the computation. Moreover, even if there were found in the Chamber of Deputies a sufficient number to initiate a summons, the participation therein of members of the Senate—whose composition is so elected as to guarantee therein a reactionary majority—is always dubious.

True, the French Constitution establishes certain guarantees for a session of parliament. The purpose of adjournment is to "quiet" the chambers when discords between them and the government are brewing. Such adjournment is for a limited time—it must not exceed one month—and it must not be repeated more than twice in one session. In the constitution it is likewise noted that both chambers must be in session at least five months during the year. Five to six months in session during a year, and extraordinary sessions as well! During this long period, however, the deputies are little occupied with legislation, as is attested by the bourgeois political scientist Barthélemy:

Exceedingly often a deputy is representative only in the commercial sense of the word—a mandatory of individual interests and claims before the government. When can a deputy work? He is always on the run. He has become a canvasser. If he is not in the legislative chamber that means that he is sitting in the reception room. If he is not carrying out state commissions, that means that he is carrying out those of private persons.[1]

Long sessions are evoked also by quarrels between the bourgeois parties. In the French Chamber of Deputies there are more than fifteen bourgeois groups, all as a rule agreed on putting tax and other burdens off on the backs of the broad masses of the people. Some must, however, be imposed on capitalists and their enterprises. Bourgeois groups, defending the interests of divers capitalist cliques, quarrel among themselves as to the division of these burdens. Every group tries to shift them away from the particular branch of industry or finance it defends and onto another. This requires time—many sessions—and evokes innumerable speeches, which delay the adoption of a budget.

The significance of sessions cannot be contemplated apart from the ever progressive decline in the influence of bourgeois parliaments. We have already noted the so-called "extraordinary legislation" and its particularly broad postwar expansion.

In France if the chambers "have sat" more than five months and discords with the government have been noted in the chambers, the President of the Republic can dissolve the chambers by his decree. Such decree is read aloud in the Chamber of Ministers, which for this purpose has the

---

[1] Joseph Barthélemy, *The Government of France* (Russian ed.), p. 75.

right to interrupt the speech of a deputy who has the floor. It should also be noted that the government has not infrequently used this closing of sessions to answer an interpellation (question) which could threaten it with a vote of "no confidence"—with dismissal. History knows not a few such examples of closing the sessions. On July 1, 1901, the head of the government, Pierre Waldeck-Rousseau, thus answered an interpellation of Deputy Zevaes. On December 31, 1920, the head of the government, Leig, similarly answered the interpellation of Deputy Ignaz. On July 10, 1930, the head of the government, Tardieu, trying to influence the Chamber, threatened to close the session, and on July 11, 1930, declared the session closed in answer to an interpellation of Deputy Amo. True, the Chamber of Deputies, assembled in a new session, can overthrow the government; but the latter, during the time the session is interrupted, ordinarily uses its rights broadly, acting at discretion.

We should also note the fact that, whatever the form of dismissing the sessions, the second chamber in France, the Senate, enjoys special privileges. It can assemble even during an interruption of a session (whereupon its sitting becomes the supreme tribunal), or when the Chamber of Deputies has been dissolved (when the post of the President of the Republic is vacant for the time being). Leaders of the directing bourgeois parties help the government get rid of parliament, especially at responsible moments. This has become particularly characteristic of France in recent years. In June, 1938, parliament ordained a recess for the summer holidays at the time when pressing demands by the Front Populaire for the establishment of pensions for aged toilers, for higher salaries for those in service, for increased relief for the unemployed, and so forth, remained without solution. The responsibility of the moment is still further increased by the international setting: the policy of fascist aggressors becomes ever more insolent and menacing. The policy of "nonintervention" in Spanish affairs works harm to the safety of France itself and the whole world. At such a moment the bourgeois majority of parliament, by 357 votes against 241—chiefly against the votes of communists and socialists—resolved to end the session so as to leave the hands of the government completely free. Such a policy evoked a burning protest from the French Communist Party which, on July 25 and August 10, 1938, addressed the Socialist Party letters as to coming out jointly, with other parties of the Front Populaire, for a renewal of the session of parliament.

All these facts characterize with sufficient clarity the parliamentary *mores* and the work of bourgeois parliaments.

The experience of the work of the first two sessions of the Supreme Soviet of the USSR established customs which will in all probability occupy a place in the future internal regulation of the chambers. Of these customs we may mention the following:

a) The method of opening sessions when the chambers are newly convened. The first session of both chambers of the Supreme Soviet of the USSR was opened by the members of each chamber senior in age. These, after an introductory speech, directed the choice of president of the chamber and his vice-presidents.[2]

b) The method of conducting the sessions. The rule of conducting the sessions of each chamber separately, and of joint sessions of both, is broadly as follows: persons reporting upon matters of the order of the day of the sittings of each chamber are recognized by the president of the chamber. Those reporting on matters of order of the day of the joint sessions of both chambers are recognized by the presidents of both. Each group of deputies of the Soviet of the Union and of the Soviet of Nationalities numbering fifty persons may put forward its own co-reporter in each chamber. The same rule of fifty persons is established also for putting forward a co-reporter at joint sessions of both chambers. Reporters are given one hour for their report and thirty minutes for the concluding speech; co-reporters thirty minutes for their report and fifteen minutes for the concluding speech. Orators are given twenty minutes for the first and five for the second occasion. Personal declarations and factual information are introduced in written form and proclaimed by the president (of the chamber or in the joint sessions of both houses) at once, or at the end of the session, according to their content. Extraordinary interrogatories are introduced in written form and proclaimed by the president at once. A speech on the order of voting is granted five minutes. Motions for voting are given three minutes.

c) The method of forming the administration. The formation of the administration at the first session of the Supreme Soviet of the USSR was preceded by a declaration of the President of the Council of the People's Commissars of the USSR, Molotov, in the name of the president of the joint session of both chambers, stating:

In accordance with Article 70 of the USSR Constitution, and having regard to the fact that the question of forming the Government of the USSR is put for consideration of the Supreme Soviet of the USSR, the Council of People's Commissars deems itself *functus officio* and lays down its plenary powers before the Supreme Soviet. It begs you to report hereof to the Supreme Soviet of the USSR.

The Supreme Soviet of the USSR entrusts to the president of the Council of the People's Commissars the composition of the government.

---

[2] The first session of the Soviet for the Union was opened by the eldest deputy, Academician Nikolay Aleksevich Bakh. The first session of the Soviet Nationalities was opened by the eldest deputy, Midha Tskhakaya.

The proposal of the first session of the Supreme Soviet of the USSR as regards this matter stated:

The Supreme Soviet of the USSR expresses confidence in the Council of People's Commissars of the USSR and entrusts to the President thereof—Molotov —the presentation of proposals concerning the structure of the government, including therein the critical remarks of the deputies expressed in the course of the debates.

The democratic character of the socialist parliament is emphasized also by the fact that delegates of the toilers, having the right to come forth upon the tribunal of the Supreme Soviet of the USSR to express their attitude toward its policy and its work,[3] have admission to its sittings.

We must also note the role of the council of the chiefs of delegations, made up of representatives of deputies of separate republics and regions aiding in the working out of the regulation and order of work of the Supreme Soviet of the USSR.

SEC. 7: STANDING COMMISSIONS OF THE SUPREME SOVIET OF THE USSR

Elaborate preliminary preparation of a law for its formulation, with a view to its consideration and adoption in chambers of the Supreme Soviet of the USSR, is demanded by the significance of Soviet law and of socialist legality.

At the first session of the Supreme Soviet of the USSR (January 12–19, 1938), each chamber chose three standing commissions for the purpose of preparing legislative proposals introduced for the consideration of each chamber. These are:

1. The Commission for Legislative Proposals, consisting of ten members in each chamber and concerned with the task of preparing legal proposals of a general character.

2. The Budget Commission, consisting of thirteen members in each chamber. The Soviet state budget assures the bases of our economic and cultural development, of the rights of citizens, and is one of the means of reinforcing the defensive capacity of our country. Its gigantic significance is characterized by the fact that in 1938 the All-Union Budget attained the figure of 132 billion rubles.

---

[3] Thus the first session of the Supreme Soviet of the USSR was welcomed by delegations of workers, kolkhoz members, and persons serving in Moscow and the Moscow region, Leningrad and the Leningrad region, the Kiev and Kharkov regions, the White Russian and Tatar ASSR, of the miners and metallurgists of the Don Basin, and of the Red Army and the Fleet.

The Budget Commission verifies the economic and political sides of the budget—income and outgo—helping the Supreme Soviet to be the sovereign master of the country's financial resources.

3. The Commission for Foreign Affairs. In the Soviet of the Union it consists of eleven persons; in the Soviet of Nationalities, of ten. It makes a preliminary examination of all matters connected with foreign affairs to be considered by the Supreme Soviet (and its Presidium). The significance of this commission may be understood in connection with international policy of Soviet authority, with the ever growing danger of war and the Soviet Union's exertions to guard peace.

Commissions are occupied with elaborate preparation of legislative proposals thereafter introduced for the consideration of the Supreme Soviet.

In addition to the foregoing commissions, each chamber of the Supreme Soviet, in accord with Article 50 of the Constitution, chooses a commission on credentials. At the first session of the Supreme Soviet of the USSR, each chamber created such a commission consisting of eleven members in each. The commission verifies the credentials of the deputies of each chamber. Upon presentation of the credentials committee, the chamber decides whether to accept the credentials or to annul the elections of the particular deputies.

According to Article 51 of the Stalin Constitution, the Supreme Soviet of the USSR appoints commissions of inquiry and investigation on any matter, when it deems such appointment necessary.

In capitalist countries, parliamentary commissions are likewise considered to be preliminary councils, studying and investigating legislative proposals destined for consideration in plenary sessions of the chambers. Bourgeois political scientists give out parliamentary commissions as a most important lever with which to control government activity. It is, however, impossible to consider the activity of parliamentary commissions without taking into account the ever shrinking influence of parliamentary legislation in general, and the ever growing role of so-called "extraordinary" or "exceptional" legislation effected independently of parliaments and parliamentary commissions.

Parliamentary commissions play perhaps their greatest part in France and in the U.S.A. They consist for the most part of representatives of dominant bourgeois parties.

The work of commissions is secret. The formal explanation of this is that through them passes a succession of important state affairs not to be given broad publicity (foreign affairs, military affairs, and the like). But secrecy is important for representatives of the bourgeoisie for the further reason that thus the practice of preparing statutes and parleying by different groups of monopolist capital remains shaded from the masses, without publicity. For this very reason, in the French Chamber of Deputies over a long period of time the admission of communists into commissions was resisted because of their supposedly "antinational policy." In reality, as everyone knows, it is precisely the ruling cliques of monopolist capital that carry on the most cynical antinational policy, as is manifested in a particularly characteristic fashion in the policy of the ruling French and English parties—especially as regards republican Spain and Czechoslovakia—in their perfidious agreement with German and Italian fascism at the expense of their own countries' national interests.

In France in the Chamber of Deputies there are twenty large standing commissions (for foreign affairs, for industry, for finance, for agriculture, and so forth) consisting of forty-four deputies chosen yearly. One deputy can be a member of various commissions. There is in addition a series of narrow, so-called nonstanding commissions chosen for a definite term (prolonged in fact for the period of the entire legislature—for the term of parliament's powers), such as the commission for universal suffrage, and so forth.

Sometimes special commissions, including commissions of inquiry, are chosen for important matters. The work of parliamentary investigating commissions may be typically illustrated by those created regarding the affairs of the speculator Stavisky and of the fascist attack of February 6, 1934. Everyone knows that in the last analysis the work of these commissions amounted in fact to no more than stifling these affairs, and absolving highly placed criminals of responsibility.

Ordinarily the membership of commissions is made up on the principle of delegating representatives from the parties. But special commissions are formed by vote of the entire chamber, which once more pursues the purpose of not allowing communists in the commission, or of limiting their role in the commission.

Commissions sit also in the intervals between sessions. As a matter of form, they hear communications from members of the administration; they can require necessary material—information from different departments—and work out their proposed legislation opposed to the administration proposal, and so on. Besides, each group of representatives of monopolist capital strives to put forward its own reporter from the committee into the plenary setting of parliament.

In France they say that parliamentary commissions furnish ministers preeminently from among the reporters of the commissions. This is understandable: various groups of monopolist capital are interested in having their creatures not merely promote this or that statute in commission but also give it practical realization thereafter as ministers. In general and as a whole, commissions in the French parliament consider almost exclusively legislative proposals which have been worked out and put forward by the administration itself, which is conditioned by the dominance in parliament of the administration and its policy.

In the U.S.A. there are committees instead of commissions. In the House of Representatives there are forty-seven committees (to 435 members) with fifteen to twenty-one members on each committee. One member may accordingly serve on various committees. Members of a committee are designated solely by the Speaker—the president of the chamber, representing a parliamentary majority. Members of the committee are the most eminent representatives of the dominant parties. For this reason, a legislative proposal passed by committee ordinarily passes through the House of Representatives without any difficulty. Woodrow Wilson wrote of the House of Representatives: "It is divided up, as it were, into forty-seven seigniories, in each of which a Standing Committee is the court-baron and its chairman lord-proprietor." [1]

Through committees of the House of Representatives the closest contact is established with secretaries—ministers—who, by virtue of the so-called "separation of powers," take no part in the work of the plena of Congress. The activity of committees better than anything else discloses how illusory is the theory of the "separation of powers," and vividly reveals the unity of the power of monopolist capital, both in legislative and in executive organs. For that which is predetermined in committee will already go automatically through the House of Representatives as well.

Furthermore, it must be added that committees enjoy a broad right of inviting to their councils "experts"—representatives of the world of finance and industry. Through the committees the influence of trusts on Congress develops most directly—unique "parliaments" behind the scenes made up of representatives, ministers, and "experts" (financiers and so on) working at a distance from publicity and in fact playing a decisive part in the enactment of this law or that. Committees are also canals through which the financial resources of the treasury often flow into the pockets of the big monopolist enterprises. Thus, Woodrow Wilson wrote that

no description of our system of revenue, appropriation, and supply would be complete without mention of the manufacturers who cultivate the favor of the Committee of Ways and Means, of the interested persons who walk attendance upon the Committee on Rivers and Harbors, and of the mail-contractors and subsidy-seekers who court the Committee on Appropriations.[2]

[1] Wilson, Woodrow, *Congressional Government* (Russian ed., p. 81; American ed., p. 92).
[2] *Ibid.* (Russian ed., pp. 157–158); (American ed., p. 190—Ed.)

The reporter of the committee is given an hour for his report in the House of Representatives, of which he can allot some minutes to the representative of the minority opinion of the committee if there is such an opinion. Consideration in plena of the House of Representatives of matters that have passed through the committees is often brief; there may even be none at all. The role of the Speaker is in this the role of a dictator. He has the right to interrupt a deputy in the middle of a word or to grant him not a single word. For ten days before the end of the session of Congress, if many legislative proposals have accumulated, the House declines to adopt the three conventional readings and usually disposes of the matter automatically in the spirit of the committee decision.

Approximately the same role is played by committees in the Senate (of which there are thirty-two). The difference is merely that members of a Senate committee are designated not by the Speaker (the Vice-President of the United States) but by the Senate. The bourgeoisie looks sharply to see that parliamentary commissions and committees are, by structure and activity, actually suitable for the tasks of the bourgeoisie; they are the "kitchen" where legislative proposals, emanating from the interests of the dominant class and thereafter given out in parliaments as "the will of the people," are ordinarily prepared.

SEC. 8: THE DEPUTY OF THE USSR SUPREME SOVIET

The Soviet system of representation, the only democratic system in the world, expresses the indissoluble and complete authority of the Soviet people. It imposes particular responsibility upon the Soviet deputy, the representative of the toiling people. "The deputy," says Stalin, "must know that he is the servant of the people, the emissary of the people in the Supreme Soviet, and he must conduct himself according to the course set for him by the mandate of the people." [1]

A deputy of the Supreme Soviet possesses broad rights. He takes part in the preparation of statutes in commissions and in the consideration and confirmation thereof in the appropriate chamber of the Supreme Soviet. He has a right to address interrogatories regarding any matter to the administration or to a People's Commissar and to have—not later than three days thereafter—an oral or written answer in the appropriate chamber. He enjoys inviolability and cannot be held to answer in court or arrested without the consent of the USSR Supreme Soviet (or of its Presidium, when it is not

[1] Speech at a preelection assembly of voters of the Stalin Elective District in Moscow (Dec. 11, 1937), p. 11.

in session). He also has obligations. He must with all energy express the true will of his electors in the appropriate chamber of the Supreme Soviet of the USSR. He must not lose contact with his electors. He must render them an account of his work and of the work of the Supreme Soviet of the USSR. He can at any time be recalled (in the method established by law) by decision of a majority of the electors. Thus the election does not terminate the mutual relations of electors and representative. "It is the obligation and the right of electors ever to hold their deputies under control and to suggest to them that they stoop in no case to the level of political philistinism but be such as the great Lenin was." [2]

The right to recall deputies is a democratic principle noted in the program of the All-Union Communist Party (of Bolsheviks) in Soviet state acts from the very first moments of the existence of Soviet authority,[3] and in the Stalin Constitution (Art. 142) and in constitutions of the Union Republics.

Soviet authority provides no representatives to fence in parliament and exchange glittering speeches while bringing about the stability and dominance of capital and the bureaucratic apparatus. Soviet authority goes out from the toiling masses themselves. It provides no parliament, but rather an assembly of worker-class representatives issuing laws which are directly executed, passing into practice and designed for the struggle with exploiters.[4]

A deputy of the Supreme Soviet is no professional politician or "legislator." He is a person connected with socialist production, science, and so forth. He is an agent of the bloc of communists and nonparty members, a man of lively experience and work, a champion of socialism.[5] He does not "fence" with glittering speeches but strives as a deputy to put all his constructive experience into the creation of laws bound to assure socialism's further strengthening and development.

Deputies of the Supreme Soviet of the USSR are guaranteed all conditions favorable for the fulfillment of the official obligations due from them to their electors. In this connection, the first session of the Supreme Soviet of the USSR directed reimbursement of deputies' expenses in connection with their execution of their official duties to the extent of 1,000 rubles a month, and 150 rubles a day during sessions of the Supreme Soviet of the

[2] *Ibid.*, pp. 14–15.
[3] Cf. Chap. X (The Elective System), p. 659.
[4] Lenin (Russian ed.), Vol. XXII, p. 239.
[5] The structure of the Chamber of the Supreme Soviet of the USSR is as follows: of the Soviet of the Union (data concerning 546 deputies): 247 workers (45.3 per cent), 130 peasants (23.7 per cent), 169 persons in service and intellectuals (31 per cent), and 77 women; 461 communists—81 per cent (out of 569) and 108 nonparty independents (19 per cent); of the Soviet of Nationalities (total, 574) 218 workers, 200 peasants, 156 in service and intellectuals; 464 men, 110 women.

USSR. In addition, they enjoy the right of free travel on all the USSR railroads and waterways.

All these conditions make it feasible for deputies to maintain intimate association with their electors, to travel out to kolkhozes and business enterprises, to central state or social organizations, in order to solve questions raised by electors, carry on constant correspondence with them, write for necessary literature, and so forth. The expenses of the presidents and vice-presidents of each chamber are special in that in the intervals between sessions they maintain constant and systematic contact with the deputies. Accordingly, the first session of the Supreme Soviet of the USSR directed that the budget estimate of the Presidium of the Supreme Soviet of the USSR provide that 300,000 rubles a year for each chamber be left at the disposal of presidents and vice-presidents of both chambers for expenses for keeping in touch with deputies and for representation.

In the parliaments of capitalist countries the role of a deputy is absolutely the opposite. The bourgeoisie establishes his formal responsibility to the "nation" or the "people," rather than to his electors, thereby freeing him from the control of the masses. During an election campaign candidates of the bourgeoisie for the office of deputy are ordinarily occupied with the advance sale of all the "advantages" in return for the vote of electors. In France bourgeois deputies take it upon themselves to bustle about, offering their adherents remunerative places, rewards and distinctions, pensions, and licenses to trade in monopolist productions (such as tobacco or matches) so as to be assured of their support.

In the U.S.A. such a system is called a "lobby" (an anteroom or passage). Formerly, persons deeming it necessary to influence the votes of a member of Congress met him in the "lobby." Now this is forbidden by a rule of the legislature, but the lobby, as a system of bribery, is preserved outside the walls of parliament. During a session of Congress, "lobbyists" finance all sorts of banquets and evening parties at which interested capitalist groups meet members of Congress and their families. "Lobbyists" penetrate even into sittings of parliamentary commissions which determine the passage of a legislative proposal through parliament. The formal explanation is the necessity of bonds between the member of Congress and the population. In reality such a "bond" is permeated by corruption, which is a constituent part of the capitalist policy characterizing bourgeois democracy. "*The more* the stock exchange and the bankers subordinate bourgeois parliaments to themselves, *the more strongly* has democracy developed." [6]

It is not at all obligatory for capitalists themselves to be present in parliaments as deputies. This matter is "democratized" in the sense that repre-

[6] Lenin (Russian ed.), Vol. XXIII, p. 348.

sentation of the interests of the capitalists or capitalist groups is entrusted to individual representatives whose passage into parliament is promoted directly by capitalist cliques through bourgeois political parties. The bourgeois party ordinarily spends colossal sums in the preelection campaign on press, agitation, and support of a staff of hired agitators and political workers. In form, a deputy of the bourgeoisie so chosen represents the interests of the whole "people," but in fact he is connected with those of banks and individual enterprises; he represents the interest of those who confirm the exploitation of popular masses. Such deputies strive to pass statutes making exploitation in this or that branch of capitalist industry easy and they are solicitous for the affairs of these enterprises before parliament, the administration, and so on. Monopolist combines of capitalists (syndicates, cartels and trusts) spare no money in promoting the candidacy of one who is necessary for them and comes forward under the auspices of some political party. The passage of only one such law—lowering the taxes on some branch of capitalist industry, or a law heightening the tariff on imports from foreign capitalist rivals—pays off with usury the campaign expenditures of monopolist cliques. Even such bourgeois political scientists as Barthélemy are constrained to speak openly of the extent of corruption under bourgeois parliamentarism.

In France lists of members of stock company councils and directorates contain more than two hundred names of members of the French Senate or Chamber of Deputies. Thus the name of "national representative" François-Marsal is encountered twenty-two times at the top of various capitalist enterprises, that of Senator Lederlan eleven times, and of Langlois ten times. Of the English parliament, 255 members occupy posts of directors in at least 713 companies with a total share capital of 1,930,968,000 pounds sterling. The capital controlled by these companies and their directors is in reality far greater.[7]

The absence of principle is characterized by bourgeois deputies frequently going over from one party to another. "During four or five years—that is to say, right down to the new elections—a deputy feels himself perfectly free, independent of the people and of his electors. He can pass over from one camp to another. He can abandon the correct—and go on an incorrect—road. He can even be implicated in machinations of a not altogether needful sort. He can turn somersaults as he likes. He is independent.' Thus Mosley, leader of the English fascists, was elected on the labor ticket in the 1931 elections. Afterwards he went over to the fascists, as everyone knows. His electors, the laborites, demanded that he resign the powers of a deputy.

[7] [A note, purporting to set out English members of parliament and the amounts of money in the companies they are supposed to control, is omitted.—Tr.]

Of course Mosley did not comply but continued to sit in the House of Commons, representing himself as responsible "to the nation." Fascism casts away democratic veils altogether. What still bears in Germany the name of "Reichstag" is no longer a legislative institution. It is convened only rarely, and then not to consider statutes but to hear fascist leaders make speeches. Fascist elections are an empty ceremonial. "Deputies" are merely those designated for the part by fascist leaders.

SEC. 9: THE HIGHEST ORGANS OF STATE AUTHORITY OF THE UNION AND AUTONOMOUS REPUBLICS

The unity of the political and economic basis of the USSR finds expression in the USSR Constitution and in constitutions of all the Union and autonomous republics. By reason of the close unity of the USSR peoples and the community of their socialist interests, the highest organs of authority in the Union and autonomous republics are built after a single type. We have already set out in detail the jurisdiction of the Union, and of Union and autonomous republics. Here our concern will be chiefly as to how the Supreme Soviets of the Union and autonomous republics are constructed. According to the USSR Constitution, the supreme organ of state authority in a Union Republic is its Supreme Soviet, elected by its citizens for a four-year term according to elective districts (Arts. 57, 58). Election rules for Union Republics are established, not by the USSR Constitution, but in the constitution of each Union Republic, with proper account taken of the special characteristics of that republic. New Union Republic constitutions, adopted in all the Union Republics in 1937, established the following rules of representation in the Supreme Soviets of Union Republics:

We will take the RSFSR Supreme Soviet as an example for the purpose of clarifying the organization of supreme state authority in Union Republics. The RSFSR Supreme Soviet is its highest organ of authority and its sole legislative organ within the bounds of its jurisdiction as a Union Republic organ. Like the Supreme Soviets of other Union Republics, it consists of one chamber chosen for four years according to elective districts, each of which sends one representative. The chamber, by simple majority vote, adopts statutes of binding force throughout the territory of the Union Republic. Starting from the community and unity of interests and tasks of defense of the whole Soviet people, each Union Republic (pursuant to Art. 19 of the USSR Constitution) acknowledges in its constitution the obligation to execute (within its territory) USSR statutes issued in accordance

Name of Union Republic	Rule of Representation to Supreme Soviet of Union Republic	Number of Deputies of Supreme Soviets Chosen for 1938
RSFSR	150,000	727
Ukrainian SSR	100,000	304
White Russian SSR	20,000	273
Kazakh SSR	20,000	300
Georgian SSR	15,000	237
Uzbek SSR	15,000	395
Azerbaijan SSR	10,000	310
Armenian SSR	5,000	256
Turkmen SSR	5,000	226
Tadjik SSR	5,000	282
Kirghiz SSR	5,000	282

with Article 14 of the Stalin Constitution. All the Union Republic constitutions so provide.

Thus, Chapter 13 of the RSFSR Constitution says:

To the end of realizing mutual aid along economic and political lines, as well as along the line of defense, the RSFSR voluntarily was united with Soviet Socialist Republics having equal rights (the Ukrainian SSR, the White Russian SSR, the Azerbaijan SSR, the Georgian SSR, the Armenian SSR, the Turkmen SSR, the Uzbek SSR, the Tadjik SSR, the Kazakh SSR, and the Kirghiz SSR) into a Union state—the Union of Soviet Socialist Republics. Wherefore the RSFSR guarantees in behalf of the USSR, personified by its supreme organs of authority and of state administration, the rights defined by Article 14 of the USSR Constitution. Outside the limits of that article, the RSFSR exercises state authority independently, preserving its sovereign rights without exception.

The jurisdiction of the RSFSR Supreme Soviet includes: the establishment of the RSFSR Constitution and control over the fulfillment of that Constitution; adoption of constitutions of autonomous republics constituting parts of the RSFSR; affirmation of boundaries and districting of autonomous republics, autonomous regions, territories and areas, and presenting (for affirmation by the USSR Supreme Soviet) proposals for the formation of new territories and areas and likewise of new republics and regions; legislation of the RSFSR; guarding state order and civil rights; adoption of a plan of national economy and of the RSFSR state budget; establishment of taxes, levies, and other income in accordance with USSR legislation; direction of the effectuation of budgets of autonomous republics, and of local budgets of territories and regions; direction of insurance and savings matters; administration of banks, industries, and trade and agricultural enterprises subject to the republic, and direction of local industry; control and supervision over the condition and administration of enterprises directed by the Union government; establishment of the regulations for utilizing land, natural deposits therein, forests, and streams; direction of housing and municipal economy, the building of dwellings and the proper arrangement of cities and other inhabited places; road building and direction of local transport and communications; labor legislation; direction of the preservation of health, social security, primary, intermediate and higher education, of cultural, educational, and scientific organizations and institutions of the RSFSR, and administration of such organizations and institutions as are of importance to the republic as a whole; direction and organization of physical culture and sport; organization of RSFSR court organs; granting rights of RSFSR citizenship; and the amnesty and pardoning of citizens condemned by RSFSR court organs (Art. 19 of the RSFSR Constitution).

Statutes of the RSFSR Supreme Soviet are of binding force throughout the territory of all the autonomous republics constituting parts of the RSFSR. If a law of an autonomous republic is inconsistent with a law of the RSFSR, the latter prevails. Manifestly, USSR laws—operative throughout the RSFSR—are binding as well upon each autonomous republic.

Fundamentally, the jurisdiction of Supreme Soviets of other Union Republics is the same as that of the Supreme Soviet of the RSFSR. Distinctions occur either by reason of a republic's special economic characteristics (thus in the constitutions of the Turkmen and Kazakh SSR there is a special provision as to their Supreme Soviets having direction of vitalizing the order of an agricultural artel and of strengthening kolkhozes) or of administrative organization. (In republics with no autonomous republics, territories or regions, management by Supreme Soviets extends immediately and directly to districts, and proposals for the formation of new districts are presented for confirmation by the USSR Supreme Soviet.)

Supreme Soviets of Union Republics each separately elect the Presidium of the Supreme Soviet, form the Council of People's Commissars, and elect the Union Republic Supreme Court. Furthermore, the Supreme Soviet of each Union Republic, as it shall deem necessary, designates commissions of inquiry and of inspection as to a specific matter. All institutions and persons are bound to carry out the requirements of these commissions and to furnish them with the necessary materials and documents.

Like the Presidium of the USSR Supreme Soviet, the Presidium of a Union Republic Supreme Soviet, accountable to the Supreme Soviet of the corresponding Union Republic, is a "collegium president." Thus, that

Name of Republic	Total Personnel of Presidium	President of Presidium of Supreme Soviet	Vice-Presidents	Secretaries	Members of Presidium
RSFSR	39	1	17 (Number of Autonomous Republics)	1	20
Ukrainian SSR	19	1	2	1	15
White Russian SSR	19	1	2	1	15
Azerbaijan SSR	17	1	2 (Number of Autonomous Republics and Autonomous Regions)	1	13
Georgian SSR	17	1	2 (Number of Autonomous Republics)	1	13
Armenian SSR	13	1	2	1	9
Turkmen SSR	15	1	2	1	11
Tadjik SSR	15	1	2	1	11
Kirghiz SSR	15	1	2	1	11
Uzbek SSR	18	1	3	1	13
Kazakh SSR	19	1	2	1	15

of the RSFSR Supreme Soviet consists of a President of the Presidium and seventeen Vice-Presidents, corresponding to the number of autonomous republics embodied in the RSFSR. This again emphasizes the right of the RSFSR peoples to participate equally in the supreme organ of authority. Furthermore, membership of the Presidium of the RSFSR Supreme Soviet includes a secretary of the Presidium and twenty members. While in other Union Republics the number of members of the Presidium of the Supreme Soviet differs, the Presidium is everywhere built on the collegium principle.

The Presidium of the RSFSR Supreme Soviet summons sessions of the RSFSR Supreme Soviet twice a year, and extraordinary sessions at discretion or upon demand by one-third of the deputies thereof. It furnishes interpretations of RSFSR statutes, issues decrees, and likewise arranges referenda of the entire people. It abrogates directives and orders of the RSFSR Council of People's Commissars and of Councils of People's Commissars of autonomous republics, as well as decisions and orders of territorial Soviets of Deputies of the Toilers in case they are not in conformity with law. In an interval between sessions it relieves of their official duties, and appoints, individual People's Commissars of the RSFSR, upon recommendation of the President of the RSFSR Council of People's Commissars and subject to later confirmation by the RSFSR Supreme Soviet; it assigns honorary titles of the RSFSR; and it exercises the right of pardoning citizens condemned by the RSFSR courts.

When the plenary powers of the RSFSR Soviet expire, the Presidium designates new elections for a date of not more than two months from the date of such expiration. The newly elected Supreme Soviet is summoned by the Presidium of the former session not later than a month after the elections.

The composition and the jurisdiction of Supreme Soviets and their Presidia in all the other Union Republics are analogous. In autonomous republics their Supreme Soviets, elected for four years by citizens of the republic according to the rules established in the ASSR Constitution, are the supreme organs of state authority of the respective republics, within the limits of the latters' jurisdiction, and the sole legislative organ thereof. The Supreme Soviet of an autonomous republic adopts the ASSR Constitution and presents it for confirmation by the Supreme Soviet of the Union Republic; it establishes division of the ASSR into districts and the boundaries of such districts and of cities, subject to confirmation by the Union Republic Supreme Soviet; it affirms the ASSR plan of national economy and budget; and it assigns honory titles of ASSR. It chooses the President of the Supreme Soviet and his two Vice-Presidents, who direct sessions of the Supreme Soviet and its internal order. Sessions of the Supreme Soviet assemble twice a year. Extraordinary sessions are convened by the Presidium of the Supreme Soviet at its discretion or upon the demand by one-third of the deputies of the Supreme Soviet. It chooses the Presidium of the Supreme Soviet. The number of members of Presidia of the Supreme Soviets differs.

The Presidium of an autonomous republic's Supreme Soviet, whose jurisdiction is defined by the ASSR Constitution, summons sessions of the ASSR Supreme Soviet, interprets ASSR statutes, publishes orders, conducts referenda, abrogates directives and orders of the ASSR Council of People's Commissars, and decisions and orders of district and city Soviets of Deputies of the Toilers of ASSR in case they do not conform with the law. In the interval between sessions of the Supreme Soviet, the Presidium of the ASSR Supreme Soviet relieves of their duties, and designates, individual People's Commissars of the ASSR upon the recommendation of the President of the ASSR Council of People's Commissars, subject to confirmation by the ASSR Supreme Soviet, and awards honorary titles of the ASSR.

The ASSR Supreme Soviet chooses a credentials commission and such other commissions as it deems necessary, and forms the government of the ASSR—the ASSR Council of People's Commissars.

Such, in brief, are the features of the composition of the higher organs of authority in Union and autonomous republics.

VI Organs of State Administration of the USSR and of the Union and Autonomous Republics

SEC. 1: INTRODUCTION

STATE ADMINISTRATION, in the strict sense of the term, is the constant, current activity of executive-administrative organs of authority, prosecuted in the interests of the dominant class and directed at guarding and strengthening the existing order—social and state. Definitive problems of state administration and its methods of realizing them, and the principles of constructing a system of administrative organs (and their relations with organs of state authority) are defined by the nature of the state and its class purposes. Each dominant class creates a mechanism after its own form and likeness.[1]

The bureaucratic apparatus of tsarist Russia was built to accord with the interests of landowners and bourgeoisie, making real autocracy's military-police dictatorship. Supreme government belonged to the tsar personally. "The authority of governing belongs in all its compass to the emperor within the boundaries of the entire Russian State" (Art. 10 of the Fundamental Laws). Subordinate government, higher and lower, was carried on by central and local administrative institutions which, in accordance with the same article, acquired a definite degree of authority from the tsar, acting in his name and by his commands. The supreme administrative institutions included:

1. *Departments and special sessions of the Imperial Council*, with jurisdiction over matters relating to the creation of landed estates, the confirmation of honorary dignities and the transfer by nobles of names, coats of arms and titles; matters relating to the responsibility of higher state officials for crimes committed by them in office, leave to build private railroads, and compulsory alienation of im-

[1] Cf. Lenin (Russian ed.), Vol. XXV, pp. 105–106.

movable property; and preliminary consideration of complaints against decisions of departments of the Ruling Senate. Members of these departments and of special sessions were appointed by the "supreme authority" of the tsar. Directives and conclusions of departments and special sessions were submitted "for the decision of the monarch."

2. *The Most Holy Ruling Synod* (founded in 1721), cooperating with the tsar in the administration of the Orthodox Church, chiefly composed of bishops designated by "supreme authority"; it was the head of ecclesiastical administration, and all matters of divorce were within its jurisdiction.

3. *The Ruling Senate,* instituted by Peter I (1711), functioned both as the supreme court and as supervisor of administration. It exercised control over the correctness of administrative orders, and the doings of ministers, the protection and certification of the rights and privileges of divers social orders, and so on. "The Ruling Senate is the supreme authority, to whose civil governance as court, administrator and executive all places in general and all establishments in the empire are subordinate" (Institution of the Senate, Art. 1).

4. *The Committee of Finances*—the highest consultative institution on matters of state credit and finance policy, including, in addition to members designated "by Imperial discretion," the president of the Council of Ministers, the Minister of Finances, and the State Comptroller.

5. *Councils: the Tutelary Council* (the highest consultative institution "on matters of special Imperial philanthropy"), and *War and Admiralty Councils* (institutions considering and referring "for Imperial decision" directives on matters concerned with the ranks and on technical and economic matters, as well as regulations and mandates addressed to institutions and officials).

6. *The Council of Ministers* (created October 19, 1905), consisting of ministers designated by the tsar and in chief command of the central institutions, and the Procurator General of the Synod. The Council of Ministers possessed extremely broad rights and powers. Every sort of matter transcending the authority of a minister came to the council. It introduced "for Imperial decision" ministerial proposals for the abrogation or change of existing laws. Its chief task was to direct and to unify actions of ministers and department heads on matters of legislation and of supreme administration of the state. It could issue binding directives, instructions, and orders. "If—during a period when the occupations of the Imperial Duma have come to an end—extraordinary circumstances are so exigent as to require consideration of a legislative character, the Council of Ministers reports thereon to the Tsar directly" (Art. 87). It had the right to permit advance credits pending the adoption of a new schedule in the established order. To the council belonged in particular the affirmation of charters of stock companies and the abrogation or change of directives of local organs of self-government.

Central organs of subordinate administration included ministries (of foreign affairs, war, navy, finance, trade and industry, internal affairs, national education, communications, justice, the imperial court, the chief administration for agrarian laws and agriculture, and state control) and administrative bodies made equal with them (His Imperial Majesty's private chancellery, His Imperial Majesty's private chancellery for institutions of the Empress Maria, and His Imperial Majesty's chancellery for the receipt of petitions to the tsar). Ministries emerged under Alexander I in 1807 and took the place of the collegia instituted by Peter I. They were the highest central governmental institutions, in charge of definite branches of state administration. At the head of each ministry was one person—a minister or chief. The right to nominate and choose ministers belonged wholly, and with no restraining conditions of any kind, to the tsar. Ministers were responsible and subordinate to him alone. They were deemed crown counselors completely independent of the Imperial Duma, which was obligated at all times to listen to them. But they had the right to deny explanations of matters which could concern only irregular actions of administrative organs and to decline to answer interpellations.

The central machinery of state administration was supplemented by a cumbrous apparatus of lower subordinate administration: (1) the governor, nominated by the tsar, the highest administrative authority and organ of the ministry for internal affairs in a guberniya; (2) the governor-general, nominated at the tsar's immediate discretion, for supreme supervision of the administration of certain guberniyas—chiefly borderlands, or otherwise specially circumstanced; (3) the guberniya administration (under the presidency of the governor) "the highest establishment in a guberniya, administering it by force of laws in the name of His Imperial Majesty" and directly subordinate to the Senate and the Ministry of Internal Affairs; (4) organs of the police administration; (5) local organs of the Ministry for Finances (the treasury, the excise administration), of the chief administration of agrarian laws and agriculture (the administration of state properties), and of state control (the chamber of control of a guberniya), subject to the supervision of the governor; and (6) sessions in the guberniya (on land and municipal affairs, and liability to military service), direction of which belonged to the governor.

This vast bourgeois-landowner machinery employed with redoubled force the methods of a police-bureaucracy. In a series of articles Lenin furnished a political characterization of governmental methods of administration in Russia. As early as 1901 he wrote that "in Russia every kind of activity—*even* that most remote from politics, such as philanthropy—leads inevitably to a clash between independent people and the arbitrary perversity of the police and measures of 'suppression,' 'prohibition,' 'limitation,' and so forth, and so forth." [2] Analyzing definitive facts, he concludes that

[2] Lenin (Russian ed.), Vol. IV, p. 280.

"illegal and savage beating by the police occurs, without exaggeration—every day and every hour in the Russian Empire." [3] In the police state of Russia "personality is nothing as against authority." [4] A vast army of bureaucrats—enjoying extraordinary freedom and independence—carried autocracy's military-police dictatorship into effect. "A handful of public embezzlers, executioners and organizers of pogroms—universally condemned and held in dishonor and public scorn—are again in full swing making mock of the people, threatening and robbing them, beating them without mercy, stopping their mouths and poisoning the air with the intolerable stench of serfdom." [5]

Most of the population of tsarist Russia was ground down by national oppression unprecedented in history. Bloody retribution wrought upon movements for national emancipation, pogroms, propagation of imperialist chauvinism, fomentation of differences between nationalities; such were the methods of the "administration" in tsarist Russia. The February Bourgeois Revolution (1917) introduced no radical changes into the police-bureaucratic state administration.

Only the great October Socialist Revolution smashed the system of arbitrary police-bureaucracy and created a new apparatus of state administration differing radically and in principle both from that of pre-October Russia and from that of contemporary bourgeois democratic states.

The Soviet state government was socialist from the first days of the great October Socialist Revolution. Its compass was, and still is, to bring to life the purposes and the problems of the worker-class dictatorship. Its task is to assure the socialist legal order against all types of internal and external encroachments upon it, to reinforce the independence of the USSR and to intensify its defensive power, to develop the socialist system of economy and to strengthen socialist property, to guard and to guarantee the rights of citizens, and to annihilate the remnants of class society and assure all the conditions precedent to the satisfaction of individuality's material and cultural needs and all-sided development.

From the first steps of its emergence, the compass of the activity of the administrative organs of the Soviet state was—as expressed by Lenin—to effectuate measures "in the name of socialism," the "positive or creative work of bringing into working order the extraordinarily complex and subtle net of new organization relationships. . . ." [6] The organs of Soviet state administration carry out the tasks from day to day, constantly and logically improving administrative methods. The guiding principle in their activity is

[3] *Ibid.*, pp. 87–88.
[4] *Ibid.*, p. 81.
[5] *Ibid.*, p. 58.
[6] Lenin (Russian ed.), Vol. XXII, pp. 225–240.

Lenin's instructions: "not to divorce administration from policy,"[7] "to aim at completely subordinating the apparatus to policy,"[8] "the apparatus *for* policy (the revision and correction of interclass relationships)—not policy *for* the apparatus!!"[9]

The fundamental principles of Soviet administration emanate from its very tenor, which corresponds completely with the problems of the socialist state, whose administration is characterized above all by the fact that its aim is to carry into effect the tasks of building socialism and strengthening the new society.

It is characteristic of our state administration, as distinguished from that of every other sort of state, that it is carried into effect on the basis of its consistently attracting the toilers to itself; it correctly expresses the interests of their broad masses, "that whereof the people are conscious."[10]

Here we see a complete contrast between the Soviet state and the bourgeois state. In the latter, those who execute the administrative function are isolated as a special group of the population, readily becoming a sort of caste. In the aggregate, professional bureaucrats form an extraordinarily powerful bureaucratic machinery of state. All the force of the bourgeois state is comprised in its state machinery—its bureaucracy and its standing army. A series of works by Marx and Engels showed the development and the increasing efficiency and strength of this bureaucratic and military machinery. Professional bureaucrats, opposed by their special privileges and irresponsibility to the majority of society, demand symmetrically regularized conduct and respect for laws while also insisting upon deference to institutions which make us lawless and replace law by arbitrary perversity.[11] The bureaucratic machinery—that "horrible parasite-organism which twines net-wise over the entire body of French society and clogs all its pores"[12]—possesses vast power. Taking France as an example, Marx proved that this machinery "holds a vast mass of interests and separate beings in constant and utter dependence upon itself."[13] Aided by this machinery, the state

entangles, controls, directs, and holds under its surveillance and tutelage civil society from the biggest to the most negligible manifestations of its life—from its most general forms of being to the particular beings of separate individuals where this parasite-body—owing to the extraordinary centralization—is as ubiquitous and omniscient, as mobile and elastic, as is the true social body helplessly dependent and absurdly amorphous.[14]

[7] *Ibid.*, Vol. XXVII, p. 252.
[8] *Ibid.*, Vol. XXVI, p. 248.
[9] *Ibid.*, Vol. XXX, p. 422.
[10] *Ibid.*, Vol. XXII, p. 256.
[11] Marx and Engels (Russian ed.), Vol. I, p. 122.
[12] Marx, *Selected Works* (1924, Russian ed.), p. 319.
[13] *Ibid.*, p. 279.   [14] *Ibid.*

Political interests of the dominant bourgeoisie compel it

ever more and more to intensify the pressure—the resources and the personnel of state authority—and at the same time to carry on incessant warfare against social opinion and, from distrust, to persecute, maim, and paralyze the independent organs of social movement, if it has not succeeded simply in amputating them.[15]

So Marx characterized the bureaucratic state machinery of the middle of the nineteenth century. That machinery, in the epoch of imperialism, was characterized by Lenin, who showed "the extraordinary intensification of the 'state machinery,' the unprecedented growth of its bureaucratic and military machinery in connection with the intensification of repressions against the proletariat—in monarchical countries, and also in the freest republican countries."[16]

This mighty bureaucratic machinery remained basically unaltered, notwithstanding the formal changes of state government. Having in view the ministries of the Provisional Government, Lenin wrote: "Even in the ministries belonging to the 'socialists' (pardon the expression!), the entire bureaucratic machinery remains essentially old—it functions in the old manner and sabotages inchoate revolutions with perfect 'freedom.'"[17] In the Third (French) Republic, an extremely significant part of this machinery long remained monarchical and hostile to the republic. The Weimar Constitution of 1919 gave Germany the forms of a bourgeois-democratic state, but in its administrative machinery directive groups who were hostile to democracy of every sort continued to be extremely influential. Undoubtedly this fact contributed to Hitler's advent to power. To the end of still further reinforcing the state mechanism, in the interests of monopolist capital, he issued a law soon after he came to power concerning the reestablishment of the professional bureaucracy (April 7, 1933), and in the statute of January, 1937, he assigned to that professional bureaucracy, which was responsible only to its superior authorities, the role of "fundamental support of the national-socialist state."

Thus in bourgeois states the gulf between the rulers and the ruled yawns daily wider and has attained the extreme limit in fascist states. In our state, however, every semblance of a barrier between the population and the machinery of state government has been effaced. The power of the Soviet state apparatus is its extremely strong bond with the masses.

There is no bureaucracy in the USSR. Our officials, our state servants of every grade, are servants of society, carrying out state trusts and obligated to act in the interests of socialist society. Fulfilling the work entrusted to

[15] *Ibid.*
[16] Lenin (Russian ed.), Vol. XXI, p. 391.
[17] *Ibid.*, p. 401.

them in the name of the state, they bear a lofty responsibility. Those in Soviet service are especially obligated, by their position and by the rights granted to them, to manifest an honorable and conscientious attitude toward the worker-peasant state, in the language of the directive of the Central Executive Committee and the Council of People's Commissars of the USSR (March 14, 1933).[18] In the Soviet state, since the first days of its emergence, the principle that officials are subject to control is in operation. They are amenable and responsible to the toilers and to the organs or authority elected by the toilers, as personified by the Soviets.

The activity of all administrative organs is subjected to social control. Broad masses of the toilers are attracted into the activity of the state through socialist plurality of offices, cooperative groups, the institute of public inspectors, and the like. This, along with the promotion of new cadres, is the most important means of improving the machinery of state government and overcoming bureaucratic perversions therein. "To struggle with bureaucracy to the end—until it is completely vanquished—is feasible only when the entire population shall participate in administration." [19]

Drawing the toilers into administration, and control over the activity of the state machinery and direct participation in its everyday work, are the most important means of simplifying the mechanics of the administrative systems, liquidating bureaucratic "mores" and "customs," clearing the road for utilization of our country's colossal reserves, heightening official responsibility, and freeing the apparatus from workmen who do not fulfill Soviet laws with complete accuracy and good faith. This is one of the means of cleansing the machinery of the remnants of the Trotsky-Bukharin spies, diversionists, and wreckers who strive to inculcate and to expand the bureaucratic perversions which are their trusted secret.

Attraction of toilers to administration of the state is thus a most important principle of our government, steadily developing with the growth and strengthening of socialism in our country. But it is ever more and more characteristic of bourgeois states to crush these masses with the aid of the state machinery made up of professional bureaucrats remote from the people.

It is further characteristic of the Soviet state government that it is made effective on the basis of the planned and conscious direction of all the processes of national economic life and the methodical putting into practice of the program purposes of the Bolshevik Party. In our state "the development of production is subordinate to the principle of planned guidance and systematic heightening of the material and cultural level of the toilers—not

[18] Cz. 1933, No. 19, Art. 108.
[19] Lenin (Russian ed.), Vol. XXIV, p. 145.

to that of competition and the guaranteeing of capital gain." [20] Here the plan becomes a binding and concrete program which includes the activity of all institutions, departments, and organizations, nonfulfillment of which is a breach of state discipline, undermining the building of the national economy.

One of the principles of Soviet state administration is the scrupulous taking into account of differences actually existing, of specific conditions of the manner of life and the special characteristics of the many peoples and tribes of the Soviet state. The entire administrative system of the USSR carries into effect the principles of the Lenin-Stalin national policy as contrasted with the principles of administration in multinational bourgeois states. Stalin says that administration in bourgeois states is a

mode when the apparatus is simplified and at its head sits, let us say, a group of men—or one man—having hands and eyes in the country in the form of governors. This is a very simple form of administration. The head—which administers the country—gets the information obtainable from governors and consoles himself with the hope that his administration is honorable and correct. Then come discords, discords pass into conflicts, and conflicts into uprisings. Then the uprisings are crushed. Such a system of administration is not our system. [21]

Soviet state administration is an indissoluble unity of administrative and economic government, a differentiation in principle of the Soviet state machinery from that of the bourgeois state. Extended to all sides of the economic and social life of the people, Soviet state administration is one of organizational creativeness.

Except in so far as its functions include the administration of economy, the bourgeois state machinery plays chiefly the part of policeman-regulator, guarding only private property's inviolability and conditions of existence, and acting—especially in fascist countries—by the methods of oppression, repressions, and overt terror. Arbitrary perversity and lawlessness characterize the bourgeois state administration.

It is clear how the very problems of administration in the Soviet state differ in principle from those of the bourgeois state, and how indissolubly the foundations of its organization and activity are bound up with these broad problems. Soviet state activity is carried into effect on the basis of socialist legality, its most important principle. This is especially clear, and was brilliantly expressed, in the great Stalin Constitution, which elevated the authority of the Soviet law to an unprecedented height. All administrative acts in the USSR must be in conformity with law. The principle of revolutionary legality penetrates the activity of all the links of our administra-

[20] Stalin, *Questions of Leninism* (10th ed.), p. 397.
[21] Stalin, *Marxism and the National-Colonial Question* (1937), p. 124.

tion from top to bottom, and the significance of this principle, always acknowledged by the Soviet state, was still more brilliantly expressed, as we have seen, in the Stalin Constitution. This raises still higher the authority and force of Soviet statutes.

On the basis of acts of the USSR Supreme Soviet and its Presidium, the Council of People's Commissars of the USSR issues its orders and directives. On the basis of all these acts, the People's Commissariats operate. The orders and instructions of People's Commissariats are binding upon organs subordinate to them. Thus an unbroken series of acts is here formed, each of which has complete force insofar as it is issued in conformity with operative laws and the acts of superior organs emanating therefrom.

The Soviet state administration, in opposition to bourgeois administration, is built on principles of democratic centralism, uniting the force of decisions of higher organs as binding upon lower organs with complete and unimpeded development "of local initiative and diversity of ways, means, and methods of moving toward the general goal." [22]

All these features of Soviet state administration manifest genuine democracy. The organization and activity of administrative organs change as the tasks confronting the worker-class dictatorship in different periods of the history of the Soviet state change. In the first months of the great October Socialist Revolution, these consisted chiefly in shattering the bourgeois-landowner machinery of state administration and creating the Soviet system of central and local administration. During this period of the socialist revolution, the first Council of People's Commissars (formed October 26/ November 8, 1917, by the Second All-Russian Congress of Soviets, to administer the country) smashed the old army and created the Red Army, took from the hands of the bourgeoisie the basic nerve of economic life—the banks—carried into effect from the beginning worker control over production and (later) the transition to direct administration, and (in place of the old and ruined provision and railroad mechanism) built in the center and in the rural areas new Soviet organs. During this period the Council of People's Commissars, in accordance with principles put at the foundation of its activity, acknowledged the independence of Finland, Armenia's freedom of self-determination, and so on.

The conditions of civil war demanded the energetic centralization of measures for the defense of the Soviet Republic and for the control of provisions, raw materials, and other resources in the interest of supplying the army, industry, and transport. Accordingly, the organs of state administration were reorganized. During this period, the administrative machinery acted upon strictly centralized principles after the system of military orders.

[22] Lenin (Russian ed.), Vol. XXII, p. 416.

The People's Commissariat of Supply (with its mechanism for accumulating and distributing provisions), the Commission for Utilization under the All-Russian Council of National Economy (which directed the distribution of industrial production), and the All-Russian Extraordinary Commission (for the struggle with counterrevolution) were advanced into the immediate foreground. Thereafter, too, the system of Soviet administration naturally reflected the basic problems of each period of the socialist revolution.

As such were successively posed (1) the rehabilitation of the economy destroyed by the imperialist and civil wars, (2) the socialist industrialization of the USSR, (3) the collectivization of agriculture and, finally, (4) the crowning of the socialist edifice. In each period Soviet administration extended to the most diversified sides of state and social life: reinforcing state defense in connection with the growth of aggressive aspirations on the part of the imperialist world with reference to the USSR; developing and strengthening of socialist economy; raising the cultural level and the material well-being of the toilers; and guarding the state order and state security. To correspond with the tasks of the Soviet state in different stages, the state apparatus was rebuilt and the jurisdiction of organs of government—Union, republic and local—modified and redistributed. As will be hereinafter shown, whole branches of the national economy were transferred from the jurisdiction of some organs to that of others, which in turn required substantial changes in the very building of the directing and governing organs in the center and in the rural areas. It is impossible to say that here were two contrasting tendencies toward centralization or decentralization; it was simply a matter of their expedient adaptation to given conditions, on the basis of the decentralization of operative functions and the simultaneous centralization of planning and guidance in fundamental matters.

SEC. 2: COUNCILS OF PEOPLE'S COMMISSARS

1. *The Council of People's Commissars of the USSR*

The supreme executive and administrative organ of the USSR state authority, uniting and directing the activity of the entire apparatus of state administration, is the Council of People's Commissars of the USSR. The Stalin Constitution delimits with complete clarity the highest organs of state authority and organs of state administration of the USSR and of the Union and autonomous republics. It establishes that legislative authority in the Union and in the republics is carried into effect only by the Supreme Soviets (Arts. 32, 59, 91), while the organs of administration are executive and directive (Arts. 64, 79). It defines with precision the jurisdiction of the sole legislative organs and of the executive organs, eliminating any possible confusion of their respective functions. This is due entirely to the insistence of our state upon the inadmissibility of functions either merging or intersecting, or executive-administrative acts being substituted for statutes, and of the effacement of the distinction between higher organs of state authority and organs of subordinate administration.

The Stalin Constitution thus eliminates the old situation where no one organ, but a series of organs, carried on legislative work: the Congress of Soviets, the Central Executive Committee, the Presidium of the Central Executive Committee, and the Council of People's Commissars of the USSR. It concentrates the legislative function in the hands of the supreme organs of the state authority—the Supreme Soviets—to promote the further growth of the incontrovertible force and authority of Soviet socialist law, to strengthen its stability and to concentrate the attention of Councils of the People's Commissars upon the tasks of directing the tremendously expanding popular economy.

The Stalin Constitution establishes the most democratic means of forming the USSR Government. "The Supreme Soviet of the USSR, at joint sitting of both Chambers, forms the Government of USSR—the Council of People's Commissars of USSR" (Art. 56), as well as the responsibility of the Council of People's Commissars to the Supreme Soviet and its accountability thereto and (in the period between sessions of the Supreme Soviet), responsibility to its Presidium and accountability thereto. Finally, it obligates the Council of People's Commissars to return, within a period of not exceeding three days, oral or written answers to questions of deputies of the Supreme Soviet (in the appropriate chamber).

All this expresses the authentic democracy in our country, and characterizes the Council of People's Commissars as an organ of administration operating in conformity with laws and on the basis of those laws, and responsible to persons chosen by the people.

The place of the Council of People's Commissars of the USSR in the system of higher state organs, and the method of its formation, differ radically and in principle from the role of a cabinet of ministers and a council of ministers in bourgeois countries. The most recent development of the bourgeois state shows how the significance of legislative organs—of parliaments and of legislation itself—is declining and the authority is ever more and more being concentrated in the hands of the government with its vast bureaucratic machinery and ever increasing irresponsibility.

The extraordinary intensification of the role of executive organs, as personified by a cabinet of ministers and ministries who have concentrated in their hands all the force of state authority, attracts ever more and more the attention of bourgeois scholars. In their most recent works [1] we see it openly admitted that parliament has no independent authority of any sort, and that the chief characteristic of "the last two generations" is the "concentration of ever greater independent authority in the hands of so-called 'bureaucracy'—the permanent bureaucrats of the administrative machinery." [2] Such bourgeois scholars and politicians of England, for example, as Muir, the most eminent member of the Liberal Party, see the essence of the British system "in a tendency to ever increasing concentration of authority and responsibility in one organ" [3]—the government—in its omnipotence. Legislation, deemed a special function of parliament, is in reality appropriated by the government. The cabinet of ministers is in practice the "Lord of Parliament." Parliament has become little more than a recording machine for orders of a military-dictatorship government.

Barthélemy admitted that "when energetic governments were in power for a long time, the dominant significance of the cabinet of ministers was so great that our regime could be called 'a regime of ministerial government.'" The French press likewise notes the extraordinary intensification of executive authority, which has once more found complete consummation in the ever encroaching power of the bureaucrats of Charles I and James II.

The omnipotence of executive authority in bourgeois states is expressed in the vastness of its plenary powers. In the person of the government, and with no control whatever on the part of parliament, that power appoints persons to all important positions. Consequently all state bureaucrats are its agents. The administrative function "goes far beyond the limits of merely carrying out statutes, and embraces a broad field of activity which has never been defined by law." [4] Governmental authority is most independent and uncontrolled in the field of foreign policy. The government makes broad use of the right of naming commissions for preparatory consideration of proposed legislation and broad application of the issuance of so-called administrative orders with the force of law, which justifies the assertion of Lord Hewart, Lord Chief Justice of England, concerning the arbitrary nature of the administration which is to come in England. The government is all-powerful in the field of finance as well; "in no single sphere is the dictatorship of the government so manifest." [5]

In the biggest bourgeois-democratic countries—the U.S.A., England, and France, to say nothing of fascist and semifascist states—the formation of

---

[1] Cf. Ramsay Muir, *How Britain Is Governed*; J. Barthélemy, *The State System of France*.

[2] Muir, *Ibid.* (Russian ed.), p. 27.

[3] *Ibid.*, p. 34.

[4] *Ibid.*, p. 39.

[5] *Ibid.*, p. 45.

cabinets of ministers is no function of representative institutions. The cabinet is composed of ministers selected either by the president (as in the U.S.A.) or by the leader of a definite political party commissioned by the king (as in England) or by the president (as in France). While the constitutional laws of some bourgeois states (e.g., the French Statute of February 25, 1875) provide in form that ministers are responsible to the Chambers—"jointly for the general policy of the government and individually for their own actions"—this so-called "joint responsibility" to parliament is in essence responsibility to a specific clique of capitalists who have put the premier and his cabinet at the helm of state life. In other countries, such as the U.S.A., where even bourgeois jurists regard the cabinet of ministers as if it were a constituent part of the "personality of the President," ministers (called secretaries of the President) are personally subordinate and responsible to the President—and not to the Congress—in everything. Even James Bryce, the bourgeois investigator of the American Constitution, wrote that "an American administration resembles not so much the cabinets of England and France as the group of ministers who surround the Tsar or the Sultan, or who executed the bidding of a Roman emperor like Constantine or Justinian." [6]

In England, according to the reliable observation of Sidney Low, the cabinet of ministers has long since become a committee, not of parliament, but of only one party "which, while it is in office, has control of legislation, administration, policy, and finance." [7]

When the executive power is thus all-powerful, the old theoretical edifice of bourgeois public-law science—the subordination of the government to parliament, the supremacy of law, and the effectuation of parliamentary control, and so on—collapse, and new "theories" are fashioned to vindicate the arbitrary conduct of the administration.

To guide the future, the Stalin Constitution confirms in clear relief that organizational principle of the Soviet Government which has already taken form and vindicated itself. The Council of People's Commissars of the USSR consists of a President, his Vice Presidents, the President of the State Planning Commission, the President of the Commission of Soviet Control, People's Commissars of the USSR, presidents of committees for higher schools and for arts formed under the Council of People's Commissars of the USSR, and the head of the administration of the state bank.

The Council of People's Commissars and each member thereof must, in the formula of Molotov in his address at the first session of the Supreme Soviet of the USSR,

[6] James Bryce, *The American Commonwealth* (Russian ed.), Vol. I, p. 101.
[7] Sidney Low, *Governance of England*, p. 73.

know how to prize the confidence of the people . . . to be worthy disciples of the great Lenin . . . to be effective helpers of the great Stalin—our teacher and the leader of the peoples of the Soviet Union . . . to be worthy of our socialist people's parliament—the Supreme Soviet . . . to be worthy of the people who, by their toilsome exertions, unselfishness, and creative enthusiasm, and despite each and every obstacle, are building communist society.

The jurisdiction of the Council of People's Commissars of the USSR is defined in general form in Article 66 of the Constitution: "The Council of People's Commissars of the USSR issues decrees and orders on the basis— and in pursuance—of laws in operation, and supervises their execution." Directives and orders must correspond likewise with decrees of the Presidium of the Supreme Soviet. They are binding throughout the territory of the USSR (Art. 67). Directives are acts establishing rules of general obligation and understood to be constantly operative until they shall have been abrogated or have lost their force by reason of having attained the result they define. Orders are acts operative on a single occasion and regulating separate and definitive cases.

The definitive content of acts of the Council of People's Commissars of the USSR is defined by Article 14 of the Constitution, which outlines the jurisdiction of the supreme organs of state authority and state administration of the USSR. Pursuant to Article 68, the most important species of acts of the Council of People's Commissars of the USSR are:

a) It issues directives and orders to unify and guide the work of All-Union and Union-Republic People's Commissariats of the USSR and other economic and cultural institutions (subject to the jurisdiction of the Council) and is concerned with the organization and activity of such institutions. Within this category are all the directives adopted by it concerning reports of separate People's Commissariats and departments containing an appraisal of their work and shaping measures for its improvement. It affirms the most important instructions prepared by separate Union departments and abrogates incorrect orders and instructions issuing from separate People's Commissariats.

b) It adopts measures for carrying into effect the national economic plan and the state budget and for strengthening the system of money credit. It affirms divers operative plans (production plans, procurement plans, and so on) and oversees their fulfillment. This includes the issuance of directives as to the state plan of agricultural works, as to a program of industrial production, as to a plan of freight movements in transportation, as to building plans, as to plans of contracting for goods for the state, and so on. So also as to directives whose purpose is to strengthen separate branches of the national economy. In the field of finances it affirms the social insurance budget and redistributes income as between the state budget and the budget of social security. It establishes turnover tax rates and rates of customs duties—defining tariffs of different kinds (for communications, for railroads, for the use of electricity, and so on). It adopts measures to regularize tax collecting. It eliminates superfluous expenses. It oversees, in general, the correct carrying out of the budget, and the improvement of the method of financing separate branches of economy and of controlling state expenses. A very important category of its directives concerns the obligatory purveying of seed cultures, meat, milk, potatoes, and wool. The institution under it of the Economic Council has led to solution by the latter of a significant number of matters touching the work of People's Commissariats of economy, the affirmance and verification of the fulfillment of separate plans, prices, funds and rates of wages, and of plans of labor.

c) It adopts measures to insure social order, the defense of state interests and the protection of civil rights.

d) It is charged with general guidance in the sphere of relations with foreign states. While the USSR Constitution refers the ratification of international compacts to the jurisdiction of the Presidium of the Supreme Soviet (Art. 49), the preliminary examination thereof takes place in the Council of People's Commissars of the USSR, which further oversees the current work of diplomatic organs, effectually directs that work and takes the necessary measures in that field.

e) It guides the general building up of the country's armed forces and, in particular, it defines the yearly contingents of citizens subject to call for active military service.

f) It appoints officials to a number of the highest posts and relieves them therefrom—in particular, vice-presidents of People's Commissars of the Union, People's Commissariats, trade representatives of the USSR, presidents of committees under the USSR Council of People's Commissars, and so on.

All these functions relate to the field of administration.

The Stalin Constitution grants full scope to the legislative initiative of individual members of the Supreme Soviet. At the same time, preparatory work in the field of legislation remains also for the Council of People's Commissars. The USSR Supreme Soviet affirms a single state budget of the USSR and a report upon the execution thereof, but, as a preliminary, the proposed budget and the reports are subjected to detailed consideration in the Council of People's Commissars of the USSR.

The Stalin Constitution establishes (Art. 69) that "the Council of People's Commissars of the USSR has, as to those branches of administration and economy within the jurisdiction of the USSR, the right to suspend directives and orders of Councils of People's Commissars of Union Republics. . . ." Rights of the USSR Council of People's Commissars in regard to Union Republic Councils of People's Commissars are more restricted than are its rights as regards Union Commissariats: orders and instructions of the latter it can abrogate, whereas directives of the former—though not in accordance with law—it can only suspend. The decision in this case belongs to the Presidium of the Supreme Soviet which under the Constitution (Art. 49, Par. *e*) abrogates directives and orders of the USSR Council of the People's Commissars as well as of Union Republic Councils of the People's Commissars in case they do not accord with the law. This is in no sense a limitation of the legal rights of a Union Republic, inasmuch as the USSR Council of People's Commissars employs this right only if there has been a violation of All-Union legislation.

2. *The commissions and committees under the Council of People's Commissars of the USSR*

According to the Constitution (Art. 68, Par. *f*), the Council of People's Commissars of the USSR, in case of need, sets up under itself special committees and central boards of administration for matters concerned with the building up of economics, culture, and defense. A recent example of this is the Council's directive of March 23, 1938, concerning the formation, under itself, of a committee on motion pictures. Presidents of such committees do not automatically become members of the Council; the structure of the latter is defined by the Constitution, and may be changed only by the established method. Under the RSFSR Council of People's Commissars, before the formation of the USSR and later under the USSR Council of People's Commissars, there was a succession of commissions for the preparation of matters considered in the Council of People's Commissars and to decide independently certain matters of secondary importance: the Small Council of People's Commissars, the Preparatory Commission, the Council of Labor and Defense (STO). To the STO particularly important significance attached; it existed down to the adoption of the Stalin Constitution. Pursuant to the enactment of August 21, 1923,[8] the goal of STO was the punctilious effectuation of the economic and finance plan and the most immediate direction of People's Commissariats in the sphere of economic measures and defense of the country. Its directives could be abrogated by the USSR Council of the People's Commissars upon its own initiative or upon departmental declarations, but otherwise they became operative without affirmation by the Council. Its jurisdiction was in fact extremely broad and it was preserved until the adoption of the Stalin Constitution.

At the present time there are, under the Council of the People's Commissars of the USSR, a number of central administrative boards, commissions and committees—some indicated in the Constitution, some organized

[8] *Herald of the Central Executive Committee, The Council of People's Commissars, and Labor-Defense Council* (1923) No. 4, Art. 106.

by the Council itself [9]—including, in the first place, *the Economic Council* under the USSR Council of People's Commissars—a standing committee, formed by a directive of the Council on November 23, 1937—whose tasks give it a certain resemblance to the Labor-Defense Council (STO). Its President is the President of the Council, and its members are the Council Vice-Presidents and the President of the All-Union Central Council of Trade Unions.

The Economic Council is charged with: (a) consideration of yearly and quarterly plans of national economy to be proposed for confirmation by the USSR Council of People's Commissars; (b) confirmation of plans for furnishing building materials and other objects of material-technical equipment, and also plans for furnishing goods of wide consumption; (c) confirmation of plans for the carriage of freight by railway and water, for seasonal economic work, and for the storage of economic products; (d) consideration of reports on the realization of the economic plans, verification of the fulfillment of government decisions on economic questions, and the adoption of measures to guarantee the same; (e) consideration of the position of separate branches of national economy and the adoption of measures to better their condition; (f) matters of prices; (g) matters of labor and wages; (h) solution of questions as to the formation and liquidation of economic agencies and of the transfer of state property from one department to another in order that it may be utilized; and (i) the solution of other economic questions of an operative character.[10]

Being by its very structure an organ which is authoritative in the highest degree, the Economic Council is not a preparatory institution. Its decisions, unless abrogated by the USSR Council of the People's Commissars, become immediately operative and binding upon all People's Commissariats of the USSR, Union Republic Councils of People's Commissars and local Soviet organs. Specifically, it is charged with affirmation of instructions on economic matters issued by People's Commissariats of the Union. Its directives may be appealed to the USSR Council of People's Commissars by Union People's Commissariats (within a period of three days) and by Union Republic governments (within the period of a month), but without stay of their fulfillment.

[9] In addition to the committees and administrative boards indicated in the USSR Constitution, the following are under the USSR Council of People's Commissars: (1) the central administrative board of the civil air fleet, (2) the central administrative board of the Northern seaway, (3) the central administrative board of forest conservation and forestry, (4) the central administrative board of the hydrometeorological service, (5) the administration of state reserves, (6) state arbitration, (7) the committee for radio and broadcasting, (8) the All-Union committee on physical culture and sport, (9) the committee for building, (10) the committee for moving pictures, and (11) the committee on measures and measuring instruments.   [10] Cz. 1937, No. 75, Art. 365.

The basic task of *the Commission of Soviet Control* (organized in 1934) [11] is "the systematic, concrete, and operative verification of the factual fulfillment of the most important government decisions by all links of the Soviet and economic mechanism from the top to the bottom" [12]—that is to say, to struggle with bureaucratism, red tape, laxity of direction, and perversions in the execution of administrative decisions; to show up specific persons who are guilty of these shortcomings; to assure correct choice and arrangement of directive cadres and to strengthen Soviet discipline. It concentrates its work on the most important sections. It cooperates closely with the Commission of Party Control. Its members are proposed by the Party Congress and confirmed by the USSR Council of People's Commissars. Its leader must be one of the Vice-Presidents of that Council. The Commission verifies the work of central and local institutions, requires their leaders to promote definitive measures, and notifies the USSR Council of People's Commissars of all cases of violation of discipline and of shortcomings in fulfilling administrative decisions brought to light by it. It can designate its agents for separate branches of economy and for separate districts.

The Commission of Soviet Control carries out a searching examination into separate matters of the utmost importance. On February 28, 1933, the USSR Council of People's Commissars proposed to concentrate attention on scrutinizing the execution of its decisions and those of the Economic Council, having separated the most pressing subjects.[13] Among the most important problems assigned to the Commission of Soviet Control by the USSR Council of People's Commissars is the study of the organization building of central and local Soviet and economic organs and of their personnel and the quality of their work, and verification of the method of receiving and turning over matters when there is change of management. The entire activity of the Commission of Soviet Control must be linked up with the activity of the State Planning Commission, which likewise searchingly scrutinizes the fulfillment of plans that have been confirmed.

The State Planning Commission is one of the most typical institutions in the Soviet state system, as distinguished from that of the bourgeois state. The elaboration, affirmation, and putting into practice of a plan of national economy were foreseen as far back as the 1918 Constitution. Historically, the planning of national economy was closely bound up with the plan of GOELRO [14]—which had to provide a new basis of electric

[11] Cz. 1934, No. 9, Art. 58.
[12] Cz. 1934, No. 12, Art. 75.
[13] Cp. 1938, No. 7, Art. 42.
[14] The State Commission for the Electrification of Russia.

power to rebuild the national economy—in whose realization Lenin saw one of the most pressing problems. The first proposal concerning a Planning Commission under the USSR Council of People's Commissars was affirmed by that Council in a directive of August 21, 1923. Thereafter both the organizational structure of the State Planning Commission and the character of its activity were subjected to a series of changes. First of all, ever increasing significance was given to scrutinizing the fulfillment of the plans of national economy. Then the plans themselves acquired a more definitive and operative character. Finally, the significance of planning on the district level increased in connection with the new allocation of the USSR production forces.

Pursuant to the directive of the Council of People's Commissars of the USSR of February 2, 1938,[15] the State Planning Commission is a standing commission of the USSR Council of People's Commissars, and consists of eleven persons individually confirmed by that Council from among leading plan workers and most outstanding specialists. The State Planning Commission works out yearly and quarterly economic plans in perspective and introduces them for the consideration of the USSR Council of People's Commissars; gives its conclusions as to plans introduced by separate departments and Union Republics; examines into the execution of settled plans of national economy; works out—according to instructions of the USSR Council of People's Commissars and upon its own initiative—individual problems of socialist economy and of the methodology of socialist planning, and directs socialist accounting. In these fields, it unites the activity of separate departments and branch organizations in order thereby to assure the properly correlated development of the various branches of the national economy. It directs special attention to scrutiny of the execution of plans of national economy. In Union Republics, regions, and territories there are agents of the USSR State Planning Commission side by side with their own planning commissions.

The Committee for Schools of Higher Learning was formed May 21, 1936, out of an All-Union committee on higher technical education originally organized under the Central Executive Committee of the USSR and later transferred [16] to the jurisdiction of the Council of People's Commissars of the USSR. The formation of the committee was due to the growing importance of scientific preparation of cadres in all branches and, on the other hand, by the necessity of actual control emanating from the Union center, to the end of improving the work of our higher educational insti-

---

[15] Cp. 1938, No. 7, Art. 41.
[16] By a directive of the Presidium of the USSR Central Executive Committee of Dec. 26, 1935: Cz. 1936, No. 1, Art. 6.

tutions. According to the regulation of the All-Union Committee for Schools of Higher Learning adopted by the Council of People's Commissars of the USSR on October 10, 1936,[17] the latter examines plans of development and estimates of expenses for the maintenance of all the higher schools (with the exception of military schools and those under the jurisdiction of committees on the arts and physical culture); establishes the nomenclature of specialties, the number and the types of higher educational institutions, the network of such institutions and a list of faculties, departments, and professorial chairs; works out and brings before the USSR Council of People's Commissars contingents of students to be received and plans for distributing them among departments; confirms the individual regulations of higher educational institutions, standard plans of study, programs and textbooks, directors and superior-professors, teachers with professorial rank and lecturers of higher schools; and, in general, directs and unifies the activity of departments in preparing and raising the qualifications of bodies of scientific teachers. The committee also controls the conferring of learned degrees.

The formation of the *Committee for the Arts* shows the high significance attributed to arts in the development of socialist culture in the USSR. Formed by directive of the Central Executive Committee and the Council of People's Commissars of USSR (January 17, 1936),[18] the committee was charged with direction of all the arts. Theaters and motion-picture organizations, musical, artistic, sculptural, and other institutions, as well as the corresponding educational institutions, were subordinated to it.

By directive of the USSR Council of People's Commissars of March 23, 1928,[19] matters concerned with motion pictures were separated from the sphere of jurisdiction of the All-Union Committee for the Arts and a special *Committee for Cinematography*, including the filming of pictures and the production and distribution of films, was formed.

3. *Councils of People's Commissars of Union Republics*

With the organization of the USSR, it was established that the internal structure of Union Republics is defined by their constitutions, while the fundamental principles of that structure were confirmed in the USSR Constitution.

The 1924 Constitution of the USSR provided (Art. 67) that the central executive committees of Union Republics form their executive organs, the Councils of People's Commissars, whose members are the

[17] Cz. 1936, No. 52, Art. 424.
[18] Cz. 1936, No. 5, Art. 40.
[19] Cp. 1938, No. 13, Art. 81.

Presidents of the Supreme Council of National Economy, the People's Commissars of Republic People's Commissariats, and likewise, with the right of consultative or decisive vote, by resolution of the Union Republic Central Executive Committees, representatives of the All-Union People's Commissariats to the Union Republic concerned.

As Soviet building developed, a number of regulations as to the organization and activity of republic and local organs was established through Union legislation.

The Stalin Constitution includes numerous general regulations defining the system of administrative organs of Union Republics (Chap. VI). Furthermore, it provides for fundamentally the same interrelations—within the limits of Union Republics—between organs of state authority and organs of state administration as exist in the USSR.

As in the USSR, the supreme executive and administrative organ of state authority of a Union Republic is its Council of People's Commissars, formed by the Supreme Soviet of the Union Republic, responsible and accountable to the latter and, in intervals between sessions, to the Presidium of the Union Republic Supreme Soviet. Its structure is precisely established in Article 83. In addition to the President and his Vice-Presidents, the structure of the Council of People's Commissars includes the People's Commissars of the republic concerned, the President of the State Planning Commission, the head of the administration of arts and representatives of the All-Union People's Commissariats.

Union Republic Councils of People's Commissars issue directives and orders on the basis and for the fulfillment of operative statutes (All-Union and Republic) as well as of directives of the USSR Council of the People's Commissars, and examine into their fulfillment. They have the right to suspend directives and orders of Councils of the People's Commissars of Autonomous Republics, and decisions and orders of territorial and area Soviets of Deputies of the Toilers, and Soviets of Deputies of the Toilers of Autonomous Regions. They can abrogate decisions and orders of executive committees of Soviets of Deputies of the Toilers of areas, territories, autonomous regions and—in republics which have no territorial division—districts, as well as of executive committees of Soviets of cities which are not subject to districts.

Directives and orders of Councils of People's Commissars are of binding force throughout the territory of the Union Republic.

In the area of legislation, Councils of the People's Commissars work out and present to Supreme Soviets proposed statutes (on the republic level) whereas, before the new Constitution, republic statutes were often issued in the form of directives of the Central Executive Committee and the Council of People's Commissars of the Union Republic.

Constitutions of Union Republics point out in greater detail the sphere of jurisdiction of Councils of People's Commissars in the administrative field:

a) They unify and direct the activity of corresponding People's Commissariats and examine into and unify the work of representatives of the All-Union People's Commissariats. The Stalin Constitution broadens their sphere of affairs in so far as it creates new (republic) commissariats of forestry, light industry, the food industry, and of state grain and livestock farms. The Union Republic Councils of People's Commissars hear reports of separate People's Commissariats as to the condition of their work and pass directives thereon.

b) They take measures for carrying into effect the plan of national economy and republic budgets, state and local. The Constitution of the White Russian SSR stipulates likewise that the Council of People's Commissars of their republic prepare a plan of national economy of the republic, the state budget of the republic, and a compilation of local budgets of the White Russian SSR, and introduce them for affirmation by the Supreme Soviet of the White Russian SSR (Art. 43, Par. *b*). Although this is not stated in other constitutions, manifestly the plan of national economy, the republic budget, and the compilation of local budgets inseparably connected therewith pass through the Council of People's Commissars of the Union Republic, and are introduced by the latter into the Supreme Soviet, which affirms them. Councils of People's Commissars adopt directives for assuring the fulfillment of plans of national economy and social culture (such as directives concerning a plan of producing building materials, the condition and the problems of work of scientific investigation in agriculture, the preparation of schools for the school year, the regularization and reduction of expenditures going into republic and local budgets, control of administrative expenses, and the like).

c) Within the limits of the Union Republic, they take measures to assure social order, to protect the interests of the state and to guard civil rights, developing in these fields the All-Union laws, directives, and orders of the USSR Council of People's Commissars as well as the acts of the supreme organs of authority and administration of the Union Republic.

d) One of the most important aspects of their activity is direction of the work of executive committees of Soviets of Deputies of the Toilers and verification thereof.

In general the 1924 Constitution of the USSR did not touch local organs of state authority. But thereafter All-Union legislation enacted a series of basic regulations concerning the organization and work of the Soviets, particularly of the lower Soviets of villages, cities, and districts. The Stalin Constitution devotes Chapter VIII to local organs of state authority, establishing the various links of the local Soviet system and defining the position of executive committees, the executive and administrative organs of the Soviet. These are charged with all the current administration and putting into practice of directives of local Soviets. Under the immediate supervision of Republic Councils of People's Commissars are the executive committees of regions and territories (of Union Republics having such division) and districts (of republics where there is no such division). These executive committees, directly subject to Councils of People's Commissars, must render an account to them, and, in accordance with their reports, Republic Councils of People's Commissars can issue directives comprising as well a general evaluation of their activity as measures for improving their work.

As to Councils of People's Commissars of Autonomous Republics, the highest executive and administrative organs of state authority of an autonomous republic, the rights of Republic Councils of People's Commissars are more restricted. The constitutions of the RSFSR (Art. 45, Par. *e*) and of the Ukrainian (Art. 43, Par. *e*), of the Azerbaijan (Art. 46, Par. *e*), Georgian (Art. 48, Par. *d*) and Uzbek (Art. 46, Par. *b*) SSR's recite that their Councils of People's Commissars guide the work of the local executive committees immediately under them and direct that of Councils of People's Commissars of Autonomous Republics. Furthermore, while Republic Councils of People's Commissars can abrogate directives of the executive committees immediately below them, they can only suspend Councils of People's Commissars of Autonomous Republics pending decision by the Supreme Soviets of Autonomous Republics (which can abrogate such directives) or a decision thereon by the Presidium of the Union Republic Supreme Soviet.

Direction of local executive committees and scrutiny of their activity by Union Republic Councils of People's Commissars are tasks of enormous significance. Many measures formerly developed at the republic level are now carried with effect by district and territorial organs. At the same time, the sphere of jurisdiction of district, city, and village organs is also broadened. In the budget of Union Republics, computation for local budgets occupies a predominant place, which enhances the significance pertaining to the direction of the activity of local executive committees.

Under Union Republic Councils of People's Commissars there are planning commissions whose tasks, at republic level, correspond with those of the State Planning Commision of the USSR at the All-Union level and which, in the methodology of planning works, must follow the latter's decrees.

There are also administrations for the arts, subordinate to the All-Union committee as well as to the government of the Union Republic, and having jurisdiction of institutions and enterprises carried on at the republic level. They must, in particular, cooperate to develop the art of the different nationalities. By a directive of the USSR Council of People's Commissars [20] (March 23, 1938), agencies to plan the filming of motion pictures are organized under the Union Republic Councils of People's Commissars, and a directive of the USSR Council of People's Commissars of April 22, 1938,[21] proposed that Union Republic Councils of People's Commissars form the chief road administrations under their own jurisdiction.

4. Councils of People's Commissars of Autonomous Republics

As we have already seen, the Stalin Constitution (Chap. VII) establishes that the Supreme Soviet of an autonomous Soviet Socialist Republic forms the Council of People's Commissars of that autonomous republic in accordance with its constitution.

According to the constitutions of those Union Republics of which autonomous republics are constituent parts, the Councils of People's Commissars of the Autonomous Republics issue directives and orders on the basis and in fulfillment of laws of the Union and of Union and autonomous republics, and also of directives and orders of the Council of People's Commissars of the USSR and of Union Republic Councils of People's Commissars, and examine into their fulfillment. They may abrogate orders and instructions of People's Commissariats of Autonomous Republics and decisions and orders of executive committees of area, city, and district Soviets of Deputies of the Toilers, and likewise suspend the decisions of Soviets themselves.

Constitutions of the individual autonomous republics define the sphere of jurisdiction of the Council of People's Commissars of an autonomous SSR in general in conformity with the sphere of jurisdiction of Union Republic Councils of the People's Commissars—but upon the scale of autonomous republics. This includes the unification and management of work of Autonomous Republic People's Commissariats, as well as unification and examination of the activity of representatives of (Union and Republic) People's Commissariats, the adoption of measures to carry into effect the plan of national economy, and the budget of the autonomous republic and its local budgets, to assure social order, to defend the interests of the state and to guard civil rights, and also direction and examination of the work of district, municipal, and (in separate republics) area executive committees. Thus, within an autonomous republic a significant proportion of the measures included in the jurisdiction of Union Republic Councils of the People's Commissars is carried out by the Council of People's Commissars of the autonomous SSR—within the limits, however, of directives and orders of the Union Republic Council of People's Commissars.

[20] Cp. 1938, No. 13, Art. 81.   [21] Cp. 1938, No. 21, Art. 133.

In precisely the same way, in so far as Supreme Soviets of the autonomous republics possess legislative power, the preparation of proposed legislation, as well as of plans of national economy and of the budget, rests upon the Council of People's Commissars of the autonomous republic. The structure of the Council of People's Commissars of an autonomous republic is itself defined in Union Republic constitutions.

The organs under the Council of People's Commissars of an autonomous SSR are the State Planning Commissions of such republics, the road administrations, and the administrations for the arts. The President of the State Planning Commission and the chiefs of those administrations are members of the Council of People's Commissars of the autonomous SSR. The sphere of activity of road administrations corresponds with that of road departments of district and territorial executive committees. The same may be said as to administrations for the arts and for planning the filming of motion pictures.

As local Soviet building expands, the activity of Councils of People's Commissars of Autonomous Republics becomes increasingly significant as regards their direction of local executive committees.

SEC. 3: PEOPLE'S COMMISSARIATS

1. *People's Commissariats as organs of state administration*

People's Commissariats of the USSR and of Union and autonomous republics are the organs of state government which carry into effect the direction of separate branches of state life within the limits of their jurisdiction and in strict conformity with statutes. Developing the will of the people as expressed in statutes, the People's Commissariats are responsible to the Supreme Soviet for their activity. They are appointed by the appropriate Supreme Soviets. In the interval between sessions of the Supreme Soviet, the right of dismissing from office, and of appointing, individual People's Commissars belongs to the Presidium of the Supreme Soviet upon the recommendation of the President of the Council of the People's Commissars, subject to later confirmation by the Supreme Soviet. A People's Commissar to whom a deputy of the Supreme Soviet has addressed an inquiry must return an oral or written answer in the appropriate chamber of the Supreme Soviet within a period of not more than three days.

Supreme Soviets appoint and remove, and effectually control and examine into the activity of, responsible directors of departments.

People's Commissars are responsible likewise to the Council of People's

Commissars as the highest executive-administrative organ of state authority.

A People's Commissar is a unitary or sole director.[1] Emphasizing the principle of unitary responsibility in carrying executive functions into effect, the Stalin Constitution (Arts. 72 and 73) establishes that the People's Commissars direct branches of state administration and issue orders and instructions. The principle of unitary responsibility establishes a solid basis for the accountability of a People's Commissar for the activity of the People's Commissariat and its organs in their entirety and, so far from contradicting the principles of socialist democracy, is a necessary condition of genuine democracy. Lenin wrote on this score:

> The mass must have the right to remove them—to know and to examine into each infinitesmal step of their activity. It must have the right to promote every single one of its worker members to administrative functions. This in no wise means, however, that the process of collective labor could remain without definite direction—without the precise establishment of a director's responsibility, without the strictest order created by the oneness of the director's will.[2]

Developing this thought at the Seventh All-Russian Congress of Soviets, Lenin said: "As the collegium form is indispensable to the discussion of fundamental questions, so are unitary responsibility and unitary direction indispensable if there is to be no red tape and no evasion of responsibility." [3]

Lenin demanded the union of the collegium principle in discussion with the unitary responsibility principle in carrying executive-administrative functions into effect. This insistence was reflected in the first Soviet Constitution (1918) and in the USSR Constitution of 1924. According to the latter, under People's Commissars, and with them as presidents, collegia were created whose members were appointed by the Council of People's Commissars. Upon his own unitary responsibility, a People's Commissar had the right to make decisions on all questions of the jurisdiction of the People's Commissariat, including the abrogation of directives of the collegium, reporting to it thereon. If it disagreed with any decision of a People's Commissar, the collegium (or separate members thereof) could, without suspending the execution of the decision, appeal it to the Council of People's Commissars. Thus a People's Commissar was assured in full compass the rights of unitary direction.

In practice, however, the principle of unitary responsibility was not infrequently violated. Down to 1934, collegia issued in their own names directives binding on all institutions subordinate to a People's Commissar.

---

[1] The expression translated by the words "unitary director" or "sole director" is intended to make it clear that such a "director" is under "sole" personal responsibility (for the operation of his commissariat) as distinguished from the "collegium" responsibility existing earlier.—Tr.

[2] Lenin (Russian ed.), Vol. XXII, p. 420.

[3] Ibid., Vol. XXIV, p. 623.

This lowered the individual responsibility of directors for decisions taken and created administrative depersonalization. Accordingly, in 1934, collegia of People's Commissariats were liquidated.[4] Such abolition, however, did not lead to increased unity of direction as to the various separate branches of People's Commissariats. Taking into account the necessity of unifying the administration of different branches of the work of People's Commissariats and of intensifying examination into fulfillment, the Council of People's Commissars of the USSR adopted a resolution (March, 1938) for reestablishing collegia in all the People's Commissariats of the USSR. Members of the collegia are appointed by that Council.

The duties of the collegia include consideration of matters of practical direction, of examining into fulfillment, of the choice of cadres, of all orders of any substance concerning the People's Commissariat, hearing reports of representatives of local organs of People's Commissariats, sending to the country representatives of a People's Commissariat to examine into fulfillment, and the like. The decision of a collegium on any of these matters becomes of binding force, however, only if a People's Commissar is in accord with it and it is developed in the form of an *order of a People's Commissar*. A collegium has no right to issue any acts in its own name. In case of disagreement between a People's Commissar and the collegium, the *People's Commissar puts into practice his own decision,* reporting to the USSR Council of People's Commissars the diversities of opinion that have arisen, and members of the collegium can, in their turn, appeal to the same body. Thus even the new collegia do not contradict the principle of unitary responsibility, but—as distinguished from the former collegia—they are so constructed as to exclude administrative depersonalization and to guarantee the feasibility of the People's Commissar carrying into effect unitary direction and examination into fulfillment.

Apart from the collegia, there are, under the People's Commissariats, councils of People's Commissariats, summoned once every two months, consisting of from forty to seventy persons, not less than half of them representing local organizations and enterprises. Such councils subserve the maintenance of bonds with the rural areas and the exchange of experience. Their decisions, if the People's Commissar agrees therewith, are put into practice by his orders.

Under the People's Commissariats there are also assemblies of active Party members, regularly summoned for the best possible utilization of the experience of the lower workmen, stakhanovites, and workers and for the promotion of criticism and self-criticism. They hear and consider the most important matters involving the work of the People's Commissariat,

[4] Cz. 1934, No. 15, Art. 103.

but adoption by the People's Commissars of decisions on the matters so considered is unitary.

We must mention also forms, such as the branch congresses and councils under the People's Commissariats, which have been broadly used during recent years.

2. *The different kinds of People's Commissariats*

People's Commissariats are divided into (1) All-Union, (2) Union Republic, and (3) Republic Commissariats.

People's Commissariats of the USSR are either All-Union or Union Republic. Each of them alike directs a branch of administration included in the jurisdiction of the USSR.

(1) All-Union People's Commissariats direct the branch of state administration committed to them throughout the territory of the USSR—immediately, or through organs appointed by them—with no People's Commissariats bearing the same name in the Union Republics.[5]

(2) As a rule, Union Republic People's Commissariats manage through People's Commissariats (of the Union Republics) bearing the same name as the branch of state administration committed to them, and administer directly only a definite and limited number of enterprises according to a schedule confirmed by the Presidium of the Supreme Soviet of the USSR.[6]

The People's Commissariats of a Union Republic are either Union Republic or Republic Commissariats, and direct the branches of administration included in the jurisdiction of the Union Republic. Union Republic People's Commissariats of a Union Republic are subordinate both to the Union Republic Council of the People's Commissars and to the corresponding Union Republic People's Commissariat of the USSR in the management of the branches of state administration entrusted to them.[7]

(3) Republic People's Commissariats—those with no People's Commissariats of the same name in the USSR—direct the branches of state administration committed to them and are immediately subordinate to the Union Republic Council of People's Commissars.[8]

People's Commissariats of autonomous republics[9] direct the branches of state administration included in the jurisdiction of the ASSR, subordinate both to the Council of People's Commissars of the ASSR and also the appropriate Union Republic People's Commissariats.

Since different branches of state administration require a different

[5] Cf. Arts. 75, 77.
[6] Cf. Arts. 76, 78.
[7] Cf. Arts. 84, 86, 87.
[8] Cf. Art. 88.
[9] Appointed by the Council of People's Commissars of the ASSR (Art. 93).

degree of supervisory centralization, it is established that some People's Commissariats are subordinate only to the center, whereas others are under a dual subordination.

Dual subordination is necessary where it is essential to know how to take into account a positively existent inevitability of diversification. Agriculture in the Kalyga Guberniya is not what agriculture is in the Kazan Guberniya—and the same is true as to all administration or government. Not to take local differences into account in all these matters would be to lapse into bureaucratic centralism and the like—to impede local workers in that evaluation of local differences upon which rational work is based.[10]

The first (1924) Union Constitution of the USSR formulated the principle of the dual subordination of People's Commissariats. In territories of the Union Republics the unified People's Commissariats of the USSR realized their functions of state administration not immediately but through Union Republic People's Commissariats bearing the same name. The latter were accordingly subordinate at once to the former and to the Union Republic Council of People's Commissars. The Stalin Constitution preserves this principle, while defining otherwise the position of the unified People's Commissariats of Union Republics. Whereas these were formerly organs of the USSR People's Commissariats bearing the same name (1924 Constitution of USSR, Art. 54), the Stalin Constitution contemplates Union Republic (formerly called "unified") People's Commissariats as organs rather of the Union Republics than of USSR People's Commissariats bearing the same name.

The dual subordination of People's Commissariats is characterized by the following elements: the precepts of Union Republic People's Commissariats of the USSR are binding upon the identically named People's Commissariats of Union Republics. According to the "General Regulation" as to USSR People's Commissariats,[11] Union Republic People's Commissariats of the USSR have the right to suspend and to abrogate acts of identically named People's Commissariats of Union Republics if these acts conflict with directives given them or with All-Union legislation— informing the Council of People's Commissars of the appropriate Union Republic of such action forthwith. This right is affirmed also by the most recent regulations concerning individual People's Commissariats. According to the Regulation of the USSR People's Commissariat for Trade of April 3, 1938,[12] that commissariat suspends and abrogates such orders and

---

[10] Lenin (Russian ed.), Vol. XXVII, pp. 298, 299.
[11] Cf. Herald of the Central Executive Committee, the Council of People's Commissars, and the Council of Labor and Defense (1923), No. 10, Art. 299.
[12] Cp. 1938, No. 15, Art. 95.

instructions of Union Republic People's Commissariats of Trade as conflict with laws and directives of the USSR Government or orders and instructions of the USSR People's Commissariat of Trade. The General Regulation does not extend this right, however, to cases where acts of Union Republic People's Commissariats are based on the exact precept of Union Republic laws or directives of the Union Republic government. In the latter case the corresponding USSR People's Commissariat enters a protest with the USSR Council of People's Commissars.

Union Republic People's Commissariats of the USSR direct and control the work of the Union Republic People's Commissariats bearing the same name.[13] They have a right to address directly any local organ of the Union Republic People's Commissariats as well as People's Commissariats of an autonomous SSR bearing the same name. Thus the directive of the USSR Council of People's Commissars (January 6, 1930)[14] granted the USSR People's Commissariat for Agriculture the right to communicate directly with agricultural organs in the rural districts on matters within the sphere of the immediate jurisdiction of the USSR People's Commissariat for Agriculture. On other matters involving the jurisdiction of Union Republics, the USSR People's Commissariat of Agriculture communicates with local organs through Union Republic People's Commissariats for Agriculture. When it communicates directly with local organs, the USSR People's Commissariat for Agriculture must forthwith inform the Union Republic People's Commissariat of Agriculture thereof.

The relations between Union Republic People's Commissariats and those of autonomous Soviet Socialist Republics are similarly organized. According to the constitutions of autonomous republics down to 1936, their People's Commissariats were divided into (1) autonomous and (2) unified. *Autonomous* Commissariats were those bearing the same name as Republic People's Commissariats of the Union Republics. These were immediately subordinate to the Central Executive Committee and its Presidium and to the Council of the People's Commissars of the autonomous republic, and actively carried into effect their directives, decrees and instructions. *Unified* autonomous Republic People's Commissariats included People's Commissariats bearing the same name as unified Union Republic People's Commissariats. The unified, autonomous Republic People's Commissariats, subordinate to the Central Executive Committee and its Presidium and to the Council of People's Commissars of the autonomous SSR, developed the directives of the corresponding unified People's Commissariats of Union Republics, formulating the measures of the latter, as a

---

[13] Art. 5 of the regulation last cited.
[14] Cz. 1930, No. 3, Art. 44.

rule, through the Central Executive Committee or the Council of People's Commissars of the autonomous republic.[15]

The old constitutions of autonomous republics thus developed a difference between autonomous and unified People's Commissariats along the line of their subordination, the former being subordinate only to supreme organs of the autonomous republic, whereas the latter were under dual subordination. In practice, however, this difference was gradually leveled out and in the final analysis the principle of dual subordination was extended to all People's Commissariats of autonomous republics. In declining to differentiate People's Commissariats of autonomous republics as "autonomous" or "unified," new constitutions effected an arrangement in complete accord with reality and established for both commissariats subordination alike to the Council of People's Commissars of the autonomous republic as well as to the Union Republic People's Commissariats bearing the same name.

3. The system of People's Commissariats

People's Commissariats were instituted on the day following the overthrow of the bourgeois-landowner Provisional Government. The decree of the Second All-Russian Council of Soviets (adopted October 26/November 8, 1917) says: "Superintendence of separate branches of state life is entrusted to commissions, whose structure must assure that the program proclaimed by the Congress—in close union with mass organizations of men and women workers, sailors, soldiers, peasants, and clerks—is put into practice." [16] These commissions, headed by members of the worker-peasant government, were the first People's Commissariats of the Soviet state. The Second All-Russian Congress of Soviets instituted the thirteen following People's Commissariats: trade and industry, justice, posts and telegraphs, labor, foreign affairs, provisioning, finances, popular education, railroads, internal affairs, agriculture, and nationalities, and the committee for military and naval affairs.[17] Soon after this Second Congress (December 2/15, 1917), the Supreme Council of National Economy was created.[18] The All-Russian Extraordinary Commission to contend with counterrevolution, speculation, and crimes in office was instituted December 7/20, 1917.

During November and December, 1917, People's Commissariats for State Control, State Welfare, Properties of the Republic and for Local Self-Government were formed (the two last being liquidated shortly after-

---

[15] See, for example, Arts. 25, 26, and 64 of the (1926) Constitution of the Chuvash Autonomous SSR.
[16] Cy. 1917, No. 1, Art. 1.
[17] Cy. 1917, No. 1, Art. 1.
[18] Cy. 1917, No. 5, Art. 83.

wards). In the beginning of 1918 the People's Commissariat for State Welfare was renamed the People's Commissariat for Social Insurance [19] for the reason that its previous name did not in fact correspond with the socialist understanding of the problems of social security. While the first Soviet Constitution was being worked out, the People's Commissariat for Railroads was renamed the People's Commissariat for Communications, in view of the prospective subordination thereto of all forms of transportation. During the course of two years, the People's Commissariat for Communications actually unified within its jurisdiction railways, water transportation, and paved and unpaved roads of state-wide importance. The Committee for Military and Naval Affairs was divided into two independent People's Commissariats: one for military affairs and one for naval affairs. In addition a new People's Commissariat for Health was created, replacing the Council of Medical Collegia—hitherto the supreme organ for the preservation of health in the Republic.

The 1918 Constitution of the RSFSR recorded eighteen People's Commissariats: foreign affairs, military affairs, naval affairs, internal affairs, justice, labor, social security, education, posts and telegraphs, nationalities, finance, communications, agriculture, trade and industry, provisioning, state control, the Supreme Council of National Economy, and public health. The Soviet state system of People's Commissariats thus took form during the first period of the October Socialist Revolution.

The People's Commissariat for Nationalities, headed by Stalin, played an extraordinarily important part in building and strengthening the Soviet federative state. Its activity was so manifold and so broad as to embrace all branches of administration amongst the nationalities. Accordingly, during the first period the structure of the Commissariat for Nationalities included departments of labor, agriculture, education, the press, military affairs, social security, forestry, and so on, as well as Armenian, White Russian, Hebrew, Latvian, Mussulman (later renamed Tatar-Bashkir) and Polish Commissariats and the following departments: Caucasian mountaineers, German, Kirghiz, Ukrainian, Chuvash, Estonian, Kalmyk, South Slav, Czechoslovak (to deal with the Czech prisoners of war), Votyak, and Komi (Zyrian).

The People's Commissariat for Nationalities addressed political proclamations to the peoples of Russia and the oppressed peoples beyond the border, exerting enormous influence upon the international movement for the emancipation of nationalities. It created the mechanism, and prepared nationalist cadres and all else that was essential, for the organization of the new Soviet Republics. It took part in the preparation and conclusion

[19] Cy. 1918, No. 34, Art. 453.

of compacts with neighbor states and between Soviet Republics. It promoted measures to assure the development of culture, national in form, socialist in content, and of production forces in the borderlands. Not infrequently it advanced the mobilization of military forces to repel counter-revolution among the national minorities, and so on.

With the formation of Soviet nationalist republics, the character of the work of the People's Commissariat for Nationalities changed somewhat, inasmuch as several branches of administration were transferred to the appropriate People's Commissariats of these republics. But even thereafter, the People's Commissariat for Nationalities exerted great influence on the activity of other People's Commissariats, directing that activity to the service of the organized national republics and assuring that the enfranchised peoples would enjoy genuine equality of rights. All the most important economic and cultural measures were promoted by individual People's Commissariats with its concurrence. It was liquidated by the directive (of July 7, 1923) of the All-Russian Central Executive Committee, having performed its fundamental and historical task in preparing the formation of the national republics and unifying them into the USSR.

A special place in the system of the central state mechanism was occupied by the Supreme Council for National Economy. Its task was to make effectual the economic dictatorship of the worker class and to centralize all the efforts of the country in its struggle against collapse and to crush the exploiters resisting revolutionary measures in the economic field. It was charged with organizing the national economy and the state finances, working out general rules and plans to regulate economic life, and bringing into accord and unity the activity of local and central regulating institutions. "All existing institutions for the regulation of economy are subordinate to the Supreme Council for National Economy. To it is granted the right to reform them." [20]

At the beginning of its existence, the Supreme Council for National Economy was a People's Commissariat of a special type in that its jurisdiction touched many branches of government. This was reflected also in its structure. At that period it included the following departments: agriculture and rural consumption, transportation, trade, state economy and banks, the economic division of the All-Russian Central Executive Committee, the All-Russian Council of Worker Control, the Committee of Economic Policy, a special council for defense, a special council for fuel, and nine subdivisions for separate branches of industry. It enjoyed broad powers. It was granted the right of confiscation, of requisition, and of sequestration. It had power to compel the establishment of worker control over the means

[20] Decree of December 2/15, 1917; Cy. 1917, No. 5, Art. 83.

and processes of production in different branches of industry and trade and to develop other measures in the field of production and distribution of industrial output and of state finances. Enjoying these plenary powers, the Council effectuated the nationalization of all industry, developed the first decisive measures to expropriate the expropriators, and made the first use of the principle of planning as a means of bringing the active influence of the state to bear upon economy. The civil war required the centralization of the entire national economy and its subordination to the interests of defending the October conquests. This the Supreme Council successfully accomplished by creating within its own structure the central and chief administrations for the various branches of industry. These managed directly all the enterprises of the Republic and had authority over the distribution of industrial output.

From 1920 on, in connection with the improved situation on the fronts and the new problems of economic building on principles of utilizing local self-help to the very utmost, all industry was divided into three groups: (1) the most important and the biggest enterprises, governed directly by the central administrations; (2) enterprises governed on principles of dual subordination: (*a*) to the central administrations and (*b*) to the local councils of national economy; and (3) enterprises completely within the jurisdiction of local councils of national economy. Parallel with these, there was a progressive narrowing of the functions of the Supreme Council for National Economy. By the beginning of 1920 it had finally become a center for the administration of industry alone, retaining only those divisions and central administrations which bore an industrial character.

Many brilliant pages were written into the history of the proletarian state by the People's Commissariat for Food Supply. While the civil war and hunger were raging, it was invoked to advance the work of the dictatorship of food supply as against the apathy of the rural bourgeoisie, deaf to the groans of the hungering workers and the poverty-stricken villagers. During this period, the consumer guberniyas were going hungry while the producer guberniyas contained great stores of grain which the kulaks, who counted on forcing the state once again to raise grain prices, concealed instead of bringing it out to the collecting stations, at the same time promoting frenzied speculation and selling the grain at fabulous figures.

The decree of the All-Russian Central Executive Committee of May 19, 1918,[21] provided: "An end must be put to this contumacy of the village kulaks—greedy and opulent as they are. The grainmasters' coercion of the

21 Cy. 1918, No. 35, Art. 468.

hungering poor must be answered by coercion of the bourgeoisie." This decree established the principle of the Soviet policy of provision-supply: the state grain monopoly, the crushing of the kulaks, and the assurance that the toilers would be supplied with provisions. A characteristic feature of the period of war communism was a provision assessment in kind in order to accumulate stores of grain. To carry these principles into effect, the People's Commissariat for Food Supply was endowed with extraordinary powers—the right to issue obligatory directives going beyond the ordinary bounds of its jurisdiction—as to the supply of provisions; the right to abrogate orders of local organs of food supply and other institutions in conflict with its own plans and actions; the right to require of all departments unimpeachable and immediate execution of its precepts; the right to apply the force of arms if the requisition of grain and other produce were resisted, and so on. Resting upon the masses, and broadly drawing workers and the poor people of the country into the administration, it carried its tasks to completion. By decree of May 27, 1918,[22] special detachments of workers, the most conscientious and most highly recommended by professional and Soviet associations for organizational-agitation work in the rural districts, were formed under the organs of supply for the struggle with the kulaks and for the storage of grain. By decree of June 11, 1918,[23] committees of the poor were instituted in the country to distribute grain and to cooperate with local organs of supply in taking grain surpluses from the kulaks and the wealthy. These mass organs united many thousands of toilers and helped the People's Commissariat for Food Supply to solve a disproportionately difficult task: to conquer hunger, to furnish bread to the Red Army, and to save millions of workers and poor folk from starvation.

In the beginning of 1921 the provision tax replaced the provision assessment in kind, and a new problem was presented, to develop agriculture on the basis of freer management of their own economic resources by the farmers and increased productivity of peasant labor. In this connection, Lenin required a change in the content and character of the work of the People's Commissariat for Food Supply, saying at the Tenth Party Congress:

We know the mechanism of the Commissariat for Food Supply. We know—by comparing it with others—that it is one of our best mechanisms. Being such, it must be preserved. But the mechanism must be made to subserve policy. What the devil good does it do for us to have the most superb mechanism for attaining food if we don't know how to harmonize our relations with the peasants? And if we don't, this most superb mechanism will serve Denikin and

[22] Cy. 1918, No. 38, Art. 498.
[23] Cy. 1918, No. 43, Art. 524.

Kolchak, and not our own class. When a decisive change—elasticity, a skillful modification—of policy is required, leaders must understand it.[24]

Accordingly, the mechanism of the People's Commissariat for Food Supply was reconstructed.

Such are the basic elements characterizing the reorganization of a number of the most important People's Commissariats which had been created by the Second All-Russian Congress of Soviets.

Prior to the formation of the USSR, there had been structural changes in the People's Commissariats in response to the conditions of the period of war communism and, later, to the transition to the New Economic Policy. By decree of June 11, 1920, the Council of People's Commissars reorganized the People's Commissariat for Trade and Industry into the People's Commissariat for Foreign Trade.[25] By reason of the creation of the Supreme Council for National Economy, in whose hands was the unified administration of industry, the People's Commissariat for Industry and Trade retained immediate jurisdiction only of matters connected with trade regulation, and trade activity had almost completely died out in the conditions of civil war and war communism. The function of distributing products was effectuated through the mechanisms of the People's Commissariat for Food Supply and cooperation. In essence, the role of the People's Commissariat for Industry and Trade dwindled to direction of foreign trade and nothing more.

In February, 1920, the People's Commissariat of State Control was reorganized into the People's Commissariat of Worker-Peasant Inspection.[26] During the first period, it had fulfilled functions solely of control—nothing more than formal verification of the money documents of Soviet institutions —which was inadequate and not responsive to the problems of the Soviet state. Accordingly, as early as 1919 (by decree of the All-Russian Central Executive Committee of April 12), the tasks of assuring factual control, and of broad attraction thereto of workers and peasants, were put forward before it "in order that State Control may cease to be an organ of formal control and become an organ of People's Socialist Control—an organ for the accumulation of experience in socialist building and for the constant improvement of the entire mechanism of Soviet authority." [27] Later decrees made these problems precise and concrete. The order of March 20, 1920, charged the People's Commissariat of Worker-Peasant Inspection to prosecute the struggle with bureaucracy and red tape in Soviet institutions, to

[24] Lenin (Russian ed.), Vol. XXVI, p. 248.
[25] Cy. 1920, No. 53, p. 235.
[26] Cy. 1920, No. 16, p. 94.
[27] Cy. 1919, No. 12, Art. 122.

intensify factual control by investigations and verification of the activity of institutions from the viewpoint of results actually achieved, to eliminate wastefulness and duplication in work, to simplify the state mechanism, and so on.

Lenin considered that the chief task of worker-peasant inspection was to collaborate in every possible way with the Soviet state in strengthening the union of worker class and peasantry. In his article, "The Best—Even if There Be Less of It," [28] he wrote:

We must try to build a state wherein workers—retaining their guidance of the peasants and the confidence of the peasants—would, with the utmost economy, hunt out of their social relationships every trace of excesses of any sort. We must reduce our state apparatus to the point of maximum economy. We must hunt out of it all traces of the excesses whereof so many remained from tsarist Russia—from its bureaucratic-capitalist mechanism.

Lenin's demands for a decisive struggle with bureaucracy and for maximum economy are reflected in all the decrees concerning worker-peasant inspection and were the foundation of its activity. To the end of enhancing its authority and strengthening its mechanism, the Twelfth Congress of the Bolshevik Worker-Peasant Party established a close connection between worker-peasant inspection and the Central Committee of the Bolshevik Worker-Peasant Party.[29]

At the end of 1919, in view of the close and immediate connection between tasks of social security and those in the sphere of the protection of labor and social insurance, the People's Commissariat for Social Insurance was merged with the People's Commissariat for Labor. Soon, however (in April, 1920),[30] by reason of the increasing scope of the work and complexity of the functions, the People's Commissariat for Labor was divided into two independent People's Commissariats, the People's Commissariat for Labor and the People's Commissariat for Social Insurance. Specifically, there was at this period a broad expansion of the social insurance of Red Army men and their families, requiring special attention. After the division, the People's Commissariat of Social Insurance was in charge of social insurance, retaining its jurisdiction until 1922 when social insurance was again turned over to the People's Commissariat for Labor.

The transition to the New Economic Policy and the tasks of strengthening revolutionary legality posed the associated question of reorganizing the All-Russian Extraordinary Commission (the Cheka). At the Ninth

[28] Lenin (Russian ed.), Vol. XXVII, p. 417.
[29] Cf. *The Bolshevik All-Union Communist Party in Resolutions* (4th ed), Pt. I, pp. 562–568.
[30] Cy. 1920, No. 28, Art. 137.

Congress of Soviets, Lenin called it "our weapon of assault upon innumerable conspiracies—innumerable attempts against Soviet authority.'[31]

Without such an institution, the authority of the toilers cannot exist so long as there are exploiters in the world who have no desire to tender workers and peasants on a platter their rights as landowners, their rights as capitalists. . . . But at the same time we say definitely that it is necessary to subject the All-Russian Extraordinary Commission to reform, to define its functions and jurisdiction, and to restrict its work to political tasks. We are now confronted with the problem of developing civil turnover—necessitated by the New Economic Policy—and this requires greater revolutionary legality. Everybody knows that we would have been pedantically playing at—and not making—a revolution, if we had then put this as our very first task in the midst of military attack—when they were holding the Soviet authority by the throat. The further we enter upon conditions of stable and firm authority, and the further civil turnover develops, the more insistently must there be advanced the strong watchword of effectuating greater revolutionary legality—and the scope of an institution giving conspirators back blow for blow becomes thereby narrower.[32]

In accordance with these instructions of Lenin, the Ninth Congress of Soviets authorized "the Presidium of the All-Russian Central Executive Committee within the briefest possible time to revise the Regulation Concerning the All-Russian Extraordinary Commission and its organs in the direction of reorganizing them, reducing their jurisdiction and intensifying the principles of revolutionary legality."[33] On this basis, the All-Russian Central Executive Committee (February 6, 1922)[34] decreed the reorganization of the All-Russian Extraordinary Commission into the State Political Administration, with Dzerzhinsky, a People's Commissar for Internal Affairs, as president, and defined its position as an organ operating under the People's Commissariat for Internal Affairs. Theretofore the Extraordinary Commission had been under the Council of People's Commissars.

The building of the system of People's Commissariats of the Union and the reorganization of the system of Union Republic People's Commissariats began with the formation of the USSR. The first Union Constitution (1924) provided (Arts. 51 and 52) for ten People's Commissariats of the USSR, including five All-Union commissariats: the People's Commissariat for Foreign Affairs, the People's Commissariat for Military and Naval Affairs, the People's Commissariat for Foreign Trade, the People's Commissariat for Transport, and the People's Commissariat for Posts and Telegraphs. In addition, it provided for five unified People's Commissariats:

[31] Lenin (Russian ed.), Vol. XXVII, p. 139.
[32] Ibid., p. 140.
[33] Cy. 1922, No. 4, Art. 42.
[34] Cy. 1922, No. 16, Art. 160.

the Supreme Council for National Economy, the People's Commissariat for Food Supply, the People's Commissariat for Labor, the People's Commissariat for Finance, and the People's Commissariat of Worker-Peasant Inspection.

Furthermore, to the end of unifying the revolutionary exertions of the Union Republics in the struggle with political and economic counter-revolution, espionage and banditry, the Constitution instituted the Unified State Political Administration (OGPU) under the USSR Council of the People's Commissars, granting its president the right of a consultative voice in that council. Through its delegates in the Union Republic Councils of People's Commissars, the USSR OGPU was charged with direction of the work of local organs of the State Political Administration (GPU).[35]

Union Republic constitutions, brought into conformity with the first Union Constitution, provided for eleven People's Commissariats, including five unified People's Commissariats: the Supreme Council for National Economy, and the People's Commissariats for Internal Trade, Finance, Labor, and Worker-Peasant Inspection; and six Republic People's Commissariats: Internal Affairs, Justice, Education, Public Health, Agriculture, and Social Security.[36]

Comparing the structure of People's Commissariats according to the first Union Constitution with their present structure, Molotov, at the first session of the Supreme Soviet of the USSR, said: "Since that time much has changed in the life of the country. The range of state work has greatly increased." [37]

The number of People's Commissariats in the USSR has increased to twenty-one, and in the majority of Union Republics to fourteen. Their structure has changed in conformity with the new tasks confronting the proletarian state.

Rehabilitation of the national economy, its reconstruction, industrialization of the country, collectivization of agriculture, strengthening of the defense of the USSR in the face of capitalist encirclement—all this demanded new organizational forms, the uninterrupted improvement of the machinery of state, and greater differentiation of state management. In all this reorganization, touching almost all branches of economy and administration, the vast growth of national economy and culture was most brilliantly reflected.

At the beginning of 1932 the administration of industry was reformed by the reorganization of the Supreme Council for National Economy into

[35] The USSR Constitution of 1924, Arts. 61, 62.
[36] Cf. the RSFSR Constitution (1925) and White Russian Constitution (1927).
[37] *First Session of the Supreme Soviet of the USSR* (1938), stenographic report, p. 109.

the All-Union People's Commissariat for Heavy Industry—light industry, forest industry, and timber manufacturing industry being withdrawn from its jurisdiction.[38] Two new commissariats were formed to direct the branches so segregated: the All-Union People's Commissariat for Forest Industry and the Unified People's Commissariat for Light Industry. The chief purpose of this reorganization was thus to eliminate the existing unwieldiness, and the inevitably ensuing remoteness from the associations and the enterprises, of the direction by the central institutions. The creation of the new People's Commissariats assured rationalization and a certain specialization in industrial administration by guaranteeing the feasibility of all exertions being focused upon the expansion of heavy industry at the necessary rate.

In the same year (1932), in connection with the reorganization of the Supreme Council for National Economy of the USSR and the creation of a Unified People's Commissariat for Light Industry of the USSR, the Union Republic Supreme Councils for National Economy were reorganized into Unified People's Commissariats for Light Industry. In order to concentrate the attention of the USSR People's Commissariat for Light Industry upon the direction of the big enterprises playing a leading part in light industry, about forty of the big enterprises and trusts were transferred to it, and around eighty enterprises hitherto under its jurisdiction were subordinated to local authorities, with the result that the USSR People's Commissariat for Light Industry ceased to be a unified commissariat and became instead an All-Union Commissariat. After such a redistribution of enterprises, the Union Republic People's Commissariats for Light Industry were reorganized (in 1934) into Republic People's Commissariats for Local Industry. To them was transferred all the local industry within the system of People's Commissariats for Heavy Industry, Forest Industry and Food Industry. This reorganization was based on directives of the Seventeenth Party Congress at which Stalin proposed "to unbind local Soviet industry— to make it feasible for it to manifest initiative in producing goods for mass consumption, and to render it all possible aid with raw materials and resources." [39]

After the adoption of the Stalin Constitution, the All-Union People's Commissariats for Forest Industry and Light Industry were reorganized into Union Republic People's Commissariats. This attested the strengthening of Union Republics and further expansion of their self-help.

At the Extraordinary Eighth All-Union Congress of Soviets the question as to the creation of a People's Commissariat for Defense Industry was decided, inasmuch as this industry, growing stupendously during the years

[38] Cz. 1932, No. 1, Art. 4.
[39] Stalin, *Questions of Leninism* (10th Russian ed.), p. 559.

of the Stalin five-year periods and being a convergence point of the most advanced technique, needed special organization and special direction. Stalin, in his report to the Congress on the draft Constitution of the USSR, analyzing the amendment and amplifications produced during the consideration of the draft by all the people, said:

The amendment of Article 77 goes further. It requires the organization of a new All-Union People's Commissariat—the People's Commissariat for Defense Industry. I think this amendment should likewise be adopted. The time is ripe to segregate our defense industry and to have for it the appropriate form of a People's Commissariat. It seems to me that this could not do otherwise than improve the defense of our country.[40]

The Extraordinary Eighth All-Union Congress of Soviets adopted this amendment and a directive of the USSR Central Executive Committee (December 8, 1936) created the All-Union People's Commissariat of Defense Industry.[41]

In August, 1937, the People's Commissariat of Machinery Building was created by separating it—after the affirmation of the Stalin Constitution—from the structure of the People's Commissariat for Heavy Industry.[42] Assigning the reason for the decision of the Central Executive Committee and the Council of People's Commissars of the USSR concerning its organization, Molotov said (at the first session of the Supreme Soviet): "Only with the aid of a special People's Commissariat can the swiftly expanding machinery building—in whose further accelerated development all branches of the national economy have so vital an interest—be correctly organized under present circumstances." [43] On the other hand, "the People's Commissariat for Heavy Industry—prior to the separation of mechanical engineering therefrom—had become a disproportionately big organization, with a vast quantity of swiftly developing branches of industry." [44]

The reorganization of the administration of transport was carried through in 1931. The enormous growth of freight turnover associated with the development of national economy, the protection of rail transportation from demands which the reconstruction period made upon it, and the extremely weak utilization and development of water transport made it necessary to reorganize the People's Commissariat of Transport, splitting off from it a separate All-Union People's Commissariat of Water Transport.[45] Thereby the forces and the resources of the People's Commissariat

[40] Stalin, *Report on the Draft of the USSR Constitution* (1936), p. 42.
[41] Cz. 1936, No. 63, Art. 461.
[42] Cz. 1937, No. 57, Art. 239.
[43] *First Session of the USSR Supreme Soviet* (stenographic report), p. 110.
[44] *Ibid.*
[45] Cz. 1931, No. 8, Art. 85.

of Transport were concentrated on bettering the work of transportation on land, by rail and otherwise. Soon, however, transport otherwise than by rail was also separated from the jurisdiction of the People's Commissariat of Transport and transferred (by directive of the Central Executive Committee and Council of People's Commissars of the USSR of June 3, 1931) to an independent central administration of paved and unpaved roads and auto transport.[46]

Defense of the country was reorganized at the end of 1937 by dividing the People's Commissariat for Defense into two independent People's Commissariats: the People's Commissariat for Defense and the People's Commissariat for the Battle Fleet.[47] Molotov said at the first session of the USSR Supreme Soviet:

It must be admitted that this is both an extremely important and extremely pressing question. We have now four battle fleets—the Baltic fleet, the Black Sea fleet, the Arctic fleet, and the Pacific fleet. . . . We must reckon with the fact that ours is a big country—washed by seas for a vast expanse, which constantly reminds us of the fact that our fleet must be strong and powerful. We are put in mind of this also by the capitalist countries—by the enormous naval construction they have carried out during recent years. . . .

The mighty Soviet power must have a sea and ocean fleet commensurate with out interests and worthy of our greatness. In order to organize this fleet with its complex technical equipment, its mighty naval ordnance, and a naval air arm worthy of the Soviet fleet, and to foster, in Soviet fashion, numerous cadres of qualified sailors and marine technicians, we need a new People's Commissariat, a People's Commissariat for the Battle Fleet. Precisely because our Red Army has grown, and because here also, enormous everyday work is indispensable for its further strengthening, for its further technical equipment, significantly better work is essential for its fostering—in the Bolshevik way—of Red Army men and commanders devoted to their country. Precisely because direction of this whole matter in the Red Army is confronted with enormous problems, and the war fleet demands special attention concentrated upon itself, we deem it necessary to have, side by side with the People's Commissariat for Defense, a People's Commissariat of the Battle Fleet.

Problems in the sphere of national communications have also multiplied and state activity in that field has been notably extended in scope. The People's Commissariat for Posts and Telegraphs acquired jurisdiction over the vast radio-telegraph economy (created during the years of the country's industrialization) in addition to that over posts and telegraphs.

[46] Cz. 1931, No. 35, Art. 258.
[47] Cz. 1938, No. 1, Art. 1. In 1934 (Cz. 1934, No. 33, Art. 256) the name of the latter Commissariat had been changed to People's Commissariat for Defense, emphasizing the Red Army's defensive function.

The name of this commissariat has ceased to reflect the scale and the content of its work and so in 1932 it was renamed the USSR People's Commissariat of Communications.[48]

The central mechanism having authority over matters of supply, collection of produce contracted to the state, and trade, passed through a very great number of reorganizations. The People's Commissariat for Food Supply contemplated by the first Union Constitution was abolished soon after the confirmation of the constitution in May, 1924. "At the present time," in the words of a directive of the Central Executive Committee and Council of People's Commissars of the USSR of May 9, 1924, "when we are passing from the natural taxation of agriculture to the imposition of a money tax thereon, and when money relationships have so developed that the population can effectively obtain supply through the market, the further existence of the People's Commissariat for Food Supply becomes superfluous." [49]

As early as July 17, 1923, the Commission for Internal Trade was instituted under the USSR Labor and Defense Council,[50] its creation being due to problems of organizing state regulation of the country's goods turnover and the market relationships called into being by the New Economic Policy. In the sequel, these problems so expanded as to necessitate the formation of a plenipotentiary organ with jurisdiction over trade matters. Such an organ was created in May, 1924, by reorganizing the Commission for Internal Trade into the Unified People's Commissariat of Internal Trade of the USSR.[51]

In 1925, with the expansion of the country's socialist industrialization and the indispensability of broadening the importation of equipment and of greater flexibility for the manipulation of resources for internal consumption and for export, the People's Commissariat of Foreign Trade and the People's Commissariat of Internal Trade were unified into one All-Union People's Commissariat of Internal and External Trade,[52] the new People's Commissariat enjoying the rights of a unified commissariat as regards the regulation of internal trade and the position of Union Republic People's Commissariats for Internal Trade being incidentally changed. In respect of foreign trade, the latter played the part of representatives of the All-Union People's Commissariat of Trade, while as to internal trade they acted as unified commissariats. They were further charged with a number of new

[48] Cz. 1932, No. 5, Art. 32.
[49] *Herald of the Central Executive Committee, the Council of People's Commissars, and the Labor and Defense Council* (1924), No. 5, Art. 163.
[50] *Ibid.*
[51] *Ibid.*, Art. 164.
[52] Cz. 1925, No. 78, Art. 590.

functions as to external trade, with the result that the need for the All-Union People's Commissariat of Trade to have its own mandatories in the republics declined. Inasmuch as the activity of Republic People's Commissariats of Internal Trade was no longer limited solely to the sphere of internal trade, they were given a new designation—People's Commissariats of Trade.

At the beginning of 1930, the government put systematization of the furnishing of food products and widely used goods to the population before the People's Commissariat of Trade as its basic task [53] and, as a practical assurance of this, the entire food industry of the Supreme Council for National Economy was subordinated to it.[54] The increased turnover in the country's internal and external trade, the swift growth of the turnover of socialized goods, the intensive proscription of the private proprietor, the increased emphasis upon the principle of planning in the sphere of trade, the new and advanced methods of storing agricultural products (understandings with the state, and so on), and the necessity of systematizing centralized supply made the tasks of the People's Commissariat extraordinarily complicated, necessitating the dichotomy of the People's Commissariat of Trade (at the end of 1930) into two independent People's Commissariats, that of Foreign Trade and that of Supply, the former being an All-Union People's Commissariat, and the latter a unified People's Commissariat.[55]

In 1931 the process of centralizing food enterprises within the jurisdiction of the People's Commissariat for Supply was completed, and the groundwork for their further development, and for the transformation of the food industry into an independent branch of national economy, thereby laid. As early as 1934 the food industry was an extremely big and complicated agglomerate of the national economy. To administer this branch of economy, confronted as it was by the enormous problems of satisfying the country's expanded demands for food products, it was necessary to organize a special People's Commissariat. At the same time, there had been radical changes in the sphere of supply. The successes of socialist industrialization and of collectivization of agriculture made it possible for the population to be supplied by the expanded kolkhoz and Soviet trade rather than by centralized distribution. The best solution of this problem required the creation of a new People's Commissariat, and to this end the People's Commissariat of Supply was separated (in the middle of 1934) into a Unified People's Commissariat of Internal Trade (renamed at the first session of the USSR Supreme Soviet the People's Commissariat for Trade), and the All-Union

---

[53] Cz. 1930, No. 17, Art. 181.
[54] Cz. 1930, No. 33, Art. 263.
[55] Cz. 1930, No. 56, Art. 592.

People's Commissariat for Food Industry [56] reorganized under the Stalin Constitution into a Union Republic People's Commissariat.

Still earlier (in 1932), the Committee for the Collection of Produce, contracted to the state, under the Labor Defense Council—later reorganized [57] into the committee bearing the same name and under the USSR Council of People's Commissars—had been charged [58] with the collection of agricultural products. Its basic task was to guide the entire work of putting into operation the directive of January 19, 1933, of the USSR Council of People's Commissars and the Central Committee of the All-Russian Communist Party (of Bolsheviks) as to the obligation of kolkhozes and individual peasant proprietors to supply grain to the state. To fulfill this task, the Committee for Produce Collection was expanded into a big organization.

In its present shape the Committee for Agricultural Produce Collection, under the USSR Council of People's Commissars, is already a typical People's Commissariat organization in the full sense, with its republic, territorial, and district organs as well as its area organs. It is in reality a great All-Union People's Commissariat for which, as you know, there is plenty of work. The organization of the matter of stores in the vast territory of the Union is a complicated and extensive affair, wherein are still more than a few serious shortcoming, the most speedy improvement of which is in the interests of the whole state as well as of agriculture itself—of the kolkhozes and their members.

A People's Commissariat which would bring genuine harmony into this matter, improving its local and central mechanism and responsible for the fulfillment of the entire matter of stores, is what is necessary. This explains the proposal to create a People's Commissariat for Produce Collection.[59]

The first session of the USSR Supreme Soviet adopted this proposal and introduced the appropriate changes into the text of the USSR Constitution.[60]

The central mechanism of administering finances was reorganized pursuant to a decision of the first session of the USSR Supreme Soviet in 1938. In view of the vast growth and continuing expansion of the scale of the work carried on by the People's Commissariat for Finance and the necessity of giving the State Bank—an independent credit-finance organization— still greater independence, it was decided to separate the State Bank from the People's Commissariat for Finance, having charged it with the administration of credit in the Union, made it directly subordinate to the Council

[56] Cz. 1934, No. 40, Art. 313.
[57] Cz. 1933, No. 11, Art. 58.
[58] Cz. 1932, No. 10, Art. 53.
[59] Molotov at the first session of the USSR Supreme Soviet, stenographic report, p. 111.
[60] Ibid., p. 199.

of People's Commissars, and given to its manager a vote, with the right of a People's Commissar as in the Council.[61]

The question of changing the methods of administering agricultural production was put on the agenda at the end of 1929 by the tempestuous growth of the socialist sector of agriculture. The period of agricultural rehabilitation, which had preeminently solved the problem of raising the individual peasant economy, was expanded and completed with essential success with the forces—and on the scale—of the separate republics. But resolute acceleration of agricultural improvement could not, for reasons associated with the attack upon capitalist elements along the whole front and the organization of socialist reconstruction of agriculture, be accomplished by the former management methods. The intense production cooperation of the poorest and middle-class economies (growing from below), having embraced entire districts with complete collectivization, and the broadly developed building of sovkhozes demanded that the gigantic reconstruction of agriculture be under one direction. To this end, a whole series of All-Union organizations was created by the USSR Government during 1928 and 1929: the Grain Trust, the Cattle Breeder, the Sheep Breeder, the Agricultural Equipment, and others. These, however, needing a unifying and directing center, still fell far short of embracing all the administrative matters involved in agricultural production.

At the end of 1929 such a center was formed—the Unified People's Commissariat of Agriculture of the USSR.[62] This was to assure for agriculture a single direction and therewith to create all conditions essential to the development of initiative and self-help by the Union Republics with reference to socialist reconstruction of the village. However, the necessity of concentrating the work of the commissariat and of the entire system of land organs—principally on the administration of the kolkhozes and the growth of the sovkhoz sector—and the consequent problems of organizing the economic reinforcement of sovkhozes, dictated the decision to divide the People's Commissariat of Agriculture into smaller units. The administration of sovkhozes was taken out of its jurisdiction at the end of 1932 and entrusted to the newly formed All-Union People's Commissariat of State Grain and Livestock Farms. Sovkhozes of republic significance were left within the jurisdiction of Union Republic Councils of People's Commissars, and delegates of the All-Union People's Commissariat of Sovkhozes were charged with their administration. Under the Stalin Constitution, the People's Commissariat of Sovkhozes was reorganized into a Union Republic People's Commissariat.

[61] *Ibid.*, pp. 112, 113.
[62] Cz. 1929, No. 75, Art. 718.

The central mechanism of regulating labor has been radically reorganized. While the struggle with unemployment and the allocation of the unemployed—the fundamental tasks of the People's Commissariat for Labor and its organs in the rural areas—prior to the first five-year period waned with the liquidation of unemployment in the USSR, the change in the system and tariff of the labor payment—the abolition of wage leveling and depersonalization—introduced into the matter of labor payment new problems apparently beyond the power of the organs of the People's Commissariat for Labor. Their solution was achieved, not by these organs, but by economic organizations with the active participation of trade unions. After the people's enemies had been eliminated from the management of trade unions, and the latter had turned to face the tasks of production, the organizing role of professional associations grew immeasurably, and their functions in practice approximated those of the People's Commissariat for Labor. The question of broadening the rights of trade unions, of transferring to their jurisdiction social insurance, the protection of labor and, in general, all the functions exercised by the People's Commissariat of Labor, was solved by the directive of the Central Executive Committee and the Council of People's Commissars of the USSR and the All-Union Central Council of Trade Unions (June 23, 1923) [63] whereby the People's Commissariat of Labor, with all its organs, was merged with the mechanism of the All-Union Central Council of Trade Unions in the center and in the rural areas, and the latter was charged with the obligations of the People's Commissariat of Labor of the USSR and its organs.

The Seventeenth Party Congress issued instructions for the intensification of control over fulfillment of the decisions of the central organs of Soviet authority, and required a reorganization of the People's Commissariat of Worker-Peasant Inspection. In his report to the Congress, Stalin said:

Correct organization of control is of supreme importance to the central directive institutions. The organization of worker-peasant inspection is not such that it can satisfy the demands of that control, properly formulated. It had its rightful place when—some years ago—our economic work was simpler and less satisfactory and when it was possible to count on the feasibility of *inspecting* the work of all the People's Commissariats and of all the economic organizations. Now, however, our economic work has expanded and become more complex and it is no longer necessary or possible to *inspect* it from one center. Worker-peasant inspection should be accordingly reorganized. It is not inspection that we need now, but checking up on the work done by way of carrying out decisions of the center—*control* over the carrying out of decisions of the center. What we need

[63] Cz. 1933, No. 40, Art. 238.

now is not an organization which sets itself the universal task of inspecting all and sundry, but one which could concentrate all its attention on work of control—on checking up on what has been done in carrying out the decisions of central institutions of Soviet authority. Only a commission of Soviet control under the USSR Council of People's Commissars—operating according to instructions of the Council and having local representatives who are independent of the local organs—can be such an organization.[64]

Accordingly, a directive of the Central Executive Committee and Council of People's Commissars of the USSR (February 11, 1934)[65] reorganized the commission of fulfillment into the Commission of Soviet Control under the USSR Council of People's Commissars, and the People's Commissariat of Worker-Peasant Inspection was abolished as *functus officio*, its mechanism being transferred to the Commission of Soviet Control.

In the sphere of popular education the chief organizational measure was the redistribution of educational institutions as between the People's Commissariats, referable to the necessity of radical improvement in the preparation of cadres and of subordinating that preparation to the tasks of the expanding national economy. Prior to the first five-year period, professional and technical education was directed exclusively by the system of People's Commissariats for Education. By 1928, such method of administering the higher technical institutes had already ceased to answer the needs of the national economy. To the end of further harmonizing the formulation of technical education with the demands of industry and transportation, the Central Executive Committee and the Council of People's Commissars of the USSR, by directive of July 27, 1928,[66] transferred to the jurisdiction of the Supreme Council for National Economy and the People's Commissariat of Communications at first thirteen educational foundations, and later (by directive of July 23, 1930)[67] charged the appropriate People's Commissariats and economic associations with administration of higher educational institutions.

Only pedagogic institutions and universities remained within the jurisdiction of the People's Commissariat for Education.

Of the utmost significance was the creation (September 19, 1932)[68] of the Committee for Higher Technological Education, under the USSR Central Executive Committee, to exercise general direction over higher technical education in the USSR and systematic control over the quality of preparation of the higher technical cadres. On May 21, 1936, this com-

---

[64] Stalin, *Questions of Leninism* (10th Russian ed.), pp. 594, 595.
[65] Cz. 1934, No. 9, Art. 58.
[66] Cz. 1928, No. 46, Art. 409.
[67] Cz. 1930, No. 38, Art. 411.
[68] Cz. 1932, No. 68, Art. 409, subdivision VII.

mittee was liquidated in connection with the creation,[69] under the USSR Council of People's Commissars, of the All-Union Committee for Higher Education, whose direction extends to all the higher institutes of learning irrespective of the department within whose jurisdiction they are—except higher institutes of learning within the jurisdiction of the Committee for Art, the Committee for Physical Culture, and the Military Schools.[70]

Changes also occurred in the system of public-health organs. In the middle of 1936 the Union Republic People's Commissariat of Public Health was formed, as contemplated by the draft of the new Constitution.[71] Previously public health had been directed exclusively in each Union Republic. Under these conditions it was impossible to solve such essential questions as a single plan for making the country healthy, the creation of a single system of public-health organs, a network for the planned distribution of medical and prophylactic benefits, and a single administration for the preparation of cadres. It was impossible to carry on within the limits of separate republics a successful struggle with epidemic diseases, and difficult to assure medical service for the leading branches of the national economy.

In the sphere of administration of internal affairs, two large organizations were carried through during this period. The first of them was realized at the end of 1930, when Union Republic People's Commissariats of Internal Affairs were abolished.[72] Until their liquidation, these Commissariats had directed the militia, criminal investigations, the communal economy and places of detention, and had fulfilled numerous other functions (recording acts of civil status, struggling with elemental disasters, supervising the issuance of binding directives by local Soviets, and so forth). In the new stage, the People's Commissariats of Internal Affairs, having united the management of different branches of administration and economy not organically connected *inter se*, "became superfluous links of the Soviet mechanism." [73]

The period of intensified attack upon city and rural capitalist elements and of socialist reconstruction of the entire national economy makes it essential that the Soviet mechanism be better adapted to the tasks of socialist building. Communal economy requires a special, planned direction and strict linking thereof with the entire local economy of the country and the tempos of its industrialization; the sharpening of the class conflict demands from organs for the struggle with criminality and for guarding social security and revolutionary order—the

[69] Cz. 1936, No. 27, Art. 250.
[70] Cz. 1936, No. 52, Art. 424.
[71] Cz. 1936, No. 40, Art. 337.
[72] Directive of the Central Executive Committee and Council of People's Commissars of the USSR Concerning the liquidation of People's Commissariats of Internal Affairs: Cz. 1930, No. 60, Art. 640.
[73] *Ibid.*

militia and criminal investigation—greater discipline as well as greater independence in administering them.[74]

When the Union Republic People's Commissariats of Internal Affairs were liquidated, their functions in the field of communal economy were transferred to the Central Administrations of Communal Economy organized under Union Republic Councils of People's Commissars. Central administrations of militia and criminal investigations, organized under Union Republic Councils of People's Commissars, were charged with administration of militia and criminal investigation. The general administration of the correctional-labor policy and the organization and administration of places of detention were transferred to the jurisdiction of the People's Commissariats of Justice. Presidia of executive committees were charged with all the remaining functions of the People's Commissariat of Internal Affairs, including jurisdiction of records of civil status.

The All-Union People's Commissariat for Internal Affairs, differing substantially from previous Commissariats of the same name, was created July 10, 1934.[75] Its structure included OGPU, which had theretofore been under the USSR Council of People's Commissars. The judicial collegium of OGPU was abolished, and matters investigated by the People's Commissariat of Internal Affairs were cognizable by court organs. To apply measures of administrative repression (exile, deportation, confinement in correctional-labor camps, or expulsion from the USSR), a Special Council,[76] acting on the basis of a regulation affirmed by the Central Executive Committee of the USSR, was organized under the People's Commissariat for Internal Affairs. The USSR People's Commissariat of Internal Affairs is charged with: assuring revolutionary order and state security, guarding social (socialist) property, guarding the borders, and recording acts of civil status. In 1934–1936 the scale of work of this commissariat was broadened in connection with the transfer to its jurisdiction (October 27, 1934) of houses of incarceration, of solitary confinement, and the like [77] and of central administration of paved and unpaved roads—hitherto an independent organ; [78] by the formation (March 17, 1935) of a fire administration, by the creation (June 15, 1935) of an administration of state survey and cartography; [79] and by transfer to the Commissariat (June 10, 1936) of Immigration, with the abolition of the All-Union Immigration Committee under the USSR Council of People's Commissars.[80] With the introduction of the Stalin Constitution, the People's Commissariat for Internal Affairs became a Union Republic People's Commissariat.

[74] Ibid.
[75] Cz. 1934, No. 36, Art. 283.
[76] Cz. 1935, No. 11, Art. 84.
[77] Cz. 1934, No. 56, Art. 421.
[78] Cz. 1935, No. 56, Art. 452.
[79] Cz. 1935, No. 49, Art. 416.
[80] Cz. 1936, No. 37, Art. 322.

Soon after its separation from the old Union Republic People's Commissariats of Internal Affairs, which had been abolished in 1930, the central mechanism for the administration of communal economy was subjected to important reorganization. With the unprecedented industrial development, which had turned the USSR from an agrarian into an industrial country, came a colossal increase in the worker class, big new cities, and expanded old ones. At the same time there was unbroken improvement in the material position of the toilers and a swift increase in their demands as to culture and living conditions. In this state of affairs, the importance of the part which the city economy was called upon to play in serving these needs of the toilers was immeasurably increased. The July (1931) plenum of the Central Party Committee noted that "the condition of the city economy in the USSR, notwithstanding notable accomplishments, cannot satisfy the growing needs of the masses." [81] To effect decisive improvement of the economic-technical administration of communal economy, the plenum proposed to reorganize the chief administrations of communal economy into Republic People's Commissariats of Communal Economy, a directive realized by the Union Republics during the second half of 1931.

Finally, the reorganization of the central mechanism of justice should be noted. In 1936 the Union Republic People's Commissariat of Justice of the USSR was formed,[82] as contemplated by the draft of the new Constitution. The organs of the prosecutor's office and of investigation were separated from the system of Union Republic People's Commissariats of Justice, and made directly subordinate to the Public Prosecutor of the USSR. Two independent systems were thereby created: (1) the court system, headed by the People's Commissariat of Justice of the USSR and the Supreme Court of the USSR, and (2) the public-prosecution system headed by the Public Prosecutor of the USSR. The purpose of making the organs of the prosecutor's office into a separate and independent system was to assure the complete independence of the prosecutor's office from all local organs whatsoever. The creation of a single court system came about because of the tasks of strengthening socialist legality in the field of court work, and the intensified interrepublic economic and cultural bonds, requiring the utmost unification of legislation and court organization.

All these reorganizations complicated the existing structure of People's Commissariats. There are in the USSR at the present time the following (twenty-one) USSR People's Commissariats: (a) All-Union Commissariats (eleven) for defense, for the navy, for foreign affairs, for foreign trade, for transport, for water transport, for post, telegraph and radio, for heavy in-

---

[81] *The All-Union Communist Party (of Bolsheviks) in Resolutions*, Pt. 2, p. 77.
[82] Cz. 1936, No. 40, Art. 338.

dustry, for defense industry, for mechanical engineering, and for stores; and (*b*) Union Republic People's Commissariats (ten) for food industry, for light industry, for forest industry, for agriculture, for state grain and livestock farms, for finance, for trade, for internal affairs, for justice and for public health.

In Union Republics there are the following (fourteen) People's Commissariats: [83] (*a*) Union Republic People's Commissariats (ten) for food industry, for light industry, for forest industry, for agriculture, for state grain and livestock farms, for finance, for trade, fcr internal affairs, for justice, and for public health; and (*b*) Republic People's Commissariats (four) for education, for local industry, for communal economy, and for social security.

Constitutions of those Union Republics which include autonomous republics provide for the formation (in each of the latter) of the following (ten) People's Commissariats: for agriculture, for finance, for trade, for internal affairs, for justice, for public health, for education, for local industry, for communal economy, and for social security. These are contemplated by the constitutions of all twenty-two autonomous republics. In addition to this, and in accordance with the special characteristics of the economy of the autonomous SSR, and with the affirmation of the Supreme Soviet of the Union Republic, People's Commissariats for Food and for Light and Heavy Industry are created in autonomous republics.

4. *The jurisdiction of People's Commissariats and the official acts of People's Commissars*

People's Commissariats "direct the branch of state administration entrusted to them," in the words of the general definition of their jurisdiction contained in the Stalin Constitution. This jurisdiction is defined in greater detail in the laws concerning the respective People's Commissariats.[84] They fulfill the tasks with which they are charged (1) through direct connection with the objects of administration and (2) through their own local organs. The objects of their administration are managed through the direct instruction and teaching of executives (by councils, active Party members, Soviets and boards under the People's Commissariats, traveling instructors and in-

[83] The Azerbaijan and Armenian SSR have no People's Commissariat for state grain and livestock farms; the Turkmen SSR has no People's Commissariat for forest industry; and the Tadjik SSR has neither.

[84] Cf. Cz. 1937, No. 76, Art. 375 for the law concerning the People's Commissariat for Heavy Industry; Cp. 1938, No. 15, Art. 95 for that concerning the People's Commissariat for Trade; and Cp. 1938, No. 22, Art. 141 for that concerning the People's Commissariat for Food Industry.

spectors, and dispatchers, as well as by the issuance of orders and instructions and checking up on their fulfillment. The Party and the government
constantly demanded—and still demand—better and improved management by the People's Commissariats.

Down to 1934 the mechanism of the People's Commissariats was built
on the basis of the functional system, whereby administration was concentrated in tens of functional divisions with consequent weakness of operative
management, bureaucratic perversions, and red tape—a mechanism that was
unwieldy, and directive organs remote from the lower links and objects of
administration. The Seventeenth Party Congress sharply criticized this
system [85] and proposed the "liquidation of functionalism" [86] as a necessary
condition precedent to improved organization work and management. To
effectuate this directive, the government of the Union and the governments
of the Union Republics adopted a series of directives, pursuant to which
the mechanism of the People's Commissariats was radically rebuilt on the
production-territorial basis, superfluous links in the administration being
liquidated, staffs reduced, the new structure and functions of the mechanism defined, and so forth. This entire agglomeration of organization measures was directed at solving one of the basic problems posed by the Seventeenth Party Congress—to bring the organization work up to the level of
political management.

Appraising the results of the reorganization of People's Commissariats
at the second session of the Central Executive Committee of the USSR,
Molotov said (in 1936): [87]

We have achieved famous successes in the work of the People's Commissariats, but these successes cannot possibly be deemed adequate. . . . Our People's Commissariats for Industry and for Transportation, as well as the People's
Commissariat for Sovkhoz Building, should actually be turned into *production-
technical staffs* to manage their enterprises. . . . To become in reality a produc-
tion-technical staff to administer a given branch of industry or transportation
means taking upon one's self actual responsibility for the technique and economy of the enterprise.[88]

Until the time of the introduction of the Stalin Constitution, People's
Commissariats—according to the general law regarding them—published
(within the limits of their jurisdiction) directives, orders, instructions, circulars, edicts, and the like.[89] According to the Stalin Constitution, People's

[85] Cf. L. M. Kaganovich, *Organization Questions* (Party and Soviet Building), 1934.
[86] *The All-Union Communist Party (of Bolsheviks) in Resolutions*, Pt. 2, p. 592.
[87] Molotov, *Articles and Speeches* (1937), pp. 166, 183.
[88] *Ibid.*, p. 166.
[89] Cf. *Herald of the Central Executive Committee, the Council of People's Commissars
and the Labor and Defense Council* (1923), No. 10, Art. 299.

Commissars (within the limits of their jurisdiction) issue orders and instructions and verify their fulfillment. People's Commissars of the USSR issue these acts on the basis and in fulfillment of operative laws and of directives and orders of the USSR Government, Union Republic People's Commissars on the basis and in fulfillment of USSR and Union Republic laws, of directives and orders of the Council of People's Commissars of the USSR and of the Union Republic, and of orders and instructions of People's Commissars of Union Republic People's Commissariats of the USSR; Autonomous Republic People's Commissars on the basis and in fulfillment of the laws of USSR, of laws of the Union and autonomous republics, of directives and orders of the Council of People's Commissars of the USSR, of Councils of People's Commissars of the Union Republic and of the autonomous SSR, and of orders and instructions of Union Republic People's Commissars.

Acts published by People's Commissars may be divided into two groups: (1) the first and more numerous group consists of acts of an operative character, comprising most frequently a series of separate orders (each regulating only one given phenomenon—some single concrete case) and consequently operative but once and completely exhausted at the moment of their issuance. Examples include orders of People's Commissars for a bonus to separate categories of workers for doing model work—typical acts of single operation. They appraise the work of specific people and create a specific legal relationship (the right of the workers to receive a definite premium) operative as to one matter only and are therewith finally exhausted. (2) The second group consists of acts of People's Commissars establishing general rules and regulating whole groups of homogeneous cases and phenomena (rather than separate cases) and so bearing the character of general regulations. They are calculated upon the future and operate until they are abrogated or until they lose their force.

A concrete example will reveal the characteristic features of these acts: on November 1, 1937, the People's Commissariat for Transport published order No. 271 providing that "for exemplary work, keeping a normal temperature constantly in railroad cars, keeping the heating apparatus, the boiler rooms, and the heating system in excellent condition and cleanliness, stokers of boilers for the central heating of trains and the senior stove tenders of passenger cars standing on sidings are to be paid a premium of 10 to 15 per cent of their monthly salary." This order establishes the bonus arrangement for a whole category of workers and requires only the occurrence of specific conditions. Had there been an order rewarding definite workmen for model work, it would have created a definitive legal relationship, whereas this order merely provides for these relationships in the future, formulating the conditions under which they can arise. Concededly such conditions may not arise at all, in which event the order will create not a single definitive legal relationship. But if the conditions contemplated by it are present, this order must give rise to a series of legal relationships—that is to say, operate for a long period and many times; whereas an order of the first sort is an act of single operation, finally exhausting itself at the moment of its publication.

Another characteristic quality of acts. establishing general rules is that they are usually realized in concrete operative actions, either of the People's Commissariat itself or of its local organs. Thus, the instruction of the USSR People's Commissariat of Finance concerning the application of the agricultural tax law presupposes that local finance organs give orders for the payment by a specific taxpayer of a definite sum by way of tax at a definite time.

This classification of acts of People's Commissars derives entirely from the meaning of the Stalin Constitution, which establishes two types of departmental acts—orders and instructions, the former being preeminently operative acts, and the latter being rules of a general character.

People's Commissars issue acts either being commissioned thereto by the legislative organ or the government in a given separate case,[90] or upon their own initiative, to realize the tasks imposed upon them in managing branches of the administration.

Acts of People's Commissars embody rules as to how—in precise conformity with its sense and content—the conditions contemplated by the statute are assured and the method of its fulfillment defined, but they can neither develop nor interpret it. The Stalin Constitution charges the Presidium of the Supreme Soviet alone with the interpretation of statutes. No single organ (except the legislature itself) has the right to develop a statute, inasmuch as any sort of development of a statute is an essential change thereof and therefore essentially the prerogative of legislative authority exclusively. During recent years the number of acts issued by People's Commissariats has markedly decreased, as a consequence of the radical reorganization of methods of directing them developed on the basis of decisions of the Seventeenth Party Congress. That Congress proposed to pass from "general," abstract directives and numerous orders to operative decisions based on study and knowledge of the details and technique of the matter

[90] For example, the Directive of the Council of People's Commissars of the USSR (of Feb. 20, 1937) Concerning the Prohibition of the Departure and Recruiting of Volunteers for Spain (Cz. 1937, No. 14, Art. 42) charges the People's Commissariat for Internal Affairs, the People's Commissariat for Transportation, the People's Commissariat for Water Transportation, the People's Commissariat for Foreign Affairs and the People's Commissariat for Defense to issue instructions for the application of the directive.

involved.[91] By directive of March 15, 1934, the Central Executive Committee and the Council of People's Commissars of the USSR made it obligatory upon "directors of the All-Soviet and economic organs to cut down the giving of heterogeneous orders and commands, and to increase the everyday, vital guidance, instruction, teaching and practical help to directors of lower organs of the Soviet economic mechanism." [92]

The functional structure of the People's Commissariats and the presence of many intermediate links (and the consequent remoteness of the central mechanism from the objects of administration) inevitably resulted in a deluge of general circulars, orders, and instructions of every sort. The liquidation of functionalism—the reorganization of the mechanism upon the production-branch principle—resulted in an increase of vital direction—of immediate instruction—of lower organs and enterprises, proximately causing a falling-off in the number of orders (particularly those of a general character). At the present time operative acts occupy a basic place among the acts of People's Commissars.

In recent years there has been a particular intensification of control by the USSR Council of People's Commissars over the publication of departmental acts. All the People's Commissariats must furnish the Council with copies of all their acts issued in execution of corresponding directives of that Council as well as of other important orders and instructions. In 1934 that Council established the method whereby all instructions, rules, and explanations for the application of existing labor legislation are issued by the All-Union Central Council of Trade Unions (with the affirmation or previous sanction of the USSR Council of People's Commissars).[93] Although this method is not in form extended to People's Commissariats, it is in recent years becoming constantly more common for People's Commissariats to transmit their most important acts for affirmation by the USSR Council of People's Commissars. Instructions of People's Commissars, confirmed by that council, are published in the collection of USSR Government directives and orders, and have the force of that council's own directives.[94]

Until the Stalin Constitution was introduced, acts of People's Commissariats of the USSR could be suspended or abrogated by the Presidium of the Central Executive Committee of the USSR and the Council of People's Commissars of the USSR.[95] Acts of Union Republic People's Commissariats

[91] Cf. *The All-Union Communist Party (of Bolsheviks) in Resolutions*, Pt. 2, pp. 592–594.

[92] Cz. 1934, No. 15, Art. 103.

[93] *Concerning the Method of Issuing Instructions, Rules, and Clarifications as Applied to Labor Legislation:* Cz. 1934, No. 43, Art. 342.

[94] *The Collection of Statutes* (Cz.) for 1934–1937 includes thirty-six acts of departments of the USSR, affirmed by the USSR Council of People's Commissars.

[95] Cf. the USSR 1924 Constitution, Art. 58.

could be suspended or abrogated by the Central Executive Committee, and by Presidia of the Central Executive Committee and the Council of People's Commissars of these republics.[96] Acts of People's Commissariats of autonomous SSR's could be suspended or abrogated by the Central Executive Committee, and by the Presidia of the Central Executive Committee, and Council of People's Commissars of the autonomous SSR.[97] The Stalin Constitution changed this arrangement. Now orders and instructions of USSR People's Commissars can be abrogated by the USSR Council of People's Commissars; those of Union Republic People's Commissars by the Council of People's Commissars of that Union Republic; and those of People's Commissars of autonomous SSR's by the Council of People's Commissars of that autonomous SSR. This arrangement is conditioned by a precise delimitation of functions as between legislative and executive-administrative organs. By the new Constitution executive-administrative functions are concentrated in full compass in Councils of People's Commissars, and the right to abrogate acts of People's Commissars, inasmuch as it expresses an executive-administrative function, belongs solely to Councils of People's Commissars.

The Stalin Constitution charges the USSR Public Prosecutor with supreme supervision, both immediately and through prosecutors of the Union and of the autonomous republics, over the exact fulfillment of laws by all the People's Commissariats and by the institutions and officials subordinate thereto. To this end the USSR Public Prosecutor and republic public prosecutors are granted the right to protest against unlawful acts of People's Commissariats to the corresponding Council of People's Commissars—but without suspending their operation.

The Commission of Soviet Control, pursuant to the regulation concerning it, conducts "systematic, concrete and operative verification of the factual fulfillment of the government's most important decisions by all the links of the Soviet and economic apparatus from top to bottom." [98] It has the right immediately to issue binding instructions to People's Commissars in the case of a manifest breach of government directives (including instructions as to the abrogation of this or that act) and brings to the attention of the USSR Council of People's Commissars all cases when it is revealed that there have been breaches of discipline and perversions in carrying out such directives.

[96] Cf. Constitution of the RSFSR (1925, Art. 43), of the Turkmen SSR (1926, Art. 46), of the Uzbek SSR (1927, Art. 54), of the White Russian SSR (1927, Art. 52), and of the Georgian SSR (Art. 54).
[97] Cf. the Constitution of the Dagestan ASSR (1926, Art. 67) and of the Chuvash ASSR (1926, Art. 67).
[98] Cz. 1934, No. 12, Art. 75.

Upon what grounds can orders and instructions of People's Commissars be abrogated? If they contradict the Constitution or statutes and decrees in force; if they contradict directives and orders of the USSR Council of People's Commissars or orders and instructions of Union Republic People's Commissars; if they contradict directives and orders of the USSR Council of People's Commissars or a Union Republic Council of People's Commissars, or the directions of People's Commissars of Union Republic People's Commissariats of the USSR or orders and instructions of People's Commissars of an autonomous SSR; if they contradict directives and orders of the USSR Council of Commissars or the Union Republic Council of People's Commissars, or the Council of People's Commissars of the autonomous SSR, or the orders of the directive of the People's Commissariat of the Union Republic.

Finally, Councils of People's Commissars have the right to abrogate any orders and instructions of People's Commissars of the corresponding commissariats.

5. Local organs of People's Commissariats

People's Commissariats manage a multitude of administrative objects scattered over the state's vast territory. To administer all these directly from one center would be impossible. Hence People's Commissariats have their local organs endowed with certain rights and enabling the former to take into account local distinctions and peculiarities and to carry on the administration, leaving the initiative and self-help of the local organs of state authority untrammeled.

According to the USSR Constitution of 1924, All-Union People's Commissariats had—with the Union Republic Councils of People's Commissars—their own fully empowered representatives subordinate to them directly. According to the general (1923) regulation of USSR People's Commissariats,[99] representatives were put forward by USSR People's Commissariats—immediately, or upon the proposal of the Central Executive Committee of the Union Republic—and confirmed by the USSR Council of People's Commissars. All the candidates put forward had to be recommended by the Union Republic Central Executive Committee, which had the right to challenge the nominee. Representatives of All-Union People's Commissariats entered the Union Republic Council of People's Commissars with a vote, consultative or decisive, according to the decision of the Union Repub-

[99] *Herald of the Central Executive Committee, Council of People's Commissars and Labor and Defense Council* (1923), No. 10, Art. 299.

lic Central Executive Committee or its Presidium. The representatives informed the Central Executive Committee, its Presidium and the Council of People's Commissars of the Union Republic concerning the activity of the All-Union People's Commissariat, and rendered an account of their work both to the corresponding USSR People's Commissariat and to the Union Republic Central Executive Committee and Council of People's Commissars. The system of fully empowered representatives of certain All-Union People's Commissariats was liquidated [100] in connection with the reorganization of the central mechanism, the liquidation of superfluous links in the system of administration, and the bringing of this mechanism near to the objects of administration. While the Stalin Constitution, as distinguished from that of 1924, does not affirm as obligatory for all the All-Union People's Commissariats the system of fully empowered representatives in Union Republics, it does establish that representatives of All-Union People's Commissariats enter the Union Republic Council of People's Commissars with the right of a decisive vote.

Aside from representatives, the All-Union People's Commissariats have local organs constructed on either the territorial or the production principle. The local organs of the People's Commissariat for Defense, the People's Commissariat for Communications, and of the People's Commissariat for Stores are built on the territorial principle. According to the Regulation Concerning the People's Commissariat for the Defense of the USSR:[101] "In order to effectuate all the measures connected with the calling up of citizens for military service, and to promote military mobilization—the People's Commissariat for Defense has its organs of military administration in the rural districts subordinate to the army commanders thereof." The local organs of the People's Commissariat for Communications are: the administrations of communications of the autonomous SSR, territory, or region, and district departments of communications.

Other All-Union People's Commissariats—the People's Commissariats for Heavy Industry, for Mechanical Engineering, for Defense Industry, for Water Transportation and for Transport—construct their organs on the production principle. Combines and trusts function as local organs of the People's Commissariat for Heavy Industry; the People's Commissariat effectually directs enterprises either immediately or through an intermediate link (the combine or trust). Similarly as to local organs of the People's Commissariats for Machinery Building and for Defense Industry. The People's Commissariat for Water Transport has local organs for seagoing vessels, for

---

[100] For liquidation of representatives of the People's Commissariat for Transportation in the Union Republics see Cz. 1934, No. 37, Art. 291; and for the liquidation of representatives of the People's Commissariat for Heavy Industry see Cz. 1935, No. 64, Art. 511.
[101] Cz. 1934, No. 58, Art. 430(b).

river vessels, for the administration of river basins, and for the administration of seaports. The local organs of the People's Commissariat for Transport are: the road administration, the district administration, the basic locomotive depot administration, administration of part of the wagon industry, the administration of stations, the road-section administration, and the administration of section signals and communications.

People's Commissariats having a production structure of administrative mechanism may also have territorial local organs. According to Union Republic constitutions—in accord with conditions of the territory (region) or area (in republics so divided) and on the basis of USSR and Union Republic laws—All-Union People's Commissariats and the People's Commissariat for Internal Affairs may form their own territorial administrations under territorial (regional) or area Soviets of Deputies of the Toilers. Local organs of All-Union People's Commissariats, both territorial and production organs, are distinguished from local organs of Republic and Union Republic People's Commissariats by the fact that the former are subject only according to a vertical line, whereas the latter are both subordinated according to a horizontal line—to Soviets of Deputies of the Toilers and their executive committees, and also according to a vertical line—to People's Commissariats.

This does not mean, however, that there is no connection between local organs of All-Union People's Commissariats and local organs of authority. This connection is expressed, for example, by means of reports to local Soviets by local organs of People's Commissariats concerning their work. According to the report of the People's Commissariat for Communications (November, 1934) the USSR Council of People's Commissars directed:

> The organs of the People's Commissariat for Communications render reports of their work to the regional, territorial, and district executive committees and familiarize all local organs of authority with the plans of development of communications undertaken by them. Local authorities (regional, territorial, and district executive committees) are bound to cooperate in every way with organs of communication in searching out and utilizing local materials and local resources to develop communications and to repair the work thereof.[102]

As a rule, Union Republic People's Commissariats of the USSR direct the branch of state administration entrusted to them through Union Republic People's Commissariats having the same name, and administer directly only a limited number of enterprises. Hence Union Republic People's Commissariats of the USSR do not have their local territorial organs; they utilize the local machinery of Union Republic People's Commissariats of

[102] Cz. 1934, No. 49, Art. 383.

the Union Republics. They have only production local organs (trusts) to direct enterprises immediately subordinate to them.

In rural areas Union Republic and Republic People's Commissariats of the Union Republics have their own territorial organs which are at the same time organs of corresponding Soviets of Deputies of the Toilers as well.

VII

Local Organs of State Authority

SEC. 1: INTRODUCTION

ONE OF the most brilliant expressions of the distinctive character of the Soviet state, as a state of a new and loftier historical type, is in the building of local organs of state authority—territorial, regional, area, district, city and village Soviets of Deputies of the Toilers—forming an indissoluble and integral part of the entire system of organs of state authority of the USSR. This system is single and monolithic (columnar) from top to bottom. All the organs of state authority, both supreme and local, are organized as Soviets, and all Soviets—from the Supreme Soviets to the village Soviet—are organs of state authority. This distinguishing feature of the Soviet state is developed with particular distinctness in the Stalin Constitution.

Article 134, defining the method of elections to the Soviets, enumerates the Soviets.

Elections of deputies to all Soviets of Deputies of the Toilers: the Supreme Soviet of the USSR; Supreme Soviets of the Union Republics; territorial and regional Soviets of Deputies of the Toilers; Supreme Soviets of autonomous republics; Soviets of Deputies of the Toilers of autonomous regions; area, district, city, and rural (Kazakh village, hamlet, farm, central Asian and Caucasian villages) Soviets of Deputies of the Toilers, are by electors upon the basis of universal, equal and direct suffrage with secret ballot.

Organs of local administration stand in no contrast to organs of state authority in the Soviet system, which is, in its entirety, an organization of the toilers' authority, so that there neither can nor could be any such antithesis within it. Accordingly, with us "all state authority has, in its entirety, become self-government, and local self-government has become state authority." [1]

[1] Kaganovich, *Soviet Local Self-Government*, p. 16.

The principle of democratic centralism is at the basis of the relations of Soviets between themselves. Fundamentally, that principle signifies that each organ of authority, being formed by a procedure at once democratic and logical, is responsible to its electors and is bound to execute their will, while at the same time it is also responsible to superior organs of authority and bound to fulfill all their orders (provided they are given within the limits of their respective jurisdiction). Defining the boundaries of centralism, Lenin pointed out that "just as democratic centralism by no means excludes autonomy and federation, so it by no means excludes—on the contrary it presupposes—that different localities, and even different communities of the state, are completely and utterly free in working out varying forms of state, social, and economic life. Nothing is more fallacious than to confuse democratic centralism with a stereotyped bureaucracy." [2]

The development of local organs of state authority has passed through a number of stages. As early as 1905, city and country toilers had begun to employ Soviets—Soviet organization—in prosecuting their struggle to overthrow the power of landowners and capitalists. Even before that, however, the worker class had created the prototype of Soviets—the Paris Commune—in its struggle to overthrow the exploiters. "The revolution of March 18, 1871, resulted in the transfer to the Commune, not merely of the city government, but of all the initiative theretofore belonging to the state." [3]

In the territory of Paris and in the (suburban) Department of the Seine, there was a merger and fusion of the state and local administration of the new type which had smashed the old government machinery and created a new one based on the election and recall of officials from top to bottom, the union of legislative as well as executive authority in administrative organs, and a whole people in arms instead of the previous armed force. The conditions and character of its activity and its successive decrees and measures make the Paris Commune a typical worker-class government. At the same time, there were also manifestations of tendencies toward state-wide development of the Paris Commune, which sought a bond of union with the communes emerging in other industrial centers (such as Lyons, Marseilles, and Toulouse) and with districts, particularly around Paris, where the peasantry sympathized with the Commune. In the Declaration of the Commune to the French People, the Paris Commune contemplated the organization of communes everywhere after its own type, down to and including the smallest hamlet. "The assembly of delegates, sitting in the chief city of the district, should oversee the common concerns of all the

[2] Lenin (Russian ed.), Vol. XXII, p. 416.
[3] Marx, *The Civil War in France* (Russian ed., 1937), p. 74.

rural communes of each district, and these district assemblies should in turn send delegates to the National Assembly, sitting in Paris." [4]

The new system of state apparatus, contemplated by the Commune after the bourgeois state machinery had been smashed, with a central delegation from federal communes, which expressed "the voluntary unification of all local initiative," [5] was the prototype of Soviet state machinery. "Already the very existence of the Commune entailed local self-government as something perfectly obvious, but no longer for the purpose of counterbalancing state authority." [6] Engels's development of this idea of Marx contemplates principles of democratic centralism whose significance in the organization of broad local self-government, without prejudice to the unity of the proletarian state, is emphasized by Lenin in The State and Revolution. [7]

The Soviets of 1905 emerged as the organs for carrying on the struggle by means of strikes by the masses and later became, with the development of the revolution, organs of the general revolutionary struggle with tsarism. Therein they became organs of insurrection, of the revolutionary struggle for authority, during which they seized the functions of organs of authority. They promoted measures to liquidate unemployment, to provide supplies, and to levy taxes as well as to organize revolutionary order and a court, and so on. The toilers gave orders to the deputies they had elected to the Soviets, heard their reports, and recommended and reelected deputies, judges, leaders of military companies and so on. The Soviets created their executive committees, organized sections and commissions for various branches of work—even created organs like the present representative groups in separate places—and published their newspapers, thereby strengthening their bonds with the broad masses of the toilers. Striving for unification, for centralization of their activity, the city Soviets were, on the one hand, connected with the Soviets and the committees beginning to emerge in the rural areas while at the same time they sought state-wide unification through the All-Russian Congress of Soviets, convening upon summons prepared by the St. Petersburg and Moscow Soviets.

Lenin generalized the experience of organizing the 1905 Soviets in his draft resolution as to Soviets of Worker Deputies, introduced by him at the Fourth (Stockholm) Congress of the Russian Social Democratic Worker Party, wherein he confirmed the directive role of the party as regards the Soviets, and of the Soviets as regards the entire revolutionary democracy.

[4] Ibid., pp. 74–75.
[5] Marx and Engels Archives, Vol. III (VIII), p. 363.
[6] Marx, The Civil War in France (Russian ed., 1937), p. 77.
[7] Cf. Lenin (Russian ed.), Vol. XXI, pp. 419–420.

The basic task of the Soviets, as he saw it, was to prosecute the armed struggle for authority and to become therein temporary local revolutionary governments under a single temporary government of the entire country.

The first Soviets developed under the conditions of the 1905 Revolution. This first (1905) revolution prepared the way for swift victory of the second (1917) revolution. Lenin has pointed out that "without the three years of extreme class conflict—and the revolutionary energy of the Russian proletariat—during the years 1905 to 1907, the second revolution could not possibly have been so swift, in the sense that its *initial* state attained its culmination within a few days." [8]

In the very first days of the Revolution the Soviets appeared. The victorious revolution rested on Soviets of Worker and Soldier Deputies. The upsurging workers and soldiers created these Soviets. The Revolution of 1905 showed that Soviets were at once organs of armed uprising and the embryo of new, revolutionary authority. The idea of Soviets lived in the consciousness of the worker masses and they brought it to realization on the very day after tsarism had been overthrown—with the difference, however, that in 1905 only Soviets of *Worker* Deputies were created, where in February of 1917—upon the initiative of the Bolsheviks—Soviets of Worker and Soldier Deputies appeared. [9]

Stalin returned to Petrograd from tsarist exile before the arrival of Lenin, and advanced before the Soviets the problem of creating a central organ of authority personified by an All-National Soviet of Worker, Soldier, and Peasant Deputies as the fundamental condition precedent to victorious revolution. The Soviets had grown swiftly and developed their organization and their work on a far wider scale than did the Soviets of 1905. The development of congresses of Soviets, of which there were none in 1905, must be particularly noted. Detachments of the Soviets, which had developed during this period, included in their activity almost all the essential branches of the work of the local administrative and Zemstvo-municipal machinery, carrying on their work along parallel lines or together with the latter (and sometimes even in place of and against them). Congresses of worker, soldier, and peasant deputies, embracing guberniyas, provinces, and regions, helped to strengthen the union between the worker class and the peasantry. An intense class struggle developed around the question of the significance of the Soviets, including local Soviets, as organs of authority. Striving to preserve capitalism, the Mensheviks and the SR's sought to pervert the Soviets into empty "talking shops" of the parliamentary type, and set off against them the organs of the bourgeois-democratic

[8] *Ibid.*, Vol. XX, p. 13.
[9] *History of the All-Union Communist Party (of Bolsheviks): A Short Course* (1938), p. 170.

Zemstvo self-government. The Bolsheviks, however, mobilized the toiling masses for a decisive struggle to achieve the transfer of *all* authority into the hands of the Soviets—to consummate the creation of the Soviet state. From the very first days of the triumphant socialist revolution and the establishment of the proletarian dictatorship, the building of a *single* columnar Soviet state mechanism developed, and all of its links (both central and local) were unified by a single great purpose—the struggle for communism.

SEC. 2: PREREVOLUTIONARY LOCAL ADMINISTRATION AND SELF-GOVERNMENT

The local administrative mechanism and local self-government by the beginning of the February Revolution.

For a better conception of the essence of the demolition of the bourgeois-landowner local state machinery achieved by the great October Socialist Revolution, familiarity with the basic features of the prerevolutionary organs of local government and self-government is essential.

In the rural areas the February Revolution of 1917 found an administrative apparatus built fundamentally on the principles of the 1775 Institutes Concerning Guberniyas. At the head of the guberniya, as representing the supreme administrative authority, was the governor appointed by order of the tsar and immediately subordinate to the Ministry of Internal Affairs. The governor's sphere of jurisdiction included in form "the publication of statutes, oversight of the entire administration in the guberniya, and the issuance of obligatory directives on matters of social quiet, order, and security." In fact the activity of almost all state organizations and institutions within the guberniya, as well as of organs of Zemstvo and city self-government and of class and social organizations, were, in some form or other, subject to him.

The governor's immediate assistant was the vice governor. Under the governor functioned the government administration (consisting of a general session,[1] chancelleries and departments, and headed in fact by the

[1] Guberniya sessions were organs of supervision and, in the opinion of certain jurists of the time, including Tarasov and Yelistratov, "reflections" of the inferior organs of administrative justice. They included, besides the governor and vice governor, the public prosecutor, the heads of the treasury and control chambers, representatives of the social orders, and representatives of organs of the Zemstvo and municipal self-government, and of institutions immediately connected with a given session as supervisory organ.

vice governor) and the chancellery of the governor (with secretarial work on matters of elections to land committees and organs of the nobility, the issuance of passports abroad, affairs of the press, civic matters concerning societies of the sessions, and matters "demanding particular secrecy and the personal disposition of the governor"). The governor (or the vice governor) presided in the sessions concerned with military affairs, provisions, Zemstvo and city affairs, and factory matters in the statistical committee, in the committee for social welfare, and in the council concerned with government schools. Besides these, there were fiscal chambers (the local organ of Ministry of Finance), the guardianship of nobles, the chamber of control, local organs of state control, the administration of excise, and the administration of state property. The police had no organ with authority throughout the guberniya except the political police, with their gendarme administration for the guberniya immediately subordinate to the Ministry of Internal Affairs. The provincial police, headed by provincial police officers, with their police inspectors, local policemen and watchmen, as well as the municipal police, were subordinate to the administration of the guberniya and to the vice governor immediately. Both capitals and a number of the largest cities were set apart into independent administrative units headed by town governors, possessing generally the rights of provincial governors. In a number of places, chiefly in the borderlands, there were guberniyas united into one general guberniya.

The inhabitants of the guberniyas were basically included in organizations of the different social orders. The order of nobility had organizations throughout the guberniya and the provinces headed by leaders of the nobility. The nobility played an important role in the guberniya, since it possessed a large part of the lands and the other immovable property, while all the ruling bureaucracy of the guberniya belonged to it. The leaders of the nobility in the guberniya were elected (by representatives of the nobility and the most eminent local officials) from among the hereditary nobility in the assembly of nobles of the guberniya. That assembly selected two candidates to be guberniya leaders and one of them was confirmed by the tsar upon the recommendation of the Minister of Internal Affairs. Provincial leaders were likewise chosen by the assembly of the nobility and confirmed by the governor. Leaders of the nobility were required to become members, and were sometimes the heads, of a number of local state organs of the collegium type. In particular, one of them presided at sessions of the Zemstvo.

The system of organizatoin of the local administrations of the guberniyas and the provinces included a peasant social organization with its village societies, with their village assemblies and elders elected by them, with a volost[2] assembly, a volost administration, volost elders, and a volost court. The peasant class and its organs of administration were essentially subordinate to the nobility. The Zemstvo chiefs, to whom the peasant social organizations were subordinate, were appointed exclusively from the nobility.[3]

Besides these two basic social orders, there was also the class of merchants, which united the merchants into three guilds, depending upon their property qualification, with an elder chosen by each guild and, in the bigger cities, an elective mercantile court; the burgher class, which elected its elders and, in the biggest cities, its court also; and finally, the craftsman class, organized in corporate form, with its own elective organs. All elective organs of all the social classes were chosen for three years.

The order of distinguished citizens, hereditary and otherwise, had no corporate organization.

The organs of local self-government were recommended by the Zemstvo of the guberniyas and the provinces, and by the municipal self-governments. The Zemstvo of the guberniyas consisted of the Zemstvo assembly of the guberniya whose members—Zemstvo town counselors—were chosen for three years, and a Zemstvo court of the guberniya under a president elected for the same period. Ordinary Zemstvo assemblies of the guberniya were summoned once a year. Extraordinary assemblies could be summoned with the permission of the governor. The organization of the provincial Zemstvo was the same. Under the law of 1890, elections to both Zemstvos were according to three *curiae* (electoral bodies): nobility, peasantry, and other qualified persons. In almost all the guberniyas the registry of the number of town councilors from each *curia* gave a majority to the *curia* of nobles over the other two. The peasants chose their own candidates for town councilor according to volosts, and from these candidates the governor appointed town councilors according to the peasant *curia*.

The jurisdiction of Zemstvos included public health, popular education, social welfare, local communications, the Zemstvo post, fire protection, mutual Zemstvo insurance of property, building, and "aid to local agricul-

---

[2] This word, the archaic form of the word *vlast*, herein translated "power" or "authority," came to mean "territory in the possession of a single person" (such as a prince), and then a district consisting of the villages or hamlets under the administration of a single "elder." —TR.

[3] By a regulation of 1889, Zemstvo district leaders were appointed by the governor "upon the counsel" of leaders of the nobility of the guberniya and province. They had the right to assess administrative imposts upon the peasants. Upon them depended the affirmation of the personnel of all organs of rural administration and of their decisions. They were also charged with supervision of the activity of the police of a given district.

ture, trade, and industry." The Zemstvo enjoyed the right of imposing taxes to carry out its functions, and Zemstvos of the guberniya had the further right to issue obligatory directives.

City self-government consisted of a city council, whose members were elected for four years, and a city administrator, chosen by the council, under the head man of the city, chosen for the period of the council's authority. Elective rights were enjoyed by persons possessing immovable property and trading and industrial enterprises. That the circle of city electors was narrow may be seen from the fact that in the elections of prerevolutionary city councils an average of about 1½ per cent of the entire city population took part. Sessions of the city council were held, as required by law, not less than four nor more than twenty-four times a year. The objects within the jurisdiction of city self-government were basically the same as those within the jurisdiction of the Zemstvo (except the post and collaboration with agriculture, but with the addition of water supply, lighting, and the like). The city self-governments, like the Zemstvo, enjoyed the right of imposing taxes and levies and issuing obligatory directives.

All directives of Zemstvo and city self-governments could be protested and abrogated by the governor not only as not in conformity with law, but also as inexpedient. A number of directives (chiefly on matters concerned with finance and credit) required to be confirmed by the Ministry of Internal Affairs and the administration. Executive organs of the self-governments required confirmation by the governor or the Ministry of Internal Affairs, and sometimes (in the capitals and Zemstvos of the guberniyas) by the tsar. During the first two weeks after he was added to the staff, the governor had the right to dismiss any employee of the local self-government if he recognized that such employee was untrustworthy and, where there was a regulation calling for intensified security protection, he could eliminate him for these reasons at any time at all.

With the beginning of the imperialist war, the Zemstvo and city self-governments issued a public declaration, summoning in Moscow their congresses (organized by the Zemstvo of the Moscow guberniya and the Moscow city council) and organized an All-Russian Zemstvo Union and an All-Russian Union of Cities under the standard of "aid for the sick and wounded soldiers." That part of the bourgeoisie which was essentially in opposition and had a majority in many organs of local self-government had long sought a state-wide unification of organs of local self-government but had encountered opposition from the bureaucracy, consisting of nobles, which had the power behind it. The Zemstvo and city unions, particularly the latter, began to pass also to measures of general economy, and later to political measures.

It is not without interest to sketch, albeit briefly, the development of local self-government from the viewpoint of the class struggle unfolding around these organs. As local self-government developed in the pre-October period, collisions of class interests and various forms of class struggle around questions of local self-government, and in the very organs of self-government, were constantly more frequent. In connection with the "struggle" of the growing Russian bourgeoisie for reform of the serf-holding state along the lines of its demands and, in particular, its struggle for the introduction of local self-government, Professors Leshkov and Vasilchikov introduced into Russia the social-economic theory of self-government created by the bourgeois science of western Europe. Its primal ancestor was the theory of "natural rights of the commune," created during the period of the French Revolution, 1789–1793 (by analogy to the theory of natural rights of man and citizen), which later became the *theory of the free commune.* This theory asserted that the commune, created earlier than the state, possesses special and inherent rights—*"pouvoir municipal"* in the words of the Belgian Constitution of 1830, which further developed the doctrine of a separation of powers. Later, when the bourgeoisie, fearful of the growing revolutionary worker movement, began to live more or less in peace with the semifeudal state, the theory created a *social-economic* theory of self-government, which asserts that, independently of questions of state activity in the rural districts, there is as well a field of local social-economic activity there, with its sphere of matters completely distinct from state activity, and necessarily carried with effect through organs of local self-government.

As the class struggle and the revolutionary movement grew, this contrast of state and communal self-government began to become less and less suited to the bourgeoisie and the agrarians. During the onset of reaction, in the 1880's and 1890's in Russia, another so-called *state* theory of self-government—also brought from the bourgeois West and fundamentally nothing more than a naked assertion that local self-government is state government—began actively to develop. As in the West, this theory was represented in Russia by two trends, political and juridic. The political, conservative trend, represented in the west by Gneist and Mayer, and in Russia by Bezobrazov, Golovin, and Korf, considered that the basic sign of self-government was that elected persons gratuituously perform all obligations through tenure of honorary offices or in conjunction with other and basic employment—a theory obviously directed against any democratic elements penetrating into directive work, into organs of self-government. The liberal juridical theory of self-government, represented in the west by Stein, Jellinek, and others, and in Russia by Gradovsky and Korkunov, started by defining self-government as a local, territorial public-law union with state functions.

This theory was later developed in detail, as one of its advocates (Gronsky) stated frankly, upon eclectic principles by the Constitutional-Democratic professors Hessen, Lazarevsky, Nolde, and others. This, which they called the Russian doctrine, combines a number of trends of European doctrines and was formulated by Gronsky thus: "Self-government is where the tasks of state administration are effectuated by the intermediation of public-law organizations whose administrative and executive organs are elected by the local populace and exercise an independent jurisdiction uninfluenced by the central authority of the state."

From the beginning of the twentieth century, matters of local self-government begin ever increasingly to be developed by Mensheviks and SR's, each of them carrying on this work under the banner of municipal socialism. The social-reformist essence of their theories may be illustrated by extracts from Kurchinsky (a teacher turned Menshevik) and the municipal theoretician of the SR's—Achadov-Danilov (later Trutovsky). According to the former,[4] "it may be thought that in communes, and especially in cities, the principles of socialism will find their realization much earlier than in state life. The city will be a hearth in which little by little (!) the society of the future will be forged." According to the latter,[5] municipal socialism is "one of the transition forms to the future socialist order." Such a resounding "revolutionary" phrase veils a petty-bourgeois opportunism which, in the process of its further development, degenerated into outright bourgeois counterrevolution.

From its very first days, the February bourgeois-democratic revolution posed the question of democratizing both the local administrative machinery and the organs of self-government, of creating a single mechanism of democratic government in the rural areas. The Provisional Government, and the conciliation parties of Mensheviks and SR's which supported it, directed their attention at organs of Zemstvo and city self-government, which, right down to their reelections on the basis of new edicts, "were becoming democratic upon their own initiative or with the cooperation of commissars of the Provisional Government" by including representatives of petty bourgeois parties, trade unions, and other social organizations and representatives of the Soviets of Worker, Soldier, and Peasant Deputies.

The Provisional Government excellently understood the danger threatening the bourgeois dictatorship—masked in a new fashion—from the swiftly growing Soviets. Preserving the state mechanism of nobles and

---

[4] In his *Municipal Socialism.*
[5] In *Socialist Party Views on Social Self-Government.*

bureaucracy to aid it, it sought to attract to its side the petty-bourgeois "socialist" parties and broad petty-bourgeois masses in the city and in the country. In the country, the Provisional Government hurriedly created a volost Zemstvo by the law of May 21, 1917, having organized therein an apex of the well-to-do peasantry and rural intellectuals of that time. Moreover, that law as to the volost Zemstvos left the class organization of the rural administration completely untouched, having subordinated it to the provincial commissars of the Provisional Government rather than to the leaders of the Zemstvo. In the cities, the Provisional Government sought support in the backward and lower levels, counting in particular on the women, the housewives, who were for the first time brought into the elections. To this end it published, as early as April 15, 1917, the law about district government (district councils) in cities with a population of more than 150,000. But the experience of elections to the district councils of Moscow, where the Bolsheviks obtained a majority of the votes, compelled the government parties to abstain from introducing district councils in a number of other cities.

The effort of the Provisional Government to preserve the former organization of self-government was clearly characterized by the fact that it did not even issue new regulations as to city and Zemstvo institutions, but confined itself to the introduction of partial corrections (by the law of June 9, 1917) in the tsarist regulations of 1890 (concerning Zemstvos) and 1892 (concerning cities). It is typical that the last to be published—in July-August, 1917—was a law concerning rural self-government. The Provisional Government was so apprehensive of the rural workers that this law was held back and was not in fact put into practice.

The new regulations relative to all the organs of local self-government took into account the fundamental principles worked out in this sphere by Western bourgeois democracy in defining their organization, jurisdiction, and functions. Fearing, however, the independence of even its own volost Zemstvos, the Provisional Government made them subordinate to the provincial Zemstvos. A series of directives issued by organs of self-government, chiefly concerned with matters of property and credit, required affirmation by the government. Single administrative judges and administrative sections of district courts were set up in rural areas to "guarantee legality" in the work of organs of self-government and to "defend legality" in administration. The system of administrative justice was headed by the first department of the ruling senate. The class interests of dominant classes were completely guaranteed by the personnel of the judiciary, headed by senators and appointed chiefly from legal specialists.

The policy of the Provisional Government in reforms of the local state machinery manifested even more clearly a bourgeois-reactionary character. Here there was nothing more than replacing governors and chiefs of police by commissars of the Provisional Government (appointed chiefly from representatives of Zemstvo courts), and replacing police by militia subject to the organs of self-government—often merely a matter of form. The entire bureaucratic machinery of officialdom and its whole system of guberniya and provincial institutions, characteristic of tsarist times, remained unchanged in what was proclaimed as "the Russian Republic." Only on October 6, 1917,[6] was the Temporary Regulation of Guberniya (Regional) and Provincial Commissars published. Only in October, at the eleventh hour of bourgeois-democratic revolution, did the Provisional Government deign, in Paragraph 3 of this directive, "to liberate the leaders of nobility (whether elected or appointed) in the guberniyas and the provinces" from the obligation to share in the organs of local government. At the same time, however, there was a further reservation to the effect that "for the time being, and pending legislative revision of the relevant statutes, leaders of the nobles in 'the guberniya and the provinces carry out their obligations in conformity with existing law, pursuant to the social institutions of nobility and the tutelage of the nobility."

Thus, on the eve of the October Revolution, the government, consisting of "socialist" ministers, preserved the self-government of the noble class. Article 6 of the directive just cited provides characteristically that the name of the governor's chancellery be changed to "chancellery of the guberniya-commissar." The entire reform of local administration by the Provisional Government was nothing more than a change of name, under which the antipopular, counterrevolutionary substance was preserved.

Renouncing the most offensive institutions—governors and police—and replacing them by commissars and militia, the Provisional Government in substance preserved the earlier administrative machinery of local government, outwardly renovated and with the center of gravity transferred to the organs of local Zemstvo and city self-government (reorganized "on democratic principles").

In contrast with this system of exploiter pseudo-"democracy" in the rural areas, the system of Bolshevized Soviets of Worker People developed in circumstances of tense class struggle, on the basis of the mass experience of which Lenin spoke as early as April, 1917. For three-quarters of this year of tense revolutionary struggle, personnel of the Soviets, both in the Soviets and in organs of Zemstvo-municipal administration, passed through a great school of local state administration. It was left for them, in the last decisive struggle for the transfer of all authority to the Soviets, to create

[6] *Collected Statutes*, No. 246.

through the dictatorship of the proletariat a new Soviet democracy for all the toilers, after destroying the "democratically" renovated state of capitalists and landowners.

The bourgeoisie directing the Provisional Government remembered well the part played by the Soviets in 1905. With class-conscious awareness of the menace involved in further development of the Soviets, the bourgeoisie strove quietly to undermine and then to smash them. One form of this struggle of the Lvov-Kerensky government against the Soviets was its feverish legislative activity on matters of local administration. Between February and October the Provisional Government issued approximately a hundred statutes on administrative matters, of which forty-four—almost half—concerned questions of local administration and self-government. By this legislation, the dominant classes sought, under the banner of democracy, to confirm their power in the rural districts and, by constantly circumscribing and limiting the activity of the Soviets, to liquidate them in the final analysis.

SEC. 3: THE SOVIETS FROM OCTOBER, 1917, TO THE ADOPTION OF THE FIRST SOVIET CONSTITUTION (JULY, 1918)

The development of the Soviets as local organs of state authority from October, 1917, to the adoption of the first Soviet Constitution in July, 1918, is most conveniently contemplated according to the periods between the All-Russian Congresses of Soviets then held almost every three months. After taking power into its hands, the Second All-Russian Congress of Soviets, addressing all the guberniya and provincial Soviets of Worker, Soldier, and Peasant Deputies, pointed out that "all authority henceforth belongs to the Soviets. Commissars of the former Provisional Government are dismissed. Presidents of the Soviets consult directly with the Revolutionary Government." [1] Another appeal of the same congress was of this tenor: "The Congress directs: all authority in the rural areas passes to the Soviets of Worker, Soldier, and Peasant Deputies. They must also assure genuine revolutionary order." [2]

These two directives also contained a basic definition of the organization and activity of the Soviets for the period immediately ensuing. Two widely promulgated addresses of Lenin directly supplemented these directives and were of enormous organizational and political significance in building the

[1] Cy. 1917, No. 1, Art. 5.
[2] Lenin (Russian ed.), Vol. XXII, p. 11.

Soviets. The first, "To Workers, Soldiers, and Peasants," we have already mentioned. The other [3] (October 26/November 8, 1917) stated that "the Council of People's Commissars summons the peasants themselves to take into their hands all authority in the rural areas."

The system of relations between various local Soviets as between themselves and the center was indicated in a circular of the RSFSR People's Commissariat of Internal Affairs (December 24, 1917/January 6, 1918): "To all the Soviets of Worker, Soldier, Peasant, and Laborer Deputies," and in the "Instructions as to Rights and Obligations of Soviets." In the first point of the "Instructions" it was said: "Soviets of Worker, Soldier, Peasant and Laborer Deputies, being organs of authority in rural areas, are completely independent as regards matters of local character, but always act in conformity with decrees and directives of the Central Soviet Authority as well as of the larger groups (province, guberniya, and regional Soviets) wherein they are included."

Here are succinctly set out the principles of democratic centralism subsequently developed in the organization and work of the Soviets. The circular notes the necessity of turning special attention to the organization of peasant Soviets and there is already characteristic emphasis upon the problem "that there be no place in those peasant Soviets for kulaks, traders, and other advocates and apostles of servile relationships." The instruction recited that "the War-Revolutionary Committees, being military organs which emerged at the time of the overturn, are annulled," thus emphasizing the existence of temporary organs of authority in the rural areas, where the bourgeois-landowner counterrevolution offered particularly stubborn resistance to the transfer of all authority to the Soviets. In such cases the Soviets of Worker and Soldier Deputies, personified by their Bolshevik factions, had put forward the military organ—the War-Revolutionary Committee—very limited in size (three to five persons) but with very great powers. To it the Red Guard of the Soviet and all the detachments of troops that had come over to the side of the Soviet were subordinate. Its tasks were: to take authority, to shatter the enemy, to smash the local apparatus of the Provisional and tsarist governments, and to administer the cities and the guberniya (or province) until the summoning of an extraordinary session of Soviets wherein normal organs of guberniya or provincial Soviets were created. Sometimes, however, a military revolutionary committee continued in existence side by side with organs created by the Congress, with resulting duality of power. The "Instruction of the People's Commissariat of Internal Affairs" also took such cases into account.

[3] Entitled "Instruction to the Peasants," in the *Herald of the Commissariat of Internal Affairs*, No. 1, Pars. 2, 4, and 8.

The decrees of the very first months of the October Revolution made a number of functions and organizational forms of local Soviets definite and precise. Thus the decree concerning the court (issued November 24/December 7, 1917) [4] established that, until the organization of direct democratic elections of local judges, they are for the time being selected by volost, city, province, and guberniya Soviets; charged local commissars of justice (selected by the appropriate Soviets) with the liquidation of the old courts and the further functioning of court affairs; and enjoined the Soviets to organize revolutionary tribunals and special prosecuting commissions (responsible to the Soviets) to contend with counterrevolutoin.

The decree concerning land [5] pointed out that all the landowners' properties and all appanage, monastery, and ecclesiastical lands pass to the jurisdiction of the provincial Soviets and the volost land committees. The regulation of worker control (adopted November 14/27, 1917) [6] stated that local Soviets of worker control are organs of the appropriate Soviet of Worker, Soldier, and Peasant Deputies, while a decree concerning the institution of the Supreme Soviet of National Economy (published December 5/18, 1917) [7] stated that the Supreme Council of National Economy unifies and directs the work of the local economic subdivisions of Soviets of Worker, Soldier, and Peasant Deputies which comprise local organs of worker control as well as local commissars of labor, trade, industry, provisioning, and so on. In case there were no appropriate economic divisions in rural areas, the Supreme Council of National Economy formed its own local organs.

During the first months after the October Revolution, the relationship of the local Soviets to organs of local self-government—Zemstvo and city— was determined by the political line taken by the latter. Where they came out against the authority of the Soviets, these resolutely entered upon the struggle, dismissing them and directing new elections (as in Petrograd) or liquidating them completely; whereas, if they occupied a neutral position as regards the Soviets, or aided them in their work, these assigned to them a definite sphere of action. The Soviet government considered it expedient to utilize the machinery of local self-government for the time being until the Soviets should grow strong as organs of authority.

The brief period from the latter part of January (in the new style) to the middle of March, 1918—from the dismissal of the Constituent Assembly and the ensuing Third All-Russian Congress of Soviets of Worker and Soldier Deputies down to the Extraordinary Fourth All-Russian Con-

[4] Cy. 1917, No. 4, Art. 50, Pars. 2, 4, and 8.
[5] Cy. 1917, No. 1, Art. 3.
[6] Cy. 1917, No. 3, Art. 35.
[7] Cy. 1917, No. 5, Art. 83, Par. 10.

gress of Soviets—was a new stage in the development of local organs of authority. The Third All-Russian Congress of Soviets adopted two state acts which were the foundation of the Soviet Constitution: the Declaration of Rights of the Toiling and Exploited People (written by Lenin, with the closest participation of Stalin) and the Directive (pursuant to the report of Stalin) Concerning the Federal Institutions of the Russian Republic. The latter set out an epitome, based on the experience of the three months just expired, of the organization and activity of the entire Soviet state machinery, and stated (in Par. 6) that "all local matters are decided exclusively by local Soviets. The right of Supreme Soviets to regulate relationships—and their decision of discords arising—between the lower Soviets is acknowledged." [8]

The further fact of the liquidation of special All-Russian Congresses of Peasant Deputies (and of the Central Executive Committee of Soviets of Peasant Deputies chosen by them), and the merging of worker and peasant Soviets in rural areas where they still existed separately, were extremely important as regards the local Soviets.

The question of the relationship to organs of the Zemstvo and city self-government was elucidated in an official clarification by the People's Commissariat of Internal Affairs: "What Is to Become of Zemstvo and City Self-Governments?" [9] Herein it was stated: "In response to the numerous interrogatories from the rural districts, the Division of Local Self-Government [to wit, the People's Commissariat of Internal Affairs] deems it necessary to point out that, with the Soviets in existence, there should be no place for Zemstvo and city self-governments. Where the organs of self-government are not ours, where they are coming out against Soviet authority, they should be dismissed. Where they work with the Soviets, they should be merged therewith, so that there be not two homogeneous organs with jurisdiction over one and the same work." In the existing conditions of the Soviet type of state, the so-called "left" SR's tried to resurrect the old social-economic theory of self-government. Under the banner of this "theory," the counterrevolutionary petty bourgeoisie tried now to entrench itself against the Soviets for the organization of uprisings against Soviet authority. During July, 1918, the "left" SR's in Moscow, in conjunction with "left communists" and Trotskyists, organized a counterrevolutionary conspiracy against Soviet authority.[10]

[8] *Gazette of the Provisional Worker-Peasant Government* (Jan. 31/18, 1918), No. 11 (56).
[9] *Herald of People's Commissariat of Internal Affairs* (Jan. 24, 1918), No. 4.
[10] In his speech during the proceedings (1938) against the anti-Soviet "right-Trotsky bloc," the USSR Public Prosecutor Vyshinsky said on this matter: "Investigation established · –and I deem it necessary here to remind you thereof, comrade judges, in its full compass—

The "left" SR's, together with the "left-communist" Bukharinists, carried on their anti-Soviet work not only seeking to preserve bourgeois self-government, but also seizing the Soviets, creating their Councils of People's Commissars and "republics" after the manner of Kaluga. They were supported also by the anarchists, who later developed in the Ukraine in their anarchist-republic in "Gulyay-Pole," headed by Daddy Makhno. The most finished expression of the insidious policy of the so-called guberniya and province Councils of People's Commissars was in the Soviets headed by "left communists" and SR's. They refused to recognize Soviet government decrees which were not to their taste. (Thus the Siberian regional Council of People's Commissars declared itself "in a state of war with Germany and Austria-Hungary" notwithstanding the conclusion of the peace of Brest-Litovsk.) It must be noted that it was almost exclusively in nonindustrial districts and guberniyas where the influence of the petty-bourgeois element was especially potent that extensive distortions of Soviet authority by local Councils of People's Commissars occurred.

After the peace treaty of Brest-Litovsk was concluded (ratified by the extraordinary Fourth All-Russian Congress of Soviets), Soviet Russia gained a breathing space and was able to be occupied exclusively with strengthening the state machinery and particularly the local machinery of authority. Especially important in the work of building the machinery of administration, including local administration, were the Theses Concerning the Immediate Problems of Soviet Authority developed by Lenin's genius in his *Immediate Problems of Soviet Authority*. The Theses proposed correct organization of administration through logical development of democratic centralism, firm safeguarding of revolutionary order, and strengthening of discipline and self-discipline and of the court as a state organ effectuating indispensable constraint; and through development of socialist emulation between the Soviets and of Soviet democracy; and through struggle against bureaucratic perversions. Adopted on April 26, in a session of the Central Executive Committee of the Bolshevik Worker-Peasant Party, the Theses were adopted on April 29 in a session of the All-Russian Central Executive Committee. An immediate consequence of this adoption was the liquidation of regional, guberniya, provincial and other People's Commissariats as

---

that in 1918, immediately following the October Revolution and while the Brest-Litovsk Treaty was being concluded, Bukharin and his group of so-called 'left communists' and Trotsky with his group, jointly with the 'left' SR's, organized a conspiracy against Lenin as head of the Soviet government. The aim of Bukharin and the other conspirators, as is clear from materials furnished by the investigation, was to frustrate the peace of Brest-Litovsk, to overthrow the Soviet government, to arrest and murder Lenin, Stalin, and Sverdlov, and to form a new government of Bukharinists (who then masked themselves under the name of 'left communists'), Trotskyists, and 'left' SR's." (Court Report of the Anti-Soviet Right-Trotsky Bloc Affair; the USSR People's Commissariat of Justice, 1938, p. 302.)

manifesting a distortion, a noxious misinterpretation, of the principle: "All power to the Soviets in the center and in the rural areas."

The class struggle, which here grew sharp in the spring, particularly furthered the liquidation of the Zemstvo self-governments in the rural districts, which culminated at this period. Of that struggle Lenin said that the October Revolution rolled into the country in the spring and summer of 1918. It was in this period that the most poverty-stricken of the rural strata formed organizations—generally under the name of "Committees of the Poor"—and took up the struggle against the kulaks who had seized authority in most of the village and volost Soviets.

Committees of the Poor, created by decree of June 11, 1918, played a great part in the struggle with the kulaks, in the redistribution of confiscated lands and the distribution of economic goods, in the storage of provision surpluses in the hands of the kulaks, and in furnishing provisions to the workers of the centers and to the Red Army. Fifty million hectares of kulak land passed into the hands of the poorest and middle peasants and a significant part of the means of production belonging to the kulaks was confiscated for the benefit of the poorest peasants. The organization of these Committees of the Poor was a further stage in the development of the socialist revolution in the rural areas. They constituted support points for the proletarian dictatorship there. To a significant degree the formation of the Red Army cadres out of the peasant population took place through them. The campaign of the proletarians into the rural districts and the organization of these committees stabilized Soviet authority there and was of enormous political significance in winning the middle peasant to the side of Soviet authority. By the end of 1918 these committees had fulfilled their tasks and ceased to exist, being merged with the Soviets in the rural areas.[11]

The first Soviet Constitution, adopted by the Fifth All-Russian Congress of Soviets on July 10, 1918, allotted a considerable place to local organs of state authority. It established new features in the territorial organization of the Soviets, stating (in Art. 11) that "Soviets of regions distinguished by a peculiar manner of life and by national structure may combine into autonomous regional unions," thus providing for the possibility of Soviets of regional unions. It confirmed the organization and practice of work of Soviets which had taken basic form in the rural areas, establishing that city and village Soviets form executive committees possessing—in the intervals between congresses—complete and entire authority within their territories. Soviets were chosen for three months and assembled to sit not less frequently than once a week in the cities and twice a week in the villages, and likewise by decision of the executive committee or as required by not less than

[11] *History of the All-Union Communist Party (of Bolsheviks): A Short Course* (1938), pp. 212–213.

half the members of the Soviet. Congresses of the Soviets were summoned by the appropriate executive committees not less frequently than twice a year by region, once in three months by guberniya and province, and once a month by volost, and likewise by decision of the executive committee or as required by Soviets representing not less than one-third of the population of a given district.[12]

The objects of jurisdiction of the organs of Soviet authority in the rural areas were defined, on the one hand, by the fact that each Soviet, Congress of Soviets, and executive committee (in intervals between sessions of Soviets or plena thereof) "is the supreme authority within the limits of the given territory" (Arts. 56, 60), and, on the other hand, by Article 61 of the Constitution, which pointed out that all local organs of Soviet authority "have as the object of their activity:

a) to put into practice all the directives of the corresponding supreme organs of Soviet authority;

b) to adopt all measures to elevate the given territory culturally and economically;

c) to solve all questions of a purely local significance (for the given territory); and

d) to unite all Soviet activity within the limits of the given territory."

This jurisdiction of local organs of Soviet authority thus broadly outlined was subsequently made more precise, both by regulations concerning individual organs, and in subsequent constitutions, particularly in the USSR Constitution of 1936.

The principles of democratic centralism, according to the RSFSR Constitution (1918) in the relations of Soviets among themselves and with the central authority, were established also in the chapter concerning objects of jurisdiction of the Soviets (Chap. XII) and in that concerning their budget laws (Chap. XVI). It was settled that regional and guberniya Congresses of Soviets and city Soviets (having a population of more than 10,000 persons) were accountable to and subject to the control of the All-Russian Central Executive Committee and the Council of People's Commissars. Thus, under Article 86, estimates of city, guberniya, and regional organs of Soviet authority were confirmed by the All-Russian Central Executive Committee and the Council of People's Commissars, while (by Art. 62) these same local organs of authority enjoyed the right "to abrogate decisions of Soviets functioning in their districts, reporting thereof in the most important cases to the Central Soviet authority." As to control of subordinate by superior local organs in general, Congresses of Soviets

[12] Arts. 54, 59.

and their executive committees, regional, guberniya, provincial, and volost, enjoyed the right to control all Soviets in the territory of the respective administrative unit, except that Soviets of cities with a population of more than 10,000 were subject only to the control of regional and central organs. "Budgets of village and volost Soviets and of city Soviets participating in provincial Congresses of Soviets, and also budgets of provincial organs or Soviet authority, are confirmed accordingly by guberniya and regional Congresses of Soviets or by their executive committees" (Art. 86).

Thus basically did the 1918 Constitution establish interrelations between the local organs of state authority. As to the working mechanism of Soviets, Article 63 granted all Soviets and executive committees the right to form appropriate subdivisions (headed by supervisory departments) in order to fulfill the tasks imposed upon them.

Thus was the first experience of building local organs of authority of the Soviet state generalized and confirmed in the Constitution.

SEC. 4: LOCAL ORGANS OF STATE AUTHORITY DURING THE FOREIGN MILITARY INTERVENTION AND THE CIVIL WAR

The experience of organizing local organs of state authority, generalized in the Constitution adopted by the Fifth All-Russian Congress of Soviets, had to be applied in the setting of civil war. To achieve uniformity in the application of the Soviet Constitution, the first All-Russian Congress of Presidents of Guberniya Executive Committees and Overseers of Guberniya Administrative Departments was summoned at the end of July, 1918. Its significance is evident from the fact of Lenin's speech on July 30. Taking into account the setting, as it was becoming more and more complex in the conditions of civil war, the Congress directed the summoning of guberniya Congresses of Soviets—not every three months (as was established by Art. 54 of the Constitution) but not less frequently than twice a year. At the same time the guberniya executive committee was granted the right to summon guberniya conferences of Soviets, with the participation of not more than three representatives from each provincial executive committee and one representative from each of the city and district Soviets, to find solutions for extraordinary matters of principle.

The Congress sanctioned the creation of presidia of executive committees to carry on the current work, and established a system of interrelations between higher and lower executive committees (and their departments) on bases of democratic centralism developed and made precise in the directive of the Seventh All-Russian Congress of Soviets. The Congress likewise established the departmental structure of government executive committees.

On the basis of the directive of the Extraordinary Sixth All-Russian Congress of Soviets, Concerning the Liquidation of Committees of the Poor (December 2, 1918), the All-Russian Central Executive Committee published (over the signature of Sverdlov) a directive Concerning the Method of Reelecting Volost and Village Soviets.[1] The second, third, and fourth subdivisions of this directive represented essentially the first instruction for elections to the Soviets. The sixth subdivision, Tasks and Organization of Village and Volost Soviet Organizations, was, as it were, the prototype of future regulations concerning these organizations. Defining the jurisdiction of village and volost Soviets by the familiar four points of Article 61 of the Constitution, the enactment amplified them further by the following six points:

e) to maintain revolutionary order in the village;

f) to calculate the population, the land, the plowing, the sowings, the hay, the seeds, the livestock and other stock and the harvest, and to communicate the information to the volost executive committee;

g) to be concerned for the correct formulation of questions relating to agriculture, particularly the reorganization thereof on communist principles (the formation of labor communes);

h) to be concerned for the correct formulation of local trades;

i) to fulfill commissions of guberniya and provincial supply divisions, particularly as to calculation of products and control of the transfer of surpluses, the distribution of certificates concerning the transfer of surpluses (or of there being none such);

j) to organize village institutions of culture and education—reading rooms, clubs, tea shops, and so forth—and to be concerned for the general well-being of the population.

As regards the organization of volost committees and village Soviets, the directive gave categorical instructions that "village Soviets do not form departments." In the volost executive committees only three departments are organized: the land department, the military department, and the department of general administration. "Other departments are formed only upon affirmation by the provincial executive committee in accordance with decrees of Soviet authority and the instructions of People's Commissariats."

Revolutionary Committees. As local organs of state authority during

[1] Cy. 1918, No. 86, Art. 901.

the civil war, from the second half of 1918 to the end of 1920, the Revolutionary Committees played a very considerable part; only one-ninth of the territory of Soviet Russia (with only one-sixth of its entire population) was not caught in the grip of military operations. In this setting, the usual apparatus of local organs of authority was inadequate or inappropriate, being too unwieldy and complex and essentially ill-adapted to this work. In this connection, on the basis of the year's experience of work of the Revolutionary Committees, the All-Russian Central Executive Committee and the Council of Labor and Defense issued (on October 24, 1919) a Regulation Concerning Revolutionary Committees,[2] whereby such committees "are formed for stubborn defense against the enemy and for the maintenance of revolutionary order: (a) in localities liberated from the enemy; (b) in the front zone; and (c) in the rear."

An important part in Soviet building was played by Revolutionary Committees of localities liberated from the enemy: into them were ordinarily recruited the best Soviet and Party workers who applied their broad experience to the rehabilitation and development of organs of Soviet authority, taking into account all that they had affirmatively gained from practice. A whole series of new organizational forms, manifested during the civil war in the local Soviet mechanism, came from districts where these Revolutionary Committees were active.

In regard to local Congresses of Soviets, the directive of the Seventh All-Russian Congress of Soviets[3] (December, 1919), Concerning Soviet Building, established the terms (when they were to be summoned) which had already been projected by the first Congress of Presidents of Guberniya Executive Committees: for province, guberniya, and region, not less frequently than twice a year; and for volosts not less frequently than once in three months. At the same time there was a special reservation as to representation in guberniya, provincial and volost Congresses of Soviets from factory and works villages, and likewise from factories and works outside inhabited places, whereby the proletarian nucleus of the congresses was strengthened. The Congress directive required that basic questions of local life, state and social, be put for the consideration of general assemblies of Soviets. In so far as the Soviets began to be isolated from practical life as the mechanisms of city Soviets merged with those of guberniya and provincial executive committees, and the tide of workers ebbed to the fronts, the Congress directive pointed out that they must work not only as a mechanism of agitation and information but also as an active mechanism, while Deputies of the Soviets were obligated to give responses to

[2] Cy. 1919, No. 53, Art. 508.
[3] Cy. 1919, No. 64, Art. 578.

voters not less frequently than once in two weeks, and the voters were reminded of their right to recall deputies who gave no account of their conduct.

The broad subdivision of the Congress directive concerning executive committees was of vital significance, containing, unlike the Constitution, a differentiated definition of the structure of departments under the executive committees. Thus, under the guberniya executive committees there were to be the following departments: (1) the department of administration, (2) the military department, (3) the department of justice, (4) the department of labor and social security, (5) the department of popular education, (6) the department of posts and telegraphs, (7) the finance department, (8) the department of agriculture, (9) the department of supply, (10) the department of state control, (11) the council of national economy, (12) the department of public health, (13) the statistics department, (14) the extraordinary commission, and (15) the communal department. Under the province executive committee twelve departments were created identical with those under the guberniya executive committee except for the absence of the extraordinary commission and the departments of justice and of posts and telegraphs. Subdivisions of departments organized under volost executive committees, Soviets of factory and works settlements, and small boroughs were to be scheduled by the guberniya executive committee.

All the local administrative-economic organs of the central administrative agencies ceased to exist independently and were merged in the guberniya councils of national economy. At the same time, the guberniya executive committee acquired the right to control and to review the activity of all administrative institutions, whether temporary or standing—not structurally identified with divisions of the guberniya executive committee although in the territory of a given guberniya—reporting immediately thereon to the appropriate central institution. Thus local Soviet organization was unified and made orderly.

The principles of democratic centralism were distinctly expressed in the so-called system of dual subordination. That system was manifested in (a) the right of the appropriate People's Commissariat to challenge a departmental supervisor chosen by the executive committee; (b) the right of an executive committee department to protest through its presidium directives of a People's Commissariat or of a higher department which are impracticable for any reason; and (c) such method of issuing orders by People's Commissariats and subdivisions thereof to lower subdivisions as would achieve the simultaneous communication of all those of particular importance to the appropriate executive committees.

The Congress directive sanctioned the creation of presidia of executive committees to direct all the current work in administering their respective territories, made up of three to five members in guberniya executive committees and of three members in the provinces. Without rendering general decision as to the method of merging the executive committees of city Soviets with guberniya of provincial executive committees, the Congress pointed out that this question is decided in each separate case by the presidium of the All-Russian Central Executive Committee.

The Seventh All-Russian Congress of Soviets entrusted to the All-Russian Central Executive Committee the development of an administrative-economic division of the RSFSR, regulations concerning the functions of the presidia of the executive committees, of village Soviets and of volost executive committees, and the organization of worker inspection.

Local Soviet administration during the civil war. Organs of village administration—the volost executive committees and the village Soviets—were the first organs of local administration whose organization and activity were established by special regulations issued in legislative form according to directives of the Seventh All-Russian Congress of Soviets. The Regulation Concerning Village Soviets (February 15, 1920) [4] bore a sufficiently brilliant imprint of its epoch. In its organizational part, the working mechanism of the village Soviet, transferred to the state budget, was put into first place. It was formulated on more efficient principles: departments were abolished, membership of the executive committee was reduced to three, and members could be chosen only in settlements with more than 10,000 inhabitants and in conformity with the population of the settlement. The role and responsibility of the president of the village Soviet were given particular importance (Sec. 9). The same degree of importance was given by this regulation to the president of the general assembly of voters, which had replaced the village Soviets in little settlements where, in the period between the sessions, he carried on the same functions as did the president of a village Soviet.[5]

Not only did the regulation cut down the number of sessions of the Soviet (two a month as against two a week under the Constitution of 1918), it also devised new methods of work for bringing the population close to the village administration through the organization (1) of nuclei of cooperation of worker-peasant inspection (which had by then attained broad development), and (2) of commissions for all branches of agricultural Soviet work from among members of the population who had the right to vote at elections to the Soviets. In the subdivision relative to the

[4] Cy. 1920, No. 11, Art. 68.
[5] On the basis of a note to Art. 57 of the 1918 Constitution.

objects of the volost executive committee's jurisdiction, the provisions most typical of the Regulation Concerning Volost Executive Committees are Section 28, the advancement of labor mobilizations and the struggle with labor desertion; Section 29, the development of correct and timely accounting, of assessment in kind according to settlements, and of produce collection to be turned over to the state according to instructions of the organs of supply; Section 30, cooperation in the work of all the economic organs of the Republic for collecting raw materials—leather, flax, and so on; and Section 31, the struggle with speculation of every sort, against the concealment and unlawful sale and export of products which should be turned over to the state according to the assessment in kind.[6] These paragraphs substantially defined the work of the volost executive committee during this period.

With regard to the remaining local organs of state authority, the city Soviets (with few exceptions) passed through a particularly severe crisis in consequence of the continuance of civil war into 1920, and were almost everywhere merged with the province and the guberniya executive committees. Nevertheless, a new work by section commissions of unified subdivisions of the executive committee and the Soviet developed in a number of unified city Soviets, and a new organ to guide the city Soviet was created, its bureau or presidium more or less closely connected with the provincial or guberniya executive committee.

At the same time guberniyas and provincial organs of Soviet authority developed and grew strong in the tense civil war setting. "The erstwhile remoteness of subdivisions of the Executive Committee from the Committee itself—and of the latter from lower Executive Committees—so sorely felt in the recent past, is now yielding to the solidarity of the government mechanism."[7] Chiefly responsible for these accomplishments were (1) the broadly expanded work of executive committee presidia resting on the work of administrative departments reorganized on the basis of the 1920 regulation, and (2) the regular sessions of councils (under the guberniya executive committees) of presidents of provincial executive committees, and of presidents of volost executive committees (under provincial executive committees, as already pointed out). Subsequently these councils developed into session plena under executive committees. During this period, the regional organizations established by the 1918 Constitution ceased to exist because of the tremendous shiftings of front lines and the necessity of intensifying the immediate bond between the center and the guberniyas.

[6] Cy. 1920, No. 20, Art. 108.
[7] From the leading editorial in *The Authority of the Soviets* (the journal of the People's Commissariat for Internal Affairs) (Aug. 1920), No. 8.

The Eighth All-Russian Congress of Soviets and Local Organs of State Authority. The Eighth All-Russian Congress of Soviets was held in December, 1920, with the civil war substantially ended. It proceeded in fact to envisage measures for peaceful building, although only one directive as to Soviet building was adopted immediately, this congress being anomalous in that most of its directives were devoted to (or associated with) the organization and activity of local organs of state authority. Such were the Directive Concerning the Working Out of a Regulation as to Regional Economic Organs and Guberniyas and Provincial Economic Councils; that Concerning Measures of Strengthening and Developing the Peasant Village Economy; that Concerning Local Organs of Economic Administration; that Concerning Local Stocks of Supply; and that Concerning the Drawing of Women into Economic Building.[8]

Inasmuch as most of these were realized already in the period immediately following, that of the rehabilitation of the national economy, they will be surveyed below. Here the first of them should be especially noted, the integrating directive concerned with Soviet building,[9] whose extensive Subdivision 4, Concerning the Interrelations of Central and Local Organs, fundamentally confirmed the goals set by the Seventh All-Russian Congress of Soviets in this regard, making them precise and amplifying them on the basis of accumulated experience. Thus, on the matter of suspending the putting of orders of separate commissariats into practice, it was pointed out that this is admissible only in exceptional cases; and furthermore that the Presidium of the All-Russian Central Executive Committee, in passing on the correctness of suspending an order, directs that the guilty party, whether People's Commissar or directors of the guberniya executive committee, be brought into court. Subdivision 5, Concerning the Work of Local Soviets and of Their Executive Committees, confirmed the obligation to further the corresponding directives of the Seventh All-Russian Congress of Soviets, and at the same time pointed out the necessity of developing regularly the reelections of the Soviets and the summoning of their congresses, and proposed the formation in all settlements of the city type, of city Soviets whose plena were to meet not less than twice a month. A regular summons of sessions of executive committees was likewise required, inasmuch as they had begun to be entirely superseded by sessions of the presidia; furthermore, expanded councils of all executive committees were established, with participation of representatives of lower executive committees and Soviets, by volost and province not less frequently than once a month, and by guberniya not less frequently than twice a month.

[8] Cy. 1921, No. 1, Arts. 1, 8, 9, 3, 6 and 12.
[9] Cy. 1921, No. 1, Art. 1.

SEC. 5: LOCAL ORGANS OF STATE AUTHORITY IN THE TRANSITION PERIOD TO PEACEFUL WORK FOR THE REHABILITATON OF THE NATIONAL ECONOMY (1921 TO 1925)

In orderly realization of the directives of the Eighth All-Russian Congress of Soviets, the Presidium of the All-Russian Central Executive Committee (February 8, 1921) issued directives Concerning Regular Reelections of Soviets and Summoning Congresses Thereof at Established Times,[1] and Concerning the Summoning of Regular Expanded Councils of Representatives of Village Soviets and Volost and Province Executive Committees.[2] At the same time the Presidium of the All-Russian Central Executive Committee adopted a Directive Concerning the Organization of City Soviets of Worker and Red Army Deputies[3] which proposed to reestablish city Soviets in all cities and factory and works villages where they had ceased to exist during the civil war, and also to create them where they had never existed previously. On March 10 the Presidium of the All-Russian Central Executive Committee distributed a "Circular Letter Concerning the Work of City Soviets"[4] devoted chiefly to improving the work of plena and of the standing committees of the Soviets which had developed during the civil-war period. The opening lines of this circular letter—to the effect that "the rehabilitation of the economy of the Soviet Republic requires the toiling people (and, in the first instance, the city proletariat) to struggle with unprecedented intensity," are, in general, the leitmotiv of the Presidium directives here enumerated. In these conditions, the work of the Soviets (and, in the first instance, of their economic organs), work which had been unified (as early as 1920 by a directive of the Eighth All-Russian Congress of Soviets) by economic councils of a regional character, took on special significance. These councils were created from the inception of the New Economic Policy upon the motion of Lenin and were associated with all the subordinate executive committees and Soviets.

Lenin's policy in the sphere of Soviet economic building at the very beginning of the New Economic Policy found brilliant theoretical and organizational expression in a "Mandate from the Council of Labor and Defense to Local Soviet Institutions," and a "Proposed Directive of the All-Russian Central Executive Committee Concerning Local Economic

[1] Cy. 1921, No. 11, Art. 72.   [3] Cy. 1921, No. 11, Art. 71.
[2] Cy. 1921, No. 12, Art. 77.   [4] Cy. 1921, No. 30, Art. 163.

Councils, Their Accountability and Leadership by the Mandate of the Council of People's Commissars and of the Council of Labor and Defense." Both these documents, written by Lenin during the last twelve days of May, 1921, were considered at the Fourth All-Russian Congress of Trade Unions and (on May 26) at the Tenth Conference of the Bolshevik Worker-Peasant Party. On June 30 they were affirmed by the Presidium of the All-Russian Central Executive Committee.[5] They have, over a period of years, defined the leading lines of Soviet economic building in the rural districts. In essence these two documents, like many other works of Lenin, are broader than their titles: the Mandate properly takes economic work—the organization of EKOSO (the Regional Economic Councils)—as the decisive link in the chain during the period under consideration, while at the same time, and particularly in its general part and "first group of questions," it presents an analysis of the problems of the state of the proletarian dictatorship during the most critical stage under review, with particular emphasis upon the tasks of local organs of authority (including those of promoting and strengthening cadres and struggling against bureaucracy).

The beginning of the policy of resuscitating the work of the Soviets. The first two and one-half years of the New Economic Policy—with its economic successes, the struggle of the worker class to confirm its union with the peasantry, the growth of the worker class in connection with the development of industry—created a sharp crisis in elections to the Soviets at the end of 1923. Thus, activity in elections to the village Soviets—which had been only 22.3 per cent of all qualified electors in 1922—had increased to 37.2 per cent in 1923. The increase of activity in elections to city Soviets was less notable—from 36.5 per cent to 38.5 per cent—but activity in elections in the worker settlements to guberniya congresses of Soviets increased greatly. Their representation grew from .3 per cent (in 1922) to 7.3 per cent (in 1923) of the entire structure of congresses.

The increased activity in elections to Soviets was a symptom of the incipient resuscitation of their work expressed in the development of the organization and work of their standing committees and of promotion, in the expansion of the work of numerous mass organizations connected with the Soviets (nuclei of cooperation of Worker-Peasant Inspection, nonparty conferences, and assemblies of women delegates), and in the development of a net of worker correspondents and agricultural correspondents, and so forth. Calculation of all these factors, noted by Stalin in his report (in May, 1924) at the Thirteenth Party Congress, was reflected in the following words of the Congress directive upon the report of Molotov, summarizing the general features of development of the Soviets during this period:

⁵ Cy. 1921, No. 44, Art. 223.

The political activity of the worker masses grows in conjunction with the country's general rise, and finds expression in the incipient resuscitation of the work of Soviets and trade-union organs, and in the growth of worker organizations, including those concerned with culture and education, and with living conditions. Of special significance is the resuscitation of the work of Soviets of Worker and Peasant Deputies (the creation under them of standing committees, commissions, and councils, and the attraction thereto of a noteworthy number of workers, peasants, and persons in service).[6]

Stalin's report at the Thirteenth Party Congress marked the beginning of a new stage in the development of the Soviets. Soon after the Congress, a revision of the regulations relating to local organs of state authority was begun, and in October of the same year (1924) a session of the All-Russian Central Executive Committee confirmed new regulations relating to village Soviets [7] and to volost and provincial Congresses of Soviets and their executive committees.[8] At that time the commission for Soviet building began its work under the Central Committee of the Bolshevik Worker-Peasant Party on the basis of a directive of its October plenum. For further development of matters connected with the policy of resuscitating the Soviets, the Presidium of the Central Executive Committee of the USSR (December 19, 1924) directed the summoning of an All-Union council on matters of Soviet building from representatives of central and local institutions; at the same time, in the course of developing the policy of resuscitating the Soviets in connection with the then campaign of Soviet reelections and the feeble activity of voters in numerous places, the Central Executive Committee of the USSR issued a directive to count as valid only elections in which not less than 35 per cent of the voters took part, and to reelect those Soviets in which less than this number of voters participated.

The first session of the All-Union Council for Soviet Building, assembling in January, 1925, planned the basic tasks of the policy of resuscitating the work of the Soviets according to the reports of Kalinin and Kaganovich, and organized a study thereof in the center and in the rural districts for which commissions for Soviet building were created under executive committees and Soviets. At the second session of the conference (in April, 1925), there were consideration—on the basis of the preparatory work aforesaid in the center and in the country districts—and confirmation of measures on matters of elections to the Soviets: as to the work of the village Soviets and the organization therein of presidia and committees of review, as to improvement of the work of meetings under the guidance of village Soviets,

---

[6] *The All-Union Communist Party (of Bolsheviks) in Resolutions* (Pt. 1, p. 584).
[7] Cy. 1924, No. 82, Art. 827.
[8] Cy. 1924, No. 82, Art. 826.

as to expanded sittings of the volost executive committees and the organization of sections (standing committees) under them, as to strengthening the bond between the lower organs as well as that between them and the higher executive committees, as to establishing quarterly oral reports of rural Soviets to electors, as to strengthening rural Soviets and volosts, and as to strengthening volost budgets, and of a series of measures for strengthening the work of city Soviets as to the work of their plena and standing committees and the broadening of their administrative and economic functions.

The decisions of the Conference for Soviet Building were approved by the Third All-Russian Congress of Soviets held in May, 1925, which, in a directive pursuant to the report of Kalinin, pointed out that "the Soviets must, as organs of authority, become in reality the head of all economic and cultural building of the Soviet Republic and direct the same"; moreover, "the Soviets can carry on this pressing and enormously important work only upon the condition of attracting the toilers themselves into Soviet building and of developing the independence of workers and peasants, male and female, guaranteeing thereby genuine proletarian guidance." [9]

In a conversation with students of the Communist university bearing the name of Sverdlov (1924), Stalin spoke of the policy (of resuscitating the Soviets) as a form of strengthening the administrative-political bond (as well as the economic and cultural bond) between the worker class and the peasantry through "implanting Soviet democracy in city and country and resuscitating the Soviets with the objects (1) of making the state mechanism simpler and less expensive and improving its moral sanitation, (2) of hunting therefrom the elements of bureaucracy and bourgeois decomposition, and (3) of effecting a complete rapprochement of the state mechanism with the millions of the masses." [10]

The counterrevolutionary Trotsky-Bukharin-Kamenev gang, then operating under the banner of the opposition, sought to combat the policy of resuscitating the Soviets, slanderously attacking the party and broadcasting their paltry anti-Lenin theories against a worker-peasant union under the guidance of the worker class, affrighted by the regeneration of the Soviets and the scourgings of the peasant element in the "lower stages" of the Soviet state mechanism, and so on and so on. With every day and every hour, however, sober reality disclosed that this anti-Soviet concoction was utterly thin and spurious.

Regulations of local organs of Soviet authority during 1924–1925 expressed the policy of resuscitating the Soviets and rehabilitating the national economy. Yet vast as was the difference between the 1924 regulations (of

[9] Cz. 1925, No. 35, Art. 247.
[10] Stalin, *Questions of Leninism* (9th Russian ed.), p. 147.

village Soviets, volost executive committees, and provincial executive committees) and those of 1922, the further reorganization during the next six months, based on the work of the All-Union Conference for Soviet Building, was hardly less enormous, particularly as regards the village Soviets and the volost executive committees.

The chief, and perhaps the most essential, characteristic of the 1924 Regulation Concerning the Village Soviets, as distinguished from earlier regulations, was that here the question of the mutual relationship of village Soviet and village meeting was put and decided. The meeting was considered a means of drawing "the entire toiling population into the building of local life." The regulation charged the village Soviet with the obligation of summoning "general assemblies of the citizens" and reporting "to higher organs, in necessary cases, all the directives of general assemblies of the citizens—their desires and petitions." [11] The directive of the All-Union Council for Soviet Building (April 1, 1925) said:

It is essential to fix strict limits to the rights and obligations of the general assembly (the meeting) and the village Soviet—not permitting either to substitute for the other in any case whatever. The village Soviet must be the sole directing organ of authority in the village. Around it are unified all the state institutions operating in the territory of the village, as well as the village society (peasant committees, cooperation, trade unions, and the like).[12]

The creation of standing committees and committees of revision was enormously significant for the strengthening of the village Soviet. In place of the halfhearted formulation in Section 4c of the 1924 regulation (whereby the village Soviet "forms commissions in necessary cases and charges separate citizens and groups of citizens with diverse matters"),[13] the council established that standing committees (sections) and committees "for fundamental branches of administrative, economic, and cultural activity" be created under the village Soviet. In sessions of the village Soviet, representatives of local social organizations as well as village officials —teachers, doctors, agriculturists, surveyors, and the like—may participate and have the right of a deliberative vote. According to Section 20 of the regulation, in large settlements the village Soviet could, with permission of the guberniya executive committee, elect an executive committee, and the council gave permission for the organization of a presidium in village Soviets of more than twenty persons. Most of the 1924 Regulation Concerning Village Soviets was taken up with an enumeration of objects of the village Soviet's jurisdiction which, in the 1922 regulation, occupied only a few

[11] Cy. 1924, No. 82, Art. 827.
[12] Cf. *The Council for Matters of Soviet Building* (1925), pp. 172–173.
[13] Cy. 1924, No. 82, Art. 827.

lines altogether. Unlike the old regulation's purely declarative catalogue of objects of the village Soviet's jurisdiction, this enumeration in 1924 generalized legislative material after three years of practical work by village Soviets under the conditions of the New Economic Policy. Linking the activity of the village Soviet with that of cooperative organizations in the village, and creating budgets showing income and outgo (which, with the enlargement of village Soviets, began to develop into village budgets) should be particularly noted.

The Regulation Concerning Volost Executive Committees [14] was no longer calculated upon the former administrative unit with a population of around 10,000, but upon an enlarged administrative-economic unit—the volost or district—with a population of 30,000 to 40,000 which had, in a number of guberniyas, begun to take the place of provinces (Tula, North Dvina, Astrakhan, Orenburg).

The Regulation Concerning City Soviets [15] was adopted by a session of the All-Russian Central Executive Committee (October 24, 1925) six months after the termination of the labors of the Council for Soviet Building, and its conclusions were taken fully into account in that regulation. Whereas the 1922 regulation had permitted the organization of city Soviets only in cities with a population of upwards of 10,000, the new regulation required them to be organized in all cities and work settlements. In cities with a population above 50,000, the city Soviets could form district Soviets. City Soviet elections took place under various rules of representation, depending on the population of the city. The city Soviet could choose its working organ, the presidium, consisting of not more than eleven persons. Communal departments were organized under the city Soviets. For other branches of the city Soviet's work, city subdivisions, or parts embodied in subdivisions of the guberniya or provincial executive committee, were formed subordinate to the city Soviet. Standing committees (sections) for separate branches of the work of the city Soviet were organized under it after the selection of their members. (Their membership must necessarily include the supervisor of the corresponding department of the executive committee, although he could not be president of the section.) Members of trade unions and of other social organizations put forward by the latter to work in sections of the Soviet were eligible as section members. Members of sections were either attached individually to different city institutions and enterprises for work and control or worked there in section brigades formed for a specific purpose.

All city Soviets were required to have certain standing committees (com-

[14] Cy. 1924, No. 82, Art. 826.
[15] Cy. 1925, No. 91, Art. 662.

munal economy, finances, popular education, public health, and cooperative trade) and could organize others as well. Directives of a standing committee (section) were affirmed and put into practice through the presidium of the municipal Soviet; if the section were not in accord with the decision of the presidium, the former had the right to present the question for consideration of the plenum of the Soviet.

Under the new regulation, city Soviets had the rights of a juristic person, including the right to issue binding directives, to impose administrative levies, and to an independent municipal budget, and a broad jurisdiction in all branches of work concerned with city government, economy, and cultural building.

The starting-point of *the development of the territorial organization of Soviets during the rehabilitation period* was the sixth subdivision of the Directive of the Eighth All-Russian Congress of Soviets for Soviet Building: "The All-Russian Congress of Soviets charges the Presidium of the All-Russian Central Executive Committee . . . to accelerate the work of developing the new administrative-economic division of the RSFSR principally on the basis of economic gravitation; to obligate all departments to finish their labors in the formation of districts within a month and to present them to the administrative commission under the All-Russian Central Executive Committee." [16] In another directive, Concerning the Working Out of a Regulation as to Regional Economic Organs,[17] the Eighth All-Russian Congress of Soviets entrusted to the Council of Labor and Defense the working out of such a regulation for the very next session of the All-Russian Central Executive Committee.

On the basis of these directives, the administrative commission of the All-Russian Central Executive Committee proceeded to work out "basis regulations" which were adopted at the March, 1921, session of the committee. But in March the Regulation Concerning Regional Economic Organs (EKOSO) was published, which pointed out that these organs are created "in order to reduce bureaucracy, accelerate the development in rural districts of measures which can and should be carried into effect by local decisions, and harmonize and intensify the activity of all the local economic organs" functioning in the territory of a given region.[18] In March of the same year (1921), a commission for the apportionment of districts was organized under the newly created State Planning Commission. To it passed the future working out of the problems of forming districts and of the entire scheme of territorial organization of the state mechanism with

[16] Cy. 1921, No. 1, Art. 1.
[17] Cy. 1921, No. 1, Art. 8.
[18] Cy. 1921, No. 27, Art. 153.

its new links, the district, the area, and the region. The organization and activity of regional economic organs, a prototype of the future administrative region in rural areas, were broadly developed in conformity with the network of districts designed by the State Planning Commission.

In March, 1922, at the Eleventh Congress of the Bolshevik Worker-Peasant Party, Lenin said in a political report to the Central Committee (his last report at a Party conference):

It is essential to broaden and develop the autonomy and the activity of the regional economic organs. We now have a division of Russia into regional districts based on scientific principles and taking into account economic and climatic conditions, ways of life, conditions of obtaining fuel and of local industry, and so on. District and regional economic organs are created on the basis of this division. Of course there will be particular corrections, but it is essential to elevate the authority of these regional economic organs.[19]

Against this policy of Lenin for the radical reorganization of the local state mechanism, the wrecker Trotsky-Sapronov "opposition" carried on behind the scenes a subversive struggle with the support of the bureaucrats of the right, in consequence of which the proposed legislation for the formation of districts, introduced at the May session of the All-Russian Central Executive Committee in 1922, was transferred from session to session and could in no wise be brought forward. The problem was solved in April, 1923, by a directive of the Twelfth Party Congress, wherein the Congress, admitting that the former administrative-economic division of republics was not in conformity with the country's new political and economic needs, found, nevertheless, that the introduction of a new system of administrative-economic division required a cautious approach as well as a long period for its final development. In a subsequent part of the directive the Congress regarded the proposed formation of districts, as put together by the State Planning Commission and the Administrative Commission of the All-Russian Central Executive Committee, as merely a tentative working hypothesis, requiring amplification, verification, and development based on experience.

The Fourteenth Congress of the Bolshevik Worker-Peasant Party (held in December, 1925) noted, in a resolution upon the report of the Central Executive Committee of the Party, that "after the partition into districts had been successfully developed, Soviet authority began to lay a material-economic foundation under the Regions and the Autonomous and Union Republics." [20]

---

[19] Lenin (Russian ed.), Vol. XXVII, p. 259.
[20] *The All-Union Communist Party (of Bolsheviks) in Resolutions*, Pt. 2, p. 47.

SEC. 6: THE SOVIETS IN THE STRUGGLE FOR SOCIALIST INDUSTRIALIZATION (1926 TO 1929)

As early as October 3–10, 1925, the plenum of the Central Committee of the Bolshevik Worker-Peasant Party, in an address, "To All Organizations and All Members of the Bolshevik Worker-Peasant Party," pointed out that in 1925 "state industry is approaching the culmination of its rehabilitation period, wherefore still more important tasks are in order—the reconstruction of industry, and therewith of the entire national economy as well, upon a new and higher technical basis." [1] In the Fourteenth Congress of the All-Union Communist Party of Bolsheviks (held at the end of December, 1925), Stalin, in a political report to the Central Committee, put before the Party and the country the task of carrying on the work in the sphere of developing national economy "along the line of transforming our country from an agricultural into an industrial country." [2] As early as April, 1926, the plenum of the Central Committee of the All-Union Communist Party (of Bolsheviks) notes that "industry is expanding far more vigorously than all other branches of the USSR economy," [3] and that "during the present year extensive investments are for the first time being made in industry for reequipment and new building, whereby the broadening of industry during the coming years becomes definitely feasible." [4] Later, at the Fifteenth Party Congress, the Party formulated the task of creating a socialist industry surpassing the technical level and compass of the advanced capitalist countries.

The task of industrializing the country put before the Soviets new organization problems in the economic sphere, as well as in that of mass work, which were solved by the method of further developing the policy of resuscitating the Soviets (as Molotov pointed out at the July plenum of the Central Committee of the All-Union Communist Party (of Bolsheviks) in 1926. On this basis a number of special problems were put forward. Thus, the directive of the April (1926) plenum of the Central Committee of the Party pointed out that "it is necessary to cooperate in every way for the development of local industry, both state industry and that of individual handicraftsmen, working especially on local fuel." The development of local industry and the precise definition and strict observance of property rights of the Soviets were intimately interrelated, and accordingly, to regularize the matter, the Central Executive Committee of the USSR issued

---

[1] Ibid., p. 43.
[2] Stenographic Report of the Fourteenth All-Union Communist Party (of Bolsheviks), p. 49.
[3] The All-Union Communist Party (of Bolsheviks) in Resolutions, Pt. 2, p. 98.
[4] Ibid.

Basic Regulations Concerning Property Rights of Local Soviets (January 9, 1929).[5] According to Paragraph 2 of those regulations, "the distribution and redistribution, as between local Soviets of different grades, of property of local significance is accomplished by means of Union Republic legislation." These regulations established in numerous later points the basic rights granted to local Soviets in organizing and exploiting their enterprises, utilizing credit, and the like.

In addition to this problem—a special problem, yet one of substantial importance for the Soviets—the tasks of developing industrialization put forward before them for solution more general problems of organization as well. The July (1926) resolution of the plenum of the Central Committee of the All-Union Communist Party (of Bolsheviks) (upon the report of Molotov) relative to reelections of the Soviets said: "It is essential to accelerate the putting into practice of the new *Regulations Concerning City Soviets*, and to work out from beginning to end the new problems of their labor, particularly in cities with a negligible proletarian population." [6] These issues were settled in accordance with the Soviet line only in 1928–1929 and, in the first instance, by the issuance by the USSR Central Executive Committee (February 8, 1928) of the Fundamental Regulations as to Organizing City Soviets of Worker, Peasant, and Red Army Deputies in the USSR.[7]

Confirming all the rights of the city Soviet set out in the 1925 regulations, the Fundamental Regulations of 1928 made those rights precise, pointing out that "all enterprises, lands, and buildings within the pale of a city and of city significance must be confirmed in behalf of the city Soviets" (Art. 16), further indicating a number of measures assuring the effectuation of this point. Article 20 is also of essential significance. It pointed out that

in cities and worker settlements which are highly developed industrially, wherein the directive organs of state enterprises carry on a significant part of the functions of rendering cultural and economic service to the worker population, legislation—of the USSR and of the Union Republics whereto they appertain—should assure to the city Soviets the directing influence in serving the workers' cultural and life needs by handing over to them (on the basis of special accords) that portion of the material resources, social-cultural institutions, and enterprises of social enjoyment not indissolubly integrated with production.

This permitted industrial enterprises to be relieved of such institutions as schools, hospitals, baths, and laundries and allowed the city Soviet to intensify its service to production in respect of culture and living conditions.

[5] Cz. 1929, No. 3, Art. 26.
[6] *The All-Union Communist Party (of Bolsheviks) in Resolutions*, Pt. 2, p. 113.
[7] Cz. 1928, No. 10, Art. 86.

Along the line of making precise the problems, referred to by Molotov, of city Soviets' work in cities with a negligible proletarian population, Article 21 of the Fundamental Regulations pointed out that, in cities not having a big city economy and an industrial proletariat, "city Soviets carry into effect the functions of social control chiefly as regards the activity of the corresponding executive committee and its different institutions and enterprises." And Article 30 must also be noted, to the effect that executive committees of a territorial unit of which a city or worker settlement is a constituent part "are bound to render an account of their work to the plena of city Soviets."

On January 27, 1929, the Presidium of the All-Russian Central Executive Committee distributed a circular to Central Executive Committees of the autonomous republics, and to territorial, regional, and guberniya executive committees, "Concerning Mass Work of City Soviets." [8] In content and significance this circular was far broader than its title would indicate. The committee pointed out that, notwithstanding the presence of definite legislative instructions, cases are observed where "city budgets remain unallocated and allocations and transfers of enterprises and properties to city Soviets having city significance are not being carried out." With regard to the Soviets turning their attention toward production, the circular said "It is essential to organize the work of city Soviets and their standing committees to conform with the immediate tasks of socialist building, particularly the tasks of rationalizing production, improving the state mechanism, struggling for a regime of economy and for cultural revolution, and so on." Furthermore, the circular gave the first official sanction to the organization of deputy groups which had been continually developing for some years: "The methods of work practiced by the city Soviets in country districts in the form of organizing deputy groups, village elders, and lists of available members of city Soviets in enterprises, have been vindicated and must be developed even further, particularly in industrial centers." The circular devoted great attention to verification of deputies' fulfillment of orders and to their accountability, as well as to the recall of deputies who did not justify themselves. The concluding part of the circular stated: "The particularly insistent task is the improvement of the interrelations between the Soviets and state industrial enterprises which have, down to the present moment, served the social-cultural and life needs of the worker." Then the circular proceeded to make concrete Article 20 which we have previously noted.

To assure that it would be possible for Soviets of territorial and regional centers (there were no longer any guberniyas) to be occupied in the broadest

[8] Published in the journal *The Authority of the Soviets*, App. 1; also in all editions of the collection *Local Organs of Authority*.

and most rational way with city economy and aid to production, the All-Russian Central Executive Committee (October 30, 1929) issued a directive, Concerning City Soviets of Cities Which Are Centers of Territorial and Regional Unions and Their Interrelations with Territorial and Regional Organs of Authority.[9] As a rule, these city Soviets had been segregated from districts and were, as regards the election of deputies to the All-Russian Congress of Soviets, on an equality with district congresses; their presidents could not at the same time be presidents of territorial (regional) executive committees. This directive sanctioned the creation by city Soviets of their own independent subdivisions: communal, finance, labor, trade, popular education, public health, and social security; and it was proposed to organize under their presidia a secretariat whose members included instructors in mass-organization work. The interrelations of city Soviets and their departments with executive committees and their departments were constructed on the principles established by the Seventh and Eighth All-Russian Congress of Soviets and the RSFSR Constitution of 1925.

Socialist reconstruction of national economy posed the problem of strengthening and developing the mass-organization work and promoting the restrained class line of the work—the village Soviets. Inasmuch as an important part in village life was played by the meeting, which merged the Soviet with local society and made it easier for kulaks to penetrate the work of the village Soviet, the All-Russian Central Executive Committee (on March 14, 1927) issued a directive, Concerning General Meeting of Citizens in Village Settlements,[10] whereby meetings were held to consider and examine matters touching the life of the village and to consider general questions of state, district, regional, guberniya, area, province, and volost significance; but village meetings had no authority to consider questions which were for the consideration of general assemblies of members of agricultural societies and vice versa, and only those who enjoyed elective rights could be present at the meetings.

On March 21, 1927, the All-Russian Central Executive Committee and the RSFSR Council of People's Commissars affirmed the Regulation Concerning Standing Committees (Sections) Under District and Volost Executive Committees and Village Soviets,[11] which were formed for separate branches of work to attract broad masses of the toilers into the practical work of the district executive committees and village Soviets and to work out in advance questions to be examined by them. Paragraph 1 contains a small but essential note inserted in 1931: "Deputy groups are organized under

[9] Cy. 1929, No. 80, Art. 784.
[10] Cy. 1927, No. 51, Art. 333.
[11] Cy. 1927, No. 39, Art. 350.

kolkhozes or production sections of the big kolkhozes, or sovkhozes or significant industrial enterprises, if such there be within the territory of a village Soviet." [12]

The role played by the agricultural standing committees of village Soviets constantly increased as the collectivization of agriculture proceeded. On December 10, 1929, the All-Russian Central Executive Committee and the RSFSR Council of People's Commissars affirmed the Regulation of Agricultural Production Councils Under Village Soviets, pointing out that

Agricultural Production Councils purpose to work out and promote measures for socialist reorganization of the agriculture of their district (the building of sovkhozes, kolkhozes and machine tractor stations, production cooperation, and so on) as well as for broadening the areas under crop, increasing harvest productivity, and developing animal husbandry and other branches of agriculture of their district in the sovkhozes and kolkhozes and in the poorest and middle economies also. They must prosecute their work on the basis of the class policy of Soviet authority.[13]

Their structure was very broad inasmuch as they could comprise representatives of kolkhozes, sovkhozes and agricultural societies, delegates of women's assemblies, activists from young communist leagues, hirelings, poor and middle peasants, agronomists, teachers, doctors, and so on, in addition to members and candidates of the village Soviet. The council for guiding its work chose a bureau of from five to seven persons and worked out a plan to accord with the plan of works of the village Soviet. The Agricultural Production Councils played a great part, as the authoritative social-mass organ of the village Soviet, in the social reorganization of the rural districts.

The new territorial organization of local Soviets. The swiftly expanding industrialization of the Soviet Union intensified the principles of planned economy in the country, and therewith the positive significance of regional organizations economically homogeneous and of adequate economic strength —with division thereof into area and particularly district—links which had everywhere ousted the obsolete province-volost (and therewith also the guberniya) system. In the middle of 1927, a great part of the RSFSR territory was already divided into regions. The presence of two systems of local organs of state authority created great difficulties in administration.

To attain the utmost unification of the work of the inferior Soviet organs connected with the economically expanding village, the People's Commissariat of Worker-Peasant Inspection worked out the draft of a directive concerning a revision of the rights and obligations of local organs of Soviet administration. This draft was adopted by the All-Russian Central

[12] Cy. 1931, No. 28, Art. 256.
[13] Cy. 1929, No. 87/88, Art. 865.

Executive Committee and the RSFSR Council of People's Commissars on July 23, 1927.[14] Embracing all the fundamental branches of economy and administration, the directive promoted a great decentralization of the work in the country districts, intensifying the operative functions of inferior organs, and relieving therefrom the superior organs, particularly the guberniya executive committees. In December, 1927, an enactment of the Fifteenth Congress of the All-Union Communist Party (of Bolsheviks), Concerning Directives for the Formation of a Five-Year Plan of National Economy, pointed out that "in order that planned guidance of the national economic life of the country may be as all-inclusive as possible, the Congress deems it necessary to complete the division of the entire country into districts during the course of the five-year period immediately ensuing." This was in fact completed during the next two years.

At a session on April 6, 1928, the All-Russian Executive Committee adopted a Regulation Concerning Territorial, Area and District Congresses of Soviets and Their Executive Committees.[15] Hitherto only regulations concerning separate territories and regions had been in operation (the Ural Region, the North Caucasus territory, and so forth). The adoption of the single regulation for all territorial and regional unions proved that the division of the country into districts was already approaching completion. On February 25, 1929, the All-Russian Central Executive Committee extended the action of this regulation to area and district organs of areas and districts embodied in autonomous republics and autonomous territories.[16] This regulation, with numerous intermediate corrections and amplifications, is operative as to territorial (regional) organs down to the present time. When areas were abolished, it naturally ceased to be in force as to area organs, except as regards a small number of areas in the RSFSR at the present time (apart from national areas, as to which a special regulation was issued, affirmed by the All-Russian Central Executive Committee on April 20, 1932).[17] It was in force as to district organs only down to January 1, 1931, when the All-Russian Central Executive Committee affirmed a special Regulation Concerning District Councils of Soviets and District Executive Committees [18] based on the Fundamental Regulations Concerning District Congresses of Soviets and District Executive Committees adopted not long before by the Central Executive Committee of the USSR (October 13, 1930).[19]

[14] Cy. 1927, No. 79, Art. 533.   [17] Cy. 1932, No. 39, Art. 176.
[15] Cy. 1928, No. 70, Art. 503.   [18] Cy. 1931, No. 11, Art. 143.
[16] Cy. 1929, No. 27, Art. 275.   [19] Cz. 1930, No. 52, Art. 545.

SEC. 7: THE SOVIETS IN THE STRUGGLE FOR THE COLLECTIVIZATION OF AGRICULTURE (1930 TO 1934)

In his report at the Sixteenth Congress of the All-Union Communist Party (of Bolsheviks) Stalin said: "Such economic upheavals have already occurred in the country as to afford complete basis for the assertion that we have succeeded in turning the village into a new path—the path of collectivization—and have thereby guaranteed the successful building of socialism in the country, and not only in the city." [1] In the same address he pointed out that the Party had proclaimed the watchword, "Collectivization," as early as at its Fifteenth Party Congress, but only during the second half of 1929 was there noted the complete turn of the peasantry to the side of the kolkhozes and the entry therein of the middle peasant masses. In this connection the Central Committee of the All-Union Communist Party (of Bolsheviks) adopted (on January 5, 1930) a directive, Concerning the Tempo of Collectivization and Measures for State Aid to Kolkhoz Building.[2] Reporting at the Party Council under the Central Committee of the Party (January 30, 1930), Molotov formulated the question of reorganizing the Soviets which had failed to keep pace with life, and turning their faces toward the kolkhoz. Thereupon the Central Executive Committee of the USSR adopted a decision to summon an All-Union Council on the matter of the tasks of the Soviets in connection with collectivization. This council opened January 20, 1930.

Agents set in motion by the kulaks, having wormed their way into the ranks of our Party, sought to utilize the very successes of kolkhoz building against the Soviets, openly or covertly posing the question: Were not the village Soviets needless in areas of complete collectivization where supposedly their functions could be carried on by the kolkhoz administrations? In the All-Union Council, with reference to the work of the Soviets in connection with collectivization, Kalinin and Kaganovich sternly rebuffed the novel liquidator-creatures of the kulaks headed by Rosit. A directive of the Presidium of the Central Executive Committee of the USSR, Concerning the New Tasks of the Soviets in Connection with the Widely Extended Collectivization in the Rural Areas,[3] issued (January 25, 1930) and based on the labors of the council, provided:

All attempts to liquidate the village Soviets and to weaken or lower their

[1] Stalin, *Questions of Leninism* (10th Russian ed.), p. 378.
[2] *Party Building* (1930), No. 2 (4), p. 72.
[3] Cz. 1930, No. 7, Art. 85.

directive role in connection with mass collectivization, whether overt or formally masked as an ostensible transfer of the rights of village Soviets to administrations of collective economies, all these attempts are essentially anti-Soviet, and reflect the moods of our class enemies, who seek to undermine the proletarian dictatorship and to weaken the power of its organs. Such liquidator efforts must be repulsed in the most decisive and pitiless fashion.

The council emphasized that village Soviets must stand "at the head of the kolkhoz movement" through "active participation in putting together and carrying into effect production plans of the collective economies; moreover, the role of the village Soviets must be particularly manifested in intensifying all the processes of socialization, of the correct organization of labor, and in seeing to it that the collective economies carry out all their obligations to the proletarian state (grain storage, contracts, imposts, and so on)." All this the village Soviets were obligated to perform on the condition that every farm laborer and poor peasant, together with the middle-class peasant, be drawn into daily work of the Soviets, liquidating the kulaks as a class, on the basis of complete collectivization. In order to enhance the role of the Soviets, the directive required that the directing Soviet cadres be examined and strengthened, ordained the introduction of a village budget in areas of complete collectivization, and provided the setting for activating all branches of agricultural work. In its concluding part, the directive stated "the necessity—in order to achieve a swift and decisive consummation—of conducting reelections of village Soviets that had manifested their incapacity to direct the kolkhoz movement."

The archaic regulation of 1924 was inadequate for the rebuilding of the village Soviets to meet the tasks of collectivization. Although it provided (in Par. 8b) that the village Soviet "cooperates in the organization and development of the collective economies and affords aid and support to the organs carrying on this work," the task contemplated by the regulation in its entirety was that of cooperating to reestablish the peasant economies ruined by years of imperialist and civil wars. The period of socialist reconstruction, of collectivization of the rural areas, presented new problems. These, the turning of the village Soviet to face toward the kolkhoz, were also indicated in the Basic Regulations for Organizing Village Soviets in the USSR confirmed by the Presidium of the Central Executive Committee of the USSR on February 3, 1930,[4] developing the principles set out in the directive of January 25, 1930, already considered.[5] In particular, Article 19 stated: "Independent budgets must be formed in all village Soviets and . . . in all districts of complete collectivization the village budgets

---

[4] Cz. 1930, No. 16, Art. 172.
[5] P. 762 previously, and Cz. 1930, No. 7, Art. 85.

must be introduced without fail beginning with the budget year 1930–1931."

At the January (1930) Party Conference under the Central Executive Committee of the All-Union Communist Party (of Bolsheviks), Molotov spoke of the necessity of reorganizing the work of the Soviets in districts and regions.[6] This reorganization found its first expression in the *new stage of district formation*—the reorganization of the territorial arrangement of the Soviet state mechanism.

In July, 1930, at the Sixteenth Party Congress, Stalin said:

There can be no doubt that we could not have achieved the enormous work in reorganizing agriculture and advancing the kolkhoz movement if we had not promoted the formation of districts. . . . The center of gravity of kolkhoz building is now shifted to the district organizations. Here the threads of kolkhoz building and of every other sort of economic work in the rural districts meet along the lines of cooperation and of the Soviets and of credit and of stores.[7]

But the district lacked sufficient people and resources as well as the immediate guidance of the territory. The path to all this was blocked by the obsolete area which was eliminated by decision of the Central Party Committee (July 15, 1930) as "an unnecessary dividing wall between the region and the districts." In its resolution upon the report of the Central Party Committee, the Sixteenth Party Congress pointed out that it "completely and entirely approves the decision of the Central Committee concerning the *abolition of areas* and the strengthening of the district as the fundamental link of socialist building in the rural districts which must result in the Party —Soviet—mechanism being brought decisively near to the village, to the kolkhozes, to the masses." [8]

According to the decision of the Central Committee of the All-Union Communist Party (of Bolsheviks), the liquidation of areas must be finished by October 1, 1930. On October 13 the Central Executive Committee and the Council of People's Commissars of the USSR affirmed the Basic Regulations Concerning District Congresses of Soviets and District Executive Committees,[9] the introductory part of which stated that "with the liquidation of areas and the transfer of their rights to districts, the latter becomes the most important link in the system of Soviet organs of authority and acquires exceptional significance—in socialist reorganization, the economic and cultural advance of the village, the drive on the kulaks, and the struggle with bureaucracy."

[6] Molotov: *Face to Face with the Kolkhoz Movement* (1930), p. 9.
[7] Stalin, *Questions of Leninism* (10th Russian ed.), p. 406.
[8] *The All-Union Communist Party (of Bolsheviks) in Resolution*, Pt. 2, Art. 405.
[9] Cz. 1930, No. 52, Art. 545.

The most essential element in this regulation concerning district executive committees was that the jurisdiction given to area district committees
by the 1928 regulation passed substantially to the districts.

The expanding socialist reconstruction of the national economy demanded a commensurate reconstruction of state mechanism to the end of
intensifying planned administration of the country's economy by the state.
The division into districts and the liquidation of the areas, which posed
anew the question of organizing the Soviets of the larger, area cities, contributed to the same end. The population of these cities was often more
numerous than that of districts, and they could not be subordinated to
district executive committees. Accordingly, on August 9, 1930, the Presidium of the Central Executive Committee of the USSR published a directive, Concerning the Organization of the Work of City Soviets in Connection with the Liquidation of Areas [10] to the effect that cities with a population exceeding 50,000—being of great industrial significance as well as cultural-political centers—are set apart into independent administrative-economic units.

Their city Soviets are immediately subordinate to presidia of the Central
Executive Committees of the USSR or of the autonomous SSR, or to the
corresponding executive committees of the territory. Into cities so set apart,
contiguous village localities, within limits no greater than one district,
could be incorporated. In these localities village Soviets are preserved, while
at the same time their population takes part also in elections of the city
Soviet which forms its own independent mechanism to administer separate
branches of government and economy. Great significance attached to Paragraph 5 of the directive, which pointed out that numerous city social-cultural institutions were relied upon to serve the rural—and not only the city
—population, wherefore it was proposed that the Central Executive Committees of the Union Republics instruct the city Soviets as to how they could
further minister to the social and cultural needs of the rural population
nearest the cities. The same paragraph directed that "the city Soviets form
standing committees for work in the villages, to the end of intensifying the
work of city Soviets in rural districts." This directive furnished the impulse
for intensification of the city's patronage work over the village and along
the Soviet line.

To intensify the turning of city Soviets to face toward production, the
All-Russian Central Executive Committee distributed (on April 30, 1930)
a circular as to strengthening the patronage of factories and works over the
state mechanism, stating that "city Soviets and their standing committees
(sections) must establish the closest connection with the patronage bri-

[10] Cz. 1930, No. 42, Art. 435.

gades, giving heed at their conferences to communications of the worker brigades as to work done in control of the state mechanism," and that "deputy groups in the enterprises must become advanced organizers of the mass patronage movement." [11]

The successful development of the socialist reconstruction of the country intensified the part played by the city and the city economy. In June, 1931, a plenum of the Central Committee of the All-Union Communist Party (of Bolsheviks) adopted a directive—upon the report of Kaganovich—Concerning the Moscow City Economy and the Development of the USSR City Economy, which stated:

In the old industrial centers, whose growth during recent years has been tempestuous . . . the question of the development and reconstruction of city economy is not merely one of service to the toiling masses now living there, but also one of accommodating and shifting hundreds of thousands and millions of workers and serving their material and cultural needs. . . . At the same time, the organization of the machine and tractor service stations of the big kolkhozes and sovkhozes, the liquidation of the areas, and the turning of numerous settlements into district centers, leads to the building of hundreds of new cities in the erstwhile settlements. All this in the aggregate puts before the party anew the problem of the city during the period of reconstruction—the problem of rebuilding old cities and building new ones. [12]

The reconstruction and building of cities enhanced the significance of the work of city Soviets and required its reorganization as applied to the new tasks. The directive of the plenum of the Central Party Committee pointed out:

City Soviets must—as organs of proletarian authority in the cities—so reorganize their work that deputies of the Soviets be drawn into each branch of city economy in the first instance for active participation in the work. Standing committees of city Soviets must actually carry into effect daily observance and guidance of the work in each branch of the city economy. It is essential to have done with the practice of triumphant parade sessions of plena of city Soviets. These plena must become centers for the efficient solution of questions of city economy on the basis of the hundreds and thousands of notes and suggestions of their electors. [13]

Great upheavals occurred in the organization and work of the city Soviets, attributable to these directives, intensifying their role in the socialist reconstruction of city and village alike. In particular, city Soviets, their standing committees, and deputy groups played an extremely notable

[11] *Izvestiya of the Central Executive Committee of the USSR and the All-Russian Central Executive Committee* (1930), No. 185.
[12] *The All-Union Communist Party (of Bolsheviks) in Resolutions*, Pt. 2, pp. 477–478.
[13] *Ibid.*, p. 479.

part in promoting shock work and socialist emulation here. Such emulation developed not only as between the standing committees and the deputy groups within a city, but also as between different cities. Moreover, there were during this period a number of conferences of cities and districts to consummate agreements of socialist emulation which decidedly raised the work of a notable number of the cities. This work also attracted lower mass organizations of city Soviets, the quarter and street committees for city welfare, which were again developing strongly.

On January 20, 1933, the All-Russian Central Executive Committee affirmed a new Regulation Concerning City Soviets,[14] generalizing the directives and legislative acts previously issued and all the experience of the work of the city Soviets. As regards the scope of their rights, the objects of their jurisdiction, under this regulation the city Soviets possessed, within the limits of the city, rights and jurisdiction precisely like those of district executive committees after areas had been abolished. Numerous new elements were introduced into the organization of the city Soviets' work.

To intensify the active role of their plena, exclusive jurisdiction was then established as to matters which must be necessarily considered by a Soviet plenum, including specifically: (a) a plan of economic and of social and cultural building; (b) a city budget and an accounting of the fulfillment thereof; (c) the effecting of loans; (d) a draft of a general replanning of the city; (e) a plan of the city Soviet's work; (f) an account of the activity of the presidium of the city Soviet; (g) a report of the mandate commission (the committee on credentials) of the city Soviet; and (h) a report as to the execution of mandates of the electors.

If, between sessions of the plenum, the presidium of a city Soviet had to adopt a directive on any of these matters within the exclusive jurisdiction of the plenum, it must—at the very next sitting of the Soviet—present such directive for confirmation by the plenum. A special chapter (4) was devoted to the organization of subdivisions and to the state mechanism of the Soviet, contemplating two types of Soviet organization: in the cities subordinate to republics and territories, as many as eleven subdivisions were, in general, created; in cities subordinate to districts, three subdivisions (communal, finance, and popular education) and three boards of inspection (labor, public health, and social security) were created, as well as a planning commission under the presidium. In defining the jurisdiction of sections (standing committees) of the city Soviet, the essential point is "that the directive of the plenum of the city Soviet can charge the standing committees with fulfillment of the individual obligations of the city Soviet departments and boards of inspection" (Art. 29). There is also the instruc-

[14] Cy. 1933, No. 29, Art. 103.

tion that "in order that they may be put into practice, decisions of a standing committee, reached within the limits of its jurisdiction, are transferred to the supervisors of departments and the heads of the boards of inspection" (Art. 33). "If he disagrees with the decision of the standing committee, such supervisor or head may, within five days, transfer the question to be decided by the president or of the presidium of the city Soviet" (Art. 33). "If a standing committee disagrees with a directive of the presidium of the city Soviet, the former can transfer the matter to be decided by the plenum of the city Soviet" (Art. 34). A special chapter (6) is devoted to deputy groups, which are regarded as cells of the city Soviets in enterprises "through which the city Soviet organizes the workers to struggle for better fulfillment of production tasks, and attracts collectives of the toilers of the given enterprise to participate in the work of the city Soviet" (Art. 36).

At the beginning of the period under review, at the December, 1930, plenum of the Central Committee of the All-Union Communist Party (of Bolsheviks), it was pointed out in a resolution (in conformity with reports of Kalinin and Molotov) concerning reelections of the Soviets that "the work of the Soviets can be reorganized only on the basis of elevating the Soviets' role as pilots of the general Party line which is irreconcilably hostile as regards the right and the 'left' opportunism alike." [15] In the years immediately following, the role of the Soviets as pilots of the general Party line increased notably and they were measurably instrumental in assuring the success of the Party policy in the rural districts. Further attacks along the entire front in the struggle to build socialism, however, required Bolshevik organization to attain still higher levels.

At the Seventeenth Party Congress, Stalin pointed out that "after the correct political line has been given, organization work decides everything, including the fate of the political line itself, its fulfillment or frustration," [16] and demanded that organization guidance be "elevated to the level of political guidance." [17] Stalin's point as applied to the matter of Soviet building was also broadly developed in Kaganovich's address upon organization questions at this Congress.

A directive of the Seventeenth Party Congress, pursuant to this report, upon organization measures in the field of Soviet building ordained with reference to the Soviets: (1) abolition of building all Soviet economic mechanisms according to the functional system and the rebuilding thereof on the production-territorial basis, starting from the lower production links

---

[15] *The All-Union Communist Party (of Bolsheviks) in Resolutions,* Pt. 2, p. 455.
[16] Stalin, *Questions of Leninism* (10th Russian ed.), p. 590.
[17] *Ibid.,* p. 595.

and ending with the People's Commissariats; (2) elevation of the role and obligations of local regional, territorial and republic organs of authority, especially in developing local industry and agriculture; (3) replacement of authorized People's Commissariats in regions and territories by creating regional and territorial administrations for heavy and light industry and for other branches of industry, having charged them with the obligation to administer all local industry and at the same time carry out the mandates of the appropriate People's Commissar; and (4) entrusting to the Central Committee the concrete working out of organizing the administration of local industry and representing Union industrial People's Commissariats in the rural areas.[18]

The same directive ordained, along the line of mass Soviet organizations,

the organization of mass control of the work of administrative organs, stern criticism by the masses of bureaucratic ulcers and mechanical shortcomings, expansion of the network of standing committees of Soviet and deputy groups in enterprises and in the settlements, the organization of subdistrict and precinct groups of deputies of the Soviets in the large cities, special attention to the drawing of activist women into the work of Soviets and their standing committees (sections) . . . and the extension and qualitative improvement of the (now vindicated) patronage of enterprises over state institutions and of socialist compatibility of work therein with work in production.[19]

On the basis of directives of the Party Congress of May 27, 1934, the Central Executive Committee of the USSR adopted a directive, Concerning Organization Work of the Soviets, which made the party injunctions definite along this line.[20] It proposed that executive committees and Soviets assure the expansion of standing committees and deputy groups as the basic forms of drawing the masses into the work of the Soviets, turning them ever more and more into a mass mechanism for carrying out the decisions of the Party and the government in the various branches of socialist building. The number of standing committees was to be increased according to a definite enumeration—by city Soviets up to twelve, and by village Soviets up to nine, in conformity with local conditions.

Thereafter the network of deputy groups, unifying the Soviet Party members, was to be more broadly developed in all enterprises and institutions being created, even if there were but one deputy present. In cities whose population exceeded 100,000, territorial deputy groups were to be organized according to the domicile of the deputies—subdistrict groups if there were district Soviets, otherwise precinct groups. Sessions of plena

[18] The All-Union Communist Party (of Bolsheviks) in Resolutions, Pt. 2, p. 594.
[19] The All-Union Communist Party (of Bolsheviks) in Resolution, Pt. 2, p. 595.
[20] Cz. 1934, No. 31, Art. 234.

of standing committees and deputy groups were arranged to be held on the same days throughout the country. This directive made a number of points aimed at strengthening the organization departments of executive committees and Soviets. By way of overcoming functionalism and bringing essentially homogeneous work to a focus, it established that, as a rule, work on cadres of Soviets, accounting-information work, and work on matters of administrative-territorial division and on rationalizing and improving the mechanism of executive committees and Soviets must be concentrated in the organization departments. It also set apart instructor groups, working under the immediate direction of the president of the district executive committee or municipal Soviet (or his vice president), in place of organization subdivisions in district executive committees and city Soviets (of cities whose population was less than 50,000). In addition appropriate departments issued directives and instructions making definite the mandates of the Party Congress relative to them.

At the end of the period under consideration, great changes occurred in the *territorial organization* of the district and the territory. In connection with the difficulties of the colossal work in the socialist reorganization of agriculture being achieved within a brief period, the plenum of the Central Committee of the All-Union Communist Party (of Bolsheviks) adopted in January, 1933 (on the report of Kaganovich), a decision concerning the organization of political subdivisions in the machine and tractor service stations and the sovkhozes. Stalin's speech, at the same plenum of the Central Committee, disclosed the shortcomings of work in the rural districts and pointed out that "political subdivisions of machine and tractor service stations and sovkhozes are among the decisive means whereby these shortcomings may be eliminated in the very shortest time." [21]

Stalin's words were justified. Numerous cadres of Bolsheviks, carefully selected by the Central Committee of the All-Union Communist Party (of Bolsheviks) and directed into the political subdivisions of the machine and tractor service stations and sovkhozes during the two years immediately following, achieved enormous work there, in the political strengthening of machine and tractor service stations and sovkhozes, the enhancement of their political role and influence in the rural districts, and the decisive improvement of political and economic work of Party cells in kolkhozes and sovkhozes, whereby a clean sweep was made of the shortcomings in rural work, mentioned by Stalin. Accordingly, a directive of the Seventeenth Party Congress concerning organization matters ordained that:

In connection with the formation of new economic centers around the machine and tractor service stations, the Central Committee create such new

[21] Stalin, *Questions of Leninism* (10th Russian ed.), p. 524.

independent districts or, at least, powerful centers of the machine and tractor service stations, and subdistricts and subdepartments thereof, as may be essential for the reorganization into district committees or subdistrict committees.[22]

The November, 1934, plenum of the Central Committee of the All-Union Communist Party (of Bolsheviks), acting upon the report of Kaganovich, pointed out that the attainments in the field of socialist reconstruction of agriculture "bring out the necessity of *completing* the division into districts begun when areas were liquidated and the bringing of organs of administration near to the *village*." The plenum further directed (1) that political subdivisions of the machine and tractor service stations be reorganized into ordinary Party organs and, for this purpose, merged with existing district committees of the Party—and particularly that large districts be subdivided into a number of new districts and that the appropriate political subdivisions be infused therein.[23] Thus, upon the successful work of Party organizations of a temporary and extraordinary order—the political divisions of the machine and tractor service stations—was based the development of permanent Party and Soviet organizations, district committees, and district executive committees.

The successes of socialist reconstruction of the national economy were, in general, powerfully reflected in the development of territorial organization of local organs of state authority. The creation (in 1932) of regions in the Ukraine and in Kazakhstan—six in each republic—was predicated upon the vast growth of cultural and economic building there. These same causes necessitated the division of a number of very large regions and territories, beginning with that of Siberia, into smaller units. During the period of collectivization, the district developed broadly. By the time the areas were liquidated in 1930, there were approximately 3,000 districts in the USSR. Then they began to be enlarged, and on January 1, 1933, their number had shrunk to 2,451. By the end of 1934 and the beginning of 1935, in connection with the creation of new districts on the basis of the machine and tractor service stations, they again numbered above 3,000. This numerical increase, in connection with the growth of economic building in rural districts, required that higher direction be brought near to them in order to improve the organization direction on the basis of decisions of the Seventeenth Party Congress. Accordingly, the number of territories and regions was notably lessened, and the number of districts in each area thereby essentially decreased, assuring a more highly definitive and differentiated administration.

[22] *The All-Union Communist Party (of Bolsheviks) in Resolutions,* Pt. 2, p. 594.
[23] *Ibid.,* p. 625.

SEC. 8: LOCAL ORGANS OF STATE AUTHORITY UNDER THE STALIN CONSTITUTION

1. *The significance of the Stalin Constitution in strengthening local organs of state authority*

The Stalin Constitution preserves the principles which were theretofore the foundation of the organization, activity, and interrelations of the local organs of state authority, the Soviets of Worker, Peasant, and Red Army Deputies. Confirming these principles and carrying their development further, the Constitution of the USSR is a powerful factor for the further reinforcement of local organs of state authority. The principles of democratic centralism and of dual subordination, as applied to local organs of state authority, are now formulated in the USSR Constitution itself. The Stalin Constitution generalizes the experience of the Union Republics as to the organization and activity of local organs of state authority, assigning to them a special chapter. The Stalin Constitution, and the constitutions of Union and autonomous republics resting thereon, define with greater precision the place of those organs in the entire system of Soviet authority. They substantially extend and make more exact the limits of the jurisdiction of Soviets of Deputies of the Toilers, defining the structure of their executive organs and establishing the rules for the election of Soviets of different grades and the interrelation of the Soviets and their executive committees with the appropriate organs, higher and lower.[1]

2. *The territorial structure of local administration*

The USSR Constitution and the constitutions of all the Union and autonomous republics devote numerous articles to the national and administrative-territorial structure of Soviet Republics.

The USSR Constitution enumerates the Union Republics (and their constituent territories and regions), the autonomous republics, and the autonomous regions. Union Republics having territorial or regional subdivisions enumerate in their constitutions the same national and administrative-territorial units as are established by the USSR Constitution. Union Republics having no such subdivisions enumerate in their constitutions

---

[1] At the moment of compiling the present work, the new regulations of local state authority, based on the Stalin Constitution, have not yet been published; accordingly, in setting out the organization and work of the Soviets, legislative acts still in force, although published before the new Constitution was introduced, have been availed of in part.

both their constituent autonomous republics and regions (as well as areas and districts) and also the cities and worker settlements segregated from the structure of districts and formed into independent administrative-economic units.

The territorial structure of Soviets and the division of the country into districts according to economic and national indices is intended to provide the best possible assurance that the Soviets will direct the socialist building in the given territory.

At the time when the economic division into districts was completed (1930), the RSFSR had 7 territories and 6 regions. At the present time (October 20, 1938) there are in 5 Union Republics (the RSFSR, the Ukraine SSR, the White Russian SSR, the Kazakh SSR, and the Uzbek SSR) 68 units in all, 6 areas (these exist only in the RSFSR), and 62 regions (including 29 in the RSFSR, counting the Permsk region, which was formed October 3, 1938). Under certain conditions the territories include autonomous regions.[2] Furthermore, the Maritime and Khabarovsk territories are divided into regions of the second order,[3] which are not found by name in the USSR and RSFSR constitutions.

When most areas were abolished in 1930, a few were preserved—those formed according to the nationality index and those whose economy, greater remoteness, or border situation sharply distinguished them from other parts of the corresponding region or republic. Their number increased from 5, at the time of the general liquidation of areas, to 30 (on October 1, 1938), including 11 national areas (all within the RSFSR).

The number of districts increased from 2,443 on January 1, 1934, when complete collectivization and the organization of the machine and tractor service stations created a firm economic basis for Soviet authority in the rural areas, to 3,463 on September 15, 1938, after the division of the districts, in connection therewith in the years 1934 to 1936, on the basis of the machine and tractor service stations.

More or less accurate data as to the number of village Soviets in the entire USSR are available only since 1928, when the process of dividing them into smaller units, beginning approximately in 1922 and 1923, was already completed. There were then reckoned 74,500 agricultural Soviets. Later they shrank to 68,209 in 1931 and 62,824 in 1934. In recent years this consolidation has stopped and some increase in the number of agricultural Soviets was actually contemplated: on September 15, 1938, there were 63,036 in the USSR.

---

[2] Directive of the All-Russian Central Executive Committee and RSFSR Council of People's Commissars (Oct. 29, 1928), Cy. 1928, No. 137, Art. 889.

[3] Decree of the Presidium of the USSR Supreme Soviet (Oct. 20, 1938).

When areas were abolished, a notable number of cities—157 out of a total of 711—were not incorporated in districts but remained administratively and economically independent units. Moreover, village localities were united with many of them. With regard to these, the city Soviets functioned as district organs of authority.[4] At the end of 1931 the number of such cities (with added village territory) was defined as 93 units; by 1937 the number had increased to 130. Now, with the complication and differentiation of city and village economy alike, these village suburban localities are either segregated into independent districts or united with the nearest districts. On September 15, 1938, there were reckoned, in the USSR, 807 cities (281 of them separated from districts), 709 worker settlements (20 of them separated from districts), and 200 acknowledged settlements of the city type. Of the cities separated from districts, 92 include village territory within their boundaries.

More than seventy of the largest cities (twenty of them with one district Soviet each, and seven with two each) are divided into districts having their district Soviets of Deputies of the Toilers. In some of them there are such Soviets only in particular sections of the city whose direct administration by the city Soviet entails some sort of difficulty. The total number of such districts in cities is by now upwards of 270.[5]

In addition to the twenty-two autonomous republics and nine autonomous regions of the USSR, formed in accordance with the nationality index, there are in the RSFSR eleven national areas set off on the same basis. Where there is the possibility that (in settlements of national minorities) nationally homogeneous districts and village Soviets may be formed in the districts, they are organized even though the population or territory of such districts or village Soviets be somewhat less than the rest. In 1934 the number of national districts inhabited by national minorities was upwards of 250, and of national village Soviets upwards of 5,300.

Establishing the method of changing the existing network of national and administrative-territorial units, the USSR Constitution provides, as to objects within the jurisdiction of the USSR (Art. 14): "(e) confirmation of changes in the boundaries between Union Republics; and (f) confirma-

---

[4] Directives of the USSR Central Executive Committee of Aug. 9, 1930 (Cz. 1930, No. 42, Art. 435) and Oct. 17, 1934 (Cz. 1934, No. 53, Art. 411) concerning the RSFSR; directives of the All-Russian Central Executive Committee and Council of People's Commissars of June 3, 1929 (Cy. 1929, No. 41, Art. 440), Oct. 30, 1929 (Cy. 1929, No. 80, Art. 784), Aug. 20, 1933 (Cy. 1933, No. 49, Art. 209) and July 1, 1933 (Cy. 1933, No. 40, Art. 150).

[5] The RSFSR has a special Instruction Concerning the Organization and Activity of District Soviets in Cities—a directive of the All-Russian Central Executive Committee and the Council of People's Commissars of April 15, 1929 (Cy. 1929, No. 35, Art. 354), as amended by the directive of July 1, 1933 (Cy. 1933, No. 40, Art. 150).

tion of the formation of new territories and regions—as well as of new autonomous republics which are constituent parts of Union Republics." All Union Republics comprising autonomous republics and regions include within their jurisdiction the affirmation of the boundaries and district division thereof. The constitutions of Union Republics include within the jurisdiction of the republic the establishment of boundaries and of district division of territories and regions if such there are—otherwise the boundaries of areas and districts. Constitutions of all autonomous republics include within their jurisdiction the establishment of the division of the republic into districts as well as of boundaries of districts and cities, their decisions to be referred for confirmation to the Supreme Soviet of the appropriate Union Republic.

At the present time the links in the organization of local organs of state authority are basically the six enumerated in the Stalin Constitution: Soviets of Deputies of the Toilers (1) territorial and regional, (2) of autonomous regions, (3) of areas, (4) of districts, (5) of cities, and (6) of rural localities (Kazakh villages, hamlets, farms, villages of Central Asia, and Caucasian villages).[6] Constitutions of Union Republics speak also of one further additional link on the same level with them—district Soviets in the cities. City Soviets are in turn divided into two types: those subordinate to a district and those set off from districts into independent administrative-economic units, subordinate immediately to one of the higher local Soviets of Deputies of the Toilers (territorial or autonomous-territorial, or even to the Supreme Soviet of the autonomous or Union Republic) rather than to the district Soviets. Some of the Soviets of cities set off from districts, in their turn, administer—directly or through their district Soviets— the village Soviets of village territory united with the city.

The structure of certain administrative-territorial units includes autonomous regions, in connection with which such division acquires the name of territory. As is shown by its very name, an autonomous region is organized on the basis of nationality. Soviets of Deputies of the Toilers of autonomous regions are independent of territorial organs of authority in numerous branches of administration, the bounds of this autonomy being defined by special regulations peculiar for each autonomous region. The autonomous region, like the entire territory, is divided into districts, cities, and village Soviets. The regional Soviets of the Primorsk and Khabarovsk territories are somewhat peculiar. In other territories the territorial Soviets are in immediate direction of the district Soviets—and in part the city Soviets—only. The constituent regions of the Maritime and Khabarovsk territories differ from all other regions in that they are not immediately

---

[6] Art. 95 of the Stalin Constitution.

within the structure of any Union Republic. In Far Eastern conditions, territories must be divided into parts whose Soviets possess almost the same rights as do all other regions—not, however, being immediately within the structure of any Union Republic but within that of a territory unifying an entire group of regions having homogeneous conditions. These regions, like all others, are divided into districts, cities, and village Soviets (and the Kamchatka region has areas as well).

Areas—formerly a normal unit of Soviet territorial organization—are exceptional at the present time. They are formed (1) on the basis of nationality, where there are several adjacent and nationally homogeneous districts, and (2) in a number of republics by reason of special conditions obtaining in the constituent districts.

A district is the most widely extended link of Soviet territorial organization. Either the Union and autonomous republics or the territories and regions where they are formed are divided into districts. Autonomous regions also are divided into districts, irrespective of their being within the structure of territories, as are the regions of the Primorsk and Khabarovsk territories and the areas (including the national areas). Only a small part of the cities, of the largest cities, are not within the structure of districts.

The district is thus so situated as to have become the nexus of socialist building in the rural areas. This was in fact the aim of the liquidation of areas carried through in 1930: to make the district into such a nexus even if it meant turning over to it the rights and obligations, the material possibilities, and even the individual structure of the liquidated area organs. It is the district organs that enact all the measures of the higher organs of state authority and administration applicable to the village and to small cities.

The local system consists most frequently of three links (territorial or regional Soviet, district Soviet, and city or village Soviet); sometimes there are only two links (territorial or regional Soviet, and the Soviet of an independent city; the district, city or village Soviet in republics with no subdivision into regions); and relatively rarely are there as many as four or five links, chiefly in autonomous regions and national areas. The greatest number of links is to be found in the national areas which are component parts of the regions of the Khabarovsk territory, where such exceptional circumstances obtain that only the five-link system guarantees that their toiling population will be broadly drawn into the building of socialism.

As to the part played by separate links in the general system of local organs of state authority, the Constitution employs a single, general formula to define the tasks of all the links of local Soviets. This does not, of course, mean that each Soviet exercises identical functions within its territory irrespective of its significance. In the performance of these tasks each has its own perfectly definite jurisdiction. Territorial and regional Soviets occupy first place among local organs of state authority. They are the highest of such organs and the task of correctly advancing Soviet policy within the limits of the territory or region rests upon them in the first instance. Territorial (regional) Soviets are chiefly planning and regulating organs. Unlike them, almost all the institutions, enterprises, and organizations of district or village significance are directly subordinate to district organs, whereby the latter become for the most part operative organs, the more so that their constituent village Soviets have no differentiated network of their own institutions and enterprises. Such a measure as that transferring the maintenance of schools completely to village Soviets showed that the latter cannot as a rule cope with the task, and the law is now abrogated. The purpose of relieving the village Soviets (in 1937) from the duties of computing and collecting taxes, insurance payments, and compulsory agricultural deliveries [7] was to focus all their work upon organization of the masses to carry out the tasks of socialist building in the rural areas, and guidance of the mounting improvement of cultural and living conditions there.

The tasks of the city Soviets in serving the masses, in respect of cultural and living conditions, and organizing them were similarly brought into sharp focus considerably earlier, and important results in this direction are already at hand. Side by side with their immediate tasks of serving the city population, city Soviets of Deputies of the Toilers, as representatives of the vanguard of the toiling proletariat, prosecute their work also among the rural population surrounding the city. This work is of the most diverse forms: direct addition to the city of the nearest agricultural territories, expanding the sovkhozes, increasing the compulsory agricultural deliveries, ministering to the village through city institutions and enterprises, aid through patronage, and the like.

3. Objects of jurisdiction

Apropos of the new tasks which had arisen in the course of the socialist construction associated with the basic building of socialism in the USSR, the reorganization of the work of all the Soviets began as early as 1934, founded on decisions of the Seventeenth Congress of the All-Union Communist Party (of Bolsheviks) (March 15, 1934) when an All-Union law, Concerning Organization Measures in the Field of Soviet and Eco-

[7] Cz. 1937, No. 22, Art. 85.

nomic Building, was issued.[8] This proposed in particular: (1) to enlarge the rights and obligations of local organs, regional, territorial, and republic, in the development of local industry and agriculture; (2) to intensify the vital guidance of lower organs and the furnishing of practical aid thereto; (3) to reinforce mass control over the work of administrative organs and to employ all means to assure that the masses are drawn into the struggle against the bureaucratic ulcers and shortcomings of the state mechanism; (4) to broaden the net of Soviet standing committees and deputy groups in enterprises and in the villages, and to organize subdistrict and precinct groups of Deputies of the Soviets in the large cities, with particular emphasis upon drawing women activists, workers, and kolkhoz members into this work; (5) to hand over to the trades unions preponderant rights in enterprises and direction of the organs in control of trade organizations; and (6) to promote the patronage of enterprises over state institutions and the socialist compatibility of work in production with work in state institutions.

As stated previously, the statute, Concerning the Organization Work of the Soviets [9] (May 27, 1934), developed the foregoing statute chiefly along the line of the Soviets' mass-organization work. It gave a model schedule of standing committees of city and village Soviets, pointed out the method of organizing standing committees, and indicated their structure and general problems, as well as the method of organizing deputy groups, both production and territorial, and their problems, and established a single Soviet day (for holding sessions of plena, Soviet standing committees, and deputy groups), and settled the basic obligations of deputies, members of standing committees, deputy groups, and the like.

The Stalin Constitution (Art. 97) defines the objects of jurisdiction of local organs of state authority: "They direct the activity of administrative organs subordinate to them; assure the maintenance of public order, the observance of laws and the protection of civil rights; guide local building, economic and cultural, and establish the local budget." Comparison of these functions with those of the Soviets as enumerated in earlier constitutions of individual Union Republics shows that the Stalin Constitution generalizes and confirms the best models of local Soviets' organization and activity. In Article 98 it speaks specifically of laws of the USSR and of Union Republics, defining the rights within whose limits Soviets of the Toilers' Deputies can adopt their decisions and issue their orders. The most essential change in the organizational structure of local organs of Soviet authority is the line of demarcation separating organs of authority—Soviets

[8] Cz. 1934, No. 15, Art. 103.
[9] Cz. 1934, No. 31, Art. 234 (p. 773).

of Deputies of the Toilers—from organs of administration—executive committees. Under the Stalin Constitution the latter become merely the executive and administrative organs of Soviets of the Deputies of the Toilers, hence the necessity of drawing the line between the functions of the Soviets and those of the executive organs. The Stalin Constitution and the constitutions of the Union and autonomous republics built on its foundation give the bases of such demarcation, to be developed by subsequent legislation in conformity with Article 98 of the Stalin Constitution. The boundary between objects within the jurisdiction of Soviets of the Deputies of the Toilers and those within the jurisdiction of their executive committees is drawn on the basis of (1) the schedule previously cited of objects within the jurisdiction of Soviets of Deputies of the Toilers and (2) the definition of executive committees as executive and administrative organs of these Soviets, elected by them and accountable to them, pursuant to Articles 99 and 101 of the Stalin Constitution.

The objects within the jurisdiction of local organs of state authority are defined above all by the fact that within their territory they are *organs of state authority* elected by the people on the basis of the most democratic law in the world, and in charge of all local economic and cultural building.

Besides drawing the boundary line between functions of the Soviets and functions of their executive organs, it is natural also to draw such a line between the functions of the various types or links of local Soviets and those of their executive organs. Therein a definitive—but not, as we have seen, the only—factor is territory: the territorial Soviet of Deputies of the Toilers functions within the geographical limits of the territory, the district Soviet within the geographical limits of the district, and the like. Again, the Soviet exercises certain of its functions throughout its territory immediately, or through executive and administrative organs directly subordinate to itself, whereas it exercises others through corresponding local Soviets of Deputies of the Toilers; furthermore, some of its functions as an organ of state authority the Soviet exercises through observing and controlling the activity of organizations and institutions present within a given territory but not directly subordinate to the Soviet itself.

The entire aggregate of institutions and enterprises directly subordinate to a given Soviet of Deputies of the Toilers or its executive organs, together with the entire aggregate of measures with whose enactment the Soviet and its executive organs are directly charged, constitute the economy of the Soviet.

Some of the individual functions of local Soviets of Deputies of the Toilers require detailed consideration.

Directing the Activity of Administrative Organs Subject to the Soviets.
The administrative organs in territories, regions, and other links of the
administrative-territorial organization are the executive and administrative
organs created by the appropriate Soviets of Deputies of the Toilers—their
executive committees. These are directly accountable to the Soviet which
selected them, an assurance that the Soviets can guide their activity. Constitutions of Union and autonomous republics fortify this proposition by
their emphasis upon the analogous subordination to Soviets of Deputies
of the Toilers of all the subdivisions thereof which are under the immediate
direction of the appropriate executive committee.

Assuring the Preservation of State Order. The task of organizing immediate measures to preserve state order is basically one for the organs of
the People's Commissariat for Internal Affairs. These, according to constitutions of Union and autonomous republics, can form their own administrations in accordance with the conditions of the territory (region) or
district, under the appropriate Soviets of Deputies of the Toilers. Such
administrations are organized in districts, subject to confirmation by the
territorial or regional Soviets of Deputies of the Toilers, or with the permission of Presidia of Supreme Soviets of the appropriate republics where
there is no division into regions. These administrations, according to the
constitutions of Union and autonomous republics, are subordinate in their
activity both to the appropriate Soviet of Deputies of the Toilers and to
the People's Commissariat for Internal Affairs.

Assuring the Observance of Laws and the Preservation of Civil Rights.
The task of supervising the precise fulfillment of laws is one for the organs
of the prosecuting magistracy, but the local Soviets, being organs of state
authority, are naturally responsible for the observance of laws and the
preservation of civil rights within their territory. They make an examination
as to how laws are carried out and how civil rights are guaranteed in the
work of all institutions, organizations, and enterprises within the territory
of the given Soviet. They arrange that new statutes shall be clarified for
the people and examine into their fulfillment by individual citizens (for
example, the timely and complete fulfillment of obligations due the state
in the matter of taxes, obligatory purveyance, obligatory education of children, and the like). They organize definite measures to effectuate statutes
completely and exactly if this is required either by the character of the
law or by provision therefor in the law itself. Soviets all along the line, right
down to the village Soviets, have the right to issue obligatory directives
pursuant to the regulation now in effect in the RSFSR, Concerning the
Publication by Local Executive Committees and Soviets of Binding Direc-

tives and the Imposition of Administrative Penalties for Breach Thereof.[10] By means of obligatory directives, obligations are established for the entire population of the territory of a given Soviet or separate parts and groups thereof, or institutions, enterprises, and organizations operating therein, nonobservance whereof renders one liable to administrative penalties and, in certain cases especially provided in the Criminal Code, to judicial penalties as well.

Furthermore, the territorial (regional) organs of authority (the regulation explicitly names executive committees and their presidia) have the right to issue obligatory directives on all matters within their jurisdiction as defined by the regulation concerning them. All inferior organs of authority issue obligatory directives only on matters precisely pointed out in the regulation itself covering each type of organ (district, municipal, village). Obligatory directives must not conflict with any statutes in force in a given territory or with any directives, instructions, or other orders of superior organs of authority and administration.

Obligatory directives may be issued for a period of not more than two years, counting from the date they became operative. (This date, as well as the period of operation, is indicated in the directive itself.) Upon the expiration of this period, the directive loses force, but the organ which issued it has the right to re-adopt it and to establish a new term for its operation. Obligatory directives indicate the territory to which they extend and contemplate a definite administrative, or in proper cases criminal, responsibility for their breach. In the RSFSR, to assure control over the legality of such directives, local executive committees and Soviets must, not later than two days after their adoption, forward them to the appropriate (local) public prosecutor, who, in case he deems them illegal, must within fifteen days file a protest regarding them with the organ of authority which adopted them. That organ must consider the protest within not more than fifteen days after its receipt, otherwise it must suspend the action of such directive. Organs of authority (other than the village Soviets) can establish imposts of an administrative character, for breach of their obligatory directives, in the form either of a warning, or of a fine not exceeding one hundred rubles, or of commitment to correctional labor for not more than one month. Village Soviets may in such cases issue warnings, and impose fines of not more than ten rubles, or sentence to correctional labor for not more than five days.

[10] Directive of the All-Russian Central Executive Committee and RSFSR Council of People's Commissars of March 30, 1931 (Cy. 1931, No. 17, Art. 186), as made more precise by instruction of the People's Commissariat for Justice of May 16, 1931, issued in conformity with the directive aforesaid and published in *Soviet Justice* for 1931, No. 16, pp. 30 ff.

Direction of Local Economic and Cultural Building. This succinct formula gives the proper and basic content of work of local Soviets of the Deputies of the Toilers in all branches of socialist building. The limitation of objects of jurisdiction to "local" matters is by no means a limitation in principle. Any phase of local building may have a significance at once purely local and also general. A question which previously had a narrowly local significance very often acquires a broader significance with a change of setting. Hence the composition of "local" economy is determined for the most part by the practical method of constructing general and sectional plans of the national economy, state and local budgets, and the like.

Satisfaction of many-sided and ever increasing demands of city and country toilers is of fundamental and first-rate significance in the work of local Soviets. Everything else is subordinated to this principal task.

The vast significance of all the work of the local Soviets in the field of communal and housing economy is manifest. A government directive (October 17, 1937), Concerning the Conservation of the Housing Fund and Improvement of the Housing Economy in the Cities,[11] notably broadens the objects under the direction of the local Soviets, giving over to their immediate jurisdiction almost all of the housing fund in the cities (which had hitherto been basically in the hands of housing cooperative associations). Changes in the external appearance of our cities and villages have been characterized by Stalin thus:

The physiognomy of our large cities and industrial centers has changed. The large cities of the bourgeois countries are inevitably conspicuous for their slums —the so-called worker quarters on the outskirts of the city—being a heap of dark, wet habitations, usually underground cellars, half ruined, where the have-nots ordinarily find refuge, swarming in the mud and cursing their fate. The Revolution in the USSR led to the disappearance of these slums here. In their place are beautiful worker quarters, newly built and filled with light—often better-looking than the center of the city. The physiognomy of the villages has changed still more. The old village, with its church in the most conspicuous place, its better houses—those of the local police official, the priest, and the kulak—in the foreground, and its half-ruined peasant huts in the background, is beginning to disappear. In its place the new village appears, with its social-economic structures, its clubs, radios, cinematograph, schools, libraries and crèches, and its tractors, combines, reapers, and automobiles. Gone are the old familiar figures of the exploiter—the kulak, the bloodsucker usurer, the buyer-speculator, and mister police official. The important people now are those active in kolkhozes and sovkhozes, schools and clubs, senior operators of tractors and combines, brigadiers

[11] Cz. 1937, No. 69, Art. 314, and No. 74, Art. 360.

in agronomy and animal husbandry, the best men and women shock-workers of the kolkhoz fields. The old contrast between city and country is disappearing.[12]

This picture shows graphically in what direction the local Soviets are expanding their work in guaranteeing the ever growing needs of the masses of city and village toilers in respect of culture and living conditions. One means of satisfying these demands is to develop local industry. This Stalin put as one of the most pressing tasks as early as 1934, in his report to the Seventeenth Party Congress: "To untrammel local Soviet industry, to make possible its manifestation of initiative in producing goods of mass consumption, and to aid it in every possible way with raw materials and means." [13]

Certain objects within the jurisdiction of village Soviets of Deputies of the Toilers must be particularly emphasized. Their responsibility, as organs of state authority, for the condition of agricultural production in their territory, and their duty to take the most active part in raising agriculture to a higher pitch and in solving the task, put by Stalin, of collecting seven to eight billion poods of grain, brings them into the closest relations with the kolkhozes. These, however, are not state enterprises subordinate or in tutelage to the Soviets, but voluntary associations of citizens who are actually and completely their proprietors. The Soviet cooperates to promote the broadest possible development of initiative and independence on the part of the kolkhozes and their members. It assures such development, seeing strictly to it that there be no departure, either by the various instiutions or by the directing organs of the kolkhozes, from the method of solving kolkhoz questions by the members themselves (as provided by the regulation of the agricultural artel). The results of economic activity of the kolkhoz make themselves felt primarily and preeminently in the members of the kolkhozes themselves. They are the persons most interested therein. Accordingly, any exercise of authority, any violation of kolkhoz democracy or administration of the kolkhoz dissociated from its members, can, and does, bring nothing but harm. Such a proposition, however, by no means relieves the Soviets of responsibility for the condition of kolkhozes within their territory, of their obligation to organize kolkhozes and their members for the fulfillment of state-wide plans and tasks, to develop and to establish their independence that they may carry to realization all the other tasks of socialist building. All of this is accomplished, however, by organizing mass work and without intrusion of the administrators in the operative work of the kolkhozes.

That the village Soviets are free from immediate work in calculating

[12] Stalin, *Questions of Leninism* (10th Russian ed.), p. 571.
[13] *Ibid.*, p. 559.

and collecting the requisitions of agricultural products in no wise means that they are not responsible for this work as it is being carried on through the instrumentality of the People's Commissariat of Supply. They must assist in every way the fulfillment of plans for collecting agricultural deliveries—above all, working along the line of clarifying them for the masses—and maintain close association with those working in the collection apparatus, being constantly in touch with the progress of the collection in their territory and eliminating, in good time, causes hampering the successful fulfillment of the plan.

Since July 1, 1933, the village Soviets have been freed from the direct conduct of work in the field of taxation and insurance, the special mechanism of the district financial divisions being charged with that activity.[14] As we have seen with regard to collection of agricultural deliveries, however, this does not mean that the Soviets must hold aloof from the work or that they have ceased to be responsible for its condition. They must carry on the work of clarification for the masses and organize the population for the swiftest possible fulfillment of all obligations due to the state. The local Soviets are immediately interested in the successful results of this work, inasmuch as their budget obtains important funds from tax receipts and from the deductions from insurance payments.

Particularly important is the significance of the work of the Soviets in administering the local budget. A special subdivision of the present chapter is devoted to this work.

Strengthening the Country's Defensive Capacity. The obligation of local Soviets to cooperate to this end is pointed out explicitly in constitutions of all the Union and autonomous republics.

Soviets of the Deputies of the Toilers effectuate their activity by making decisions and giving orders within the limits of the rights granted to them by the laws of the USSR and of the appropriate Union Republic (similarly in autonomous republics, by the laws of the appropriate autonomous republic). Obligatory directives of local Soviets, of which mention has already been made, are one of the forms of such orders.

4. *Drawing the masses into the work of Soviets of Deputies of the Toilers*

The reorganization of the work of Soviets on the basis of the Stalin Constitution, on the basis of their further democratization, creates conditions propitious for drawing far greater numbers of the masses into the work of administration and for the broadest utilization of various methods of achieving that result. The Stalin Constitution directly establishes the obligation of each deputy of any Soviet of Deputies of the Toilers to render

---

[14] Cz. 1937, No. 22, Art. 85.

an account to his electors both of his work and of the work of the Soviet of which he is a member. According to the RSFSR regulation of the municipal Soviets issued in 1933, deputies are bound to render an account to their electors not less frequently than twice a year, "illuminating therein both the activity of the Soviet and its organs and also of their own activities as members of the Soviet."

Moreover, the rights of electors are by no means confined to offering suggestions and listening to reports concerning their fulfillment. Under Article 142 of the Stalin Constitution, "any deputy may at any time be recalled pursuant to the decision of a majority of the electors in the manner established by law." In almost none of the capitalist countries is there any such right to recall deputies, and where it does exist, its effectuation is hedged around by excessively complicated formalities and is in practice almost never used. The new system of elections to the Soviets now establishes also a new method of recall which must be further settled by a special law.

Particular methods of drawing the entire electorate into the work of administration are: (1) participation of the toilers in sessions of the Soviets and their mass organizations, for which reason such special sessions are often called "itinerant" sessions because of journeys away into collectives where the consideration of a given question can lead to the best results; (2) the formulation in print, at the mass meetings for enterprises, institutions, organizations, and kolkhozes of the most important questions to be decided by the Soviet; (3) efficiently organized acceptance and consideration of complaints of the toilers, and more profound study of the causes thereof, against the various institutions, organizations, and organs of the press; and (4) systematized receipt of written and oral suggestions for improving the work of this or that organ, and eliminating shortcomings therein, and so on. This enumeration is far from complete; it cannot be exhaustive for the reason that the activity of the Soviet constantly reveals new methods whereby the masses can participate in state administration. Standing committees (sections) of the Soviets, the special form of mass work which is time-honored and proved, are created according to branches of the Soviet's work and to a certain degree parallel the divisions of the executive committee, except that a standing committee (section) is a mass organ of the Soviet, with a nucleus of Soviet deputies who combine work in the section with work in production.

Deputy groups are another form of organizing the work of the masses. The Seventeenth Party Congress acknowledged the necessity of "broadening the network of standing committees (sections) of Soviets and of deputy groups in enterprises and in the villages, organizing subdistrict and precinct

groups of deputies of Soviets in the large cities, and devoting special attention to drawing activist women and women workers and kolkhoz members
into the work of the Soviets (sections) and their standing committees." [15]

Deputy groups are thus organized upon two heterogeneous principles:
(1) the production principle, such as deputy groups in enterpises, in institutions, in kolkhozes and sovkhozes, and so on; and (2) the territorial principle according to the domicile of the deputies, such as settlement groups
(in separate settlements which are component parts of a given village
Soviet), and subdistrict and precinct groups (in separate parts of the large
cities). Deputy groups differ from standing committees as being formed
on the basis of the place where deputies work or dwell and not according
to administrative branches. The term "deputy group" is ordinarily understood to be more than a group of deputies. Such groups unify around themselves the entire Soviet active membership working in the different areas
of Soviet work within a given enterprise or territorial precinct. Deputies
are the organizing and directing nucleus of the deputy group.

The paramount functions of deputy groups are (1) to exercise control
over the fulfillment of orders and decisions of the Soviets and of superior
organs of authority; (2) to cooperate with every type of local organization
to the end of fulfilling their production tasks; (3) to cooperate for improvement in service to the toilers in respect of culture and living conditions;
(4) to participate in working out problems concerned with the work of
the Soviets; and (5) to systematize deputies' accountability to the people.

Beginning in 1933, street committees were formed on the basis of
energizing the masses to act for themselves in improving the communal
and living conditions of our cities and worker settlements. As the work
of the committees expanded, it was manifest that their tasks completely
paralleled those of territorial deputy groups. They had, in fact, to be occupied
with ministering to the people in all branches of Soviet work and were
consequently the nuclei of the Soviets nearest to them. They were accordingly included within the system and are, in fact, the links of territorial
deputy groups. Their organization upon the territorial principle, as well
as their very title (they are still called quarter committees, commissions of
cooperation for good street conditions, and the like), shows that their basic
function is the satisfaction of popular demands connected with the domicile
of the electors: above all, to care for the cultural condition of streets, yards,
lodgings, for yards and streets to be kept green, for playgrounds, schools,
grocery stores, and so on.

Among the other forms of organizing mass work, the socialist compatibility of work in production with the fulfillment of definite functions

---

[15] A directive pursuant to the report of Kaganovich, *Organization Questions*.

in the state mechanism is particularly significant, as is also the patronage of worker collectives over separate state institutions which has proved to be a firm basis as well for the promotion of such socialist compatibility. There are also numerous mass organizations under such institutions as schools (assemblies and committees of parents), libraries (library councils), administrations of houses of local Soviets (cultural and sanitary commissions), trade enterprises (shop commissions of consumer cooperatives where still preserved), and the like. All this vast and variegated net of mass organizations takes under its control all sections of the work of our state mechanism and at the same time actively cooperates with the mechanism in the execution of all its tasks.

5. How local organs of state authority work

When regularly functioning organs, personified by Soviets of Deputies of the Toilers, take the place of congresses of Soviets assembling for but one session, this introduces radical changes into the order or work of all the local organs of authority except the primary (city and village) organs. The work of Soviets of Deputies of the Toilers is carried on in a session. They convene from time to time for a longer or shorter period, the date when individual links of the Soviets are summoned being defined by constitutions of the Union and autonomous republics. In most of the Union Republics, territorial and regional Soviets are convened not less frequently than four times a year (in the Kazakh SSR, not less freqently than twice a year); area and district Soviets not less frequently than six times a year, with a few exceptions (in the Kazakh SSR, not less frequently than three times a year); and city and village Soviets not less frequently than once a month (in the Kazakh SSR, and in the nomad districts of the Kirghiz SSR, in the Yakutsk and Kalmyk ASSR and the Komi ASSR, the village Soviets are convened not less frequently than once in two months). A president and secretary are elected to conduct the meetings, such election being for the term of that session only, except as regards village Soviets, whose session meetings are conducted by the permanent president of the village Soviet (who is at the same time president of the executive organ of the village Soviet as well). All sessions of the Soviets are convened by their executive committees (in the village Soviet by its president).

Constitutions indicate certain special functions exercised by sessions of the Soviets: (a) the establishment of a local budget; (b) elections of executive organs of Soviets; (c) elections of president and secretary to act during the session; (d) the abrogation of decisions and orders of lower Soviets of Deputies of the Toilers; and (e) the formation of departments of their executive committees.

Aside from this, the regional and territorial Soviets of Deputies of the Toilers, and also of Deputies of the Toilers of autonomous regions and of national and administrative districts, choose for a period of five years the appropriate territorial and regional courts, courts of autonomous regions, and courts of national and administrative areas.

In carrying out the tasks enumerated in the Constitution, Soviets of Deputies of the Toilers have the right to set down for consideration any questions of local cultural-political and economic building and reports as to the activity—as a whole and with regard to particular matters—of their executive organs and their subdivisions of lower Soviets, of their deputies, and of various mass organs, and can abrogate and amend their decisions and orders. As organs of state authority within their territory, they may form standing and temporary commissions of every kind and upon any matter or any branch within their jurisdiction and establish relations of such commissions with executive organs of the Soviets, with their subdivisions and with other institutions and organizations. Standing commissions may be illustrated by such tested forms of organization as sections (standing committees) or deputy groups of the Soviets.

6. Executive organs of the Soviets of Deputies of the Toilers

Prior to the Stalin Constitution, the highest organs of authority in the territory of a given administrative unit (such as a territory, region, or district) was admittedly the appropriate Congress of Soviets. But when the last session of the Congress came to an end, its members lost their authority. This passed to the executive committees chosen by the congresses. The regulation concerning local congresses of Soviets and their executive committees provided expressly that "during periods between congresses of Soviets, executive committees are the highest organs of Soviet authority in the appropriate territory and enjoy all the rights of congresses of Soviets with the exception of such matters as are referred to the exclusive jurisdiction of the latter." [16] Inasmuch as over a period of years a Congress of Soviets was summoned for but one session of some days, however, the compass of its executive jurisdiction was not very large: elections to higher congresses, elections of an executive committee, the report of the executive committee, and a budget. (When conferences were not called every year, the authority of the Congress of Soviets over the budget naturally dropped.) Regulations concerning local organs ordained that, during the period between sessions of the executive committee, its presidium possesses all the rights of the committee except that of adopting a local budget.

[16] Cy. 1928, No. 70, Art. 503.

The Stalin Constitution draws strict lines of demarcation between the various local organs as regards the exercise of directive and executive functions. Soviets of the Deputies of the Toilers are the organs of authority with the right to adopt directive orders as to all objects within the jurisdiction of local organs of state authority. Executive committees of these Soviets are only their executive and administrative organs, completely accountable to the Soviets which elected them and directing the cultural-political and economic building throughout the territory solely upon the basis of decisions of the Soviets of Deputies of the Toilers (who elected them) and of superior state organs. They are not themselves organs of state authority; they may be considered local organs of state administration.

The Stalin Constitution [17] points out that elective executive committees consist of a president, vice presidents, secretary, and members, and executive organs of small village Soviets consist of a president, a single vice president, and a secretary.

Constitutions of Union and autonomous republics assign a very important place to the mechanism of local Soviets, particularly to the subdivisions of executive committees: they set out all of these subdivisions (and establish special conditions for the organization of some of them) and their relations with executive committees, Soviets, and appropriate subdivisions, higher and lower. Subdivisions are formed, as are People's Commissariats, according to branches of state administration. Their organization in all except village Soviets is contemplated, whereas formerly they were generally not formed in city and settlement Soviets subordinate to districts (namely, the overwhelming majority). Thereby the organization of executive organs of the Soviets is made distinct, clear, and complete.

All subdivisions may be divided into two groups: (1) those which the Constitution itself requires to be organized and (2) the subdivisions and administrations whose organization depends upon the conditions of a given territorial unit. Most of the subdivisions of the former category are organized in the executive committees of all the links, in the territorial (regional), district and municipal executive committees, and include: (1) finance, (2) trade, (3) popular education, (4) public health, (5) social security, (6) general, (7) planning commission, and (8) the sector of cadres under the president of the executive committee.

The remaining five subdivisions, agriculture, local industry, communal economy, roads, and the arts, are formed as constituent parts of territorial (regional) executive committees; moreover, there are agricultural and road subdivisions within the structure of district executive committees, and a subdivision of communal economy within the structure of municipal execu-

[17] Arts. 99, 100.

tive committees. Furthermore, some of these subdivisions may be formed also in conformity with local conditions: the agriculture and local industry subdivisions within the structure of municipal executive committees (by direct decision of the appropriate city Soviet of Deputies of the Toilers), and the local industry and communal economy subdivisions within the structure of district executive committees (if confirmed by the higher Soviets—territorial and regional Soviets in territories and regions, the Supreme Soviet of the appropriate Union or autonomous republic in republics not so subdivided).

In addition, constitutions of Union Republics also provide for representatives or administrations of the All-Union People's Commissariat for Supply under the executive committees of territorial (regional) Soviets. Other All-Union People's Commissariats form their administrations only under certain territorial (regional) Soviets in conformity with local conditions. The Union Republic People's Commissariat for Internal Affairs also forms its local administrations in the same manner; it can form them, in conformity with local conditions, not only in territories (regions), however, but also in districts. (Here their organization must be confirmed by a higher Soviet.)

Also, and likewise in conformity with special characteristics of the economy of the territory (region), territorial (regional) Soviets may, with the confirmation of the appropriate Union Republic People's Commissariats, form subdivisions of administrations of light industry, food industry, forest industry, and state grain and livestock farms. With regard to the Soviets of administrative areas, the RSFSR Constitution establishes neither the number nor the method of organizing subdivisions, merely pointing out that they are formed on the basis of laws and decrees of the supreme organs of the Union Republic and decisions of territorial (regional) Soviets of Deputies of the Toilers. The constitutions of other Union Republics having areas —the Uzbek and Turkmen SSR's—contain such directives, whereby the subdivisions of executive committees of area Soviets are the same as in the territory (region), save only as to the subdivision of local industry and (in Uzbekistan) the road subdivision. From the number of the administrations formed in conformity with local conditions, these constitutions contemplate the possibility of forming administrations of All-Union People's Commissariats and the People's Commissariat for Internal Affairs.

Subdivisions of executive committees of Soviets of Deputies of the Toilers of autonomous regions are mentioned in the constitutions of all the Union Republics (having such regions) except that of the RSFSR, which contemplates the issuance of special regulations for each autonomous region. Constitutions which speak of the formation of subdivisions in autonomous regions (the constitutions of Azerbaijan, Georgia, and Tadjikistan) establish therein the organization of all the thirteen subdivisions formed under executive committees by territorial (regional) Soviets. The Azerbaijan and Georgian SSR's contemplate the organization of one further subdivision, that of forest economy. Moreover, in all three of these Union Republics there are, under Soviets of Deputies of the Toilers of autonomous regions, the administration of stores (formerly the representative of the Committee for Supply) and the administration of the People's Commissariat for Internal Affairs.

National areas are found only in the RSFSR, whose constitution contains no reference to the mechanism of executive committees of Soviets of the Deputies of the Toilers of these areas contemplating the issuance of a special regulation, Concerning National Areas, by the Supreme Soviet of the Republic.

Constitutions of Union Republics say nothing concerning the mechanism of executive committees of district Soviets of Deputies of the Toilers in districts of the large cities for the reason that these Soviets are equated with city Soviets, and their executive committees have the same subdivisions as do the city Soviets. The constitution of the Armenian SSR indicates this plainly.

No subdivisions are formed within the structure of village Soviets, irrespective of whether or not a village Soviet has an executive committee, or a president with his vice president and secretary, as its executive organ.

7. The material basis of local Soviets

That local Soviets can fulfill their numerous and diverse functions in all the fields of socialist building is assured by granting all local Soviets of Deputies of the Toilers the rights of a juristic person, consisting, in particular, of the right to possess or to use, to acquire or to sell, to take or to lease, properties of a certain sort; to form economic enterprises; and to assume obligations and the like within the limits and in the method established by special laws. Moreover, all property within the jurisdiction of local Soviets is admittedly state property, in the management of which local Soviets execute the functions of organs of state authority.

The transfer of a portion of the state properties to be administered by local Soviets takes place because of the very nature of the latter as local organs of state authority, bringing the economic objects close to the directing organs, and insuring and stimulating the development of local initiative and self-help. It puts under the work of the Soviets a stable basis, material and financial, indispensable to the unfolding of the creative self-help of the Soviets and of the masses of the toilers they unite. This basis, which includes receipts from taxes and from other sources, permits local Soviets to create a local budget whose expense entries assure that the many and extremely varied demands of the population as to schools, hospitals, social security, welfare, and so on, will be satisfied. The segregation of local economy and the creation of local budgets guarantee the drawing of the greatest possible number of the masses into practical administrative work.

Within the system of local Soviets as a whole, properties are differentiated as being of territorial-regional, area, district or city significance, and each administrative-territorial link has, accordingly, its own budget which is a constituent part of the general system of the local budget.

Distribution and redistributon between the Soviets of different links occurs in the legislative process of the Union Republics on the basis of the Union law [18] and with a view to economic expediency: there can in principle be nothing in the nature of isolation of local properties from state properties. These properties can be exploited by local organs *either* by direct administration thereof (without segregating them into special management units), carrying all the income therefrom and disbursements therein in their entirety to the appropriate local budgets, or by segregating them, each separately or by groups, into special management units and exploiting these enterprises more or less independently on bases of economic computation according to the net cost principle—the budget including only the final financial result (the balance or a definitive part of the income). Less frequently local properties are exploited by hiring them out to other economic or social organizations (such as kolkhozes or voluntary societies). In these cases the budget includes only the rent reserved.

Special laws and instructions govern the preparation of an inventory of all the property of local Soviets. Liquidation of basic properties included in the inventory, as well as the acquisition of new properties to be included therein and the organization and conditions of managing and liquidating independent units (trusts, societies, combines, or separate enterprises), can take place only in situations defined by special laws and in the established method. A special statute declares the times within which, prior to the beginning of the budget year, changes in the redistribution of properties and other sources of income and expenditure must be effectuated as between separate Soviets and their budgets, to the end that such changes may not catch the Soviet by surprise after the beginning of the budget year.

When any new institutions are transferred to be maintained by a Soviet, or any new expenses are charged upon it, an increase of the expense portion of the budget must be compensated by a corresponding increase of the income portion thereof. If, during the course of the budget year, a Soviet has dis-

[18] Cz. 1929, No. 3, Art. 26.

closed new sources of income or exceeded the receipts contemplated by the approved budget, all the additional receipts are likewise counted into its budget and may, with certain exceptions, be disbursed for measures financed thereby. The proceeds of self-taxation, though not included in the local budget, form a considerable part of the economy of lower, district, and particularly village Soviets. They are spent, pursuant to the directives of general assemblies, either for new measures not included in the local budget at all, or for increasing budget allocations for measures particularly important to a given settlement or group. No budget allocations for any measure can be reduced upon the assumption that it will be financed by self-taxation. These proceeds are spent in developing and repairing roads, building and repairing schools, bridges, wells and public bath houses, and repairing hospitals, village reading rooms, and other cultural institutions, and thus have a strictly specific function.

The local budget itself contains also the proceeds of levies for specific purposes. Thus, the income from each specific assessment on trade must be applied to maintain the markets. Income from the municipal building fund and the communal enterprises must go toward the needs of building and communal economy; in the first instance, to the repair of dwelling houses and communal enterprises. The budget develops no special resources accruing to certain institutions and enterprises on the basis of special legislation, and disbursed by them according to particular estimates (of special resources) affirmed in the same method as is the budget itself.

Local Soviets have the right to conclude loans on the basis of special legislation and with the permission of superior organs. Loans are entered upon for purposes of a special function precisely defined, and may not be undertaken in order to cover budget deficits. Responsibility for loans rests only on the Soviets which conclude them, and such responsibility is limited to property upon which the existing legislation permits imposts to be levied. In actual practice of the work of local Soviets, loans are applied for very rarely, and are chiefly short-term loans.

As juristic persons, the Soviets are under property responsibility as well for all their other operations. Certain state properties belonging to them may, in the method provided by special legislation, be applied to extinguish their debts and other obligations. For incorrect management, for wasting property entrusted to them, workers of the Soviets are politically responsible to their electors as well as to the higher organs of authority, and are criminally responsible also.

The budgets made up by all the local Soviets of Deputies of the Toilers must contain no deficits. All the expenses contemplated by the budget must be paid by definite budget income. But the economy of separate administra-

tive-territorial units is extremely diversified: thus, irrespective of administrative-territorial boundaries, all the trade and industrial centers amass the
resources of the important territory which gravitates to them, while there
must be a certain minimum satisfaction of the needs of the entire Soviet
population, for schools, for medical aid, and so on, without reference to
the resources ordinarily entering into the local budget. For this a number
of types of income, chiefly of the character of income from taxes, become
regulatory, entering not only into the various local budgets but also into
some one budget—for example, the budget of a district—and being defined
in differing amounts for different districts, according to receipts from firmly
stabilized income, to the end that each separate budget be in balance without any deficit. At the present moment the basic regulatory income is the
tax on turnover, which is sometimes figured in the district and village budget
at 100 per cent, and in other cases at 10 per cent or even less. The same is
true of such taxes as agricultural and income taxes and the levy for culture.

The percentages of receipts from each regulatory income in each given
local budget are defined in advance by the superior organs, with the result
that each Soviet, when making up its budget, is dealing with receipts from
each type of such income that have already been made definite. In addition
to regulatory incomes, there are also regulatory funds from which grants are
made to separate local budgets (chiefly village budgets) when regulatory
income alone does not produce a budget in balance and without a deficit.
The regulatory funds are entered in the income account from other, and
stronger, local budgets, and these are special charge-offs into this fund from
the budgets of superior Soviets.

Special legislation provides for the creation of funds for unanticipated
disbursements and budget reserves in local budgets.

Village budgets must be confirmed by district organs of authority. All
other budgets, if made up without deficits, are affirmed by the appropriate
Soviets directly. Furthermore, each link of the Soviets, except the primary
links, makes a compilation of local budgets (comprising the budget both
of that Soviet and of all the inferior Soviets), and forwards this compilation
to the superior Soviet. Since the budget defines the material possibilities of
the given Soviet's work for the entire budget year in all fields of social building, the Soviets should devote the closest attention to its correct preparation
and effectuation and to the organization of control over its fulfillment. Since
the budget includes all the phases and all the branches of the Soviets' work,
all the departments and administrations, and all the standing committees
(sections) of the Soviets, should be drawn into its operation. Finance subdivisions and sections merely generalize, bringing the budgets formulated
by separate branches into the single budget of the given Soviet. All subdi-

visions and administration, all mass organizations of the Soviets (and, in the first instance, their standing committees), must daily follow the course of budget fulfillment, aiming at the complete disclosure and utilization of all sources of income and the most expedient and thrifty disbursement of each Soviet ruble.

Such in basic features is the structure, and such are the tasks and forms of activity, of the local organs of state authority in the USSR.

VIII

The Court and the Prosecutor's Office

SEC. 1: THE COURT AND THE PROSECUTOR'S OFFICE IN
THE SOCIALIST STATE OF WORKERS AND PEASANTS

THE COURT and the prosecutor's office occupy a special place in the
system of organs of state authority in the USSR. The principles underlying the organization and activity of the Soviet court and the Soviet prosecutor's office are confirmed in Chapter IX of the Stalin Constitution and
in the law, Concerning the Judicial System of the USSR and of the Union
and Autonomous Republics. Appropriate chapters devoted to the court and
the prosecutor's office are found in the constitutions of all the Union Republics. Both these systems of organs of state authority, the court system and
the prosecutor's office, are powerful and actual levers of the proletarian dictatorship by means of which it assures the fulfillment of its historical tasks,
strengthens the socialist legal order, and combats those who violate the laws
of Soviet authority.

The court in the USSR is an organ preserving the interests of the socialist state and Soviet citizens. Under socialism the interests of the state and
those of the vast majority of citizens are not, as they are in the exploiter
countries, mutually contradictory. "Socialism does not deny individual interests—it amalgamates them with those of the collective," as Stalin re-
marked in his conversation with H. G. Wells. "Socialism cannot be isolated
from individual interests. It is only socialist society that can most completely
satisfy those individual interests. Furthermore, socialist society represents
the only stable guarantee that the interests of personality will be safeguarded." [1] Safeguarding the interests of the socialist state, the court thereby
safeguards also the interests of citizens for whom the might of the state is
the primary condition essential for their individual well-being. Safeguarding

[1] Stalin, *Questions of Leninism* (10th Russian ed.), p. 602.

497

the interests of separate citizens, the court thereby safeguards also the interests of the socialist state wherein the development of the material and cultural level of the life of the citizens is the state's most important task.

In this sense the tasks of socialist justice are defined in Article 2 of the law concerning the judicial system of the USSR and the Union and autonomous republics.

The task of justice in the USSR is to defend from encroachments of every character: (a) the social and state organization of the USSR established by the USSR Constitution and by the constitutions of the Union and autonomous republics, and the socialist system of economy and socialist property; (b) personal and property rights and interests of USSR citizens, their political rights and interests, and those which they possess in their labor, their dwellings, and otherwise, guaranteed by the USSR Constitution and by the constitutions of the Union and autonomous republics; and (c) rights and legally protected interests of state institutions, enterprises, kolkhozes, cooperatives, and other social organizations.

The task of justice in the USSR is to assure the precise and unswerving fulfillment of Soviet laws by all the institutions, organizations, officials, and citizens of the USSR.

This the court accomplishes by destroying without pity all the foes of the people in whatsoever form they manifest their criminal encroachments upon socialism. At the present moment that task is in the first instance to cooperate for the final extinction of the trashy Trotsky-Bukharin bands and for the merciless repression of the criminal activity of spies and diversionists, agents of fascist reconnaissance, and to struggle against those who would misappropriate state property, the economic basis of the Soviet order. Again, the court struggles against crimes inherited from the capitalist social order, against pillagers, thieves, hooligans, and other criminals. It safeguards the rights of citizens by entertaining actions brought by individual citizens to reestablish rights which have been violated and by punishing persons admitting criminal encroachment upon those rights. All the activity of the court exerts a broad and fostering influence not only upon persons to whom the court applies corrective measures, but also upon great masses of the toilers who, following its work and participating therein, are imbued with respect for Soviet laws and learn the rules of socialist life together.

The prosecutor's office also participates directly in all this work.

The bonds joining court and prosecutor's office are of the closest possible character and they act united by an indissoluble and organic bond. Their tasks are identical although they employ different methods of work. Accordingly, matters relating to them are united in a general chapter (IX) of the USSR Constitution.

The court is the organ which administers justice.[2] Dispensing justice is one of the state's most important functions. In the socialist state it consists in resolving matters, transferred to be considered by the court, on the basis of Soviet laws and the socialist legal consciousness of the judges, independently of any influence whatever exerted by any party. Accordingly the judges are independent, and subordinate to law alone.[3] In the trial of a specific court matter, the court establishes the attendant facts of the case and decides the inferences to be drawn therefrom on the basis of Soviet law and socialist legal consciousness. This is socialist justice carried into effect. The task of justice in the USSR is, above all, to safeguard and defend the socialist state from all encroachments whatsoever. Defense of the social and state organization established by the USSR Constitution and by the constitutions of the Union and autonomous republics, of the socialist system of economy, and of socialist property is of primary importance. Justice has the further task of defending the rights and interests of citizens guaranteed by the Constitution and by all the Soviet laws, and the rights and legally protected interests of state institutions, enterprises, kolkhozes, cooperatives, and other social organizations.

The position of the Soviet court in the system of organs of Soviet authority is defined in conformity with the character of socialist justice thus delineated. The court is not an organ of state administration like the executive and administrative organs, central and otherwise, which are the subject matter of Chapters V and VIII of the USSR Constitution. It does not itself administer; instead, it decides specific court cases, criminal (concerned with crimes) and civil (concerned with civil disputes), participating thereby in state administration, but in its own unique fashion and not at all in the way in which other organs of authority participate in such administration. Article 4 of the law relative to the USSR judicial system reflects this difference, which consists in the fact that (1) matters are tried in the courts by the method of public court process, wherein (2) both sides take an active part (accuser and accused, plaintiff and defendant), the law guaranteeing them all the rights essential to the protection of their interests in court.

Thus, by trials of criminal and civil matters in court sessions, the court fulfills the tasks of socialist justice hereinbefore indicated.

In criminal trials the court applies legally established measures of punishment directed against traitors, wreckers, pillagers of socialist property, and other foes of the people who betray their country, as well as against robbers, thieves, hooligans, and other criminal elements and derangers of socialist

---

[2] Constitution of the USSR, Art. 102.
[3] *Ibid.*, Art. 112.

society. In civil trials the court decides controversies touching the rights and interests of citizens and of state and social institutions and organizations.

A court of whatever sort is an organ of the authority of the class dominant in a given state, defending and guarding its interests. The bourgeois court is one of the keen weapons for repressing the toilers and resisting encroachments upon the system of capitalist relations, upon private property. In the original sketch of his article "The Immediate Tasks of Soviet Authority," Lenin wrote: "In capitalist society the court was preeminently a mechanism of oppression, of bourgeois exploitation." [4] Addressing the Third All-Russian Congress of Soviets in January, 1918, Lenin said that the bourgeois court "figured as the defender of order, whereas it was in reality a blind and subtle instrument for the pitiless repression of the exploited, protecting the moneyed interests." [5]

Bourgeois theorists strive to depict the court as an organ above classes and apart from politics, acting, supposedly, in the interests of all society and guided by commands of law and justice common to all mankind, instead of by the interests of the dominant class. Such a conception of the court's essence and tasks is, of course, radically false. It has always been an instrument in the hands of the dominant class, assuring the strengthening of its dominance and the protection of its interests. Some bourgeois scholars go so far as to acknowledge this with reference to the court of historical epochs of the past, but not as to the court of the bourgeois state. Thus Bacot, a French jurist of the last century, studying the court organization of ancient Rome, wrote: "If one would understand the power of the court of the ancients, he must entirely forget its significance at the present time. Now there is a breach between the court and politics, whereas in antiquity there was the closest bond between them. The authority of the court of the ancients, being in the hands of the dominant classes, served everywhere as a means of influence and exploitation." [6] The author very correctly defines the class character of the court of ancient Rome, but holds that only the court of antiquity was a class court and that this is not so as to the modern bourgeois court which, in his opinion, has nothing in common with the politics of the dominant class. Such handling of the bourgeois court and similar denial of its class character are typical of bourgeis jurisprudence, which strives to shade off and to mask the fact that it is essentially an instrument of class policy and actually a keen weapon for the repression and exploitation of broad masses of the toilers in the interests of the dominant exploiter minority.

[4] Lenin (Russian ed.), Vol. XXII, p. 424.
[5] *Ibid.*, p. 212.
[6] Bacot, *The Organization of Criminal Justice in the Principal Epochs of History* (Russian ed., 1867), p. 23.

Engels wrote of the English courts:

When a rich man is summoned, or rather invited, into court, the judge expresses regret that the rich man had to inconvenience himself and tries in every way to turn the matter to the rich man's advantage; and if he must, despite everything, condemn him, he again expresses his infinite regret, and so on. The result is a negligible fine which, as he departs, the bourgeois gentleman contemptuously throws on the table. But if some one of the poor has to come before that judge, he is looked upon from the very beginning as guilty. He is shouted at, and all his attempts to justify himself are met by a contemptuous "Oh! we know these excuses!" The bias of Justices of the Peace, particularly in the rural districts, actually exceeds all description, and is such a common phenomenon that all cases not outstanding are reported in the papers perfectly quietly and without comments of any kind. And how could it be otherwise? On the one hand, these Dogberries [Justices of the Peace] interpret the laws only in the sense contained therein. On the other hand they are themselves bourgeois, and see the chief foundation of every kind of true order preeminently in the interests of their class.[7]

Where these interests require the condemnation of one known to be innocent or, conversely, the vindication of one known to be guilty, the bourgeois judge takes such a perversion of the idea of justice in his stride. Many cases of this sort have acquired world-wide notoriety. Here are some of them.

1. In 1895 a coterie of anti-Semitic elements from among the reactionary militarists in France falsely accused an officer of the general staff, Dreyfus, a Jew by birth, of espionage in aid of Germany. Although proof was completely lacking, the military court, by order of the minister of war, condemned Dreyfus to life exile. In 1897, it was manifest that the acts of espionage unjustly ascribed to Dreyfus were committed by Major Esterhazy. The matter was on every tongue and Esterhazy had to be turned over to the court. To condemn Esterhazy would have been to admit that the condemnation of Dreyfus was without justification. Accordingly, the military court vindicated Esterhazy notwithstanding manifest proof of his guilt. Emile Zola, the author, addressed an open letter to the President of the republic, headed "J'Accuse," in which he unmasked this entire court comedy. Upon complaint by the military authorities, Zola was handed over to the court for libel. The law required the court to ascertain whether or not the information communicated by Zola in the open letter was known to be false—that is to say, to examine the fundamental question: Is it true that the military court condemned Dreyfus and vindicated Esterhazy upon order "from above"? In the teeth of the direct meaning of the statute, the

[7] Marx and Engels (Russian ed.), Vol. III, pp. 558–559.

president of the court permitted no consideration of this basic question upon whose decision depended the further decision of the question as to whether or not the information communicated by Zola was defamatory. Nevertheless, Zola was condemned. The press compaign associated with *L'Affaire Dreyfus* did not abate, however, and the court of last resort in France (the Court of Cassation) abrogated the sentence in 1899. Upon fresh examination of the matter in the military court, the court again adjudged Dreyfus guilty but "deserving of lenience," whereupon he was pardoned by the President.

2. Another less notorious case of court comedy occurred in tsarist Russia in 1913. A Jew, Beilis, serving in one of the works in Kiev, was handed over to the court on an accusation, known to be false and grotesque, that he slew the boy Yushchinsky in order to obtain the blood of a Christian boy to fill the needs of a religious cult. The absurdity of this accusation was clear from the very outset. It was directly indicated that the murder of Yushchinsky was perpetrated in one of the vile dens in Kiev, which were under police protection. Nevertheless, the tsarist prosecutor's office proceeded against Beilis, striving to play upon the ignorant and benighted masses and to develop their proclivities for pogroms against the Jews (thereby distracting them from revolutionary activities against tsarism). The outcome of this proceeding was different from that of the Dreyfus affair, however. Beilis came on for trial before a jury and, notwithstanding all the exertions of the prosecutor's office, including the falsification of evidence and special expert testimony arranged behind the scenes, the jurors acquitted him. The court comedy cooked up by tsarist justice collapsed. Even the hand-picked jurors proved unreliable!

When class interests of the bourgeoisie require the innocent to be condemned, even a court and jury, the most democratic form of court possible under capitalist conditions, is no guarantee against injustice. In 1927, in the U.S.A., a jury condemned two Italian worker-Communists, Sacco and Vanzetti, to death upon a charge of murder. An alibi was indisputably proved in behalf of the accused in court. At the moment when the murder was perpetrated they were in a different place. This did not save them from the death sentence, inasmuch as they were Communists—and consequently enemies of the jurors representing the bourgeoisie.

On the other hand, under the conditions of bourgeois democracy, the democratic forms of the organization of the court (such as jurors) and of criminal process (publicity, adversary proceedings, and the like) make it difficult to accomplish such manifest injustice. Bourgeois procedural democracy, notwithstanding all its unilateral character and hypocrisy, does nevertheless allow the accused to defend himself, to struggle against an irregular indictment. In certain circumstances this struggle may prove to be successful, as was shown by the foregoing affair of Beilis. The situation is different in states where the bloody dictatorship of fascism is dominant. Fascism studiously annihilates everything formerly democratic in the bourgeois-democratic state organization, including the court. This in fascist countries becomes merely a subdivision of a police district, an organ to deal without any nonsense with all antifascists. Fascists find no need even to keep within the external forms of decency serving, in a bourgeois democracy, to mask the class nature of the bourgeois court. Abolishing jury courts in favor of extraordinary tribunals of every sort, depriving the accused of every kind of procedural rights, and dealing out arbitrary punishment on a large scale, with the aid of the court and otherwise, fascism brings about a monstrous terror as regards all the toilers.

The Soviet court is radically different from any court to be found in exploiter states. It is a new type of court, precisely as the socialist worker-peasant state is a completely new type of state. For the first time in the history of mankind, the court in the USSR is not an instrument for the enslavement of the vast majority of the population in the interests of the exploiter apex, but a genuine people's court, defending the true interests of the people against all their foes, all those who would disorganize the building of socialism.

The Soviet court was organized in the very first days of the victory of the great October Socialist Revolution, which smashed the old bourgeois-landowner machinery of state and the old court, and erected upon its ruins a new, Soviet people's court. The fundamental principles of its organization were formulated in the decree—worked out with the immediate participation and guidance of Lenin and Stalin—Concerning the Court (No. 1), issued November 24/December 7, 1917.[8]

In "The Immediate Tasks of Soviet Authority" (previously referred to), Lenin defines the task of the Soviet court thus:

Above all, a new court was indispensable to the struggle against the exploiters striving to reestablish their dominance or to defend their privileges (or furtively to insinuate, or fraudulently to get advance payment on some portion thereof). But there is another and still more important task resting upon the courts if they are in reality organized upon the principle of Soviet institutions—to assure the strictest development of the toilers' discipline and self-discipline.[9]

These tasks of the Soviet court, to struggle against the people's foes and their agents, and to exert its influence to educate the unstable elements among the toilers, have been ever before it during all the stages of the

[8] Cy. 1917, No. 4, Art. 50.
[9] Lenin (Russian ed.), Vol. XXII, p. 424.

development of the socialist revolution, and are before it even in the present epoch when the Stalin Constitution is being carried into effect and socialist society is being basically constructed.

Inseparably integrated with the court is the Soviet prosecutor's office, an organ of state authority obligated to oversee that socialist legality is observed. It was organized in 1922 by a decision of the third session of the All-Russian Central Executive Committee at its ninth convocation.[10] When the country had passed to the reestablishment of the national economy after the triumphant termination of the civil war, Soviet authority was confronted with the task of further reinforcing revolutionary legality. The Soviet office of prosecutions was created under the immediate guidance of Lenin and Stalin, who decided the fundamental matters of principle involved in its organization. In May, 1922, Lenin, in his letter addressed to Stalin, Concerning "Dual" Subordination and Legality, set out the problems and the role of the Soviet prosecutor's office, pointing out that "legality cannot be the legality of Kaluga or the legality of Kazan, but must be one single All-Russian legality, even one single legality for the entire federation of Soviet republics," wherefore the task of the prosecutor's office is "to see to the establishment of a truly uniform understanding of legality in the entire republic irrespective of any local differences whatsoever and regardless of any local influences whatsoever"; furthermore "the prosecutor is responsible that not a single decision of a single local authority be divergent from the law. From this point of view alone is it incumbent on him to protest an unlawful decision of any sort." [11]

In such activity the Public Prosecutor is indissolubly bound up with the court inasmuch as, to be decided by the court, he transfers proceedings instituted by him and involving breach of legality.

SEC. 2: PRINCIPLES OF SOCIALIST DEMOCRACY IN THE ORGANIZATION AND ACTIVITY OF THE SOVIET COURT

The court organization is inseparably embodied in the state organization as a constituent part of that organization. Accordingly, directives of the USSR Constitution concerning the court rest on the same principles as does the entire USSR Constitution.

The Stalin Constitution is the most democratic Constitution in the world. These principles of socialist democracy are placed as the foundation of the law, Concerning the Judicial System of the USSR and of the Union

[10] Cy. 1922, No. 36, Art. 424.
[11] Lenin (Russian ed.), Vol. XXVII, pp. 298–299.

and Autonomous Republics, adopted by the second session of the USSR Supreme Soviet. Erected on the basis of this law, which defines the tasks and the organization of the Soviet court, that court is the most democratic court in the world. Only a court resting upon such principles and guided thereby in its activity can—simultaneously with the task of crushing the foes of socialism—effectuate the most important role of educator which must pertain to the court in socialist society, a society which, while assuring to citizens the maximum of rights, requires also the maximum of discipline and self-discipline. How highly Lenin esteemed this role of court institutions in his time is manifest from his insistence that their activity be extended "over the entire working life of the country." At the same time he pointed out that courts will know how "to bring it to pass that the wishes of discipline and self-discipline remain not merely empty wishes" only "upon condition that the broadest masses of the toiling and exploited population participate therein" and, moreover, that their action be "in democratic forms in conformity with the principles of Soviet authority." [1]

Article 5 of the law concerning the judicial system establishes the principle that there is one and the same court for all citizens, whatever be their position as regards society, property, or service, and irrespective of the nation and race to which they belong. In tsarist Russia there was a whole line of special courts for different categories of citizens. Thus, officials accused of official crimes were judged in the privileged court with representatives of the social orders taking part, while for peasants there were special volost courts which, unlike all other courts, could, almost down to the revolution of 1905, apply corporal punishment.

Soviet courts are built and operate upon the principles of logical socialist democracy which, in their lowest terms, require (1) that each member of the population take part in the functioning of justice, (2) elective courts, (3) judges who are independent and subordinate to the law alone, (4) the consideration of matters in court in the national language, (5) publicity and immediacy, and (6) court procedure based on adversary proceedings and the right of the accused to defend himself.

All these principles are expressed and confirmed in the Stalin Constitution and in the constitutions of the Union Republics.

Lenin formulated the proposition: "The court is an instrumentality to attract every individual member of the poorest classes to state administration." [2] The same proposition was established also in the program of the All-Union Communist Party (of Bolsheviks):

In order to attract the very broadest masses of the proletariat and poorest

[1] Lenin (Russian ed.), Vol. XXII, p. 425.
[2] Lenin (Russian ed.), Vol. XXII, p. 460.

peasantry to the functioning of justice, the participation in the court of temporary court-assessors, constantly replaced, has been introduced and mass worker organizations, trade unions, and the like have been drawn into the make-up of the lists. . . . The All-Union Communist Party, defending the further development of the court along the same line, should strive that all the toiling population without exception be attracted into the functioning of court obligations.[3]

This is confirmed in the Stalin Constitution (Art. 103) as a *constitutional* principle: "People's assessors participate in the consideration of matters in all courts, except in cases specifically provided for by statute." The fundamental rule established by Article 14 of the law concerning the judicial system is that the consideration of any court matter, whether criminal or civil, is conducted by a collegium composed of a single permanent judge and two people's assessors. This method is operative in all courts, from the people's court to the Supreme Court of the USSR, with exceptions permitted in cases when, according to law, consideration of the matter by three members of the court and without people's assessors is contemplated. The three-man court also considers appellate matters, when complaints and protests against sentences and decisions are being reviewed.

The participation of people's assessors, obligatory in all courts, assures the solution of two problems: (1) to attract the people into the administration of the state, into the fulfillment of the most important state functions through their participation in the decision of court matters; and (2) to introduce into the functioning of justice a genuine popular principle, the people's socialist legal consciousness, convictions, and conscience. Such a method guarantees the true socialist democracy of Soviet justice, the bond of the court with the people, and the court's authority in the eyes of the people.

The court structure known to bourgeois law is that wherein nonprofessional judges, representing the "people" so-called, are drawn to participate. The classical form of the bourgeois court is the "court with jury" (a court with participation of sworn assessors) existing in the capitalist countries that preserve the bourgeois-democratic forms of state order. In such a court the jurors (ordinarily twelve) decide the guilt of the accused, and, on the basis of that verdict, permanent judges (appointed by state authority) apply the law and designate the punishment. In its modern form, such a court was created by the bourgeoisie in consequence of its victory over feudalism and was progressive as compared with the bureaucratic and caste courts of the noble-landowner state. While bourgeois democracy flourished, such a court undoubtedly served as a bulwark of the political freedoms proclaimed by

[3] *Program and Statute of the All-Union Communist Party (of Bolsheviks)* (1936), pp. 39–41.

the bourgeoisie at the time of its triumph over the power of the feudal monarchy. But jurors are now, as they were formerly, the bulwark of that order of social relationships which rests on private capitalist property. The class character of such a court is an index as well of the class direction of the justice to which the jury gives effect. Chosen chiefly from the circles of the middle and petty bourgeoisie, and predisposed by their own social position to see the buttressing of the existing social order as their function, jurors are captivated by the views, even as to concrete matters, enunciated by the press, which is in the hands of the biggest capitalists.

This is the court of bourgeois democracy protecting the interests of persons of wealth and substance, characterized by Marx as "a caste court of the privileged classes instituted to plug the law's loopholes with the latitudinarian bourgeois conscience." [4]

Engels analyzed the English court with jurors, the most finished and developed form of bourgeois-democratic court, and laid bare the falsity and hypocrisy masking its true class nature. It "is essentially a political rather than a juridical institution but, since every sort of juridical being has an innately political nature, the *truly* juridical element is manifested therein; and the English court of jurors, as the most developed, is the culmination of juridical falsehood and immorality." [5] The class character of the court with jurors had to be acknowledged even by some of the most conscientious bourgeois scholars. An outstanding representative of bourgeois procedural science (Garraud) asserts "the direct and striking" absence of impartiality among jurors. He condemns the justice of the jury which ought to be popular justice, the justice of all classes and all citizens, as having "become egoistic justice, defending the juridical interests of one class only. Everyone knows that jurors reserve their severity for crimes which seem to threaten the class of petty proprietors or petty traders where they themselves belong), and are happy to tolerate—to the point of justifying—crimes with no apparent bearing upon their own safety." [6]

As compared with the bureaucratic and caste courts of the feudal-servile state, the court of jurors was undoubtedly a progressive form of court and a great step forward historically. The very fact that citizens who were not professional, official judges participated in the court, having fulfilled their judicial obligations within a brief period and having decided the question of the guilt of those before the court without the cooperation of permanent, official judges appointed by the government, gave this court a democratic

[4] *The Köln Proceedings Against the Communists Exposed*, Marx and Engels, *Collected Works* (Russian ed.), Vol. VIII, p. 558.

[5] F. Engels, *The English Constitution*, Marx and Engels, *Collected Works* (Russian ed.), Vol. II, p. 383.

[6] Garraud, *Traité d'instruction criminelle*, Vol. IV, p. 459.

character. The jurors were far less guided in their decisions by "views of the government" than were the permanent judges and sometimes brought their opposition moods into the court's activity. Of such a court, Lenin wrote that "for public representatives to participate in the court is undoubtedly a democratic principle." [7] But for this democratic principle to be logically applicable, it is essential that "there shoud be no *qualification* which jurors must satisfy in order to be eligible, no limitation based on conditions of learning, property, domicile, and the like." [8] This, however, is precisely what is lacking as to bourgeois jurors: they comprise, for the most part, the petty and middle bourgeoisie, townsfolk, traders, shopkeepers, kulaks, and so on, rather than true representatives of the people, workers and peasants.

Precisely for the reasons that such a court is a bourgeois-democratic organization, it was under constant attack by every sort of reactionary element. The famous nineteenth century German jurist, Professor Mittermaier, favored the court with jurors in his treatise on the subject in the middle of the last century, writing that "of all the criminal institutions of modern times, it enjoys the greatest popularity," but noting withal "a morbid distrust thereof on the part of the legislators themselves as well as of the judges." In his opinion the fundamental occasion for this distrust was that the jurors too often acquitted persons tried before them. All those hostile to the court, from the reactionary circles of bourgeois society, gleefully parroted this idea as to its clemency or leniency. Of course the jury court was never clement or indulgent to persons accused of encroaching upon bourgeois social relationships, upon private property, but it is true that its very character made it a less facile instrument in the hands of the administration than a court made up solely of official judges, and that its activity reflected, in a greater degree than did that of the latter, the moods which were being molded in society. For this very reason the reactionary circles of bourgeois society desired ever more ardently to abolish the jury court.

One bourgeois jurist—like Mittermaier, friendly to such courts—could not refrain from setting out the following phenomenon: "The chief procedural problem of the present time is whether to preserve or to abrogate the jury court. There are outspoken expressions in favor of abolishing it and putting a special form of *Schöffengericht* [9] in its place; the construction of the latter, however, hangs in the air and seems completely impractical." [10]

---

[7] Lenin (Russian ed.), Vol. XXX, p. 194.

[8] Mittermaier, *European and American Jury Courts* (Russian ed., 1869), Pt. 1, pp. 5, 6.

[9] *Schöffengericht*: a "mixed" court having jurisdiction over minor crimes, and consisting of one judge and two lay assessors (later, in more important cases, of two judges and three lay assessors), all participating equally in deciding the issue of guilt and fixing the appropriate sentence.—TR.

[10] Josef Kohler, *Moderne Rechtsprobleme* (1913), p. 70.

While, as will be manifest later, the Schöffengericht was extremely "practical" for bourgeois states which had abolished the bourgeois-democratic parliamentary forms, the attention of bourgeois politicians and jurists had long been focused upon the abolition of the jury court. It was energetically attacked by representatives of the so-called anthropological school of criminal law, which proposed to turn the court into a "social clinic," [11] forcing representatives of society out of the court under the pretext of employing more rational methods to cure "social diseases" (criminality) and eliminating social control of the court, and being thus relieved of all restraint in dealing with elements dangerous to the bourgeoisie.

In prerevoutionary Russia the court with jurors was introduced by the court regulations of 1864, but as early as the 1870's its jurisdiction was steadily diminishing under the influence of mounting political reaction. Katkov, a well known reactionary publicist of the past century, called it contemptuously a "street-corner court." Lenin paused more than once to consider the part played by the prerevolutionary Russian court with juries, investing the expression "street-corner court" with a completely different content. "The street-corner court is valuable precisely because it introduces a living current into the spirit of official formalism whereby all governmental institutions are impregnated through and through." Characterizing the advantages of the court with jurors as a democratic court in comparison with the court with class representatives, he said: "For this reason reactionary publicists and a reactionary administration hate—and cannot do otherwise than hate—the street-corner court." [12]

Jurisdiction of the court with juries did not include authority over political or official crimes, encroachments upon representatives of authority, or the like.

How the jurisdiction of the court of jurors was narrowed and its role and authority declined is noted in all the capitalist countries, even those that have preserved bourgeois-democratic forms of state administration (the U.S.A., England, and France). As class contradictions become acute in bourgeois states and the ground under the feet of the exploiter classes becomes less and less firm, the most reactionary cliques of the capitalist classes jettison bourgeois-democratic forms, freedoms, and guarantees and conduct an attack also upon the court with jurors, which is, as we have seen, the court's classic bourgeois-democratic form. Upon the program of a single national front—to defend the bourgeois-democratic forms of state administration against reactionary attempts to trample them under foot and destroy

---

[11] Enrico Ferri, *Criminal Sociology* (Russian ed., 1908), pp. 436, 488.
[12] Lenin (Russian ed.), Vol. IV, p. 84, the article, "Beat, But Not to Death."

them—is also the struggle to preserve the court with jurors from attempts to supplant it by crown courts and such courts as the Schöffengericht.

In fascist countries like Italy and Germany, the court with jurors, like all bourgeois-democratic forms, has been abolished and the basic form of court is the so-called Schöffengericht court (known in Italy as the court of assessors) wherein assessors and permanent (crown) judges constitute a single collegium and jointly decide questions of guilt and of punishment alike. In Germany the Schöffengericht court supplanted the court with jurors as early as 1924, signifying that it is easier for the permanent judges in this court to exert influence on the assessors, to subordinate and depersonalize them, than it is where there are juries. Under the fascist regime the assessors in the Schöffengericht type of court usually represent fascist organizations. This court can in no wise be called an instrument of justice, even in the bourgeois significance of the word, inasmuch as it has become a police instrument to deal with revolutionaries and antifascists—with the toilers—shamelessly applying the methods of accusations brought about by fabricated indictments and falsified proofs. This, of course, is not justice; it is an outrage upon the very essence of justice.

Popular participation in the functioning of justice in the Soviet Union is utterly different from that in the bourgeois states. In the Soviet court all the judges are judges from the people. Judges of the people's court are called people's judges. All judges are elected, not appointed. There are no official judges in the Soviet court. Accordingly, in our court antithesis of assessors to permanent judges on the hypothesis that the former are of the people would be simply absurd. The antithesis of society to the state—traditional in bourgeois science—is meaningless as regards the Soviet state, since the latter expresses and defends the interests of all the laboring people.

In the Soviet court the permanent judges and assessors constitute a single collegium wherein both are elected from the Soviet people. Article 19 of the law concerning the judicial system of the USSR and of the Union and autonomous republics establishes that in case the people's judge is temporarily absent by reason of illness or leave of absence, one of the people's assessors is charged to execute the duties of a judge.

A people's assessor, participating in the consideration of a case, enjoys all the rights of a judge. All questions, whether arising in the consideration of the case or in formulation of the sentence or decision, are decided by a mere majority vote, and the vote of the president is no more weighty than is that of a people's assessor.

The Stalin Constitution establishes the most solemn guarantee assuring the independence of people's assessors in their decision of court matters; they are chosen in the same manner and for the same term as are the permanent judges. According to the Constitution, the people's courts are elected by the citizens through universal, direct, and equal suffrage with secret ballot for the term of three years.[13]

An edifying history lies back of the definition of the method of choosing our judges. At its Second Party Congress (1903) the adopted program minimum of the Russian Social-Democratic Party forecast the "immediate tasks" before the Party in view of the increasing bourgeois-democratic revolution, and in its eleventh point it provided that "judges were to be elected by the people." In the "Proposal for Remaking the Theoretical, Political, and Certain Other Parts of the Program" introduced by Lenin in 1917 at the All-Russian April conference, Section 11 again required that judges be elected by the people.

After the victory of the proletariat in October, 1917, the Decree of Soviet Authority Concerning the Court (No. 1) abolished the old courts and laid the foundations of the new Soviet court, proclaiming the principle that judges be elected on the most democratic basis by universal and direct suffrage. A succession of historical conditions (the resistance of exploiter classes to the measures of Soviet authority, the civil war, intervention, the struggle of the kulaks against the policy of collectivizing agriculture, and so forth) prevented the realization at that time of this principle of universal and direct suffrage, and during the years which followed, judges—including popular judges—were elected by the Soviets. In cities people's judges were elected by the city Soviets; and in the rural localities by the local district executive committees of the Soviets. To the end of strengthening the independence of people's judges as regards local organs of authority, the law of June 25, 1932, Concerning Revolutionary Legality,[14] established that the people's judges could be recalled only pursuant to directives of the district or regional executive committees of Soviets.

Members of regional and district courts, of supreme courts of autonomous and Union Republics, and of the USSR Supreme Court, were chosen, and were recalled by the appropriate executive committees of the Soviets.[15] Since the Soviets thus electing the judges were themselves strictly democratic organizations unifying all the toilers, this method of electing judges was many times more democratic than the method employed in capitalist states to man the court mechanism—the administrative appointment of the judges. Now, with socialism conclusively victorious and no exploiter classes in the Soviet state, the principle of universal, direct, and equal suf-

[13] USSR Constitution, Art. 109; Judicial Code, Art. 22.
[14] Cz. 1932, No. 5, Art. 298.
[15] Prior to the confirmation of the Stalin Constitution, these courts were called "the chief courts of the autonomous republics."

frage to elect the people's court with secret ballot is made real and is the foundation of the judicial system now in force (Art. 109 of the USSR Constitution).

Articles 22 to 25 of the law concerning the judicial system ordain that elections of the people's courts be held according to elective districts embracing the entire population domiciled in the territory wherein the people's court operates. The right to put forward candidates for the position of people's judge is granted to social, party, and professional organizations and societies of the toilers. The method of electing people's judges (registering candidates, publishing lists, and so on) is defined in detail by the legislation of the Union Republics.

The Stalin Constitution ordains the election (for a term of five years) of judges of the higher courts (territorial, regional, and areas) and of courts of the autonomous regions, by the appropriate Soviets of Deputies of the Toilers.

In the vast majority of the countries of capitalist Europe, including those which have preserved the bourgeois-democratic forms of administration, judges are appointed, not elected. Thus in France, at the time of the bourgeois revolution (1791), it was established that judges were to be elected—upon principles of property qualification, however; but as early as 1799 the Constitution abolished the elections of officials, including judges—excepting judges of the lowest courts and of the commerce courts. Election of the judges of the lowest courts was abolished in 1802. Thereafter the appointment of judges was entrusted to the head of the state.[16]

The consequence of judges in bourgeois countries being appointed is that such appointees of the administration become officials giving effect to its will. Bourgeois legislation usually seeks to obviate this result by making judges irremovable. Once appointed by the administration, a judge cannot be removed but remains in office for life or until he reaches the age limit. As to judges being irremovable, Lenin wrote: [17]

The irremovability of judges—over which the liberal bourgeois in general and our Russian bourgeois in particular are kicking up such a fuss—is only an item in the account of medieval privileges between the Purishkeviches and the Milyukovs, between the serf owners and the bourgeoisie. In *reality* it is impossible completely to develop irremovability, and it is nothing less than absurd to defend it as applied to unsuitable, careless, and bad judges. In the middle ages the appointment of judges was exclusively in the hands of the feudal lords and absolutism. The bourgeoisie, having now attained broad access to judicial circles,

---

[16] Cf. Art. 3 of the constitutional law of Feb. 25, 1875, and now in force in France: "The President of the Republic . . . appoints to all civil and military offices."

[17] Lenin (Russian ed., 1912), Vol. XXX, p. 195, the article, "The International Congress of Judges."

defends itself from the feudal lords by means of "the principle of irremovability" (because in most cases appointed judges will inevitably come from the bourgeoisie since most of the "educated" jurists belong to the bourgeoisie). So—defending itself from the *feudal lords* by maintaining that judges should be appointed—the bourgeoisie is at the same time defending itself *from democracy*.

Nowhere is the irremovability of judges in fact developed completely. In any capitalistic state the administration finds grounds to remove any judge whose activity does not conform with the views of the directing capitalist groups. In fascist countries the irremovability of judges is completely abolished. Thus, in Italy judges may at any moment be dismissed from their posts because of unsuitability and so on (Statute of January 30, 1923, and Regulation of March 23, 1923, Concerning Judges of Assize).

How remote the appointment of judges by administrative authority is from meeting the needs of true democracy needs no demonstration. But even where—as in Switzerland and in the U.S.A.—judges of the lower judicial ranks are chosen by the people, it is under such conditions as to be only nominally a choice by the people. Necessarily attendant upon the election are all the obstacles impeding the manifestation of the majority will in countries of bourgeois democracy, all the influences of directing capitalist cliques irresistible in capitalist society, in consequence whereof the majority will is subordinated to the will of the negligible minority making up the apex of the social ladder. In the U.S.A., where capitalism is most broadly developed, the vices of the capitalist system in elections of judges are so conspicuous that even observers who are wholeheartedly on the side of bourgeois ideology cannot remain silent. Thus, James Bryce wrote that "in some states it is not only learning and ability but also honesty and impartiality that are lacking. The party organizations which nominate candidates for the Bench can use their influence to reward partisans or to place in power persons whom they intend to use for their own purposes." [18]

Article 112 of the Stalin Constitution establishes the principle of judicial independence: "Judges are independent and subject only to law." Herein the Constitution has in view their right and obligation to reach their sentence or decision in each individual case upon their own inner conviction based on their socialist legal consciousness, in strict conformity with the circumstances of the case and with the mandate of the law.

At the end of the eighteenth century, the principle of the independence of judges was proclaimed by the bourgeoisie, but in the sense of their independence of feudal authority, of the ruling apex made up of the nobility. In the legislation of bourgeois-democratic states, the principle of judicial independence is in the nature of a screen, masking the true class nature of

[18] Bryce, *Modern Democracies* (1921), Vol. II, p. 386.

the bourgeois court. In *The Civil War in France,* Marx wrote with reference to measures of the Paris Commune relating to the judicial system: "Court officials have lost their seeming independence, which merely concealed their subordination to the alternately shifting governments; to each government they took an oath of fidelity, and to each government they proved faithless." [19]

Bourgeois judges, representing and defending the class interests of the exploiter class, cannot be genuinely independent. Even though it be declared that they must decide matters according to their conviction and upon their conscience, this conviction and this conscience are nevertheless defined by their class position, by the class content of the bourgeois court's activity. In "The Proceeding against Gottschalk and His Comrades" (1848), Marx wrote that the court of jurors would not serve to assure the correct decision of this matter.

"But the *conscience* of the jurors," their expostulation will run, "their *conscience* . . . is any greater guarantee necessary?" Ach, mon Dieu! Conscience depends on consciousness, on the entire form of a man's life. A republican has a different conscience from that of a royalist. A "have" has a different conscience from a "have-not." A thinker has a different conscience from that of one who has never had a thought. When property or other qualification alone decides who is called to obligations of a juror, his conscience is likewise a "qualification" conscience. That is the point: the "conscience" of the privileged is a privileged conscience.[20]

Only the Soviet court, the court of the socialist worker-peasant state, expressing the will of the entire toiling people of the Soviet Union, is truly independent in the authentic and direct sense of the word. Soviet judges are independent, inasmuch as the Soviet court, being subordinated only to the law, which sets forth the will of the entire people, is independent of all influences and inducements whatsoever in deciding specific court matters. In arriving at their sentences and decisions, judges are subordinate only to demands of the law, and rely upon their inner judicial conviction formed upon a consideration of all the circumstances of the case. In this sense the Soviet court, the court of the people, the court of the toiling masses, is a genuinely independent court.

The law, Concerning the Judicial Structure of the USSR and of the Union and Autonomous Republics, establishes such guarantees of judicial independence as not a single bourgeois country knows or has ever known. Judges are relieved from office and people's assessors from their obligations only upon recall of the electorate or by virtue of a court sentence concern-

[19] Marx, *Selected Works* (Russian ed., 1933), Vol. II, p. 396.
[20] Marx and Engels (Russian ed.), Vol. VII, pp. 495–496.

ing them (Art. 17). Criminal proceedings against judges are initiated—and they are dismissed from office in connection therewith and handed over to the court—only upon a directive of a Union Republic Public Prosecutor sanctioned by the Presidium of the Union Republic Supreme Soviet. Similar action in regard to members of special courts (military courts, courts of rail and water transportation) and of the USSR Supreme Court is upon directive of the USSR Public Prosecutor sanctioned by the Presidium of the USSR Supreme Soviet.

For toilers of the Soviet Union, the Soviet court is their people's court not only as to the structure of the judiciary but also as regards its accessibility; it is always close to the people in the language in which legal proceedings are carried on and explanations may be made to the court. Article 110 of the USSR Constitution requires that "judicial proceedings be conducted in the language of the Union or autonomous republic or autonomous region, guaranteeing that persons ignorant thereof be made completely cognizant of the materials of the matter through an interpreter and have the right to use their own language in court." It is interesting to compare this directive, a realization of the Lenin-Stalin nationalist policy in the functioning of justice, with Article 3 of the prerevolutionary Fundamental Laws, which reproduces the despotic policy of autocracy: "The Russian language is the language of the entire state and is obligatory in the army, the fleet, and all state and social establishments." And contemporary fascist states go still further in this matter. Under Article 137 of the Italian Code of Criminal Procedure, operative in 1931, court proceedings are carried on in the Italian language only, and a person refusing to use the Italian language in court (and unable to prove that he does not understand it) is punishable by a fine of from 500 to 2,000 lire. Only the overthrow of tsarism and of the exploiter classes (who had crushed the national culture of the many peoples shackled in the iron ring of tsarist despotism) could disclose the way to the free development of national languages; only Soviet authority could give effect to the demand that all languages have rights completely equal.

Article 110 of the Stalin Constitution guarantees that the court be accessible and intelligible to the people where it is held, while, at the same time, it assures the rights of persons ignorant of the language in which the matter is there being considered. Pursuant thereto, Union Republic constitutions designate the language of the respective Union Republics—Russian in the RSFSR (Art. 114), Ukrainian in the Ukraine SSR, and so on. Furthermore, in the case of a number of constitutions, in the articles concerning language, there are designated the autonomous republics and the autonomous regions which make up the Union Republics as well as the languages of these republics and regions: under Article 117 of the Constitution of the Azerbaijan SSR, court proceedings in the Nakhichevan autonomous SSR are conducted in the Azerbaijan language and in the Nagorno-Karabakh autonomous region, in the Armenian language; under Article 109 of the Constitution of the Uzbek SSR, in the Kara-Kalpak autonomous SSR, in the Kara-Kalpak language. The constitutions of the RSFSR and of the Georgian SSR, which likewise embody autonomous republics and autonomous regions, reproduce without specific enumeration the general formula of the Union Constitution to the effect that court proceedings are carried on in the language of the autonomous republic or autonomous region.[21] With regard to the RSFSR Constitution, the general formula of the Union Constitution concerning the language in which a matter is examined in court (including therein only the designation of the state language of the Union Republic) is retained by reason of the great number of constituent autonomous Soviet Socialist Republics and autonomous regions (enumerated in Art. 22 of the Union Constitution).

Furthermore, Union Republic constitutions enact supplementary rules for carrying on court examination in the language of the nationality, starting from the national conditions of the given republic. Thus the RSFSR Constitution, aside from the language of the autonomous republic or autonomous region, designates also the language of the national area (Art. 114), while the Constitution of the Ukraine SSR establishes for the Moldavian autonomous SSR two languages: Moldavian or Ukrainian, "depending on the national structure of the majority of the population of the district" (Art. 109). The Constitution of the Azerbaijan SSR (Art. 117) provides that in districts where the majority of the inhabitants are Armenian or Russian or Talysh, the proceedings are to be conducted accordingly, in the appropriate language. Numerous other constitutions contain the same proviso to the effect that in individual districts proceedings are to be conducted in the language of the numerically predominant population.

Among numerous directives of the chapter (IX) of the USSR Constitution relative to the court, Article 111, establishing the principle of publicity in the consideration of court matters, is enormously significant. Such publicity is indispensable to the people's control of the administration of justice by their elected judges. At the same time, nothing better guarantees legality than to investigate cases publicly. Article 111 of the Constitution accordingly directs that "the examination of cases in all USSR courts be open." To this rule the law admits but few exceptions, cases when the court, in investigating a matter, has to touch upon questions which are military or other state secrets, or matters concerning sex crimes.

[21] The RSFSR Constitution, Art. 114; the Georgian Constitution, Art. 124.

Justice, public and open, contributes more than all else to an understanding of the court's authority and assures that its activity will achieve social and educational results. Concerning one court proceeding, Lenin wrote with reference to the public consideration of matters involving persons guilty of official procrastination. (It is perfectly clear that this refers in like measure to other crimes also.) "From the point of view of principle, it is necessary not to leave such matters within the confines of bureaucratic institutions, but to carry them out into the public court—not so much for the sake of strict punishment (possibly a reprimand will be enough), but for the sake of public notoriety and to dispel the universal conviction that the guilty cannot be punished." [22] Without the public administration of justice, the Soviet court would be in no condition to fulfill one of its most important tasks: to be *"an instrument to inculcate discipline,"* [23] a task which Lenin called "enormous." [24]

Addressing the active members of the Leningrad Party organization (April 13, 1926), Stalin directed particular attention to the necessity of a decisive struggle against thievery, against pilferers of social property. He pointed out that to contend successfully with those who misappropriate social property it is not enough merely to catch the thief; a measure more effective and decisive is essential. Such a "measure consists in the creation of an atmosphere of general moral boycott and hatred of such thieves on the part of the public round about them, in waging such a campaign, and creating such a moral atmosphere amongst workers and peasants as would make thievery—and the life and the existence of thieves and pilferers of the people's goods—impossible." [25] The public investigation in open court of cases where thieves and pillagers of social property are held to responsibility is a mighty instrument for creating the moral atmosphere of which Stalin spoke.

Bourgeois legislation concerning the court establishes the principle of publicity, of the investigation of cases in court, but the conditions of capitalist society rob broad popular masses of the possibility of being in fact present in court and in control of its work. Bourgeois courtrooms are ordinarily filled with representatives of the substantial strata of society. In its time, in the eighteenth and early nineteenth centuries, when it was struggling against absolutism and the order of feudal nobles, the bourgeoisie put forward the demand that the court be public and open as a means of limiting the arbitrary perversity of the feudal judges. After taking authority into its own hands, the bourgeoisie preserved the form of this democratic principle

[22] Lenin (Russian ed.), Vol. XXIX, p. 412.
[23] *Ibid.*, Vol. XXII, p. 460.
[24] *Ibid.*
[25] Stalin, *The Soviet Union's Economic Position* (1937), pp. 16, 17.

of public proceedings but did not assure its effectuation through guarantees making it possible for the broad popular masses actually to control the work of the court, and such is the form in which it is retained at the present time in bourgeois-democratic states. Fascist states have brought it to naught.

In fascist Germany the overwhelming majority of criminal matters of political significance is examined by so-called "extraordinary courts" in conditions incompatible with the possibility of citizens being present in the court (order of March 21, 1933). The laws of fascist Italy (Code of Criminal Procedure, 1931) give the court the right to close the doors in any matter capable of arousing "culpable curiosity," and also provide that persons "known to be inclined to perpetrate crimes against persons and property," as well as persons "indecorously attired," may be excluded from the courtroom. It is perfectly clear that any toiler, worker, revolutionary or anti-fascist could be thus excluded upon such ridiculous allegations.

Article 111 of the USSR Constitution requires that the accused be guaranteed the right to defend himself. In procedural science there is a distinction between defense in the material sense and defense in the formal sense. Defense in the material sense means the sum total of all the guarantees observed in the accused's interests and of all the rights granted to him by law to enable him to defend himself from the charges contained in the complaint against him. Defense in the formal sense means the representation of the accused's interests in court by a particular person, a defender. When it speaks of the accused's right to defense, the USSR has in view both formal and material defense.

In this matter of the accused's right to defend himself, bourgeois democracy deems it enough to establish equality in form by giving each accused the right to invite a defender if he wishes to do so and can. It is the exception (for example, in matters of the utmost importance) and not the rule for bourgeois statutes to contemplate so-called public defense by a court directive charging counsel with such a duty. It was of England, where the principles of bourgeois democracy found their earliest realization in the organization of justice, that Engels wrote: "He who is too poor to provide a defender is lost if his case is at all doubtful." [26] Only in 1903 did England pass a law for the defense of poor persons who were accused, and the most conscientious bourgeois jurists must admit that the application of this law has become in most cases a complete farce and that under the established practice it is the criminal rather than the innocent man who will know how to obtain a defender. [27]

[26] Engels, The English Constitution, Marx and Engels, Collected Works (Russian ed.), Vol. II, p. 385.
[27] Solicitor, "English Justice" (1932).

In fascist countries nothing remained of the accused's right to defend himself, even in the formal sense in which the principle is ordinarily understood in bourgeois democracies. In a fascist court the accused is deprived of rights and guarantees of every sort which would assist him to defend himself, to contend with the indictment prepared against him; the examining magistrate assiduously employs the barbarous methods of the middle ages—torture and the falsification of evidence—against which the accused is completely defenseless. As to formal defense, the creation of the so-called "unified" (fascist) bar has turned the formal defender into a fascist accuser of the person under his protection.

The Stalin Constitution for the first time elevated the right to defend oneself from a procedural rule into constitutional principle as, indeed, ought to be the case in socialist society, which "represents the only stable guaranty that the interests of personality will be safeguarded." [28] In the Soviet state the accused's right of defense is embodied in the system of principles underlying socialist democracy and is carried into effect in the principle of adversary procedure, that method of investigating criminal and civil cases in court wherein the accused or a party possesses procedural rights as the opponent or adversary of the accuser or the other party and can contest the indictment or affirm the opposite side before the court. Our procedure is adversary procedure. In a criminal proceeding the accused is granted, and is truly guaranteed, the right of defense. "The adversary nature of proceedings in the Soviet court is one of the principles of that court democracy which cannot but embody in itself the features and special characteristics embodied in the entire Soviet socialist democracy." [29]

To guarantee the accused his right of defense, to represent the interests of both sides in court, and to give juridical aid to the entire population there is the bar, organized in 1922 in the form of collegia of defenders in the territories and regions. The collegium is a social organization carrying out functions important to the state wherewith it is charged to promote socialist justice and to defend the rights and interests of citizens. Collegia of defenders are organized on principles of self-government. The presidium of the collegium, chosen (by secret ballot) by a general assembly of advocates of the territory or region, directs the activity of the collegium and admits new members. The activity of the collegia of defenders is under the general direction of the People's Commissariat of Justice of the USSR and of People's Commissariats of Justice of the Union and autonomous republics.

[28] Stalin, *Questions of Leninism* (10th Russian ed.), p. 602.
[29] Vyshinsky, *The Position on the Legal Theory Front* (1937), p. 40.

SEC. 3: THE USSR COURT SYSTEM IN OPERATION

In conformity with Article 102 of the USSR Constitution, "the administration of justice in the USSR is by the Supreme Court of the USSR, the Supreme Courts of Union Republics, territorial and regional courts, courts of autonomous republics and autonomous regions, area courts, special courts of the USSR established by directive of the USSR Supreme Soviet, and people's courts."

On August 16, 1938, the second session of the Supreme Soviet of the USSR adopted a law, Concerning the Organization of the Courts of the USSR and of the Union and Autonomous Republics, which established an organization of the court system to conform with the USSR Constitution.

In studying the organization of the court system, it is necessary to distinguish between courts of original jurisdiction and courts of appellate jurisdiction. The former investigate the matter and render a sentence (in a criminal case) or decision (in a civil case); the latter consider complaints and protests against sentences or decisions handed down by courts of original jurisdiction. One and the same court may have original jurisdiction as to some cases and some categories of matters, and appellate jurisdiction as to others.

In capitalist states there are from this point of view for the majority of matters three types of court: (1) a court of original jurisdiction, which decides the matter in the first instance; (2) an appellate court, which considers the matter in its essence for the second time, provided either side takes the proper steps to that end; and (3) the court of last resort, which makes certain that the appellate court has observed the law, reconsidering the matter from the purely formal point of view and making no reexamination in substance. In the Soviet court system as organized, there is no appellate court; a matter is examined in two courts, the first and the second. The higher court in the USSR cannot be limited, as are courts of last resort in bourgeois states, to a mere formal verification of the sentence or decision of the first court. Article 15 of the 1938 statute requires the higher court to verify both the legality and the basis of the sentences and decisions appealed from—the fundamental soundness thereof in substance as well as in form. For matters decided by the people's court in the first instance, the appellate court is that of the region, territory, or area; for matters decided by the regional, territory, or area court in the first instance, the appellate court is the Republic Supreme Court. In autonomous republics, the appellate court for matters decided by the people's court is the Autonomous Republic Supreme Court and for matters decided by the Autonomous Republic Supreme Court in the first instance, the appellate court is the Union Republic Supreme Court. Sentences and decisions of the Union Republic Supreme Court sitting as a court of original jurisdiction are final and not subject to appeal. Where it has been established in individual cases that the matter has been decided incorrectly in the two normal courts (exercising original and appellate jurisdiction), their decisions thereupon may be protested through the method of court supervision by the Union Republic or USSR Public Prosecutor, or by the President of the Republic or USSR Supreme Court.

1. *The people's court*

The people's court is the court nearest to the people. Through it passes the basic bulk of criminal and civil matters. Its activity is enormously important for the realization of socialist legality and the protection of civil right.

By establishing that the people's courts are elected for a three-year term by citizens of the district by secret ballot on the basis of universal, direct, and equal suffrage, the Stalin Constitution elevated the role and significance of the people's court to a lofty political height. The party and the government have unswervingly fought to bring the court as close as possible to the people, to strengthen its bond with the masses, to accelerate its disposition of cases and to improve the quality of its work. It is a court of original jurisdiction; only it considers the substantial majority of criminal and civil matters, all criminal and civil matters (excepting those assigned by special directives of the law to the jurisdiction of higher courts) being within its jurisdiction as a general rule.[1]

Included in the civil matters investigated by the people's courts are those arising out of labor relations in connection with violations of labor laws, collective and labor contracts, and office and factory regulations. The rules for investigating such matters are established by a special law.[2]

Recently the jurisdiction of the people's courts was extended still further. They were charged with the extremely important task of guarding the election rights of Soviet citizens. They examine complaints by citizens against decisions of Soviets of the Deputies of the Toilers that names of toilers have not been entered, or have been entered incorrectly, in the list

---

[1] Cf. Art. 21 of the 1938 statute previously cited. The jurisdiction of the people's courts and of higher courts is ordained by the law, Concerning the Judicial System, and by the Codes of Procedure—Civil and Criminal.
[2] Cz. 1928, No. 56, Art. 495.

of voters, and the decision of the people's court in this case is final.[3] Finally, they are charged with the investigation of matters relative to diverting property levies to deficits for taxes, obligatory insurance and obligatory supplies in kind, and fines.[4]

By Section 29 of the law concerning court organization, a people's judge is charged with the duty of rendering to the electors an account of his work and of the work of the people's court.

2. The territorial (regional) and area courts and the court of the autonomous region

In each territory or region, autonomous region or area there is a corresponding court elected for a term of five years by the Soviet of Deputies of the Toilers of the territory (region), area, or autonomous region. The territorial (regional) or area court, or the court of the autonomous region is: (1) a court of original jurisdiction for the more important civil and criminal affairs within its jurisdiction; and (2) an appellate court as regards all people's courts of the territory (region) or autonomous region, examining complaints and protests against sentences, decisions, and judgments rendered by the people's courts.

The territorial (regional) and area courts, and the court of the autonomous region, consists of a president, vice presidents, members of the court and people's assessors summoned to take part in consideration of matters therein, and embodies a court collegium for criminal matters and a court collegium for civil matters.

Complaints of the parties, and protests of the prosecuting officers, against sentences, decisions, and judgments of the people's courts are examined by the three permanent members of the court. Consideration of matters by the court sitting as a court of original jurisdiction is by a tribunal under the president—or a member of the court—presiding and two of the ordinary people's assessors elected by the corresponding Soviet of Deputies of the Toilers for a period of five years to participate in court sessions.

As courts of original jurisdiction, these courts examine (1) criminal matters (referred by law to their jurisdiction) concerned with counter-revolutionary crimes,[5] with crimes against administrative order of particular danger to the USSR—the pillaging of socialist property, and with important official economic crimes; and (2) civil matters (referred to their jurisdiction) concerned with controversies between state and social institutions, enterprises, and organizations.

[3] Regulation Concerning Election to the USSR Supreme Soviet, Arts. 18, 19; Regulation Concerning Election to the RSFSR Supreme Soviet, Arts. 19, 20.

[4] Cz. 1937, No. 30, Art. 120.

[5] Arts. 58 (2), 58 (14) of the RSFSR Criminal Code.

3. *The Autonomous Republic Supreme Court*

In the autonomous republics, Supreme Courts, elected by the Supreme Soviet of the Republic for five years, are courts of original jurisdiction as to matters referred to their jurisdiction, and appellate courts as to matters decided by the autonomous republic people's courts. Their structure and jurisdiction are like those of the territorial (regional) courts.

4. *The Union Republic Supreme Court*

The highest judicial organ of each Union Republic is its Supreme Court, an organ to oversee the court activity of all court organs of that Union Republic, with the right to exercise that oversight by way of abrogating any sentence, decision, or judgment of any Union Republic court. It has appellate jurisdiction also as to matters examined by area or territorial (regional) courts, by Autonomous Republic Supreme Courts, and—in Union Republics not subdivided into regions—by people's courts.

The Union Republic Supreme Court is chosen by the Union Republic Supreme Soviet for five years. It consists of a president, vice presidents, members of the court, and people's assessors summoned to participate in the consideration of court matters. Organized on the collegium principle, it acts in criminal matters and in civil matters. As to criminal and civil matters of special importance, it exercises original jurisdiction.

Complaints and protests against sentences, decisions, and judgments of courts, and protests addressed to its supervisory jurisdiction are considered by a tribunal consisting of three permanent members of the Supreme Court.

Consideration of matters by a Union Republic Supreme Court exercising its original jurisdiction is by a tribunal under the president or a member of the Supreme Court, and two of the people's assessors especially chosen by the Union Republic Supreme Soviet to participate in sessions of the Supreme Court.

5. *Special courts*

According to Article 102 of the USSR Constitution, special courts can be created by directive of the USSR Supreme Soviet. Their structure is defined by Chapter VI of the law of 1938.[6]

In conformity with Article 105 of the USSR Constitution, special courts are elected by the USSR Supreme Soviet for a period of five years. Special courts at the present time include:

1. The system of military tribunals having appellate jurisdiction as the military collegium of the USSR Supreme Court. Military tribunals are

---

[6] Hereinbefore cited, Concerning the Judicial System of the USSR and of the Union and Autonomous Republics.

formed in connection with military formations (armies and fleets, military areas, military fronts, military bodies and other military formations and militarized institutions). The jurisdiction of military tribunals [7] includes authority over military and counterrevolutionary crimes and over crimes against administrative order or particular danger for the USSR, if perpetrated by persons in military service or obligated thereto or held up to the same responsibility (such as workers of the civil air fleet), as well as over crimes of treason, espionage, terror, arson, and other diversionist acts, irrespective of the perpetrator.

2. The system of courts of the railroad transportation lines,[8] exercising appellate jurisdiction as the railroad collegium of the USSR Supreme Court, and the system of courts of the water transportation lines,[9] exercising appellate jurisdiction as the water-transport collegium of the USSR Supreme Court. Line courts thus organized on lines of railroads and of water communications have jurisdiction over crimes directed at undermining labor discipline in transportation and other crimes subversive of normal work therein.

6. The Supreme Court of the USSR

In accordance with Article 104 of the USSR Constitution, the Supreme Court of the USSR is the highest court organ in the Union. Pursuant to Article 105, it is elected by the USSR Supreme Soviet for a term of five years. It is charged with overseeing the official action of all the court organs of the USSR and the Union Republics. It exercises this supervision through consideration of protests of the USSR Public Prosecutor and of the president of the USSR Supreme Court against court sentences, decisions, and judgments having the force of law, and by considering complaints and protests against sentences of military tribunals and courts of railroad and water transportation lines. Furthermore, it acts as a court of original jurisdiction in criminal and civil matters of All-Union importance.

The USSR Supreme Court consists of a president, vice presidents, members of the Supreme Court and people's assessors summoned to participate in the consideration of court matters. It acts through five collegia: (a) the judicial collegium for criminal affairs; (b) the judicial collegium for civil affairs; (c) the military collegium; (d) the railroad collegium; and (e) the water transport collegium.

At the present time it is composed of members chosen August 17, 1938, at the second session of the USSR Supreme Soviet.

[7] Cf. Regulation Concerning Military Tribunals (Cz. 1926, No. 57, Art. 413) as amended.
[8] Cz. 1930, No. 57, Art. 601; Cz. 1933, No. 55, Art. 324.
[9] Cz. 1934, No. 33, Art. 251.

The USSR Supreme Court examines matters in the appropriate collegia. Sitting as a court of original jurisdiction, it investigates matters acting under a president or member of the Supreme Court and two people's assessors. In considering protests and complaints against sentences, decisions, and judgments of other courts, it consists of three members of the Supreme Court.

Unlike other courts [10] the structure of the USSR Supreme Court embodies a plenum, convened not less frequently than once every two months, consisting of president, vice presidents, and all the members of the USSR Supreme Court. The USSR Public Prosecutor must take part in sessions of the plenum, in which the USSR People's Commissar for Justice also participates. The plenum considers protests brought to it by the President of the USSR Supreme Court and the USSR Public Prosecutor against sentences, decisions, and judgments of collegia of the USSR Supreme Court, and also gives directive instructions on matters of court practice on the basis of decisions adopted in court matters considered by the USSR Supreme Court, thus assuring that court practice will be uniform and will meet all the requirements of the single socialist legality obtaining throughout the entire USSR.

SEC. 4: FUNDAMENTAL PRINCIPLES UNDERLYING THE ORGANIZATION OF THE SOVIET PROSECUTOR'S OFFICE

The basic principles for the organization of the Soviet prosecutor's office were formulated in 1922 by Lenin in his famous letter to Stalin, "Concerning 'Dual' Subordination and Legality," [1] to which we have previously referred. From the principle that there is a single legality obtaining throughout the Republic "and the entire federation" (Lenin), and from the obligation of the Public Prosecutor to see to it that no single decision of local authority deviates from the law, Lenin deduced all the most important principles for the organization of the prosecutor's office. In order that it might be possible to defend the truly unitary state-wide legality, "notwithstanding any local differences and despite local influences of whatever sort" (Lenin), the prosecutor's office must be *centralized* and completely *independent* of local organs of authority.

In order for it to be a powerful and flexible instrument in the hands of the worker classes' dictatorship in its struggle for communism, the prosecu-

---

[10] Pursuant to Art. 75 of the law, Concerning the Judicial System of the USSR and of the Union and Autonomous Republics (1938), hereinbefore referred to.
[1] Lenin (Russian ed.), Vol. XXVII, pp. 298–301; cf. Sec. 1 previously cited.

tor's office had necessarily to work, as Lenin said, "under the closest supervision and in the most immediate contact with the three Party institutions which constitute the maximum guarantee against local and individual influences: the Organizing Bureau of the Central Committee, the Political Bureau of the Central Committee, and the Central Control Committee. In order that this centralized mechanism, directed from above, should not supplant local organs of authority (Soviets of Deputies of the Toilers—the political basis of the Soviet order of society), the prosecutor's office must not be an administrative organ, must not itself govern, must not itself have the final decision of matters of state administration. It must merely see to it that local organs of authority decide such matters in conformity with law. If anyone should issue an illegal order, or if there should be illegal actions on the part of anyone whatsoever, the prosecutor's office must protest the illegal order by transmitting the matter for the decision of the superior organ of authority. If the decision by the latter was not in accordance with law, it could in its turn be protested by the prosecutor's office, and the question can thus reach the supreme organs of state authority, whose decision is final. If the violation of law is in the nature of a criminal act, the duty of the prosecutor's office is not limited to filing a protest; it must see that the persons who have violated the law are held to criminal responsibility. Even here, however, it makes no decision which is final.

The prosecutor's office initiates and investigates a criminal matter, but thereafter its "sole right and obligation is to transfer it to be decided by the court." [2]

The prosecutor's office appears in court with the right of a party, upholding the indictment in the name of the state, but has no part in the final decision of the matter, the sentence being that of the court. Even here, however, the prosecutor's office sees to it that the sentence be in conformity with the law and is obligated to file a protest as regards every sort of unfounded and illegal sentence to be considered by the higher court, whose judgment is, in turn, subject to protest by the prosecutor's office.

These principles of Lenin were the foundation of the organization of the Soviet prosecutor's office in 1922. The law of June 20, 1933,[3] organized the USSR prosecutor's office with the USSR Public Prosecutor at its head. The law of July 20, 1936,[4] and later the USSR Constitution, separated the organs of the prosecutor's office from those of Union Republic People's Commissariats of Justice in whose system they had theretofore been. Centralization of the prosecutor's office upon an All-Union scale completed and

[2] *Ibid.*, p. 299.
[3] Cz. 1933, No. 40, Art. 239.
[4] Cz. 1936, No. 40, Art. 338.

assured its entire independence from all local (including republic) organs of authority.

Under the Stalin Constitution, the prosecutor's office is a strictly centralized mechanism. Article 113 charges the USSR Public Prosecutor—not the prosecutor's office—to exercise supreme supervisory power. Hence Union Republic constitutions establish no independent supervision unrelated to that of the USSR Public Prosecutor. "Supreme supervision over the strict execution of laws by all People's Commissariats and all institutions subordinate thereto, as well as by individual officials, persons and citizens within the territory of the RSFSR, is exercised both by the Public Prosecutor of the USSR directly and also through the Public Prosecutor of the RSFSR." [5] The matter is dealt with in precisely the same way in the constitutions of the other Union states.

Article 117 of the Constitution of the USSR establishes the rule that all organs of the prosecutor's office are subordinate to the USSR Public Prosecutor alone.

An inevitable consequence of the methodical effectuation of the principle of centralizing the prosecutor's office is that its organs are independent of local organs of authority. It is no mere chance that the same article (Art. 117) of the USSR Constitution which establishes that all organs of the prosecutor's office are subordinate to the USSR Public Prosecutor stipulates that they are independent "of all local organs whatsoever." Only under conditions of such independence can they accurately carry out directives of the USSR Public Prosecutor, and maintain the struggle against all sorts of attempts to destroy the law under color "of local peculiarities."

The prosecutor's office, as distinguished from the court, is built on the principle of strictly unitary responsibility. Whereas all the more serious matters are decided in court by the collegium of judges by majority vote, all questions are always decided in organs of the prosecutor's office by the order of the Public Prosecutor alone, the head of the given organ of prosecutor's office empowered to decide the given matter. This by no means eliminates the possibility of the broadest criticism and self-criticism in organs of the prosecutor's office. Each worker therein has the right to come forward at assemblies and in the press with criticism of incorrect actions of his superior, the Public Prosecutor. Moreover, each such worker has the right and the duty to communicate to his superior, the Public Prosecutor—up to and including the Public Prosecutor of the USSR—concerning each action of his immediate chief which he considers incorrect.

A natural sequel of these principles of building the prosecutor's office is also the method of recruiting its mechanism—based not on the elective

---

[5] Constitution of the RSFSR, Art. 117.

but on the appointive principle. Subordination of all organs of the magistracy solely by vertical line from below upward inevitably presupposes also a method of appointing and dismissing workers likewise by vertical line from above downward. Under Article 114 of the USSR Constitution, the USSR Public Prosecutor is appointed by the highest organ of authority in the state, the Supreme Soviet of the USSR, for a term of seven years. So long a term, exceeding all the other terms established by the Constitution for tenure of any office, is explained by the fact that stability of direction is of particularly important significance for an organ which guards legality. "Stability of the laws is necessary to us now more than ever before," said Stalin at the Extraordinary Eighth All-Union Congress of Soviets. The requirement of stability of laws concerns not only their publication but their application as well, and supervision of the application of laws constitutes a fundamental obligation of the prosecutor's office. The appointment of all the remaining workers of the prosecutor's office issues from the USSR Public Prosecutor. Public Prosecutors of Union and autonomous republics and of territories and regions are appointed directly by the Public Prosecutor of the USSR (Art. 115).

Area, district, and city Public Prosecutors are appointed by Union Republic Public Prosecutors subject to the approval of the USSR Public Prosecutor (Art. 116). All Public Prosecutors except the USSR Public Prosecutor are appointed for five years.

Centralization of the prosecutor's office—the principle of unitary responsibility whereon direction of the work of the prosecutor's office and the method of appointing Public Prosecutors are built—in no degree whatsoever eliminates the democracy of the Soviet prosecutor's office and its indissoluble bond with the broad masses of the toilers. It is democratic first of all because it obtains its plenary powers from the most democratic organ in the world, the USSR Supreme Soviet, and also because it works, as we have already pointed out, indissolubly associated with the directing organs of the Communist Party, the vanguard of the most democratic portion of the Soviet people, the worker class. It is democratic in its structure, inasmuch as the vast majority of its cadres are representatives of the most democratic strata of the population, workers and peasants. It is democratic in its tasks, which can be reduced in the last analysis to defense of the interests of genuine socialist democracy. It is democratic in the methods of its work, which are calculated upon its organs being most closely bound up with broad masses of the toilers. All the organs of Soviet community, the Young Communist League, the trade unions, worker correspondents and peasant correspondents, and so on, take an active part in the work of the Soviet prosecutor's office, in its struggle to strengthen socialist legality.

But in addition to utilizing the aid of all organs of the Soviet community, the prosecutor's office in its work relies as well on its own Party social workers in the form of cooperation groups and sections of revolutionary legality. A very important form of participation by the community in the work of the prosecutor's office is through active, public-spirited workers appearing as Public Prosecutors in court upon warrants of the prosecutor's office.

The active social members of the prosecutor's office are a reserve for filling the cadres of the workers therein. The Soviet prosecutor's office, unlike that in bourgeois countries, is not separated by an impassable wall from the popular masses; it is flesh of their flesh and bone of their bone. The passing of active social workers, who have revealed themselves in social work, into the ranks of permanent workers of the Soviet prosecutor's office is a graphic manifestation of the actual democracy of the Soviet prosecutor's office, its indissoluble connection with the Soviet people.

Even in the most democratic of the bourgeois states, the prosecutor's office is always separated by an impassable abyss from the true people, the toiling masses; even where (as in the U.S.A.) the local prosecutors are elected, they are connected not with the people, but with the capitalist concerns which join forces for their election—and sometimes with professional criminals.

The compilers of the official American report on law observance write: [6]

Criminal justice and local politics have an intimate connection which aggravates the bad features of state prosecution already considered. Notoriously this connection between the prosecutor's office and politics is the bane of prosecution. There is a close connection between corrupt local political organizations and criminal organizations. The former exploit and the latter organize law-breaking and vice. Campaign funds are derived from what amounts to licensed violations of law. Often such things, however, cannot go far under an efficient system of administering criminal justice. Hence it is vital to a combination of corrupt politics and organized crime to control the prosecutor's office, or if that cannot be done, to render its activities nugatory. Thus the prosecutor's office, with its enormous power of preventing prosecutions from getting to trial, its lack of organization, its freedom from central control, and its ill-defined responsibility, is a great political prize. Under the political conditions which obtain in large cities, except for occasional outbursts of popular indignation, prosecutors are likely to be selected with reference to the exigencies of political organizations rather than with reference to the tasks of law enforcement. The system of prosecutors elected for short terms, with assistants chosen on the basis of political patronage, with no assured tenure yet charged with wide, undefined powers, is ideally adapted to misgovernment. It has happened frequently that the prosecuting attorney withdraws wholly from the courts and devotes himself to the political side and sensa-

[6] National Commission on Law Observance and Enforcement, *Report on Prosecution* (Washington, 1931), pp. 13–15.

tional investigatory functions of his office, leaving the work of prosecution wholly to his assistants. The "responsibility to the people" contemplated by the system of frequent elections does not so much require that the work of the prosecutor be carried out efficiently as that it be carried out conspicuously.

It is unnecessary to speak of the prosecutor's office of the remaining bourgeois countries, where its workers are appointed.

It is typical of the organization of the bourgeois prosecutor's office as distinguished from that of the socialist state, that in no single bourgeois country is the head of the prosecutor's office appointed by parliament and independent of the administration as he is in the USSR. In most bourgeois countries, including France, Germany, and imperial Russia, a member of the administration, the Minister of Justice, who at the same time directs the work of the courts, was charged with direction of the prosecutor's office. All persons working in the prosecutor's office are appointed by him, and he directs their work. Attempts to weaken the dependence of Public Prosecutors upon Ministers of Justice—to give that office even a semblance of independence—have always been unsuccessful in bourgeois countries.

The original draft of the so-called Institutes Concerning Court Establishments (the regulation concerning court organization) of tsarist Russia included Article 82 to the effect that "the personnel of the Direction of Public Prosecutions are untrammeled by any orders in declaring their opinions in cases." This evoked objection by Zamyatin, the Minister of Justice. He wrote in his notes on this article:

Complete independence of the judges [7] is indispensable. It is essential to support the dignity of the court's authority—to eliminate altogether any suspicion of prejudice and flunkeyism. The principle of independence of the personnel of the Direction of Public Prosecution, however, is incongruent alike with the principle that such direction is strictly unitary and with the rule that, throughout the Direction, younger members are subordinated to elder. [8]

But aside from their "official" dependence upon the Minister of Justice, workers in the prosecutor's office in most bourgeois countries are unofficially, but in a very real sense, dependent upon the police. Lenin frankly termed the tsarist Prosecutor an official whose relations with the police were most intimate. [9] In "The Köln Proceedings Against Communists Unmasked," Marx said:

The police, who during the investigation had performed the duties of an examining magistrate, had to come forward as witnesses at the time of the pro-

---

[7] We have already seen what this "independence" really means.
[8] *Journal of the State Council* for 1864, No. 48, pp. 17-18, cited in H. Muravyev, *Direction of Public Prosecutions* (Moscow, 1889), p. 395.
[9] Cf. Lenin (Russian ed.), Vol. IV, p. 84.

ceedings in court. Side by side with the ordinary Prosecutor, the government had to put on an extraordinary Prosecutor as well; side by side with the prosecutor's office it had to put on the police; side by side with Sedt and Sekkendorf (official Prosecutors) it had to put on Stieber (chief of the secret police, an organizer of German espionage in the middle of the last century) with his agents Wermuth, Vogel, Greif, and Holdheim. The third state authority had inevitably to intrude into the court in order that the wonder-working forces of the police might constantly purvey for the juridical accusation facts for whose shadows it vainly hunted. The court so well understood this position that the president, the judge, and the prosecuting attorney, with the most praiseworthy humility, yielded their respective parts, one after the other, to the police counselor and witness, Stieber, and constantly hid behind his back.[10]

But at a time when the bourgeoisie still found it necessary to utilize the *décor* of democracy to conceal the oppressive part played by their state mechanism, the close bond between the prosecutor's office and the police rarely came out openly. The prosecutor's office was required to be relentless in defending the interests of the dominant class but to observe therein certain decencies. The wishes expressed with reference to the prosecutor's office by the Imperial Minister of Justice Muravyev, then Public Prosecutor of the Moscow Court Chamber, are extremely typical in this regard. The Public Prosecutor must "observe legality strictly, but not to the point of a formalism which would fetter the prosecution; and humanity, but not to the point of sentimentality which would extenuate the crime; impartiality, but not to the point of insensibility; and tranquility, but not to the point of flaccidity, always losing to the adversary. In the prosecuting magistrate, society requires active force to maintain the conflict with internal foes [11] circumspectly, yet operating legally, rationally with boldness and decision, neither heedful of obstacles nor disturbed by reproaches." [12]

When, however, under the pressure of the swelling wave of revolution, the bourgeoisie casts off all the democratic *décor* and goes over to the methods of open and frantic terror, the methods of fascism, the prosecutor's office is freed even from these requirements of outward decency.

Kasper Anrath, the Düsseldorf lawyer, frankly puts forward the proposition of subordinating the prosecutor's office to the Ministry of Internal Affairs.[13] Georg Damm asserts that the Public Prosecutor sustains the concept of "der Führer" in criminal proceedings inasmuch as he effectively "takes into consideration practical and political needs" therein; in other

[10] Marx and Engels (Russian ed.), Vol. VIII, p. 505.
[11] *Scil.*, representatives of the revolutionary movement of the oppressed classes (Compilers).
[12] Muravyev, *op. cit.*, p. 530.
[13] K. Anrath, *Die richtige Gestaltung des Strafverfahrens entwikelt aus dem Wesen des Menschendenkens*, Berlin, 1934.

words, he preaches the idea of arbitrariness and lawlessness carried into effect by the hands of the Public Prosecutor.[14] The most recent legislation of fascist Germany (such as the law of June 28, 1935) gives the fascist prosecutor's office the right to conduct an uncontrolled investigation of criminal affairs unconstrained by any procedural forms whatsoever. The practice of "preventive arrests," widely employed in fascist Germany, makes it possible for the prosecuting officer to hold anyone at all, even though he has committed no crime of any nature, under guard and without judicial examination for a practically unlimited time. An example is the "affair" of Thälmann whom fascist jailers have already held in prison for five years, notwithstanding the fact that even the Hitler "people's" court did not decide to hand him over for legal proceedings.

The position of the prosecutor's office is the same in fascist Italy. In an explanatory note to the Italian Code of Criminal Procedure of 1931, it is stated frankly that the prosecuting officer is in no sense an organ for observing legality; he is merely an accuser. This code forbids him to undertake any actions whatsoever to defend the rights of the accused. In the lowest link of the court-prosecutor system, the pretor, the functions of prosecuting officer and judge are blended into one. The pretor himself initiates criminal cases, himself investigates them, and himself examines them as judge.

Thus, in the countries of fascist dictatorship the prosecutor's office loses its most characteristic feature: it ceases to be an organ of supervision and gathers into its hands enormous administrative powers, while in fact it becomes a mere appendage of the fascist secret police, one of the instruments for the carrying on of woefully arbitrary and unrestrained terror.

Only in the socialist worker-peasant state is the prosecutor's office built on the foundation of Lenin's teachings and actually the guardian of legality, an instrument to defend the true interests of the people.

SEC. 5: THE TASKS AND FUNCTIONS OF THE SOVIET PROS-ECUTOR'S OFFICE

Article 113 of the USSR Constitution charges the USSR Public Prosecutor with "supreme supervision over the precise fulfillment of laws by all the People's Commissariats and all institutions subordinate thereto, as well as by individual officials and citizens of the USSR." This supervision he effectuates directly, and also through the machinery of the prosecutor's office in the governing center and in the rural districts. The methods whereby

[14] G. Damm, "Bemerkungen zur Reform des Strafverfahrens," *Zeitschrift für gesammte Strafrechtswissenschaft*, B. 44, 4.

this supervision is achieved are defined by individual laws: the Regulation of the USSR Prosecutor's Office [1] and the Codes of Criminal and Civil Procedure.

Supervision by the prosecutor's office is expressed, first of all, in seeing to it that not a single organ of authority, not a single state or social organization, either issues orders or puts into practice measures not in conformity with the law. It is obligated to protest each unlawful order or measure upon its own initiative as well as upon complaint by citizens whose rights are thereby invaded.

These obligations are among the differences most characteristic of the Soviet prosecutor's office as against that of capitalist states. In bourgeois countries state authority was never interested that its own mechanism observed legality strictly to assure conditions propitious for the utmost realization of exploitation. The basic task of that mechanism was to hold the exploited in obedience. In fulfilling this task, organs of state authority of capitalist countries must here and there violate the laws of their own bourgeois state. Many statutes, including so-called "factory legislation" for safeguarding the labor of workers in capitalist enterprises, are issued by bourgeois states under pressure of the masses, and the bourgeoisie is altogether without interest in strict oversight of the actual observance of these laws being established. "When the report [2] of the Church of England Commission on Child Labor was presented in parliament, Lord Ashley hastened to introduce a bill categorically prohibiting the employment of women—and very much restricting that of children—in mines. The bill was passed, but in most localities it remained a dead letter since no mine inspectors were appointed to see to its fulfillment." [3]

In a long line of cases, the supreme organs of state authority of capitalist countries were directly interested that police and other local organs of authority should not be scrupulous about the law in crushing the oppressed classes. Accordingly, in capitalist countries the prosecutor's office is either removed entirely from overseeing the legality of actions of organs of authority or its oversight is confined to a narrow category of relatively unimportant matters and is exercised merely in form.

In considering the part to be played by the reformed tsarist prosecutor's office in overseeing the activity of organs of authority, the Minister of Justice wrote to the State Council (November 27, 1865): "Supervision by the prosecutor's office of all matters performed in offices is far from being so

[1] Cz. 1934, No. 1, Art. 2.
[2] This report of the shocking exploitation of children by industry produced a great impression on social opinion.
[3] *The Position of the Worker Class in England*, Marx and Engels, *Collected Works* (Russian ed.), Vol. III, p. 530.

indispensable, inasmuch as the correct course and solution of these matters is assured by the activities of the members and, in general, of those in the service of each establishment and, above all, by the supervision of the immediate chief." [4] This meant that supervision of the activity of organs of authority must be effectuated only by the method of hierarchic subordination. Marx explained the import of this supervision: "The hierarchy punishes the official in so far as he sins against the hierarchy or commits a sin unnecessary to the hierarchy, but takes him under its own protection in so far as his sin is its own sin." [5]

If we look below the surface, these reflections of the Imperial Minister of Justice mean that arbitrary and illegal action is made legal. What even ministers of tsarist Russia found it necessary to hide under obscure and grandiose ratiocination, fascism says openly. In justification of the rule that permission of the Minister of Justice is a condition precedent to holding fascist police and black shirts responsible for crimes committed by them in prosecuting measures "for the protection of order," A. Rocco, a former Minister of Justice of fascist Italy, one of Mussolini's closest companions-in-arms, wrote: "Appointed officials and agents cannot be expected to carry out their duties with proper speed and energy unless the law frees them from the danger of criminal prosecution every time performance of their duties requires them to commit an act which—in the abstract—the law regards as a crime." [6] Thus those guilty of openly arbitrary action are guaranteed in advance legal immunity from punishment for any crime, provided only that it shall have been committed in the interests of preserving fascist "order."

Only in a socialist state, where the law is actually the expression of the people's will, can effective supervision of the exact and steadfast fulfillment of the law be established. To exercise such supervision is one of the most important tasks of the Soviet prosecutor's office. In cases when a breach of law is a crime, the prosecuting officer is bound to hold those who are guilty thereof to criminal responsibility.

To ferret out every single crime for punishment while carrying on, in association with the organs of the People's Commissariat of Internal Affairs and the court, a decisive struggle with all the remnants of the Trotsky-Bukharin bandit gangs, with the hirelings of fascist reconnaissance, with spies and diversionists, with pillagers of socialist property, and with robbers, thieves and hooligans—in a word, with all species of criminality—is the first task of the prosecutor's office. While performing it with utter Bolshevik resoluteness and inexorability as regards enemies of the people, the Soviet

[4] Muravyev, *op. cit.*, p. 432.
[5] Marx and Engels, *Collected Works* (Russian ed.), Vol. I, p. 574.
[6] Cf. p. 10 of the explanatory note to the (1930) draft of the Italian Code of Criminal Procedure.

prosecutor's office is bound at the same time to be on the lookout that measures calculated for criminals do not affect irreproachable citizens; that a scrupulous investigation of every criminal case from every side be assured, so that it shall be guaranteed to every citizen held to responsibility that he can effectuate his constitutional right to defense and prove his innocence if the proceedings against him are without foundation. This task the prosecutor's office fulfills by initiating criminal proceedings and by supervising investigation thereof, and by participating in the work of the court. The prosecutor's office oversees the correctness and the legality of the investigation of criminal matters. Article 127 of the USSR Constitution specifically requires the prosecuting officer to guard the legality of arrests. A USSR citizen may be arrested only at the instance of the court or with the sanction of a prosecuting officer.

After a criminal matter has been investigated, it can be transferred to court only with the sanction of the prosecuting officer, except as regards the most insignificant cases.

In court the prosecuting officer appears in support of the state's indictment. His obligation is to adduce proofs to convict the guilty in court, to lay bare, in the court proceedings and in his speech as accuser, the crimes being investigated therein. But even in court he remains the accuser only so long as he retains his conviction that the accused is guilty; even in court he must be on the lookout to see that the law is observed punctiliously and that the matter is investigated completely and correctly. If the court proceedings do not sustain the indictment, the prosecuting officer is bound to withdraw his support. In capitalist states the law seeks to limit the possibility of such withdrawal by the Public Prosecutor. Thus in such a bourgeois-democratic country as France, the prosecuting officer may so withdraw his support from an indictment only in the so-called corrective police courts in which matters of moderate importance are examined. In the assize courts, where all matters concerning most important crimes are investigated, the prosecuting officer has no right to withdraw his support from an indictment, whatever the possible results of the court investigation.

Coming forward as the state accuser, the Public Prosecutor cannot give the court any instructions binding upon it; he enjoys the same rights as does the defense. In the stage of court investigation, the prosecuting officer is the court's assistant. By his participation in the court examination, and by his speech as accuser, he aids the court to decide the matter correctly. On the other hand, even here he does not cease to be an organ to oversee legality, assuring constant fulfillment of all that the law requires in investigating the matters in court.

While the principle that the parties are on an equality in court is pro-

claimed in bourgeois countries as a matter of theory, it is disregarded in fact
—not merely in practice but even in legislation. Thus, for example, the code
of criminal procedure of tsarist Russia termed the prosecutor's remarks to
the court on the calling of witnesses and expert testimony and the like,
"demands," and recognized that they were binding upon the court, whereas
remarks to the court by the accused and his defender on the same matters
the law termed "petitions," and left within the court's discretion.[7] Moreover, in presenting his "demands," the prosecutor was not limited by any
periods of time, whereas the accused and his defender must present his
"petitions" within a seven-day period which began when the defender was
appointed. The prosecutor was not bound, as was the accused or his defender, to explain why he needed a given witness. So manifest a departure
from the principle that the parties stand upon an equality was motivated by
the following reasoning:

> The parties do not stand in altogether similar relationships to the matter; the
> prosecutor adduces proofs of a crime in the name of a law of a type which finds
> the condemnation of an innocent person even more repellent than is the vindi-
> cation of one who is guilty. . . . Such is not the accused's relationship to the mat-
> ter. Even an innocent defendant, in his natural desire to be vindicated by all
> means within his power, will fail to distinguish between the essential and the
> unessential facts of the case, and will certainly wish to confirm both by the
> testimony of witnesses.[8]

Actually this meant an effort to make it difficult for the accused with complete freedom to effectuate his defense, whereas the prosecutor was completely free to frame his indictment as he wished.

In the bourgeois-democratic countries of western Europe, where the
oppressive character of the proceedings is more skillfully and subtly masked,
the same end is achieved by the rule that, while the right of the accused to
call supplementary witnesses and experts is conceded, its exercise is conditioned by his obligation forthwith to tender in cash down the amount of
the court expenses, making it definitely clear that bourgeois democracy is
essentially democracy for the rich.

In the USSR, the principle that the parties stand upon an equality in
court is developed with complete logic and with no limitations of any sort.
Furthermore, the prosecutor is obligated to protest to higher courts all court
sentences and decisions rendered in violation of the law or upon inadequate
foundation. A special characteristic of the Soviet prosecutor's office in the
sphere of its court work is the extensive part taken by the prosecuting officer
in civil proceedings. In capitalist countries its participation in civil proceed-

---

[7] Regulations of Criminal Procedure, Arts. 573–576.

[8] Explanatory note to the Proposed Code of Criminal Procedure (1863), pp. 286–287.

ings is extremely limited. In the USSR, it has the right to initiate a civil court proceeding, or to intervene in one already begun, in all cases when the interests of the state or of the toilers so require. Participation by the prosecutor's office in civil proceedings is one of the highly effective methods of defending the rights of Soviet citizens, and this side of its activity, in matters of alimony, for example, is very important.

Finally the prosecutor's office is bound to supervise the fulfillment of court sentences. This is not limited merely to the moment when the sentence is being executed (as by the arrest of one condemned to lose his liberty), but extends to the entire period during which the sentence imposed by the court is being served out. In particular, supervision by the prosecutor's office of the fulfillment of sentences involving loss of liberty is of great significance.

The work of the prosecutor's office with reference to complaints by citizens is enormously important. Each citizen who considers that his rights have been infringed by anyone may file a complaint with the prosecutor's office, which the prosecuting officer is bound to examine. If it seems well founded, he is required to take immediate measures to guard the rights of the complainant; and if the violation of these rights is of a criminal character, he must bring the guilty person to criminal responsibility. To the organs of the prosecutor's office come complaints of workers and kolkhoz members regarding the violation of their political, labor, housing, personal, and property rights. No prosecutor's office in any bourgeois state carries on such work; resort to the prosecutor's office is there limited solely to petitions for the inception of criminal prosecutions.

All the functions of the Soviet prosecutor's office thus depicted are indissolubly connected among themselves. Whether initiating or investigating criminal matters, or coming forward as accuser in court, or examining complaints, or filing protests against the illegal directives of any organ of authority, the Soviet prosecuting officer is the watchman of socialist legality, the leader of the policy of the Communist Party and of Soviet authority, the champion of socialism.

IX The Fundamental Rights and Obligations of USSR Citizens

SEC. 1: INTRODUCTION

CLARIFICATION OF the rights and obligations of citizens, in the light of a truly scientific approach thereto, discloses the true position of personality in the state being studied, and thereby makes it possible to demonstrate the class essence of that state. This explains the fact that, in the bourgeois doctrine of state law, the subdivision concerned with so-called personal rights is the most false and hypocritical of all, the furthest removed from the tasks of truly scientific investigation. That bourgeois theories of personal rights are highly complex and intricate and extraordinarily abstract is due to the fact that precisely here are the contradictions between reality and the rights proclaimed by the bourgeois constitutions particularly sharp. It is not surprising that, for all the wealth of bourgeois literature on the matter of civil rights, that problem is, by the admission of bourgeois jurists themselves, the least worked out.[1] Even such a matter as that of the juridical significance of constitutional rules concerning civil rights in bourgeois public laws is still in dispute. A notable proportion of bourgeois political scientists conclude that these constitutional rules have no juridical significance and are merely promissory.[2]

Only in the USSR does socialist reality afford the possibility of completely unfolding a doctrine of civil rights and obligations without fear of coming upon a hiatus between reality and theory, between the factual position of personality on the one hand and the civil rights and obligations established by the Constitution on the other.

[1] Gambarov, *Freedom and Its Guaranties* (St. Petersburg, 1910).
[2] Cf. Thoma's article (in the three-volume commentary on the Weimar Constitution), *Die Grundrechte und Grundpflichten der Reichsverfassung* (1929). See also Esmein, *Éléments de droit constitutionnel* (1925), Vol. I, pp. 561–562.

Assuring the manifold rights of the citizens of socialist society, the Stalin Constitution, the Constitution of socialism triumphant, reflects the full flowering of personality characteristic of socialism.

Bourgeois scholars have long broadcast malicious fictions to the effect that socialism means the complete absorption of personality by the collective, the abolition of all individual freedom of every kind. Thus Hauriou, one of the most eminent representatives of modern bourgeois political science, declares that under collectivism (socialism) "individual freedom disappears." In complete accord with Bourgain, a well known bourgeois critic of socialist theories, he writes: "We must be grateful to Bourgain for insistently pointing out that this (socialist) social order would eliminate freedom to all intents and purposes and put in its place the most burdensome slavery." [3]

In his conversation with Roy Howard, an interview touching among other things upon the freedom of personality in the USSR, Stalin made it completely clear that such views were entirely nonsensical and false.

Implicit in your question is the innuendo that socialist society negates individual freedom. That is not so. . . . We have not built this society in order to cramp individual freedom. We built it in order that human personality feel itself actually free. We built it for the sake of genuine personal freedom, freedom without quotation marks. What can be the "personal freedom" of an unemployed person who goes hungry and finds no use for his toil? Only where exploitation is annihilated, where there is no oppression of some by others, no unemployment, no beggary, and no trembling for fear that a man may on the morrow lose his work, his habitation, and his bread—only there is true freedom found. [4]

Bourgeois traducers of socialism fervently wish to affirm that the factual equality effectuated by socialism must mean a leveling of wants and ways of living as regards individual members of the society, that differences in individual characters, tastes, and needs are completely ignored. [5] In reality socialism, in annihilating man's exploitation of man, affords such a high degree of social and economic equality, and creates such conditions for the all-sided development of all the capacities and creative forces of the individual, that man's complete freedom and happiness are assured for the first time in his history.

Bourgeois theories to the effect that, under socialism, personality is absorbed in the collective, start from a hypothesis which assumes that the individual and society are constantly and irreconcilably antithetical. Only in exploiter societies is such antithesis inherent; to socialism it is foreign.

---

[3] Hauriou, *Principles of Public Law* (Russian ed., 1929), p. 410.
[4] Stalin, Interview with Roy Howard (1937), pp. 12–13.
[5] Hauriou, *op. cit.*, p. 412.

There neither is nor should be an irreconcilable contrast between the individual and the collective, between the interests of the individual personality and those of the collective. There should be none forasmuch as collectivism—socialism—does not deny individual interests; it amalgamates them with the interests of the collective. Socialism cannot be dissociated from individual interests. Only socialist society can furnish the most complete satisfaction of personal interests. Moreover, socialist society represents the only stable assurance that the interests of personality will be safeguarded.[6]

In a society divided into opposing classes, individuals "find the conditions of their lives already fixed in advance: the class defines their position in life and, at the same time, their personal fate as well; the class subordinates them to itself."[7] In exploiter society there is a necessary connection between the prosperity of the individual and his affiliation with the privileged class, and possession of the privileges of wealth, connections, and so on. Woodrow Wilson declares bitterly in his The New Freedom that in the U.S.A., the one country where for decades individual success has been said to be decided by the qualities of that individual, these play no such part in reality for the reason that everything is determined by mighty organizations—trusts, syndicates, societies, and others having the disposal of capital.[8]

In the USSR, personality occupies a diametrically opposite position: "One's place in society is defined by his personal capacities and personal labor, and not by his material circumstances, or his national origin, or his sex, or his position in service."[9] The Stakhanovites, the Papaninites, the hero-airmen, and so on, became famous in the land, and gained universal honor and respect by reason of their individual toil and capacities and not for any other cause.

Because it reflected the actual position of personality in the USSR, the Stalin Constitution is a graphic proof that socialism creates all the conditions precedent to the complete satisfaction of individual interests. The greatest civil rights recorded in the Stalin Constitution are: the right to labor; the right to rest; the right to material security in old age, disease, or loss of working capacity; the right to education; freedom of conscience; truly democratic freedoms of speech, of assembly, of the press, and of meetings; and the right to be united in social organizations. All these rights, guaranteed by the Soviet social order itself, attest before all the world "the

[6] Stalin: Questions of Leninism (10th Russian ed.), p. 602.
[7] Marx and Engels (Russian ed.), Vol. IV, p. 44.
[8] Cf. Woodrow Wilson, Die neue Freiheit (1924), pp. 41–46.
[9] Stalin, Report on the Draft of the USSR Constitution (1936), pp. 20–21.

facts of the triumph in the USSR of democracy unfurled and infinitely logical," [10] the authentic socialist democracy of the Soviet state.[11]

SEC. 2: THE FUNDAMENTAL RIGHTS AND OBLIGATIONS OF CITIZENS IN BOURGEOIS STATES

Demands for rights and civil freedoms are encountered for the first time, in primitive form, of course, in cities in the Middle Ages.[1] Influenced by the animation of trade and industry in the cities, a movement directed at obtaining civil rights, through accord with the feudal seigneurs or by armed force, had its inception in the eleventh and twelfth centuries. Citizens of the Middle Ages were still limited to demands commensurate with the framework of small-trade production. The program of the eighteenth century bourgeoisie, which had created the vast potentialities of a world market, included liberation of the peasantry from fulfilling serfs' obligations and of workers from the guild orders, abrogation of the nobles' immunity from taxes, and destruction of political privileges. Coming forward in the name of all society, it declared equality to be a *right of man*.

The first document to become part of the history of bourgeois constitutionalism as a model of bourgeois declarations of fundamental civil rights is the Virginia Declaration of Rights of 1776 (U.S.A.). John Adams, who drafted this Declaration, wrote in one of his letters: "Not a single constitution is built so completely on the principle of the people's rights and equality. It is chiefly the doctrines of Locke, Sidney, Rousseau, and Mableu that have been put into operation." [2] Starting from the proposition that "all men are by nature free," the Declaration proclaimed their right to life, liberty, security, property, and happiness. It declared the sovereignty of the people,

---

[10] *Ibid.*, p. 45.

[11] Even persons very far removed from communism cannot but admit this. Thus, in the preface to the English edition of the draft of the USSR Constitution, the person most active in the Labor movement in England, George Hicks, points out that "under this Constitution, USSR citizens have rights which, in capitalist countries, are no more substantial than dreams. . . . This Constitution is undoubtedly the charter of socialist civilization. It is a symbol of mankind's intellectual progress consequent upon the authority of the worker class. . . . It is the beginning of the new order not only in Europe but in all the world. It is the legislative ancestor of the constitution of a world federation of socialist republics, of a mighty union of the peoples of the world."—*The Draft Constitution of the Soviet Union* (London, 1936), p. 17.

[1] "That Greek and barbarian, free man and slave, *civis* and *aliens*, Roman citizen and Roman subject (in the broad sense) can assume to be of the same importance politically would have seemed an insane idea to the ancients."—Marx and Engels (Russian ed.), Vol. XIV, p. 103.

[2] Hagerman, *Die Erklärungen der Menschen und Bürgerrechte der ersten amerikanischen Staatsverfassungen* (1910), p. 18.

the freedom of elections, the equality of political rights, the freedom of the press, and the inviolability of the person—and introduced the separation of powers to assure them. Later, however, the Constitution of Virginia gave rights only to the apex of the bourgeoisie. Slavery continued to exist; equal political rights, elective rights in particular, were limited by high property qualifications; and personal inviolability remained a fiction.

The lauded Virginia Declaration proved an exemplar of the false promises of bourgeois declarations. Similar declarations were adopted also in certain other North American states and included, as in Virginia, in the text of their constitutions. The first act of the United States was the Declaration of Independence, adopted by the Congress on July 4, 1776. This differed from the declarations of the separate states in that it speaks of unalienable rights of citizens only in a general way and without precise definition or enumeration, saying: "We hold these truths to be self-evident, that all men are created equal; that they are endowed by their Creator with certain unalienable rights; that among these are life, liberty, and the pursuit of happiness." [3] However, the Declaration of Independence, like other similar declarations, remained mere promises which the bourgeoisie, having assumed authority, neither fulfilled nor even set about fulfilling. Popular agitations began. In Massachusetts a former captain of the Revolutionary Army, Shays, raised a revolt, "the delegates [of the Congress] seeming to fear a triumphant American army almost as much as they did the soldiers of George III." [4] Events compelled the bourgeoisie, interested in creating a powerful administration, to set about the creation of a federal constitution.

The convention which assembled to work out the Constitution consisted of the biggest financiers and merchants, and owners of land and slaves; of course, the Constitution worked out by such people meticulously guaranteed the interests of capital. The Constitution does not include a single one of the fundamental civil rights depicted in such detail in the constitutions of numerous states. It is not surprising that there was a wave of indignation against ratifying the Constitution drafted by the convention, chiefly on the part of small farmers, city laboring people, and the population burdened with debts. Notwithstanding the powerful opposition of the masses, the Constitution was adopted by legislative assemblies of states with an overwhelming majority of representatives from the "have" classes. In all, 160,000 citizens expressed themselves for affirmation of the Constitution, less than 5 per cent of the population of the thirteen states. [5] A great wave of dissatis-

[3] The Declaration of Independence, the Articles of Confederation, the U.S. Constitution (Russian ed., 1919), p. 3.
[4] Charles A. Beard, *The Rise of American Civilization*, Vol. I, p. 233.
[5] Beck, *Die Verfassung der Vereinigten Staaten* (1926).

faction compelled the state legislators to adopt a series of amendments, chiefly proposals as to fundamental civil rights. Within two months after the storming of the Bastille in Paris, and one month after the National Assembly in France had adopted the Declaration of Rights of Man and Citizen, the Congress of the United States assembled for final formulation of the Constitution. The influence of these events on the decision of Congress is indubitable. The first session adopted the Bill of Rights in the form of ten amendments to the Constitution. The first five confirmed freedom of conscience, freedom of speech, freedom of the press and freedom of assembly; the right to bear arms; a prohibition against billeting soldiers in private houses without consent of the owner; the inviolability of the person, dwelling, and papers of citizens; and responsibility of citizens to the court, and the right to life, liberty, and property. The remaining five speak of measures of criminal punishment, legal procedure, and so on.

Unlike the American Bill of Rights, which was adopted by way of amendment to the Constitution, the French Declaration of Rights of Man and Citizen (1789)—that most brilliant memorial of the classic bourgeois revolution—is a single document, preceding the Constitution. Its principles became the watchwords of the bourgeois constitutional movement in other states. Starting from so-called natural rights of man and citizen, the Declaration established in seventeen articles an enumeration of the inviolable rights of the individual, rights supposedly not to be abrogated or destroyed either by constitutions or by ordinary statutes. "People are born free and equal in their rights. Social differences can be based only on the general welfare. The goal of every sort of political union is to preserve man's natural and inalienable rights: freedom, property, security, and resistance to oppression.[6] . . . Inasmuch as property is an indestructible and sacred right, no one can be deprived thereof except in cases where this is manifestly required by social necessity, legally attested, and upon condition of just payment in advance."[7] Private property was thus the alpha and omega of this showy schedule of rights.

The combination of "equality in rights" with "social differences" in Article I of the Declaration shows that even then the French bourgeoisie foresaw the future paths of its political practice. Even then the bourgeoisie understood that this "equality in rights" or, as it was formulated in later declarations and constitutions, "equality before the law" will be constantly violated in so far as it conflicts with the "inviolable and sacred" right of property. The bourgeoisie's policy after winning power proved that the rights proclaimed by the Declaration are fundamental rights and privileges

[6] Declaration, Arts. 1, 2.
[7] Declaration, Art. 17.

of the bourgeois alone, formal, hypocritical promises made in order to crush the majority of the population. Everywhere, upon its access to power, the first steps taken by the bourgeoisie to strengthen its domination disclosed the difference between the abstract watchword "of all mankind," proclaimed by the bourgeoisie, and the definitive content of bourgeois legislation—indeed all the activity of the bourgeoisie as the dominant class. The abstract personality, of whose rights bourgeois declarations and constitutions prate, turned out to be in reality the bourgeois personality, whose basic and inalienable right was the sanctified and inviolable right of private property rather than freedom and equality.

The bourgeois demand of equality was embodied in the form merely of equality before the law which, in the ironic words of Anatole France, "in its stately righteousness forbids rich and poor alike to sleep under a bridge, to beg for alms in the street, and to steal bread." [8] As to freedom, as early as the *Communist Manifesto* there was an exhaustive characterization of freedom in bourgeois society under modern bourgeois conditions of production in the following words: "Freedom means freedom of trade, freedom to buy and sell." [9] So it is as to fundamental rights of man and citizen, since all the other rights comprised in the so-called catalogue of freedoms are definitive manifestations of these general and fundamental rights. In other words, while declaring that personality, man in general, bears natural and inalienable rights, and noting a whole catalogue of these and of rights of personality in general, in its Constitution the bourgeoisie, when it came to power, actually did nothing but make a formal acknowledgment that individuality in general possesses these rights, but defended the possibility of utilizing these rights in fact only in its own behalf, putting upon the toilers the entire burden of the obligations. "Freedom and equality in the bourgeois social order, so long as private property in land and in the means of production is retained, remain, even in bourgeois democracy, empty forms signifying in reality the *hired slavery* of the toilers (who are free in form and have in form equal rights) and the *omnipotence of capital*, the weight of capital upon labor." [10] The practice of the bourgeoisie in all countries has shown that bourgeois declarations and constitutions are not "abstractions subserving happiness" like the "legality," the "legal order," and the "general welfare" of the liberal professors and their kind.[11] They are a new arena or scene of action, a new form of class struggle between the bourgeoisie and the numerous (and ever growing) worker class. "The bourgeoisie cannot

[8] The French Constitution of 1785 (Art. 6) defined equality as "consisting in the fact that the law, whether defending or punishing, is the same for all."
[9] Marx and Engels, *Manifesto of the Communist Party* (1938), p. 43.
[10] Lenin (Russian ed.), Vol. XXIV, p. 310.
[11] *Ibid.*, Vol. XIV, p. 18.

win its political dominance, cannot express this political dominance in a constitution and laws, without at the same time putting weapons into the hands of the proletariat." [12]

In declarative form, the basic rights of citizens are variously formulated in constitutions of the different European countries. The Declaration of Rights of Man and Citizen was embodied in the French Constitution of 1791 and then, somewhat changed and expanded, in the Jacobin Constitution of 1793 (which never became operative). The right to resist oppression was eliminated in Article 22 of the Constitution of 1795, adopted after bourgeois reaction had triumphed, while at the same time the obligation of citizens was stressed. In subsequent French constitutions, right down to 1848, the Declaration of Rights was no longer included in its original form. The so-called Constitution of the Year VIII (1799) included only certain individual rights, while the Charters of 1814 and 1830 merely introduced subdivisions dealing with "public rights of the French."

The Revolution of 1848 compelled the bourgeoisie again to include a special subdivision concerning fundamental civil rights, and to introduce universal suffrage for men. Marx showed how these "fundamental rights of citizens," written into the Constitution of 1848, were nullified by subsequent reservations usually issued in the form of laws or orders of the executive authority.[13] The Constitution of the Empire of Napoleon III (1852) contained nothing more than a general phrase in Article I: "The Constitution acknoweldges, affirms, and guarantees the great principles proclaimed in 1789, the basis of the public law of the French." [14] In the constitutional laws of 1875, issued after the Paris Commune had been crushed, there is no word of the great principles of the Declaration of Rights of Man and Citizen.

In England a newspaper tax was introduced in 1702, after the "great revolution," to retard the development of the press and to limit the possible circulation of newspapers among the masses. In 1716 the term of parliament's plenary powers was extended from three to seven years, so as to avoid the frequent preelection agitations. In 1728 publication of the text of parliamentary debates was forbidden. In 1738 censorship of the theater was introduced. As worker agitations against the unprecedented exploitation mounted, the Habeas Corpus Act was suspended and a series of extraordinary statutes was passed. Only the pressure of the English worker class, which had created the revolutionary party of Chartists, compelled the government to reestablish the Habeas Corpus Act, to annul (in 1824) the laws

[12] Marx and Engels (Russian ed.), Vol. XIII, Pt. 1, p. 74.
[13] Marx, *The Eighteenth Brumaire of Louis Bonaparte*, p. 21.
[14] *Les constitutions d'Europe et d'Amérique, recueillies par Laferrière* (Paris, 1869), p. 17.

against freedom to organize workers' associations, to carry through (in 1832) an elective reform, to adopt the first laws limiting the work day for children (and later for workers), and to abrogate the tax on advertising and on newspapers (1852).

In Germany the reaction after the 1848 Revolution abrogated (in 1851) the Constitution of the Frankfort National Assembly, which had proclaimed the fundamental rights of citizens. In individual German states, such as Prussia (1852), paragraphs concerning the rights and freedoms of citizens were introduced into the Constitution, but all these were later abrogated by the "law against socialists." Workers were deprived of the right to assemble and to organize unions, of freedom of the press and of agitation, during the years from 1878 to 1890. Only the heroic tenacity of the workers broke the resistance of the government and compelled it to repeal this extraordinary law. The first Imperial Constitution of Germany (1871), which lasted until 1918, did not even include articles concerning the fundamental rights of citizens. Fascist Germany has completely liquidated all "civil rights" of every sort.

In the U. S. A. it took decades of struggle to gain for the workers the right to organize associations and to abrogate property qualifications in a number of states (in some they still exist), and it took the protracted Civil War (1861–1865) to abrogate slavery in the Southern states and a century and a half of struggle to gain suffrage for women.

In bourgeois states the category of fundamental civil rights has no constitutional standing, and is in fact annulled through the issuance of a vast quantity of ordinary laws and orders regulating the enjoyment thereof. Bourgeois political science has renounced the theory of the natural and inalienable rights of man and citizen. The enormous bourgeois mechanism, judicial and administrative, effectually suppresses and works violence upon the toilers. In bourgeois society based on the principle of private property, the dictatorship of capital is complete in all spheres of life; all the privileges and political freedoms in society are in fact confirmed in behalf of the dominant bourgeois class, and all obligations are foisted off upon the shoulders of the exploited. Having all the force of the state mechanism, the police, the army, the prisons, and the clergy, at its disposal, the bourgeoisie has set this entire system of class repression to work to subserve its interests, to guard its rights, and to force the toilers to perform unprotestingly the obligations established for them by the bourgeoisie. This inexorable law of the development of "civilization" was very brilliantly formulated in his time by Engels: "Civilization will explain so that even a complete fool will understand, the difference and the contrast between rights and obligations, granting one class almost all the rights and foisting off upon the other almost all the obligations." [15]

This woeful contradiction between reality and the principle (proclaimed in bourgeois declarations and constitutions) that all citizens are equal as regards rights and obligations—the contrast between the rights and the obligations of citizens—has compelled, and still compels, bourgeois political scientists to avoid in every way an expanded formulation of the character and class essence of civil obligations. To illustrate this, and how they evade the disclosure of the definitive content of those obligations, reference may be made to a political gazette, published in Leipzig in 1923, which altogether declines to enumerate the civil obligations in constitutional acts: "All civil obligations of citizens may be reduced to the single general obligation to obey. Every sort of obligation, like every sort of right, issues from the state. An enumeration of civil obligations is therefore impossible." [16]

Russian prerevolutionary political scientists are no exception. In their courses on public law they likewise confused and shaded in every way the class character of the problem of rights and obligations. Thus the bourgeois jurist Kuplevasky, in his chapter "General Obligations of Subjects," [17] puts as the primary obligation participation in the court as a juryman or class representative. Here, however, he enumerates how much property or income must be at one's disposal in order for him to be entered on the list of jurors. Another famous Russian bourgeois jurist and historian, Chicherin, in his chapter "The Obligations of Citizens," [18] enumerates the basic obligations of Russian subjects, which he divides into personal and political. The former is nothing more than unconditional obedience to supreme authority, the obligation "to have a form of thought and of actions inclined to preserve the state and to sustain existing authority," and to carry out the assessment on land consisting in "furnishing the state with the means necessary for it." Political obligations include liability for military service and functioning in various state offices such as juror or police officer.

Particular note should be taken of the trend, originating in dicta of Comte, the father of bourgeois sociology, which would shade out the cleavage between the rights and the obligations of citizens in capitalist society by eliminating the very idea of personal rights of citizens in favor of the idea of duty or social function. Reflecting the bourgeoisie's craving to shut the door upon the theory of inalienable and natural rights which it had proclaimed during its struggle for authority, Comte asserted as early

[15] Marx and Engels (Russian ed.), Vol. XVI, Pt. 1, p. 152.
[16] *Politisches Handwörterbuch* (7th ed., 1923), p. 973.
[17] H. O. Kuplevasky, *Russian Public Law* (2 vols., Kharkov, 1902), pp. 322–344.
[18] B. Chicherin, *A Course of Political Science*, Vol. I, pp. 237–238.

as 1850 in his *System of Positive Policy,* that the essence of the matter was that no one had any rights of any kind, merely an obligation to perform his duty. According to his idea not even the representatives of the dominant class have rights, inasmuch as each person, whatever the place he occupies in society, is only performing some obligation or other, his duty.

These assertions of Comte attained their profoundest development at the beginning of the twentieth century in the works of Duguit, a very eminent French political scientist, who asserted that neither man nor the collective has any rights whatever in society, but, in keeping with the position he occupies, the obligation of each man is to fulfill this or that social function. "Each individual is bound to fulfill a certain function in society, directly depending upon the place he occupies therein." [19] Property itself becomes one of the social functions according to Duguit's theory, the proprietor, like all persons, being bound to fulfill obligations: "The proprietor has an obligation, and by the same token plenary powers as well, to use the thing he possesses to satisfy individual demands, particularly his own personal demands, for the development of his moral, physical, and intellectual activity." [20] In his effort to efface all the boundaries separating rights and obligations by an impassable abyss, Duguit defines the rights of the bourgeoisie, its parasitic existence, the price whereof was the exploitation of the proletariat, as its fulfillment of a social duty. The proletariat, working for its oppressor, possessing nothing but its hands, minus guarantees of every sort and living in gloomy indigence, is fulfilling its social duty (Duguit opines) in a situation where it has equal rights with the bourgeoisie.

Unmasking the efforts of bourgeois ideologists to confuse all ideas concerning rights and obligations, Engels wrote ironically that all these hypocritical ratiocinations were directed toward a single assertion: the exploiter class exploits the oppressed class simply and solely in the interests of the exploited class itself; and "it is the foulest ingratitude toward the exploiter-benefactors if the exploited class does not understand, and even begins to resent, this." [21]

Hauriou, another bourgeois theoretician, expressing the views of the reactionary portion of the French bourgeoisie, formulates a series of proposals finally revealing the class essence of the capitalist state. His conclusion is that only the proprietor truly participates in civil society, while the class whose obligation is to labor stands beyond the bounds of the country's social and political life. Although the heaviest work is fobbed off on them,

---

[19] Duguit, *The General Transformations of the Civil Law Since the Time of the Code Napoleon* (Russian ed., 1919), p. 87.

[20] *Ibid.,* p. 90.

[21] Marx and Engels (Russian ed.), Vol. XVI, Pt. 1, pp. 152–153.

Hauriou acknowledges that the toilers are nevertheless not citizens in fact, since civil life is based on the principle of private property and not on labor. Existing "civil society is class society . . . created chiefly for the .class of the bourgeoisie, which in its entirety lives by utilizing its property. . . . That society takes very much less account of persons of the worker class."[22] After further emphasis upon the difference between the contemporary order and earlier social-economic forms, Hauriou concludes that society was in the last analysis so organized that the heavy labor rested upon the class predestined therefor and idleness remained the lot of the privileged class.

These assertions of Hauriou show that the woeful hiatus between rights and obligations in capitalist society is becoming so manifest that even individual bourgeois political scientists are constrained to chatter about it aloud with cynical openness such as that of Hauriou in the foregoing treatise.

In all bourgeois constitutions, as in all courses on public law, the matter of civil obligations is formulated in extremely blurred generalities and veiled in every way by sundry pedagogic and ethical norms.

A typical specification of civil obligations is that in the French Constitution of August 22, 1795:

All obligations of man and citizen flow out of the following principles inscribed by nature on every heart: Do not do to others that which you do not wish them to do to you; constantly do to others the good that you wish them to do to you. The obligations of each with regard to society are to defend it, to serve it, to live in conformity with its laws, and to respect its organs. No one can be a good citizen who is not a good son, a good father, a good brother, a good friend, a good spouse. . . . Every citizen should serve his country and safeguard freedom, equality, and property whensoever the law demands it.[23]

French constitutions following that of 1795 furnish no definition of obligations; only the 1848 Constitution (in Art. 7 of the introduction) points out that "citizens must love their country, serve the Republic, defend it even at the price of their own lives, and participate in state obligations in proportion to their condition."[24]

The fullest—and least clear-cut—formulation of fundamental civil obligations is that of the Weimar Constitution now abrogated by fascist Germany. Bourgeois constitutions presently in force speak of obligations (if at all) by way of indicating generally the obligations of citizens to fulfill the laws of the state, to perform military service, to pay taxes, and to serve the interests of the state in general. Thus the Japanese Constitution obligates all Japanese subjects to serve in the army or fleet (Art. 20) and to pay

[22] Hauriou, *Principles of Public Law,* pp. 366, 367, 374, 553.
[23] Laferrière, *op. cit.,* p. 17.
[24] *Legislative Acts of France* (Russian ed., 1905), p. 87.

taxes (Art. 21) according to legal directives. Similar obligations are enumerated in the constitutions of Yugoslavia, Bulgaria, Portugal, and others.

Herein it must be taken into account that, while for the toilers the importance of the rights proclaimed by the bourgeoisie is that of a preeminently formal announcement, inasmuch as the pressure of capital does not permit the toilers actually to realize a single one of them, the obligations charged upon the toilers have, nevertheless, an utterly real meaning and significance. There is nothing unreal about the performance of military service, or the payment of taxes, or the fulfillment of statutes. . . . At the same time, there is nothing fluctuating about rights and privileges in society possessed by the bourgeoisie; their reality is guaranteed by the fact that all political and economic power is in the hands of the bourgeoisie. The bourgeoisie is thus saved from the fulfillment of obligations, which it evades in every possible way, and succeeds, with the aid of money, numerous agents, and wide connections, in getting its children exempted from military service, its taxes reduced, and all sorts of exemptions and privileges for itself.

In his famous work *The Position of the Worker Class in England,* Engels shows that the bourgeoisie, with the power of the state at its disposal, is not only incapable of contributing anything to the country but is bent exclusively on pillaging the whole nation for the sake of its own private interests. "As a member of the ruling class, responsible for the situation of the whole nation and bound to observe the general interests because in *its hands is the power of the state,* it has not only done nothing that its position required it to do but it has robbed the entire nation for its own private interests." [25]

So when it is a matter of whether or not the bourgeoisie shall perform its obligations to the state or some duty in the interests of society, it sets itself up not only as against all society but even as against the collective capitalist, the state. In every way it gets around the institutions established by its regime, "in so far as it can succeed in doing so in each separate case, although it wishes everyone else to observe them." [26]

· Characteristic of the postwar period, with its extraordinary intensification of all the incongruities of capitalism, are the imperialist bourgeoisie's open renunciation of its own democracy and, because it is fearful of the idea of the storm maturing in the consciousness of the masses, its craving to annul the entire body of bourgeois-democratic freedoms which the toilers could use for their own ends. [27]

[25] Marx and Engels (Russian ed.), Vol. III, p. 414.
[26] *Ibid.,* Vol. IV, p. 161.
[27] Stalin, *Questions of Leninism* (10th Russian ed.), pp. 544, 545.

The ultimate materialization of this universal tendency of the financial bourgeoisie toward reaction is in the countries of fascist dictatorship. Typical of fascism—that regime of criminality in power—is the liquidation of all fundamental civil rights and all bourgeois-democratic freedoms, the destruction of trade unions, of cooperatives, and of all the legal organizations of workers, as well as of all other nonfascist political and cultural organizations; arbitrary savagery and violence as to the broadest masses of the population, and physical extermination of the flower of the worker class, its leaders and organizers. It openly denies that citizens stand upon an equality of rights. By its Nuremberg "laws" against the Jews and its savage Jewish pogroms, fascism has demonstrated to all the world that there are no limits to the cynicism and ferocity wherewith it mocks at legality and law.

Fascist legislation in Germany parcels out the population into two categories: persons of merely German nationality (the so-called "inhabitants"), and persons "of German blood." Only the latter possess all the rights of German citizenship, the former being considered elements that are tolerated and no more, being defenseless in fact as against organs of authority. Under the law for reestablishing professional officialdom (April 7, 1933), persons of non-Aryan origin are dismissed from the posts they have held. The law concerning communities gives the right of carrying on functions within the mechanism of the community "administration" to "citizens" only and not to "inhabitants." But although imperial citizens, as distinct from inhabitants, enjoy a number of rights, there are fundamental rights—freedom of speech, freedom of the press, freedom of assembly, freedom of demonstration, freedom of association—enjoyed by neither the one nor the other. By directive of February 28, 1933,[28] various articles [29] of the Weimar Constitution proclaiming the inviolability of the person and of the dwelling, the privacy of correspondence, freedom of opinion, freedom of the press, freedom of unions and freedom of assemblies were declared no longer in force.

For words incautiously spoken, the Decree Concerning the Defense of the Government of National Renaissance from Insidious Encroachments (March 21, 1933) threatens a prison sentence of not more than two years or a fine of not more than 10,000 marks, with an eloquent reservation as to the possibility of more severe punishment under other laws. For an attempt aimed at creating a new political party or supporting any of the parties persecuted by fascism, the Law Against Forming New Parties (July 14, 1933) imposes a penalty of not more than three years in a house

[28] V. O. des Reichspräsidenten zum Schutz von Volk und Staat, R. G. Bl. I, p. 83.
[29] Arts. 114, 115, 117, 118, 123, 124, 153.

of restraint or a prison sentence of from six months to three years, with the same proviso as to the possibility of more severe punishment.

Having destroyed the trade unions, the National "Socialists" hunted the workers in coercive fashion into fascist organizations of "the labor front" aimed, as was stated in the law concerning councils of representatives, at "making the employer again master in his own house."

Inviolability of a person and dwelling, and legality are ideas eliminated in fascist Germany, as in all countries of the fascist dictatorship. An instruction for judges issued in Germany teaches that their duties do not include defense of the accused from arbitrariness; the judge should "base his decision on what should be the national spirit."

The worker class of capitalist countries struggles on heroically against fascist barbarism for the democratic freedoms betrayed by the bourgeoisie in the person of monopolist capital. It struggles for them because they are necessary postulates of the successful struggle to free mankind from the chains of capitalist slavery, of the successful struggle for socialism. It defends these freedoms because, for all they have been so curtailed, they represent progress as compared with fascist barbarism, in the struggle against which all that is advanced and best in human society is united.

The great Stalin Constitution, attesting the breadth and genuineness of the rights and freedoms of USSR citizens, is "the moral help and the true succor of all who now carry on the struggle against fascist barbarism." [30]

SEC. 3: THE FUNDAMENTAL RIGHTS AND OBLIGATIONS OF CITIZENS OF THE USSR

1. *The genuineness and breadth of the rights of the toilers from the very first days of the existence of the Soviet state*

Only the victory of socialist revolution made true political freedoms and equality of civil rights possible. That victory gave over to the worker class state power torn from the hands of the exploiters to the end of annihilating man's exploitation of man and the very basis thereof—private property in the means of production—and the division of society into antagonistic classes. The annihilation of private property in the means and instruments of production, and the creation of socialist property in the means of production, signifying the emancipation of the toilers from the chains of capitalist slavery, mean thereby the creation of a firm basis for true democracy, for true political freedoms and equality of civil rights.

[30] Stalin, *Report on the USSR Draft Constitution* (1936), p. 46.

From the very earliest days, the great October Socialist Revolution, having overthrown in Russia the dominance of landowners and bourgeoisie, shattered the bourgeois state machine and established a state of worker dictatorship, created for the overwhelming majority of the population "such possibility in fact of utilizing democratic rights and freedoms as never existed, even approximately, in the very best and most democratic bourgeois republics." [1]

The transfer of authority into the hands of the Soviets—those exceedingly comprehensive organizations of the toilers—and the metamorphosis of the Soviets into the political basis of the worker-dictatorship state signified a complete break with bourgeois democracy and the realization of a democracy of a new and higher type, democracy of a breadth and logic unprecedented in history. "It is precisely the masses, who were excluded in fact by countless methods and tricks from participating in political life and utilizing democratic rights and freedoms, even in the most democratic bourgeois republics, although possessing equal rights in legal theory, that are now drawn into constant and stable and more decisive participation in the democratic administration of the state." [2] It is precisely these toiling masses who, for the first time in the world, have become genuinely possessed of freedom of assembly, freedom of speech, freedom of the press, freedom of demonstration, freedom of unions and so on.

That the rights of the popular masses were genuine and real was due to the fact that the only logically revolutionary class, the proletariat, had taken possession of state authority and had, from the very first days, begun the realization of its historical mission to abolish private property in the instruments and means of production and to make the means of production socialist property. The first decrees of Soviet authority, such as those concerning land, worker control, and the nationalization of banks, had already laid the granite foundation of socialism and created indestructible guarantees that the toilers would enjoy the rights granted to them by the state.

The logic and breadth of democracy made real by the socialist state, from the earliest period of its emergence, were brilliantly reflected in the fact that one of the first measures of Soviet authority was to make all nationalities,[3] as well as men and women,[4] equal in rights, to abolish social orders and to eliminate class privileges and civil limitations of every sort.[5]

---

[1] Lenin (Russian ed.), Vol. XXIV, p. 13.

[2] Ibid.

[3] Declaration of Rights of the Peoples of Russia (Nov. 2/15, 1917), Cy. 1917, No. 2, Art. 18.

[4] Cf. decrees concerning the dissolution of marriage (Cy. 1917, No. 10, Art. 152), and concerning civil marriage, children, and the keeping of records of civil status (Cy. 1917, No. 11, Art. 160).

[5] Cy. 1917, No. 3, Art. 31.

For centuries the bourgeois democracy had proclaimed the equality of human beings irrespective of sex, religion, race, and nationality; but nowhere had capitalism permitted this equality of rights to be carried actually into effect and had, in its imperialist stage, led to an extreme exacerbation of racial and national oppression. Only because Soviet authority is the authority of the toilers could it, for the first time in the world, utterly and in all spheres of life, develop this equality of rights to the point of achieving the complete annihilation of the last traces of woman's inequality as regards marriage and family rights in general.[6]

Thus the first two or three months of the existence of the state of the worker dictatorship already manifested the entire breadth and logic of the democracy of the socialist state.

The special characteristics of this new and higher type of democracy—the new content and form thereof and of its constituent institutes, as differing from those of bourgeois democracies, and the new content of the ideas of freedom and equality—were brilliantly expressed in proletarian declarations of rights, and in the first Soviet Constitution which noted the numerous rights won by the toilers as the result of the triumph of the socialist revolution.

2. *Proletarian declarations of rights*

Proletarian declarations of rights are built on principles diametrically opposed to the bourgeois declarations which speak hypocritically of personality in the abstract, and of man and citizen in general, while in reality they have in view the specific personality of the bourgeois individual, the property owner, and his interests and requirements. Proletarian declarations of rights cast aside the spurious generalities whereby bourgeois declarations seek to obscure the class essence of the rights they proclaim, and speak either of the peoples of the USSR, of the numerous nationalities formerly oppressed under tsarism, or of the toiling and exploited people as a whole, irrespective of national distinctions. In each case the concept "people" is employed with the precise interpretation of the word required by the context on each occasion, and not in the indeterminate sense of population in general (the mathematical total of all the citizens of the state). Proletarian declarations of rights frankly manifest their class essence, reflecting nothing of the desire of bourgeois declarations to shade off and mask the class character of the rights they proclaim.

In point of time, the first proletarian declaration of rights was the historical Declaration of Rights of the Peoples of Russia written by Stalin, and published November 2/15, 1917, over the signatures of Stalin and

[6] *Program of the All-Union Communist Party (of Bolsheviks)* (1936), p. 26.

Lenin. This is a document of the greatest historical significance, reflecting with unparalleled brilliance the socialist character of Soviet democracy, and of the rights established thereby.

Everyone knows that bourgeois declarations and constitutions are nationalist in character, defending dominance in behalf of a definite nation.[7] Such nationalist character of bourgeois declarations, of bourgeois "rights of man," is emphasized by Marx and Engels in their immortal works. Thus: "The specifically bourgeois character of these rights of man is attested by the fact that the American Constitution, the first which acknowledged them, at the same time confirmed the slavery of the colored races which still exist in America: class privileges were abolished, race privileges were sanctified."[8]

The French Constitution of 1791, containing the 1789 Declaration of Rights of Man and Citizen, pointed out in a special article that "although the colonies and the French possessions in Asia, Africa, and America form part of the French Empire, the Constitution aforesaid still does not extend to them," an admission that the Declaration of Rights of Man and Citizen was meant only for the dominant nation; namely, the French.

The Declaration of Rights of the Peoples of Russia proclaimed the equality of nations, their sovereign self-determination up to and including the right to withdraw and form an independent state; the abolition of all sorts of national-religious privileges and limitations, and the free development of national minorities and ethnographic groups inhabiting Russia.

These rights were not inferred from any fable as to man's inherent and inalienable rights. They were all contemplated by the victorious proletariat as necessary consequences of the fact of the socialist revolution, under a common banner calling for the emancipation of the toilers, as an inalienable part of the general task of abolishing man's exploitation of man. The Declaration of Rights of the Peoples of Russia confirmed in legislative form the foregoing rights of the peoples as definitive principles of administrative policy and thereby guaranteed the authenticity of all those personal civil rights granted to citizens by the socialist revolution and later fixed in the first (1918) Soviet Constitution.

Written by Lenin and adopted by the Third All-Russian Congress of Soviets (January, 1918), the Declaration of Rights of the Toiling and Exploited People summarized the activity of the socialist state for the first two and a half months and formulated the basic principles at the foundation of the socialist state which had been created.

[7] Cf. Stalin, *Report on the Draft of the USSR Constitution.*
[8] Engels, *Anti-Dühring,* Marx and Engels, (Russian ed.), Vol. XIV, p. 106.

By its announcement that "at the moment of the decisive conflict" of the proletariat "with its exploiters there can be no place for them in a single organ of authority," the Declaration confirmed the political social order which alone could assure the toiling masses—and from the very beginning—real political freedom." [9]

By its announcement that the Soviet Russian Republic, set up as a federation of national republics, was founded on the free union of free nations, and by granting to the workers and peasants of each nation the independent decision in their Congresses of Soviets of the question of their participation in federal government and as to the forms thereof, the Declaration confirmed the break with the policy of oppressing weak nations and of national privileges and limitations, and accordingly created a basis for the complete legal equality of citizens irrespective of their nationality.

Reinforcing by legislation the abrogation of private property in land, declaring the entire stock of land, all forests and natural deposits, and waters of state-wide importance to be national property to belong to the people as a whole, and confirming the law as to worker control as the first step to the complete transfer of basic means of production into state property, and the law annulling loans, the Declaration thereby corroborated the basis of the socialist social order, the most important guarantee of the rights and freedoms granted to the toilers by the socialist revolution.

The same Declaration, however, proclaimed universal liability to labor service, to the end of abolishing the parasite strata of society and organizing economy, as well as the arming of the toilers by the formation of the socialist Red Army of Workers and Peasants, and the complete disarming of the "have" classes in the interest of guaranteeing in behalf of the toiling masses authority entire and complete.

The Declaration speaks of fundamental civil obligations side by side with fundamental rights of the toiling and exploited people. Therein is one of the differences between proletarian declarations and bourgeois declarations. As a rule the bourgeoisie avoids speaking about obligations in declarations, preferring to speak of them in ordinary laws rather than in the ostentatious declarations invoked to adorn the façade of the bourgeois democratic state. The Declaration of Rights of the Toiling and Exploited People, having confirmed the bases of the Soviet social order which had by then been created and were guaranteeing the stability, completeness, and reality of civil rights and freedoms, was later included in its entirety in the first Soviet Constitution, that of the RSFSR (1918).

[9] Cy. 1918, No. 15, Art. 215.

3. *The provision of the Constitution of the RSFSR (1918) concerning civil rights and obligations*

The numerous rights and freedoms of the toilers attained legislative formulation in their entire breadth in the second subdivision of the first Soviet Constitution, that of the RSFSR (1918). That Constitution noted the actual freedoms won by the toilers through the victory of the socialist revolution: freedom of conscience, freedom of the press, freedom of assembly, freedom of unions, freedom of access to knowledge, as well as equality of civil rights regardless of race and nationality (Arts. 13–17, 22). It noted the bestowal of the political rights of Russian citizens upon toiling foreigners, and the right of asylum to all foreigners persecuted for political and religious crimes in bourgeois states (Arts. 20, 21). By legislative confirmation of the fact that all the technical and material resources essential to their enjoyment had been transferred into the hands of the worker class and the poorest peasantry, it guaranteed—for the first time in history—the rights bestowed by the state. "To the end of assuring in behalf of the toilers actual freedom to express their opinions, the RSFSR abolishes the dependence of the press upon capital, and gives into the hands of the worker class and the poorest peasantry all technical and material resources to publish papers, brochures, books, and other products of the press of every sort, and guarantees their free dissemination throughout the land" (Art. 14).

All the other rights hereinbefore noted are guaranteed by the Constitution in the same manner. Thus the first Soviet Constitution, as contrasted with all bourgeois constitutions, had already shifted the center of gravity with reference to civil rights to guarantees of those rights.

Side by side with rights, the Constitution noted also the fundamental obligations of USSR citizens; namely, the obligation to toil and the obligation to defend the socialist fatherland (Art. 18, 19).

The Constitution of 1918 did not proclaim freedom in general—freedom of conscience, freedom of opinion, freedom of assembly, and freedom of unions—in behalf of all citizens without exception. Having proclaimed the watchword: "He who does not toil does not eat," it has nothing in common with the hypocrisy of bourgeois constitutions and declarations which proclaim freedoms and rights supposedly possessed by all people in equal degree, whereas at the same time the social order itself, as well as ordinary bourgeois legislation, makes the rights thus widely heralded inaccessible in fact to the toiling masses. The Soviet Constitution frankly and openly declared that freedom to express opinions, freedom of assembly, freedom of unions, and so on, are granted only to the toilers, signifying in fact the overwhelming majority of the people. Even in establishing the obligation of all citizens of the republic to defend the socialist fatherland, the Constitution granted toilers alone "the honored right to defend the revolution with arms in their hands," pointing out that "the nontoiling elements are charged to perform other military obligations" (Art. 17). And as if to emphasize still more sharply the complete difference between the freedom and equality afforded by the socialist state and those existing in bourgeois understanding, the Constitution of 1918 provides (in Art. 23, the last article of the subdivision concerned with general propositions of the Constitution) in developing the point of the Declaration of the Rights of the Toiling and Exploited People (already mentioned): "Guided entirely by the interests of the worker class, the RSFSR deprives individuals and separate groups of rights utilized by them to the detriment of the interests of the socialist revolution."

"This paragraph," as Lenin said at the First All-Russian Congress concerning education outside the schools, "is known to all the world. . . . We introduced it into the Soviet Constitution, and have drawn to it already the sympathies of the workers of the entire world." [10]

The 1918 Constitution expressed the proletarian understanding—differing in principle from the bourgeois understanding—of freedom of equality. Realizing the worth of political freedoms and legal equality, the proletariat neither makes a fetish thereof nor reduces the (whole) concept of freedom and equality thereto. Comprehended in the proletarian demands of freedom and equality are freedom from capitalist slavery and equality in the sense that classes are abolished. "Freedom gainsaying the liberation of labor from the oppression of capital is a delusion." [11] These are the criteria of the proletariat as it comes to appraise political freedom and legal equality.

The liberation of the toilers from the chains of capitalist slavery, the annihilation of the landowner and bourgeois classes, was precisely what made it possible to carry into effect—even from the first days of the worker class dictatorship and to an extent unprecedented in history—political freedom and equality of civil rights, regardless of sex, race, nationality, or religion. At the same time, however, the interests of freedom and equality, in the profound senses in which the proletariat comprehended these concepts, imperatively required, in the conditions in which the class struggle was then going on, that the political rights of exploiters be limited and a certain inequality (in aid of the worker class) in regard to rules of representation be confirmed. [12] These unprecedentedly broad civil rights and freedoms, synchronizing with open limitations upon the rights of exploiters

[10] Lenin (Russian ed.), Vol. XXIV, p. 307.
[11] Ibid., pp. 289, 293.
[12] For details cf. Chap. X.

and certain limitations—in aid of the worker class—upon legal equality as regards the rules of representation, reflected the socialist character of our democracy as it definitively materialized at that point of our history.

The great October Socialist Revolution practically and graphically demonstrated the genuineness of what had been declared long before by the Marx-Lenin theory: "Only under the proletarian dictatorship can the exploited be truly 'free,' proletarians and peasants actually participate in the administration of the country." [13] The Soviet Constitution of 1918 reflected this in its Articles concerning civil rights and freedoms.

The 1925 Constitution of the RSFSR, like the new Union Republic constitutions adopted in connection with the formation of the USSR, reproduced without change the civil rights and obligations formulated in the first Soviet Constitution.

4. *Fundamental rights of citizens of the USSR under the Stalin Constitution*

The Stalin Constitution—that genuine charter of the rights of emancipated humanity—reflected the fact that democracy had developed mightily in the process of socialist building and confirmed the results of that development. Notwithstanding all its breadth and depth since the very first days of its existence, Soviet democracy is not set or immutable. As socialist reorganization proceeds, socialist democracy goes along the road of ever greater development and expansion. "It is also the power of socialist democracy that, having emerged as a result of the victory of the proletarian dictatorship, it grows and broadens with each day, particularly in conjunction with the growth of culture among the masses. This reflects the mighty growth of our powers." [14]

Clarification of the entire depth of socialist democracy's development necessitates a review of the conditions in which the state of worker-dictatorship that had emerged as a result of the victory of the socialist revolution began its colossal activity in the reorganization of society upon socialist principles. Coming to authority, the proletariat found the national economy in utter ruin, disorganized by the predatory management of landowners and bourgeoisie and worn out by four years of an exhausting imperialist war. Ruin everywhere, hunger threatening to wipe out the primary productive force—the worker class; unemployment, "a boundless ocean of tiny, individual peasant holdings with their backward, medieval technique," [15] the kulaks in the village, the culture of the masses on an extraordinarily

[13] Stalin, *Questions of Leninism* (10th Russian ed.), p. 29.
[14] Molotov, *Socialism's Constitution* (1936), p. 15.
[15] Stalin, *Report on the Draft of the USSR Constitution* (1936), p. 8.

low level, a tremendous percentage of illiteracy, women in the position of serfs in domestic economy, a great number of nationalities economically and culturally backward by reason of the chronic rapacity of tsarist Russia's colonial policy—such were the conditions in which proletarian democracy began to develop. These conditions, themselves extraordinarily difficult, were still further complicated by the uninterrupted and extremely savage conflict which, in various forms and from the very first days, the Soviet state was compelled to carry on against the numerous enemies of the toilers: the White Guards, the interventionists, the Mensheviks, the SR's, and other counterrevolutionary anti-Soviet parties, the cleverly masked Trotsky-Bukharin agents of fascism, the wreckers, and so on.

Naturally, then, notwithstanding the fact that the rights enumerated in the first Soviet Constitution were guaranteed, the broadest masses of the toilers could not in an instant make them completely their own. If they were all to be able to make these rights, bestowed upon them by the Constitution, their own in full measure; if they were to learn how to utilize them, unemployment must be liquidated, the cultural level of the masses must be raised, illiteracy must be abolished, women must be emancipated in fact, enormous work in uniting the toilers of the formerly oppressed nationalities to a life of political consciousness must be carried through, and the general material level of life of the city and village toilers must be raised. There was but one way to achieve this: by the socialist reconstruction of the entire national economy, by the socialist reorganization of society.

The triumphant socialist building in the land, the elimination of the remnants of the urban bourgeoisie and of the kulak class, the raising of the material level of the toilers, the expansion of cultural revolution in the country, the flowering of the national republics, the improvement of the state mechanism and the rooting of that mechanism in the national republics and regions—all this resulted naturally in the ever increasing utilization of their rights by the toilers. The sharp increase in newspaper circulation from year to year, the quantity of books produced in all languages, the number of students in all the schools and higher educational institutions, the enormous growth of membership in different social organizations (trade unions, cooperatives, and voluntary societies, and the numerical growth of the party—all this confirms the sweeping assimilation of rights and of freedom of assembly, freedom of the press, freedom to form unions, and so on,[16] typical of the period between the first Soviet Constitution and the Stalin Constitution of socialism victorious.

As the riches of our socialist country increased, so did the material basis

[16] For further details, see paragraphs devoted to individual civil rights.

systematically grow and increase, assuring the toilers the beneficial utilization of their rights: printing establishments and their equipment, paper stocks, public buildings for assemblies, schools, higher educational institutions, funds earmarked for scholarships, and so on. Concurrent with the same process of triumphant socialist building was the implementation also of the rights possessed by the toilers by virtue of their being bestowed upon them by the Soviet legislation. Such are the rights to rest and to material security, and the inviolability of person, dwelling, and correspondence preserved by laws established by the Soviet state. Finally, the same process of socialist building guaranteed, as early as 1931, the abolition of unemployment and thereby created all the conditions precedent to the realization of the most valuable of human rights—the right to labor.

The right to labor is one which the proletariat has long demanded.[17] It is impossible of realization under the conditions of capitalism, which rest on the exploitation of another's toil, remaining thereunder either an empty fancy conceived by the toiling masses, or an inflammatory watchword utilized by the dominant class for its own purposes. The proletariat, having taken into its own hands authority in our country, having overthrown the dominance of capital, created the basic essentials for the realization of this age-old dream of mankind. The ruin of the national economy in the first stage of socialist revolution, and the resulting unemployment, however, afforded no possibility of guaranteeing the right to all citizens at one stroke. Such a guaranty became possible only with the victory of socialism, which has forever liquidated unemployment and assured to all citizens the application of their powers in productive labor.

The development and strengthening of Soviet democracy was further expressed in the fact that limitations on the enjoyment of political rights by former nonlabor elements were abolished; the elimination of exploiter classes in the land made superfluous the limitations upon rights which had been established as early as the first Soviet Constitution of 1918, and affirmed by subsequent Union Republic constitutions and by the election laws of the USSR and of the Union and autonomous republics alike.

As early as 1931, the Presidium of the Central Executive Committee of the USSR [18] issued a special directive concerning the reestablishment of the dispossessed kulaks in all their civil rights (upon the expiration of five years from the moment of their eviction) and the grant to them of election rights, provided, during this period, they "shall in reality demonstrate that they have ceased to struggle against the peasantry organized into kolkhozes and against measures of Soviet authority directed at raising

[17] Cf. the paragraph following on the right to work.
[18] Cz. 1931, No. 44, Art. 298.

agriculture . . . and shall show themselves in reality honorable and conscientious toilers." In 1934 and 1935 the Central Executive Committee
of the USSR adopted directives [19] indicating in greater detail the method
of reestablishing the former kulaks, as well as their children, in all rights.
Molotov, speaking at the Seventh All-Union Congress of Soviets, in his
report concerning the changes of the Soviet Constitution in respect of
these directives, declared: "All this proves that in the Soviet Union the
door to a life with complete rights for all honorable toilers stands open
and that the group of the disfranchised is constantly narrowing." [20]

The Stalin Constitution, reflecting the fact that exploiter classes had
been eliminated in our country and the class structure of Soviet society
changed, confirmed in behalf of all citizens, as participants in socialist
society possessing equal rights, identical rights and obligations, noting in
Chapter X the fundamental rights of USSR citizens and enumerating those
civil rights which, as is emphasized by their very designation in the text
of the Constitution, constitute the *foundation* essential to all the many
remaining rights of USSR citizens pointed out in other chapters of the
Constitution or regulated by separate codes and current legislation. There,
in first place among the basic civil rights, is put the group of rights guaranteeing the material conditions of civil existence and assuring them for the
morrow: the right to labor (the right of citizens to obtain guaranteed work
and to be paid for their toil in accordance with the quality and quantity of
that toil), the right to rest, and the right to material security in old age as
well as in case of sickness or loss of working capacity. A special characteristic of the Stalin Constitution, as of all the earlier Soviet constitutions,
is that it is not (as are bourgeois constitutions) "limited to the mere drafting
of formal civil rights; it transfers the center of gravity to guarantees of those
rights and to means of effectuating them." [21] In each article attention is
directed to such guarantees, established by the Constitution, equally with
the corresponding right. In this legislative guarantee that civil rights are
genuine and real, the socialist character of the democracy of the Stalin
Constitution finds its most brilliant expression.

Chapters dedicated to the basic rights and obligations of citizens in
new constitutions of the Union and autonomous republics reproduce the
text of Chapter X of the Stalin Constitution; that chapter is organically
connected in its entirety with Chapter I of the Constitution and is the
logical development of the basic principles therein confirmed.

Any contrasting of individual civil rights with the state is alien to

[19] Cz. 1934, No. 33, Art. 257; Cz. 1935, No. 7, Art. 57.
[20] Molotov, *Changes in the Soviet Constitution* (1935), p. 26.
[21] Stalin, *Report on the Draft of the USSR Constitution* (1936), p. 21

socialist public law; this is a particularly clear-cut distinction between the Soviet Constitution and constitutions of bourgeois states, as Soviet public law is distinct from bourgeois public law.[22]

This history of the socialist state, which from the very first days of its emergence granted to the toilers rights of unprecedented breadth, proves incontrovertibly that the source of these numerous civil rights is to be sought in the socialist social organization rather than in any myth as to man's natural and inherent rights. Confirmation of the might of the socialist state, the confirmation and development of the socialist organization of society, are the basis assuring the authenticity, breadth, and systematic confirmation of civil rights and the full flowering of socialist democracy.

a) The Right to Work

The right to work is the foundation whereon the Soviet citizen's rights and freedoms rest. The watchword: "The right to work," put forward by the revolutionary proletariat at the time of the bourgeois revolution in France at the end of the eighteenth century, and remaining as the war cry for decades thereafter, expressed an elemental protest against capitalist society, against the exploitation and unemployment predominant therein, but did not constitute a demand that capitalism be overthrown. The worker folk demanded of the bourgeois state only measures directed against beggary and unemployment. In accordance with the then bourgeois ideology of natural law, this slogan was not infrequently formulated as "man's natural right to existence."

In 1789, while the committee of the National Assembly was considering the proposed Declaration of Rights of Man and Citizen, Deputy Target proposed to include therein a recital that "the state must guarantee to each man the means of existence by assuring him property, work, or aid in general." [23] Notwithstanding the extremely widespread unemployment and agitation in Paris, this proposal found no support in the National Assembly. *The Declaration of Rights of Man and Citizen contains not a single word*

[22] Bourgeois theories of fundamental rights—subjective public rights as they are called—ordinarily begin with the antithesis of personality and state, contemplating the rights of personality as a limitation upon the state and the essence of the chief civil rights as freedom from the state, nonintrusion by the state on the basis of the sovereignty of rights of personality. Cf. Hatschek, *Deutsches und preussisches Staatsrecht* (1922), Vol. 2, p. 9; Meyer, *Lehrbuch des deutschen Staatsrechts* (1914), Vol. 1, p. 38; Ripport, *Le régime démocratique et le droit civil moderne* (Paris, 1936).

The same antithesis of personality to the state is at the basis of the bourgeois theories which deny that the freedoms and rights granted by the constitutions are to be characterized as individual rights, and define them not as rights but as rules of objective law, as rules of public law established by voluntary self-limitation on the part of state (and subject to annulment by it at any time), and making it possible for citizens to act without hindrance in certain fields (Laband, Zorn, Seidel, and others and, in detail, Giese, *Die Grundrechte*, 1906).

[23] Cited in Prochownik, *Das Angebliche Recht auf Arbeit* (1891), p. 39.

either about work or about aid to the unemployed. Fearing demands by organized workers for higher wages, the victorious bourgeoisie (February 14, 1791) deprived workers even of the right of coalition. During consideration of the proposed Constitution (1793), the convention rejected Robespierre's proposal to include in the text of the Constitution an article establishing the obligation of the state to guarantee the existence of all citizens by furnishing either work or appropriate relief. Article 21 of the Declaration of June 23, 1793, speaks only of furnishing work or aid to unfortunate citizens. It is perfectly clear that subsequent French constitutions and charters contained nothing in the nature of aids or assurance to persons without the means of existence.

The expectations of the workers were reflected in the works of socialist-utopians, chiefly Fourier and his pupils, who more than once declared that the right to work is the only valuable right possessed by the unfortunate. "We have lost whole centuries in petty quarrels about the rights of man with absolutely no thought concerning the acknowledgment of the most essential rights, such as the right to work, without which all the others come to naught." [24] Notwithstanding the correctness of these assertions, neither Fourier nor the other utopians comprehended the utopian character of this right, that it cannot be effectuated unless capitalist property and the capitalist system of economy are abolished and man's exploitation of man destroyed.

Influenced by the doctrines of the utopians and reformist politicians, the workers did not unite their demand of the right to work with the struggle to abolish capitalist order, as may be seen from the 1848 revolution in France, when the proletariat, with the participation of the petty bourgeois reformist, Louis Blanc, put forward the right to work as the demand of its program. The bourgeoisie, faced with a proletarian uprising, at first disingenuously acknowledged that it was bound to assure the worker his existence through work, but, having gained time, it drowned the uprising of the workers in blood and cancelled all its promises in their behalf. The Constitution of November 4, 1848, included only the right to social philanthropy.

All the illusions of the worker class as to the possibility of realizing the right to work under capitalist conditions were thus dispelled. Marx says of these demands for the right to work that they represented "the first impotent formula of the proletariat's revolutionary demands," [25] while Lenin, in his *Agrarian Program of Social Democracy in the First Russian Revolution of 1905 and 1907*, wrote on this score that "in the right to work

[24] Fourier, *Théorie de l'unité universelle* (1841), Vol. II, p. 180.
[25] Marx and Engels (Russian ed.), Vol. VIII, p. 33.

possessed by the French citizens and by workers of the middle of the nineteenth century was nothing but spurious socialist theory." [26]

In the following decades the "right to work," which the bourgeoisie and the reformists had distorted into the "right to social philanthropy and defense of work" and so on, was under consideration inside parliament and out: in 1848 and 1849 in sessions of the Frankfort National Assembly, in 1884 in the German Reichstag, in Switzerland during the plebiscite of 1894, in the English House of Commons in 1905, and in Germany in 1919 (during the adoption of Article 157 of the Weimar Constitution).[27] In all these debates even the representatives of the bourgeoisie acknowledged on each occasion that logical development of "the right to work" means "a socialist state," a state control, unconditional and complete, over the entire production mechanism.[28] The bourgeoisie and its representatives understand that the right to work and the right of private property in the instruments and means of production are incompatible rights.

Capitalism cannot exist without a vast reservoir army of unemployed ever lowering the pay for work and service. Manpower must—under capitalism—remain a market commodity the same as any other commodity. Even in the years of "prosperity" (so-called), there were millions of unemployed, in the U.S.A., England, Germany, Austria, Poland, Japan, and so forth. The average annual number of the unemployed in the thirty-two chief capitalist countries in the years 1929–1936 was 19 millions. At the beginning of 1938 the unemployed reached the number of 26 millions.

During the universal crisis of capitalism, the conditions of slave labor thereunder further deteriorate in consequence of the unprecedented rise of unemployment, the lowering of wages, and the introduction (in a number of countries) of forced labor service and military discipline. The "labor front" in fascist Germany, the labor camps in Germany, Poland, and Bulgaria, and the "closed communities" for workers in Japan put millions of workers in these countries into the still more intolerable position of slaves of monopolist capital and the militarists. Such is the inevitable consequence of the progressive collapse of the capitalist system. A process diametrically opposed in principle is being carried to accomplishment in the USSR, where the brilliant growth of the socialist economy assured the transformation of work into a "matter of *honor*, a matter of *glory*, a matter of *valor* and *heroism*" (Stalin).

Work in the USSR ceased to be an instrumentality for enslavement

[26] Lenin (Russian ed.), Vol. XI, p. 473.

[27] This slogan was reflected in the same mutilated form in the Polish Constitution of 1921 (Art. 102), in the Constitution of Yugoslavia of the same year (Art. 23), in the Constitution of Esthonia (Art. 25), and of Finland (Art. 6), and in others.

[28] Speeches of Bismarck and Richter in a session of the German Reichstag, May 9, 1894.

and became "an instrumentality for emancipation, making it possible for each personality to develop in all directions and to manifest all its capacities both physical and spiritual." [29] The most notable manifestation of the new character of work, of the mounting awareness of those taking part in the socialist production process, is the development of diverse forms of socialist competition and the broadly expanded Stakhanovite movement, the highest form of socialist competition.

The right to work in the USSR is guaranteed by the socialist system of economy under which production is directed by a state plan of national economy in the interests of the entire people. Socialist planning guarantees at once the growth of production equipped with the newest technique, a rise in the employment of the toilers in all branches of Soviet life, and no unemployment. The number of those at work and in service in the USSR increased from 11.6 million in 1928 to 26.3 million in 1937, with concurrent and constant increase in wages. "The enormous success of socialist industrialization of the country and the swift tempo of collective farms and state farm building led to the complete abolition of unemployment in the Soviet Union and required supplementary hundreds of thousands of workers." [30] A notable date on the road to realization of the right to work was the instruction of Stalin, set forth in his speech at the Congress of Industrial Administrators in June, 1931, in particular, that with reference to the organized recruiting of man power. The instructions of Stalin were embodied in legislative rules concerning the organized recruiting and distribution of man power.

In all the stages of the development of the socialist system of economy, the legal regulation of work was one of the most effective instrumentalities at first to limit and at the same time to dislodge, and later to eliminate, the capitalist elements.

The socialist state created a single system of socialist labor law, expressed in legislation regulating not only the labor of persons at work and in service but also labor in collective farms and industrial cooperatives. Most important among these laws is the Model Charter of the Agricultural Artel; the Stalin Charter of the Agricultural Artel of 1935 is the greatest legal document of the socialist organization of work in the collective farms.

Constitutional guarantees of the right to labor find their concrete formulation in legislative rules in the code of labor laws, in collective farm and industrial-cooperative legislation, and in the civil and criminal codes.

Side by side with the socialist labor of those at work and in service,

---

[29] Engels, *Anti-Dühring* (1936), pp. 212–213.

[30] Directive of the All-Union Communist Party (of Bolsheviks) Central Executive Committee (Oct. 20, 1930), *Pravda*, Oct. 22, 1930, No. 292.

of members of the collective farms and of the industrial cooperative artels, the Stalin Constitution admits the minute private economy of individual peasants and craftsmen based on personal work and not including exploitation of the labor of another.

Confirmed in the USSR Constitution, the right to work guarantees labor, the source of comfortable and cultural existence, to all workers, peasants, and intellectuals. It guarantees payment to each citizen for his toil, based on the logical application of the socialist principle of payment according to the quality and quantity of the work. The socialist system of wages is the most important instrumentality for raising labor productivity, for better employing the work day, for elevating the worker's qualification, for improving the quality of the work, for achieving complete mastery of the technique of production, and for bettering the workers' material position.

Under the conditions of capitalism, wages—apparently and in form payment for the entire labor—comprise payment only for the part thereof going to rehabilitate the worker's strength. Latent under the form of the wages is capitalist exploitation. The capitalist has no fear of the worker being worn out before his time. Outside the gates of enterprises there always stands a vast army of the unemployed from which the capitalist can obtain a new worker to replace one who has absented himself. "The capitalist constantly strives to reduce wages to their physical minimum and to prolong the work day to its physical maximum, while the worker constantly exerts pressure in the opposite direction, and it is merely a question of the correlation of the forces of the opposing sides." [31]

The proletariat's struggle to raise wages in capitalist lands was directed chiefly toward schedules guaranteeing a minimum wage and the acknowledgment of such schedules as binding all workers and proprietors in a given line. Laws as to minimum wage rates existed in England, Austria, and a number of other countries before the war. In the postwar period, wage agreements and wage legislation developed in all the countries of Europe, most strongly in Germany, where wage agreements covered approximately 65 per cent of the workers. These laws and agreements, however, initiated by the pressure of the revolutionary mass movement of 1918–1919, were being constantly violated by the employers who, concurrently with the wage agreements, brought about a whole system of individual contracts raising or lowering wage schedules in accordance with the economic situation, with the growth or decline of unemployment in the country. When fascism came to power, the consequence was—in Germany as in a number of other countries—to wipe out even the insignificant conquests won by the proletariat of these countries in the prolonged struggle for wage standards.

[31] Marx, *Wages, Price and Profit* (Russian ed., 1932), p. 74.

The October Revolution radically changed the essential character of wages, and the system and form thereof. It proclaimed the principle of socialist payment, payment according to the quality and quantity of the work. Accordingly, as early as the first half of 1918, a scale of wages was worked out, based on the principle of allocating all persons at work and in service to five groups (each subdivided into fifteen categories). In January, 1919, this system was revised, its basic features having been retained until the introduction of the New Economic Policy.

The necessity, during the civil war, of insuring supplies to towns and, in the first instance, to those at work and in service in the leading branches in production and transport, prompted the introduction of payment in money and in kind. In *The Immediate Tasks of Soviet Authority*, Lenin wrote (in the beginning of 1918): "It is essential in the first instance to set up, apply practically and test payment by the job, to apply much that is scientific and progressive in the system of Taylor: to make the wage commensurate with the general totals of the product's yield or of the exploitation results of railroad and water transport, and so forth, and so forth." [32]

The policy of the Party and of Soviet authority after the civil war assured the rehabilitation of industry, transport, and agriculture, a higher standard of living for the toiling masses. A single wage schedule of seventeen categories was introduced in 1922. The anti-Party and antistate policy of the direction of trade unions at that time—due to the petty-bourgeois interpretation of socialist equality—led, however, to the schedule being so applied in a number of cases as to violate the basic principles of socialist wages. The wage scales and the qualification manuals existing prior to Stalin's historic speech at the Congress of Industrial Managers in 1931 were so framed as to establish equalitarianism in the pay of workers doing simple and qualified labor. This position, as Stalin showed in that speech, led to apathy on the part of the worker as regards his qualifications, to fluctuation of man power, and the like. "To destroy this evil, it is necessary to abrogate equalitarianism and to destroy the old wage system. To destroy this evil, it is necessary to organize a system of wage scales that would take into account the difference between qualified and unqualified labor, between heavy labor and light labor." [33]

Stalin's instructions as to the six conditions prerequisite to the development of our industry served as a program of action in the planning and regulation of wages. In the USSR the Party and the government define an increase of the work wage pursuant to prepared plans of national economy whose basis is the increasing needs of workers, material and cultural,

[32] Lenin (Russian ed.), Vol. XXII, p. 454.
[33] Stalin, *Questions of Leninism* (10th Russian ed.), p. 451.

and the unbroken growth of labor productivity. Specifically, an increase of wages depends on quantitative and qualitative indices calculated on the basis of technical standards of output that are established. Vast work has been, and is being, carried on for the correct formulation of correlations in the amounts of the wage schedule according to various fields of the national economy and categories of labor. A brilliant example of such work is the directive of the Council of People's Commissars of the USSR and the Central Committee of the All-Union Communist Party (of Bolsheviks) on May 21, 1933, Concerning the Wages of the Workers and the Technical Engineering Forces of the Coal Industry of the Don Basin.[34]

The establishment of technical standards corresponding to a given level of the toilers' technique and qualification in each stage of the development of our economy is of the greatest significance for the correct planning of wages. "Technical rules constitute the great regulating force which organizes in production the broad masses of the workers around the forward elements of the worker class."[35]

The Stakhanovite movement smashed the old technical rules and posed the question of new and higher technical rules to replace them. Accordingly, the plenum of the Central Committee of the All-Union Communist Party (of Bolsheviks) in its directive of December 25, 1935, condemned the former practice, based on obsolete technical rules, of standardizing labor and required the establishment of new rules which should take into account the advanced production experience of Stakhanovites. The new technical rules which have been, and are being, worked out are the foundation of the national economic plan, and, at the same time, of the state planning of the work wage.

The legal regulation of all species of work wage in the USSR is the very best assurance that the principle, established in the Constitution, of socialist payment for work is being put into practice. At the same time the Soviet state[36] guarantees a minimum wage of 115 rubles, exclusive of premiums and other additional wages, for those at work and in service in all factories and works and in rail and water transportation. State funds for providing the cultural and living conditions of workers and those in service (for the preservation of health, for building worker dwellings, and so on) constitute a real and important addition to the working wage.

Violations of labor legislation concerning wages—cheating the workers—are among the most grievous crimes in the USSR, and the Soviet state accordingly visits stern punishments upon the guilty. Such violations are

[34] Cz. 1933, No. 31, Art. 183.
[35] Stalin, Speech at the First All-Union Congress of Stakhanovites (1935), pp. 22-23.
[36] Directive of the Council of People's Commissars of the USSR, Nov. 1, 1937.

often the means employed by the class enemy with careful calculation in the attempt to evoke dissatisfaction among workers. In order to contend successfully with such violations, trade unions and directors of enterprises are charged with the duty not merely of clarifying for the workers the basic principles of socialist payment for labor but also of achieving the result that each worker and person in service know his standard output, his value, and his schedule rate.

The right to work requires the socialist relationship toward work. Fostering this new relationship toward work was the principle task of the Soviet state from the earliest days when the proletariat won authority. In *The Immediate Tasks of Soviet Authority,* Lenin posed this question with all keenness and sharpness: "It is necessary to make secure what we have ourselves won, what we have decreed, legalized, considered, projected—to make it secure by entrenching it in the stable forms of *everyday work discipline.*" [37]

Work discipline consists in the scrupulous and conscientious fulfillment by the toilers of all the obligations resting upon them with reference to the work they perform. The steady growth of a conscious and conscientious attitude on the part of citizens toward their own and others' work is an index of the success being attained in conquering the remnants of capitalism in the economy and consciousness of the people. The best model of the development of the socialist relationship toward work is socialist competition, shock work, the Stakhanovite movement. "The most significant thing in competition is that it produces a complete reversal of people's views toward work; it turns work—formerly deemed a shameful and grievous burden—into a matter of *honor,* of *glory,* of *valor and of heroism.*" [38]

Any weakening of work discipline in our enterprises, collective farms, and institutions plays into the hands of enemies of the socialist state. Against those who violate Soviet laws and work discipline the Party and the state carry on an irreconcilable struggle. Hence the obligation of an honorable attitude toward the social duty and discipline of work inscribed in Article 130 of the USSR Constitution. The struggle in behalf of the new discipline of socialist work is prosecuted through the education of citizens by state organs and by Party, trade union, and other social organizations. Against those who disorganize production, and those who undermine the discipline of work, the state has established a number of criminal measures applied by Soviet courts as dictated by the gravity and the consequences of the crime or violation. The struggle against infraction of work discipline not constituting criminal offenses is actively carried on also by social courts composed of fellow workers. Furthermore, upon the basis of applicable decrees, directors

[37] Lenin (Russian ed.), Vol. XXII, p. 464.
[38] Stalin, *Questions of Leninism* (10th Russian ed.), p. 393.

of enterprises, institutions, administrations, and general assemblies of collective farms and the like may impose disciplinary penalties upon persons guilty of a breach of discipline. Work enthusiasm, socialist consciousness, and the lofty feelings of a state duty to the fatherland and to the Soviet people, however, decide questions of work discipline among us—not penalties or the threat of criminal punishment, as in capitalist countries.

b) The Right to Rest

The right to rest is inseparably connected with the right to work. Like the right to work, it is confirmed and guaranteed only in the USSR by the Constitution of the socialist state. Such a right is possible only with a social order which tolerates neither exploitation nor exploiters, where man himself is a valuable capital, where rest is developed and organized for the constant strengthening of the forces, and the physical and cultural development of the toiler. The right to rest is essentially repugnant to capitalism, which constantly needs a reserve army of the unemployed ready to work on any conditions, and is politically interested to have the worker class culturally backward, being indifferent to the health, the fate, and the life of toiling man.

Hundreds of years of stubborn struggle by the worker class in capitalist countries were needed to achieve an infinitesimal shortening of the working day. Only under the pressure of the Chartist movement was the working day shortened in England from twelve hours to eleven.[39] Statutes of 1844, 1847, and 1848 gradually established in England a shortening of the working day for children and then for workers in their teens. Statutes for the protection of child labor had been issued somewhat earlier (in 1802, 1816, 1819, and 1833). Laws introduced at first only for the cotton industry were extended (in 1854, 1864, and 1867) to other enterprises employing more than fifty persons. Throwing light upon the worker class struggle to shorten the working day in England, Marx and Engels showed the abominable methods of deceit applied by factory owners, with the blessing of the government, to circumvent these laws.

The same picture is repeated in other capitalist countries. In France the influence of the Lyons weavers led to the issuance in 1841 of a decree forbidding child labor up to the age of eight and night labor for children up to the age of thirteen. The working day for children (between the ages of eight and twelve) was confirmed at eight hours, and for juveniles (from twelve to sixteen) at twelve hours. But this law was not put into practice:

---

[39] Chartism, from the word "charter," was a revolutionary mass movement of English workers in the 1840's for political rights and for improving the material conditions of their existence, set out in a charter.

the 1848 Revolution resulted in the establishment of a ten-hour working day in Paris and an eleven-hour working day in the provinces. After the worker uprising had been put down, the bourgeoisie revoked these "concessions" and lengthened the working day. Laws issued in 1874 and the following years prohibiting the labor of children under the age of twelve, and shortening to some extent the working period of adults, were constantly violated by the entrepreneurs. The manner of their transmutation into life is evidenced by the speech of the "socialist" minister Millerand: he declared that "execution of the law is unthinkable."

With the growth of proletarian resistance and the sharpening of the class struggle at the end of the nineteenth and beginning of the twentieth centuries, the bourgeoisie of all countries was constrained to make a number of further concessions in this matter. The shortening of the working day, painfully won by the workers in a tireless struggle, did not put an end to the exploitation or save them from unemployment, beggary, and hunger, or satisfy the most essential physical needs, or protect their health from barbarous exploitation by the manufacturers.

In Russia, where capitalism developed much later, laws to safeguard child labor were issued in 1882, after the series of big strikes in the 1870's and 1880's. To regulate the effectuation of the statute, there were for all of Russia twenty (!) inspectors who "observed"—in the interests of the manufacturers of course. Right down to 1897 there was no general limit on the working day; only the strike of 1896 compelled the government to issue (in 1897) a law limiting the working day to eleven and one-half hours.[40] This law, however, was essentially nullified by a circular of the Minister of Finance permitting the application of overtime work without limit, although, as a result of hundreds of strikes between 1897 and 1905, the mean length of the working day already amounted in fact to ten and one-half hours. During the Revolution of 1905–1907 a certain shortening of the working day was attained in many branches of the national economy. The fruits of these victories were lost during the onset of reaction from 1908 to 1912. In 1913 the mean length of the working day was ten hours—nine and two-thirds for women and juveniles; only 8½ per cent of all the workers enjoyed an eight-hour working day whereas 15½ per cent of them worked from eleven to twelve hours. During the imperialist war, the position of the workers grew very much worse.

The history of the struggle for the eight-hour day, the history of the issuance and violation of the relevant legislative acts under capitalism, shows how right Lenin was when he wrote:

[40] Cf. *A History of the All-Union Communist Party (of Bolsheviks): A Short Course* (1938), p. 19.

It has always seemed that, several years after the issuance of some "solicitous" —some would-be solicitous—law concerning the workers, the matter again reverted to its former position; the number of dissatisfied workers has become larger, the ferment has increased, and the agitations have become more intense, and again a "solicitous" policy is put forward with clamor and hullabaloo. There are resounding and showy phrases about heartfelt concern for the workers, and some new law is issued containing a pennyworth of benefit for the workers and a pound's worth of empty and lying words, and then after some years the old story is repeated.[41]

This characterization of the legislation of tsarist Russia is entirely applicable to the so-called labor law of all the bourgeois-democratic countries.

After the February Revolution in Russia, the eight-hour day, under pressure of the revolutionary masses, was introduced, but only in Petrograd, Moscow, and a number of localities where the workers were more strongly organized and powerful. This situation continued to exist down to the October Revolution itself since, during the eight months of the existence of the Provisional Government, the Menshevik Ministers of Labor, to gratify the capitalists, put the brakes on the issuance of the appropriate law.

The political and socialist dominance which it had won in the great October Socialist Revolution enabled the worker class *"itself to defend its labor."* [42] Organized into a state, the worker class itself defines the length of the working time and the regime of its labor. In the very first days of the revolution, Soviet authority established the shorter working day; by the decree of October 29/November 11, 1917 [43] the eight-hour work day was introduced; and for persons engaged in office work and intellectual labor, six hours. The decree concerning leaves of absence was issued in November, 1917.

Over a period of ten years, as a result of the resuscitation of industry and of increased labor productivity, a seven-hour day has been established, without lowering wages, for persons employed in factories and works. A working day of six, four, or even three hours has been ordained for those employed in heavy or dangerous work. For juveniles, who are not, as a rule, allowed to work under the age of sixteen, a shortened working day is established, and they are forbidden to engage in injurious production work. Overtime is strictly limited. Marx's prophetic words are realized: "The very working time—being limited to a normal span and existing in my own behalf and not in behalf of another, and because social contracts between masters and slaves, and so forth, have been abolished—as genuine social labor, and,

[41] Lenin (Russian ed.), Vol. IV, p. 159.
[42] Marx and Engels (Russian ed.), Vol. VIII, p. 100.
[43] Cy. 1917, No. 1, Art. 10.

finally, as the basis of free time, acquires a completely different, a freer, character." [44] The putting into practice of authentic labor legislation has resulted in preserving the health of the citizens, of the workers in all branches of national economy, and is assuring their rest and a higher level of culture. In addition to rest after the end of the day's work, there must be a recess, during the work period, of from half an hour to two hours, during which the toiler not only eats but can also read the newspaper and take part in conversations organized by Party and social organizations. The vast majority of enterprises work a six-day week, and when production operations are continuous a five-day work week has been introduced. Under the six-day work week, the toilers have sixty days' rest, and under the five-day work week, seventy-two days' rest, during the year, not counting revolutionary holidays. Furthermore, each worker and person in service is given yearly leave, with pay, consisting of not less than twelve work days, and for juveniles, or persons working in injurious conditions, twenty-four days. Individual categories of toilers (for example, teachers and scientific workers) have leave for a month and a half or even two months. Including the days of rest, each worker has about eighty free days during the year.

The Soviet state not only grants, it also guarantees, the worker's enjoyment of days of rest and leave so that he may restore his strength and develop his physical and intellectual capacities. To this end a number of rest houses, sanatoria, clubs, tourist sites and parks have been built and organized, and the radio network is constantly being extended. As early as the civil-war period, the first houses of rest and sanatoria were organized in palaces and in private residences taken from exploiters. After the defeat of Wrangel, Lenin (in December, 1920) signed a decree, Concerning the Use of the Crimea for Treating the Toilers. In May, 1921, the Council of People's Commissars issued a decree, over the signature of Lenin, Concerning the Broad Organization of Rest Houses for the Toilers.

The state social-insurance budget reveals capital expenditures for houses of rest, sanatoria, and health resorts prior to the first five-year period amounting to 27.3 million rubles. During the first five-year period such expenditures amounted to 175.5 million rubles, and during the second five-year period to 556.3 million rubles. Trade union organizations spent 475 million rubles in 1935 on rest houses, sanatoria, and tourist purposes, and 671 million rubles in 1936, and allocated 1,060 million rubles for these purposes in 1938. From 1933 to 1937 social insurance alone paid for more than 8.5 million persons sent for rest to rest houses and sanatoria. Of exceptional significance for cultural and healthful rest is the broad development of physical culture and tourist activity. The budget of social insurance shows

[44] Marx, A Theory of Surplus Value (Russian ed., 1932), Vol. III, p. 199.

the disbursement by trade unions for tourist and excursion work of 3.25 million rubles in 1935, 14.2 million in 1936, and 38.6 million in 1937; 50 million have been allocated for 1938.

For cultural advancement during rest periods, the toilers enjoy a constantly increasing network of theaters and motion-picture houses. In 1914 Russian had only 153 theaters and 1,412 motion-picture houses. In 1936 the USSR had 770 theaters and circuses and 29,758 motion-picture houses. In 1935 there were 147 collective farm theaters; in 1937, 207. In 1933 there were 42 children's theaters; in 1936, 104. At the beginning of 1937, 74 radio stations and approximately 8,000 radio hookups were functioning. To serve the toilers, 81,000 palaces of culture and worker and collective farm clubs were created and approximately 250 municipal and village parks of culture and rest had been opened down to 1937. The number of museums increased from 180 in 1914 to 757 in 1936.

The material guarantees of the right to rest created a mighty basis for the improvement of sanitary conditions for the benefit of the entire population and for the bringing of national talents to the light and to fruition. The right to rest is a complete assurance of the right to healthy and creative toil.

c) The Right to Material Security in Old Age and in Case of Illness or Loss of Working Capacity

The USSR is the only country in the world in which all workers and persons in service are covered by social insurance at state expense. In the USSR social insurance is designed to elevate and strengthen the material and cultural level of workers, persons in service, and the members of their families, and to improve and rebuild their way of life upon socialist principles.

From the second half of the nineteenth century on, workers in capitalist countries, in periods of strikes and demonstrations, put forward in an important way demands for state insurance. In numerous countries (including some of the states of the United States, England, France, Austria, Belgium and Norway) group-insurance legislation was achieved after a savage class struggle. In Germany, after the failure of the so-called law regarding socialists, invalidism and old-age insurance was introduced in 1891 to distract the masses from revolutionary struggle and to create illusions of reform.

The 1905 Revolution in Russia stimulated the bourgeoisie of certain European countries to satisfy the partial demands of the workers: in France partial insurance for illness and old age was introduced; in England insurance against accidents, illness, and unemployment; in Austria, for invalidism and old age, and for the benefit of widows and orphans; and in

Norway in case of disease and maternity and so on. But only a negligible proportion of workers was covered by these species of insurance. In Russia, in the period of the 1905–1907 Revolution, the struggle to introduce the social insurance of workers played an important part as one of the most essential of the partial demands of the proletariat. Not until the Third Duma were laws—which had been in course of preparation by the tsarist government over a period of several years—presented for legislative action; they were issued in June, 1912, in the form of two mandatory statutes requiring the insurance of workers in case of personal injury and in case of disease. As to insurance covering loss of wages by reason of old age or invalidism, or for the benefit of widows or children, or in case of unemployment, the statutes had not a syllable. Moreover, the statutes extended only to one-sixth of the persons engaged in working for hire. The tsarist government thought by the shabby gift of such paltry statutes to halt the growing revolutionary movement.

While these statutes were in preparation, Lenin wrote a program of state social insurance of workers which was adopted by the Conference of Bolsheviks in Prague, 1912. Therein he wrote that state insurance must guarantee the worker in all cases of loss of working capacity (personal injury, disease, old age, invalidism, pregnancy and childbirth) as well as in case of unemployment. Insurance must embrace all persons engaged in working for hire, and their families, providing for their widows and orphans. All disbursements for social insurance must be borne by the employer and the state. Such complete social insurance, responsive to the needs of workers, there neither is nor can be in any capitalist country whatever. That is understandable. "The capitalist cannot divert his income to elevation of the well-being of the worker class. He lives for gain. Otherwise he would not be a capitalist." [45]

After the February Revolution the bourgeoisie, together with the Menshevik ministers, failed to satisfy the demands of the workers for promotion of the social insurance of workers through legislation. Lenin's program of social insurance was carried into effect by the victory of the October Revolution. In the very first days after the victory, November 1/14, 1917, the Soviet government issued a communication over the signature of Lenin to the effect that it was losing no time in setting about the issuance of decrees for complete social insurance on the basis of worker-insurance watchwords. The decree of November 16/29, 1917,[46] handed over to the state the factory hospital funds and all the medical foundations and enterprises thereto-

[45] Stalin, *Questions of Leninism* (10th Russian ed.), p. 185.
[46] Cy. 1917, No. 3, Art. 34.

fore under the jurisdiction of industrialists. On December 11/24 [47] a decree was published concerning insurance in case of unemployment. Eleven days later [48] insurance in case of sickness was introduced. For the first time in the world, social insurance embraced all whose source of income was wages, freeing the toilers from fees of every sort. Complete self-government of the insured was advanced with the wide participation of the trade unions. In all the land the broad work of putting these decrees into practice was expanded.

The great October Socialist Revolution in Russia compelled the bourgeoisie of foreign countries, under pressure of their workers, to make a series of concessions along the line of social insurance against unemployment (Germany, Austria, Italy, and Poland).

At the present time, data of the International Labor Office in the League of Nations reveal that, of 77 capitalist countries, only 22 have social insurance against disease, 22 against invalidism and old age, and 20 against accidents. Only 8 have unemployment insurance. Only in 1935 did the U.S.A. adopt a mandatory old-age security law, by virtue of which pensions will be paid only as from 1942.

Insurance laws in capitalist countries comprise so many limitations that they nowhere embrace all those who work for hire. Bourgeois professors work out in all its variations the so-called "limit theory" of state social insurance, invoked to justify these limitations.

In bourgeois states the basic fee for insurance comes from the insured themselves. Under the conditions of capitalism, therefore, social insurance is a form of cutting wages. During the world crisis—that is to say, in the very period when the workers most needed aid—their position further deteriorated. In fascist Germany workers pay two-thirds and employers pay only one-third of the insurance fees for insurance in case of illness. In Poland the workers pay three-fifths and the employers two-fifths.

Aid to the insured is extremely meager, always less than the full wage. To obtain a pension for invalidism and old age requires a sizable insurance record: in France and England the payment of insurance fees over a two-year period is essential; in fascist Germany, payments over a period of 250 weeks (almost five years) in case of invalidism and 750 weeks (about fifteen years) in case of an old-age pension. The fascists liquidated the elective factory hospital funds; all these resources passed into the hands of the employers and the fascist bureaucrats.

The history of social insurance shows that only under socialism is radical improvement in the workers' position possible. This is confirmed by the

[47] Cy. 1917, No. 8, Art. 111.   [48] Cy. 1918, No. 13, Art. 188.

development of true social insurance in the USSR from the very earliest days of Soviet authority. During the war communism, social insurance was replaced by social security, which embraced all the toilers of city and country and the members of their families. The decree of October 31, 1918,[49] was extended to all cases of inability to work and unemployment by reason of having lost the means of existence. Social security was developed at the expense of the state. The People's Commissariat for Social Insurance was charged with sole direction of its being put into practice.

With the introduction of the New Economic Policy, social insurance was reestablished by a decree issued November 15, 1921.[50] In the USSR, insurance fees are paid by institutions and enterprises, and the workers and those in service are free of them.

The development of socialist building and the successful fulfillment of the first five-year plan evoked essential changes in the structure of the social insurance budget. Pensions and aids made up a considerable item in this budget. Right down to 1930, large sums were spent on social insurance in the form of unemployment payments. Since 1930 unemployment in the USSR has entirely ceased and this item has accordingly disappeared.

For the four years of the first five-year plan, disbursements for social insurance exceeded 10 billion rubles, and for the four years of the second five-year plan, increased to 26.5 billion rubles. The income side of the budget of state social insurance in 1938 was affirmed by the government in the figure of 6,323 million rubles.

The transfer (in 1933) to the trade unions of the whole matter of social insurance, as included in the functions of the People's Commissariat for Labor, which have been abolished, is the best expression of socialist democracy of the Soviet social order and brilliantly demonstrates the part played by the trade unions in the system of the worker-class dictatorship. Harmonizing their activity completely with socialist building, the organs of social insurance devote special attention to raising the level of life of the basic worker bodies occupied in the leading branches of our economy (metals, coal, basic chemistry, transportation, machine building). The system of paying aids during temporary working incapacity and pensions in cases of invalidism contemplates many privileges for Stakhanovites, shock workers, engineering technicians, and workers of the leading branches of economy. For these categories of insured persons, higher standards of aids and pensions are established and the formal requirements are eased, giving the right to one or other type and amount of security payment (seniority and so forth).

[49] Cy. 1918, No. 89, Art. 906.
[50] Cy. 1921, No. 76, Art. 627.

The socialist state affords all toilers the right to material security in case of illness, to free medical aid, and to qualified treatment, including treatment at a health resort. Relief for temporary loss of working capacity is paid to all insured persons from the first day of illness. Members of the trade union with a three-year record, including not less than two years of continuous labor in the given enterprise, receive on the basis of their full wages from the very first day of illness.

As regards aids for temporary disability, all persons in service and non-industrial workers have, since August 1, 1937, been on the same footing as employees of industrial enterprises.[51] Stakhanovites and shock workers obtain relief from the very first day of illness on the basis of their full wages under a general production record of not less than a year, irrespective of the length of work in the given enterprise and the record of their shock work.

State social insurance guarantees the insured pensions in case of invalidism from common maladies as well as when it is due to industrial disablement or occupational disease. Insurance legislation concerning invalidism has established higher rates of pensions for labor invalidism in the case of workers in the leading branches of the national economy, with an increase for seniority, and so on. Besides giving relief in the form of money, the state takes all steps to enable one who retains some remnant of his working capacity to be engaged in labor according to his strength. The cooperation of individuals, furnishing to the country production amounting to 692 million rubles in 1935, attained broad development. From 1920 to 1936, more than one million invalids were rehabilitated in the RSFSR, approximately 140,000 in 1936. In 1936 the state paid out 28 million rubles for retraining individuals. As to the pension rate for invalidism, those now in service are (since August 1, 1937) on the same footing as workers.[52]

Aside from pensions for invalidism, the USSR has established as well old-age pensions for certain categories of workers—pensions after having worked a certain number of years, personal pensions, academic pensions, and pensions to surviving members of families of insured persons. Old-age insurance is extended to all workers and, since August 1, 1937, to all in service who have ceased to work after this date or who continue to work.[53]

The state's provision for invalids of the civil war and also of the imperialist war and for invalids of military service has been established. Members of the families of these persons are also provided for. In January, 1937,

[51] Cz. 1937, No. 49, Art. 204.
[52] Cz. 1937, No. 49, Art. 203.
[53] Ibid.

a law was issued for increasing the pension of invalids of the civil war and of military service within the ranks of the Worker-Peasant Red Army, former Red Guards, and Red Partisans and also of members of their families.[54]

Women are objects of special concern and protection on the part of the state. Possessing rights equal in every respect to the rights of men, a woman has the same rights to social insurance as does a man. Provision is also made for her during pregnancy and maternity.

The Stalin Agricultural Artel has afforded broad possibilities of improving the work and way of life of millions of kolkhoz members. On the basis of this decree, funds are created in the kolkhozes by the decision of a general assembly to aid invalids, the aged, those who have temporarily lost their working capacity, and needy families of Red Army men, and to support crèches for children and orphans—all this by deductions amounting to 2 per cent of the gross output of the kolkhozes. Mutual benefit clubs of members are invoked to carry on the work of affording material aid to the needy members thereof. According to Point 14 of the Stalin Agricultural Artel law, kolkhozes are obligated to devote special attention to kolkhoz mothers.

The Stalin Constitution guarantees the unbroken development and improvement of Soviet social insurance. The organs possessing immediate jurisdiction over insurance are: the All-Union Central Council of Trade Unions (the social insurance of workers and persons in service), the People's Commissarait for Social Insurance (kolkhoz mutual benefit clubs and the insurance of invalids), and the People's Commissariat for Health (assuring medical aid for the toilers).

New forms of attracting to the immediate administration of social insurance broad masses of workers and persons in service have emerged. The elective organs carrying on all the practical work of social insurance in a given enterprise or institution are the insurance councils organized under factory works and local trade union committees which, during the brief time of their existence, have justified their role in attracting the broadest masses of the toilers to the administration of this most important state concern.

d) The Right to Education

The right to education means the genuine, state-guaranteed possibility for every citizen to raise the general level of his culture and also to obtain special knowledge through study in educational institutions from the lowest to the highest.

[54] Cz. 1937, No. 9, Art. 30.

The right of citizens to an education is unthinkable in the conditions obtaining in a bourgeois state,[55] where education is the privilege of the narrow minority. The utmost that bourgeois states can accomplish is universal elementary education, which has at the present time been introduced by almost all the European states, by the largest states of the U.S.A, and by Australia and Japan. Such universal compulsory education is often a fiction, however. Thus, for example, it was proclaimed in Poland as early as the 1921 Constitution and was not in form abrogated even by the new fascist Constitution of 1935. Free education was abolished, since actually the incredible spread of beggary among the toiling masses of Poland decided the fate of this "universal" instruction. In reality, as is evident from information contained in the Polish press itself (including even government organs), not only is the percentage of illiteracy not diminishing, it is increasing in Poland. Mass illiteracy is shown to be as high as 60 to 70 per cent among the adult population in a number of localities.

And even in those countries where universal elementary education is not a fiction, it is in fact a limit which the broad masses can overstep only in rare cases and under a favorable concurrence of circumstances. In England only 1.4 per cent of the children finishing the elementary schools receive further professional instruction thereafter. In Germany, for example, prior to the coming of the fascists, the children of workers in higher educational institutions amounted only to 2.9 per cent, and the children of small peasants to 2.2 per cent, of the total number of students. "The higher school in bourgeois countries is not only inaccessible to the toilers, in many cases it has even suffered a decline in comparison with former years." [56]

Mass unemployment in all the capitalist countries has led to the result that even one holding a diploma in higher education cannot find work; unemployed persons having a diploma from a higher educational institution are a common phenomenon in bourgeois countries.

Especially grievous is the position of the students, teachers, and scholars in lands of fascist dictatorship where freedom of instruction, like all the other fundamental civil rights formerly noted in constitutions, is abolished. Ignorance is the instrument of fascism. In fascist Germany the schools, from the lowest to the highest, have been turned into unified barracks, the teacher into a sergeant major, and the students into soldiers. According to the official declaration of one of the eminent "fascist "leaders," Hans Schemm, the entire fascist program of education reduces to four ideas: "Race, arms, Führer and religion. . . . The basic thing is the inculcation

[55] Not even in form do bourgeois states proclaim the right to education. In those bourgeois constitutions which speak of education in general, the reference is chiefly to freedom to teach, not of the right to an education.

[56] Molotov, "The Higher School," *Bolshevik* (1938), No. 10–11, p. 5.

of race consciousness." Fascist legislation on matters of education brilliantly reflects fascism's veritable campaign against culture and enlightenment. One of the first laws enacted when the National "Socialists" came to power in Germany was that concerning institutions of higher education, sharply diminishing the number of pupils in them, and establishing percentage standards for the acquisition by women of certificates of maturity (not more than 10 per cent of the number of men obtaining such certificates) and rules of admission for "non-Aryans" (1.5 per cent). In fact, Jews were denied entrance to higher educational institutions even within the limits of this rule.

It is not surprising that after three years, from 1932–1933 to 1935–1936, the number of students in Germany was reduced to one-half; and in 1938 the largest German universities could admit only one-third of the number of students admitted in 1932.

Only in the USSR have the toiling masses gained free access to education, including higher education.

The proletariat, having taken authority into its hands, had to deal with a burdensome legacy from tsarism, the monstrous percentage of popular illiteracy amounting to approximately 70 per cent. The official governmental *Russian Yearbook for 1910* reveals that in 1908 there were fewer than 46.7 students to a thousand inhabitants. Approximately four-fifths of the children and juveniles in tsarist Russia remained outside the walls even of primary schools. "No other country so savage, wherein the masses of the people were so *plundered* in the sense of education, enlightenment and knowledge, is to be found in all Europe," wrote Lenin in 1913. "And this savagery of the national masses, particularly of the peasants, was not fortuitous. It was *inevitable* under the pressure of the landowners who had seized tens and tens of millions of acres of land as well as state power both in the Duma and in the State Council—and not alone in these institutions which are relatively still the *lower* institutions." [57]

Enormous work was devoted to cementing a union between the masses and knowledge and culture from the very earliest days of the victory of the October Socialist Revolution. An official document in the form of an address to the people (October 29, 1917) by the People's Commissar for Education enumerated the tasks which Soviet authority set itself in the field of education: [58] (1) to secure within the shortest time universal popular literacy through organizing a network of properly placed schools and introducing universal compulsory instruction, (2) to create a single secular school for all citizens, and (3) to organize schools for adults. These were

[57] Lenin (Russian ed.), Vol. XVI, p. 410.
[58] *Gazette of the Worker-Peasant Provisional Government* (1917), No. 3

the most important tasks which Soviet authority set itself from the very first days of October. One of the first measures for their realization was the decree concerning the separation of the church from the state and of the school from the church,[59] whereby the school became purely secular. Article 9 stated: "The school is separated from the church. The teaching of religious doctrines in all state and social and private institutions of learning where matters of general instruction are taught is not permitted."

The RSFSR Constitution of 1918 ordained (Art. 17): "To the end of insuring genuine access to knowledge in behalf of the toilers, the RSFSR sets itself the task of furnishing workers and the poorest peasants, without cost to them, an education complete and comprehensive." Thereby the fundamental law of the land strongly reinforced the general direction of the Soviet state policy in the sphere of education. The doors of educational institutions, including the highest, were opened wide to the worker-peasant youth. But many conditions precedent to the utilization of such free access were lacking. Entrance into the higher educational institutions required preparation of the scope of that in an intermediate school, which, prior to the revolution, was inaccessible to the masses of worker-peasant youth. Furthermore, the civil war had naturally drawn off a vast number of youth from their studies. Accordingly, during the years immediately following the revolution, the higher educational institutions continued to have a low percentage of workers and peasants. The ending of the civil war resulted in a mass influx of workers and peasants within the walls of educational institutions.

As early as September 17, 1920, a decree was issued over the signature of Lenin concerning worker faculties (worker higher schools), intended to make it possible for the worker-peasant masses to realize broadly the right of free access to higher educational institutions noted in their behalf in the Constitution. "The fundamental task of the worker faculties is to achieve a broad attraction of the proletarian and peasant masses within the walls of the higher school" (Art. 1).[60] Article 3 pointed out that the worker faculties receive workers and peasants (from the age of sixteen) delegated by production unions, factory committees, party work sections in the rural districts, and executive committees of volosts, districts, and guberniyas, and even persons recommended by People's Commissariats or their local organs or any of the enumerated higher organs. The creation of the worker faculties played a great part in renewing the student body in the higher schools, in creating its intellectuals.

Since 1920 the work—begun as early as October, 1917—of abolishing

[59] Cy. 1917, No. 18, Art. 263.
[60] Cy. 1920, No. 80, Art. 381.

illiteracy among the adult population has developed on a broad scale. A decree (of July 19, 1920) of the Council of the RSFSR People's Commissars over the signature of Lenin (to effectuate an earlier decree [61] of December 26, 1919, for abolishing illiteracy) created a new organ: The All-Russian Extraordinary Commission to Abolish Illiteracy.[62] Only the complete ending of the civil war and the rehabilitation of the national economy made it possible, however, to set directly about the realization of all the tasks above noted in the sphere of popular education and to achieve decisive successes.

In this regard 1930 was a notable year, being the year when universal compulsory instruction was introduced. The initiative in this vast work was supplied by Stalin. After pointing out what had been achieved in raising the cultural level of workers and peasants, the enormous numbers of children and youth in schools, technical institutions, and institutes of higher education, and the achievement of 62.6 per cent literacy in the USSR, he declared:

The important thing now is to pass to compulsory primary instruction. I say "important" because such a transition would signify a decisive step in the cultural revolution. The time to pay attention to this matter is long past; in the overwhelming majority of districts of the USSR we now have everything necessary for the organization of universal primary education. Hitherto we have been constrained to "economize in everything—even schools" so as to "save—to reestablish —heavy industry" [Lenin]. Recently, however, we have completed the reestablishment of that industry, and are developing it still further. Consequently the time has come when we must set our hands to the organization of universal compulsory primary education.[63]

The law of the Central Executive Committee and the Council of People's Commissars of the USSR (August 14, 1930),[64] issued in accordance with the decision of the Sixteenth Congress of the All-Union Communist Party (of Bolsheviks), introduced throughout the USSR, as from the 1930–1931 school year, universal compulsory instruction for children to the extent of not less than a four-year primary school course, a six-year course in industrial cities, works and factory areas and worker settlements.

The reorganization of higher educational institutions and higher technical schools, developed in 1928–1929 upon the initiative of Stalin, resulted in a notable increase in the network of such institutions and in the number of their students, a renewed enrollment therein from children of workers, and general improvement in the formulation of their teaching.

[61] Cy. 1919, No. 67, Art. 592.
[62] Cy. 1920, No. 69, Art. 312.
[63] Stalin, *Questions of Leninism* (10th Russian ed.), p. 384.
[64] Cz. 1930, No. 39, Art. 420.

The logical realization by the Party and by the Soviet government of the task, proclaimed as long ago as the first Soviet Constitution (that of the RSFSR, in 1918), of giving workers and the poorest peasants complete and comprehensive education without cost to them, resulted in the attainment by the USSR in 1932 of first place in the world as regards the number of students. The total number of students in the USSR in the 1936–1937 school year exceeded 38 millions, and was 4.7 times the 1914 figures.

Higher education has expanded enormously in the USSR. The end of the twenty-year period of Soviet authority in the land saw 700 higher educational institutions already created, in which approximately 550,000 children of workers, peasants, and Soviet intellectuals were taught without charge. The overwhelming majority of Soviet students—around 90 per cent, and in a number of the higher educational institutions 100 per cent—are assured of a state stipend. Tsarist Russia possessed a total of 91 higher educational institutions, where education was attained only by the children of the bourgeoisie, the landowners, the bureaucrats, the clergy, and the kulaks. In the range of its higher education, especially of its technical and agricultural education, the USSR occupies first place in the world. Each year up to 100,000 specialists leave the halls of our higher schools. "The worker class, the peasantry, and the intellectuals of the Soviet Union may be proud that our higher school stands on a lofty plane of development, that the worker-peasant state manifests a concern for this matter above and beyond what the honored bourgeois states are up to." [65]

During the last four years alone the budget for the higher educational institutions of the USSR has grown 2.2 times—from 986 million rubles in 1934 to 2,195 million rubles in 1938. Salaries of workers in the higher schools for these years increased from 229 to 675 million rubles; the scholarship fund for students of the higher institutions from 388 to 801 million rubles; and school expenses from 115 to 228 million rubles.

The USSR has given wide effect to the system of acquiring general and special education without breaking off production. A network of schools for general adult education has been created. There workers and members of the kolkhozes obtain intermediate education without an interruption of production. Technical studies of workers, broadly expanded in connection with the Stakhanovite movement, on the basis of the directive of December, 1935, plenum of the Central Party Committee, have been pursued by millions of people. A single, integral system of forms of instruction without interruption of production has been created in the

[65] Molotov, "The Higher School," *Bolshevik* (1938), Nos. 10–11, p. 4.

rural districts.[66] In city and rural districts alike, free technical and agricultural instruction includes a series of links from elementary technique up to and including the preparation of qualified organizers and specialists.

Education, including the highest education, is accessible for all citizens in the USSR.[67] In noting (in Art. 121) the right of USSR citizens to education—"citizens of the USSR have the right to education"—the great Stalin Constitution reflected a right already achieved and won. This right is assured by universal compulsory primary education, by the fact that education, including higher education, is free; by the system of state scholarships to the overwhelming majority of students in the higher schools; by teaching in schools in the native language of the district; and by the organization of free production technical and agricultural training of the toilers in factories, sovkhozes, machine and tractor service stations and kolkhozes.

In the same fashion the right to education has been formulated, as among the fundamental rights of USSR citizens, in the constitutions of all the Soviet Union and autonomous republics.

e) The Equality of the Rights of Men and Women

The question of the complete equality of rights of women and men is essentially the broad question of the equality of civil rights and freedom in general considered in a concrete setting. This is clearly so, inasmuch as a society wherein woman is without rights cannot be free. The degree of woman's emancipation in any given society is the natural measure of the general emancipation therein.[68]

To say that women have no rights, or to set bounds to their rights, is to exclude more than half the population from the number of citizens with equal rights; in other words it is to turn civil rights into the privileges of men alone.[69] The juridical inequality of women, the actual enslavement of female personality, is a general law of the exploiter states. The bourgeois

[66] Compare directive of the RSFSR Council of People's Commissars (Cy. 1932, No. 87, Art. 389).

[67] As early as 1936, in connection with the liquidation of exploiter classes in the land, a statute was issued abrogating the rules theretofore regulating admission into higher educational and technical institutions and not permitting the entrance therein of the children of nonlabor elements (Cz. 1936, No. 1, Art. 2).

[68] Compare Marx and Engels (Russian ed.), Vol. III, p. 229, where this thought of the great socialist utopian, Charles Fourier, is developed.

[69] Woman without rights, or with limited rights, is in form, as well as in essence, no citizen. The eminent French reactionary political scientist Hauriou admits this. He wrote in The Fundamentals of Public Law: "The enjoyment of political rights is a sign of citizenship . . . A citizen is a subject of the male sex, a Frenchman by origin, or by virtue of the law of nationailty or of naturalization. This excludes foreigners, French women, and French subjects who are not French by nationality and have not been naturalized (the aborigines of certain colonies and of Algiers)." Cf. pp. 486–487; italics supplied.

revolution and the bourgeoisie's access to power merely resulted in a change in the definitive juridical forms of this inequality of rights, leaving the law itself without change. In this sphere the progress achieved by capitalist means of production as against feudal means of production consisted in drawing broad strata of women out of conditions of isolation within the four walls of the domestic economy into industry and trade, and thereby creating the basis for the struggle of women for equal rights with men.

As early as the period of the French Revolution of 1789, a movement emerged among the women taking an active part in political events for making them equal with men in respect of rights. In 1789 two petitions, setting forth a series of demands, were presented to the king. Quickly upon the acceptance of the Declaration of Rights of Man and Citizen, which contained not a word about women, a Declaration of the Rights of Women [70] was formulated by a famous woman active in the feminist movement of the time, Olympe de Gouges. Its chief demands were that women be given active and passive suffrage and admitted to all offices. "Woman has the right to ascend upon the scaffold," exclaimed Olympe de Gouges, meaning that woman has the right to ascend upon the orator's tribune.

Notwithstanding the broad sweep of the feminist movement of the time, the leaders of the French bourgeois revolution, expressing the general bourgeois attitude toward the equality of women in respect of rights, not only did not grant women the rights they demanded but, in course of time, closed all the women's clubs that had then come into being. The reactionary epoch which rapidly set in long stifled the feminist movement in France, and it developed anew and broadly only after the 1848 Revolution. From the very time of its emergence, the feminist movement disintegrated into bourgeois and proletarian currents. While the former set the struggle for suffrage as its only task, the "female worker movement puts as its chief task the struggle for economic and social, and not merely the formal, equality of women."

The entire history of the feminist movement shows clearly that all the partial successes attained in one bourgeois-democratic country after another through giving women the suffrage, admitting them to some professions, and the like, became possible only as a result of the broad revolutionary movement of the proletariat. International experience of the struggle for the equality of women with men in respect of their rights completely confirmed

[70] Cf. text of this Declaration in *Famous Women of the Revolution*, by Lairtullier (Paris, 1840), Vol. II, pp. 137 ff. This is an incomplete translation into Russian: Lili Braun, *The Woman Question* (1903), p. 73.

the Marxist-Leninist proposition that such complete equality, the actual emancipation of women, can occur only upon condition that the socialist revolution is successful.

Hitherto, however, women have not been made equal with men in respect of their rights in a single capitalist state—not even in the most democratic. Constitutions of most of the states are true to the tradition established as far back as the Declaration of Rights in the U. S. A. and in France at the end of the eighteenth century; they have not a single word to say about women, indicating thereby that the civil rights they grant are destined exclusively for men.[71]

At the present time only twenty-two states of eighty-four states and great colonies enjoying self-government grant women equal suffrage with men; and in seven of these such right is given only to isolated and narrow categories of women and on conditions other than those obtaining as to men.[72] And even in states where women, or a small part of them, are given suffrage, they are limited in their civil rights: property rights, domestic rights, and so on. Even in the oldest countries of bourgeois democracy, like England and the U. S. A.—to say nothing of France—the legal position of women is sharply distinguished from that of men.

In England, for example, it was only in 1928 [73] that women were granted elective rights to vote on an equality with men, and even now women are under legal limitations as regards a whole series of civil rights. Particularly great are the limitations on the right of a married woman—specifically termed "feme covert" in English civil law [74]—since her personality is in the eyes of the law submerged in that of her husband. If a woman in England leaves her husband for another man, the law gives the husband the right to institute action for abduction.[75]

Women in England have no right to occupy diplomatic or consular positions, or to sit in the House of Lords, or to work in a long line of pro-

[71] For a selection of materials, cf. Grinberg, La femme et les constitutions nouvelles (1935).

[72] This computation was made on the basis of data cited in the Journal Beyond the Frontier (1937). Moreover, we must not lose sight of the fact that the formal grant of suffrage in bourgeois states is remote indeed from signifying that women utilize it. A brilliant example is the Philippines; there, in form, women have suffrage, but they have not yet taken part in elections on a single occasion.

[73] An act of parliament of 1918, and the so-called Sex Disqualification Act (1919), granted women in England the right to vote, but on conditions not equal with men. One may speak of equality in the elective rights of women and men in England only since the enactment of the Equal Franchise Act of 1928.

[74] Cf. Arthur Curti, Englands Privat-und Handelsrecht (1927), p. 20.

[75] "The husband's injuries" are said by Blackstone "to be principally three: abduction . . . adultery or criminal conversation . . . and beating or otherwise abusing her." Biga-ouette vs. Paulet, 134 Mass., 123.—Tr.

fessions.[76] A common phenomenon in England as in all the capitalist countries is the inequality of women's wages as compared with men's. For the same work as men, women get 20 per cent—and in many fields of labor even 50 per cent—less than men with the same qualifications. Unemployed women get relief on a smaller scale than men, while their living expenses are not taken into account at all. The woman worker or servant in England is so oppressed in fact that she cannot exercise the right of joining a union, which is in form granted to her equally with men. Out of 4,567,000 trade unionists by the end of 1934, only 736,000 were women. Of the entire army of women laborers, 90 per cent are outside the trade unions.[77]

Women acquired the right of suffrage in the U. S. A. in 1920. Up to the present time the legislation of all the states includes around 1,000 statutes which in greater or less degree restrict the rights of women in the most diverse fields. In twenty-seven states they cannot be judges. In all states woman is bound by law to live where her husband demands. There are calculated to be some sixty species of legal inequality confirmed by legislation in the U. S. A.[78]

Women still have no right to vote in France and are placed in a position of dependence upon their husbands, parents, or brothers in the sphere of property, family, and other rights. Without her husband's permission a married woman has no right to enter either service or an institution of learning in France.[79]

The foregoing limitations on the rights of women are, of course, characteristic not only of the countries indicated but also of bourgeois-democratic countries in general.[80]

If such is the position of women in bourgeois-democratic countries, however, their position in fascist countries which have destroyed all the remains of bourgeois democracy in general, and all the conquests of the feminist movement in particular, is no longer to be described by the term "limitation of rights," but must be defined as the formal and factual absence of right, as a return to the Middle Ages. Women in Germany have been driven out of the Reichstag and out of civil self-governments, and are

[76] See *Encyclopaedia Britannica* under the article "Women." In particular it reproduces a significant part of the text of the Sex Disqualification Act of 1919.

[77] Cf. Jean Beauchamp, *Women Who Work* (London), 1937.

[78] Brief information as to the legal position of woman in the U. S. A. and the history of woman's struggle for suffrage may be found in the article on "Women" in the *Encyclopaedia Americana*.

[79] When the world-famous Madame Curie was invited to enter the government being formed in France after the victory of the popular front in the parliamentary elections of 1936, she was required by French law to obtain her husband's official permission to accept.

[80] Cf. Dame Ethel Smyth, *Toward Equal Rights for Men and Women* (Washington), 1929.

in fact devoid of either passive or active right of franchise. A number of professions are closed to them.[81] For women there is established a special and lowered quota in higher educational institutions, and not a single one of these institutions has the right to increase that quota. Feminine organizations—other than fascist, of course—are dispersed.

In all the other fascist countries as well, where malfeasance holds sway and every right of personality is trodden under foot, woman occupies an analogous position. In the colonies the native woman is completely without rights of any kind, being, in most of them, a slave wherein her husband or father has a property interest (Cameroons, Cyprus, the African possessions of France, Rhodesia, and so forth).

Only in the USSR did the "October Socialist Revolution, which initiated the abolition of every sort of class exploitation—the abolition of classes themselves—initiate at the same time the complete and final emancipation of women as well." [82] The first steps in this field were the abolition of the relevant tsarist laws solicitously preserved by the bourgeois Provisional Government, and the attraction of women to the gigantic work of building the Soviet state on an equality with men. Typical of the results of the first year of Soviet authority was the complete equalization of women with men in respect of their rights. Lenin wrote in 1919:

Not a single democratic party in the world in any of the most advanced bourgeois republics has in decades accomplished in this respect even a one-hundredth part of what we have done in the very first year of our authority. In the strict sense of the word, we have not left one stone upon another of those bad laws relative to the inequality of women, restraints on divorce, the abominable formalities surrounding it, the nonacknowledgment of children born out of wedlock, the searching out of their fathers, and the like, laws whose remnants—to the shame of the bourgeoisie and of capitalism—are numerous in all civilized countries.[83]

Clarification of the entire range of this work, carried on by Soviet authority during the very first year and under general conditions incredibly difficult, requires a knowledge of the legal position of women in prerevolutionary Russia. According to the laws of the former Russian Empire, women were not only without political rights, they were limited as well in all other civil rights. Of course in speaking of the legal position of women in any bourgeois state, it is essential not to lose sight of the difference, which legislation has developed, between the position of the "have" classes in this regard and that of the "have-not" classes. Most completely without

---

[81] For details cf. a publication of the International Labor Office of the League of Nations, the *I. L. O. Yearbook* for 1934–1935, 1935–1936, and 1936–1937.

[82] In the words of the June 27, 1936, directive of the Central Executive Committee and Council of People's Commissars of the USSR (Cz. 1936, No. 34, Art. 309).

[83] Lenin (Russian ed.), Vol. XXIV, p. 343.

rights in tsarist Russia was a woman of the toiling classes. To women of the "have" classes, tsarist legislation granted numerous advantages over women toilers. Thus, for example, after the 1905 Revolution the tsarist government permitted women who possessed the requisite qualification in immovable property, and had the legal right to vote in the election to the Duma, to transfer their votes to husbands or sons.

In the field of domestic relations, the limitation of the rights of women was clearly expressed in Articles 106 to 108 and Article 179 of the Russian Imperial Code, requiring wives to obey their husbands.[84]

Tsarist laws allowed a divorce to be obtained upon petition by one party in strictly limited cases (where a spouse was absent and not heard from, or where a spouse was deprived of status rights, and so on). In all other cases divorce proceedings were extraordinarily complicated and were surrounded by degrading formalities. Moreover, the prohibitive cost made divorce unavailable to toiling women.

If a wife voluntarily left him, the husband had the right to demand her through the police, as if she were a transported convict.[85]

The law preserved the father's superior rights to the children. Children "born out of wedlock" were in a special situation. They had no rights to the name of their father or to inherit from him after his death. Women were forbidden by law to seek out the father of an "illegitimate" child.

Without the husband's consent the wife could not be engaged in industry or trade.[86] Even the right of the daughter or wife to inherit was far smaller than that of the husband.[87]

With rare exceptions (the telegraph and hospital service) women were not admitted to the state service down to the time of the revolution. In 1912 the Duma passed a proposed law admitting women to the bar, but the State Council refused its sanction.

[84] "A wife is bound to obey her husband as the head of the family; to reside with him in love, honor, and unlimited obedience; and to show him, as master of the house, every sort of complaisance and devotion" (Art. 107).

[85] Passport Regulations, Code of Laws, Vol. XIV (1903).

[86] It is altogether typical that, at the same time, in the sphere of effectuating a married woman's property rights, tsarist legislation gave her in form the appearance of independence—out of concern for the capital, of course, and not out of tenderness for the personality of the woman. At all events, this was the basis for Pobedonostsev's characterization of tsarist legislation regarding women (in Vol. II of his *Course of Civil Law*, and after an elaborate comparison with the foreign legislation of his time) as advanced, and the position of Russian women as enviable in the eyes of foreign women. The futility of this attempt to elevate tsarist legislation to the rank of progressive law-making is obvious. All of Pt. I of Vol. X of the Code of Laws (legalizing an individual's loss of legal personality) made this formal independence of the married woman the merest fiction as regards her realization of property rights.

[87] Under the tsarist law of June 3, 1912, the wife, like daughters who had brothers, inherited only a 1/7 share of landed property outside the cities. Of movable property the widow could take by inheritance only a 1/14 share.

The utter absence of legislative protection for the labor of women and for maternity, the legalization of prostitution, the savage laws concerning "illegitimate children," and so on, beat with their full force upon the toiling women.

The February Revolution merely granted women the right of suffrage to the Constituent Assembly, doing nothing to equalize women with men in respect of any other rights. Abrogation of the abominable statutes cited above, and others like them, was due solely to the October Socialist Revolution.

From the very first days of the establishment of Soviet authority, women received election rights to all organs of authority on an equality with men. This complete equality in the election rights possessed by women and men was later confirmed by the first Soviet Constitution, the 1918 Constitution of the RSFSR (Art. 64). Equality of the sexes in the sphere of family relationships was accomplished by the issuance of laws concerning marriage, family, and guardianship and divorce in the very first months after the establishment of Soviet authority (December, 1917).[88]

The first Soviet code, the Code of Laws Concerning Acts of Civil Status, and the Law of Marriage, Family, and Guardianship, was published in October, 1918.[89] It accepted and developed the propositions comprised in the December laws of divorce, marriage, family, and guardianship aforesaid and was, in the full sense of the word, the code of rights of the emancipated woman.

Having guaranteed the juridical equality of both sexes in respect of their rights, Soviet legislation has, from the very first days after the October Revolution, provided for the planned development of an integrated system of measures for the safeguarding of maternity and infancy, for preferential protection of women's toil,[90] for drawing women into socialist production and administration, and for promoting women to skilled work and commanding posts in all the fields of labor and administration.[91]

"Equality by law is still not equality in life." [92] The juridical equality

---

[88] The Decree of the All-Russian Central Executive Committee and Council of People's Commissars (Dec. 19, 1917), Concerning the Dissolution of Marriage (Cy. 1917, No. 10, Art. 152); Decree (of the same organs) Concerning Civil Marriage, Children, and the Keeping of Records of Acts of Status (Dec. 18, 1917; Cy. 1917, No. 11, Art. 160).

[89] Cy. 1918, No. 76–77, Art. 818.

[90] The bourgeois-feminist treatment of sex equality, denying the preferential protection of women as a matter of principle and in whatever province, under the pretext that this is supposed to destroy the equality of the sexes, was always alien to Soviet legislation, which constantly lays down special rules for the particular protection of women in all cases where equal labor conditions are in fact harmful to the female organism or where woman needs greater aid in general.

[91] *Ibid.*

[92] Lenin (Russian ed.), Vol. XXV, p. 40.

of women and men in respect of their rights, introduced by Soviet authority from the very beginning, still did not eliminate the factual inequality of their rights. Lenin spoke of this more than once during the first years of Soviet authority, pointing out that this juridical equality is only the first step in the actual emancipation of women in all spheres.

But the *cleaner* we made the ground by sweeping away the rubbish of the old bourgeois laws and institutions, the more manifest it became that this was only clearing of the ground for a structure and not yet the building itself. In spite of all the liberating laws, woman still remains a *domestic slave*, crushed, stifled, dulled, and debased by *petty domestic economy* which ties her down to kitchen and nursery, stealing her labor by work that is unproductive to the point of savagery, petty, enervating, stupefying, and oppressive.[93]

The true emancipation of women, as Lenin pointed out more than once, is to be found only where women are drawn into productive work, in the mass creation of social dining halls, public crèches, and playgrounds. So long as the great mass of women continue to be tied down to private domestic economy, they naturally cannot utilize all the exceedingly broad rights granted to them equally with men by the socialist revolution.

The socialist reconstruction of the entire national economy was of decisive significance in the assimilation in their completeness of the rights granted to women by the Constitution. The collectivization of agriculture resulted in the inclusion, in the social and political life of the country, of vast strata of women who had theretofore taken no part therein, having spent all their strength on the petty economy of the individual peasant homestead and being in fact economically dependent upon husbands, fathers, or adult sons. As Stalin said when he received the kolkhoz shock workers of the beet fields (1935):

By its work days, the kolkhoz has liberated woman and made her independent. No longer does she work for her father while she is a young girl and for her husband after her marriage; she works, above all, for herself. This means the emancipation of the peasant woman. It means the kolkhoz system, which makes the working woman the equal of any working husband.[94]

As the triumphant socialist building proceeded, the USSR women of all nationalities, including those formerly the most backward, completely assimilated, under the guidance of the Communist Party, the rights granted them by the Soviet state in all the multiform phases of our socialist life. The mere enumeration of the directives of the Central Committee of the Party and of the higher Soviet organs of authority, concerned with drawing women into production, with teaching, state administration, guarding the

[93] *Ibid.*, Vol. XXIV, p. 343.   [94] *Pravda* (Nov. 11, 1935), No. 310.

interests of the mother, and (especially) with work among women of the
East and so on, gives the most brilliant idea of the concern for man, for
the highest humanity, so characteristic of socialist society.[95] This concern
for USSR women is eloquently manifested by the directive of the Central
Executive Committee and Council of People's Commissars of the USSR of
June 27, 1936.[96]

Organizational forms of the daily systematic work carried on, especially
among women, by the Party and by the Soviet organs included sections of
Party organizations for social and political work among women,[97] delegates'
assemblies, councils and congresses of women workers and peasants, women
deputies, women's agricultural production councils, commissions for improving the work and living conditions of female workers and peasants,[98]
women sectors in organizational branches of executive committees, and
so on.

The results of this enormous work, the political growth of women, their

[95] A partial list of some of the most important of the relevant directives and decrees
(1927-1934): Drawing Women into the Practical Work of the Soviets: a directive of the
USSR Central Executive Committee (Dec. 16, 1937); The Results of the All-Union Conference of Committees for Improving the Work and Living Conditions of the Women of
the East: a directive of the USSR Central Executive Committee, Protocol No. 37, Par. 8;
Measures to Draw Women into Agricultural Cooperation: a directive of the USSR Central Executive Committee (Oct. 13, 1929; Cz. 1929, No. 66, Art. 619); Reservation of a
Place for Girls in Higher and Other Technical Schools and Workers' High Schools: a
directive of the Central Committee of the Bolshevik All-Union Communist Party (Feb.
22, 1929; Central Committee Izvestiya, No. 7); Promoting Women to Directive Work:
a directive of the Central Committee of the Bolshevik All-Union Communist Party (Party
Building, Nos. 3-4, 1930); Cadres of Women Members of Soviets: a circular of the
USSR Central Executive Committee (May 19, 1930; Cz. 1930, No. 29, Art. 326); Prac-
tical Measures for Preparing and Promoting Women Kolkhoz Members: a directive of the
Central Committee of the Bolshevik All-Union Communist Party (Party Building, Nos.
19-20, 1930); Utilizing Women's Labor in Production in the State and the Cooperative
Mechanisms: a directive of the RSFSR Council of People's Commissars (Dec. 8, 1930;
Cy. 1931, No. 2, Art. 14); Work Among Women Nationalists in Autonomous Soviet
Socialist Republics, Autonomous Regions, National Areas and Districts: a directive of the
All-Russian Central Executive Committee (June 20, 1933); Reorganizing the Work of
Committees to Improve the Work and the Living Conditions of Female Workers and
Peasants: a directive of the All-Russian Central Executive Committee (July 10, 1932; Cy.
1932, No. 61, Art. 271); and Preparing Cadres of Women for Promotion to Directive Work
in the Soviet Electioneering Campaign of 1934; a directive of the All-Russian Central
Executive Committee (Protocol No. 129, Par. 1).

[96] Cz. 1936, No. 34, Art. 309, Concerning the Prohibition of Abortions, Increasing
Material Aid to Women in Childbirth, the Establishment of State Aid to Large Families,
Expansion of the Network of Lying-in Homes, Crèches and Playgrounds for Children, Increasing the Criminal Punishment for Failure to Pay Alimony, and Certain Amendments
of Divorce Legislation.

[97] After playing a most important part, these were replaced in 1929 by sectors of mass
work among women workers and peasants in the Party organs.

[98] Commissions for improving the work and living conditions of women workers and
peasants within the structure of Soviet organs (beginning with the Central Executive
Committee of the USSR) were replaced in 1932 by women's sectors within the organizing
divisions of the executive committees and the city Soviets which have such branches.

assimilation of rights, was clearly expressed in the Seventeenth Party Congress by Kaganovich as follows: "Woman has now so grown that it is becoming awkward to speak of specific work among women."[99]

Beginning with 1934, work among women is conducted not by special organizations created for the purpose, but by all the divisions of the Party and Soviet mechanism in the field, and for this special advisors are set apart.

In 1936 women comprised one-third of all those at work and in service in the USSR; and, whereas in tsarist Russia (1897) 55 per cent of the women working for hire were servants and day workers and 25 per cent were poor farm day laborers, and, whereas in the U. S. A. (according to the 1930 census) considerably more than half of all the working women are domestic servants, in the USSR only 2 per cent of the women working for hire are in domestic employment. All the others work in industry, transportation, trade, education and care of the public health, state and social institutions, sovkhozes, machine and tractor service stations, and so on. There are no poor female farm day laborers in the USSR; the socialist reorganization of agriculture has expunged this species of most onerous female toil. Women have filled the halls of institutions of learning, including higher institutions of learning. The general percentage of women in all higher institutions of learning in the USSR on January 1, 1937, excluding industrial academies and communist institutions for higher education, was 41 per cent.[100] Hundreds of thousands of women are commanders of industry: engineers, technicians, and experts,[101] commanders of agricultural production: members of kolkhoz administrations, managers of kolkhoz goods farms, brigadiers and agriculturists. In the USSR, woman also participates as director, organizer, investigator, and teacher in any of the scientific fields. Equality of payment for the labor of women and men of the same qualification has been an unwavering law of Soviet authority from the very beginning.

In elections of the city Soviets in 1934–1935, 90 per cent—and in elections of the village Soviets 80.3 per cent—of the women voters took part. In the 1934–1935 elections the general percentage (for the USSR) of women deputies returned was 26.2.

Especially important is the fact that women of the eastern nationalities, who had in the past been the most downtrodden and miserable, have been drawn into socialist production and administration. As early as 1926 only

[99] *Stenographic Report of the Seventeenth Party Congress* (1934), p. 550.

[100] This figure may be compared with the percentage of women students in capitalist countries: in England (1933–1934) 24.2 per cent, in Italy (1935–1936) 15.2 per cent, in Germany (1935–1936) 13.9 per cent.

[101] On July 1, 1936, there were 82,300 women members of engineering technical sections.

7.8 per cent of the women electors of the Uzbek SSR, and only 2.5 per cent of them in the Turkmen SSR in 1927, took part in the elections of the village Soviets. In the 1934 elections of the village Soviets, 73.5 per cent of the women electors of the Uzbek SSR and 69.4 per cent of those of the Turkmen SSR took part. These figures reflect what a great way the women of the East have come—from the veil to state administration. With the veil, the women of the Soviet East have cast away the abominable precepts of the shariat [102] and the adat,[103] which impose upon them an infinite number of obligations and deprive them of all sorts of rights. Thus the shariat makes the woman bride an object of, instead of a party to, the marriage agreement. It does not suffer her to appear in public places without important reasons and requires her to wear a veil or "parandzha" which strangers' eyes cannot pierce. The husband can at will, and without any explanation whatsoever, be divorced from his wife, whereas the shariat denies the possibility of the wife's securing a divorce against her husband's will.

Although the precepts of shariat regulating family and property relationships ceased upon the confirmation of Soviet authority to have the force of law, yet in the struggle with Soviet authority the rich landowners, the counterrevolutionary kulak bandits, the bourgeois-nationalist groups, the various types of wreckers from among the agents of foreign reconnaissance, and others boldly made use of the shariat, taking advantage, at the same time, of what remained of the tribal manner of life, superstition and prejudice among certain (the most backward) strata of the toilers of the East, and also of the traditional seclusion and servility of women. The socialist reconstruction of the Soviet East, as indeed of all the USSR, extirpated the influence of the shariat and the adat upon the toilers. The woman of the Soviet East now broadly enjoys all the rights granted to Soviet women.

Soviet law stands vigilantly on guard for the rights of Soviet woman. The RSFSR Criminal Code, for example, contains a special chapter, "Crimes Constituting Survivals of the Tribal Manner of Life," as well as a number of articles in other chapters (Arts. 140, 155) protecting woman from all encroachment upon her rights and independence. A directive of the Presidium of the RSFSR Supreme Court (February 13–14, 1936) specifically contemplated increased protection of the rights of women

[102] Shariat is the religious law of Islam, based on a theological-juridical interpretation of the Koran and of religious tradition, the sum total of the rules regulating the family, civil, and criminal, as well as the religious, relationships of Mussulmans.

[103] Adat is the customary law among Mussulman peoples, the sum total of popular customs and popular juridical practice in the sphere of property, family, and other relationships.

members of kolkhozes from encroachments calculated to hamper their production and social activity or forcibly to lessen their role in the kolkhozes. It depends upon the circumstances of the case and the personality of the accused whether such encroachments are dealt with according to the articles as to counterrevolutionary crimes (Art. 58, Par. 10, and in case of attempts on the life of these women Art. 58, Par. 8 of the RSFSR Criminal Code) or under Article 73, Part 2, of the Criminal Code providing for loss of liberty for a period not exceeding five years. A law issued by the Central Executive Committee and the Council of People's Commissars of the USSR [104] (October 5, 1936) established criminal responsibility for refusal to accept women to work and for paying them lower wages because of pregnancy.

The Stalin Constitution reflected and confirmed the equality of women's rights in our land.

Women in the USSR are granted rights equal with the rights of men in all spheres of economic, state, cultural, and social-political life. That these rights of women can be carried into effect is assured by giving women rights equal with those of men to work and to payment therefor, to rest, and to social insurance and education, and by state protection of interests of mother and child, by granting a woman leaves with full pay during pregnancy, and by a broad network of maternity homes, children's public crèches, and kindergartens.[105]

Furthermore, Article 137 says: "Women have a right to elect and to be elected on an equality with men." The participation of almost every woman in elections to the Supreme Soviet of the USSR, and the election to the Supreme Soviet of 187 women, brilliantly illustrate the operation of these articles.[106]

Constitutions of Union and autonomous republics have reproduced these notable articles in their entirety. In certain eastern Soviet republics where formerly the situation of women was particularly void of rights, and where it is still necessary to prosecute the struggle with survivals of the tribal manner of life, the constitutional articles concerning the equality of the rights of women and men contain a rider to the language of Article 122 of the Stalin Constitution: "Resistance to the woman's enfranchisement in fact [handing over those of tender years in marriage, selling a bride for a price, or the organization of resistance to the drawing of women into studying, agricultural and industrial production, state administration and social-political life] is punishable by law." This is stated in the last part

---

[104] Cz. 1936, No. 51, Art. 419.

[105] Stalin Constitution, Art. 122.

[106] The following figures are significant for purposes of comparison: the 1935 elections returned nine women to the English House of Commons and the 1934 elections six women to the U. S. House of Representatives.

of Article 121 of the Constitution of the Uzbek SSR, and similar riders
are found in constitutions of the Tadjik SSR (Art. 107), the Kazakh SSR
(Art. 100),[107] the Kirghiz SSR (Art. 93), and the Turkmen SSR (Art. 99).

The position of women in the USSR (the only country in the world
which has completely equalized men and women in respect of their rights,
guaranteed the equality of women's rights actually as well as legally, and
also realized the emancipation of woman's personality) is a brilliant manifestation of the general enfranchisement of personality, of the freedom,
equality, and completeness of the rights of citizens of the USSR, confirmed
by the great Stalin Constitution.

f) The Equality of Rights of Citizens of the USSR Regardless of their Nationality and Race

The complete and unconditional equality of citizens, irrespective of
nationality and race, is one of the basic principles of the Soviet system. In
the matter of national equality of rights, the contrast between socialist and
bourgeois public law is outlined with extraordinary brilliance; the hypocrisy
of bourgeois democracy and the unbridled and arbitrary misanthropy of
fascism stand revealed no less brilliantly. "The existence of capitalism without national oppression is just as unthinkable as is the existence of socialism
without the emancipation of downtrodden nations, without national freedom." [108]

The bourgeois formulation of the matter of national rights is characterized by dissociating the civil rights and native language on the one hand
from the equality of nations—their right to self-determination and to the
formation of an independent state—on the other. The grant of formal
equality of rights is here contemplated basically as a means of reducing
the entire national question as a whole to one of "minorities," of removing
the question of national self-determination, and of "providing a 'solution'
to the question which presses nations mechanically into the Procrustean
bed of the state's entirety." [109] Tiny and partial reforms are designed to
strengthen and improve the system of national oppression represented by
the bourgeois state. The bourgeoisie of dominant nations has always in
reality sought the maximum curtailment, or reduction to a mere formality,
of even these truncated civil and language rights of the population of a
different nationality, considering them a limitation upon its "right" to
complete and unlimited dominance in the state. When the bourgeois state

---

[107] In enumerating the forms of resistance to woman's emancipation in fact, Art. 100
of the Constitution of the Kazakh SSR points out likewise: entering into marriage with
persons of tender years, polygamy, and "amengerstvo."
[108] Stalin, Marxism and the National Colonial Question, p. 67.
[109] Ibid., p. 23.

turns fascist, this leads to open renunciation of the principle of the formal equality of rights of citizens, irrespective of their nationality. This is brilliantly evidenced by the fanatical and misanthropic policy of Hitler's Germany with reference to "non-Aryans." Bourgeois states have returned to their starting point, feudal barbarism of the Middle Ages, having thrown overboard, like old clothes, outworn and good for naught, those principles upon which the bourgeoisie relied when it came to power in its struggle with feudalism.

In the socialist state national equality of rights is a conclusion from the general principle of proletarian internationalism which affirms the solidarity of all toilers, irrespective of race and nationality, establishes the equality and the sovereignty of nations, and finds expression in the right of nations to separate and to form their own states. This right is the most brilliant expression of genuine national equality. In savage conflict against common enemies, the toilers of the formerly oppressed nationalities availed of rights proclaimed by the socialist revolution to create their own national statehood on the basis of Soviets. The Lenin-Stalin national policy, after leading to the national emancipation of formerly oppressed peoples, made it a concurrent condition that they be indissolubly united within the framework of a single Soviet Union State. This policy is brilliantly expressed in the fact that the USSR consists of eleven Union Republics having rights and, in their turn, uniting twenty-two autonomous republics, nine autonomous regions, and eleven national areas.[110] This fact, typical of the Soviet multinational state, is supplemented by the guaranty of complete equality of rights in behalf of those national groups which, by reason of their small numbers and their geographical dissociation, cannot form a Union Republic or use the right to state-territorial autonomy: that is to say, national minorities in the strict sense of the word.

The rights of national minorities, in connection with the general question of the equality and sovereignty of nations, were formulated with entire distinctness by Stalin before the war in his *Marxism and the National Question*, where he advanced the following basic principles in a program of solving the national question: (1) acknowledgment of the right to self-determination, including withdrawal and the formation of an independent state; (2) acknowledgment of the right to regional autonomy; and finally (3), in behalf of national minorities, *national equality of rights in all the forms thereof (language, schools, and so on) as a necessary point* in the solution of the national question." [111]

These principles were transmuted into the Declaration of Rights of

[110] Cf. Chap. IV previously cited, "The State Organization."
[111] Stalin, *Marxism and the National Question*, p. 43.

the Peoples of Russia, which, side by side with the proclamation of the equality and sovereignty of Russian peoples and their right to self-determination (including withdrawal), contemplated the annulment of each and every one of the national and national-religious privileges and limitations and "the free development of the national minorities and ethnographic groups which inhabit the territory of Russia." [112] They were fixed in the first (1918) Constitution of the RSFSR, which, while reproducing the text of the articles of the Declaration of the Rights of the Toiling and Exploited People concerning the fact that the Russian Republic is instituted as a "Federation of Soviet National Republics," and asserting in Article 11 the right of national regions to autonomy, asserted at the same time (in Art. 22) that the RSFSR, acknowledging equal rights in behalf of citizens, irrespective of their race and nationality, declares "the establishment or tolerance on the basis thereof of any privileges or advantages, as well as any suppression of national minorities or limitation upon their equality of rights, incompatible with the basic laws of the Republic." This article was reproduced in the constitutions of other Soviet republics. Not a single bourgeois constitution contains such a broad interpretation of the rights of nationalities.

Article 13 of the 1925 Constitution of the RSFSR (after changes introduced by the Fourteenth All-Russian Congress of Soviets in 1929) contained the principles of the right of nations to self-determination (including withdrawal) and a formula of Soviet autonomy, an affirmation of the principle "of the equality of rights of citizens irrespective of their race and nationality." At the same time, it guaranteed that "free use of the native language in congresses, court, school, administration, and social life was unqualifiedly possible." In one form or another, these formulations were likewise reproduced by the constitutions of the other Union Republics.

The Stalin Constitution, and constitutions of the Union and autonomous republics constructed in accordance therewith, formulated and settled the matter of the national equality of rights most completely and with classical lucidity. Chapter II of the Stalin Constitution "On State Organization" confirms the voluntary character of the Soviet Union State, the equality of rights of its constituent Union Republics. Section 123 of the Constitution affirms the national equality of rights in the most categorical form: "The equality of rights of citizens of the USSR, irrespective of their nationality and race, in all fields of economic, state, cultural, and social-political life is an immutable law. Any limitation of rights of whatsoever sort, and whether direct or indirect, or, conversely, any establishment of

[112] Cy. 1917, No. 2, Art. 18.

civil privileges, direct or indirect, on account of race or nationality, as well as any advocacy of race or national exclusiveness, hatred, or contempt is punishable by law." This article excludes the establishment not only of any direct national privileges or limitations, but also of indirect privileges and limitations of any sort which could arise; for example, in case the right to a native language was inadequately taken into account. Furthermore, the right to the native national language is especially guaranteed by Article 40 of the USSR Constitution, pursuant to which USSR laws are published in the languages of the Union Republics. Article 121 contemplates instruction in the schools in the native language as one of the conditions essential to effectuation of the right to education. Article 110 establishes the carrying on of court proceedings "in the language of the Union or autonomous republic or autonomous region, guaranteeing, in behalf of persons ignorant thereof, complete familiarity with the materials of the case through an interpreter as well as the right to address the court in their native language."

Constitutions of the Union Republics do not merely reproduce Articles 121 and 123 and make Article 110 of the USSR Constitution definitive; they contain as well further details of the rights of national minorities with reference to conditions of the separate republics. Equality of rights of USSR citizens, irrespective of nationality and race, is defended and assured by legislation in force in the USSR and in the Union and autonomous republics.

In all Soviet legislation and in all Soviet life, national equality of rights is developed in an absolutely methodical way. Our legislation knows no laws which would introduce any limitation of any sort whatsoever upon any persons whatsoever in consequence of their national or racial origin. The practice of discrimination (the employment of special limitations) in the work of any organ in relation to persons belonging to national minorities, or toleration of such discrimination, or encroachment of any sort upon national equality of rights is punished as a counterrevolutionary crime, falling within the operation of Article 58, Paragraph 1, of the RSFSR Criminal Code and the corresponding articles of criminal codes of other Union Republics, which declare that action of every sort aimed at undermining or weakening the national conquests of the proletarian revolution is counterrevolutionary.

The right to one's own language is assured by special legislative acts of the USSR and Union Republics. School in one's own language is one of the basic principles of the Soviet school system. Confirmed by the RSFSR Council of People's Commissars, the Law of the Primary, Junior Intermediate, and Intermediate School establishes (since 1934) that "all pedagogic work in the Soviet polytechnical school be carried on in the native language of the students." [113] With equal logic this principle is developed in the legislation and school organization of other Union (and autonomous) Republics. A state school in the native language for all nationalities is among the most important cultural conquests of the great October Socialist Revolution. Assuring all nationalities of the USSR of schools in their native language required enormous work in preparing teaching bodies, putting together textbooks, and so on. There was the question of creating a system of writing, of working out a literary language for a whole series of nationalities. At the present time nationalities and national minorities are assured of school in their native languages.

The use of one's native language in court is confirmed by Article 110 of the Stalin Constitution and Article 7 of the law, Concerning the Judicial System of the USSR, the Union and the Autonomous Republics, adopted at the Second Session of the Supreme Soviet of the USSR. It is provided for likewise by Articles 22 and 241 of the RSFSR Code of Civil Procedure, by Article 9 of the RSFSR Code of Civil Procedure and by corresponding articles of the codes of the other Union Republics. (Compare the chapter on the court and the Public Prosecutor's Office.)

A whole series of administrative directives in all the republics aims at implanting the system securely. The most important acts are the directive of the All-Russian Central Executive Committee, Concerning Measures for Translating the Business Correspondence of State Organs in National Regions and Republics into Local Language (April 14, 1924),[114] and a series of analogous acts of other republics. These establish the principle that all business correspondence of state organs of a republic should be translated into the language of that republic, with a guaranty of the interests and rights of national minorities. Special commissions were created in the republics to establish the system in practice and to translate business correspondence into national languages.

An important element in serving national minorities was the formation of national village Soviets and districts, with business correspondence in the languages of the national minorities and promotion of workmen from the local population to the structure of their organs. In all the Union Republics there is a great quantity of national districts and Soviets: Tatar, German, Bulgarian, Hebrew, Greek, Armenian, Mordvinian, Chuvash, and so on. The constitution of the Uzbek SSR makes special provision for the formation of two national districts within the framework of the republic.

In a number of republics, bourgeois nationalists—agents of foreign recon-

[113] Cy. 1934, No. 42, Art. 263.
[114] Cy. 1924, No. 41, Art. 371.

naissance—tried to take advantage of the progress achieved in securing the state apparatus and school to local roots for purposes of alienating the peoples of the Soviet Republics, as to culture, ideas, and language, from the Russian population. This was an important element in their treasonable plans to dissociate the national republics from the USSR. As early as 1926, Stalin pointed out:

> With the native communist cadres in the Ukraine weak, this movement, headed here and there by noncommunist intellectuals, may in places take on the character of a struggle to alienate Ukrainian culture and Ukrainian society from those of the Soviet Union as a whole—a struggle against "Moscow" in general, against Russians in general, against Russian culture and Leninism, its highest attainment. I will not demonstrate that such danger is becoming ever more and more real in the Ukraine.[115]

To further their counterrevolutionary aims, the bourgeois nationalists carried on a struggle against Russian culture and the Russian language, excluded the teaching of the Russian language from national schools, and so on. The destruction of Bukharin-Trotskyists and bourgeois-nationalist nests was the finishing stroke to the wreckers in this field.

The Russian language enjoys vast affection among all the peoples of the USSR as the general property of the Soviets. The peoples of the national republics do not set their native languages off against the Russian language. There has been in all the national republics an extraordinary and increasing movement toward study of the Russian language, whereas formerly, prior to the revolution, Russian in the national republics was the exclusive monopoly of a negligible exploiter apex of non-Russian population. Assuring the right of each nationality to its own language and the strengthening of mutual confidence and friendship between the people promotes a broader expansion of knowledge of the Russian language, a mighty instrument for the cultural uplift of all the USSR peoples, among the toiling masses of all the USSR nationalities.

The Russian language is the language of the great Russian people, which, by its heroic struggle against oppressors and exploiters, has shown all the peoples of the former Russian Empire the road of emancipation, the road to socialism.

An exceedingly important element in the national policy of Soviet authority is the struggle against nationalism of every sort, against the preaching of national hatred and dissimilarity. Such dissimilarity, fanning the flame of national antagonisms, has always served as one of the most dangerous instruments in the hands of exploiter classes for enslaving the

[115] Stalin, *Marxism and the National-Colonial Question*, p. 173.

masses and contesting the revolutionary movement. In the USSR, advocacy of national enmity is one of the most dangerous forms of the class
struggle of the shattered exploiter classes and their remains against the
Soviet state. It is characteristic that as early as July 27, 1918, the RSFSR
Council of People's Commissars issued over the signature of Lenin a
decree, Extirpation of the Anti-Semitic Movement, which declared that
movement "a catastrophe as regards the Worker-Peasant Revolution" and
directed that "those who carry on and participate in pogroms be put beyond
the pale of law." [116]

In 1931 Stalin, answering an inquiry of a foreign telegraph agency, declared:

Anti-Semitism is profitable for the exploiters, a lightning conductor as it
were, bringing capitalism out from under the stroke of the toilers. It is dangerous
for the toilers, a false path, leading them astray out of the correct road and into
the jungle. Hence, as logical internationalists, Communists cannot but be the
unreconciled and mortal foes of anti-Semitism. In the USSR it is most sternly
prosecuted as a phenomenon profoundly inimical to the Soviet social order.
Under the laws of the USSR, active anti-Semites are punished by death.[117]

Advocacy of national hatred or contempt is a criminal encroachment
upon the honor and worth of the Soviet citizen and is not to be tolerated.
The problem of the struggle with national dissimilarity is expressed in its
most brilliant form in the Stalin Constitution, which punishes by law "advocacy of race or national exclusiveness or hatred or contempt of any sort"
(Art. 123). Under the criminal codes of the RSFSR and other Union Republics, propaganda or agitation directed at the incitement of national or
religious enmity or dissimilarity are among the particularly dangerous
crimes against administrative order, punishable by loss of freedom for a
period not exceeding two years; in a military setting, or where there are
mass agitations, by loss of freedom for not less than two years and by confiscation of all, or part, of the property of the guilty party; and if circumstances are particularly serious, the punishment is more severe and includes
execution by shooting and confiscation of property (Art. 59, Par. 7 of the
RSFSR Criminal Code).

The principles of the Lenin-Stalin national policy by no means comprise legal equality and nothing more; that which is an unattainable ideal
under capitalist conditions is, under the conditions obtaining in the USSR,
only a beginning, a key to the solution of the national question. "National
equality of rights is per se a very important political acquisition. There is,

[116] *The Policy of Soviet Authority on the National Question During Three Years*
(1920), p. 32.
[117] Cited in Molotov, *The Constitution of Socialism*, p. 27.

however, the risk that it will continue to be merely an empty sound if there are not at hand adequate resources and possibilities for the utilization of this extremely important right." [118] Herein is manifested with perfect clarity a special characteristic of Soviet democracy: it "does not merely tabulate formal civil rights—it transfers the center of gravity to the matter of guaranteeing them." [119] The Bolsheviks introduced a new element into the national question, that of the factual, as distinguished from the merely legal, equalization of nationalities. This policy of factual equality, of abrogating factual inequality, is developed both as regards Soviet national republics and with reference to national minorities. It embraces the entire aggregate of measures of a political, economic, and cultural order directed at raising the welfare of nationalities, elevating their cultural level, and unifying them most completely with socialist building, drawing them into the administration of the state. In the first stages special commissions and committees, working under the immediate control of the Central Executive Committee of the USSR (or of central executive committees of Union Republics) and with their organs in the rural areas, were created to direct and develop this work among national minorities. Such was the character, accordingly, of commissions for the affairs of national minorities and departments of nationalities under central executive committees of Union Republics, delegates for matters of national minorities under local executive committees, and special committees for the education of national minorities under People's Commissariats for Education. The publication of literature for national minorities was concentrated in the Central Publishing House of the Peoples of the USSR, and the like. At the present time the work in serving national minorities is carried on by all Soviet organs as an important and integral part of their labors.

g) Freedom of Conscience

Freedom of conscience, as a rule of public law, signifies the assent of the state that each person has the right to observe any religion, change from one religion to another, carry out the essential religious ceremonies prescribed by the cult, and the right, as well, to follow no religion of any sort and to carry on antireligious propaganda.

True freedom of conscience can be realized only upon the following conditions: that church and state—and school and church—be completely separated, that the state be altogether neutral as regards all religions, that there be no dominant church, that the state not intrude into religious convictions of the citizens and the internal affairs of the church, and that every

---

[118] Stalin, *Marxism and the National-Colonial Question* (1936), p. 85.
[119] Stalin, *Report on the Draft of the USSR Constitution* (1936), p. 21.

legal limitation and civil privilege whatsoever connected with religion be abolished.

The separation of the church from the state, and of the school from the church—by its character a constituent part of the bourgeois-democratic revolution—relates to those measures "which bourgeois democracy puts forth in its programs, but has nowhere in the world brought to a conclusion, thanks to the various factual bonds between capital and religious propaganda." [120]

Even in the few states where church and state are separated in form (U.S.A., France, and others), the church actually enjoys the support of the state and possesses tremendous influence in the spheres of popular education and the upbringing of children. Thus, for example, in the U.S.A.—though constitutions in a number of states grant parents the right to bring up children not only in any religion whatever but also outside any religion—the upbringing of children in a religious spirit is in reality predetermined by the facts that religion is taught in schools, that atheist teachers are hunted out of the schools, that court proceedings are instituted where Darwinism is taught, and so on.

The Constitution of the state of Arkansas says frankly: "No one denying the existence of God can occupy a place in state institutions or be admitted to testify in court." Thus it is impossible to speak of freedom of conscience in the United States in the true sense of the word; and if this is the state of affairs in a country which has in form separated church and state, much less can there be talk of true freedom of conscience with regard to countries where the system of a state or dominant church is preserved (as in England, Rumania, and so forth). There a dominant and privileged position is secured in behalf of a definite church. The clergy play a considerable part in institutions of popular education, and a notable proportion of the schools, more than half of them in England, are entirely in their hands. Even in the state schools and the private schools, the teaching of "the Divine Law" is mandatory. In many of these countries all the citizens, irrespective of whether or not they are believers, are compelled to pay an ecclesiastical tax. Some constitutions which announce the proposition that civil rights do not depend on a profession of religious faith immediately add that the state makes an exception to this rule in respect of service in the schools.

The proletarian revolution in Russia shattered the union of church and state by destroying the exploiter state and completely separating the church from the new state created by the revolution—the socialist state—and the school from the church.

The state should not be concerned with religion, nor should religious societies be linked with state authority. Every person should be completely free to profess

[120] *Program of the All-Union Communist Party (of Bolsheviks)*, Sec. 13.

whatever religion he pleases or to profess no religion at all—to be an atheist, which every sort of socialist ordinarily is. No distinction whatsoever is to be made as between citizens in respect of their rights as dependent upon their religious faiths.[121]

These propositions of Lenin, formulated as early as 1905, were at the foundation of the Soviet state policy with regard to religion. The Declaration of Rights of the Peoples of Russia (November 2/15, 1917) proclaimed the abolition of national-religious privileges and limitations of every sort. Having a negative attitude toward religion, carrying high the banner of militant atheism, having initiated from the very earliest days a planned and decisive struggle with religion, and aspiring, in the words of Marx, "to liberate the conscience from religious superstition," [122] the triumphant proletariat, organized into a state and guided by the Communist Party, was tolerant toward the religious beliefs of the toilers in the knowledge that the genuine struggle with religion is not a struggle with believers, and that the prohibition of religion or the forcible abrogation of a cult (as the anarchists proposed) would lead merely to the artificial fanning of fanaticism. "The All-Union Communist Party is guided by the conviction that only the effectuation of planned development and awareness in all the social-economic activity of the masses will bring to pass the complete withering away of religious prejudices." This is the statement in Section 13 of the Party program. This proposition lies at the foundation of all the legislation of the Soviet state on the matter of religion.

Sensitivity to the religious convictions of the toilers is brilliantly evidenced by the directive of the Council of the People's Commissars of December 9/22, 1917, Concerning the Transfer of the Sacred Koran of Osman, a religious relic of the Mussulmans, being at that time in the State Public Library, to the Regional Mussulman Congress at the request of the latter. At the same time, incidental to planned realization of measures in the struggle with religion, a decree of the Council of People's Commissars (January 23, 1918) [123] concerning the separation of the church from the state, and of the school from the church, effectuated such separation and gave legislative confirmation of freedom of conscience. "The issuance within the limits of the Republic of any local laws or directives which would embarrass or limit freedom of conscience, or establish any advantages or preferences whatsoever on the basis of the faith which citizens profess, is forbidden. Each citizen can profess any religion he likes—or no religion at all. Any deprivation of rights on the basis of the profession of any faith what-

---

[121] Lenin, *Socialism and Religion*, Vol. VIII, p. 420.
[122] Marx and Engels (Russian ed.), Vol. XV, p. 286.
[123] Cy. 1918, No. 18, Art. 263.

soever, or with the profession of no faith, is abrogated" by Sections 2 and 3 of this decree. A note to Section 3 pointed out that any indication of the religion to which citizens belonged, or did not belong, was to be expunged from all official acts. The decree permitted believers the free use of religious ceremonies provided they neither violated social order nor were attended by encroachments upon the rights of citizens of the Soviet Republic.

Granting citizens complete freedom of conscience, the right freely to determine their relationship to religion, the decree at the same time pointed out in a special article that no one can on the plea of his religious convictions decline to fulfill his civil obligations, permitting an exception to this proposition only if one civil obligation be replaced by another in each separate instance in accordance with the decision of the people's court. The decree thus took into account the presence of religious sects which on religious grounds forbid their members to take part in military service.[124] The keeping of records of civil status was transferred from ecclesiastical to civil authority. Religious organizations were deprived of their juristic personality and, in particular, of the right to possess property, and were put into the position of private societies enjoying neither advantages nor grants of any kind from the state. All the property of churches and religious societies was declared the property of the people. The gratuitous use of buildings and of the necessary objects of their cult was granted to the appropriate religious societies for the holding of divine services.

The school was separated from the church and the teaching of religious beliefs in schools was forbidden. Citizens could, if they wished, teach and be taught religion privately.

By the time of the adoption of the first Soviet Constitution, the separation of the church from the state, and of the school from the church, was already an accomplished fact. The 1918 Constitution (Art. 13) confirmed this guaranteed freedom of conscience in the following words: "To the end of assuring actual freedom of conscience in behalf of the toilers, the church is separated from the state and the school from the church; but freedom of religious and antireligious propaganda is conceded in behalf of all citizens." For the first time in the world, the basic law of a state confirmed freedom of antireligious propaganda, without which genuine freedom of conscience is impossible. The 1925 Constitution of the RSFSR completely reproduced the text of this article. Analogous formulae were found in all constitutions of the Union and autonomous republics.

The legal position of religious organization is defined at the present time

[124] By directives issued in the development of this point in the decree, such persons were granted the right, according to a decision of a court, to substitute sanitary service or other work of general utility (at the choice of the person summoned) during the period of call of people of their age for military service.

by a directive of the All-Russian Central Executive Committee and the Council of the People's Commissars of RSFSR (April 8, 1929, with subsequent amendments), Concerning Religious Societies,[125] granting believers the right to be united into religious societies or into groups of believers [126] for joint satisfaction of their religious needs. These organizations do not enjoy the rights of a juristic person. The law requires religious societies and groups of believers to be registered in local Soviets in a special manner distinct from the method applicable to social organizations of the toilers. Duly registered religious societies or groups are granted the right to use without charge special buildings and objects of devotion destined exclusively for religious purposes. They are also granted the right to organize general assemblies with the permission of the local Soviets, to choose—for the immediate fulfillment of functions connected with the administration and utilization of cultural property, as well as for the purpose of external representation—executive organs from among their members (to the extent of three persons for a religious society, and one representative for a group of believers) and also committees of inspection (consisting of not more than three persons) to verify the property and money resources of the cult obtained by collections or from voluntary offerings. Religious organizations are forbidden to create funds for mutual assistance, cooperatives, or production units, to organize other than religious assemblies, groups, excursions, libraries, reading rooms or the like—anything, that is to say, not immediately related to the basic functions of religious organizations. The law makes no difference between the numerous faiths.

The state does not intrude in the internal affairs of organizations of church folk of the different trends and cults. Local Soviets supervise the activity of religious organizations. Closing churches is appropriate only if the toilers themselves have passed a directive concerning it.

Encroachment of any sort upon the freedom of conscience of citizens, any breach of the rules concerning the separation of the church from the state and of the school from the church, is subject to prosecution by law (compare RSFSR Criminal Code, Arts. 122–127, and corresponding articles of the criminal codes of other Union Republics).

What has been said discloses how nonsensical are the scurrilous aspersions appearing from time to time in the bourgeois press as to supposed persecution of religion by the government of the USSR. The struggle with religion is there carried on, not by administrative repressions, but by the socialist refashioning of the entire national economy which eradicates reli-

[125] Cy. 1929, No. 35, Art. 353.
[126] A "religious society" is a local organization of not less than twenty citizens of one and the same cult, who have attained the age of eighteen years; organizations with less than twenty members are called "groups of believers."

gion, by socialist reeducation of the toiling masses, by antireligious propaganda, by implanting scientific knowledge, and by expanding education. The mass exodus of USSR toilers away from religion is directly due to these measures taken in their entirety.

Great work in the matter of antireligious propaganda is carried on by the mass society of the toilers, the Union of Militant Atheists. Stalin, speaking of freedom of conscience in the USSR, points out:

> The legislation of the country is such that each citizen has the right to profess any religion he wishes; this is a matter for his own conscience. For this very reason we carried through the separation of the church from the state. In carrying through that separation, after our proclamation of freedom of belief, however, we have at the same time preserved in behalf of each citizen the right to struggle by persuasion, propaganda, and agitation against this or that religion or against any religion at all.[127]

The Stalin Constitution (Art. 124) reflected and confirmed by law the actual freedom of conscience possessed, together with the other fundamental rights, by every citizen of the USSR. "To the end of assuring freedom of conscience in behalf of citizens, the church is separated from the state, and the school from the church, in the USSR. Freedom for religious cults to function and freedom for antireligious propaganda are conceded in behalf of all citizens." All the extremely broad rights enumerated in Chapter X of the USSR Constitution are granted to all citizens utterly irrespective of their religion. Article 135 specifically points out that elective rights are granted to all citizens irrespective of their religion. Similar formulae are to be found in all the new constitutions of the Union and autonomous republics.

h) Freedom of Speech, of the Press, of Assembly, of Meetings, of Street Parades and of Demonstrations

Freedom of speech, of the press, of assembly, of meetings, of street parades and of demonstrations, being natural and indispensable conditions precedent to the manifestation of freedom of thought and freedom of opinion, are among the most important political freedoms. No society can be called democratic which does not afford its citizens all of them. Only in a state which actually guarantees these most important political freedoms, and in behalf of all citizens without exception, is expanded and completely logical democracy to be found.

While constitutions of bourgeois-democratic states ordinarily make a formal grant of these freedoms to all citizens without exception, every sort of limitation thereupon and all the capitalist social order in its entirety, have

---

[127] Stalin, *Questions of Leninism* (10th Russian ed.), p. 192.

turned what are, in form, rights possessed by all citizens into rights actually possessed by a narrow and privileged minority only.[128] Freedom of assembly, "even in the most democratic bourgeois republic, is an empty phrase, since the rich have at their disposal all the best dwellings, social and private, as well as sufficient leisure for meetings (and protection thereof by the bourgeois mechanism of power). Proletarians of city and country, and small peasants, the vast majority of the population, have none of the three." [129]

And all the sharpness of even the formal limitations in the bourgeois state is directed against the toilers enjoying the benefit of freedom of assembly, of meetings and of demonstrations. The requirements of bourgeois legislation as to street parades as well as open-air meetings—mass meetings of the toilers, whom this form of meeting suits better than meeting indoors because of their lack of proper premises and the great number of those taking part—are usually particularly strict, including a complicated method of obtaining a permit, while the police, present under the pretense of protecting social order, are given broad powers, under diverse specious pretexts, to close these meetings when they find it necessary. The entire hypocrisy of bourgeois legislation regarding such "freedoms" is clearly expressed in the fact that in England, for example, it was impossible to assemble upon private property without the permission of the owner or upon state property without the permission of state organs.[130] Under such conditions the "right" of assembly requires per se no permit; permission is required only for the temporary occupation of a parcel of earth. The result necessary for the bourgeoisie is attained, while the semblance of "freedom" is not touched. Legislators of contemporary England have decided, nevertheless, to fill the existing gap in the sphere of legislative regulation of "freedom" of assembly, and in 1936 issued a special law (the Public Order Act) [131] concerning meetings and demonstrations. This law officially charged the police, after the example of continental bourgeois countries, with the duty of dispersing undesirable meetings and demonstrations and arresting those taking part in them—functions hitherto unofficially exercised by the English police.

In France the law of October 23, 1935, forbade street assemblies and required, as to street processions and demonstrations, a preliminary declaration concerning them, having granted to trustworthy organs of authority the right to forbid the proposed demonstration or street parade if they shall find

---

[128] Even in Japan, a country where thought in an undesirable direction is per se subject to legal prosecution, the Constitution contains a hypocritical declaration as to granting freedom of the press to *all* citizens.

[129] Lenin (Russian ed.), Vol. XXIV, p. 9.

[130] Ivanovsky, *Manual of Public Law* (1910), p. 265.

[131] Cf. Albert Crek, *The Law Relating to Public Meetings and Processions* (London, 1937).

that it may violate social order. For an inaccurate declaration, or for taking part in the organization of manifestations not declared, the law provides for the imprisonment for from fifteen days to six months and a fine up to 2,000 francs.[132] Freedom of assembly, meetings, and demonstrations in capitalist countries is most brilliantly illustrated by the numerous police attacks upon peaceful demonstrations of workers, the dispersal of the latter and the beating or shooting of those who took part in the demonstrations.

To turn freedom of meetings from a right which is mere form into an actual right of the toiling masses, "it is necessary at the outset to take from the exploiters all the social and elegant private buildings, to give leisure to the toilers, and to have the freedom of their meeting preserved by armed workers, not by petty nobles or capitalist officers with broken-down soldiers." [133]

Freedom of the press stands no better in countries of bourgeois democracy, inasmuch as "this freedom is a delusion so long as capitalists commandeer the better printing establishments and the largest stores of paper, and capital retains its power over the press—a power manifested throughout the world with a cynicism brilliant and cutting in proportion to the development of democracy and the republican social order, as in America." [134]

Bourgeois public law ordinarily regards the absence of preliminary censorship as the most essential and fundamental indication of freedom of the press. Thus, from this viewpoint, the U.S.A. or England, where such censorship has long since been abrogated, are rated as countries where the press is absolutely and completely free. In reality, in these countries the bond between the press and capital, the enslavement of the press by capital, appears perhaps more clearly than in any others. Thus in England the most influential conservative daily, the *Times*, is the organ of banks, connected through its directors with Lloyd's Bank, with the largest railroad companies, with insurance companies and with a number of the biggest capitalist firms (Armstrong, Vickers, and others). The *Daily Telegraph*, the other very powerful organ of the press, likewise conservative, is considered the organ of heavy industry The newspaper enterprises of Lords Rothermere and Beaverbrook uniting a number of newspaper trusts, dictate to their papers the direction in which social opinion is to be molded.[135]

[132] *Journal officiel* (1935), pp. 11,203.
[133] Lenin (Russian ed.), Vol. XXIV, p. 9.
[134] *Ibid.*, p. 10.
[135] Lord Northcliffe, owner of one of the newspaper trusts in England, in his pamphlet, *Newspapers and Their Millionaires*, openly declares: "Certain provincial papers, like certain London papers, are maintained by rich persons in order to strengthen their political or social position. There is nothing strange in this. . . . *The Westminster Gazette* was always a 'kept' paper, passing—over a long period of years—from one millionaire to another."

Newspapers in the U.S.A. are still larger capitalist enterprises connected with specified banks and trusts in whose stock the capital of the newspaper owners is invested. Hearst, for example, a big American capitalist connected with war industry, banks, and concerns which are exploiting the countries of Latin and South America, owns twenty-nine papers with a total circulation of ten million readers. These papers, by order of Hearst, carry on a bloodthirsty agitation against the Communist Party, the revolutionary workers' movement and the USSR. How the freedom of the press in the U.S.A. looks in practice, and by what mechanism social opinion in the U.S.A. is shaped—how all the newspapers except the worker press are maintained by capitalists—is brilliantly told in the recent book of the talented American journalist George Seldes.[136] Freedom of the press consists essentially in the possibility of freely publishing the genuine, not the falsified, opinions of the toiling masses, rather than in the absence of preliminary censorship. This was clearly shown in the experience of the press in tsarist Russia.

The Revolution of 1905 compelled the tsarist government to abrogate a number of Draconian laws against the press, including that requiring editors to make a large preliminary deposit, that granting the administration the right to impose assessments on editors without court proceedings, and likewise that providing for the preliminary censorship of periodical publications in the cities and—from and after April 26, 1906—of "other than periodical" issues also. This by no means left the press free, however. The abolition of preliminary censorship was accompanied by increased strictness of subsequent censorship threatening, on the basis of Temporary Rules Concerning the Press (November 24, 1905), editor-publishers and authors with imprisonment for every sort of attempt to take seriously the freedom of the press declared by the "imperial" manifesto and by the very "rules" themselves.[137] Preliminary censorship was abolished, but confiscation, enormous fines, and the closing up of newspapers, which took on the character of an open epidemic from 1905 on, put such a noose around the neck of the press that it appeared strangled.[138]

To make the press actually free "it is necessary at the outset to take away from capital the possibility of hiring writers, buying printing houses, and

---

[136] George Seldes, *Freedom of the Press* (1937, Russian transl. by Kalmer).

[137] E. A. Vallo de Barr, in his *Freedom of the Russian Press After October 17, 1905* (published in Samara in 1906), writes bitterly that the Temporary Rules (above referred to) involuntarily recall the famous words of Figaro, replete with irony, as to establishing the freedom of the press on condition that the press should not touch the powers nor the church nor policy nor morality nor officials nor honorary classes nor anybody who has any connection with anyone.

[138] Cf. *Martyrology of the Russian Press*, appended to Vallo de Barr's text.

bribing papers, to which end it is necessary to overthrow the yoke of capital and to overthrow the exploiters and crush their resistance." [139]

Even before the October Revolution, Lenin, by way of preparing the masses to seize power, wrote (October, 1917):

Only the Soviet government could have successfully struggled with such pitiful injustice as the seizure by capitalists—with the aid of millions pillaged from the people—of the biggest printing presses and most of the newspapers. It is necessary to shut down the bourgeois counterrevolutionary papers,[140] to confiscate their printing establishments, to declare private advertisement in newspapers a state monopoly, and to transfer them to the administrative paper published by the Soviets, and telling the peasants the truth. Only in this way is it possible and our boundless duty to knock out of the hands of the bourgeoisie a mighty instrument for lying and defaming with impunity, for deceiving the people, for leading the peasantry into error, and for preparing counterrevolution.

The victory of the Socialist Revolution in the USSR, which transferred to the hands of the worker class, along with the basic means and instruments of production, buildings for meetings, printing houses, and stores of printing paper, meant the broad realization of freedom of speech, of the press, of assembly, and of meetings. For the first time in the world, these became genuine freedoms of the masses.

To the end of assuring in behalf of the toilers actual freedom of assembly, the RSFSR, conceding the right of its citizens freely to organize assemblies, meetings, processions, and the like, grants to the worker class and the poorest peasantry the use of all premises suitable for the organization of popular assemblies, together with their furniture, lighting, and heat (Art. 15 of the RSFSR Constitution, 1918).

Having given the toilers freedom of speech, assemblies, street parades, press, and so on, the Soviet government explicitly excluded the nonlabor classes from enjoyment of this freedom. Lenin spoke on this matter at the First Congress of the Comintern: Any class-conscious workman who has not broken with his class will understand immediately that it would be folly to promise freedom of meetings to exploiters at a time (and in a setting) when the latter are resisting their overthrow and defending their privileges. When the bourgeoisie was revolutionary it did not give "freedom of assembly" to monarchists and nobles who had summoned foreign troops and had "assembled" to organize attempts at restoration either in England in 1649 or in France in 1793. If the present bourgeoisie, long since turned

[139] Lenin (Russian ed.), Vol. XXIV, p. 10.
[140] Naming Rech, Russkoe Slovo, and the like.

reactionary, demands of the proletariat that, notwithstanding the future resistance of capitalists to their expropriation, the proletariat guarantee in advance freedom of assembly to the exploiters, the workers will merely smile at the bourgeoisie's hypocrisy.[141] Having assured genuine freedom of the press to the toilers, the Soviet government did not extend this freedom to nonlaboring strata. Concerning freedom of the press, the first Soviet Constitution, of 1918, said:

> To the end of assuring in behalf of the toilers actual freedom to express their opinions, the RSFSR annuls the dependence of the press upon capital and hands over to the worker class and poorer peasantry all the technical and material resources for publishing newspapers, pamphlets, books, and all sorts of other productions of the press, and guarantees that they may circulate freely throughout the land (Art. 14).

One of the first and most important measures of the Soviet government in assuring actual freedom of the press in behalf of the toilers was the closing—by the War-Revolutionary Committee in the very first days after the revolution in Petrograd—of numerous organs of the counterrevolutionary press. Enemies of the proletariat raised a hullabaloo on this occasion, screaming about violation of the freedom of the press. In sanctioning these actions of the War-Revolutionary Committee, the decree concerning the press, issued by the Council of People's Commissars (October 27/November 9, 1917),[142] made it clear to the toilers that the liberal screen of "free press" is actually a cover for the freedom for the "have" classes (after possessing themselves of the lion's share of all the press) to poison the minds of the masses and introduce confusion into their consciousness without let or hindrance. "Everyone knows," the decree said further, "that the bourgeois press is one of the bourgeoisie's most mighty weapons. Particularly was it impossible at the critical moment when the new authority, the authority of the workers and peasants, was only in the process of being stabilized to leave this weapon —at such moments no less dangerous than bombs and machine guns—entirely in the hands of the foe.

This decree evoked sharp attacks from the "Left" SR's as well as from the Trotskyists and Bukharinists who, traitors to the socialist revolution, masked themselves under the name "Bolsheviks." It is extraordinarily important to note that it was at the very session of the All-Russian Central Executive Committee, November 4/17, 1917, when this decree concerning the press was under consideration, and after the Bolshevik resolution completely approving this step of the Council of the People's Commissars had

[141] Lenin (Russian ed.), Vol. XXIV, p. 9.
[142] Cy. 1917, No. 1, Art. 7.

been adopted by majority vote, that the "Left" SR's, in token of their protest, declared that they refused to accept responsibility and recalled their
representatives from the War-Revolutionary Committee and other organs.
In alliance with the "Left" SR's, a group of strikebreakers—fascist hirelings
in the persons of Rykov and others—came out with a vehement declaration
about leaving their posts, allegedly because of the Bolshevik Party's refusal
to come to terms with the tolerationist parties and also because of the supposedly "terrorist" policy of Soviet authority (an allusion to the closing of
counterrevolutionary organs of the press).

The great October Socialist Revolution destroyed each and every possibility of the rich bribing the press and capitalists being free to employ
their wealth to fabricate social opinion. It created in the Soviet state, for
the first time in the world, a truly free press, a means of expressing the
opinions of the toilers with genuine freedom. Guided by the Bolshevik All-
Russian Communist Party, the press in the USSR became a mighty instrument for the true education of the masses, for their self-organization, for
fostering new discipline among them, for criticism and self-criticism, and
for mobilizing the masses to eliminate all shortcomings in state and social
building—for the building of socialism.

Paralleling the growth of our socialist land, our press has increased and
grown strong. In 1936 the number of copies of our papers struck off at each
issue was 37,971,000, almost fourteen times greater than that in 1913. The
total number of newspapers was 9,250, almost eleven times as many as in
1913. The total number of books struck off was 571,071,000, more than
six and one-half times the number of 1913. Newspapers in the USSR appear in 69 languages, and books in 111 languages, of the USSR peoples.[143]
Hundreds of thousands of worker correspondents and peasant correspondents take an active part in all types of periodicals.

Soviet law stands on guard for the Soviet press. The law, Concerning
the Chief Administration for Literature and Publication (June 6, 1931),[144]
provides for political-ideological control of productions of the press and
obligates the Administration, a constituent part of the RSFSR People's
Commissariat for Education, "to prohibit the issuance, publication, and circulation of productions: (a) containing agitation and propaganda against
Soviet authority and the proletarian dictatorship; (b) publishing state secrets; (c) arousing nationalist and religious fanaticism; or (d) of a porno-
graphic character."

The RSFSR Criminal Code (Arts. 182, 185) prosecutes those who violate Soviet legislation concerning the press.

[143] Cf. *Twenty Years of Soviet Authority* (1937), pp. 103–104.
[144] Cy. 1931, No. 31, Art. 273.

A number of circulars of the USSR Public Prosecutor's Office have instructed prosecutors as to the necessity of the utmost endeavor to have the courts apply stern punitive measures to persons persecuting worker and peasant correspondents and thereby encroaching upon the freedom of the press.[145] The first assemblies of the organizations and societies of the toilers take place according to the plan of these organizations and societies and upon the call of the proper executive organs thereof without any permission whatsoever from the organs of authority. District, area, and regional (territorial) councils, conferences, and congresses are called with the permission of the regional (territorial) executive committees and the Council of People's Commissars of the Autonomous SSR. Republic congresses, conferences, and councils, with the participation of representatives of the localities, are summoned with the permission of the appropriate Republic Council of People's Commissars. Congresses, conferences, and councils summoned by state organs of the USSR, by All-Union cooperatives and by social organizations are summoned with the permission of the Council of People's Commissars of the USSR.[146]

Full initiative as to street parades and demonstrations in the USSR is given to the social organizations and societies of the toilers and, in the first instance, to the Communist Party as the directing nucleus of all these social (as well as of state) organizations. Rules of the People's Commissariat for Internal Affairs relative to the organization of these parades and demonstrations contain rules of a purely technical character touching the observance of social order, supervision over which is a responsibility of the worker-peasant militia.

In our state, naturally, there is and can be no place for freedom of speech, press, and so on for the foes of socialism. Every sort of attempt on their part to utilize to the detriment of the state—that is to say, to the detriment of all the toilers—these freedoms granted to the toilers must be classified as a counterrevolutionary crime to which Article 58, Paragraph 10, or one of the corresponding articles of the Criminal Code is applicable.

Freedom of speech, of the press, of assembly, of meetings, of street parades, and of demonstrations are the property of all the citizens in the USSR, fully guaranteed by the state upon the single condition that they be utilized in accord with the interests of the toilers and to the end of strengthening the socialist social order. Their breadth and genuineness and the

---

[145] Cf. the circular of Dec. 3, 1933, "Concerning the Struggle with the Persecution of Worker and Peasant Correspondents" (*For Socialist Legality*, 1934, No. 1).

[146] Cf. directive of the USSR Council of People's Commissars (May 15, 1935, Cz. 1935, No. 26, Art. 209) and of the All-Russian Central Executive Committee and RSFSR Council of People's Commissars (June 20, 1935, Cy. 1936, No. 6, Art. 29).

assuredness of their socialist character are confirmed in Article 125 of the Stalin Constitution:

In conformity with the interests of the toilers and to the end of strengthening the socialist social order, citizens of the USSR are guaranteed by law: (a) freedom of speech, (b) freedom of the press, (c) freedom of assembly and meetings, and (d) freedom of street parades and demonstrations. These civil rights are assured by granting to the toilers and their organizations the uses of printing establishments, stocks of paper, public buildings, streets, means of communication, and other material conditions essential for their realization.

i) The Right of Citizens to Unite in Social Organizations

One of the fundamental signs of a democratic state organization is the concession by the state in behalf of citizens of the right to unite in unions and societies, in party, professional, cooperative, scientific, technical, cultural, and similar social organizations. Characteristically, this right of unification in societies and unions was acknowledged by bourgeois-democratic states later than all the other civil rights ordinarily proclaimed in bourgeois declarations and constitutions. Thus in England—considered the birthplace of bourgeois freedom to organize or join unions and societies, and where as early as the second half of the eighteenth century such a large political association as the Society to Support the Bill of Rights could legally exist— severe laws were passed at the end of the eighteenth century and at the very beginning of the nineteenth, threatening not only a long term in prison but even death for organizing or participating in a society pursuing ends undesirable to the administration. A large number of societies and unions—beginning with worker organizations—were closed down on the basis of these laws. Gradually the pressure of the worker class led to their repeal during the first quarter of the nineteenth century. Although thereafter there were in England no special limitations in form upon the freedom to organize or join unions and societies, not a single statute, down to the present day, speaks of granting citizens such a freedom.

Considerably later the so-called freedom (in the formal sense) to organize or join unions and societies was established in France. Not a single declaration or constitution of France, right down to 1848, proclaimed such freedom. On the contrary, an attitude of hostility toward this species of civil freedom was manifested from the very beginning of the French Revolution. A whole series of laws either directly forbade citizens to organize or join unions and societies or put every sort of obstacle in the way of their being organized. Such was the law of May, 1791, which forbade existing associations to publish formal reports of their sessions, to present joint petitions to the government, or to agitate among officials; the law of Chapelier

(1791), which under penalty of imprisonment forbade every sort of association of workers; and the law of 1793, which forbade the organization of women's political clubs and societies, and so on. During the Empire, the position of unions and societies was regulated by none other than the Code Pénal (Arts. 291–294), making them completely dependent upon the administration, which could arbitrarily disband those already existing and refuse to approve the organization of any others.

Freedom to organize and to join unions and societies, including political societies, was declared for the first time in the French Constitution of 1848 (Art. 8), whereby "citizens have the right to be united"; no law permitting citizens to utilize this right was passed until 1901, however. Only in 1864 was the Chapelier law against worker associations repealed, and not until twenty years thereafter was a law passed legalizing professional unions. The date of the formal grant in France of freedom to organize or join associations is the passage of the law of July 1, 1901, which gave the right to organize societies and unions without preliminary permission and even without filing the bylaws, and required the filing of a declaration and bylaws only as regards societies and unions desiring to acquire the rights of a juristic person.[147]

In Germany, likewise, "the freedom of unions" was proclaimed for the first time in 1848 and (likewise) remained a fiction because no statute common to all the states incorporated in the German Empire was passed. More or less "freedom" was enjoyed only by societies and unions possessing no political character. Worker unions, which had begun to form in 1848, were dissolved after the victory of reaction. Only from the 1860's on do worker organizations in the shape of trade unions and the Social-Democratic Party emerge in Germany.[148] As early as 1878, however, the law against socialists, which forbade every sort of worker organization associated with socialist propaganda, led to the liquidation of these legal worker organizations, while the Social-Democratic Party went underground. The worker class of Germany carried on a great struggle for the right of coalitions before achieving the repeal of this law (in 1890). But even that repeal, leading to the legalization of worker organizations, did not entail a declaration of freedom to organize and join unions and societies: formal concession of such freedom in Germany was first made in the law of April 19, 1908.

In Russia the very formula "freedom of unions" was treason in the eyes of the tsarist administration right down to 1905. Only the revolution of that

---

[147] Compare A. Esmein, *Éléments de droit constitutionnel* (1921), Vol. 2, pp. 582–586; Esmein, *Précis de l'histoire du droit français de 1789 à 1814*; and Duguit, *Traité de droit constitutionnel*, Vol. V.

[148] The worker unions (Vereine) theretofore existing had narrow cultural and educational purposes and were entirely under bourgeois influence.

620   THE LAW OF THE SOVIET STATE

year wrested from the tsarist administration the promise, among others, to "bestow" freedom of unions. Prior to the issuance of the manifesto of October 17, 1905, not a single political party, not a single union or society aiming at political goals, could legally exist. The very societies and unions which were admitted—philanthropic, scientific and the like—were subordinate to a cruel regime and depended entirely upon the caprice of the administration and the police. Characteristically, and like the regime in France during the Empire, the legal position of societies in Russia was defined by a law for averting and suppressing crimes. The Temporary Rules of March 4, 1906,[149] as to societies, issued after the manifesto of October 17, 1905, which proclaimed the freedom to organize and join unions as the "steadfast foundation of civil freedom," were so put together that even such an exceedingly "well-meaning" political scientist as Professor Ivanovsky, after setting out these rules, was compelled to observe: "From what has been hereinbefore set forth, it manifestly follows that the Temporary Rules of March 4, 1906, concerning societies, establish no guarantees whatsoever of the freedom of forming societies." [150] In particular these rules, being constrained to legalize the professional societies which had emerged during the revolutionary storms, forbade their unification into unions[151] and deprived all those working in governmental institutions, or on public or private railroad and telephone enterprises of general utility, of the right to organize professional societies or to enter those already existing except by the permission of the authorities.

The subsequent reaction was accompanied by a sharp deterioration even in respect to conditions established by the Temporary Rules aforesaid (of 1906), by more than one destruction of trade unions, and by driving underground and prosecuting the party of the proletariat and the other worker-class organizations.

As a rule, postwar bourgeois constitutions proclaim freedom to organize and join unions and societies, thereby undoubtedly giving expression to the influence of the October Socialist Revolution and of the wave of revolutionary proletarian battles which rolled across bourgeois countries in 1918–1919. But while constitutions or individual laws in almost all bourgeois states proclaim freedom to organize and join unions and societies, no single one of them contains any reliable guarantees of such freedom. Even in the most democratic bourgeois countries, where Communist Parties and other organizations of the toilers legally exist, the utilization by broad masses of the freedom of union granted to all citizens in form involves incredible diffi-

---

[149] *Collection of Decrees of the Ruling Senate* (1906, No. 48, Art. 308).

[150] Ivanovsky, *Manual of Public Law* (Kazan, 1910), p. 494.

[151] According to the terminology conventional in public law, a union is the name used to designate a unification of societies.

culties in the conditions of political and economic bourgeois domination. Nevertheless, for all its truncated and merely formal character and despite the utter absence of guarantees, freedom to organize and join unions and societies in bourgeois democratic countries is a vast political conquest by the worker class, permitting it to rally its ranks, create its organizations, clarify its tasks to all the toilers, and strengthen its union with them in the struggle against capitalist exploitation—against capitalism. Wherefore the worker class, and all the toilers in capitalist countries, cannot but esteem highly the freedom won to organize and join unions, cannot but defend it, together with all the democratic institutions confronted by fascist reaction.

Wherever fascism comes to power it annihilates freedom to organize and join unions and societies along with all democratic institutions. All worker organizations and party, professional, and other organizations are smashed and their members are hunted. The history of the bourgeoisie as the dominant class thus starts with a prohibition of freedom of unions and the prosecution of all workers and all political organizations, and returns at the end to the same procedure, now accompanied by methods even more barbarous—those of fascism.

Only the socialist worker-peasant state affords genuine freedom to organize and join unions and meetings, the genuine, state-guaranteed right of the toilers to be united into social organizations. As early as the first Soviet Constitution, the RSFSR Constitution of 1918, it was declared: [152] "To the end of assuring in behalf of the toilers actual freedom to organize and join unions, the RSFSR, having shattered the economic and political power of the 'have' classes and thereby eliminated all obstacles hitherto impeding [in bourgeois society] the utilization by workers and peasants of freedom of organization and action, collaborates with the workers and the poorest peasants in every way, material and otherwise, for their unification and organization." Constitutions of all the other Union Republics have formulated in precisely the same fashion the right of the toilers to unification. Where the state has thus completely guaranteed the right of toilers to be united in social organizations, the latter have acquired, in the Soviet land, a development unprecedented and beyond the imagination of the capitalist world.

With each year these mass unions of the toilers in the Soviet state have grown broad and strong, constantly embracing new strata of the population, drawing them in to take active part in socialist building and in the defense of the Soviet state. The manifold forms of these unions, the content and sweep of their activity, and the very number of the USSR toilers embraced by them indicate most brilliantly the essence of Soviet democracy as democracy of a new type, immeasurably better than that of the bourgeoisie. Their

[152] Art. 16.

character and role, and the tasks fulfilled by them in the system of the worker-class dictatorship, lead to the classification of these numerous unifications of the toilers as follows: professional unions, cooperative organizations, youth organizations, voluntary societies (for sport, for defense, and cultural, technical, and scientific societies), and the Party.

Professional unions make up the largest organization of the worker class, numbering, at the beginning of 1938, more than twenty-two million members. "Trade unions may be called a 100 per cent organization of the worker class, which is dominant among us." [153]

The great October Socialist Revolution radically changed the position and the tasks of trade unions in our land. In capitalist countries their basic task is to struggle against capital, to defend the worker class from capitalists. In the socialist state, trade unions work hand in hand with the economic and Soviet state organs, setting as their goal the further development of production forces, raising the level of the material, living, and cultural conditions of the worker masses, defense of the latter from bureaucratic perversions of Soviet labor legislation, and drawing the worker masses into state administration and production. Soviet trade unions "are the school of communism. From their midst they segregate the best people for directive work in all branches of administration. They constitute the bond between the forward and the backward members within the structure of the worker class. They unite the worker masses with the vanguard of the worker class." [154] These words of Stalin bear the impress of the vast role of trade unions in the system of the worker-class dictatorship. "Trade unions must act in the most intimate and constant collaboration with the state authority" in the words of a resolution of the Eleventh Congress of the Russian Communist Party of Bolsheviks. Throughout the entire history of the Soviet state, trade unions have been its most trustworthy support, the most important instrumentality for socialist building, aids to the state in all its undertakings. This was assured by the decisive struggle carried on by the Party and, under its guidance, by the trade-union masses themselves against all the many attempts by the masked foes of the worker class—enemies of the people, agents of fascist reconnaissance, including Trotsky, Bukharin, Tomsky and other Judases—to pervert the role of trade unions in the Soviet state.

As socialist building proceeded, the role of trade unions grew and became complicated. Thus, in 1933, a directive of the Central Executive Committee and Council of People's Commissars of the USSR, adopted jointly with the All-Union Central Council of Trade Unions, transferred to the latter functions previously charged upon the USSR People's Com-

---

[153] Stalin, *Questions of Leninism* (10th Russian ed.), p. 114.
[154] *Ibid.*

missariat for Labor,[155] and thereby Soviet authority transferred to the hands of the trade unions such mighty instrumentalities for improving the life of the worker class as state social insurance and control over the effectuation of laws concerning the protection of labor and safety techniques. The inner organization of trade unions and the methods of work are defined by trade-union law and by directives of All-Union trade-union congresses and, in the interval between them, of the All-Union Central Council of Trade Unions.

If trade unions are the most numerous organization of the worker class, we have in the shape of the cooperative, with its different species (kol-khozes, and consumer and industrial cooperatives), the most numerous organization of all the toilers in general. The cooperative is found in various forms—chiefly in that of the consumer cooperative—in bourgeois countries also. There, however, it inevitably grows into the system of capitalist enterprises, inasmuch as only upon that condition is its existence possible. The overthrow of the bourgeoisie's domination and the establishment of the worker-class dictatorship naturally effect a radical change in the role of the cooperative and open up before it the broadest perspectives. In 1926 Stalin wrote of the cooperative: "It acquires special significance after the stabilization of the proletarian dictatorship, during the period of broad building. It facilitates the connection between the vanguard of the proletariat and the masses of the peasantry, and makes it possible to attract the latter into the stream of socialist building."[156]

The most important types of cooperative organizations—possible, however, only if there are no landowner or bourgeois classes—are the kolkhozes, that socialist form of agricultural organization resting on the principle that the toiling peasants voluntarily unite agricultural·production resources with their toil. They thus lead to socialist refashioning and a higher level of all agriculture, and to the annihilation of beggary, the liquidation of the kulaks, a comfortable life for the peasant, and radical change in his living conditions and his psychology. Thanks to the logical policy of the Party and of the Soviet government, to the creation—as a result of socialist industrialization of the country—of a mighty basis for equipping agriculture with complicated machines, to the patient elucidation of the advantage of this form of organizing agriculture over the single peasant homestead economy, and to the aid of every sort[157] which, from the very beginning of its existence,

[155] Cz. 1933, No. 41, Art. 238.
[156] Stalin, *Questions of Leninism* (10th Russian ed.), p. 115.
[157] Cf. Cy. 1917, No. 7, Art. 105, Instruction Concerning the Regulation of Land and Economic Relations by Land Committees; Cy. 1918, No. 43, Art. 524, Decree of the All-Russian Central Executive Committee Concerning Committees for Peasant Poverty; and Cy. 1918, No. 81, Art. 856, Decree of the Council of People's Commissars of Nov. 2, 1918, Concerning the Formation of a Special Fund for Measures to Develop Agriculture.

the Soviet state furnished to accomplish the transition to collective forms of agricultural production, in 1937 these forms of unifying the toilers embraced 18½ million (93 per cent) of the peasant homesteads.

The purposes and the tasks of. these organizations of the toilers were clearly set out in the Model Charter of the agricultural artel adopted by the Second All-Union Congress of Kolkholz Shock Workers and affirmed by the USSR Council of People's Commissars and the Central Committee of the Bolshevik All-Union Communist Party (February 17, 1935): [158]

> The toiling peasants of the village (of the Kazakh village, of the hamlet, of the farmstead, of the Central Asia village, of the Caucasian village) . . . of the district . . . are voluntarily united into an agricultural artel to the end that, employing common resources of production and common organized labor, they may build a collective, that is, a social, economy; assure a complete victory over the kulak, over all exploiters and foes of the toilers, and over need and darkness, and over the backwardness of the petty, individual peasant economy, create high labor productivity, and thus assure the best life for the kolkhoz members.

On the basis of the Model Charter, adopted by the Second Kolkhoz Congress and endorsed with the force of law by administrative affirmation, the kolkhozes drew up their own regulations, which are registered with the district executive committees. State organs direct these organizations of the toilers upon the basis (a) of unconditional observance of the principle that their organization is voluntary, and (b) of the law of the agricultural artel, a law built in complete accord with the propositions of the stable law of kolkhoz life (the Model Charter). The All-Union Lenin Young Communist League plays an important part, under the direction of the Communist Party of Bolsheviks, in the socialist building and education of youth. "This is a mass organization of worker and peasant youth, not a Party organization but a Party adherent. Its task is to help the Party in educating the young generation in the spirit of socialism. It provides youthful reserves for all the remaining mass organizations of the proletariat in all branches of the administration." [159]

The law of the All-Union Lenin Young Communist League, adopted by the Tenth Congress of the Young Communist League (April 21, 1936), reproduces these thoughts of Stalin concerning the role and the tasks of this form of unifying the toilers in the system of worker-class dictatorship. The Young Communist League is a most active assistant of the Party and of the Soviet state in educating the young, working among children in the school, strengthening the family, caring for children, and otherwise. It participates in the everyday work of Soviet organs and aids in making those

---

[158] Cz. 1935, No. 11, Art. 82.
[159] Stalin, *Questions of Leninism* (10th Russian ed.), p. 115.

organs strong. It carries through great and honorable tasks in defending the socialist fatherland and fostering youth in the spirit of Soviet patriotism, actively cooperating with the state in strengthening and developing the armed forces.

The bond between the Young Communist League and the trade union and Soviet organizations is specifically insisted upon by regulations which point out that organs of the League set apart, for the purpose of joint work, representatives who collaborate with the trade unions, the organs of national education, and the other institutions carrying on work concerned with the interests of youth. "Representatives from the Young Communist League to the trade union, Soviet, and other organizations put into practice decisions of the Party—of the Young Communist League—see after the fulfillment of laws of the government concerning youth, take part in the general work of the appropriate organizations, and render regular accounts of their work to the Young Communist League organizations which have sent them" (Art. 44 of the regulations).

The general characterization of the tasks of the numerous voluntary societies and their unions is furnished by the statutes concerning them, adopted by Republic Central Executive Committees and Councils of People's Commissars. A directive of the All-Russian Central Executive Committee and Council of People's Commissars of the RSFSR, July 10, 1932, says:

Voluntary societies and their unions, being organizations of social self-help of the toiling masses of city and country, aim at active participation in the socialist building of the USSR as well as cooperation in strengthening the defense of the country. . . . Voluntary societies and their unions carry on their activity in accord with the plan of national economy and social-cultural building, taking a practical part in effectuating the immediate tasks of Soviet authority in the corresponding branches of socialist building. The work of voluntary societies in scientific research is conducted on the basis of the Marx-Lenin method.[160]

Such societies are organized upon the initiative of the toilers in the following manner: a declaration concerning the affirmation of the regulations of the society or union, together with the proposed regulations, is given to the appropriate state organ (depending on the proposed scale and character of the activity of the society or union), and, upon affirmation of the regulations by this organ, the society is considered organized and acquires the rights of a juristic person to the extent necessary to effectuate the tasks put upon it by the regulations.[161]

[160] Cy. 1932, No. 74, Art. 331.
[161] Cf. Cz. 1933, No. 61, Art. 362, a directive of the Central Executive Committee and Council of People's Commissars of the USSR (Sept. 27, 1933): the Production and Commercial Activity and the Lottery Work of Voluntary Societies.

Local subdivisions of voluntary societies are registered in local (regional, district, city, and agricultural) organs of authority. State organs, having affirmed the regulations and likewise having registered the subdivisions of the society, exercise supervision and control with reference to these societies and unions and their subdivisions. Liquidation of voluntary societies and unions may occur either (a) by virtue of a directive of congresses or assemblies of these societies to that effect or (b) by virtue of a directive of organs of state authority exercising supervision over them in case (1) of a breach of existing legislation by the society or union, or (2) of deviation by the society or union from the aims and purposes indicated in the regulations.

Of the many existing voluntary societies, the most numerous, embracing millions of the toilers, are the Society of Collaboration for the Defense of the Soviet Union and for the Development of its Aviation and Chemical Industries, the International Organization to Aid Revolutionary Fighters, and the Society of the Godless. In the system of the worker-class dictatorship, all the organizations of the toilers that have been examined—each having its own specific tasks—play the part of unique instrumentalities furnishing leverage or driving power and assuring the successful work of this system in its entirety.

The directive force in the system of the worker-class dictatorship in its entirety is the All-Union Communist Party (of Bolsheviks) which exercises direction in the USSR over state organs (personified by the Soviets and their ramifications in the center and in the rural areas) as well as over all the other "levers" personified by the previously enumerated organizations of toilers. The Communist Party is likewise an organization of toilers, but by a special sort of organization—the highest form of organization.

Its force is that it absorbs all the best people of the proletariat from all the proletarian mass organizations. Its function is to *unify* the work of all the proletarian mass organizations without exception and to *direct* their actions to a single goal—the emancipation of the proletariat. Such unification and direction along the line of a single goal is absolutely essential. Otherwise neither unity of the proletarian struggle nor guidance of the proletarian masses in their struggle for authority, for the building of socialism, is possible. Such unification and direction only the vanguard of the proletariat, the party of the proletariat, is competent to achieve. Only the party of the proletariat, of the Communists, is capable of fulfilling such a role as that of basic guide in the system of the proletarian dictatorship.[162]

Being an advance detachment of the worker class, the Party is also at the same time an advance detachment of the toilers in their struggle to

[162] Stalin, *Questions of Leninism* (10th Russian ed.), p. 115.

strengthen and develop socialist society, inasmuch as it has always set before itself the goal of freeing not only the worker class, but all the toilers as well, from the pressure of exploitation—the goal of building socialism wherein all the toilers are interested.

In connection with the annihilation of exploiter classes in our country, the gradual effacement of the boundary between the worker class and the peasantry, this role of the Party as an advance detachment of all the toilers in their struggle to strengthen and develop the socialist social order comes out particularly clearly. In the USSR there is only one party, the Party of the Bolsheviks.

The position of our Party as the sole legal Party in the country—the monopoly of the Communist Party—is not artificial or studiously excogitated. Such a position cannot be created artificially through machinations of the administration and so on. Our Party's monopoly grew from life, developed historically, as a result of the fact that the SR and Menshevik Parties finally went bankrupt and passed from the scene, whereas we were actively operating.[163]

One single Party of Bolsheviks, the Party of Lenin and Stalin, directing all the levers of the system of the worker-class dictatorship in the USSR and resting on the undivided faith and love of all the toilers: therein is the pledge of communism's victory.

The Soviet state, in granting freedoms to citizens, starts from the interests of the toilers and naturally does not include freedom of political parties in the enumeration of these freedoms granted, inasmuch as this freedom, in the conditions prevailing in the USSR, where the toilers have complete faith in the Communist Party, is necessary only for agents of fascism and foreign reconnaissance, whose purpose is to take all freedoms away from the toilers of the USSR and to put the yoke of capitalism upon them once more. The victory of socialism, the liquidation of the exploited classes in the land, has finally removed the ground upon which new parties could emerge independently of the All-Union Communist Party (of Bolsheviks).

Several parties and, accordingly, freedom for parties as well, can exist only in a society where there are antagonistic classes with hostile and irreconcilable interests, where there are, let us say, capitalists and workers, landowners and peasants, kulaks and the poorest peasantry. In the USSR, however, there are no longer such classes as capitalists, landowners, kulaks, and the like. There only are two classes, workers and peasants, and their interests not only are not hostile, they are, on the contrary, amicable. Accordingly, there is in the USSR no ground for the existence of several parties, and so none for freedom for these parties, either. In the USSR there is ground for one Party only—the Communist

[163] Stalin, *Questions of Leninism* (9th Russian ed.), p. 275.

Party; and in the USSR only one party can exist—the Communist Party, boldly defending to the end the interests of workers and peasants.[164]

The All-Union Communist Party (of Bolsheviks) is the directive force in the system of the socialist state, the directing nucleus of all the organizations of the toilers both social and state. As early as the Eighth Party Congress, a resolution as to the matter of organization recited: "The Communist Party sets itself the task of winning decisive influence and complete guidance in all the organizations of the toilers: in trade-union organizations, cooperatives, rural communes, and so forth. Particularly does it aim to promote its program and its complete dominance in contemporary state organizations such as the Soviets." [165] Undivided direction of state and all other organizations of the toilers in the USSR by the Communist Party is a logical consequence of the fact that the All-Union Communist Party (of Bolsheviks), as an advance detachment of the worker class, is for that very reason an advance detachment of all toilers. The Stalin Constitution (Art. 126) reflected and confirmed the broadest utilization by the toilers of the right, guaranteed to them by the Soviet state from the very beginning of its history, to be united in social organizations.

In conformity with the interests of the toilers, and to the end of developing the organizational initiative and political activity of the popular masses, citizens of the USSR are assured the right to be united in social organizations: trade unions, cooperative organizations, youth organizations, organizations for sport and for defense, cultural, technical, and scientific societies; and the most active and politically conscious citizens from the ranks of the worker class and other strata of the toilers unite in the All-Union Communist Party (of Bolsheviks), the advance detachment of the toilers in their struggle to strengthen and develop the socialist social order, and the directive nucleus of all the organizations of the toilers, both social and state.

The Stalin Constitution is thus the only constitution in the world which frankly declared the directing role of the party in the state. Everyone knows that not a single bourgeois constitution up to the present speaks of the role of parties in the bourgeois state. This is understandable, with the class character of the governing parties on the one hand, and the aspiration to obscure the class essence of the bourgeois state on the other.[166] Article 126 of the Stalin Constitution, which has reflected with astonishing distinctness

---

[164] Stalin, *Report on the Draft Constitution of the USSR* (1936), pp. 29–30.
[165] *The All-Union Communist Party (of Bolsheviks) in Resolutions*, Vol. I, pp. 314–315.
[166] In bourgeois states not only constitutions but ordinary laws, and even rules of parliament, avoid the very word "party." Cf. Pelloux, "Political Parties in Postwar Constitutions" (*Revue du droit politique*, No. 2, 1934); and Franz Adler, "The Legal Place of Political Parties in the Modern State" (*Zeitschrift für Politik*, No. 3, 1932).

the rights to unification—realized by citizens of the USSR with unprecedented breadth—and the role of the Communist Party, that highest form of unification of the toilers, is directly supplemented by Article 141 which assures, in behalf of the enumerated social organizations and societies of the toilers, the right to nominate candidates to the Supreme Soviets. The language of these articles is reproduced in the constitutions of all the Union and autonomous republics.

The brilliant victory of the block of Communists and non-Party candidates at the elections to the Supreme Soviet of the USSR and to Supreme Soviets of the Autonomous and Union Republics most eloquently illustrates Article 126 of the Stalin Constitution.

j) The Inviolability of the Person and of the Home—The Privacy of Correspondence

The right of personal inviolability must be understood to mean the legally established guaranty of a citizen against unlawful arrest, and against searches, seizures, and inspections of personal correspondence and other measures illegally limiting the citizen's personal freedom. The right, ordinarily called "the right of civil liberty," is in bourgeois countries the exclusive privilege of the dominant classes, the exploiters. Only in the socialist state is inviolability of the person of citizens, and their equality before the law, truly guaranteed, for only here is "the equality of rights of USSR citizens, irrespective of their nationality and race, in all fields of economic, state, cultural, and social-political life, an immutable law. Any limitation whatsoever, direct or indirect, upon rights or, conversely, any establishment whatsoever of civil advantages, direct or indirect, which depend upon the race or nationality to which citizens belong, as well as any advocacy of race or national exclusiveness, or hatred or contempt, are punished by law" (USSR Constitution, Art. 123).

Where people are divided into oppressed and oppressors, exploited and exploiters, there can be no personal inviolability.

What can be the "personal freedom" of an unemployed person who goes hungry and finds no use for his toil? Only where exploitation is annihilated, where there is no oppression of some by others, no unemployment, no beggary, and no trembling for fear that a man may on the morrow lose his work, his habitation, and his bread—only there is true freedom found.[167]

Only in socialist society, where man is "the most precious capital," where the actual flowering and genuine freedom of human personality are assured, where there is no "irreconcilable contrast either between the individual and

[167] Stalin, Interview with Roy Howard (1936), p. 13.

the collective or between the interests of the separate personality and those of the collective," [168] where the interests defended by the state are at the same time the interests of all the toilers—only in these conditions is the actual protection of the individual inviolability of citizens possible. Only "socialist society reliably guarantees protection of the interests of personality." [169] The genuine right of personal inviolability has its source in the abolition of class inequality, of exploitation, and the victory of the socialist manner of economy. Only the Constitution of the USSR, the Constitution of socialism triumphant, truly guarantees personal inviolability. Article 127 says: "Citizens of the USSR are guaranteed personal inviolability. No one can be subjected to arrest except by directive of the court or with the sanction of the Public Prosecutor." To the end of protecting USSR citizens, in the interests of state security, actual criminals may be subjected to arrest, but, to forestall the possibility of arbitrary arrest, a method is introduced into the USSR whereby arrest may be made only upon court directive or with the sanction of the Public Prosecutor. The court and the Public Prosecutor, in issuing a warrant for arrest, verify the necessity and legality of the application of this measure. Having in view that the Soviet court and the Soviet prosecutor represent the authority of the socialist state and express and defend the interest of all toilers, their verification of the correctness of the arrest is a true and real guarantee that citizens are not being deprived of their freedom illegally and without adequate foundation. Every state is cognizant of arrest applied as a means of holding the accused in check, to obviate the possibility of his escaping from the court and the prosecution, and to isolate him, since if he were found at large prior to the pronouncement of sentence, the safety of society and of the state would be threatened.

The reality and the scope of the guarantees against unfounded arrests are always defined by the political regime of the state proclaiming them. The degree and the reality of guarantees against unjustified arrest depend directly upon the degree to which democracy has developed. It is impossible likewise not to note that laws of bourgeois countries regulating the making of arrests do not as a rule know of preliminary sanction therefor, requiring merely verification after the event of the propriety of the arrest. Only in the USSR, where the actual inviolability of the citizens is truly guaranteed, is a method established pursuant to which preliminary sanction is a prerequisite to arrest and no one may be arrested before either written permission therefor shall have been given by the Public Prosecutor or a directive shall have issued from the court.

[168] Stalin, *Questions of Leninism* (10th Russian ed.), p. 602.
[169] *Ibid.*

Bourgeois laws defining the method of arrests are replete with sundry reservations and loopholes making possible the broad application of arbitrary arrests. Thus Article 113 of the French law, Concerning Guarantees of Individual Freedom, regulating arrest procedure, says:

The accused after his first interrogation by the investigating judge may in no case be imprisoned or left under guard if he has a definite domicile, provided the penalty to which he is subject is less than two years' imprisonment. This directive is inapplicable to an accused already condemned for crime, or to one condemned to prison for an offense everywhere regarded as criminal for a period of more than three months without the application of a suspended sentence. In all cases in the corrective court other than those contemplated by the preceding subdivision of this Article, and in cases of crimes, there must be provisional release within five days after the interrogation. This rule may be rendered inapplicable, however, and the preliminary imprisonment may be prolonged by a directive of the court (in writing and with supporting reasons) in the following cases: (1) if the accused has no definite domicile in France; (2) if he was previously convicted of an offense everywhere regarded as criminal for a term of more than three months' imprisonment without the application of suspended sentence; (3) if there is reason to apprehend that he will escape from the court; (4) if he is a threat to social security; or (5) if leaving him at large may impede disclosure of the truth.[170]

It is easy to understand that all these "ifs" make it possible for arrests to be made in all cases when this is necessary for the French bourgeoisie. Each unemployed person with no definite place of abode, everyone who is a menace to social security from the viewpoint of the dominant class, if only he has committed a crime for which ordinarily arrest is inadmissible as a restraining measure may, merely by virtue of the reasons aforesaid, be kept under guard.

In fascist countries arrest is a greatly extended form of settling accounts with people displeasing to the fascists. The abrogation of all guarantees of personal freedom in the fascist state is reflected also in fascist legislation. Thus in Germany the law of April 24, 1934, abrogated the obligation of court to review, upon its own initiative and within definite times, extension of the period of holding the accused under guard. This means, in essence, that the period of arrest, applied as a measure of restraint, is unlimited. But fascist practice goes further even than fascist "law." Those arrested over a period of years are held under guard without preliminary accusation, as is best proved by the case of the leader of the German proletariat, Thälmann, who has already been held under guard for years without being indicted for any crime. Reaction of every sort is linked with the expansion of despotic

[170] The law in the form of Feb. 7, 1933; cf. *Journal officiel* No. 34 of Feb. 11, 1933, p. 1354: the Law Relative to Guarantees of Individual Liberty.

conduct expressed in the broadening of arbitrary arrests. Actual personal inviolability, the complete guarantee of individual freedom, can exist only in the socialist state, where arbitrary arrest is barred, being punishable as a most serious crime.

Man cannot feel himself free unless his home is secure from arbitrary invasion, unless the privacy of his personal correspondence is guaranteed. Hence it is natural that, guaranteeing the personal inviolability of a citizen of the USSR, the Constitution says: "The inviolability of the homes of citizens and the privacy of their correspondence are preserved by law" (Art. 128). Inviolability of the citizens' homes consists chiefly in their homes being guaranteed against any violent invasion whatsoever. Only representatives of the state may, in cases defined by law, enter a citizen's home without his permission when this is necessary to assure state security. Everyone knows that the search is the most widely extended means of invading the homes of the toilers in capitalist countries. Bourgeois legislation contains limitations upon the right of search. Thus a forced penetration into the habitation of a citizen is possible under English law only when so decided by a criminal court. These limitations have a purely formal character, however, (1) because bourgeois courts always and unreservedly hand down such a decision when the interests of the bourgeoisie require it, and (2) because, side by side with the basic laws supposed to limit the violent invasion of citizens' homes, there are various subsidiary rules which reduce the basic law to nought. Laws in force in most bourgeois states permit a search for the purpose of "eliminating possible danger" as well as on the basis of a completed crime. Such principle in particular operated in prerevolutionary Russia, where the method of conducting a search was governed by the regulation (of March 12, 1888) concerning police supervision, which, for the purpose of eliminating possible danger, permitted a search "upon suspicion," which obviously opens up broad possibilities for arbitrary invasion of the citizen's habitation.

Preserving the inviolability of the Soviet citizen's home, the Soviet law strictly regulates the method of conducting the search, permitting it only at the inception of a criminal proceeding.[171] In the USSR, a search may be conducted only by prosecuting organs, and only in cases when there is adequate basis to suppose that objects of vital importance for the disclosure of crime or the detection of a criminal are to be found in some lodging or in the possession of some person. A warrant is issued as to the necessity of conducting this search and pointing out the basis for holding that it is essential. The results to be attained by the search are specified in the war-

---

[171] Rules for conducting searches are established by the Union Republic codes of criminal procedure.

rant. Before proceeding with the search, the one conducting it is bound to make demand that the objects to be taken be voluntarily turned over, and if this is done, he may be limited to taking away the objects thus voluntarily produced for him.

Persons conducting a search unlawfully, or without adequate basis therefor, are held responsible.

All this guarantees in the USSR the inviolability of citizens' homes from arbitrary searches. Searches may be carried out only in the homes of persons who criminally violate the order established by the state and thereby threaten social security. Protection of the inviolability of homes can be truly guaranteed only where all the legal rights of the person occupying the habitation are preserved.

To the end of assuring the inviolability of the person of the Soviet citizen in the USSR, the privacy of personal correspondence is preserved by law. No one may familiarize himself with a citizen's personal correspondence, with one exception only: in case this is necessary in order to disclose crime and detect a criminal, and even then it is permitted only to investigating organs acting pursuant to special directives sanctioned by the Public Prosecutor. Without the permission of the Public Prosecutor, no one—not even investigating organs—has the right to familiarize himself with a citizen's personal correspondence.

k) The Right of Asylum

Article 129 of the USSR Constitution established that "the USSR grants the right of asylum to foreign citizens persecuted for defending the interests of the toilers or for scientific activity or for their struggle in behalf of national liberation." The same articles are included in the constitutions of certain Union Republics (as in Art. 133 of the RSFSR Constitution).

The practice in international relations of granting persecuted foreigners the right of asylum rests on an international custom, of over a thousand years' standing, for a state in whose territory a persecuted foreign citizen has found shelter to refuse the request of the authorities of the persecuting state that the fugitive be handed over.

Not a single one of the basic capitalist states establishes the right of asylum in its constitution; the right is determined by them through internal legislation and international compacts concerning the extradition of criminals. Persons persecuted for political reasons usually enjoy the right of asylum, a principle apparently won by the bourgeois-democratic revolution against feudalism and formulated for the first time in the French Constitution of 1793 (Art. 119): "The French people gives asylum to foreigners expelled from their own country in consequence of their struggle for freedom." Subsequently it was introduced into legislation (as in the Belgian law of 1883 and the Swiss law of 1892), into international compacts (for the first time into that between France and Sweden in 1831), and into acts of international law (the resolution of the Institute of International Law of 1882, the Havana Code of Private International Law of 1928), and so on.

In capitalist countries the right of asylum is a privilege of the exploiter classes preeminently; its utilization by the oppressed classes is made extraordinarily difficult. Under the conditions of the capitalist world, the grant of the right to politicians of the exploiter classes struggling for power for their clique frequently becomes a means of effectuating the political purposes of the state granting the asylum; for this, reference may be made to the utilization of the Russian White Guard for the anti-Soviet struggle in Germany, Poland, Japan, and other countries; the utilization by German fascists of Austrian and Czechoslovakian Hitlerites; and the utilization by imperialist Japan, of persons who had fled from China after the Revolution of 1912, and the like. Such abuse of the right of asylum on the part of states affording it was pointed out particularly by Zhdanov in his address at the first session of the USSR Supreme Soviet (January 17, 1938).

Bourgeois states create every possible obstacle to the utilization of the right of asylum by toilers and by politicians struggling for their interests, as well as by persons active in the struggle for national emancipation. Thus, as early as the 1890's, there were many attempts to deny the right of asylum to persons who had struggled against the very social and political basis of the contemporary capitalist society. The resolution of the Institute of International Law (1882) noted above expressed this spirit, and this element was reflected later in certain international compacts concerning extradition (compacts between South American states) and in the legislation of individual countries (for example, the American law of May 1, 1917, forbidding the entry into the states of "extreme elements . . . advocating the violent overthrow of governments"). In one of his addresses at Geneva, Litvinov noted: "The very states which give the broadest hospitality to emigrants of a definite political coloration, forget the right of asylum when it is invoked by emigrants of another political coloration." [172] Such forgetfulness "reaches the point of handing antifascist champions over directly to be dealt with by fascist states. Thus, in 1936, the Belgian authorities handed over two antifascist political émigrés to the Gestapo. It goes without saying that fascist states grant no right of asylum to foreigners persecuted for defending the interests of the toilers. The German-Japanese-Italian compacts of 1936 and 1937 establish the direct collaboration by the police

[172] M. Litvinov, *The Foreign Policy of the USSR*, p. 88.

and secret police of those countries to prosecute the struggle against "communism."

The Stalin Constitution, establishing as a basic law of the USSR the grant of a right of asylum to foreign citizens persecuted for defending the interests of the toilers, in reality and in fact makes it broadly and genuinely possible for toilers of the whole world to utilize the "right of asylum," and so is in this regard the most democratic constitution in the world. The right of asylum established in the Stalin Constitution is a development and a confirmation of the principles noted in constitutions of individual Union Republics as early as the years immediately after the great October Socialist Revolution (compare Article 21 of the RSFSR Constitution of 1918, Chapter 14 of the White Russian Constitution of 1919, and others). The corresponding articles of these constitutions established the right of asylum in general form for persons persecuted "for political and religious crimes," but contained no indication that the right was granted to persons persecuted for scientific activity.

Practical application of these articles proved that only two categories of persons persecuted for their convictions seek asylum in the USSR: those persecuted for defending the interests of the toilers and those participating in the struggle for national emancipation, the very persons to whom the formal law of asylum of bourgeois-democratic countries affords no protection. During the twenty years of the existence of Soviet authority, thousands of foreign citizens have found asylum in the USSR after struggling in their fatherland for the interests of the toilers or for national emancipation, true representatives of advanced and progressive humanity, like those who—as all will remember—took part in the Asturian uprising in Spain in 1934. Thousands of workers, persons in service, and intellectuals were received in the USSR as class brothers, whereas in any other country in the world they would have been greeted as a heavy burden at best, as undesirable foreigners harried by police, unemployment, and hunger.

Bourgeois theorists in international law (e.g., Fauchin) concede that the right of asylum cannot be exercised to the detriment of the state's interests, of the state's "right to self-preservation." Naturally the USSR, a single socialist state amidst hostile capitalist encirclement, cannot grant the right of sojourn in its territory to persons who, though hostile to this or that order of capitalism, nevertheless remain antagonistic to socialism. This of course does not mean that individual persons or even groups of this sort may not be allowed entry into Soviet territory, and of course the Soviet state is under no obligation whatsoever to surrender them to the authorities of the persecutor state.

The USSR makes an exception to "the right of asylum" as regards a single category of political criminals—terrorists. On May 19, 1938, it signed in Geneva a convention, Concerning the Prevention of Terrorism and the Struggle Therewith, obligating the signatories to take repressive measures against persons taking shelter in their territories after complicity in terrorist acts. The attitude of the USSR toward political crimes of this sort is illuminated with exhaustive fullness by Litvinov in working out the proposed convention.[173]

The inclusion in Article 129 of the USSR Constitution of the proposition as to the right of asylum of persons persecuted for scientific activity has the most profound political meaning and reveals the complete contrast of the socialist and capitalist systems, the fundamental contrast of our time. Reactionary obscurantism and frantic fascist banditry persecute science and scholars in the countries of decaying capitalism, close scientific institutions, burn books, and destroy the culture created by the ages. The USSR, granting the right of asylum to persons of the capitalist world active in science, defends human culture from fascist fanaticism and saves those living forces, which can serve the toiling national masses, from being physically exterminated by the moribund class.

5. The Basic Obligations of USSR citizens according to the Stalin Constitution

a) The Inseparability of Rights and Obligations of USSR Citizens

All the great rights of citizens of the USSR established in the Constitution are inseparably connected with obligations resting upon them. All the power in our land belongs to the toilers of our socialist society. It is they who are the masters of all the blessings of our state. For the very reason that they are the all-powerful masters of their country, they must fulfill with regard to their country a number of obligations. In his notes on the draft of the Erfurt program, Engels proposed the formula: "For the equal rights and *equal obligations of all*" in place of the formula: "For the equal right of all." "*Equal obligations*," he wrote, "are for us a particularly important addendum to bourgeois-democratic *equal rights*, an addendum removing the specifically bourgeois meaning from the latter." [174]

The scientific foresight of Marx and Engels of a society in which equal rights and equal obligations would be transmuted has been brought to actual realization in our country. It has confirmed "the equal obligation of all to labor according to their capacities and the equal right of all toilers

[173] *Ibid.*, p. 87.
[174] Marx and Engels (Russian ed.), Vol. XVI, Pt. 2, p. 107.

to obtain therefor according to their toil." [175] The obligations of all USSR citizens include: observance of the USSR Constitution, fulfillment of the laws, observance of labor discipline, an honorable attitude regarding social duty, respect for the rules of socialist life in common, protection and confirmation of social socialist property, discharging the honored obligation of military service in the Worker-Peasant Red Army, and defense of the fatherland as a sacred duty of each citizen. Each of the obligations enumerated in the Stalin Constitution is responsive to the life interests of the USSR peoples; therein is their force. By the blood of their most devoted and valorous sons shed in battles on numerous fronts of the civil war, the peoples of our country have won a free and joyous life, and have themselves become interested in the fulfillment of each of these obligations due their fatherland. When the rights and the obligations of USSR citizens are placed side by side, the indestructible bond between them is graphically evident, particularly as exemplified by the right to labor. The Soviet state has granted citizens the right to get guaranteed work, with payment for their labor in accordance with its quantity and quality. At the same time Article 12 of the USSR Constitution says: "Labor in the USSR is an obligation and a matter of honor as regards every citizen capable thereof, in accordance with the principle: 'He who does not work does not eat.'" The socialist social order is unthinkable without the observance of labor discipline. At the First All-Russian Congress of Kolkhoz Shock Workers, Stalin noted: "Socialism is built on labor. Socialism and labor are inseparable." [176]

Each citizen's fulfillment of his obligations to the socialist fatherland, as established in the Stalin Constitution, sustains the strengthening of the USSR wealth and might, the full flowering of a comfortable and cultured life for the toilers, the defense of our fatherland from any encroachment upon its conquests on the part of its foes, and the transition from the lower phase of communism to its highest phase, the condition most essential to all our forward movement.

In bourgeois society individual interests and state interests are dissociated and mutually contradictory. This even Jellinek, one of the greatest bourgeois jurists, was constrained to admit. In a number of his works, *A System of Subjective Public Rights, General Doctrine of the State,* and others, he develops the thought that man, in so far as he is subordinate to the state, ceases to be a personality (a subject of rights) and becomes only a subject of obligations. The power and might of any state are, in his

[175] Stalin, *Questions of Leninism* (10th Russian ed.), p. 583.
[176] *Ibid.*, p. 533.

opinion, based exclusively upon the obedience of the subjects, and power can be realized only if individuals *sacrifice themselves for the state*.[177]

The nature of capitalist society is such that not only the interests of the toiling people but also the interests of the entire progressive development of society as a whole are matters of no concern whatsoever to the ruling class of the bourgeoisie. For the bourgeoisie the decisive and sacrosanct principle, the chief incentive to action, is the acquisition of gain. Within the camp of the bourgeoisie there is no unity as between individual capitalists; they are disunited by the discords and strife between diverse groups of the dominant class. "Ceaselessly hostile within themselves, the bourgeoisie constitute a class only in so far as they have to carry on a common struggle against some other class; in other respects they are, as rivals, in enmity and in opposition as between themselves."[178] The construction of capitalist society is such that capitalism cannot exist and develop without these irreconcilable contradictions.

The indissoluble unity of the peoples of the USSR and their socialist state, the inseparability of civil rights from civil obligations responsive to blood and life interests, turn the USSR into a mighty and indestructible force with no equal in the world, past or present.

Even in his time Engels foresaw the might of the communist social order and warned the gentlemen of the bourgeoisie of the woeful result inevitably awaiting them if they clashed with it: "Take into account, gentlemen, that in the event of war—which of course can be carried on only *against anticommunist* nations—a member of such a (communist) society must defend the *actual* fatherland, the *actual* hearth, and will therefore struggle with an enthusiasm, a steadfastness, and a valor before which the mechanical training of the modern army must scatter like straw."[179]

What has been said above does not mean that the adoption of a new constitution automatically guarantees that all citizens will voluntarily and consciously fulfill their obligations. The process of overcoming the survivals of capitalism in the consciousness of people in our country is still incomplete. The repellent features of the old society, ensconced in the consciousness of the people through the ages, are not yet completely eradicated: bureaucracy, sycophancy, selfishness, trying to lay hands on a bit more, an unbecoming attitude to each other or toward woman or toward one's family,

---

[177] Jellinek, *A General Doctrine of the State* (Russian ed., 1903), p. 278. While this is true of any antagonistic society, it is inapplicable to socialist society, where what is personal and what is social—civil rights and obligations—are not only not mutually contradictory, but are mutually conditioned upon and organically linked with each other.

[178] *The German Ideology*, Marx and Engels (Russian ed.), Vol. IV, p. 44.

[179] Marx and Engels (Russian ed.), Vol. III, p. 278.

and so on. Lenin in his time pointed out that "the most fearful force is the force of habit of millions and tens of millions."[180]

The further struggle to conquer once and for all the survivals of capitalism, "the forces of habit," means also the solution of the problem of all citizens fulfilling their obligations, a direct and vital necessity for all the members of socialist society.

While emphasizing the connection between the rights and the obligations of USSR citizens, we must not lose sight of a difference between them, evident if only from the fact that a USSR citizen can, at his own discretion, use or not use this or that right and is subject to no responsibility if he does use it; whereas his nonperformance, refusal of performance of obligations imposed upon him, entails legal responsibility.

b) Observance of the Constitution, Fulfillment of the Laws, Observance of Labor Discipline, an Honorable Attitude Toward Social Duty, and Respect for the Rules of Socialist Community Life

Article 130 enumerates the fundamental obligations charged upon USSR citizens by the Stalin Constitution: "Every USSR citizen is bound to observe the USSR Constitution, fulfill the laws, uphold labor discipline, maintain an honorable attitude toward social duty, and honor the rules of socialist community life." The great Stalin Constitution contains no declaratory or program affirmations but, as "a conspectus of a path already traversed, of conquests already won," it is the "recording and legislative confirmation of that which has already been gained and won in fact."[181]

This fundamental law of the USSR confirms the political and economic foundations of the socialist worker-peasant state, the principles and forms of state organization and the building of organs of authority, as well as civil rights and obligations, and is the basis of all the USSR legislation. The same propositions, on the scale of the Union and autonomous republics, are confirmed by their constitutions. The stability of the USSR Constitution, and of Union and autonomous republic constitutions, is a most indispensable condition precedent to the full flowering of our socialist state and the complete utilization by citizens of all the exceedingly broad rights granted to them.

It is natural that the very first obligation of USSR citizens is the observance of the USSR Constitution and those of the Union and autonomous republics. Accordingly, Article 130 and the corresponding articles of Union and autonomous republic constitutions begin their enumeration of

[180] Lenin (Russian ed.), Vol. XXV, p. 190.
[181] Stalin, *Report on the Draft of the USSR Constitution* (1936), p. 17.

the fundamental obligations of Soviet citizens with the obligation to observe the Constitution.

Soviet laws, the only laws in the world truly expressing the will of the people, are directed at strengthening the socialist economy and Soviet discipline and educating citizens in the spirit of communism, and at pitiless struggle against all the foes of the great Soviet people, against the traitors, betrayers, and agents of fascist reconnaissance, and against each and every encroachment upon the interests and rights of the people. In the hands of the socialist state, they are a mighty instrument for the reorganization of society, for refashioning human consciousness, and for strengthening socialist society. Their power consists in the fact that they express the interests of the people and are put into practice with the aid of the people themselves. Therefore, from the very first days of its emergence, the Soviet state, having abrogated bourgeois legality and created a new (socialist) legality, requires that all citizens, institutions, and officials observe Soviet laws precisely and without protest.[182] In complete accord with their role and their significance, the Stalin Constitution in Article 130, and constitutions of all the Union and autonomous republics in the corresponding articles, define the fulfillment of Soviet laws as one of the very first of the basic obligations of USSR citizens. Education of the toilers in the spirit of respect for the laws of the socialist state and unswerving fulfillment thereof by all the People's Commissariats, official and individual citizens of the USSR is a potent instrumentality for further strengthening the might of our socialist state.

The USSR is the only country in the world where labor is surrounded with honor and the individual's position in society is entirely defined by his labor, where honorable labor brings people fame, glory, and esteem, and has become a "matter of *honor,* of *glory,* of *prowess,* and of *heroism.*" [183] The great October Socialist Revolution enfranchised labor and declared it to be an obligation of all citizens, and initiated as well a new attitude toward labor, a new, socialist discipline of labor, which had come to replace the old punitive discipline of the labor of capitalist society. During the socialist refashioning of the entire national economy, socialist labor discipline expanded and grew strong in the process. The sprouts of this new socialist discipline of labor, of the new attitude toward labor, were noted by the genius of Lenin in the first communist gatherings for social work in the civil war epoch. In time this attitude toward labor became common to the Soviet people and found expression in the mighty growth of mass socialist

---

[182] Cf. for example, Cy. 1917, No. 1, Art. 12, the Extraordinary Sixth All-Russian Congress of Soviets (stenographic report, pp. 13–14); Lenin Collection, Vol. XXI, p. 264, Lenin (Russian ed.), Vol. XXIV, pp. 433–434.
[183] Stalin, *Questions of Leninism* (10th Russian ed.), p. 393.

rivalry and, finally, in the Stakhanovite movement. Articles 12 and 130 of the Stalin Constitution reflected and confirmed the position assigned to labor in our society. The former says that "labor in the USSR is an obligation and a matter of honor of each citizen capable thereof in accordance with the principle: 'He who does not work does not eat.'" In the USSR the socialist principle: "From each according to his capacity, to each according to his toil" is carried into effect.

That conscious and disciplined labor is the obligation of each citizen is emphasized in Article 130, which includes the observance of labor discipline among the fundamental obligations of USSR citizens. Similar formulae are contained in constitutions of all the Union and autonomous socialist republics.

The enumeration in the Stalin Constitution of the obligations of USSR citizens manifests brilliantly the honored and lofty role of a citizen of socialist society. The Soviet citizen is a citizen of a state of a higher type, of a socialist state that has obliterated the opposition between personality and the collective which is characteristic of capitalism, and harmoniously united their interests. Socialist society elevates the idea of social duty to a lofty height. Taking a direct and active part in socialist building, the USSR citizens must possess a highly developed idea of social duty and must realize that each citizen's fulfillment of his social duty is the basis upon which society in its entirety, and therefore the personal welfare of the citizens, may flourish. The Stalin Constitution has reflected this relationship toward social duty in the USSR, having confirmed (in Art. 130) as one of their fundamental obligations an attitude of honor on the part of citizens toward social duty. The same is true in constitutions of all the Union and autonomous Soviet socialist republics. Thereby an honorable attitude toward social duty became not only a rule of morality but also an unchanging law of the state, deviation from which is deemed a breach of the fundamental law with appropriate consequences flowing therefrom.

Among the fundamental obligations of citizens of the USSR pointed out by Article 130 is respect for rules of socialist community life. At any given moment of history, the rules of community life are defined by the principles of the then social order. Capitalist means of production, based on private property and exploitation of the majority by the minority, accordingly creates compatible social arrangements, the rules of community life in bourgeois society. The dull greed of the private proprietor, stimulated by avid aspirations to be rich and to win the possibility of escaping from labor, of becoming richer, and so more powerful, than his rival, leads to that unrestrained repression and exploitation of the toiling masses which is the inevitable concomitant of capitalist society. The principles of bourgeois community life, and the customs, *mores* and views of bourgeois society are all qualified and colored by the capitalist means of production, with its irreconcilably antagonistic contradictions. Science, art, and printing, the school and the church, all are enlisted to inculcate in the consciousness of the masses, tastes and rules of conduct agreeable to the bourgeoisie, given out officially as principles common to all mankind, whereas in reality the bourgeois reasons: "Society—I am society; morality—that means my tastes and my passions; law—that is what is for my advantage." [184]

In complete accord with the laws of the bourgeois social order, principles are advocated that people must act according to such rules as: "Each for himself and God alone for all," and "Every man is a wolf to his fellow man," to the effect that victory in the struggle is his who appears stronger. "Such is already the law of the exploiters—to beat the backward and the weak—the wolf law of capitalism. You are backward, you are weak; that means you are wrong and may therefore be beaten and enslaved." [185] But this unlimited individualism, the savage struggle for "a position in society," the egoism, the competition wherein each is ready to gnaw a rival's throat— these are the most characteristic features developed by a social order of oppression and exploitation among men.

The bourgeoisie has vulgarized and perverted the best ideas of advanced mankind. In bourgeois society everything is measured in money. Everything is dominated by cupidity, calculation, and ubiquitous venality. Everything—not only inanimate objects—but human personality and conscience, love and science—everything inevitably becomes a subject of purchase and sale so long as the power of capital holds. Deceit, hypocrisy, and sanctimoniousness are the outstanding characteristics of bourgeois morality. Bourgeois preachments concerning the sanctity and inviolability of the family and of property are in woeful contradiction with reality, where prostitution flourishes and the children of millions of proletarians are turned into mere objects of trade and instruments of toil, where only a fraction of 1 per cent of the population possesses property, while the rest are "free" of property, and where all society is based on hired slavery, on exploitation of millions of the toilers.

The great October Socialist Revolution accomplished an overturn unequaled in the world's history of the social life of mankind. From that moment the basis of the life of millions upon millions of people, and therewith all the order and all the rules of life and of community living, began to change. But the creation of new forms of social life, of new orders of community living, is an extremely protracted process. New order and rules

[184] P. Lafarge, *Collected Works* (Russian ed.), Vol. III, p. 374.
[185] Stalin, *Questions of Leninism* (10th Russian ed.), p. 445.

of community living could not appear at a single stroke, since this new society was not yet emancipated, and could not at a stroke be emancipated, from the survivals of the social order from which it had only just emerged. Even under the first phase of communism—socialism—this new society "in all respects, economic, moral, and intellectual, still preserves the birthmarks of the old society from whose womb it has issued." [186] Addressing the workers, Marx wrote that they would themselves have "to survive fifteen, twenty, or fifty years of civil war and international battles in order not only to change existing conditions, but that they might themselves change and become capable of political domination." [187] In their earlier work, *The German Ideology*, Marx and Engels wrote of the fact that only in revolution can the worker class "be liberated from all the old filthiness," and the same thought was expressed more than once by Lenin.[188]

Only in a protracted struggle with the old world were the new people of socialist society, those who are establishing new forms of socialist comunity life, created. This process began in the land from the very earliest days of the proletarian revolution. As Lenin teaches us, "We will work to delete the accursed rule: 'Each for himself, and God alone for all!' . . . We will work to instill in consciousness the habit, in the everyday intercourse of the masses, the rule: 'All for one and one for all'; the rule: 'Each according to his capacities, to each according to his needs,' so as to introduce communist discipline into communist labor gradually but unswervingly." [189] In the stubborn struggle with survivals of the way of life and *mores* of the capitalist past, new people were wrought out in all spheres of our life from the very first years of Soviet authority.

Genuine elevation of the masses' creative activity, like the broad flowering of human personality, was made real upon the stable substructure of a socialist society.

Among us, socialism is not merely something constructed; it has already entered into the way of life, the everyday way of life, of the people. Ten years ago it would have been possible to debate whether or not socialism could be constructed among us. Now this is no longer a debatable question. Now it is a matter of facts—of a living life, of a way of life—which penetrate the entire life of the people.[190]

Only in the land of socialism, where there is no private property in instruments and means of production, is man freed from the pressure and

[186] Marx and Engels (Russian ed.), Vol. XV, p. 274.
[187] *Ibid.*, Vol. VIII, p. 506.
[188] Lenin (Russian ed.), Vol. XXIII, p. 490.
[189] *Ibid.*, Vol. XXV, p. 256.
[190] Stalin, "Speech at the Preelection Assembly of Electors of the Stalin Election District of Moscow" (Dec. 11, 1937).

serfdom and the external forces of society dominant over him. Socialism turned man into a true lord of the forces of nature, an individual perfecting his intellectual and spiritual capacities.

Stalin again emphasised in 1934, in a conversation with the English writer H. G. Wells, that only socialist society guarantees the most complete freedom of personality, and he returned to the same thought in his well known conversation with Roy Howard, pointing out that we build communist society for the sake of the true freedom of human personality. Only the communist social order guarantees the full flowering of the inner content of personality as the bearer of moral and cultural values, and makes complete freedom from the traditions, habits, and mud of the old society possible for man. These ideas of the founders of scientific communism, Marx and Engels, were brought to life in our country by their mighty successors, Lenin and Stalin. Among us, the new material basis, social, socialist property, is the foundation for new relationships between people, a new attitude to labor, social duty, family, and children, and for new rules of socialist community life in the spirit of communist morality. At no other time or place has human personality, the worth of the Soviet citizen, been raised to such a height as in our land. The relationship to people, to man, in the socialist country was thus expressed through the lips of Stalin: "Of all the valuable capital to be found in the world, the most valuable, and the most determinant, is people—cadres." [191] The laws of the jungle: "Every man is a wolf to his fellow man"—"Every man for himself," are forever thrust out from our socialist way of life.

The heroic epic of the rescue of the Chelyuskinites, the magnificent exploit of the bold Papaninites on the drifting ice floe "The North Pole," the unprecedented flight and exploits in the vast Siberian forests of the heroic three, Grizodubova, Raskova, and Osipenko, and the fraternal and friendly love and concern for them manifested by the entire Soviet people, have most brilliantly demonstrated to all the world that only in the land of socialism is man man's friend, that only on the basis of socialism can people attain such a degree of friendship, collective support, organized aid, and unity. These socialist principles in action enter into life every day and become ever more and more characteristic of our contemporary socialist reality. In our days the vision of Lenin is being realized:

Only from socialism will a swift, insistent, and genuinely mass movement forward in all spheres of social and personal life begin, with a *majority* of the population, and then the entire population, taking part.[192]

[191] Stalin, "Speech at the Kremlin at the Graduation of the Red Army Academicians" (Party Publishing House, 1935), p. 14.
[192] Lenin (Russian ed.), Vol. XXI, p. 439.

Morality is that which serves to destroy the old exploiter society and to unify all the toilers around the proletariat which is creating the new society of communists. Communist morality is that morality which serves this struggle, which unites the toilers against every sort of exploitation. . . . At the foundation of communist morality lies the struggle for the strengthening and consummation of communism.[193]

Communist morality, of which Lenin spoke in 1920, penetrates into ever broadening strata of our society. The actions, the entire conduct, of the honorable Soviet citizen to social and personal life is dictated by the interests of our socialist revolution, the interests of the people, and by the task of the triumphant consummation of communism. For this reason implacable hatred for enemies of the revolution, struggling against foes of the people, against Trotsky-Bukharin spies and diversionists who acted for the bourgeoisie in striving to overthrow the existing socialist social order in the USSR and to reestablish capitalism, is one of the most important principles of communist morality.

Before us still lies protracted and systematic work, "the most grateful and most noble" work, in Lenin's words, on the final liquidation of the heavy heritage still remaining to us from the old society and the education of all citizens in a spirit of respecting and fulfilling all the rules of socialist community life. For this reason respect for the rules of socialist community life is an obligation of each citizen of the USSR under Article 132 of the Stalin Constitution. Each citizen is thereby obligated to such conduct in society as would promote the further strengthening of socialism; and this means an honorable and conscientious attitude to his labor, his social obligation, the strengthening of socialist discipline, the fulfillment of Soviet laws, the protection and strengthening of the community's socialist property, implacable opposition to foes of socialism, honor and truth as regards others, and advancement of his own socialist culture.

Respect for the rules of socialist community life and the fulfillment thereof by all citizens of the USSR strengthens the might of our socialist state which is, in turn, the true pledge of the further brilliant triumphs of socialism, of further triumphs of communism in the history of the entire world.

c) The Obligation to Safeguard and to Strengthen Socialist Property

Article 131 of the USSR Constitution says: "It is the duty of every citizen of the USSR to safeguard and to strengthen social socialist property." This is one of the sacred obligations of the Soviet citizen wherewith he is charged by the great Stalin Constitution. The realization of the prole-

[193] *Ibid.*, Vol. XXX, pp. 411–413.

tarian revolution signifies the abrogation of bourgeois property and the creation of the conditions for establishing the socialist organization of society,
whose economic basis is socialist property. The dominant system of production and appropriation always finds complete expression in the corresponding system of property relations. "The contemporary bourgeois
private property is the last and most complete expression of such production and appropriation of products as is based on class contradictions, on the
exploitation of some by others." [194] The nature of socialist property is entirely different. The affirmation of socialist property signifies the victory of
the socialist system of economy, the abolition of man's exploitation of man,
and for this reason the obligation to safeguard and to strengthen socialist
property is an indispensable condition of the struggle for communism.

Emphasizing the necessity of pitiless struggle against those striving to
encroach upon socialist property, Lenin calls such encroachment a most
serious breach of discipline, and points out that foes of the revolution who
make attempts upon social property must be pitilessly punished. He always
emphasized that every pood of grain and fuel belonging to the Soviet state
is a veritable holy of holies,[195] the loftiest of all; that the struggle to defend
this property must be carried on with implacable resolution, and that each
of the toilers is obligated to safeguard and to strengthen socialist property.
"The struggle to safeguard social property, the struggle by all the measures
and all the means put at our disposal by the laws of Soviet authority, is one
of the basic tasks of the Party" [196] is the teaching of Stalin.

The proletarian revolution deprived the bourgeoisie of the instruments
and means of production, destroyed bourgeois property relations, and
created socialist property. Socialist property grows and is strengthened, and
at the same time the hatred of the foes of Soviet authority for socialist property grows also. They understand all too well that with each forward step
in the development and strengthening of socialist property they become
weaker, and that the growth and strengthening of socialist property lead to
their final ruin. Socialist property is the economic basis of the Soviet social
order, and for this reason the foes of socialism have tried, and are still trying,
above all to undermine this basis, to annihilate and to pillage socialist
property.

The main point in the "activity" of these bygone folk is that they organize
mass thievery and plundering of state property, of cooperative property, of kolkhoz property. Thievery and plundering in factories and works, of railroad
freight, in warehouses and trade enterprises—particularly in sovkhozes and kol-

[194] Marx and Engels, *Communist Manifesto* (Russian ed., 1938), pp. 41–42.
[195] Lenin (Russian ed.), Vol. XXIII, p. 30.
[196] Stalin, *Questions of Leninism* (10th Russian ed.), p. 509.

khozes—such is the basic form of their activity. They sense, as by a class instinct, that the foundation of Soviet economy is social property and that it is this foundation that must be caused to totter in order to befoul Soviet authority, and they actually try to cause social property to totter by organizing mass thievery and plundering.[197]

To the savage attempts of the class foe to undermine socialist property, to cause it to totter, the Party and Soviet authority responded by intensifying a most decisive and stern struggle to safeguard socialist property. The law of August 7, 1932, says in that regard:

Socialist property (state, kolkhoz, and cooperative) is the basis of the Soviet social order, sanctified and inviolable. Persons making an attempt upon it must be deemed enemies of the people, wherefore a decisive struggle with pillagers of social property is the very first obligation of organs of Soviet authority. . . . The supreme measure of social defense shall be applied by the court to put down pillaging (thievery) of kolkhoz and cooperative property; guilty persons shall be shot and all their property confiscated, although if there are extenuating circumstances, the sentence may be commuted to imprisonment for not less than ten years and to confiscation of all property.[198]

As the attempts of enemies to undermine socialist property, to cause it to totter, became more intense, the struggle to safeguard such property became proportionately more active. The words of Lenin were brilliantly vindicated: "The more diverse the attempts and the travail of exploiters to defend the old order of things, the more rapidly will the proletariat learn to drive its class foes out of their last refuge." [199]

Nonetheless, it would be a serious mistake to suppose that at the present time all the toilers without exception manifest a conscious and genuinely socialist attitude toward national property. It must not be forgotten that the toiler, while emancipated from the yoke of capitalism, is far from being emancipated at one stroke from the survivals of the psychology of capitalist society. In his speech at the Second All-Russian Congress of Trade Unions in 1919, Lenin said on this score: "No Chinese wall ever separated the worker from old society; he, too, preserved much of the traditional psychology of capitalist society. The workers are building a new society without having been turned into new people free from the mud of the old world. They are still standing in this mud up to their knees." [200]

As early as 1926, in his speech at the plenum of the Central Committee of the All-Union Communist Party (of Bolsheviks), Stalin, emphasizing the necessity of intensifying the struggle for socialist property, noted at the same

[197] *Ibid.*, pp. 507–508.
[198] Cz. 1932, No. 62, Art. 360.
[199] Lenin (Russian ed.), Vol. XXII, p. 157.
[200] *Ibid.*, Vol. XXIII, p. 490.

time that all the people in our land have not yet shaken off the view that socialist property is something alien, something impersonal:

> When a spy or a traitor is caught, the indignation of the people knows no bounds. It demands that he be shot. When, however, a thief operates before the eyes of all, pillaging state property, the public around about merely laughs good-humoredly and claps him on the shoulder. Yet it is clear that the thief, who pillages the people's property and undermines the interests of the people's economy, is just as much a spy and a traitor, if not worse.[201]

In this address Stalin emphasized with particular clarity the significance of the struggle with the pillagers of socialist property. He views an attempt upon socialist property as a political crime, and persons perpetrating that crime as foes of the people, spies, traitors. At the same time he emphasizes the antisocial conduct of all those whose attitude to socialist property is as if it were the property of another and they didn't care what became of it.

The final triumph of the socialist economy, the affirmation of socialist property as the firm foundation of the Soviet social order, is a factor which has radically changed not only the economy of the country, having made it socialist, but also the psychology of millions of Soviet people. That which the founders of Marxism, Marx and Engels, foresaw is taking place before our eyes. Setting out the principles of communism, they wrote:

> As in the last century the peasants and the workers in factories changed their entire form of life and became altogether different people when they seemed drawn into big industry, precisely so the carrying on of production in common by the forces of all society, and the new development of production resulting therefrom, will need—and will create—utterly new people.[202]

A new Stalin generation of people grew up, Stakhanovites, honorable citizens loving their toil and understanding that the safeguarding of socialist property is their sacred obligation inasmuch as socialist property is the inviolable basis of the Soviet social order, the source of the fatherland's wealth and might and of the comfortable and cultured life of the toilers.

The aspiration to safeguard and to strengthen socialist property became an aspiration of the Soviet people defending the bulwarks of socialism, and it was therefore natural that, in defining the fundamental rights and obligations of citizens, the USSR Constitution legislatively confirmed the obligation of the Soviet citizen "to safeguard and to strengthen social socialist property." At the same time the Constitution warns all those seeking to encroach upon socialist property that they will be regarded as enemies of the people: "Persons making attempts upon social socialist property are

---

[201] Stalin, *The Economic Position of the Soviet Union* (1926), p. 16.
[202] Marx and Engels (Russian ed.), Vol. V, pp. 477–478.

enemies of the people" (Art. 131). Precisely for this reason, the law of August 7, 1932, establishes severe punishment for those guilty of this most serious crime. Precisely for this reason, the law imposes serious responsibility as well upon those whose violation of their duty and criminal attitude toward their obligations create conditions favorable for thieves and pillagers of socialist property.

Socialist property is safeguarded not only by means of the criminal punishment against pillagers, however, but also with the aid of a broad system of measures of a social-organizational and preservative character. The presence of a broad network of social control organizations, the broad activity of the people of our land, and the lofty feeling of Soviet patriotism —these are the guarantees of the methodical fulfillment of the Soviet citizen's sacred duty to "safeguard and strengthen social socialist property." The safeguarding of Soviet socialist property is in the hands of the Soviet people themselves. They guard the people's property as the apple of their eye.

Socialist property is a great cultural force, completely reflecting the force of the Soviet state and of the new socialist culture. Private property in the means and instruments of production is opposed to it in principle. The entire history of the development of private property as an institution is the history of the bloody oppression, sufferings, and deprivations of the toilers. How the struggle to safeguard private property was conducted may be demonstrated by a whole series of examples. In antiquity, long before our era, we find extraordinarily cruel laws directed toward the defense of private property. Under legislation of the Babylonian king, Hammurabi, *circa* 2000 B.C., the punishment commonly ordained for a crime against private property was death by drowning, burning, or hanging, however insignificant the size of what had been stolen and irrespective of the motives of the thief. In Germany in the sixteenth century, the death sentence was applicable to theft (regardless of the amount) and to all crimes against property. In England as late as the eighteenth century, the death sentence was imposed for such crimes as the unauthorized felling of timber and larceny. In the reign of Henry VIII, 70,000 persons were punished in England as "thieves" and "robbers" in the course of a few years, whereas in reality they were simply paupers and ruined peasants.

In Russia as many as 20,000 persons were punished because of the Rebellion of 1662. It occasioned the capitalists no embarrassment to hand over to be executed for the theft of a kopeck persons whom they had themselves spent their entire lives in robbing. When the bourgeoisie came to power, it always put forward into first place in all its documentary declarations the principle of protecting private property as the foundation of the social order. The Declaration of Rights of Man and Citizen of the French bourgeois revolution said: "The goal of political union of every sort is the preservation of man's natural and inalienable rights. These are: freedom, property, security, and resistance to oppression." Private property was thus declared a "natural, inalienable" right of man, whereas it is utterly beyond question that "property is for the capitalist, the right to appropriate another's unpaid labor or the product thereof, and is for the worker the impossibility of appropriating to himself his own product." [203] Accordingly, in whatever forms bourgeois property was proclaimed as "sacred" and "inviolable," and however insistently it was declared a natural and inalienable right of a citizen, it will always be merely a right of the capitalist to appropriate the unpaid labor of another and so will always be hateful to the toilers as instrumental in their exploitation. On the other hand the obligation to defend socialist property is, for citizens of the USSR, a sacred obligation, since the issue concerns property in the instruments and means of production, the affirmation of which destroys man's exploitation of man once and for all and guarantees the victory of socialism.

d) Universal Military Service and the Defense of the Fatherland

The army is one of the basic institutions of the state.[204] From the moment it comes into existence, the state, the organization of the dominant class, creates special armed forces which are summoned to safeguard it both from encroachments by other states upon its independence and integrity and, in the first instance, from forces within the country hostile to the dominant class.

It is characteristic of exploiter states that the army is isolated from the people, stands opposed to them, a menacing, blind force entirely in the hands of the dominant class. Independently of the method of organizing the armed forces, whether by enlistment or by conscription, and notwithstanding the fact that the rank and file of the army is collected from the broadest masses of the toilers, it appeared—and still appears—in exploiter society as a weapon directed entirely toward defense of the interests of the dominant class.

In the capitalist states of Western Europe and America, there are different systems of organizing the army. (Formerly they existed also in tsarist Russia.) As a rule the capitalist world nearly everywhere still keeps to the system of universal military service introduced in most states, beginning in the second half of the nineteenth century. The establishment of this method was due to various causes, including particularly the development of mili-

---

[203] Marx, *Das Kapital* (Russian ed., 1937), p. 641.
[204] Engels, *The Origin of Family, Private Property and the State,* Chap. 9.

tary technique, the growth of the means of communication, the complexity of army organization, and the necessity of introducing distinctness and planning into preparation for war; and it became the generally acknowledged method in all countries except England and the U.S.A.[205]

An army organized on the principle of universal military service is based on regular units consisting of cadres. Most of the army command—filled in bourgeois countries from the "have" classes—remains as a rule in military service for life. The rankers or "lower officers," according to the terminology of the tsarist army, are called into the ranks upon attaining a definite age, ordinarily twenty to twenty-one, for a period of one to four years, and are thereafter dismissed to the reserve, where their status continues for an average term of around twenty years. In case of war, the reserve is called up for actual military service. Reserves are divided into bodies of cadres which are thus developed into wartime staffs.

The system of universal military service, removing citizens, as it does, for a definite period from their ordinary occupations and, in bourgeois states, exposing them to the discomforts of barrack drill and entailing limitations on their civil and political rights, becomes extremely burdensome and oppressive for the people of capitalist countries. Proclaiming, with typical hypocrisy, that military service is a duty of each citizen, the bourgeoisie has none the less done everything to put the chief burdens of this service on the shoulders of the toilers and to be themselves freed from them so far as possible. This purpose is attained by granting numerous exemptions carrying freedom from military service—of a sharply defined class character, as a rule. Thus, there are exemptions on the basis of property and economic position, deferring for a number of years the call into the army of persons themselves directing trade, factory, or works enterprises. Exemptions on the ground of education, which in capitalist countries is accessible chiefly to the substantial strata of the population, are of the same class character. The basis of the army thus is, and always has been, the toiling masses.

The untrustworthiness, from the class point of view, of an army so constituted is exceedingly obvious. The bourgeoisie tries to assure the army's reliability first of all by choosing a trustworthy staff to be in command of it. The staff of officers of bourgeois countries is, as a rule, chosen from among the privileged classes, and officers are given various advantages and are a

[205] England and the U. S. A. build their armies on the basis of enlistment. Moreover, the period of service in England varies from three to nine years, and in the U. S. A. from one to three years and more. Constrained during the first imperialist war to pass to universal military service, these countries returned thereafter to the method of enlistment. The countries vanquished in the imperialist war (Germany, Bulgaria, Turkey, and Hungary) were even constrained by the Treaty of Versailles to pass to the enlistment system, but, as everyone knows, they annulled these articles of the treaty and now man their armies by the system of universal military service.

special caste, all of whose welfare is closely linked with the welfare of the dominant class. Then, still in order to assure the army's obedience, the bourgeoisie isolates it from the people and from the life of the country, shutting up in barracks those called and subjecting them to rigorous barrack adaptation and drill. Life under the barrack regime in capitalist countries —reminiscent of prison regime—and the establishment of barbarous responsibility for the smallest delinquency are calculated to destroy the soldiers' capacity to reason and to make the soldier mass-obedient. By way of reinsurance, the bourgeoisie creates specially chosen privileged units enjoying special advantages and granted numerous exemptions. Their commanding staff is likewise chosen from the most privileged strata of the population, and the aim of their existence is to support the dominant classes at a critical moment. Since the army manifestly cannot be relied on as an instrument of the struggle against the toiling classes, the bourgeoisie is compelled to create their own armed class forces. Coordinate with the army are armed detachments made up exclusively of members of the bourgeoisie. Such forces are formed in Germany, Italy, Poland, Latvia, Esthonia, Finland, Bulgaria and elsewhere. At the necessary moment they act independently, or are partially merged in the ranks of the army.

The army of the socialist state is organized on diametrically opposite principles, being indissolubly linked with the people, enveloped by the love of the people, and living a full-blooded political life together with the people.

The Worker-Peasant Red Army is destined to defend the socialist Worker-Peasant State. It is called to guarantee under all conditions the inviolability of the boundaries, and the independence, of the USSR. Any attack upon the socialist Worker-Peasant State will be beaten off with all the might of the armed forces of the Soviet Union, and military action will be transferred to the territory of the aggressor-foe.

This first point of the field order of the Worker-Peasant Red Army discloses with extreme clarity and fullness the tasks and the purposes set before the army of the socialist state.

Created in January, 1918, by decree of the Worker-Peasant government over the signature of Lenin, the Red Army passed through a long and complicated process of preparation prior to its formation into the mighty organized armed force of the world's first socialist state.

In his article, "The War Program of the Proletarian Revolution," Lenin wrote (as early as 1916):

An oppressed class which does not strive to learn to possess, to have, a weapon, such oppressed class would deserve only to be treated like slaves. But we cannot, without becoming bourgeois pacifists or opportunists, forget that we live in a class society, and that therefrom there is, and can be no way out other than class struggle. . . . Our watchword must be: "Arming the proletariat to vanquish, expropriate, and disarm the bourgeoisie." [206]

By the time of the great October Socialist Revolution, the forces of the Red Guard in Petrograd alone numbered 40,000. In the October days in Moscow, the Red Guard, together with the revolutionary parts of the old army, struggled heroically during eight days with White Guards, shattered the officer-junker regiments, and compelled them to surrender.

After grasping authority, the Red Guard was the first armed support of the proletarian dictatorship. Wearied by the imperialist war, the old army had collapsed of its own motion. Soldiers, mostly peasants, strove to scatter to their homes and to take the land from the landowners. Meantime a stubborn and protracted armed struggle against the forces of international imperialism and internal revolution was impending. A mighty army of the proletarian dictatorship was needed. Immediately after the establishment of the proletarian dictatorship, the party took in hand the organization of that army. A decree concerning the creation of the Red Army was issued in January, 1918, as follows: (1) The Worker-Peasant Red Army is created out of the most class-conscious and organized elements of the toiling classes; (2) its ranks are open for the entry of all citizens of the Russian Republic who have attained the age of eighteen years. [207]

The Red Army was originally composed of voluntary workers, hired labor, and the poorest peasants. With the old bourgeois-landowner war machine entirely smashed and in ruins and the old army disbanded, a new army could be created only by recruiting volunteers. The principal attention of all the Party, Soviet, and professional organizations was devoted to recruiting and forming the units of the Red Army. By the spring of 1918, the armed forces of counterrevolution had encircled the Soviet Republic. The fierce armed struggle which developed required the transition from forming the army on a voluntary principle to that of universal military service. On May 29, 1918, the All-Russian Central Executive Committee adopted a decree, Concerning Compulsory Recruiting into the Worker-Peasant Red Army, [208] the first step in this direction. On the 10th of July, 1918, the Fifth Congress of Soviets adopted a directive concerning the introduction of universal military service. Article 19 of the RSFSR Constitution, adopted by the same congress, said:

To the end of defending by all measures the conquests of the great Worker-

---

[206] Lenin (3rd Russian ed.), Vol. XIX, p. 326.
[207] Cy. 1918, No. 17, Art. 245.
[208] Cy. 1918, No. 41, Art. 518.

Peasant revolution, the RSFSR acknowledges the obligation of all citizens of the Republic to defend the socialist fatherland and establishes universal military service. The honored right to defend the revolution arms in hand is granted only to the toilers: nonlabor elements are charged with carrying out other military obligations.

The Red Army of workers and peasants produced by Lenin and Stalin achieved miracles. It shattered all the numerous and armed forces of Russian counterrevolution led by experienced generals and officers and under the tutelage and inspiration of foreign states which had supplied them with money and armament.

With destructive blows the Red Army shattered all the foreign conquerors who tried to drown the proletarian revolution in blood and to turn the Soviet Republic into a colony. It was victorious because the Party of the Bolsheviks, guided by Lenin and Stalin, stood at the head of the masses and organized the victory; because it struggled for the interests of the broadest masses and had strong and invincible support in the rear which provided the front with everything down to the last lump of sugar; because in its struggle it invariably obtained aid and support from the international proletariat and the toilers of the entire world; and, finally, because it struggled for the right to liberate the toilers from the yoke of capitalism, and went strongly along the line pointed out by the revolutionary Marx-Engels-Lenin-Stalin theory. Under the conditions of capitalist encirclement, the mighty Worker-Peasant Army is the very first condition essential to the existence of the socialist state. Thanks to the tireless concern of the Party and of the Soviet government, our army, equipped with advanced technique and strong on a lofty plane of political consciousness, is a menacing and invincible force, guarding our frontiers and preserving our peaceful labor.

Our army is organized on the principles of universal military service; in the conditions obtaining in a socialist state, however, such service is not, as it is in capitalist states, a burdensome obligation but an honored duty, fulfilled by USSR citizens with conscious pride. According to the law concerning obligatory military service (wherein changes were introduced in 1936 as regards lowering the age of call from twenty-one years to nineteen, which answers the interests of Soviet youth by affording it thereafter the possibility of working at a chosen specialty, or of studying without interruption, and is explained by the enhanced physical development of the toilers during the years of Soviet authority), all the toilers of male sex from nineteen to forty years of age are bound to pass through military service. Military service is made up of (1) precall training, passing through educational preparation; in place of the precall training, higher educational institutions and technical schools have introduced higher nonarmy training, consisting of a theoretical course and educational preparation over a period of from three to four months; (2) actual military service for a period of five years passed (*a*) as member of a cadre, (*b*) in a shifting body of territorial troops, and (*c*) in nonarmy assignments; and (3) the status of a reservist up to the age of forty.

Actual military service as a member of a cadre consists of (*a*) uninterrupted service in the ranks of from two to four years (four years in the fleet, three years in parts of the shore defense and air fleet, two years in the infantry and other troops); (*b*) long-term leave during the balance (from one to three years) of the five years; and (*c*) educational preparation during such long-term leave. For citizens who have finished higher educational institutions in which higher nonarmy preparation has not been introduced, the term of actual military service in the army is shortened to one year, and in the fleet to two years, upon the expiration of which they (the citizens) go in for a test for the rank of intermediate reserve command. For citizens who have finished technical schools in which higher nonarmy preparation has not been introduced, and likewise for those who have finished worker faculties, schools of the second degree (with a period of training of not less than nine years), and educational institutions corresponding thereto, the period of uninterrupted service in cadres of the Worker-Peasant Red Army is fixed at two years. In the first year of service these persons are appointed as a rule to military schools and there prepared for positions of junior command. Having successfully finished the military schools, they pass the second year of service in offices of junior command and are prepared for the position of intermediate reserve command and, after passing examinations, are dismissed on long leave.

The actual military service in the shifting body of territorial units consists of three months' training during the first year of service, educational preparation generally continued for not more than eight months (depending on the type of troops), and being on leave for the entire remaining period of actual military service.

Actual military service passed in nonarmy assignments consists of periodical educational preparation generally continued for not more than six months, and being on leave during the entire remainder of the time of actual military service. Citizens subject to ordinary call for actual military service may be granted exemptions on the basis of family-property position. These consist of freeing those who are called from service in cadres during time of peace and replacing it by service in the shifting body of territorial units or of service passed in nonarmy duties. Such exemption is granted in a case when the call relates to the only member of the family able to work where there are one or more members of the family unable to work and supported by his labor. A person called up loses the right of exemption for family-property position if it is established (by court proceedings) that he has avoided, or sought to avoid, the call to actual military service.

Deferment of call to actual military service is granted (a) to students not passing higher nonarmy preparation; (b) to scientific workers; (c) to schoolteachers in rural localities; (d) to migrants and persons being settled in different places; (e) to agricultural emigrants and immigrants; and (f) to qualified specialists in kolkhozes, sovkhozes, and machine and tractor service stations.

Students not passing through the higher nonarmy preparation are granted deferments of call until the end of their course in the educational institution. Toilers studying in higher educational institutions and technical schools pass through higher nonarmy preparation which is actual military service, replacing for them the term of service in the cadres.

Extraordinarily indicative of the attitude of the population toward the army and universal military service are the numerous cases of refusal of USSR citizens to take advantage of the immunities they could rightfully enjoy.

Article 132 of the Stalin Constitution says: "Universal military service is the law. Military service in the Worker-Peasant Red Army is a duty of honor of USSR citizens." These words of the fundamental law are a concentrated expression of the principle upon which defense of the socialist fatherland has been organized. This article is inseparably linked with the next (Art. 133): "Defense of the fatherland is the sacred duty of each USSR citizen."

Ideas of the fatherland, and of its defense as the duty of each citizen, may be found in any bourgeois state, in its constitution or in the appropriate laws, and of course in a wealth of political literature; and it is hard to find a more empty or false idea than these anywhere in the capitalist world. As early as the *Communist Manifesto*, Marx and Engels stated of capitalist society: "Workers have no fatherland. That which they have not cannot be taken from them." The idea of the fatherland is utilized by the bourgeoisie to exploit the feeling of devotion on the part of the broad masses of the toilers to the earth whereon they and their forebears have toiled, and to the country where everything is the creation of their labor, to exploit their feeling of love for their people and of hatred for attempts to enslave their country. In critical moments this great feeling has compelled the masses to forget their position as slaves in their own country and to pour out their blood to save their "supposed" fatherland (being in fact a fatherland only for the dominant classes) from hostile attack.

The dominant class of bourgeois countries has turned the idea of the fatherland into an instrument to deceive the masses. "Phrases concerning the defense of the fatherland, beating off enemy aggression, a defensive war, and the like from both sides are absolutely nothing but bourgeois deceit of the people," as was said in a resolution of the conference of the foreign sections of the Russian Social Democratic Workers' Party (in 1915), adopted at the climax of the imperialist war.[209] "It is impossible in twentieth century Europe, even in far-eastern Europe, to 'defend the fatherland' otherwise than by struggling with all revolutionary means against the monarchy, the landowners, and the capitalists of *one's own* fatherland—that is to say, the *worst* foes of our native land," [210] said Lenin, writing under the conditions of tsarism. As a result of the socialist revolution, which cast down the power of the landowners and the bourgeoisie, the USSR toilers finally acquired their fatherland, and since that time the watchword: "Defense of the fatherland," is the highest law for each citizen of the USSR. "In the past we had, and could have, no fatherland. But now, when we have overthrown capitalism, and authority among us is worker authority, we have a fatherland and will defend its independence." [211]

The years of the civil war showed with what heroism the people know how to defend their fatherland. Referring to the attempted bourgeois revolution at the end of the eighteenth century in France, Engels long ago wrote: "Recall what marvels the enthusiasm of the revolutionary armies achieved from 1792 to 1799, struggling only for an *illusion*, for a *supposed fatherland*, and you cannot fail to understand how powerful must be an army which struggles for true reality and not for an illusion." [212] During the years of the civil war, the Worker-Peasant Red Army manifested the indestructible force historically envisioned by Engels, and proved to the entire capitalist world what people are capable of when they are struggling for a real, and not for a supposed, fatherland. Brilliantly and pitilessly it shattered the Japanese samurai who sought to burst into our territory at the island of Khasan, demonstrated all the might of its Soviet patriotism, all the grandeur of its heroism, and the all-destroying force of the Soviet state's defensive capacity.

Article 133 of the Stalin Constitution reflected and legally confirmed the attitude toward defense of the fatherland engendered by the great love of the toilers for their fatherland that they had won, for the country drenched with their blood in battles with the exploiters and turned by them into a land of socialism under the wise guidance of the Bolshevik Party. Article

[209] *The All-Union Communist Party (of Bolsheviks) in Resolutions,* Vol. I (1936), p. 225.
[210] Lenin (Russian ed.), Vol. XVIII, p. 82.
[211] Stalin, *Questions of Leninism* (10th Russian ed.), p. 445.
[212] Marx and Engels (Russian ed.), Vol. III, p. 278.

133 reflected and turned into law the sacred feeling of hatred conceived by the USSR toilers for all the loathsome traitors to their fatherland: "Defense of the fatherland is a sacred duty of each USSR citizen. Treason to the fatherland—violation of the oath of allegiance, desertion to the foe, inflicting damage on the war might of the state, and espionage—are punished with all the severity of the law as the most heinous of crimes."

Such are the essence and the principles of the fundamental rights and obligations of citizens according to Soviet socialist public law.

The Elective System of the USSR

SEC. 1: INTRODUCTION

THE RIGHT to vote, like every sort of right, expresses the will of the dominant class. Parliament, national representation, national sovereignty, and national suffrage were in their time the chief political watchwords of the bourgeoisie put forward by it in the struggle against the feudal regime and absolutism. As early as the first bourgeois revolutions (the English and the French), the most revolutionary part of the bourgeoisie declared the right to vote "the natural right of all persons to freedom and equality." During the English Revolution (1640–1660) the council of the revolutionary army more than once posed the question of introducing universal suffrage into elections to the House of Commons. The French bourgeoisie, at the moment when it was arousing the people to a decisive attack upon feudalism in its Declaration of the Rights of Man and Citizen (1789), likewise proclaimed that "people are born free and equal in their rights" (Art. 1) and that "law is the expression of the general will. All citizens have the right to take part, individually or through representatives, in the making of laws" (Art. 6). Thus the bourgeoisie identified its class interests with the interests of the people in order to arouse the people for the struggle with the feudal nobility, to win political power. In reality the bourgeoisie was pursuing its class purposes, the assurance of its dominance.

In England, after the execution of Charles I (1649) and the creation of the English Commonwealth (1649–1660), the right to vote was transferred into the hands of proprietors, and after the restoration of royal power (1660) all political power passed into the hands of the great landowners and the great traders. In France the bourgeoisie rejected the principles of "natural law" after its victory. Individual bourgeois philosophers and thinkers "proved" that only proprietors, the bourgeoisie, have the right to represent "the entire people" in parliament. The first election law was very far from giving the right to vote to all French adults, violating thereby the Declaration of Rights of Man and Citizen. Under the Constitution of September 3, 1791, the first written constitution on the continent of Europe, half the adult population of France, chiefly the "have-nots," were deprived of the right to vote. Excluded from the number of those having the right to vote were women. Men could enjoy the right to vote upon attaining the age of twenty-five, provided they paid a direct tax measured by three days' work pay, did not occupy the position of servant, and had been domiciled in one place for not less than a year. Citizens satisfying these requirements obtained the designation of "active citizens," while the rest were called "passive citizens."

The same constitution established a system of two-stage elections. In order to have the right to be elected to the second assembly of electors, where deputies were elected, it was necessary to pay a direct tax and to be the proprietor or lessee of property yielding an income equal to wages for from 150 to 200 work days. Only five deputies voted for universal suffrage, one of them being Robespierre. In general the active inhabitants, those with full rights, numbered around four million out of twenty-five million inhabitants of France at that time. Even the most democratic constitution of France (the Jacobin Constitution of 1793) granted election rights only to men twenty-one years of age and domiciled in one place for not less than six months. Women have never enjoyed election rights in France and do not enjoy them at the present moment.[1]

After the suppression of the Jacobins, the bourgeoisie still further curtailed election rights. In 1795, in the constitutional commission, Boissy d'Anglas, the reporter on the matter of the right to vote, said: "If you grant persons who do not own property the right to vote and if they appear at some time on the parliamentary benches, they will stir up insurrections without fear of the consequences." The most eminent bourgeois ideologists, Royer-Collard (1763–1845), Guizot (1787–1874), Constant (1767–1830), and others, have demonstrated that national representation cannot be a comptometer to count "individual wills"; that a distinction must be made between "natural rights" and political capacities; and, finally, that these capacities are possessed only by the bourgeoisie, free from concerns of a material order, enlightened, possessing leisure and living a settled life. Only the bourgeoisie is interested in preserving the "reasonable" legal order personified by the bourgeois state. All the most recent bourgeois political scientists strive likewise to vindicate the special rights of the dominant bourgeoisie as opposed to the toilers. The state, some of them have proved, is the source of law and so cannot be subordinate to the will of the very

[1] Woman's suffrage was made law in France in 1945.—ED.

people whom it fashions. The chief bourgeois political scientist, Jellinek, has said that the state, in the manner established by law, draws on the individual wills called to perform its functions. French political scientists of the later period—Hauriou, for example, and others—reckoning with the "universal" right of suffrage already existing, point out that it is not a right but a "social function," a function subordinate to the interests of the bourgeois legal order.

The bourgeois right of suffrage neither did nor could rescue the proletariat from exploitation and oppression; it always expressed the will of the bourgeoisie and served as an instrument of its class domination. Throughout the course of its class struggle, the proletariat enjoyed the right of suffrage only in so far as it won it in stubborn conflict. Only by reason of this struggle did the bourgeoisie introduce universal suffrage in certain capitalist countries. Fear of the worker class compelled the bourgeoisie of America, England, France, Belgium, and other countries to leave in their constitutions "universal" suffrage, albeit in a curtailed and falsified form. In a letter to Engels, Marx noted that universal suffrage is only a concession made to the workers and, of course, in a very extreme case.

During the course of the agitation for parliamentary reform in England in 1832, the workers making up the radical wing of the Reform Party set out their demands in the so-called "national charter" and organized the first worker party under the name of Chartists. The Chartists and the strike movement organized by them played an important part, compelling the dominant classes to enter upon a series of concessions with regard to the voting system, abolition of the so-called "rotten boroughs," and effectuation of certain points in the charter. Chartism played an historical role which was by no means unimportant. It impelled one part of the dominant classes to enter upon certain concessions, upon reforms, for the sake of avoiding great convulsions.[2] Landlords lost a number of privileged places ("rotten boroughs"),[3] and the number of deputies chosen in the new industrial cities was increased, as was the number of voters from 400,000 to 900,000. But the new election law did not admit the worker class to the elections (this class had grown immensely in England during this time) nor did it make it possible for the middle bourgeois strata to get into the House of

---

[2] Stalin, *Questions of Leninism* (10th Russian ed.), p. 611.

[3] "Rotten boroughs" were little cities and places, numbering not infrequently some tens of inhabitants. In some of them there were scarcely ten electors. Sometimes there was only one. The boroughs, preserving in form the rights of a city, were in the complete possession of the big landowners, who sold seats in the House of Commons representing them. Even the famous economist, Ricardo, got a place in the House of Commons in 1819 from Portarlington after furnishing the possessor of this rotten borough a large loan without interest. According to the stories of his contemporaries, Ricardo never saw his electors, of whom there were twelve in all.

Commons, since it established a high property qualification for the right to be elected (the passive right of suffrage): 300 pounds sterling for a city deputy and 600 pounds sterling for deputies of the shires. As a result of this, not more than one person in twenty-four possessed the suffrage.

In the Revolution of 1848 in France, the bourgeoisie, for the first time in the history of a bourgeois state, developed universal suffrage under the influence of a revolutionary outburst of the proletariat. The number of electors increased from 241,000 in 1846 to 8,222,000 in 1848. But after the bloody suppression of the worker uprising in June, 1848, the bourgeoisie again moved backward. In 1850 a law was introduced establishing the three-year domiciliary qualification, on the basis of which the number of voters shrank from 9.618 million to 6.809 million—almost 30 per cent. In 1851 Louis Napoleon again introduced "universal" suffrage. But this was the cunning of the old fox. With the aid of this demagogic measure, he attracted the middle classes, particularly the kulak part of the peasantry, to his side and prepared to have himself proclaimed emperor. With the help of his bureaucrats, the state mechanism, the soldiers' bayonets and the moneybags, he and the dominant part of the bourgeoisie had obtained a majority in parliament. The bourgeoisie was persuaded that with "universal" suffrage it could manage very well if only capital and the power in the state remained in its own hands.

The experience with "universal" suffrage in France was availed of by the bourgeoisie in Germany somewhat later (in 1866). Bismarck introduced it as a temporary measure only, with a view to set the people off as against individual German princes who had opposed unification around Prussia, as well as to draw the masses into the war at first against Austria (1866) and then against France (1870). But the worker class construed universal suffrage in its own way, taking advantage of it to organize its ranks. In the struggle against this worker movement, Bismarck later introduced extraordinary laws against socialists (1878–1890), declared worker organizations unlawful, shut down the worker press, and so forth. With "universal" suffrage in Germany in such a position, the possibility of free elections was completely excluded.

"Universal" suffrage in bourgeois countries was so completely adapted to the bourgeois manner of administration as to become a constituent part of it. "The class of 'haves' dominates immediately with the aid of universal suffrage," said Engels.[4]

The greatest events in the history of the struggle of the proletariat in the nineteenth century were the seizure of power by the Paris workers

[4] Marx and Engels (Russian ed.), Vol. XVI, Pt. 1, p. 148.

(March, 1871) and the formation of the Paris Commune. "The Commune was formed from town counselors chosen by universal voting in various districts of Paris. They were responsible and could be replaced at any time. Most of them were very manifestly workers or acknowledged representatives of the worker class. The Commune was bound to be a working, and not a parliamentary, corporation legislating and executing laws at one and the same time." [5] In the hands of the Paris proletariat, universal suffrage was a means of destroying bourgeois parliamentarism and creating organs of worker-class authority, the first experience of creating the organs of authority of a proletariat dictatorship. The bourgeoisie succeeded in annihilating the Commune, having drowned it in the blood of French workers, and (having returned to power) again introduced its methods, which were advantageous and gratifying to itself. Nevertheless, however brief the existence of the Paris Commune, it showed that the worker class put concretely the question of winning power and creating its own state. Notwithstanding a succession of defeats inflicted upon the worker class by the bourgeoisie in different countries, the pressure of the toiling masses could no longer be withstood and the bourgeoisie was constrained gradually to expand its elective system. After Germany's victory over France (in 1871) and the unification of Germany, universal suffrage was extended also to elections to the Reichstag of the German Empire. In England in 1884 and 1885, suffrage was extended to certain strata of the worker class (the worker aristocracy), which increased the number of electors by as much as 15.9 per cent of the entire population. In France (1875) the Constitution confirmed universal suffrage though, we repeat, in truncated form. The proletariat had, however, attained its purpose, and deputies of proletarian organizations appeared for the first time in the bourgeois parliament. Engels wrote:

Universal suffrage had long existed in France, but it had acquired a bad reputation there because it had been abused by the Bonaparte government. After the Commune, there was no worker party in existence which could have used universal suffrage. In Spain it was also introduced from the times of the republic, but all the serious opposition parties had from of old refrained from taking part in elections as a general rule. Least of all could the Swiss experiment with universal suffrage encourage the worker party. Revolutionary workers of the Latin lands were accustomed to consider the elective right a snare, an instrument of administrative deceit. In Germany matters were different. Already the *Communist Manifesto* had proclaimed the winning of universal suffrage, the winning of democracy, as one of the first and most important tasks of the struggling proletariat. . . . When Bismarck seemed constrained to introduce this measure

[5] Marx, *Selected Works* (1935, Russian ed.), Vol. II, pp. 394–395.

as the only means of interesting the popular masses in his plans, the workers forthwith took the matter seriously and sent August Bebel into the first constitutive Reichstag, and thenceforward so used the suffrage that it brought enormous benefit to themselves and became a model for the workers of all lands.[6]

The extension of suffrage in a number of states, and the first successes of worker organizations in elections, created petty-bourgeois illusions as to the possibility of a proletarian victory through "winning" a majority in the bourgeois parliament. Accordingly Marx and Engels carried on an irreconcilable struggle against a tolerationist policy, issuing their first warning to the German social democrats that, if they should be successful at the elections, they must not forget that the worker class can annihilate capitalism and build socialism only by means of a proletarian revolution and the creation of a proletarian dictatorship. Universal suffrage can be utilized by the proletariat only as one of the means of struggling for their emancipation. It is, in the words of Engels, "an index of worker-class maturity. It cannot, and will never, give more in the present state."[7] On the basis of bourgeios parliamentarism, universal suffrage makes it possible for the workers to carry on agitation, cast up their forces, and furnish to representatives of the workers a parliamentary tribune from which they can address the masses. "The democratization of the elective system expresses the confidence of the bourgeoisie in the growth of its own forces and in the capacity of bourgeois authority to subordinate the masses to itself, as if it were in accord with their own will, the will of the electors."[8]

In reality the unequal and privileged franchise of the "haves" remained in form and in fact the basis of the elective system in bourgeois lands.

The great proletarian October Revolution of 1917, and the revolutionary movement evoked by it throughout the world, were decisive strokes which compelled the bourgeoisie, in fear of the revolution, to go so far as to grant, in form, universal suffrage to broad masses of the population in England, the U.S.A., Holland, Germany, and so forth. Even now, however, the dominant bourgeois classes, with the aid of every conceivable machination, direct "universal" elections into the channel of their interests.

Stalin says that "they who rule, not they who elect and vote, have the power."[9] When the class struggle reaches higher tension, the bourgeoisie prefers fascism to democracy. Fascism destroys democratic rights and every sort of elective quality. In fascist Germany so-called "non-Aryans" are deprived of the suffrage on the basis of the race theory. The whole procedure

[6] *Ibid.*, p. 145.
[7] Marx and Engels (Russian ed.), Vol. XVI, Pt. 1, p. 148.
[8] Molotov, *Changes in the Soviet Constitution* (1935), p. 33.
[9] Stalin, *Articles and Speeches on the Ukraine* (1936), p. 38.

of elections takes place under the fierce terror of the storm troopers. More-over, "elections" are only an empty ceremonial; the "deputies" are in fact appointed by the fascists at their discretion. Fascists and their Trotsky-Bukharin accessories—those agents of fascist reconnaissance—direct their frantic hatred "against the Soviet Union, against the great country of social-ism, as the most mighty bulwark of the peace, freedom, and progress of all mankind—the greatest obstacle in the path of fascist aggression." [10]

The great proletarian revolution which gave mankind a new and higher type of state, the Soviet state, initiated genuine socialist democracy, genuine universal Soviet suffrage, developed in conditions where there are no con-tradictions between the state and society, between general interests and individual interests. Only in the USSR is there universal suffrage, the genuine right of all USSR citizens to elect their organs of authority.

The democracy of a state is expressed with particular clarity in its elec-tive system. The democracy of an elective system is measured by the degree to which it is actually possible for the people to elect their representatives, those who enjoy the people's confidence, whom the people themselves freely nominate. The system and the practice of elections constitute an integral part of the entire system of a given state. In bourgeois countries elections match perfectly the bourgeois system of state administration, being directed toward strengthening the dominance of the ruling bourgeois class, deceiving the broad masses of the people in order to thrust them aside from elections, and assuring a "majority" for the bourgeois clique which administers the country.

The Soviet elective system rests on the great principles of socialist democ-racy affirmed in the USSR by the Stalin Constitution. In the Soviet land, elections to the Soviets are the broadest form of attracting the masses into state administration. The role and significance of the Soviets as organs of state administration define also the Soviet system of elections, which are radically different from the elective system in bourgeois states. The Soviet elective system has always promoted, and still promotes, the principles of the broadest attraction of the toilers to state administration, to socialist build-ing. From the first day of its existence, Soviet authority granted elective rights to all the adult toiling population. In his pamphlet, *The Proletarian Revolution and the Renegade Kautsky*, Lenin says: "Proletarian democracy is a million times more democratic than any sort of bourgeois democracy. Soviet authority is a million times more democratic than the most democratic bourgeois republic." [11] Throughout its more than twenty years of existence,

[10] Dimitrov, "The Unity of the International Proletariat—the Supreme Imperative of the Present Moment." *Pravda* (May 1, 1937), No. 120.
[11] Lenin (Russian ed.), Vol. XXIII, p. 350.

the Soviet state has systematically and undeviatingly expanded the democracy of its franchises. The Stalin Constitution provided an elective system which is the most democratic in the world.

SEC. 2: UNIVERSAL SUFFRAGE

Marxism-Leninism contemplates universal suffrage as one of the most important conquests achieved by human society. Universal, direct, and equal suffrage with a secret ballot was the chief political watchword of bourgeois parties in the best years of the development of bourgeois democracy and parliamentarism (in the nineteenth century and the early twentieth century). The bourgeoisie was then confident of its power, of the ability of its authority to subordinate the masses to itself. But, as we have hereinbefore said, the growth and rise of the worker revolutionary movement caused the bourgeoisie to be seized with anxiety for the morrow. During recent times, it narrowed universal suffrage in every way, and fascism has passed frankly to the undisguised terrorist power of capital over the toilers and to the complete annihilation of universal suffrage as of other bourgeois democratic principles.

The Soviet Union proceeds by an utterly different path. From the very beginning of its existence, the Soviet state has embodied a higher type of democracy, assuring the attraction to state administration of broad masses of the toilers in unprecedented numbers.

As early as the first Soviet Constitution, written under the guidance of Lenin and Stalin and adopted July 10, 1918, the toilers were assured the broadest franchise, without a parallel in history. According to this Constitution, all the toilers had, upon attaining the age of eighteen years, the right to elect, and to be elected, to the Soviets. Cast away was the division of voting rights into active and passive (the right to elect, and the right to be elected). Abolished once and for all were limitations according to nationality or religious profession, or based on property, domicile, or other qualifications. Women acquired elective rights identical with those of men. Limitations on the voting right of persons in the ranks of the army were abolished. The initial disfranchisement of the bourgeoisie was only a temporary measure and not an inevitable concomitant in all cases of the development of the proletarian revolution.

Depriving the bourgeoisie of the suffrage is not a necessary and indispensable sign of the proletarian dictatorship. Even in Russia, the Bolsheviks, who had put forward the watchword of such a dictatorship long before the October Revolution, did not speak in advance of taking the franchise away from exploiters.

This constituent part of the dictatorship developed spontaneously during the course of the struggle. . . . It did not come to light "according to the plan" of any party.[1] . . . The disenfranchisement of exploiters is a *purely Russian* matter and not a matter of the proletarian dictatorship in general.[2]

If in certain stages of the revolution our election law did exclude specific and negligible strata of the population from the elections, this was only because of the bourgeoisie's resistance to socialism. "The animosity of the bourgeoisie against the independent and omnipotent (because all-embracing) organization of the oppressed, its struggle—a most shameless, selfish, mercenary and grimy struggle—against the Soviets, and finally its manifest participation, from the KD's[3] to the Right SR's, from Milyukov to Kerensky, in the theories of Kornilov—that is what prepared the formal exclusion of the bourgeoisie from the Soviets."[4]

The bourgeoisie's own action put it outside the ranks of Soviet citizens enjoying voting rights. The exclusion of the bourgeoisie from the body of voters became necessary to assure the complete triumph of the toilers over exploiters who, immediately after the overthrow of their power, still had at their disposal vast forces with which to struggle against the new power just established. Not for nought did the Mensheviks and SR's, who had passed entirely to the side of the bourgeoisie, demand "freedom" and "equality" within the bounds of the "labor democracy." They saw that their admission into the Soviets would create a convenient springboard for the struggle against the Soviets. Lenin decisively rebuffed these counterrevolutionary demands, pointing out that "he who talks about freedom and equality within the limits of a labor democracy—upon condition that the capitalists are overthrown while private property and freedom of trade still remain—is a champion of the exploiters."[5]

Loss of the franchise was not introduced as a measure established once and for all in the struggle of the workers with the class foe. As early as 1919, Lenin demanded

that it be made clear to the toiling masses, to avoid incorrect generalization from transitory historical exigencies, that in the Soviet Republic the disfranchisement of part of the citizens by no means touches, as it did in most bourgeois democratic republics, a definite category of citizens declared rightless for life; it relates only to exploiters, those who, despite the basic laws of the Socialist Soviet Republic, stubbornly defend their exploiter position and preserve capitalist rela-

---

[1] Lenin (Russian ed.), Vol. XXIII, p. 369.
[2] *Ibid.*, p. 355.
[3] Konstitutsionale Demokraty (Constitutional Democrats), commonly called "Cadets." —ED.
[4] Lenin (Russian ed.), Vol. XXIII, p. 369.
[5] *Ibid.*, Vol. XXV, p. 470.

tionships. Consequently in the Soviet Republic, as, with each day that socialism grows stronger, the number of those objectively able to remain exploiters or to preserve capitalist relationships shrinks, the percentage of those deprived of the suffrage automatically grows less. The abatement of attack from without and completion of the expropriation of the expropriators can in certain circumstances create a position where proletarian state power will choose other means of crushing exploiter resistance and will introduce universal suffrage with no limitations of any sort.[6]

The principles of the Soviet election system were established in the very first days after the October Socialist Revolution, and were expressed with particular distinctness in the Declaration of Rights of the Toiling and Exploited People adopted by the Third All-Russian Congress of Soviets on January 25, 1918, in the statement that, at the moment when the proletariat was locked in decisive struggle with its exploiters, "there can be no place for exploiters in any one of the organs of authority." The declaration and the directive (adopted by the Third All-Russian Congress of Soviets), Concerning the Federal Institutions of the Russian Republic, confirmed the general bases of the organization of Soviet authority and the method of Soviet elections which had defined universal elective suffrage for the toilers and pitiless struggle with the bourgeoisie. The practice of the past indicated to the worker class that there would and should be no place for the bourgeoisie in the Soviets; there could be no talk of granting the suffrage to it at the very moment when it was meeting the formation of Soviet authority by armed struggle. Its exclusion from the Soviets made it easier for the worker masses to be able to be freed from bourgeois influence. It was necessary for the confirmation at that period of the victory of the toilers over the exploiters, for the final abolition of capitalism, and for the stabilization of the Soviet social order and the destruction of the exploiter classes.

Only the toilers, without distinction of sex, who are not exploiting another's toil—that is to say, workers, peasants, and the toiling intelligentsia—elect and can be elected to the Soviets: such was the basic proposition of the first Soviet Constitution. Into the practical work of the Soviets and into the administration of the entire state were drawn thousands and tens of thousands of toilers. The principles of the Soviet elective system were preserved even after the formation of the USSR and the adoption of the first Union Constitution of the USSR (1924).

Convinced of the stability of Soviet authority and of the impossibility of overthrowing it in open contest, the capitalists continued to struggle against it secretly. Capitalist elements sought in every way to slip surreptitiously,

[6] Ibid., Vol. XXIV, p. 94.

or to smuggle their own people, into the Soviets and from there to do harm to socialist building. In 1925, when the New Economic Policy was the basis of intensified class stratification in the Soviet village, the kulak tried to get an attack under way somehow or other. The "work" of counterrevolutionary groups became animated. Mensheviks, Trotskyists, and like elements that had sneaked into the Party for counterrevolutionary purposes brought forward the demand that election rights be granted to counterrevolutionary parties, while—for the same counterrevolutionary purposes—the Trotskyists demanded that the middle-class people be expelled from "the lower stories" of Soviet authority (the Soviets) and deprived of their franchise. They defamed Soviet authority, accusing it of being degenerate and the Soviet state of being nonproletarian. Employing every possible instrument of provocation, crudely violating Soviet laws, trying by their illegal administration to incense the population against Soviet authority, these gentlemen sought in every way to befoul and injure the Soviet state. However, these hostile machinations, too, the Party unmasked and destroyed.

Since 1924 the Party and the administration have gone over to the policy of vitalizing the Soviets. The development of the elective system during this period was concretely expressed in the election instructions of the Central Executive Committee of the USSR (January 16, 1925, and September 28, 1926), emphasizing the necessity of promoting a more decisive class policy. A minimum was established—at first 35 per cent and later 50 per cent—as requisite for an elective assembly to be considered legal. Work with the poor, with women, and with the young was greatly expanded. A more elaborate and strict approach to the disclosure of disfranchised persons was developed. All this intensified the activity of the electors. Whereas the percentage of city and country electors appearing at the polls prior to 1924 was not more than 40 per cent and was not constant, it was notably higher after 1924 and continued to increase steadily with each year, as is clear from the table on the following page. Women evinced a constantly increasing activity. Up to 1924 there was no calculation of the women appearing at elections. Thereafter their number constantly increased.

Throughout the entire ensuing period the systematic curbing and ouster of the profiteer-tradesman and kulak continued on all the fronts of socialist building.

The extinction of kulaks as a class on the basis of complete collectivization led to the result that as early as 1930–1931 the lists of Soviet electors were more than ever purged of kulaks, profiteer-tradesmen, and other alien class elements. Many kulak families disintegrated. Some of the kulak children entered an honorable life of toil. The proportion of capitalist elements in trade turnover shrank from 20 per cent in 1928 to 5.6 per cent in 1930.

| YEARS | VOTERS APPEARING AT THE POLLS (IN PERCENTAGES) | | | |
| | City | | Country | |
	Total	Women	Total	Women
1922	36.5	No information	22.3	No information
1923	38.5	No information	37.2	No information
1924	40.5	16.6	28.9	10.8
1925	48.7	25.8	36.9	19.9
1926	52.0	42.9	47.3	28.0
1927	58.4	49.8	48.4	31.1
1928–29	70.8	65.2	61.8	48.5
1930–31	79.6	75.3	70.4	63.4
1934–35	91.6	88.2	83.3	80.3

The network of retail private trade contracted sharply. According to data of the State Planning Commission concerning the achievement totals of the first five-year plan, the number of localized units of private trade shrank from 163.9 thousand in 1929 and 47.1 thousand in 1930 to 17.7 thousand for 1931.

The method of reestablishing certain categories of people in voting rights of which they had been deprived (kulaks, traders, and the like) was made simpler. Down to 1930, these groups could be reestablished in their voting rights only by directive of the Central Executive Committee of the autonomous SSR, guberniya, territorial and regional executive committees. From and after 1930, this right was granted to district executive committees. A law was passed forbidding the disfranchisement of persons who had attained their majority in 1925 and, later, of children of disfranchised persons (provided the children were engaged in independent and socially advantageous toil). Further successes of socialist building afforded a basis for the Central Executive Committee of the USSR to issue a law concerning the method of reestablishing in their elective rights expelled kulaks who proved in fact that they had ceased to struggle against Soviet authority (July, 1931). According to the election instructions of 1934, district executive committees and city Soviets obtained the right to restore to their voting rights children of kulaks whether found in special settlements and places of exile or elsewhere. The Central Executive Committee of the autonomous SSR, territorial and regional executive committees were granted the right to restore kulaks to their elective rights upon the expiration of the five-year term of exile, provided they had become shock workers in production work and taken an active part in social work. All this led to a lessening of the number of persons disfranchised. Whereas in 1930–1931 the number of such persons in the rural areas was 3.7 per cent and in the city 4.9 per cent, in 1934–1935 the former figure was 2.6 per cent and the latter only 2.4 per cent. These data attest the fact that in the 1934–1935 elections "not only the entire mass of the toilers, but also a certain proportion of the citizens formerly disfranchised took part." [7] Speaking of this at the Seventh All-Union Congress of Soviets, Molotov emphasized:

In the Soviet Union the way to a life embodying complete rights is open to all honorable toilers. . . . We move toward the complete abrogation of limitations of all sorts upon elections to the Soviets. Such limitations were introduced in their time as "temporary measures of the struggle with the exploiters' attempts to defend or to reinstate their privileges," in the words of the program of the All-Union Communist Party (of Bolsheviks).[8]

Disfranchised persons during the elections to the Soviets in 1934 were only around 2.5 per cent of the entire population, showing that the elective system in the USSR was incomparably higher than the most democratic bourgeois elective system. Methodically confirming the proletarian dictatorship, building socialist society, and destroying the resistance of exploiters, the Soviet state has arrived at the complete abrogation of particular limitations in the elective system. Lenin had constantly emphasized the temporary character of those limitations. To the end of further developing socialist democracy, the Soviet state had proceeded to the complete realization of universal suffrage. As Molotov said at the Seventh All-Union Congress of Soviets:

It may now suit the bourgeoisie in the lands of capital to cast a slur upon that which its own manuals and its own literature and social science record as the highest attainments of the borugeois state, but Soviet authority takes everything that is best in the development of the contemporary state and boldly makes it living and incarnate, in the interests of the toilers and against the exploiters, in the interests of the building of socialism. . . . If there is no longer faith in the camp of the bourgeoisie even in their own democracy and their own parliamentarism, we can well understand it. The bourgeois social order is looking now at its own grave. On the other hand, we are confident that not only by the toilers of our country but also far beyond the boundaries of the Soviet Union the significance of the further democratization of our elective system, of the all-sided democracy realized by us, will be correctly understood.[9]

[7] Molotov, *Changes in the Soviet Constitution* (1935), p. 20.
[8] *Ibid.*, p. 21.
[9] *Ibid.*, pp. 27–28.

The Soviet socialist worker-peasant state was convinced of its strength and therefore abrogated the preexisting limitations on the Soviet right to vote and introduced genuinely universal suffrage. The principles of Soviet universal suffrage found classical expression in Articles 135, 137, and 138 of the Stalin Constitution. They have no parallel in any other constitution or elective law in the world. Article 135 of the Stalin Constitution provided that: "Elections of deputies are universal: all USSR citizens who have attained the age of eighteen years, regardless of race, nationality, religious profession, educational qualification, domicile, social origin, property status or past activities, have the right to participate in the election of deputies, and to be elected, with the exception of insane persons and persons condemned by a court of law to a sentence which includes deprivation of election rights." Article 137: "Women have the right to elect and to be elected on equal terms with men." Article 138: "Citizens in the ranks of the Red Army enjoy the right to elect and to be elected on equal terms with all citizens."

The Soviet elective system, built on the basis of Article 135 of the Constitution, seeks not only to grant universal suffrage to citizens of the USSR, but also to make it easier for them to be able to take advantage of their right to vote and to express their will by taking part in the election of organs of state authority. Wherever he may be, in the city or in the country, in a train or on a boat, on a mission or in a hospital, each citizen who has not been disfranchised is assured that he can appear in the election precinct and fulfill his civic duty in accordance with the great principles of the Stalin Constitution.

Bourgeois countries likewise proclaim "universal" suffrage in their constitutions, but not a single capitalist state has truly universal suffrage. Universal suffrage presupposes that the entire population of the country, having attained a certain age, participates in the election. A system of universal suffrage should guarantee the right of this population to elect and to be elected without distinction of sex and irrespective of property status or race or nationality, or profession of faith, education or domicile. With the aid of (direct and indirect) restrictive addenda, amendments, and appropriate "interpretation" of the principle of universality in capitalist countries, however, large masses of the toilers were, and still are, excluded.

Bourgeois jurists are themselves compelled to admit that in bourgeois countries the expression "universal suffrage" in bourgeois juridical language is most indefinite and subject to many interpretations. Thus the French professor Barthélemy writes:

In political language the expression "universal suffrage" has only a conditional significance, indicating that suffrage is not a prerogative of a limited circle of people privileged by birth, condition, or abilities. It must not be supposed, however, that all take part in elections: even under the system of so-called universal suffrage, the body of electors represents only a certain select part, although this selection is made on an extremely broad scale. French laws are extraordinarily liberal in this regard. They require only French nationality by birth or by naturalization. The foreigner becomes a voter immediately upon his naturalization. Only persons of the male sex can vote. This rule, accepted in all Latin countries, is ordinarily explained by the requirement of a definite intellectual and moral level, based moreover on the supposed superiority of the male sex.[10]

Bourgeois election laws establish an election which makes it in fact impossible for the laboring masses of "have-nots" to participate in elections. The bourgeoisie does not reckon on the support of the toilers because, by various instructions appended to the statute concerning universal suffrage, it bars them from this "universal" suffrage.

Speaking of "universal suffrage," the bourgeoisie in many countries—about forty of them—deprive women of voting rights. Among these countries are France, Bulgaria, and Switzerland. In Hungary women are admitted to elections only if they have three living children (a son slain in battle being counted as alive). Meanwhile women constitute half the population. In England women finally acquired the right to vote in 1928, in the U.S.A. in 1920.[11]

In fascist countries (Italy, Germany, and Japan) women do not even dare to think about voting rights. The "family hearth," the kitchen, and children fall to their share. Here the election principle is in general liquidated.

In a number of the largest capitalist countries (England, the U.S.A., France, and others) at the present time, with "universal" suffrage present there, hundreds of millions of the colonial population are not admitted to take part in elections to the representative organs of those countries.[12]

In a number of countries (France, Czechoslovakia, and others) soldiers

[10] J. Barthélemy, *The State Social Order of France* (Russian ed., 1936), p. 52.

[11] Of 153 deputies returned in the lower chamber in Ireland (in the elections of 1927), there was only one woman; in Esthonia (in the elections of 1929) there was one woman out of 100 deputies; in Belgium in the elections of 1929, there was one woman out of 187 deputies; in Denmark in the elections of 1929, there were three women out of 143 deputies; and in Switzerland (in the elections of 1928) there were three women of 230 deputies. In the upper chambers there are almost no women at all.

[12] In France there is a population of around 42 millions, and in the French colonies and mandated countries 60 millions; but these latter, with rare exceptions, take no part in the elections of the French parliament. In Belgium there is a population of 8.3 millions, and in the Belgian Congo 9.3 millions; the colonial population takes no part in parliamentary elections. In Holland there is a population of 8.4 millions, and in the Dutch colonies (Dutch East India) there are more than 60 millions; but the latter is completely without elective rights. In the British Empire there are around 485 millions, hundreds of millions of whom take no part in elections.

—that is, the youth—an overwhelming majority of them city and country toilers, are barred from elections under the "universal" suffrage existing there. A number of other indirect limitations make it impossible for the proletarian strata of the population, against whom these limitations are chiefly directed, to utilize election rights. Such are the age qualifications, the domicile qualification, the property qualification, the educational qualification, race and nationality qualifications, and so on. Aside from these "general" qualifications there are in bourgeois countries a number of special limitations as to elections to second (upper) chambers and as to elections to local organs of administration. As a result, in the U.S.A., for example, not more than 40 to 45 millions out of 72 million citizens of voting age systematically took part in the presidential elections during the last ten years, and in elections to the Senate and House of Representatives not more than 25 to 30 millions; in Japan under "universal" suffrage (universal only for males) this right is taken advantage of by only around 21 per cent of the population, women, military personnel, and those having no definite domicile and so on being barred. In India, where the population numbers 350 millions, the right to vote is enjoyed by only 35 million—10 per cent of the whole population—and so on. Even the system of elections to the Russian Constituent Assembly, deemed most democratic as compared with that of other bourgeois countries, did not guarantee truly universal suffrage. These were conducted according to a proposition worked out by a "special council" created by the Provisional Government in March, 1917. The very method by which this council was created is itself eloquent of bourgeois machinations, most of the places in the mechanism of the "special council" being given to KD's, and the Party of the Bolsheviks getting one place. The "special council" required the granting of election rights to members of the House of Romanov. Fearing the revolutionary move of the Petrograd proletariat, most members of the "special council" proposed to summon the Constituent Assembly in Moscow or at the quarters of the supreme commander in chief in Mogilev. The "council" dragged out its work on the proposal until September. The fundamental principles of the elective system of elections to the Constituent Assembly were: (1) universal, equal, secret, and direct voting: (2) an age qualification of 20 years; (3) the proportional system of elections; and (4) deserters were to be deprived of suffrage.

The last point was directed against workers and peasants who by their desertion from the front protested against the imperialist war. The system of election precincts was so constructed by the "special council" that the peasant guberniyas gained the chance to choose a preponderance of deputies in comparison with the industrial centers. Direction of the election precinct commissions was in the hands of representatives of the Zemstvos and the cities. The elections themselves took place on November 12, when Soviet authority was not yet everywhere established; in the country, and especially in the villages, the elections occurred (almost everywhere) in the immediate presence of the SR-KD administration, which by various promises and deceit "persuaded" the electors to put SR ballots into the ballot boxes. The part of the population, particularly in the remote villages, which was not class-conscious yielded to these "persuasions." The peasantry was not familiar with the machinery of elections, and analyzed but feebly the programs of the various parties, which numbered as many as 22 and even 80 (Zhitomir).[13]

The KD-SR elective committees resorted to a whole series of abuses: in a number of cases women were not admitted to the ballot boxes; votes were noted by a simple mark on a piece of paper; only ballots of anti-Soviet parties were distributed; Bolshevik agitation was forbidden; lists of candidates were given out only to literate persons; lists of Bolsheviks were destroyed; the workers of many factories and the peasants of many villages were deprived of their vote; instances of buying ballots, of confiscating Bolshevik literature, of forbidding the election of Bolshevik deputies, and so on, were noted. A significant part of the workers and peasants, however, particularly in the industrial districts, voted for Bolsheviks. In the Moscow guberniya the Bolsheviks got 56 per cent of the votes and the SR's 25 per cent; in the Tver guberniya the Bolsheviks got 54 per cent and the SR's 39 per cent; in Tula the Bolsheviks got 97.8 per cent and the SR's none, and so on. Altogether, the Constituent Assembly should have had approximately 815 deputies. Upon incomplete data 707 were elected. The SR's knew how to smuggle in their deputies to the number of 370; the Bolsheviks occupied second place with 175; then came the "left" SR's with 40; and then the Mensheviks with 16. Both the metropolitan and the industrial centers, and likewise the army, having given their votes to the Bolsheviks, were the deciding factor in the political struggle of the people, notwithstanding the SR majority in the Constituent Assembly. Lenin wrote on this score: "The force of the proletariat in any capitalist country is incomparably greater than the share of the proletariat in the sum total of the population."[14]

The Bolsheviks exposed to the workers and peasants the machinations of the bourgeoisie. They demanded the immediate convocation of the Constituent Assembly. They knew that such a summons would, on the one hand, entail a struggle in behalf of the masses who had not yet outlived their illusions concerning the Constituent Assembly but took their cue blindly from the tolerationist parties. They must be shown that the Con-

[13] Town in the Volhynia guberniya, southwest Rusia.—ED.
[14] Lenin (Russian ed.), Vol. XXIV, p. 648.

stituent Assembly was essentially bourgeois; on the other hand, to summon the Constituent Assembly was to unmask the policy of the bourgeoisie which was battling against such a summons and putting it off indefinitely. Having assumed authority, the Bolsheviks guaranteed that the Constituent Assembly would be convened forthwith.

The Constituent Assembly was opened on January 5, 1905, in Petrograd in the name of the All-Russian Central Executive Committee by Sverdlov, who at the same time proclaimed the Declaration of Rights of the Toiling and Exploited People and demanded that Soviet authority and the decrees of the Council of People's Commissars be acknowledged. By a majority of the SR votes, the Constituent Assembly declined to consider the matter of the Declaration proposed by the Bolsheviks. The latter—and later the "left" SR's, who had stood on the Soviet platform—left the assembly. The remaining counterrevolutionary part of the Constituent Assembly was dispersed by the guard of the Tavris Palace. Broad masses of the toilers at once turned their backs on the Constituent Assembly. On January 6, 1918, the Council of People's Commissars, and on January 7, the All-Russian Central Executive Committee, issued a decree dissolving it.

This decree was later affirmed by the Third Council of Soviets.

That "universal" suffrage in bourgeois countries is far from being universal will be manifest upon even slight familiarity with the essence of the qualifications.

Age Qualifications. Age qualification means that admission to participate in elections is conditioned upon the attainment of a certain age: the higher the age the later the right to participate in elections comes, and the narrower and more limited the democracy of the right to vote. In capitalist countries the right to elect (active franchise) is ordinarily acquired by citizens upon the attainment of 20 to 25 years. Thus the youth from the age of 18 to 20 to 25 is barred from elections. Such exclusion bears a definitely expressed class character. The toiling youth of 18 is already entirely independent and, having experienced all the burdens of an unsecured existence under capitalism, is familiar with the conditions of the struggle for existence. At this age he has by general admission already attained complete intellectual and political maturity. At the same time, youth from 18 to 25 is ordinarily the most impulsive part of the population and the most dangerous to the bourgeoisie in terms of revolutionary moods. It is to the advantage of the bourgeoisie to be saved from toiler voters of this age, comprising as they do a sufficiently significant proportion of the voting public: for example, in the U.S.A., according to the 1930 census, around 6 million; and in England, according to the 1931 census, 2.3 million. The right to be elected (passive franchise) is acquired by citizens of bourgeois countries upon their attaining the age of 21 or even 30. Bourgeois legislators consider that citizens of this age, possessing certain property and having a family and so on, yield to the "influence" of the bourgeois administration. Such age qualification is established for elections to the lower chamber.

For the upper chamber the bourgeoisie strives to assure a most select membership. The age qualification is, accordingly, fixed still higher as regards the upper chamber: the active franchise at 21, 25, 30 or even 40 years; the passive franchise at 40—and in Czechoslovakia, at 45.

Independently of age, the acquisition of passive franchise requires the fulfillment of supplementary conditions along the line of domicile, property qualification, and so on. Obviously the number of electors to the upper chamber is much less than to the lower: of the 42 million population of France, the right to vote in elections to the lower chamber is possessed by 12 million and in elections to the upper chamber by 75,000.[15]

The age qualification for active and passive franchise for the elections to lower and upper chambers of bourgeois countries is set out in the table on page 678.

Such age qualification furnishes select representatives of the bourgeoisie in parliament. The masses are limited in the elections in such cases. The average age of members of the lower house in France is 54, and of the upper chamber 63.7 (1931). The "youngest" membership is that of the upper house in Poland—53. In Italy the average age of members of the upper house is 69.2. Engels said of the English House of Lords: "The sneers unfailingly showered upon the upper house for more than one hundred years have gradually so entered into social opinion that this branch of legislative power is regarded by all as a rest house for statesmen who have served out their time." [16]

Only for persons of very "lofty" origin is the age lowered. Thus in Belgium a senator must be not less than 40, but sons of the king—or, if there are none, Belgian princes of the branch of the royal family called upon to govern—are by law automatically senators upon attaining the age of 18. In Italy princes of the royal house sit in the senate upon attaining the age of 21. In Japan members of the imperial family of the male sex may sit in the senate after attaining the age of 20.

The USSR has the lowest voting age in the world, a direct result of a democratic elective law which is the most logical in the world. In the

[15] The election of senators in France is conducted by special collegia of electors consisting of (1) deputies of the lower chamber elected in a given department; (2) members of the general council (the organ of self-government of the department); (3) members of the district councils; and (4) delegates elected by municipal councils ("many-stage" elections).

[16] Marx and Engels (Russian ed.), Vol. II, p. 371.

Name of the Country	The Lower Chamber		The Upper Chamber	
	Active Franchise	Passive Franchise	Active Franchise	Passive Franchise
Switzerland	20	20	Age qualification varies	
Great Britain	21	21	Appointed	
Ireland	21	21	30	30
Belgium	21	25	21	40
France	21	25	25	40
U.S.A.	21	25	21	30
Turkey	22	30	No upper chamber	
Spain	23	23	No upper chamber	
Greece	21	25	21	40
Rumania	21	25	40	40
Czechoslovakia	21	30	26	45
Yugoslavia	21	30	21	40
Sweden	23	23	27	35
Norway	23	30	23	30
Poland	24	30	30	40
Denmark	25	25	35	35
Holland	25	30	24	35
Japan	25	30	30	30

USSR every citizen has the right to vote, and to be voted for, upon attaining the age of 18; there is no division into active and passive suffrage.

Property qualification also is designed to limit the elective rights of persons not possessing the required property and unable to pay the required taxes. All the remaining qualifications of domicile, education, and the like, depend in some degree on the property qualification, which (openly or otherwise) has always been, and is still, favored by bourgeois legislators (through requiring supplementary votes, a deposit for the right to put forward candidates, and so forth).

In a number of states of the U.S.A. (such as Alabama and Oregon), the elector must possess definite property, lacking which a citizen cannot be an elector. In some states (such as Massachusetts, Mississippi, and others) the elector must pay a definite poll tax, otherwise he is not admitted to elections. The highest property qualification is in Southern Rhodesia (an income of 100 pounds sterling) where only 22,000 Europeans and 70 negroes—out of a population of 996,000, of whom 42,000 are Europeans—have the vote. Victoria (Australia) has a property qualification of 10 pounds sterling, and New South Wales of 50 pounds sterling. In England a voter may be a person with an independent income—or paying rent—of not less than 10 pounds sterling. In Bolivia the property qualification is expressed in terms of a yearly income of 200 boliviano (around 400 gold francs); in Colombia a yearly income of 300 pesos or real worth of 1000 pesos. Property qualification exists in Egypt and other states.

This limitation becomes particularly oppressive where the masses are beggared under imperialism because of overexploitation, chronic unemployment, and so forth. In particular states of the U.S.A., persons who have not paid for lodgings are not admitted to elections. Such persons are very often unemployed, of whom there are millions in the U.S.A.

The USSR requires no property qualification.

The qualification of domicile, likewise one of the peculiarities of the bourgeois elective system, means that an elector must be a citizen resident for not less than a certain time in a given election precinct, and is officially established in all bourgeois countries. Of course it flatly contradicts the principle of "universal" suffrage proclaimed by bourgeois constitutions. It differs in different countries. Active suffrage requires domicile in one place: in Great Britain and Czechoslovakia, for three months; in France and Belgium, for six months; in the U.S.A., for from three months to two years (depending on the laws of separate states); in Sweden, in addition to the ordinary formalities for putting on the voting lists persons taking part in repeated voting, it is required that they shall have been entered on the voting list in the preceding elections; in Norway, for five years.

Passive suffrage is acquired by citizens domiciled in a given locality for a longer time. For example, in the U.S.A. and Denmark, a permanent domicile is necessary; in Norway, domicile for ten years and so on.

On the basis of this qualification, moving from one dwelling place to another deprives a citizen of his suffrage. With reference to it Lenin wrote as early as 1905, that it "makes the franchise *not universal* in fact because anyone can understand that it is the workers, the hirelings, the day laborers that most often have to wander from city to city, from province to province, without having a stable domicile. Capital casts the working masses from one end of the country to the other, deprives them of domicile, and *for this* the worker class must lose part of its political rights." [17] On the basis of domicile qualification, millions of citizens, chiefly toilers, are barred from the elections. In the U.S.A., in the state of California, there are around 250,000 agricultural workers, one of the most active and militant detachments of the worker class. There is no possibility of their voting, however, because of the requirement of a definite domicile. They have to pass from

[17] Lenin (Russian ed.), Vol. VII, p. 245.

place to place, and not infrequently live within the area of a given precinct for three months in all, and not for the longer period required by law.

The only country in the world which knows of no distinction between the rights of citizens domiciled and those of citizens not domiciled is the USSR.

The qualification of nationality and race is a means whereby the bourgeoisie in all capitalist countries oppress nationalities and races. It finds its ultimate expression in multinational states. Thus, in the South African Union (a British Dominion), only English citizens of European origin enjoy the franchise. Of the states making up the South African Union, Cape Colony alone has, since 1853, granted the negro population the franchise, albeit with a very high property qualification. Even this negligible "election right" is highly dangerous, however, and in 1936 the South African Union adopted a statute depriving these negroes of their election rights and granting them in lieu thereof the right to send three European deputies to the lower chamber. The local "colored" population was barred from participation in elections. The same is true also in Canada (another British Dominion.)

In the U.S.A. elective rights of citizens of oppressed nationalities are taken away or otherwise limited. According to the Constitution of the U.S.A., diversity of race, color, or other physical peculiarities cannot serve as a basis for taking away elective rights; but individual states deprive national minorities of elective rights indirectly by setting up qualifications: domicile, payment of taxes, property qualification, education, "orderly life," and the like.[18] On the basis of these legislative enactments, such matters as education, good behavior, and knowledge of the English language are taken into account in defining rights of suffrage. These abundantly suffice to deprive millions of the toilers and the exploited from among the oppressed nationalities and races of election rights. In 1928 in Louisiana, the voting lists included 25 per cent of the whites, and ¼ of 1 per cent of the negroes, of the total population. In five Southern states (South Carolina, Georgia, Alabama, Mississippi, and Louisiana) the right to vote is enjoyed by around 20,000 Negroes, whereas 2,225,000 were disfranchised "for illiteracy." In individual New York precincts in 1922, up to 20 per cent of the voters failed to pass tests "in the English language."

To the end of depriving citizens belonging to the oppressed nations of their election rights, bourgeois states have established a special method of organizing districts to the advantage of the bourgeoisie of the dominant nation. Thus in Poland, in the Polish district of Cracow, 124,000 voters elected four deputies; whereas in the Ukraine district of Volyn

[18] A. Esmein, *Basic Principles of Public Law* (1928), p. 214.

250,000 voters elected only five deputies; that is to say, one Polish vote was apparently equal to nearly two Ukrainian votes. In India, where the menacing sweep and force of the national revolutionary movement has forced imperialism to make concessions, the new (1935) constitution especially assures representation of the European and Anglo-Indian minority, both in provincial assemblies and also in federal legislative organs, by creating special *curiae* for these elements. The curial elective system was introduced in India and there are three *curiae*: professional, religious, and according to sex—aside from special representation for Europeans and Anglo-Indians.

Only in the USSR is the elective system international. In his *Report on the Draft Constitution of the USSR*, Stalin says that the draft

starts from the proposition that all nations and races have equal rights; that no difference in color or language, in the level of cultural or of political development, or in any other respect as between nations and races, can serve as a basis to justify national inequality of rights; and that all nations and races, independently of their past and present position and irrespective of their strength or weakness, must enjoy like rights in all spheres of the economic, social, political and cultural life of society.[19]

The educational qualification was likewise introduced by the bourgeoisie to promote its class policy for restricting the toilers in their use of the suffrage. On the basis of this qualification, citizens lacking this or that degree of education are barred from elections. Inasmuch as there is no possibility that the workers of capitalist countries and exploited persons will in general enjoy these degrees of education, the whole point of this qualification is directed specifically against them. At the same time persons possessing a higher education (such as a learned degree acquired in one of the English universities not located in the district wherein the given voter is domiciled) enjoy the right of two votes in the elections of a deputy to parliament. Inasmuch as education in bourgeois countries is broadly accessible only to the bourgeoisie, these two extra votes enure entirely and exclusively to the bourgeoisie.

When the appropriate election organs are testing the education, many arbitrary interpretations and requirements are admissible. For example, in the U.S.A., negroes are required to interpret complex and little understood articles of the Constitution.

Ignorance of language, illiteracy, serve as reasons for barring the population from elections to parliament. To test knowledge of the English language, a judge who suspects a worker of sympathy with the revolutionary movement puts to him a series of questions on "civil law," questions of this

[19] Stalin, *Report on the Draft Constitution of the USSR* (1936), pp. 19-20.

sort: Who was the fourteenth President of the United States? What is the name of the First Assistant Attorney General? What is the Fifth Amendment to the Constitution? Such an examination not even persons thoroughly conversant with the English language could always pass.[20]

According to the law of the state of New York, the literacy test for voters takes place under rules established by a special board (the State Board of Regents). Each new voter must present to the registration authorities as proof of his literacy a diploma (or other equivalent attestation) showing that he has finished the eighth grade, or a verification of his literacy issued according to rules established by the State Board of Regents. Between 1923 and 1928, 500,000 persons took these tests and 15 per cent of them failed to pass. In certain states it is possible, however, to buy one's way out of the educational qualification by paying a specific sum or higher taxes.

At the present time there is an educational qualification in England, the U.S.A., Japan, Hungary, and Bulgaria and other capitalist countries.

In the USSR there is no educational qualification.

SEC. 3: EQUAL SUFFRAGE

The Soviet Constitution, in contrast to bourgeois constitutions, grants equal election rights to all citizens. Equal suffrage signifies that in elections each elector has an equal vote with all the other electors, one vote only, and no preference or advantage over other electors. The election law of the USSR says: "On the basis of Article 136 of the USSR Constitution, the elections of the deputies are equal: each citizen has one vote; all citizens

[20] A test for verifying the literacy of voters in New York: "Read this and write your answers. You may read this as many times as necessary. 'Mary was waiting for the coming of the Fourth of July. On that day her father and mother were preparing to take her to the park. On that day her father was not supposed to work, because it was a holiday. In school it was explained to Mary why we celebrate the Fourth of July. On that day in 1776, the Declaration of Independence was signed. The declaration was drafted by Thomas Jefferson. It is called the Declaration of Independence because it proclaimed the independence of the thirteen American colonies from England. The Fourth of July is celebrated as a national holiday by all forty-eight states.'

"Answers to the following questions must be taken from the foregoing paragraph: (1) What day was Mary waiting for? (2) Where were Mary's parents going to take her? (3) Why did Mary's father not have to work? (4) Where did Mary learn why we celebrate Fourth of July? (5) When was the Declaration of Independence signed? (6) Who drafted the Declaration of Independence? (7) From what country were the thirteen American colonies proclaimed independent by the Declaration of Independence? (8) How many states celebrate the Fourth of July as a national holiday?"

This is cited as a typical example in Magruder, *American Government* (1936), pp. 574–575.

participate in elections on equal terms." [1] On the basis of Article 137 of the USSR Constitution, "women enjoy the right to vote and to be elected equally with men." [2] On the basis of Article 138 of the USSR Constitution, "citizens being in the ranks of the Red Army enjoy the right to vote and to be elected on an equality with all citizens." [3] Equal suffrage is likewise further assured by the fact that each elector is entered in only one voting list. [4] The Soviet election system further assures the actual equality of electors and actual equal suffrage by reason of the fact that the Supreme Soviet of the USSR is elected by USSR citizens according to election precincts, and each such precinct sends to the Supreme Soviet only one deputy. [5]

Election precincts for elections to the Soviet of the Union are equal among themselves. Everyone knows that, prior to the adoption of the Stalin Constitution in 1936, the worker class had advantages in the rules of representation in elections to the Soviets. Article 25 of the RSFSR Constitution (1918) established that the All-Russian Congress of Soviets consists of representatives of city Soviets on the basis of one deputy to 25,000 electors and of representatives of guberniya Congresses of Soviets on the basis of one deputy to 125,000 inhabitants. The Constitution established a varying correlation for the representation of city and village to the regional and guberniya Congresses of Soviets (Art. 53). Prior to the adoption of the Stalin Constitution, the following rules were preserved: to district Congresses of Soviets (RSFSR)—city Soviets, sovkhozes, machine and tractor service stations, factories and works situated outside city settlements sent one delegate for each 60 electors, and rural Soviets one delegate for each 300 inhabitants. In elections to territorial (regional) Congresses of Soviets—city Soviets, sovkhozes, and so on sent one delegate for each 2,500 electors, and the rural population one delegate for each 12,500 inhabitants.

In addition to this, the city population enjoyed two further advantages in representation in Congresses of the Soviets. The constitutions of Union Republics contemplated the direct representation of cities and worker settlements in the higher Congresses of the Soviets. Starting from this point, cities and worker settlements in the RSFSR, for example, electing deputies to the volost Congresses of Soviets, at the same time elected also their own deputies to the provincial congresses (one deputy for 200 electors) and to the regional congresses (one deputy for 5,000 electors). The cities sent their delegates directly even to the All-Russian Congresses of Soviets (one deputy for 25,000 electors). As a result of the districting which was put

<hr />

[1] Propositions Concerning Elections to the USSR Supreme Soviet, Art. 3.
[2] Ibid., Art. 4.
[3] Ibid., Art. 5.
[4] Ibid., Art. 11.
[5] Ibid., Arts. 20–22.

into effect, the rules of representation were somewhat changed but the direct representation of cities continued until 1930. Under the instructions of October 20, 1930, and October 1, 1934, direct representation to higher Congresses of Soviets was granted only to the few cities which had been segregated into independent administrative-territorial units and subordinated to territorial regional executive committees. From the remaining city Soviets, representatives to the higher Congress of Soviets came to be elected at district Congresses of the Soviets and not at plena of the city Soviets.

Furthermore, the cities sent deputies to the higher Congresses of the Soviets not only through plena of the appropriate city Soviets, but also through trade-union and Party organizations. In 1920 the number of delegates from social organizations comprised 7.6 per cent of the total number of deputies of provincial Congresses of Soviets, and 6.3 per cent of the total number of delegates of the guberniya congresses. This representation had already begun to shrink in 1921 and had been completely abolished by 1925.

Life itself brought about the differences in the rules of representation. Everyone knows that by the time of the adoption of the first Soviet Constitution by the Fifth All-Russian Congress of Soviets (July 10, 1918), the Soviet state was going through a difficult period. The chain of counterrevolutionary conspiracies within the country, the foul designs of the SR's and the Bukharinists against Lenin and Stalin, the Czechoslovakian uprising, the beginning of intervention, the acute shortage of provisions—all this contributed to the setting in which the first Soviet Constitution was worked out and adopted. In the rural areas the kulaks were struggling stubbornly against the proletarian dictatorship; the middle-class peasant was still wavering; and the poorest peasants had only begun to be organized into committees of the poor. Of this period Lenin wrote: "For the village our revolution still continued to be a bourgeois revolution, and only later, six months later, were we constrained, within the framework of this state organization, to initiate the class struggle in the villages, to institute in each village committees of the poor, semiproletarians, and to struggle systematically with the village bourgeoisie." [6]

A month before the adoption of the Constitution (on June 11, 1918) a decree concerning the organization of committees for the country poor was adopted. It was only in the second half of 1918 that, with the aid of these committees of the poor, the village Soviets and the volost executive committees were purged of the kulaks who had infiltrated in a number of places. Under these conditions the worker class had to direct the building of the state, to reeducate the peasantry, to organize the defense of its state, to

[6] Lenin (Russian ed.), Vol. XXIV, p. 20.

obtain provisions, and so on, and even in the Constitution, the proletariat enjoyed certain preferences in the political life of our country. As to this Lenin wrote:

Our Constitution acknowledges an advantage possessed by the proletariat over the peasantry. . . . Measures such as the inequality between workers and peasants are emphatically not prescribed by the Constitution. The Constitution has noted them *after* they had been put into practice. . . . The organization of the proletariat progressed much more swiftly than did that of the peasantry. This made the workers the support under the Revolution, and gave them preeminence in fact. Beyond us stands the task: to move gradually away from these advantages and toward their equalization.[7]

Many years have passed since that time, and the gigantic changes occurring in our country in the interim have eliminated the matter of the advantages of workers as compared with peasants in the election system. Their inequality has disappeared. Molotov characterized the causes of the differing election rights of workers and peasants thus:

These advantages on the side of the workers were introduced when the peasants were all still petty proprietors and while the influence of the kulaks was still great in the rural areas. . . . But after the peasants, too, followed the workers up into the ranks of direct builders of socialism, the way was cleared for the abolition of differences of every sort as between the workers and peasants and, above all, for the elimination of differences in election rights. Workers and peasants were now occupied with a single *general concern*—the building of socialism on the basis of the Soviet social order; and Soviet authority has grown unprecedentedly strong, wherefore the earlier reasons for the existence of differences in election rights as between workers and peasants must disappear.[8]

Stalin, conversing with Roy Howard, said that our elections will be equal "because neither the difference (which still exists in part) in respect of property nor race nor national origin shall confer any privilege or cause any detriment. Women shall enjoy the franchise, active and passive, on an equal basis with men." [9]

The Stalin Constitution eliminated the erstwhile temporary distinction between workers and peasants in respect of election rights, having established in the election system the complete equality of the entire population of the country.

Bourgeois countries and bourgeois jurists have much to say as to the equality of citizens in bourgeois society. During the seventeenth and eighteenth centuries, they proclaimed "the national equality of man and citizen,"

[7] *Ibid.*, p. 146.
[8] Molotov, *Changes in the Soviet Constitution* (1935), pp. 23–24.
[9] Stalin, Interview with Roy Howard (1937), p. 14.

the "natural" right of all citizens to participate in creating the law, and the like. When, however, the bourgeoisie emerged victorious, "natural equality was limited to the equality of citizens before the law, and the most essential of man's rights was declared to be the right of bourgeois property." [10] Property defines man's position in bourgeois society.

Equal suffrage signifies the right of each elector to enjoy only one vote, whereas in bourgeois countries rich people may have more. In England, for example, electors domiciled in one election district, and possessing land or a business in another, acquire in the latter a supplementary, second vote. In the election district of the City of London, the center of the English and world banks and of the largest enterprises, the lists enumerate 44,000 electors, whereas the entire population there domiciled is calculated at around 11,000, and the population of voting age at around 7,000. The other 37,000 acquire the right to vote here only because they possess a trading or banking enterprise, a house, land, or the like in this election district. In London in 1931 there was an enumeration of 137,731 electors enjoying such a supplementary vote. [11]

With reference to "equality" in bourgeois countries, Lenin write that this is a lie, that there is no equality there "if it contravenes the liberation of labor from the pressure of capital [12]. . . because the gorged grain speculator and the hungry toiler are not equal." [13] At the Extraordinary Eighth All-Union Congress of Soviets, Stalin said: "They talk about the equality of citizens but forget that there can be no actual equality between master and workman, between landowner and peasant, if the former is wealthy and has political weight in society whereas the latter lacks both the one and the other; if the former is an exploiter and the latter is exploited." [14]

Even the most democratic suffrage in bourgeois countries accommodates a negligible quantity of capitalists. Capitalists hold in their hands the power and the state mechanism. Enjoying these, the bourgeoisie attaches such provisos to a democratic law that it is completely abrogated; but the mechanism obligingly fulfills a definition of election method and techniques agreeable to the bourgeoisie, with the result that not infrequently in bourgeois countries the proportion of voters of one single election district is one-tenth of that of the voters of another. In Poland, for example, the Cracow election district sends one deputy from 48,000 voters, while the Kreshmenets district, with a population predominantly Ukrainian, sends one deputy from 96,000 voters. In France in the first precinct of a bourgeois election district

[10] Engels, *Anti-Dühring* (Russian ed., 1934), p. 12.
[11] *Census of England and Wales* (1932), p. 12.
[12] Lenin (Russian ed.), Vol. XXIV, p. 293.
[13] *Ibid.*, p. 309.
[14] Stalin, *Report on the Draft of the USSR Constitution* (1936), p. 21.

of Paris, there are 8,000 voters that send one deputy. The second precinct of the same district, Corbeil, having 50,000 voters and situated in a proletarian suburb of Paris, likewise sends one deputy. Marseilles, with 500,000 inhabitants, sends to the Chamber of Deputies twenty-four deputies, and seventeen little places of the same department, with 30,000 inhabitants, also send twenty-four deputies.[15] Such "election geography" attests the absence of equality from bourgeois countries. Vast masses of workers inhabiting a definite territory are artificially combined into one district and return one deputy. Territories with a much smaller, but bourgeois, population are likewise combined into one election district and likewise return one deputy. As a result the bourgeoisie acquires more seats in parliament than do representatives of the workers. In 1932, at the time of the elections of the French parliament, the communists assembled 800,000 votes and obtained twelve mandates. The Radical-Socialists (the bourgeois party) assembled 1,850,000 votes. It would seem that they should acquire no more than twice as many mandates; in fact, however, they acquired 157 mandates—thirteen times as many.

A crude policy of inequality was followed by the government of tsarist Russia during the elections to the Imperial Duma.[16] The population of entire regions was disfranchised (Akmolinsk, Transcaspia, Samarkand, Semipalatinsk, Semirechye, Syr-Daria, Turgay, Ural, Fergana, Yakutsk). The toilers of the national borderlands were limited: in European Russia one deputy was returned for 279,000 inhabitants as against one for 1,000,000 inhabitants in Siberia. Women in tsarist Russia were without rights and had no franchise. The same is true of all so-called "nomad foreigners," Kalmyks, Kirghiz, Yakuts, and others. No persons not familiar with the Russian language were elected. Young people up to the age of twenty-five—approximately 14,000,000 persons, not counting women—were without election rights. Students, irrespective of age, were barred from elections. Of the peasants only "householders," not including hired laborers, enjoyed the right to vote. Workers—only males—elected on the basis of one delegate from an enterprise with 50 to 2,000 employees and one from each full thousand thereafter. (If there were 999 workers, they had no right to a delegate.) This was done with the aim of excluding from elections the most class-conscious workers of the big enterprises. To have a right to be elected delegate, a worker must have worked continuously in a given enterprise for not less than six months. The workers of handicraft establishments had no right to vote in the worker *curia*. Thus only approximately 15 per cent of

[15] J. Barthélemy, *The State Social Order of France* (Russian ed., 1936), p. 5.
[16] Special reference should be made to the Regulation of Elections to the Imperial Duma of June 3, 1907.

the population took part in elections to the Duma (in the 51 guberniyas of European Russia, only 17,000,000 out of 112,327,000). As a result of such measures, the landowners (being one-fifth of the population) had 51.3 per cent of the persons elected, the first municipal *curia*, 13.2 per cent; the second, 11 per cent; the peasants (being 90 per cent of the population), 22.4 per cent, and the workers, 2.1 per cent.

The disparity between the equality of the population proclaimed by the bourgeoisie and reality comes out particularly distinctly if we compare the social structure of the population of socialist countries with that of representative organs. According to a computation made by English economists and statisticians in 1924–1926 on the basis of the English census of 1921, 3.7 per cent were entrepreneurs, 76 per cent received wages, 14 per cent were in private and state service, and 6.3 per cent lived on their own account (local landowners, craftsmen, petty tradesmen, and the like).

After 1921 in England, there were, of course, significant changes in the proportion of the workers and salaried employees in the direction of increasing their number. The social structure of the English parliament remained the same, however. In 1929, when the laborites came to "power," the 615 members of the House of Commons was made up as follows: 25 per cent were big entrepreneurs, 9 per cent big landowners, 27 per cent members of the liberal professions, expressing the interests of the bourgeoisie, and 39 per cent represented the "worker" party, including only a few workers. In 1935 members of the House of Commons included 139 persons of independent means, 27 landowners, 37 industrialists, 114 bankers and other businessmen, 21 literary people, 110 engineers, teachers, doctors, and lawyers, 32 officials and accountants, 3 clerics, 8 members of cooperatives, 99 representatives of trade unions and persons attending to serving the mechanism of the Labor Party, and only 5 workers. Approximately one-third of the deputies of the country areas in the House of Commons belong to the titled nobility: 1 duke, 11 lords, 12 sons of lords, 3 marquises, 1 son of a marquis, 1 earl, 5 sons of barons, 113 knights and baronets, and 10 sons of knights and baronets.[17] The same parliamentary social structure, with its oil kings and the like, is found in other capitalist countries also (such as France and the U.S.A.), not to speak of fascist countries, inasmuch as in Italy the "parliament" is simply appointed by Mussolini, and in Germany by Hitler. Moreover, in Germany persons of non-Aryan blood are completely excluded from the concept of "citizens."

These data show that in bourgeois countries a negligible minority of

[17] This computation of the structure of the House of Commons is based on the tables of Prof. Harold Laski published in the *New Statesman and Nation* (Nov. 30, 1935), p. 805.

capitalists has an overwhelming number of representatives in parliament and decisive influence in these organs. The woeful inequality in the franchise is obtained by employing every possible machination permitted by the bourgeoisie in the election of its representative organs (bribery, sending voting warrants to the wrong address, "mistaken" omission of workers from the voting list, the creation of unequal election districts, and so on) and by resorting to all sorts of reservations in the law. And this inequality of suffrage is constant and inevitable so long as the power of the bourgeoisie exists. Only the overthrowing of the power of the bourgeoisie and the establishment of the proletarian dictatorship can give genuinely equal suffrage.

SEC. 4: DIRECT SUFFRAGE

Direct suffrage means the right of voters to elect deputies directly. In the election system such elections of deputies are called direct (immediate or single-stage elections). In the USSR, direct elections are established by the Stalin Constitution (Art. 139): "Elections of deputies are direct; elections to all Soviets of Deputies of the Toilers, from the village and city Soviet of Deputies of the Toilers up to and including the Supreme Soviet of the USSR, are by the citizens immediately by means of direct elections."

Prior to the Stalin Constitution only city and village Soviets were elected by means of direct elections. In their election assemblies the toilers of the city and the village elected deputies to the said Soviets immediately (directly, by one stage). The higher organs of Soviet authority were elected by indirect elections (in many stages). Delegates to district Congresses of the Soviets were elected by the plena of city and village Soviets, not by the electors directly. Delegates to the territorial (regional) Congresses of Soviets were elected at district Congresses of the Soviets and at plena of the city Soviets subordinate to the territory (region). Most delegates to the All-Russian and All-Union Congresses of Soviets were elected at territorial (regional) Congresses. Elections of executive committees were conducted in the appropriate Congresses: the district executive committee was elected by the district Congress of Soviets; the territorial or regional executive committee by the territorial or regional Congress of Soviets; the All-Russian Central Executive Committee by the All-Russian Congress of Soviets; and the Central Executive Committee of the USSR by the All-Union Congress of Soviets.

Thus we have (1) one-stage or direct elections (the electors elect agricultural and city Soviets); (2) two-stage elections (plena of the agricultural and city Soviets elect delegates to district Congresses and their executive organs); (3) three-stage elections (the district Congress elects delegates to the territorial-regional Congress and the district executive committee); (4) four-stage elections (territorial and regional Congresses of Soviets elect delegates to the Union Republic Congress of Soviets and All-Union Congress of Soviets and the territorial executive committee).

This system was necessary. It was produced by life itself even before the adoption of the first Soviet Constitution of 1918.

The economic condition of the country, the character of the link between city and country, the cultural level of the population, the degree of mass activity, and so forth, made such a system of elections necessary at that time. Lenin then said of it: "Indirect elections to nonlocal Soviets facilitate Congresses of Soviets, and make the *entire* apparatus cheaper, more mobile, and more accessible to the workers and peasants in a period when life boils, and it must be feasible with no loss of time to recall one's local deputy or to send him to the general Congress of Soviets." [1]

Of course multiple-stage elections had their shortcomings, the basic one being that electors did not take a direct part in elections of delegates to Congresses of the Soviets, to say nothing of their executive committees.[2] But during the civil war and for a number of years thereafter, the economic, cultural and social-political position of the country made the transition from indirect to direct elections difficult. In practice the members of the All-Russian Central Executive Committee were very closely linked with the electors, even under the system of indirect elections. The very nature of the Soviet state is such that a deputy of the Soviet cannot work successfully without a close bond with the electors of the district where he works. By the time of the adoption of the Stalin Constitution, the conditions favorable to the introduction of direct elections had been created and the country passed to direct election of the Soviets from top to bottom. According to the existing Soviet election system, each elector elects his deputy directly in his election precinct. Clearly this method of elections provides still greater assurance and guaranty of the bond between deputies and electors. The elections to the Supreme Soviet of the USSR, which were held December 12, 1937, and later the elections to Supreme Soviets of Union and autonomous republics, created a firm and living bond between deputies and their electors.

Elections under the Soviet election system are by election districts divided into election precincts, assuring the electors all conveniences for giving effect to their election rights.

In bourgeois countries where "universal" suffrage has been introduced,

---

[1] Lenin (Russian ed.), Vol. XXIII, p. 350.
[2] By a regulation, Concerning Members of the All-Union Central Executive Committee, the latter were chosen and recalled by directive of the All-Russian Congress of Soviets.

the deputies of lower chambers, and likewise of organs of local self-government, are elected immediately by the people by direct vote of the select part
of the population, as we have already seen. The situation is different as to
the upper chamber of parliament; its members are either altogether appointed (as in England) or partly appointed (as in Japan), or they are
elected by indirect elections (and, in a lesser degree, by direct voting, as in
the U.S.A.). In such states as the U.S.A., France, Czechoslovakia, Poland,
and others, indirect elections are employed in electing a president. Indirect
elections have diverse forms. Thus the President of the U.S.A. is elected as
follows: the people of each state choose special electors who in a special
session give secret votes for one or the other of the candidates for the presidency. A formal record of these sessions, indicating the number of votes
obtained by each candidate, is sent to the Capital at Washington. Here
the total votes for each candidate in all the states throughout the country
are compiled. In this case indirect elections are effectuated through special
electors who assemble only for the purpose of voting.

In the French and Czechoslovak republics, a joint session of the
Senate and House of Deputies is assembled for the election of a president,
at which there is a secret vote upon all the previously nominated candidates
for president, the parliament itself acting as elector. In Italy members of
the upper chamber are appointed by the king for life. In Japan [3] the House
of Peers is composed partly of appointees of the emperor, partly of persons
acquiring the position by inheritance. In Yugoslavia, half the members of
the Senate are appointed by the king. In Canada, all the members of the
senate are appointed for life. In Great Britain [4] part of the membership of
the House of Lords is appointed by the king, part acquires its position by
reason of holding office (judges of the highest court, bishops, and archbishops) and part by inheritance. In Iran all members are appointed by
the king. In Hungary the upper chamber consists mostly of representatives
of ancient noble families who keep their "mandates" for life.

In bourgeois countries multiple-stage elections serve the class purposes
of the bourgeoisie. A characteristic example of this is the multiple-stage
system of elections [5] to the Imperial Duma in tsarist Russia under the law

[3] At the present time in Japan the Senate, the House of Peers, consists of 16 members
of the imperial family, 15 princes, 30 marquises, 18 earls, 66 viscounts, 66 barons, 125
persons appointed for life by the emperor from the important representatives of Japanese
aristocracy, 4 persons chosen by the Imperial Academy of Sciences, and 6 persons chosen
from among those who pay not less than 200 yen in direct taxes.—*The Statesman's Yearbook* (1935), p. 1071.
[4] The House of Lords in England consists of 25 dukes, 27 marquises, 129 earls, 75
viscounts, 460 barons, 26 archbishops and bishops, and 16 titular representatives of Ireland.
—*The Constitutional Yearbook* (1936), p. 87.
[5] "Method of Election to the Imperial Duma," cf. the paragraph entitled 'Organization
of Election Districts."

of June 3, 1907. Under this law direct elections occurred only in five cities (St. Petersburg, Moscow, Kiev, Odessa, and Riga). In all the remaining localities, elections were in multiple stages; two stages for provincial land-owners, three stages for workers, and four stages for peasants. The latter two were established by Stolypin's law in order to sift out candidates from the workers and peasants dangerous to the tsarist government and to en-able the greatest number of landowners and capitalists (representing a minority of all the population of the country, the exploiters) to pass into the Imperial Duma.

SEC. 5: SECRET BALLOT

Article 140 of the Stalin Constitution says: "Voting at the elections for deputies is secret." Secret voting means that the voting is conducted by fill-ing in ballots with absolutely no other voters or bystanders present, guaran-teeing that the voter manifests his will freely and independently. Such method of voting assures the voter against unpleasantness on the part of bureaucrats blackballed and therefore feeling offended. Stalin sees the force of Bolshevik guidance in the bond between this guidance and the masses, in readiness to listen to the voice of the masses. If the leader does not answer to these required qualities, the masses will not vote for him. Thus secret elections (secret voting) are not only one of the most important means of expressing criticism, of exerting control from below, but also very often a very heavy "whip in the hands of the population against poorly working organs of authority." [1]

Being one of the most important principles of the Soviet election system, secret voting is assured by appropriate premises for elections and a special room for filling in ballots into which no one, not even members of the elec-tion commission, is admitted, except the voters during the election. If sev-eral voters are admitted into the voting room at the same time it must be equipped with partitions or screens according to the number of voters so admitted. The Soviet election system admits an exception to this rule in case of illiterate voters or those under some physical infirmity, in consequence of which outside assistance is indispensable to filling out a ballot. He may, in that case, invite into the room for filling out the ballot any other elector he chooses to help him fill out his ballot. This measure, in no wise violating the secrecy of the election, accords in the fullest degree with the promotion of the principle of universal voting.

[1] Stalin, Interview with Roy Howard (1936), p. 15.

The Soviet Constitutions of 1918 and 1924 did not define the means of voting; it could therefore be open or secret. As a rule, however, the elections of Soviets were in practice conducted by open voting, and instructions concerning these elections so noted. Soviet election law most strictly forbade that any pressure whatever be exerted on electors, assuring thereby the initiative of the masses which were always drawn widely into the work of administering the Soviet state. Nevertheless, in individual cases the bureaucratic and opportunist elements in the Soviet and trade-union mechanisms tried to utilize the open voting for the surreptitious promotion of the candidates agreeable to them. With the adoption of the Stalin Constitution, this possibility was eliminated. The growth of political mass consciousness, the suppression of the exploiter classes in the land, the destruction of counterrevolutionary-wrecker-spy organizations, the raising of the cultural level of the population—all these made it possible to do away with open voting completely and to establish secret voting as a binding rule of law. Why did we introduce secret voting? "Because we wish to give the Soviet people complete freedom to vote for those whom they wish to elect, those to whom they entrust the assurance of their interests." [2]

The transition to secret voting thus signified the further growth of worker-socialist democracy in the Soviet Union and, as Molotov has pointed out, the aspiration of Soviet authority to place the work of its organs under the intensified control of workers and peasants.

In bourgeois countries secret voting does not exist everywhere. Thus in Yugoslavia open voting was legalized under "universal" suffrage. In Hungary the secret ballot is admitted only in large city election districts; in all other districts, voting is open. We may judge of the dimensions of open and secret voting in Hungary from the fact that out of 244 members of the Hungarian parliament, only 40 were elected by secret voting. [3]

Even in the bourgeois countries where secret voting has been introduced in form, we must speak of it with reservations inasmuch as the bourgeois classes there dominant employ all sorts of means to reduce this right to nought. "Bourgeois parties dominate in an enormous degree by reason of their deceit of the masses of the population." [4] The system, which includes the direct purchase of votes, terror, violence, and pressure, creates such conditions in the bourgeois countries that individual voters have no power to resist them. Giddings, an American professor, considers that by reason of the terror occurring at elections, only 5 per cent of the voters of the country vote freely.

[2] *Ibid.*
[3] Karl Braunias, *Das parlamentarische Wahlrecht*, (Berlin, 1932), Vol. I, pp. 603–604.
[4] Lenin (Russian ed.), Vol. XXIV, p. 647.

Particularly illusory is the secret voting in fascist countries. The mere fact that lists of candidates for parliament in Germany are made up only by the National-"Socialist" Party attests in itself that the "secret" of elections is known in advance to the fascists and that the will of the people there amounts to nothing. The terror of the fascists makes the "secret" a fiction. In Germany electors are persecuted by the fascists if they take it into their heads to discuss the candidates of the official fascist list, to say nothing of proposing candidates of their own. Those who avoid "elections" are accused of treason and subjected to torture.[5] During the elections in 1933, voters in many districts in Germany were given official ballots already marked "Yes," and in other cases transparent envelopes were used through which their votes could be seen. There was also a practice of giving numbered envelopes whereby it was possible to determine who voted for whom, inasmuch as the envelopes were given out according to a list. Ballot boxes were so constructed that the ballots dropped in them formed in the order in which the votes were given, thus making it possible to establish how a given voter had voted. In the concentration camp at Dachau, notorious for its cruelties and murders, there were in August, 1934, 1,517 votes for Hitler, 8 against him, and 10 void. The fascists led the "voters" and made them "voluntarily" fill out their "manifestation of will." Such a system of "secret" voting terrified the broad masses who were constrained to "vote" for fascists.

From information furnished by one German voter, published in the English paper The Daily Worker (April 20, 1936), it is clear that German fascists in the election room have one booth, guarded by fascists. It is so constructed that the fascists who "guard" it can look freely over the shoulder of the voter and see how he votes—"for" or "against." "There was nothing to do," writes this voter, "one had to vote Yes," and when certain workers—on the evidence of this same paper—voted against the fascist creatures, they were cruelly beaten. Elections in the other fascist countries (Italy, Japan) are conducted in like fashion.

"Secret" voting in bourgeois countries thus comes to nought. The bourgeoisie uses every device to substitute the unlimited power of a comparatively small group of magnates of capital for the will of the masses of the toilers. All this attests the weakness of the bourgeoisie, which can no longer govern by the old parliamentary methods and resorts to terror.

The transition to secret voting in the Soviet Union attests to its strength, to the fact that "Soviet authority draws its powers from the growth of the active participation by the masses in all state administration and from the

[5] The (British) Daily Worker, April 20, 1936.

intensified mass control of the work of the entire state mechanism from top to bottom." [6]

SEC. 6. THE ORGANIZATION OF ELECTIONS

Organization details in the election system (the technique of elections) are of enormous political significance. Such organization questions in the Soviet election system of elections to the Supreme Soviet include: the compilation of voting lists and election commissions, the organization of election districts and precincts, the nomination of candidates for Deputies of the Soviet, the method of voting, and the determination of the results of the voting. Organization matters of the Soviet election system for elections to the Supreme Soviet of the USSR and Supreme Soviets of Union and autonomous republics are defined by the Regulations Concerning Elections to Supreme Soviets.

1. *Voting lists*

The Soviet voting system assures that every citizen possessing the right to vote may participate completely in elections. Therefore registration of voters, the compilation of lists, is serious and responsible work constituting the first step in the preparation for elections to Supreme Soviets and Soviets of the Deputies of the Toilers in general. Lists of voters are made up by city and village Soviets [1] according to election precincts (lying-in-hospitals, sanatoria, hospitals, except the scarlet fever and diphtheria wards and hospitals for lepers, whose inmates take no part in elections, and the like) in alphabetical order on the basis of house lists, lists of members of collective farms making the rounds of the population of a given election precinct, and so forth. No documents are prerequisite to inclusion in the voting lists. "All citizens having the suffrage and residing, permanently or otherwise at the time the lists are compiled, in the territory of the given Soviet, having attained the age of eighteen years by election day, are entered in the lists." [2]

In the Soviet state there is nothing whatever of the so-called domicile qualification, requiring a citizen to have lived in a given election district for a definite period. Article 15 of the Regulations contemplates the pos-

---

[6] Molotov, *Changes in the Soviet Constitution* (1935), p. 26.

[1] In military units and formations, lists of voters are made up by the command and signed by the commander and the military commissar. All other persons in military service are entered on lists of electors by Soviets of Deputies of the Toilers according to their place of residence.

[2] Regulations Concerning Elections to the USSR Supreme Soviet, Art. 8.

sibility of a voter changing his domicile in the interval between the making up of the list and election day, in which event the Soviet of the Deputies of the Toilers issues to the elector a special "attestation of the right to vote."

On the basis of this attestation, the elector can vote in any new place of residence in the USSR even though he arrived there on the voting day. He is there entered on the list of those voting "according to attestations of the right to vote." However, "no voter may be entered upon more than one election list." [3]

Persons deprived of election rights by the court are not entered on the voting lists during the period set in the sentence of the court, but thereafter the condemned person again acquires election rights.[4] Persons duly declared to be feeble-minded are also not entered in the lists of voters.[5]

For thirty days before the elections, the lists of voters are posted for general information (or the Soviet guarantees that voters may become familiar with them on the premises of the Soviet). Each citizen has the right to complain to the Soviet of the Deputies of the Toilers of his incorrect noninclusion in, or exclusion from, the lists of electors, of the distortion of any of his names, and of the inclusion upon the lists of persons deprived of the franchise. The executive committee of the Soviet must consider the complaint within the period of three days. If the declarant is dissatisfied with the decision of the Soviet of Deputies of the Toilers, he can appeal it to the people's court, which must consider the complaint within three days. A complaint is considered in the people's court with the assurance of all the guarantees that the decision will be correct, in open court session and with both the declarant and a representative of the Soviet summoned to appear. Thus each citizen can defend his franchise and correct the mistaken inclusion among the number of voters of persons deprived of the franchise. The decision of the court is final.

In bourgeois countries likewise, election lists are made up according to defined election precincts. But the bourgeoisie so frames its election lists that tens of thousands of "unreliable" electors, chiefly workers, are not

---

[3] *Ibid.*, Art. 11.

[4] On the basis of the directive of the Central Executive Committee of the USSR (Oct. 16, 1937, Cz. 1937, No. 69, Art. 315), persons who have been convicted or are serving a court sentence (but without deprivation of election rights and without being in confinement), as well as special colonists, are entered in election lists, as are also persons under surveillance but not held under guard (if they are not deprived of election rights by the court).

[5] Nonentry in the voting lists, or exclusion therefrom, of individual citizens as feeble-minded by Soviets of the Toilers rests on a determination or sentence of a court, based upon appropriate certification by court psychiatric experts, or upon lists presented by the regional (territorial) or municipal subdivisions of public health regarding persons under treatment in psychiatric hospitals and colonies.

included therein; payment of a special tax is required for being put upon the voting list (as in many states of the U. S. A.), or all sorts of information and attestation (the acquisition of which involves great expenditure of time, money, and so forth) must be furnished. The election law of the state of Virginia contains the following article: "One wishing to acquire the right to vote must answer under oath all questions bearing on his acquisition of that right." In the state of Florida, the election law requires that a citizen give information under oath as to his age and domicile, and swear that he has never been convicted of crime. The giving of false information may be punished by twenty years in prison. For making up lists of voters, a definite time—two or three days in the year—is established. Voters not appearing at this time are not included in the list. Various sorts of qualifications likewise exclude enormous masses of the adult population from the number of electors. On the other hand, according to the bourgeois political scientist Bryce, persons who have no right to take part in elections are entered upon the lists of voters, including persons who have long since moved away or died, [6] and the like. Tens of thousands of such persons are to be counted in lists of bourgeois electors. The bourgeoisie has to employ forgers so that the election warrants of those non-existent "voters" may be presented for use (through venal individuals) in voting for candidates of bourgeois parties. Bryce writes that these forgeries "are perpetrated so frequently as to constitute one of the important social evils."

2. The organization of election districts and voting precincts

Election districts in the USSR were introduced by the Stalin Constitution (Art. 141): "Candidates for elections are nominated according to election districts," and that Constitution defines the election rule (Arts. 34 and 35): "The Soviet of the Union is elected by USSR citizens according to election districts on the basis of one deputy for each 300,000 of the population. The Soviet of Nationalities is elected by USSR citizens, according to Union and autonomous republics, autonomous regions, and national areas, on the basis of twenty-five deputies from each Union Republic, eleven from each autonomous republic, five from each autonomous region, and one from each national area." The list of election districts is published by the Presidium of the Supreme Soviet of the USSR at the same time it designates the day of elections.

Prior to the Stalin Constitution, elections to the Soviets took place chiefly according to production units (factories, works, shops, mines, collective farms, and so forth). Only in the village and among the unor-

[6] James Bryce, *The American Commonwealth* (Russian ed., 1890), Pt. 2, p. 412.

ganized population in the cities was the territorial principle of organizing elections employed. This was necessary to the end of completely barring nontoilers and persons deprived of election rights from participating in the elections, and it was a measure assuring the directing role of the worker class in elections to organs of state authority. Under present conditions, with the exploiter classes in the country liquidated, man's exploitation of man finally abolished, socialism fundamentally built, and universal suffrage introduced, there is no necessity to organize elections according to production principles. Under the given conditions the organization of elections according to election districts is a further step in the development of Soviet socialist democracy in the most comprehensive realization of universal suffrage.

Election districts for elections to the Supreme Soviet of the USSR are formed by the Presidium of the Supreme Soviet of the USSR. Election districts for Union Republic Supreme Soviets are formed by the Presidia of Union Republic Supreme Soviets, and for elections to the Supreme Soviets of Autonomous Soviet Socialist Republics by the Presidia of Supreme Soviets of such autonomous republics. Each election district sends one deputy.

The constitution of each Union Republic, in accord with the manifested will of the people thereof, has established its rules for forming districts: the RSFSR, 150,000 population to one election district; the Ukraine SSR, 100,000; the White Russian SSR, 20,000; the Azerbaijan SSR, 10,000; the Georgian SSR, 15,000; the Armenian SSR, 5,000; the Turkmen SSR, 5,000; the Uzbek SSR, 15,000; the Tadjik SSR, 5,000; the Kazakh SSR, 20,000; and the Kirghiz SSR, 5,000. The difference in dimensions of districts in the Union Republics is defined exclusively by the number of the population of these republics.

The organization of election districts upon such a principle serves to attract the masses to the elections. The number of deputies in the Supreme Soviet is also defined in terms of the rules established by Union Republics for organizing election districts. The first elections of the Supreme Soviet of the USSR and of Union Republic Supreme Soviets defined this number of districts: the USSR, 569 election districts for elections to the Soviet of the Union and 574 districts for election to the Soviet of Nationalities (25 districts in each of the 11 Union Republics—275 districts; 11 in each of the 22 Autonomous Soviet Socialist Republics—242; 5 in each of the autonomous regions; and one in each of the 12 national areas.) In the RSFSR the number is 727 election districts, in the White Russian SSR, 273; in the Ukraine SSR, 304; in the Tadjik SSR, 283; in the Uzbek

SSR, 395; in the Kazakh SSR, 300; in the Kirghiz SSR, 284, and in the Turkmen SSR, 226.

For the formation of election districts for elections of Supreme Soviets in Autonomous Soviet Socialist Republics, the following rules are established by the constitutions of these ASSR's (members of the RSFSR unless otherwise indicated):

1. Karelian *	5,000 population to a district,	111 districts
2. Kalmyk	3,000	65
3. Mordvinian	12,000	107
4. Komi	4,000	79
5. Crimean	10,000	105
6. Chuvash	12,000	96
7. Tatar	20,000	143
8. Bashkir	20,000	150
9. German-Volga region	4,000	127
10. Daghestan	8,000	113
11. Udmurt	7,500	142
12. North Ossetian	4,000	79
13. Chechen-Ingush	6,000	112
14. Mari	6,000	93
15. Buriat-Mongolian	6,000	89
16. Karbardino-Balkarsk	4,000	85
17. Yakutsk	3,000	130
18. Abkhazian (Georgian SSR)	5,000	104
19. Adjarian (Georgian SSR)	3,000	63
20. Moldavian (Ukraine SSR)	6,000	104
21. Nakhichevan (Azerbaijan SSR)	2,000	66
22. Kara-Kalpak (Uzbek SSR)	3,000	144

From this it is clear that the election districts within each autonomous SSR are likewise equal among themselves. The varying norms for forming election districts, and consequently the varying quantity of districts in different republics, is explained by the number of the population in such autonomous SSR's.

To elect one deputy to the territorial or regional Soviet the following rules are established: in the RSFSR, from 15,000 to 40,000 population (depending on the dimensions of the territory or region); in the Ukraine SSR, from 25,000 to 35,000 population; in the Kazakh SSR, from 4,000 to

* In connection with the order of the Presidium of the Supreme Soviet of the USSR of May 28, 1938, concerning the formation of the Murmansk region and the inclusion therein of the Kandalaksha district of the Karelian ASSR, the number of districts in the latter was diminished to nine.

8,000 population. To elect one deputy to the regional Soviet of an autonomous region the following rules are established: in the RSFSR, 1,500 to 2,000 population; in the Azerbaijan SSR, 1,500; in the Georgian SSR, 2,500 (the South Ossetian autonomous region); and in the Tadjik SSR, 500 (the Gorno-Badakhshan autonomous region).

Area Soviets consist of one deputy from 2,000 to 10,000 population in the RSFSR; from 2,000 to 3,000 in the White Russian SSR (in 1938 the areas were liquidated); 5,000 population in the Ukraine and Uzbek SSR's; 2,000 population in the Kazakh SSR; and 1,500 population in the Turkmen SSR. One deputy is sent to Soviets of national areas from not less than 100 nor more than 500 inhabitants, depending on the population of the area. One deputy is sent to the district Soviet,[7] depending on the size of the district: in the RSFSR, the Ukraine SSR, the White Russian SSR, from not less than 500 nor more than 1,500; in the Azerbaijan SSR and the Armenian SSR, from 300 to 1,000; in the Turkmen SSR, from 250 to 600 of the population; in the Kirghiz SSR, from 150 to 1,000; in the Tadjik SSR, from 150 to 600 population; in the Georgian SSR, from 300 population; in the Uzbek SSR a district with population of up to 30,000 sends one deputy from 500 population; with a population of from 30,000 to 40,000, one deputy from 650 population; with a population of from 40,000 to 50,000, one from 800 population; with the population of from 50,000 to 60,000, one deputy from 900 population; with a population of above 60,000, one deputy from 1,000 population. Municipal and district Soviets (in cities) elect one deputy on the basis of the following rules: in the RSFSR and the Ukraine SSR, from 100 to 1,000 (from Moscow and Leningrad 3,000); the White Russian SSR, 150 to 300; the Armenian SSR, 100 to 1,000; Azerbaijan SSR, 100 to 750; and for Baku, 1,000; the Uzbek SSR, 100 to 600, and for Tashkent 1,000; the Tadjik and Kirghiz SSR's, 100 to 500; the Kazakh SSR, 100 to 400, and in Alma-Ata, 500; the Georgian SSR, the city of Poti, one deputy from 200; the city of Kutaisi, one deputy from 400; the city of Tiflis, one deputy from 700; the remaining cities with a population up to 10,000, one deputy for 100; with a population above 10,000, one deputy for 150.

The rules of representation to the village, settlement, and Caucasian hamlet Soviets in the RSFSR, the White Russian SSR and the Ukraine SSR call for one deputy from 100 to 250; in the Azerbaijan and Armenian SSR's, 100 to 250; in the Kazakh SSR, one deputy from 50 to 250; in the Uzbek SSR, one deputy from 75 to 100; in the Turkmen and Tadjik SSR, one deputy from 50 to 100; in the Georgian SSR, one deputy from 20 to 150; and in the Kirghiz SSR, one deputy from 50 to 200.

[7] In the Buriat-Mongolian ASSR and the Oirot autonomous region, to the Aimak Soviet.

The rules of representation to the district Soviet of the Toilers of an autonomous SSR do not exceed the limits of the rules established by the corresponding Union Republic; the electors of all the autonomous SSR's which are component parts of the RSFSR and the Ukraine SSR, send to the district Soviets of the Deputies of the Toilers [8] one deputy from a population of not less than 500 nor more than 1,500; district Soviets of the Nakhichevan autonomous SSR send one deputy from 250 to 1,000; in the Adjarian and Abkhazian autonomous SSR's, one deputy for 300; in the Kara-Kalpak autonomous SSR, one deputy from 500 to 1,000. The same may be said also with reference to the rules of representation to city Soviets and district Soviets of the big cities. They are elected according to the rules of the corresponding Union Republics. The Abkhazian, Adjarian, Nakhichevan and Kara-Kalpak ASSR's have their rules within the limits of those of their respective Union Republics, the first: one deputy from 100 to 200 population; the second and fourth, one from 100 to 300; and the third, one from 100 to 350.

The village Soviets in an autonomous SSR are elected according to rules somewhat deviating from those of their Union Republics. In the Karelian, Kalmyk, Komi, Daghistan, North Assetian, Chechen-Ingush, Buriat-Mongolian, Kabardano-Balkarian, and Yakutsk ASSR's, one deputy is sent from 50 to 250 population, and the same rules obtain in the Udmurt ASSR for settlement Soviets (in the RSFSR, 100 to 250); the nomad village Soviets of the Yakutsk ASSR are elected according to rule—one deputy from 15 to 50 of the population. In the remaining autonomous SSR's making up the RSFSR, the rules of the Union Republic are preserved. The village Soviets of the Kara-Kalpak autonomous SSR are elected on the rule of one deputy from 50 to 200 of the population (in the Uzbek SSR, 75 to 200). The village Soviets of the Abkhazian, Adjarian, Nakhichevan, and Moldavian autonomous SSR's follow the rules of their Union Republics in their entirety.

Both the organization of the areas in the USSR and the establishment of rules of representation to all organs of authority, from the village Soviet to the Supreme Soviet, pursue one purpose: to carry into effect genuine Soviet democracy. "Elections of the Soviets in the USSR are the only actually free and actually democratic elections in the whole world." [9] The organization of election districts and the establishment of rules of repre-

[8] In the Kalmyk autonomous SSR, to tribal (Ulrus) Soviets of Deputies of the Toilers; in the German-Volga autonomous SSR, to canton Soviets of Deputies of the Toilers; in the Buriat-Mongolian autonomous SSR and the Oirot autonomous region, to Aimak Soviets of Deputies of the Toilers.

[9] Stalin, "Speech at the Preelection Assembly of Voters of the Stalin Election District of Moscow" (Dec. 11, 1937), p. 9.

sentation create the conditions essential to the effectuation of such elections.

To promote the greatest convenience for the receipt of ballots and the counting of votes, the entire territory of cities and districts making up an election district is divided according to the Soviet system into election precincts, whose creation brings the election place near the elector and assures the realization of truly universal elections. In the USSR there are districts, in the north, for example, which embrace enormous territory, whereas elections must take place within a single day between 6 A.M. and 12 midnight. Without dividing the territory of the district into election precincts, it would be difficult to conduct the elections.[10]

Election precincts are created as follows: worker settlements, villages, and the territory of village Soviets containing more than 2,000 inhabitants are divided into precincts on the basis of 1,500 to 2,500 persons. In each station, village, and Caucasian hamlet of from 500 to 2,000 inhabitants a separate election precinct is organized. In accordance with the directive of the Central Executive Committee of the USSR of October 3, 1937,[11] election precincts may be formed in settlements or a group of settlements having a population of less than 500 but not less than 300 whenever the distance between such settlements and the center of the election precinct is more than ten kilometers. In individual northern and eastern districts, where tiny settlements predominate, election precincts can be organized if the inhabitants number 100 persons. For national areas of the north, and likewise for mountain and nomad districts, election precincts with a population of less than 100, but not less than 50, persons may be organized with the permission of the Presidia of Union Republic Supreme Soviets.

To guarantee the greatest convenience of voting in military units and formations, separate election precincts with a number of voters not less than 50 nor more than 1,500 are created as constituent parts of election districts according to the place where the unit or formation is located. Election precincts are likewise created in hospitals, sanatoria, lying-in hospitals, and in invalid homes containing not less than 50 electors. Election precincts are created on boats which are cruising on election day, if there are not less than 25 electors on them, such precincts being constituent parts of the district of the boat's port of registry. Passenger trains which are in

[10] The number of election precincts is: in the RSFSR, 93,927 (2,047 of them on boats and steamers); in the Ukraine SSR 21,070; in the White Russian SSR 3,878; in the Uzbek SSR, 5,104; in the Georgian SSR, 2,932; in the Azerbaijan SSR, 2,692; in the Kirghiz SSR, 1,527; in the Tadjik SSR, 1,520; in the Turkmen SSR, 1,220; and in the Armenian SSR, 1,204.

[11] Cz. 1937, No. 67, Art. 306.

the course of a journey [12] on election day create their election precincts ascribed to the election districts in whose territory the trains will be, according to schedule, at the beginning of the voting on the day of election. In big stations at junction points, election precincts are organized to receive ballots from passengers in transit.

Election precincts are formed forty-five days prior to the election of the Supreme Soviet by district Soviets of Deputies of the Toilers in cities divided into districts, by city Soviets in cities not so subdivided, and by district Soviets of the toilers in village localities.

In capitalist countries the organization of elections according to election districts was, in its time, directed against the system of class representation established during the dominance of feudalism: the States-General in France, the Parliament in England, the Cortes in Spain, the Land Committees in Russia, and the like. Under the class system of representation, the biggest feudal lords, spiritual and temporal, were generally not elected but invited to the session of these organs by personal letters of the king (France, England). The system of class representation sustained the dominance of the feudal orders and afforded no means whereby the young and growing bourgeoisie could emerge into the political arena. The bourgeois-democratic system of elections according to election districts, supported by the workers, the petty urban bourgeoisie, and the peasantry was directed against this privileged system.

In individual capitalist states a division of the population according to *curiae*, the curial system, was long preserved. It was directed at furnishing to the tiniest groups of the population, comprising the wealthiest taxpayers, broader representation than was furnished to the petty proprietors. Separate groups made up *curiae*. Workers and peasants had almost no representatives of their own in parliament. An example of the curial system is the method of election to the Imperial Duma in tsarist Russia under the law of June 3, 1907. Electors corresponding to a definite qualification were divided into four *curiae*: the land owning *curia*, the *curia* of the city bourgeoisie—subdivided in turn into big proprietors (one city *curia*), the medical proprietors (two city *curiae*)—the peasant *curia*, and the worker *curia*. For the first *curia*, one person was elected for 230 voters; for the first city *curia*, one person was elected for 1,000 members; for the second city *curia*, one person for 15,600; for the peasant *curia*, one person was elected for 60,000; and for the worker *curia*, one for 125,000.

Furthermore, these were multiple-stage elections. Peasants assembled

[12] If a train is on a journey for more than four hours (directive of the Central Election Commission of the RSFSR, *Izvestiya*, May 15, 1938).

at the volost meeting, where they chose delegates; the delegates chose electors; and the electors were sent to the guberniya assemblies, where they too took part in the general elections. (There were thus four stages.) [13] By three-stage elections workers sent their electors. Such a method of elections was established so that, with the aid of police selection, candidates from the workers and peasants who were dangerous to the tsarist government could be sifted out and candidates of landowners and capitalists could pass into the Duma.

In bourgeois countries the division into districts is employed by the bourgeoisie at the present time for all sorts of machinations to the end of assuring to the bourgeois parties success in the elections. In most bourgeois countries this "election geography" in fact destroys election equality of every sort. In France, for example, the district of Florac has a population of 22,000, while the district of Corbeil has 137,000; Briançon has 25,000, while Grenoble has 120,000, and the second district of the 18th arrondissement of Paris has more than 115,000.[14] In England, at the 1935 elections, the district of Epes in Surrey had 105,855 electors; the district of Southwark North, 28,695; the district of Ramford, 167,393; and Vernard Castle, 27,309. In the 1931 elections, one labor deputy obtained 154,406 votes while one conservative deputy received 22,262.[15] Districts with a smaller population are bourgeois and those with a larger population are worker. Each district, however, sends one deputy.

In the U. S. A., the apportionment into election districts takes place within the states and is conducted in the interests of the bourgeoisie. This division in the U. S. A. acquired the peculiar name of gerrymandering, named after Governor Gerry, who was, at the beginning of the nineteenth century, a "specialist" at so patterning election districts [16] that his adversaries were tucked away into a small number of them and his adherents could come out as winners in the elections. Election machinations in the U. S. A. result in a sharp difference in the number of electors in individual districts. During the congressional elections of 1934, from 210,000 to 240,000 votes were cast in the first, second, and eighth districts of New York, while in the twelfth, thirteenth, fourteenth, fifteenth and twentieth districts of the same state the number of votes varied from 20,000 to 30,-000. During the 1936 elections to the House of Representatives, from 202,730 to 222,217 votes were cast in the second, eighth, and twenty-third districts as against 19,280 and 18,722 in the twelfth and twentieth

[13] Badaev, How the Toilers Voted for the Tsarist Duma (1937).
[14] Manuel électoral (Paris, Dalloz, 1928), p. 345.
[15] The Times, House of Commons (1935), p. 171.
[16] Frank A. Magruder, American Government (1936), p. 13.

districts.[17] The formation of this sort of election district helps the election of candidates belonging to the ruling parties but lacking support from the majority of the population. For such majority, one or two big districts are created in which the majority of the population is tucked away, while the minority, supporting candidates agreeable to the ruling party, is cut up into small election districts whose number is increased. Inasmuch as each district sends only one candidate, the party of the minority is assured of victory in that event.

The bourgeoisie thus organizes election districts to the end of "shoving out" the proletariat, the toilers, from the administration and assuring their own domination. The same purpose of barring workers from elections is pursued by the bourgeoisie when it creates its own election precincts (communes, sections) in the center of the town far from the worker borderlands. Election precincts are often placed side by side with police stations, frightening away broad masses of the toilers.

The organization of election districts and precincts in the USSR on the basis of the Stalin Constitution starts from the point that the elections to all organs of authority are conducted on the basis of universal suffrage and are direct and equal, wherefore it is essential to create conditions for the complete participation of the voters in the elections. In the USSR "there are no capitalists, no landowners, and no exploitation, and actually there is no one to oppress the people in order to distort their will." [18] Accordingly, in the USSR, completely equal districts and precincts are organized near the voters, creating a setting for the collaboration of workers, peasants, and intelligentsia in mutual confidence and friendship.

3. Election commissions

To carry on truly democratic elections to the Supreme Soviets of the USSR and of the Union and autonomous republics, as well as to make genuine national control over the course of elections effective, election commissions are formed, made up of representatives of social organizations and societies of the toilers. The Central Election Commission is confirmed by the Presidium of the appropriate Supreme Soviet at least two months prior to the elections, at the time when the date of the elections is published. Election commissions for elections to the Soviet of Nationalities are created in each Union and autonomous republic, autonomous region and national area, and are confirmed by the Presidia of the Supreme Soviets of the Union and autonomous republics and by Soviets of

[17] *Congressional Directory*, 74th Congress (April, 1935), pp. 244–245.
[18] Stalin, "Speech at the Preelection Assembly of Voters of the Stalin Election District of Moscow" (Dec. 11, 1937), p. 9.

Deputies of the Toilers of autonomous regions and national areas at least fifty days before the elections.

Area election commissions for elections to the Soviet of the Union are confirmed by the territorial (regional) Soviet of Deputies of the Toilers and, in republics with no territorial (regional) subdivision, by Presidia of the Supreme Soviets of the Republics at least fifty-five days before the elections. Area election commissions for elections to the Soviet of Nationalities are affirmed by Presidia of the Supreme Soviets of Union and Autonomous Republics, and by Soviets of Deputies of the Toilers of autonomous regions, at least fifty days before the elections. Precinct election commissions are confirmed by municipal or district Soviets of Deputies of the Toilers at least forty days before the elections.

The Central Election Commission consists of a president, a vice president, a secretary, and twelve members. They oversee the unswerving fulfillment of the election law during the course of the elections throughout the USSR territory; consider complaints of incorrect actions by election commissions and hand down final decisions thereupon; establish models of election boxes, documents (attestations of the right to vote, ballots and envelopes, lists of voters, records of the total vote, warrants of election); register deputies who have been elected; and perform for commissions on credentials of the Soviet of the Union and the Soviet of Nationalities the secretarial work on the elections.

Election commissions of Union and autonomous republics, of an autonomous region and of a national area, for elections to the Soviet of Nationalities consist of a president, vice president, secretary, and from six to ten members. These commissions oversee the fulfillment of the election law in their territory, and consider complaints of incorrect actions in elections to the Soviet of Nationalities.

Area election commissions for elections to the Soviet of the Union consist of a president, vice president, secretary, and eight members. These commissions oversee the timely organization by executive committees of election precincts, the seasonable compilation and bringing to general attention of voting lists; register candidates for election as deputies; furnish precinct election commissions with ballots and envelopes; count the votes for candidates and establish the results of the election for the area; furnish the secretarial work in connection with elections to the Central Election Commission; and give the elected deputy a warrant of election.

Area election commissions for elections to the Soviet of Nationalities consist likewise of a president, vice president, secretary, and eight members. They register candidates to be deputies to the Soviet of Nationalities; furnish precinct election commissions with ballots; count the votes; establish the results of elections; furnish the secretarial work in connection with elections to the Central Election Commission and to the appropriate republic election commissions concerning elections to the Soviet of Nationalities or to the election commission of an autonomous region; and furnish the elected deputy with a warrant of election.

Precinct election commissions consist of a president, vice president, secretary, and from four to eight members, acting in connection with elections to the Soviet of the Union and to the Soviet of Nationalities alike. These commissions receive the ballots by precincts from the electors, count the votes given for candidates for deputies of the Soviet of the Union and the Soviet of Nationalities, and furnish the secretarial work in connection with the elections to the area election commission (for elections to the Soviet of the Union and to the Soviet of Nationalities). During the last twenty days before elections, they daily broadcast to the electors the date and place of the elections.

All matters are decided in election commissions by a simple majority vote, the vote of the president being decisive if the votes are equally divided. More than half the general membership of the commission constitutes a quorum for the transaction of business. Each commission has its own seal. All expenses connected with the conduct of elections are charged to the state.

Thus, in the USSR, the conduct of elections and supervision over their propriety is in the hands of representatives of social organizations and societies of the toilers.

The structure of the election commissions may be judged by the example of the election commissions of the RSFSR. During the 1938 elections of the RSFSR Supreme Soviet the structure of election commissions was as shown on page 708.

In precinct election commissions there were 7,666 (8.4 per cent) women presidents of commissions; 12,930 (14.1 per cent) women vice presidents; 22,059 (24 per cent) secretaries. The rest were members of election commissions. In area election commissions women carried on the following work: 65 women were presidents of area election commissions, 122 were vice presidents, and 167 were secretaries of area election commissions. The rest were members of the commissions.

Such democratic methods of elections is unknown in any bourgeois country. Thus in England and the U. S. A. there are no election commissions of any sort. The authorities simply appoint an official for the elections (a commissar) who himself appoints individuals to be in charge of the election precincts. In France elections are under the general direction of the

Precinct Election Commissions

Total Election Commissions	Total Membership of Election Commissions	Of These		Nonparty	Social Structure					Participation of Women
		Members of All-Union Communist Party of Bolsheviks	Members of All-Union Lenin Young Communist League		Workers	Peasants, Kolkhoz Members	Individual Peasants	Clerks	Others	
91,880 (aside from 2,047 on boats)	609,993	135,597 22.2%	141,733 23.2%	333,663 54.6%	101,796 16.7%	284,127 46.6%	11 0%	220,601 36.2%	3,458 0.5%	158,919 26.1%

Area Election Commissions

727	7,993	4,189 52.4%	1,391 17.4%	2,413 30.2%	2,383 29.8%	1,991 24.9%		3,411 42.7%	208 2.6%	2,458 30.8%

Ministry of Internal Affairs, and in election precincts the elections are directed by the mayor and by his appointees, who constitute the bureau of the election section. In Czechoslovakia a bureaucrat of the Ministry of Internal Affairs is appointed president of the election system. In Norway the election bureau is formed of members of the municipal council, and so on. In Germany, along with an election commission selected by the fascists with great care, there is an institute of commissars attached to the police and defining the presence of "Aryan" blood in the electors.

In a number of countries, such as England, a policeman accompanies each voter in the election premises. "There is nothing particularly reprehensible in unarmed firemen being brought in to keep order, or even gendarmes circulating between the voters and the ballot boxes" according to Rabany,[19] author of the French election guide. In England an official directing elections can declare a crazy man sane or a drunken man sober, and admit them to vote,[20] and actually casts their votes for blind persons and for deaf mutes.[21]

These data suffice to establish the fact that elections in bourgeois countries are compressed within the framework of the Ministry of Internal Affairs. Officials of this department are in command during elections. Police restrictions keep the toilers down, and there are frequent scuffles between the police and the voters as a result. In order that possible outbursts of the voters may be swiftly crushed, election premises always have a third exit through which "officials can quickly appear and leave the premises." For this very reason election premises are required in England to be built on the first story.[22]

The management of elections in the USSR is radically different from that in bourgeois countries. Here elections, and the control of their course by the entire people, are effectuated jointly by the whole population of the country and by their representatives on election commissions who have been dispatched especially for this work by social organizations and societies of the toilers.

4. Nominating candidates to the Supreme Soviet

One of the elements characterizing the infinitely expanded Soviet socialist democracy is the right and method of nominating candidates to the Supreme Soviet. The Stalin Constitution and the election law formulated on the basis thereof assure the right of nominating candidates in

[19] Charles Rabany, *Guide général des élections* (1928, 1935), Sec. 412.
[20] Braunias, *Das parlamentarische Wahlrecht*, p. 236.
[21] Parker, *Gazetteer for Supervisors and Other Officials Acting in Elections to the House of Commons*, Sec. 26.
[22] *Ibid.*, Chap. 16.

behalf of social organizations and societies of the toilers, in behalf of Communist Party organizations, trade unions, cooperatives, youth organizations, cultural societies, and other organizations registered in legal form.[23]

The right to nominate candidates is possessed both by the central organs and by the republic, territorial, regional and district organs of these societies, as well as by general assemblies of workers and those in service in enterprises, of Red Army men according to military units, of peasants according to collective farms, and of workers and those in service in state farms according to such farms.[24] Candidates are thus nominated not by individual persons but by collectives, general assemblies, wherein each citizen of the country may, according to his dwelling place or place of work, be present.

The Stalin Constitution directs basic attention to the factual assurance of rights and not to their formal proclamation. The right to nominate candidates in the USSR is a truly democratic right, guaranteeing in fact the attraction of the entire population of the country into this responsible political work.

Each citizen of the USSR who has attained the age of eighteen, not having been deprived of his election rights by judgment of a court and not being feeble-minded, may be a candidate for any elective organ of authority of the USSR. There is no division into active and passive suffrage. The Soviet election system knows no "qualifications" of any kind. "Neither his property status nor his national origin, neither sex nor position in service, but the personal capacities and personal labor of each citizen define his position in society." [25]

A candidate for Deputy of the Supreme Soviet is nominated at least thirty days before the elections and recorded for that period in the district election commission,[26] which, at least twenty-five days before the elections, publishes in the press, for the information of all, the names, age, occupation, and party of the candidate and the name of the organization nominating him. The only requirement is that such candidate give his written consent to be voted for in a given election district.

A candidate for election to be a deputy cannot be a member either of the district or of the precinct election commission of the district where

[23] Regulations Concerning Elections to the USSR Supreme Soviet, Art. 56. No right to nominate candidates as deputies is enjoyed by sectarian or religious societies in general, being organizations created only "to satisfy their religious requirements" (Directives of All-Russian Central Executive Committee and the Council of the People's Commissars of the RSFSR, April 8, 1929; Cy. 1929, No. 35, Art. 353).

[24] Regulations, Art. 57.

[25] Stalin, *Speech on the Draft of the USSR Constitution* (1936), pp. 20, 21.

[26] Regulations Concerning Elections to the Supreme Soviet of the USSR, Arts. 59, 60, and 61.

he is nominated as candidate for the Supreme Soviet. He can vote only in one election district (Regulations, Art. 62). In elections of Union Republic Supreme Soviets, one and the same candidate may be nominated at the same time in different republics.

The district election commission is bound to record the candidates nominated by social organizations and societies of the toilers if the documents forwarded to them correspond with the requirements of the Stalin Constitution and of the Regulations. It can decline to record candidates who have not attained the age of eighteen or lack election rights for other reasons, and likewise if the appropriate documents (the formal record of the meeting or session which nominated the candidate and the written consent of the latter) are not forthcoming. Upon the refusal of the district commission to record a candidate, a complaint may, within the period of two days, be presented to the Central Election Commission, whose decision is final. The refusal of the district election commission for elections to the Soviet of Nationalities may be appealed within the same period to the election commission of the Union or autonomous republic or autonomous region. The decision of the latter may be appealed to the Central Election Commission, whose decision is final.

Candidates recorded by the district election commission are entered upon the ballot according to the place of the voting. Not later than fifteen days before the elections, district commissions print in the language of the population of the corresponding election district, and distribute among the precinct commissions, a sufficient number of election ballots to make sure that all the voters will be furnished with them.

Factual assurance of the democratic rights of the toilers is expressed also in Article 70 of the Regulations: "Each organization which has nominated a candidate recorded in the district election commission, and each citizen of the USSR, is guaranteed the right to campaign without let or hindrance in behalf of his candidate in assemblies, in the press, and by other means in accordance with Article 125 of the USSR Constitution." Anyone who shall obstruct a citizen in the exercise of his election rights is subject to legal punishment.

In the USSR there neither are nor can be opposing parties, as there neither are nor can be opposing classes. There is but one Party, the Bolshevik All-Union Communist Party, which is the advance detachment of the toilers in their struggle to confirm and to develop socialist order.

The experience of the 1937 elections to the USSR Supreme Soviet showed that the non-Party masses of our country have nominated candidates to the Supreme Soviet in a bloc with the Communists. This bloc is guaranteed by the correctness of the policy of the Party and the un-

limited confidence of the entire toiling population of the country which
the Party enjoys.

In capitalist countries an election campaign takes on the character of
a commercial enterprise. As late as the last quarter of the nineteenth century
the legal right to buy elections continued in the U. S. A. and was employed by the two parties then existing, the Republicans and the Democrats. Now, notwithstanding the laws against corruption, the bourgeois
parties widely practice the bribery of voters at elections. We have already
pointed out the different qualifications amounting to *chevaux-de-frise*
against the toilers' nominating candidates from among the youngest and
most energetic people. But aside from this, candidates for parliament are
under an obligation (in certain bourgeois countries) to pay part of the
election expenses, particularly of the cost of the ballots (France, Czechoslovakia). In Japan a candidate for deputy is bound to furnish a pledge
in the sum of 2,000 yen,[27] and if he fails to obtain 10 per cent of the total
number of votes cast at the time of the election, divided into the number of
parliamentary seats in the given district, the pledge is foreclosed in favor
of the treasury.[28] In Ireland this pledge amounts to 100 pounds sterling, in
England to 150 pounds sterling, and in Albania to 100 francs.

In England special commissions are created to conduct elections. The
entire preparation for elections is in the hands of these commissions, and
the rank and file of the population does not know how it is going. "Inasmuch as elections entail very large disbursements, these election commissions often give preference to someone ready to assume these expenses
himself, even though he is not sufficiently suitable," in the words of the
leader of the English Liberal Party, Muir. "In certain cases, if there is confidence that a given party has a manifest majority in a given election district, there is often only one candidate nominated. These 'guaranteed
mandates,' if they are not necessary to party leaders, are often given to
people who contribute large sums of money to the secret party funds
therefor. . . . In such election districts, all the electors who are not
devoted adherents of the party having a majority are, in fact, deprived of
the possibility of voting."[29] In the U. S. A. the original nomination of
candidates is made at the first assemblies of the parties (the primaries).
From there candidates are sent to the "convention" (assemblies of the delegates of a specific bourgeois party, elected at the primaries). Who shall
be entered as a candidate in the official list is decided, not by the majority,

[27] G. S. Quigley, *The Administration and Political Life of Japan* (Russian ed., 1934),
p. 245.
[28] In 1930 the total sum obtained by the Japanese government from such fines
amounted to 743,000 yen.
[29] R. Muir, *How Britain Is Governed* (Russian ed., 1936), p. 165.

however, but by the so-called bosses, agents of the bourgeois parties. It is for the popular assembly to affirm candidates nominated by the boss.

For nominating a candidate, workers have to collect money among themselves for campaigning in behalf of their candidates and making the required deposit, as well as for paying the necessary expenses for printing and distributing various sorts of preelection bulletins, circulars, and so on. Much money has to be spent on hiring the premises, since the bourgeoisie does not give premises for preelection assemblies free. The printing of articles, advertisements, and the like also requires enormous resources. All this the workers pay out of their own scanty wages. Of course in such cases it is very difficult to compete with the bourgeoisie. Consequently an enormous number of workers take no part in the voting (absenteeism). Everyone knows that a majority of the successful candidates are the representatives of the bourgeoisie. Workers are rarely elected to the lower chamber and never to the upper.

In the English parliament there were only five worker members among the 615 deputies after the 1935 elections. The nobility constituted one-third of the membership of the House, and representatives of the bourgeoisie came next. The chambers of other states also present a similar picture.

We have already cited information as to the membership of upper chambers in bourgeois states. There is no need to speak of fascist countries (Germany and Italy). There the "parliament" is simply appointed at the discretion of Hitler and Mussolini. By order of Hitler in fascist Germany, "a Reichstag deputy loses his mandate if he abandons the National-Socialist Party or is expelled from it. His successor is appointed by the leader of the National-Socialist faction of the Reichstag." In Italy the lists of candidates for parliament are compiled by the "grand fascist council." No one else has the right to propose candidates for parliament. The voter is given a ballot containing a list of candidates and the question: "Do you approve of the list prepared by the grand fascist council?" The voter must answer by a single "Yes" or "No" to the entire list. Opponents of the regime are ordinarily barred entirely from voting, and doubtful persons are taken under observation. In such circumstances a great deal of courage is required to vote "No." In Poland, the right to propose candidates is granted to district election commissions which are subordinate to the government.

5. *The method of voting and the determination of the results thereof*

On the basis of the USSR election law, elections of the Supreme Soviet of the USSR are conducted during a single day common to the entire

USSR, and this day must be announced at least two months before the date of the elections. This period completely guarantees the preparation for election. Elections are conducted on a nonworking day from 6 A.M. to 12 midnight so that all voters can be sure of appearing at the ballot box. The date of elections is established by the Presidium of the Supreme Soviet of the USSR.

The election law establishes a strict method of voting which admits of no abuses or incorrectness whatsoever. The law covers the verification and sealing of election boxes, the giving out of ballots upon the presentation of documents, and the verification of the election list, the filling in of the ballots in a special room (where the presence of any other person whatever is forbidden), the sending of the ballot in a sealed envelope, the necessity of voting in person, the prohibition of campaigning in the election premises, and the maintenance therein of complete order. The election law guarantees the correctness of the determination of election results no less completely. When the votes are totaled in the precinct election commission, representatives of social organizations and societies of the toilers, as well as of the press, are present.

The method of counting the votes in the precinct election commission is established in precise detail in the election law: the collation of the number of envelopes given out with the number of persons participating in the election, the entry of the result of the verification in a formal record, the opening of the envelopes by the president of the precinct commission and the publication of the result of voting according to each ballot in the presence of all the members of the election commission, the writing of the results separately for the Soviet of the Union and the Soviet of Nationalities, the preparation of two copies of the final computation for each candidate, the conditions invalidating a ballot, the method of solving doubtful cases, the preparation of a detailed report of the voting (including all the elements of determining the result thereof), the publication of the result of the totaling of all the votes, timely communication of one copy of the formal record of the voting to the district commission, and the sealing and handing over of all ballots for safekeeping to the Soviet of Deputies of the Toilers.

The same detailed rules are established also in totaling the votes in the district election commission on the basis of the formal records of the precinct election commissions.

A candidate who has obtained an absolute majority of votes, more than half of all the votes cast in the district and conceded to be genuine, is deemed elected (according to Art. 104 of the Regulations) and receives official intimation of that fact from the district election commission. If no single candidate has obtained an absolute majority of votes, the district commission communicates this fact to the Central Election Commission and at the same time declares a reballoting of the two candidates who have received the greatest number of votes, designating a day for such reballoting not later than two weeks from the expiration of the first holding of the election.

But it may happen that less than half of all the voters of the district took part in the voting in that district. The district election commission forthwith informs the Central Election Commission of this; the Commission declares the election invalid, and designates a new election within a two-week period. The reballoting for candidates for deputies in the new election (to take the place of that declared invalid) are conducted according to the lists of voters compiled for the first election and in complete conformity with the election law.

If for any reason a deputy quits the membership of the Supreme Soviet, then there must, within two months thereafter, be an election of a new deputy to be held within a two-week period as designated by the Presidium of the Supreme Soviet of the USSR.

Soviet law strictly guards the method of conducting elections. Article 3 of the Regulations says: "Everyone who by violence, fraud, threats, or corruption shall obstruct a USSR citizen in the exercise of his right to elect and to be elected to the Supreme Soviet of the USSR may be punished by the loss of his freedom for not more than two years." The following article provides that "an official of the Soviet or member of the election commission who counterfeits election documents, or knowingly renders an incorrect total of the votes cast, may be punished by the loss of his freedom for not more than three years."

Enemies of the people, enemies of socialism, followers of Trotsky, Zinovyev, Bukharin, and Rykov—those hirelings of German-Japanese fascism, spies, wreckers, and diversionists—sought to sap the might of the land of socialism. But they did not succeed—nor will they. The peoples of the USSR, by elections to the Supreme Soviet of the USSR and to the Supreme Soviet of Union and Autonomous Republics, have shown that they go steadily toward communism, sweeping from the road all who obstruct their path.

In every bourgeois country, without exception, the most shameless system of machinations of every sort, lying, bribery and fraud, holds sway during the period of elections. Property, capital, dictates its will: "Money is the mightiest voter," they say in America. The election of but one President of the U. S. A. cost the country $30,000,000. Not in vain did Lenin say: "Nowhere is the power of capital, the power of a handful of millionaires over all society, manifested so crudely and with such open venality as in America." [30]

In fascist countries terror is added to bribery. Any sort of campaigning against "candidates" nominated by the fascist party is deemed a state crime. Only candidates who have passed according to the list of the fascist party can be members of the Reichstag. Only German citizens can vote. And "German" citizens are considered to be only citizens belonging to the German state by German or kindred blood, who had the suffrage at the moment the law concerning imperial citizenship took effect (Hitler's decree of December 14, 1935). By the same order the imperial Minister of Internal Affairs may for a time deprive anyone not agreeable to him of imperial citizenship and so bar him from elections. The same is true in fascist Italy.

In bourgeois countries preparation for elections is often so brief that it is difficult for the broad masses to become duly familiar with the candidates. Elections are often designated for working days when the masses of toilers, particularly the workers, are occupied with work.

Various sorts of qualifications, the requirement of all possible information, the organization of examinations for the right to vote, and so on— all this leads to the result that millions of the masses of the toilers take no part in the voting. The American bourgeoisie frequently discharges voters if they vote against candidates supported by their masters. Accordingly, under various pretexts, the toilers not infrequently avoid taking part in the voting for bourgeois candidates.[31]

Concerning venality, bribes, during election time, highly illuminating facts are furnished by the famous American writer Upton Sinclair.[32] When he was nominated for the office of governor of California, various sorts of propositions, being essentially bribery proposals, began to come to him from all quarters. One oil capitalist offered him $400,000, having in view to obtain support in the future in obtaining a lease of oil properties from the governor-to-be. A representative of "Tango Players" in California

---

[30] Lenin (Russian ed.), Vol. XXIV, p. 375.

[31] After the 1923 elections for the mayor of Chicago, 5,310 electors were interrogated by a questionnaire as to why they had not appeared at the election. These causes were: illness, 12.1 per cent; absent on a journey, 11.1 per cent; inability to leave a member of the family without assistance, 2.2 per cent; obstacles put in the way of women by their husbands, 1 per cent (54 cases); distrust of elections (distrust of voting, aversion to politics, disillusionment with their own party, conviction that there was corruption), 17.7 per cent; insufficient period of residence, 5.2 per cent (274 cases); fear of losing a job, 5.5 per cent (289 cases); the poor situation of the booths, fear of a crowd at the elections, 1.9 per cent; apathy as regards elections, 27.9 per cent; lack of information concerning the election and fear of voting, 7.1 per cent (378 cases); carelessness, lack of preparation and the like, 9.3 per cent. These data are from the *Encyclopaedia Britannica*.

[32] Upton Sinclair, "The American Plutocracy," *Pravda* (July 8, 1938).

gave him a "decent sum" for "protection." The same representative in San Francisco proposed to give $16,000 a week for the four years of his tenure of office. During the fourteen months of the campaign, Sinclair spent more than $1,000,000 for the necessities of the campaign, and his representatives in Los Angeles and San Francisco spent two or three times as much. By the end of the campaign he was himself completely ill and entirely in debt. He obtained 879,000 votes but was not elected governor.

By means of corruption, the capitalists and their monopolist associations put their own people into responsible posts in the state. In the *Eighteenth Brumaire of Louis Bonaparte*,[33] Marx wrote that "all state institutions are becoming institutions of purchase and sale: the senate, the state council, the legislative assembly, the Order of the Legion of Honor, the soldiers' medal, the laundries, the state buildings, the railroads, the general staff of the National Guard (which has no rank and file), and the confiscated properties of the Orléans family. Every sort of place in the army and in the government machine is an object of purchase." While the forms of this corruption are various, the system is the same. Notwithstanding the laws forbidding it, corruption exists in fact even now. Thus, there is a law in England forbidding agents of a candidate of a given election district to bring voters in a hired carriage or automobile; it is forbidden likewise to pay the fare of electors on the railroad. But if the bourgeois party mobilizes wagons to bring the purchased electors, it is not considered unlawful; the carriage is not a hired carriage. In precisely the same way, it will be lawful if the fare of electors on the railroad is paid by an agent of the neighboring election district. Bribery, entertainment of electors by a deputy, is forbidden by law; but if this is done by somebody else and not by the deputy himself, then the English law is silent.

According to a law of the U. S. A. of 1925, preelection expenses in senatorial elections must not exceed $10,000 and for a member of Congress, $2,500. But in the very next year the elections of three senators in Pennsylvania and Illinois cost $2,500,000—all spent on bribing voters.

Election practice includes:

1. The holding of a single election in all districts. The person elected is he who in a given district gets the most votes out of all those cast in that district, even though the number be less than half the total number of electors (a relative majority).

2. The holding of two elections, when the voting is done twice: in the first he is deemed elected who obtains absolute majority, that is, more than half the votes cast. In those districts in which there are no candidates with an absolute majority, a second election is held. In this, votes are cast

[33] Marx, *Selected Works* (Russian ed., 1935), Vol. II, p. 333.

for all the candidates voted for in the earlier election, and he is deemed elected who receives a relative majority. Sometimes on the second occasion votes are cast only for the two candidates receiving the most votes on the first occasion.

3. Multiple elections. Elections are repeated a number of times until one of the candidates obtains an absolute majority of the votes cast.

The election practice of England, France, and the U. S. A. often shows that the parties victorious in the elections have received a number of votes less than half the number of voters. This is explained by the fact that in these countries not an absolute but a relative majority is required for an election. Why such a method of voting suits the bourgeoisie may be graphically shown from the elections in the distict of Northing in England, where in the elections the Conservatives received 15,477 votes, the Labor Party, 15,473, and the Liberals, 14,163. The Conservative was elected, although his adversaries together totaled 29,636 votes.

In 1935, in England, the Conservatives received 10,488,000 votes and obtained 387 seats; the Laborites, 8,325,000 votes and 154 seats. It is clear how vast is the voting significance of each extra vote, and why the bourgeoisie grants a certain category of the bourgeois population the right to have two votes.

In France the person elected at the first election held is the candidate who has obtained more than half of all the votes cast in a given district, and the total number of votes in the district must be not less than 25 per cent of the total number of electors of the district. If no one candidate obtains the necessary majority, new elections are designated, in which event the person elected is he who obtains a relative majority. If the votes are equal, the elder candidate is declared elected. Thus parliament is occasionally elected by a minority of the electors of the country. In 1928 the elected deputies received 4,830,000 votes, and the remaining candidates 6,565,000; in 1932 the elected candidates got 5,245,000, and the remaining candidates, 6,315,000. This is a very graphic illustration of the fact that parliament is not an expression of the will of the entire people and that the bourgeois democracy does not represent a majority of the people.

Bourgeois election practice has worked out a number of systems of defining the majority, all of which become generalized in majority and proportional election systems. Under the majority election system, only votes cast for the candidate who obtained a majority (absolute or relative) are taken into account. In countries where numerous parties with different platforms participate in elections and contend for a place in parliament, the majority system of representation leaves no possibility for representatives of the minority parties to reach the elective organs; their votes are ordinarily lost. With the proportional election system, seats in parliament are distributed among all the parties in proportion to the number of votes cast for each.[34]

In bourgeois countries workers struggle for the latter system, under which it is possible to send a number of worker deputies, although a small number, to parliament. In Switzerland the election system contemplates both a majority system and a proportional system; in some cantons of the Swiss Union (Zurich, Berne, Geneva, Schwys, Glarus, and others) the proportional election system obtains; in Unterwalden, Obwalden and other cantons, the majority election system.

6. *The recall of a deputy*

One of the most important principles of the Soviet election system is the right, and the method, of recalling a deputy. This right is expressed in the fact that electors can at any time and of their own volition recall a deputy from the election organ before the term of his authority has run out. According to Article 142 of the Stalin Constitution: "Each deputy must account to his electors in respect to his work and the work of the Soviet of Deputies of the Toilers, and may at any time be recalled by a decision of the majority of the electors in the manner established by law." The question of the recall of deputies from the Soviets was posed in the very first months of the existence of Soviet authority. As early as December 4, 1917, a Proposed Decree Concerning the Right of Recall, introduced by the Bolsheviks at a session of the All-Russian Central Executive Committee, was adopted unanimously: "Any elective institution whatsoever or assembly of representatives whatsoever may be considered truly democratic and actually representative of the will of the people only upon the condition that the right of the electors to recall those whom they have elected be conceded and applied." [35]

This decree was broadly utilized by the masses for the first time to recall the SR's and Mensheviks who had sneaked into the Soviets. In the 1918 RSFSR Constitution the right of electors to recall "at any time" a deputy whom they had elected was noted as one of the basic propositions for the organization of Soviet authority. In the sequel it was reflected in the Bolshevik Worker-Peasant Party's program adopted at the Eighth Party Congress (March 18–28, 1919) and in a succession of other most

[34] Under the proportional election system, voting is carried on according to lists of the candidates taking part in the voting of the parties. From each list as many representatives are considered elected as the number of votes necessary for obtaining a single seat divides into the total number of votes obtained by this list.

[35] Lenin (Russian ed.), Vol. XXII, p. 92.

important Party and Soviet documents. Until 1921 Article 58 of the RSFSR Constitution was in operation, to the effect that the Soviets must be reelected each three months, and there was, therefore, no practical necessity for employing the right to recall deputies prior to the Congress of the Soviets. Nor was this situation changed by the war-political setting of 1918—1921.

In connection with the ending of the civil war and the extension of the period of the plenary powers of the Soviet, especially during the animation of the work of the Soviets after 1924, the right of recall begins comparatively often to be applied in practice, and by 1928, after the special instruction of the Fifteenth Party Congress as to verifying the effectuation of this right, it was broadly applied.[36]

The right of recall acquired special significance during the expanded socialist attack along the entire front. As this attack was proceeding, it was essential "to arrange the reorganization of all the practical work . . . of the Soviets and of other mass organizations of every sort with a view to the needs of the reconstruction period; to create in them a nucleus of the most active and revolutionary workers, having excluded and isolated the opportunist trade-union, bureaucratic elements; to hunt out of them the alien and degenerate elements, and to advance new workers from below." [37]

The most important stage in the reconstruction of the Soviets in this direction was "the year of the great crisis," 1929, and the subsequent reelections of the Soviets in 1930–1931. But even after these reelections, membership in the Soviets included not a few deputies unequal to their functions, wherefore even during the first six months of 1931, almost immediately after the elections, approximately 23,000 deputies were recalled from the rural Soviets of the RSFSR (aside from the autonomous parts thereof), and more than 1,000 from the city Soviets.[38]

After the reelections of 1934–1935, which notably improved the membership of the Soviets, the number of recalls of deputies was far lower, although Soviet electors broadly employed the right of recall even at this time. Thus, during the first six months of 1935, according to data of 36,078 rural Soviets of the RSFSR, 30,165 deputies, or approximately one deputy for each village Soviet, were recalled, and it must be borne in mind that the number of persons recalled does not include those who had left the Soviets

---

[36] As to the recall of deputies, cf. *Circular of the All-Russian Central Executive Committee of July 23, 1928* (Cy. 1928, No. 104, Art. 657) and supplements thereto (Cy. 1931, No. 28, Art. 256, and Cy. 1933, No. 40, Art. 150).

[37] Stalin, *Questions of Leninism* (10th Russian ed.), pp. 391–392.

[38] The recall of deputies took place in general assemblies of the voters of the election precinct from which they had been elected. The recall of deputies who were members of executive committees took place in the appropriate Congresses of Soviets.

for various other reasons. This, on the one hand, attests the fact that inadequate attention was paid during the election of the Soviets to the choice of candidates for deputies and, on the other, demonstrates the attentive regard for the work of deputies on the part of electors who strictly and methodically developed the directive of the December, 1930, unified plenum of the Central Committee and the Central Control Committee of the All-Union Communist Party (of Bolsheviks) concerning the fact that "the reelections of the Soviets must introduce radical improvements into the very structure of the Soviets" where "the first place necessarily belongs to the best shock workers."

The practice of recalling deputies is encountered very rarely in certain cantons of Switzerland and in individual states of the U.S.A. An American political economist, Bird, says that there are in California more than fifty different statutes concerning the recall of municipal officials, and more than forty statutes concerning the recall of officials of autonomies in the village localities. These laws are so complicated, so confused, that it is utterly impossible to use them, and their broad application in practice is therefore not feasible. Data as to the recall of deputies in California show that the citizens of California cities, having the right of recall, use it in fact about once in fifty years, during which they recall not more than one elected official. The electors of rural autonomous organizations use the right of recall still more rarely.

Upon the evidence of the famous French political scientist, Hauriou, the matter of recalling deputies stands no better in the Swiss cantons than in the U.S.A.: "Swiss citizens have for a long time ceased to employ the right of recall." Another expert of public law, Karl Braunias, asserts that the right of recall has lost its significance in the Swiss cantons.[39]

Electors in bourgeois countries, even in the most "democratic" countries, do not know in fact how their deputy works. He is not connected with them, for in such countries "the people have a right to vote once in two years but often decline to exercise it since their votes elect those who crush them, and there is no democratic right to sweep them away, to take effective measures to repress them."[40]

Attributing vast significance to the right of recall, Lenin at the same time emphasized that only Soviet electors enjoy it. The right is likewise noted in constitutions and in various sorts of supplementary laws in bourgeois countries, but the electors of those countries almost never use it. "By thousands of dodges, cleverer and more truly effective the more developed the

[39] Karl Braunias, *Das parlamentarische Wahlrecht*, Vol. II, p. 268.
[40] Lenin (Russian ed.), Vol. XXII, p. 96.

'pure' democracy is, the capitalists *repel* the masses from participation in administration." [41] For these reasons the masses of toilers in the bourgeois countries cannot even reach "their" deputy.

"So long as elections are going on, deputies flirt with the voters, fawn upon them, swear that they will be faithful, and make a multitude of promises of all sorts. The dependence of deputies upon electors is seemingly complete. As soon as the elections are held and candidates have become deputies, relations radically change. Deputies, instead of depending on electors, become completely independent." [42] The right of recall is confirmed in the Stalin Constitution:

> Electors have the right before the end of their terms to recall their deputies if they begin to shuffle, if they turn aside from the path, if they forget their dependence upon the people, upon the electors. . . . A deputy must know that he is the servant of the people, the people's emissary to the Supreme Soviet, and he must conduct himself according to the line commanded by the people. Should he turn aside from the path, the electors have the right to demand that new elections be designated and to throw to the dogs the deputy who has turned aside from the path. [43]

The Soviet election system is a mighty instrument for further educating and organizing the masses politically, for further strengthening the bond between the state mechanism and the masses, and for improving the state mechanism and grubbing out the remnants of bureaucratism.

Under the new Stalin Constitution elections to the Supreme Soviet of the USSR and to the Supreme Soviets of Union and Autonomous Republics have shown that the entire population of the land of the Soviets are completely united in spirit, have demonstrated an unprecedented democracy. The days of elections have actually been festive days of the entire people, when the block of Party and non-Party Bolsheviks have elected their best people to the Supreme Soviets. The call of the Bolshevik Party to the Soviet people, to all the electors, the vote for candidates of the bloc of the Communists and the non-Party members had exceptional results. In the voting for candidates to the Supreme Soviet of the USSR, 91,113,153 electors out of 94,138,159 took part—96.8 per cent of the entire number of citizens having the right to vote.

The percentage of those participating in the voting for elections for the Supreme Soviet of the USSR in individual Union Republics is as follows: the RSFSR, 96.8; the Ukrainian SSR, 97.8; the White Russian SSR, 97.4;

[41] *Ibid.*, Vol. XXIII, p. 349.
[42] Stalin, "Speech at the Preelection Assembly of Voters of the Stalin Election District of Moscow (1937), p. 10.
[43] Address of the Central Committee of the All-Union Communist Party (of Bolsheviks), Dec. 5, 1937.

the Azerbaijan SSR, 95.6; the Georgian SSR, 96.2; the Armenian SSR, 96.2; the Turkmen SSR, 94.2; the Uzbek SSR, 93.5; the Tadjik SSR, 95.3; the Kazakh SSR, 96.9; and the Kirghiz SSR, 94.3. Of this number the following percentages voted for the candidates of the Communist non-Party bloc: in the RSFSR, to the Soviet of the Union, 98.4 to the Soviet of Nationalities, 97.5; in the Ukrainian SSR, 99 and 97.9; in the White Russian SSR, 98.7 and 98.4; in the Azerbaijan SSR, 99.2 and 98.6; in the Georgian SSR, 99.1 and 99; in the Armenian SSR, 99.2 and 99.3; in the Turkmen SSR, 99.3 and 98.8; in the Uzbek SSR, 99 and 98.6; in the Tadjik SSR, 98.7 and 98.4; in the Kazakh SSR, 99.4 and 98.7; in the Kirghiz SSR, 97.1 and 97.3; and in the entire Soviet Union, 98.6 and 97.8.

Elections to the Union Republic Supreme Soviets showed the still greater, the almost infinite, activity of the voters. The number of voters taking part in voting and casting their votes for candidates of the Communist-non-Party bloc is expressed in the following percentages: [44] in the RSFSR, 99.3, of whom 99.3 voted for candidates of Communist non-Party bloc candidates; corresponding figures in other republics were: in the Ukrainian SSR, 99.62 and 99.55; in the White Russian SSR, 99.65 and 99.19; in the Azerbaijan SSR, 99.36 and 99.59; in the Georgian SSR, 99.2 and 99.6; in the Armenian SSR, 99.06 and 99.6; in the Turkmen SSR, 99.55 and 99.8; in the Uzbek SSR, 97.93 and 99.57; in the Tadjik SSR, 99.5 and 99.64; in the Kazakh SSR, 99.2 and 99.5; and in the Kirghiz SSR, 98.23 and 99.1.

To the Supreme Soviet of the USSR, there were elected altogether 1,143 deputies (569 to the Soviet of the Union and 574 to the Soviet of Nationalities). Of these, 946 (83.5 per cent) were men and 187 (16.5) were women; members of the All-Union Communist Party (of Bolsheviks) numbered 870 (76.1), and 273 (23.9) were non-Party. Out of 546 deputies of the Soviet of the Union, 247 (45.3) were workers, 130 (23.7) were peasants, and 169 (31) were in service. Of 574 deputies of the Soviet of Nationalities, 218 (37.9) were workers, 200 (34.9) were peasants, and 156 (27.2) were in service.

The ages of deputies of the Supreme Soviet were: up to the age of 20, 13 deputies; 21 to 25, 84; 26 to 30, 187; 31 to 35, 292; 36 to 40, 255; and above 40, 312. Of ages up to 40 there were 831 deputies (71.8 per cent); of ages above 40 there were 312 deputies (28.2 per cent). Fifty-four nationalities are represented in the Supreme Soviet of the USSR.

[44] The first elections were: to the Supreme Soviet of the USSR, Dec. 12, 1937; to the Supreme Soviets of the Georgian and Armenian SSR's, June, 1938; of the Azerbaijan, Tadjik, Uzbek, Kazakh, Kirghiz and Turkmen SSR's, June 24, 1938; and of the RSFSR and of the White Russian and Ukraine SSR's, June 26, 1938. Elections in the various Autonomous Soviet Socialist Republics were on corresponding dates.

Never in a single country did the people manifest such activity in elections as did the Soviet people. Never has any capitalist country known, nor can it know, such a high percentage of those participating in voting as did the USSR. The Soviet election system under the Stalin Constitution and the elections of Supreme Soviets have shown the entire world once again that Soviet democracy is the authentic sovereignty of the people of which the best minds of mankind have dreamed.

RUSSIAN TRANSLITERATION TABLE

(Based on the new Russian orthography)

This scheme is designed for the convenience of readers who do not know Russian. It is intended primarily for the rendering of personal and place names—mostly nouns in the nominative case.

The aim is to produce words as "normal" in appearance as possible, without the use of diacritical marks, superscripts or apostrophes, but at the same time to approximate the sounds of the Russian words, so that if spoken by an educated American they would easily be identified by a Russian.

Names which are a part of English cultural tradition, such as Moscow, Archangel, Tolstoy, Tchaikovsky, are given in their customary English spelling.

Extended phrases or entire sentences involving verb forms and case endings, which occur in footnotes for the convenience of students who know Russian, are given in a somewhat more complex transliteration which is reversible.

Russian		*English*	
А	а	*a*	
Б	б	*b*	
В	в	*v*	
Г	г	*g*	except in genitive singular where it is *v*, as in Tolstovo.
Д	д	*d*	
Е	е	(1) *ye*	when initial, and after ь, ъ, and all vowels, except ы, и: Yekaterina, Izdanie, Nikolayev.
		(2) *e*	elsewhere, as in Lenin, Vera, Pero.
Ё	ё	*yo*	but after ж and ш = *o*.
Ж	ж	*zh*	
З	з	*z*	
И	и	*i*	but after ь = *yi*, as in Ilyich.
Й	й	*y*	in terminal diphthongs, but *i* medially, as in May, Kochubey, Kiy, Tolstoy, but Khozyaistvo.
К	к	*k*	
Л	л	*l*	
М	м	*m*	
Н	н	*n*	
О	о	*o*	
П	п	*p*	
Р	р	*r*	

Russian		*English*	
С	с	*s*	
Т	т	*t*	
У	у	*u*	
Ф	ф	*f*	
Х	х	*kh*	as in Kharkov.
Ц	ц	*ts*	Tsargrad.
Ч	ч	*ch*	Chapayev, Vaigach.
Ш	ш	*sh*	Shakhta.
Щ	щ	*shch*	Shchedrin.
Ъ	ъ	Omit	
Ы	ы	*y*	Mys, Tsaritsyn.
Ь	ь	Omit	
Э	э	*e*	Ermitazh.
Ю	ю	*yu*	
Я	я	*ya*	

Adjectival Endings

Plural	ЫЙ,	ИЙ	ый,	ий	both simply *y*, as in Dostoyevsky, Grozny.
Singular	ЫЕ,	ИЕ	ые,	ие	both simply *ie*.

The English letter *y* serves both as vowel and as consonant (as it does in English): (1) as a vowel *within* words, as in Mys, Tsaritsyn, and also (2) as an adjectival terminal vowel, as in Khoroshy, Razumovsky, May, Kochubey, Tolstoy, and (3) with consonantal force to soften vowels, as in Istoriya, Bratya, Yug.

Index

Abbreviations:
CC of CP and CCCPSU—Central Committee of Communist Party of Soviet Union
CEC—Central Executive Committee
CP—Communist Party
CPC—Council of People's Commissars
NEP—New Economic Policy
RSFSR—Russian Soviet Federative Socialist Republic
USSR—Union of Soviet Socialist Republics